Lecture Notes of the Institute for Computer Sciences, Social Informatics and Telecommunications Engineering 219

More information about this series at http://www.springer.com/series/8197

Guanglu Sun · Shuai Liu (Eds.)

Advanced Hybrid Information Processing

First International Conference, ADHIP 2017
Harbin, China, July 17–18, 2017
Proceedings

 Springer

Editors
Guanglu Sun
Harbin University of Science
  and Technology
Harbin
China

Shuai Liu
Inner Mongolia University
Hohhot
China

ISSN 1867-8211   ISSN 1867-822X (electronic)
Lecture Notes of the Institute for Computer Sciences, Social Informatics
and Telecommunications Engineering
ISBN 978-3-319-73316-6   ISBN 978-3-319-73317-3 (eBook)
https://doi.org/10.1007/978-3-319-73317-3

Library of Congress Control Number: 2017962886

Printed on acid-free paper

This Springer imprint is published by Springer Nature
The registered company is Springer International Publishing AG
The registered company address is: Gewerbestrasse 11, 6330 Cham, Switzerland

Preface

We are delighted to introduce the proceedings of the first edition of the 2017 European Alliance for Innovation (EAI) International Conference on Advanced Hybrid Information Processing (ADHIP). This conference gathered together researchers, developers, and practitioners from around the world who are leveraging and developing theories and methods for hybrid information compression, classification, and recognition. The theme of ADHIP 2017 was "Data-Driven Theory, Method, and Application in the Real World."

The technical program of ADHIP 2017 consisted of 65 full papers in oral presentation sessions of the main conference tracks. The conference tracks were: Track 1, "Advanced Methods and Applications for Hybrid Information"; Track 2, "Real Applications of Aspects with Hybrid Information."

Aside from the high-quality technical paper presentations, the technical program also featured two keynote speeches given by Dr. Guoru Ding, IEEE Senior Member, from the National Mobile Communications Research Laboratory of China and Dr. Wanxiang Che from the Research Center for Social Computing and Information Retrieval, Harbin Institute of Technology.

The steering chairs and all members of the Program Committee were essential for the success of the conference. We sincerely appreciate their constant support and guidance. It was also a great pleasure to work with such an excellent Organizing Committee and we thank them for their hard work in organizing and supporting the conference. In particular, we also thank the Technical Program Committee, led by our TPC chair, Xiaochun Cheng, who completed the peer-review process of technical papers and compiled a high-quality technical program. We are also grateful to conference manager, Lenka Bilska, for her support and all the authors who submitted their papers to the conference.

We strongly believe that this ADHIP conference provides a good forum for all researchers, developers, and practitioners to discuss all science and technology aspects that are relevant to hybrid information processing. We also expect that future ADHIP conferences will be as successful and stimulating, as indicated by the contributions presented in this volume.

November 2017

Shuai Liu
Guanglu Sun
Yun Lin
Guohui Yang

Organization

Organizing Committee

General Co-chairs

Guanglu Sun	Harbin University of Science and Technology, China
Shuai Liu	Inner Mongolia University, China

Technical Program Committee Co-chairs

Xiaochun Cheng	Middlesex University, UK
Yun Lin	Harbin Engineering University, China
Bo You	Harbin University of Science and Technology, China

Web Chair

Houbing Song	West Virginia University, USA

Publicity and Social Media Chair

Guohui Yang	Harbin Institute of Technology, China

Workshops Chair

Ruolin Zhou	Western New England University, USA

Sponsorship and Exhibits Chair

Xiaochun Cheng	Middlesex University, UK

Publications Chair

Shuai Liu	Inner Mongolia University, China

Panels Chair

Jingchao Li	Shanghai Dianji University, China

Tutorials Chair

Guodong Wang	South Dakota School of Mines and Technology, USA

Demos Chair

Qi Wang	Nanjing Normal University, China

Posters and PhD Track Chair

Zhiping Zhang   Wright State University, USA

Local Chairs

Jiazhong Xu   Harbin University of Science and Technology, China
Suxia Zhu   Harbin University of Science and Technology, China

Conference Coordinator

Lenka Bilska   EAI (European Alliance for Innovation)

Technical Program Committee

Yun Lin   Harbin Engineering University, China
Guanglu Sun   Harbin University of Science and Technology, China
Liang Zhang   Jimei University, China
Zheng Pan   Inner Mongolia University, China
Xuefei Ma   Harbin Engineering University, China
Shanshan Li   Harbin Engineering University, China
Chao Wang   Harbin Engineering University, China
Seng Wang   Harbin Engineering University, China
Meiyu Wang   Harbin Engineering University, China
Zhigang Li   Harbin Engineering University, China
Yuan Liu   Western New England University, USA
Weina Fu   Inner Mongolia Agricultural University, China
Jiazhong Xu   Harbin University of Science and Technology, China
Yongjun He   Harbin University of Science and Technology, China
Kuang Zhang   Harbin Engineering University, China
Guodong Wang   South Dakota School of Mines and Technology, USA
Shuai Liu   Inner Mongolia University, China
Zhiqiang Wu   Wright State University, USA
Guohui Yang   Harbin Institute of Technology, China
Zhutian Yang   Harbin Institute of Technology, China
Guoru Ding   Pla University of Science and Technology, China
Ao Li   Harbin University of Science and Technology, China
Jingchao Li   Shanghai Dianji University, China
Xiaochun Cheng   Middlesex University, UK
Gihog Min   Pai Chai University, South Korea
Jing Qiu   Harbin University of Science and Technology, China
Xumin Ding   Harbin University of Science and Technology, China
Suxia Zhu   Harbin University of Science and Technology, China
Bo You   Harbin University of Science and Technology, China

Wei Wang   Harbin University of Science and Technology, China
Liu Shuai   Inner Mongolia University, China
Gaocheng Liu   Inner Mongolia University, China
Meng Ye Lu   Inner Mongolia University, China
Fanyi Meng   Harbin Institute of Technology, China

Contents

Application of Improved RFID Anti-collision Algorithm in Cylinder Inflation System

You Bo, Wu Kun[(⊠)], and Xu Jiazhong

School of Automation, Harbin University of Science and Technology,
Harbin 150080, China
youbo@hrbust.edu.cn, haerbin_wukun@163.com

Abstract. An improved design of an inflatable system based on RFID smart cylinder and an improved algorithm for preventing the collision of multiple electronic tags during the recognition process are solved. The continuous filling of the unmarked and discarded cylinders is solved, and the cross charging of the cylinders is solved. And customer churn and other issues. Through the RFID radio frequency identification technology and GPRS wireless communication technology to achieve the inflatable terminal can be real-time upload the cylinder of RFID coding and filling information to the database server. In this paper, a new improved algorithm is proposed, which is based on the binary tree search algorithm, which improves the number of collisions and transmission faults of the reader in the recognition process. Information. The system has carried out the filling test, the real-time monitoring and testing of the cylinder data and the historical data query test. The test results show that the system can control the continuous filling of the non-seized and discarded cylinders and the cross filling of the cylinder to realize the accurate and fast of the network transmission, to meet the requirements of the safety management of the barrel of things.

Keywords: RFID · Algorithm · GPRS · Database · Objects of Internet styling

1 Introduction

With the fine management of liquefied petroleum gas companies and the state to improve the management of liquefied petroleum gas, cylinder safety management has always been a very headache for managers. Cylinder safety management is mainly reflected in: whether the control is not seized, scrapped cylinders continue to fill; can control the cross-filling cylinder; can control the loss of scrap cylinders; can control the loss of customers and other phenomena [1–3]. In order to solve the above problems, to achieve the safety management of the Internet of things, the system depends mainly processing. On the cylinder on the smart angle valve device, the smart angle valve embedded with RFID smart chip and limit control device. RFID smart chip so that each cylinder has a unique RFID code, that is, ID information. The inflatable gun is equipped with an RFID identification device and a control inflator. The identification device is composed of a reader and an STM32 controller. The control device on the intelligent angle valve can only be opened after the reader and the identification. And

© ICST Institute for Computer Sciences, Social Informatics and Telecommunications Engineering 2018
G. Sun and S. Liu (Eds.): ADHIP 2017, LNICST 219, pp. 1–11, 2018.
https://doi.org/10.1007/978-3-319-73317-3_1

then open the inflatable operation. When the cylinder inflated after the end of the filling information (cylinder inspection, filling, release, validity, specifications, cylinder code) through the GPRS wireless communication module uploaded to the database server, easy to monitor the center for statistical, query and other data applications. The inflatable system is through the RFID technology to control the cylinder is not seized, scrap cylinders continue to fill and cylinder filling, to eliminate expired, not seized, dangerous cylinders are used again, through the cylinder RFID coding means for each cylinder to wear a Helmet, so that people's lives and property from the threat [4–6]. But the core problem of the system is the reader in the identification of cylinder ID, there will be RFID tag collision phenomenon, resulting in the reader can not correctly identify any one of the label information, reducing the reader's recognition efficiency and read and write Speed, seriously affecting the normal operation of the system.

There are two kinds of anti-collision algorithms in RFID system. ALOHA-based uncertainty algorithm and deterministic algorithm based on binary tree (BT, binary tree). ALOHA algorithm is a random algorithm, its operation is simple but random, low throughput, there will be a label in a very long time can not be identified, that is, "label hunger" phenomenon. The binary tree algorithm is a deterministic algorithm. The algorithm does not have the phenomenon of "label hunger and thirst", its recognition rate is high, and the advantages of throughput are applied in the RFID system, but the algorithm is relatively complex and the recognition time is long. In the improved binary tree algorithm, Fikenzeller proposed a binary search algorithm [7], the advantage lies in the idea of simple thinking, but there are many requests and return the amount of data larger shortcomings. On this basis, Zhang Hang proposed a return binary search algorithm [8], the advantages of the algorithm can be ordered to read and reduce the number of requests, the disadvantage is that the amount of data returned to the label is still large. The dynamic binary search algorithm proposed by Hsuei has improved the first two algorithms, and the problem of reducing the number of requests but the large amount of data returned by the tag still exists [9]. In this case, Bingcai proposed based on the stack storage anti-collision algorithm, which reduces the amount of data returned by the label has improved, but the number of requests for the reader did not change a lot [10]. Above the binary search algorithm still exists too many times the number of reader requests and the amount of data returned by the label is too large and so on [11–13].

In this paper, based on the binary search algorithm, an improved algorithm based on stack is proposed, which can reduce the number of times of reader/writer while ensuring the redundancy of data redundancy, and effectively solve the problem that many cylinders are embedded in the filling process RFID tag collision problem.

2   System Solutions

2.1   System Composition

With pneumatic system based on RFID intelligence cylinder design mainly consists of four parts, respectively, inflatable terminal layer, data layer, data processing layer and application management. The system structure diagram is shown in Fig. 1.

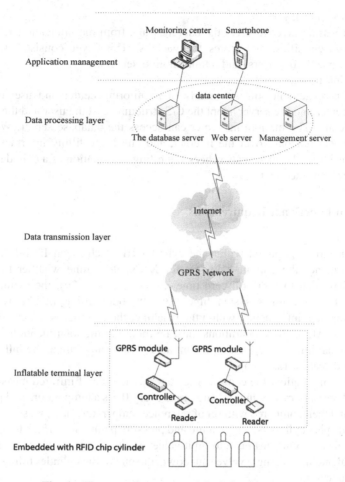

Fig. 1. The overall structure of the inflatable system

(1) Inflatable terminal layer
Before filling operation, first by identifying the device within the cylinder RFID chips on ID information verification, if the verification through, start control pneumatic device, the intelligent Angle on the cylinder valve limit device filling valve opened, the air gun to the cylinder air. If not, the buzzer alerts the alarm and indicates which identity information is not passed on the LCD. Fill in the filling and then upload the cylinder's filling information to the database via GPRS module.

(2) Data transfer layer
The data transmission layer is located between the inflatable terminal layer and the data processing layer, which is used to carry out the downstream transmission of the cylinder information and control information. In order to meet the requirement of data collection and transmission, the GPRS network is used to transmit data.

(3) Data processing layer

The data processing layer receives the data message from the inflatable terminal layer and interprets, classifies, and stores the packets. This layer consists primarily of database servers, Web servers, and administrative servers.

(4) Application management

Application management consists mainly of monitoring center and user center, the monitoring center and the server adopt the C/S structure, and the user and the server are the B/S structure. The monitoring center can access the database server, Web server, and management database over the Internet, and check the filling information of the cylinder in real time. Users can also check the filling information of a cylinder by using a smartphone login account.

2.2   System Functional Requirements

(1) Validation

First identification equipment within the cylinder RFID chips on ID information for validation: whether the current cylinders for XXX, determine whether the cylinder using time has been to scrap (discard time < system time + 30), the cylinder testing time is due (detection time < system time + 30), the bottle filling number is consistent with the filling data information within the machine, the cylinder is in accordance with the provisions. All of these conditions must be met, and the identification device will activate the charging device, turn on the inflatable valve and inflate the inflatable gun.

(2) Run the detection function

In the process of aeration, the controller to start the module of infrared measuring temperature and pressure measuring modules, read every 0.5 s a temperature and pressure in a cylinder, and then compared with set of reference temperature and pressure, your LCD screen time display cylinders, temperature and pressure parameters. If the temperature or pressure inside the cylinder to rise to limit value, an alarm signal, the controller immediately signal intelligent Angle valve shut down, the end of the cylinder filling operation.

(3) Query function

Administrators monitor the data and view historical data in real time, and generate data reports that facilitate the analysis, statistics, and application of data.

3   Algorithm Principle

Role of read and write in the RFID system, if there are multiple electronic label, the same time there can be multiple tags for energy and send information to the read/write device that will interfere with each other, causing the cylinder embedded RFID encoding can't correct recognition. In this adopted a stack-based RFID binary tree anti-collision algorithm, the principle of which is to read and write device using the detected conflict into the stack to the current request sequence, when the conflict a greater than 1, through the stack decide next time to read and write device sends the request instructions, avoid the request each time from the base of the tree in the process of identification is insufficient [14, 15]. The algorithm can reduce query times and improve recognition efficiency.

3.1 Basic Binary Search Algorithm Principle

The algorithm requires that each tag have unique ID information, and the information is encoded in Manchester to quickly locate the location of the data conflict location. In this code, the increase along the encoding logic "0" indicates the descent along the encoding logic "1". In the process of receiving data, there is no jump in the state level, and the data bit is in conflict. For example, it identifies the collision process by bit, as shown in Fig. 2.

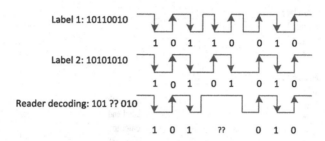

Fig. 2. The Manchester code identifies the conflict bits

3.2 Introduction

(1) Request(ID) Request: abbreviated R(ID), within the read-write scope, the label of all the active status is received and the ID information is returned. For example, the R(11111111) directive, which removes the tag outside of the silent state, returns its own ID information from the tag.
(2) Rw-data read-write Data: the reader reads and writes to the selected TAB.
(3) Push (data) into the stack: Push data into the stack.
(4) Pop () the stack instruction: the sequence of the previous entry stack.
(5) Select the ID tag.
(6) UnSelect(ID) to select: the selected tag causes it to enter the silent state and does not respond to any instruction from the reader.

3.3 Algorithm Process

The whole improved anti-conflict algorithm's ideas and processes, as shown in Fig. 3.

Assume that there are four tags in the scope of the writer's scope, whose ID information is encoded in eight bits, and its tag ID information is shown in Table 1.

Table 1. The tag ID number

The tag	ID number
Tag 1	(highest) 10111001 (lowest)
Tag 2	(highest) 10011000 (lowest)
Tag 3	(highest) 11011001 (lowest)
Tag 4	(highest) 11011000 (lowest)

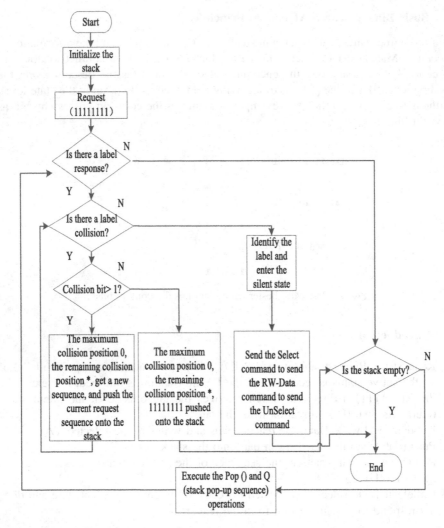

Fig. 3. The framework of the conflict prevention algorithm

Use these four labels to specify the process:

a. The reader sends the R(11111111) instruction, and the status tag returns its own ID. Label at 0, 5 and 6 clashed, received 1xx1100x serial number is 1, according to the rules of algorithm, when conflict digit is greater than 1, the sequence of read/write device receives the highest conflict location to 0 and the rest of the conflict to *, 10*1100*, get the next new send sequence onto the stack, and then sends the current sequence that Push(11111111).

b. Send R(10*1100*) instruction, received the command of all labels, comparing their ID number and request serial number, its scope is at the highest level to the highest * bits of data between bits. Within this range, the same data to a tag to make reply and return with * a corresponding data, namely the tag 1 and 2 is selected, and the tag 1 and 2 data returned 11, 00 respectively, the conflict is still greater than one, then the current sequence onto the stack, which Push(10*1100*), according to the highest position 0 conflict rules, get the next sends the request sequences of R (1001100 *).

c. Send R(1001100*) instruction, only 2 tags TAB is selected and no conflict occurs, read and write device sends the Select(10011000) instructions and RW - Data command, read the label 2 Data, at the end of the operation, send UnSelect (10011000) instruction will be set to silent mode. Because no conflict has occurred, it is possible to determine whether the stack is empty. When the stack is not empty, the stack instruction Pop() is called, and the stack sequence pops up, and the next request sequence, R(10*1100*) is sent.

d. Send R(10*1100*) instruction, 1 is selected, the tag Data returned 11 and there is no conflict, and then to read and write device sends the Select(10111001) instructions and RW - Data operation, upon the completion of the read and write, send UnSelect (10111001) order will tag 2 set of silent state. Because no conflict has occurred, it is possible to determine whether the stack is empty. When the stack is not empty, the stack instruction Pop () is called, and the next request sequence, R(11111111), is sent.

e. Send the R(11111111) instruction, tag 3 and tag 4, and only one conflict occurs, and the reader receives a new sequence of 1101100x. The highest conflict location 0 and the remaining conflicts are *, and the next time the sequence is R(11011000) and Push(11111111).

f. Send R(11011000), the only label 4 response, Select(11011000) to be selected and corresponding RW-Data instructions after the completion of the operation, send UnSelect(11011000) order will tag 4 set of silent state. View the stack not empty, and send the next instruction R(11111111).

g. To send R(11111111), because the tag 1, tag 2, and tag 3 are blocked, only the tag 3 response, the read-writer, reads and writes to it, and the recognition process is over.

3.4   Analysis

In the VC++ simulation platform, the process of transceiver and electronic tags is implemented, and the read-write process is simulated by a large amount of data. Label bits digit, which represeanted by $K = 8$, $K = 16$, $K = 32$ three conditions, the basic dynamic binary, backward binary binary, and improved algorithm to identify the total number of read and write, transfer the total digits are simulated, the simulation results as shown in Figs. 4, 5, 6, 7, 8 and 9.

Figure 4 through Fig. 6: (1) when the tag number is certain, the total number of reads and reads increases as the number of tags increases; (2) the label number, tag number are at the same time, the basic dynamic binary algorithm to identify the total number of binary and almost unanimously, the improved algorithm based on stack and backward binary total number. So the stack based improvement algorithm and the backward binary are better than the basic binary and dynamic binary algorithm.

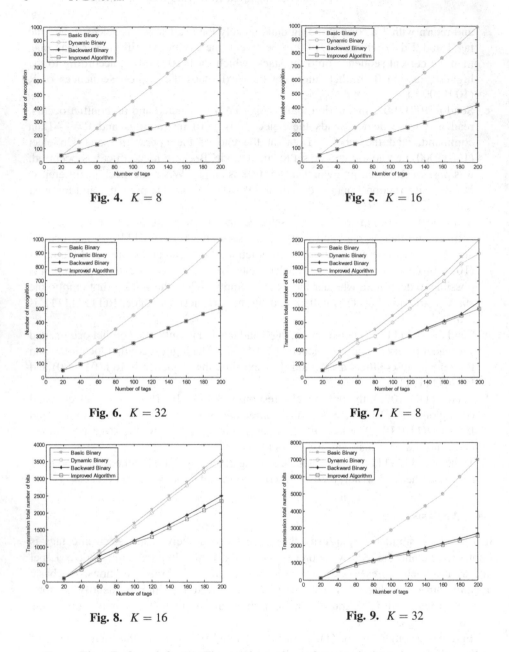

Fig. 4. $K = 8$

Fig. 5. $K = 16$

Fig. 6. $K = 32$

Fig. 7. $K = 8$

Fig. 8. $K = 16$

Fig. 9. $K = 32$

From Figs. 7, 8 and 9: (1) The total number of transmissions increases as the number of tabs increases, as the number of tags increases. (2) When the number of tags is certain, the number of total digits transferred by the four algorithms increases as the number of tabs increases. (3) When the number of tabs and the number of tags is identical, the total number of bits of the stack based improvement algorithm is the smallest.

By Figs. 4, 5, 6, 7, 8 and 9, it is so easy to get: (1) under the same conditions, the improved algorithm and backward binary algorithm based on stack in the identification of the total number of almost the same, but the improved algorithm in the data transmission is far less than backward binary algorithm. So according to the total number of identification number and transmission of the simulation result shows that the improved algorithm is superior to the basic binary, dynamic binary, backward binary algorithm.

4 Monitoring System Design and Testing

4.1 Monitoring System Design

The monitoring center consists of the upper machine software and the database. The top machine software was written in the Visual Studio 2010 development environment with the c# language, using SQL Server 2008 as a database, and its application interface was implemented using ADO through the OLE.db technology. The entire monitoring system structure diagram is shown in Fig. 10.

The monitoring system is established by GPRS communication module, cylinder information management module, user information management module and cylinder information. GPRS communication module is responsible for RFID read-write device collecting information in accordance with the agreement of cylinders packing backwardness to monitor and control system, monitoring system based on protocol analysis data, in every field in the database table. The information about the cylinder

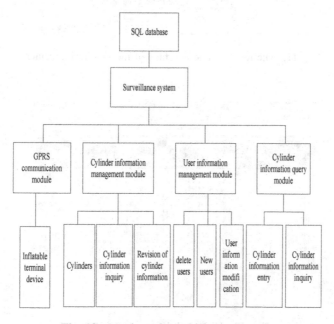

Fig. 10. Monitors the architecture diagram

information in the database includes the information such as the RFID number of the steel bottle, the time information for filling, the time of scrap, the charge record, the filling station number of the cylinder, etc.

4.2   Monitor System Real-Time Data Test

The previous real-time monitoring interface is shown in Fig. 11. Interface display basic information refilling station, shows the number of cylinders filling and filling, query the total gas filling gun number, and the data in the form of real time curve display. Adjust the amount of charge and fill the total amount of gas in real time according to the requirement.

You can query the full history of the filling and display the user's detailed cylinder information, as well as the historical data for a certain period of time. Its historical data query interface is shown in Fig. 12.

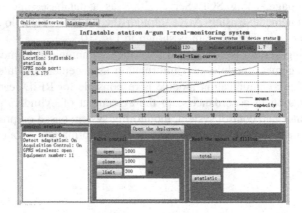

Fig. 11. The top machine interface of the monitoring center

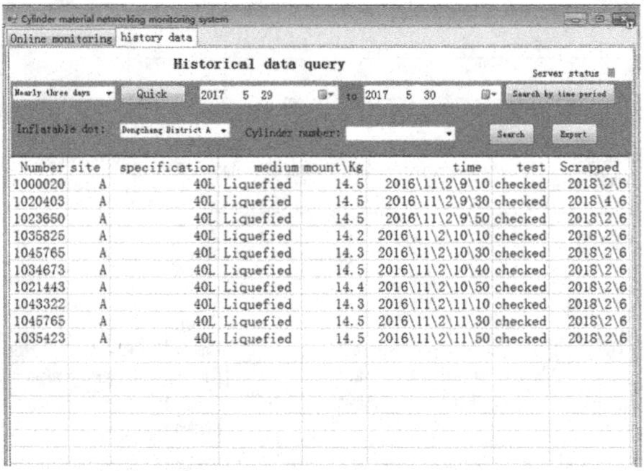

Fig. 12. Historical data query interface

5 Conclusion

An improved algorithm designed to prevent multiple electronic tags from colliding in the identification process is designed based on RFID. According to the result of simulation shows that the improved algorithm is superior to the binary tree search algorithm, decrease the number of collisions and consult for the recognition process of the cylinder, and the cylinder data information upload real-time test, the test results show that the system can realize the cylinder accurately and fast network transmission of information, the administrator can query the cylinder filling data real-time information and historical data, and meet the requirements of the cylinder iot security management.

References

1. Shijie, X.: Design and implementation of the RFID based cylinder management system. Xiamen University (2007)
2. Rong, H.: Application of radio frequency identification technology in cylinder safety traceability. China Autom. Ident. Technol. **02**, 72–74 (2013)
3. Chao, Z., Shouyuan, C., Zengzhen, S., Jian, L., Lijuan, L., Lin, L.: Development of logistics tracking system based on RFID, GPS and GPRS. Electron. Des. Eng. **05**, 147–149 (2015)
4. Jin, T., Yahui, W., Xuemei, F., Shujun, Z., Donghui, C.: Fresh agricultural products cold chain logistics status monitoring information system. J. Jilin Univ. (Eng. Sci.) **06**, 1707–1711 (2015)
5. Lin, L.: Design and implementation of IT - based network operation and maintenance management system. Huazhong Normal University (2012)
6. Jedda, A., Khair, M.G., Hussein, T.M.: Decentralized RFID coverage algorithms using writeable tags. Comput. Netw. **07**, 257–261 (2016)
7. Finkenzeller, K.: Radio Frequency Identification Technology. Electronic Industry Press, Beijing (2006)
8. Hang, Z., Minghao, T., Hui, C.: Improved backplane binary anti-collision algorithm. Comput. Eng. Appl. **25**, 208–211 (2011)
9. Chuiyi, X., Yigang, H., Bing, L., Gefeng, F.: Improvement of dynamic binary tree search algorithm. Comput. Eng. (02), 260–262+265 (2015)
10. Bingcai, C., Dongsheng, X., Guochang, G., Lili, G.: An RFID anti-collision algorithm based on stack storage. Comput. Appl. (06), 1483–1486 (2009)
11. Xue, W., Zhihong, Q., Zhengchao, H., Yiman, L.: Research on RFID anti-collision algorithm based on binary tree. J. Commun. **06**, 49–57 (2014)
12. Bo, F., Jintao, L., Weimin, Z., Ping, Z., Zhenhua, D.: A new anti-collision algorithm for RFID tag identification. J. Autom. **06**, 632–638 (2008)
13. Duroc, Y., Vera, G.A., Martin, J.G.: Modified RSSI technique for the localization of passive UHFRFID tags in LOS channels. Int. J. Microwave Wirel. Technol. **55**, 27–32 (2013)
14. Zhenya, C., Tai, J.: An Ethernet-based anti-trailing elevator access control system. Comput. Eng. Appl. **22**, 232–237 (2016)
15. Hsu, C.-H., Chen, Y.-M., Kang, H.-J.: Performance-effective and low-complexity redundant reader detection in wireless RFID networks. EURASIP J. Wirel. Commun. Netw. **1**, 12–16 (2008)

User-Controlled Encrypted Data Sharing
Model in Cloud Storage

Yuezhong Wu[1,2], Shuhong Chen[3,5(✉)], Guojun Wang[3],
and Changyun Li[2,4]

[1] School of Information Science and Engineering, Central South University,
Changsha 410083, China
yuezhong.wu@163.com
[2] School of Computer Science, Hunan University of Technology,
Zhuzhou 412007, China
lcy469@163.com
[3] School of Computer Science and Educational Software,
Guangzhou University, Guangzhou 510006, China
shuhongchen@gzhu.edu.cn, csgjwang@gmail.com
[4] Intelligent Information Perception and Processing Technology,
Hunan Province Key Laboratory, Zhuzhou 412007, China
[5] School of Computer and Communication, Hunan Institute of Engineering,
Xiangtan 411104, China

Abstract. Cloud storage services provide us convenience for storing and sharing vast amounts of data by its low cost, high scalability and other advantages while it brings out security risks as well. A user-controlled encrypted data sharing model in cloud storage (UESMCS) is put forward hereby. It pre-processes user data to ensure the confidentiality and integrity based on triple encryption scheme of CP-ABE ciphertext access control mechanism and integrity verification. Thus, the reliability and safety for data sharing can be achieved provided the trustworthy third party being brought in. The experimental results show that UESMCS ensures data security in cloud storage services platform and enhances the operational performance for data sharing. The security sharing mechanism perfectly fits the actual cloud storage environment.

Keywords: Cloud storage · Data confidentiality · Ciphertext access control

1 Introduction

A substantial number of people, in their learning, working and living store, share their information through an open network. Cloud storage services, a new form of network application model, emerged and gathered numerous different types of storage devices through the application of software co-functioning to realize external data storage and business access services through using clustering applications, grid technology and distributed file systems and other functions, ensures data security and saves storage space effectively [1–3]. Users can store their data in remote cloud storage stored centers, access on-demand and user-friendly for enterprises to save costs, improve availability and reliability. However, corporate users lost a fundamental physical

© ICST Institute for Computer Sciences, Social Informatics and Telecommunications Engineering 2018
G. Sun and S. Liu (Eds.): ADHIP 2017, LNICST 219, pp. 12–20, 2018.
https://doi.org/10.1007/978-3-319-73317-3_2

control for their data stored in the cloud, which will doubt their confidentiality and integrity of the data, and inevitably raises its concerns about data security and privacy aspects. There are two points about the reason: First, the cloud service providers are facing a wide range of internal and external attacks following malicious enemies deleting or destroying user data. Second, the cloud service providers may be dishonest, they may seek to save their reputation or interests while trying to hide the information of theft or destruction of the data stored in the cloud. Thus, based on the complexity of the dynamic and open cloud storage environment and other features, users rely entirely on untrusted cloud storage providers and other data storage and management factors, how to securely share data in the open cloud storage environments is a problem need to be solved for cloud storage applications.

To have these problems worked out, and to guarantee a safe cloud storage service of data sharing for general users or business users, a secure storage for cloud sharing model is proposed based on CP-ABE technology. It is functioning actively by user and systems with triple encryption to secure user-controlled access for the data in cloud storage.

The main contributions of this paper are:

(1) User-controlled encrypted data. Based on symmetric encryption, CP-ABE and MD5 technology, it is triple encrypted and integrities checking for the data. It promises access permissions of the encrypted data by user-controlled, ensuring the security of data stored and shared in the cloud storage.
(2) Trusted third party. The introduction of a trusted certification authority as a third party authorized purposed to store key information, monitor and audit user access data to achieve security data sharing.

The remainder of this paper is organised as follows: Sect. 2 introduces the terminology and the related work. Symbol description is in Sect. 3, and we also introduce the proposed the data sharing model and application scene. In Sect. 4, we detail the security encryption and algorithm design. In Sect. 5, we present the results and analysis for the experiment. Finally, we conclude in Sect. 6, and briefly touch on the future work.

2 Related Work

Ciphertext access control mechanism is a cloud storage data security approach, which uses the data encryption keys, and achieves the access control target through the control key access permissions. It is an important solution for protecting the privacy of user data in the untrusted server-side scene. CP-ABE uses a set of attributes to represent a user, generates user's private keys in accordance with their properties set, and associates with the ciphertext and the access control policy. The user can decrypt the ciphertext only when the user's private key attributes meet the ciphertext access control policies. It is a suitable ciphertext access control mechanism in cloud storage environments, encrypted data for user groups satisfied certain conditions, and does not encrypted by determining the user groups individually. The authors proposed CP-ABE mechanisms, which are flexible to satisfy the requirements for customizing access policy by the data owner in cloud storage environment [4, 5]; Jung et al. proposed a multi-authorities mechanism for preserving privacy data in cloud storage environments with CP-ABE access control program, which uses globally unique identifier for the user to prevent users conspiracy [6]; The authors proposed the CP-ABE programs for multi-authority in cloud storage to solve the key escrow problem [7, 8]. In this paper, the authors adopt CP-ABE access control policies to encrypt plaintext file encryption key, improving encryption efficiency, while add a trusted third party to solve the key escrow problem.

After obtaining the ciphertext, it also needs to be considered to provide users with data integrity verification. The techniques in this research field include: hash functions, public key cryptography, digital signatures, Merkle hash trees, and so on. The authors proposed some more efficient data integrity verification methods, making use of these methods, the client will be able to verify the integrity of the data being damaged only through exchanging minimal data with the cloud platform [9, 10]; the authors proposed a data integrity dynamic authentication service, which processed blocks and generated verification labels before storing the data, then stored the processed data into the cloud server, and verified the integrity of the data by selecting the method of random sampling [11, 12]. In this paper, the authors adopt MD5 data integrity verification program, which can verify whether data integrity suffered damage through a series of simple digest value.

3 Data Sharing Model

3.1 Secure Sharing Model

Based on the network application scene storing and sharing unstructured documents in the cloud, the authors proposed a user-controlled encrypted data sharing model in cloud storage. There are three-layer architecture in this model: the cloud user layer, the system service layer and the cloud storage layer. Respectively including: the cloud client, the authentication servers (AS), the system servers (SS) and the cloud server provider (CSP), as shown in Fig. 1.

(1) The cloud client is made up by the document owner and user. By operating the application directly, the clients upload document, retrieve document and other resource sharing services. It interacts with the AS and SS. The cloud client has the following functions: ①Creating index for a plaintext uploaded by the user, and encrypting the index keywords; ②Encrypting the plaintext and the key respectively according to encryption keys and user access policy set by the user; ③Packaging ciphertext, and uploading them to the SS; ④Getting the ciphertext and decrypting from the SS, and getting the detection and audits for the encytped data from the AS.

(2) The authentication servers (AS) is used as a trusted third-party. It interacts with the cloud client, stores user information and encryption policy, and provides key services to help users complete the encryption and decryption; It reviews and monitors access relevant data from the SS; It verifies MD5 digest value of documents generated by the cloud client and SS.

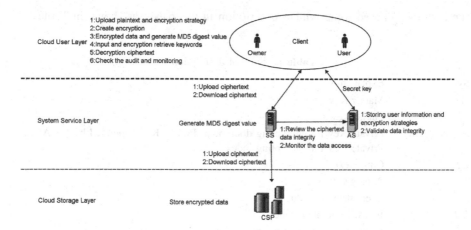

Fig. 1. User-controlled encrypted data sharing model in cloud storage

(3) The system servers (SS) supports the interaction between the cloud client and the cloud server provider. It generates MD5 digest value of ciphertext, uploads the ciphertext to the cloud server provider or downloads ciphertext and returns to the user.

(4) The cloud server provider (CSP) is as a cloud storage layer. It interacts with the main SS, and provides storage services.

3.2   Application Scene

Assumption: the SS and CSP are services to be allowed to purchase, also can belong to the same service provider. We assume that they are honest but curious in this paper. The application scene of this article is network document sharing application in cloud storage [13]. An employee of a company uploaded a confidential document, and set the access policy of this document for the designation users getting. The access structure is as shown in Fig. 2.

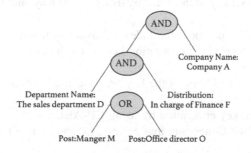

Fig. 2. A user access structure example of CP-ABE

The authors proposed some symbol description in this paper, as shown in Table 1.

Table 1. Symbol description

Symbol	Explanation
MK	Master Key
PK	Public Key
SK_f, SK_c, SK_i	Private Key for encrypting document, Private Key generated by CP-ABE, Private Key for encrypting index
CT	Ciphertext
T	Access structure
S	User attributes value
I, I'	Index, Encryption Index
AES	Symmetric data encryption
DV, DV'	Message digest value by cloud client, Message digest value by the SS
Key, Key'	Query keywords, Encryption Key with SK_i
$File, File', File''$	User file, user encryption file in cloud client, user encryption file from CSP
$Flog$	Log Analysis

4   Encryption

4.1   Security Encryption

Security encryption includes two aspects in this paper: user initiative setting and system active monitoring service.

(1) Users active: It mainly uses the triple encryption scheme based on symmetric encryption and CP-ABE in this stage. It can be better assured that allowing users to submit data to the cloud storage service through this scheme.

(1) Index encryption

①GenerateStrategy()-> SK_i: After completing to create the index for the document uploaded by the user in the cloud client, then it needs to encrypt the index. The AS generates a unified secret key of the index by using UUID way, and return them back to the cloud client.

②$AES(I, SK_i)$-> I': Encrypted the index by using symmetric encryption method after the cloud client obtains the encryption key of the index.

(2) File encryption

$AES(File, SK_f)$-> $File'$: Users set the key SK_f, and used symmetric data encryption their uploading documents.

(3) The symmetric key encryption by using CP-ABE

①Setup->(MK, PK): Generating master key MK and system public key PK;

②Encrypt(*PK, SK$_f$, T*)->*CT*: Used PK and access structures *T* to encrypt plaintext data *SK$_f$*, to generate a ciphertext *CT*;

③KeyGen(*MK, S*)->*SK$_c$*: Used *MK* and user attributes value *S*, to generate the corresponding user private key *SK$_c$*;

④Decrypt(*CT, SK$_c$*)->*SK$_f$*: Used *SKc* to decrypt the private key *CT*, and get plaintext data *SK$_f$*.

(2) System active: This stage is mainly aim at the audit and inspection of the SS by the AS, and verifies integrity of ciphertext data, and obtains available access data by the log analysis.

(1) Ciphertext integrity verification by MD5

①Cloud client and SS respectively generated message digest value for ciphertext by using MD5

a. MD5(*File '*)->*DV*: Cloud client encrypted ciphertext to generate message digest value *DV* by using MD5, and passed AS to store;

b. MD5(*File ''*)->*DV'*: SS encrypted ciphertext to generate digest value *DV'* by using MD5, and passed AS;

②AS verified data integrity

```
If DV=DV'
    return true       // If DV = DV', returns true, the data
is integrity
  Else
    return false      // Otherwise, it returns false, the
data has been tampered with
  End If
```

(2) Log analysis for user access operations

Analytics (Id, Unit, Username, IP, Action, Date)->*Flog*: AS analyzed log of user access operations in SS, and returned the data available to the document owner.

4.2   Algorithm Design

The functions of the ciphertext storage scheme designed in this paper include: (1) Users upload documents in cloud client: uploading files, create plaintext index, set file encryption key and CP-ABE user access policy. (2) The cloud client uses triple encryption with AS: encrypt the file, encrypt file encryption key by using CP-ABE, and encrypt new indexes. (3) SS Uploades ciphertext to CSP: SS uploaded ciphertext to CSP.

The pseudo-code of the ciphertext storage algorithm

```
Input: File, Key
Output: DEK(File, SKf)->File', and MD5(File')->DV
        If DV is null
            CreateIndex(File), and DEK(I, SKi)
        Else
            CP-ABE(SKf)
            Upload(File') and Upload(I')
            MergeIndex(I') and Update the index, then
Upload(File') to CSP
            Record data storage case in AS
        End
        AES(Key, SKi)->Key'
        Search(Key')
        Get the ciphertext File'' and MD5(File'')->DV'
            If DV' = DV
                Decryption with CP-ABE and AES
            Else
                Ciphertext data has been tampered with
            End
            Record available user data in AS, and Return
the available data to the data owner
```

5   Experiment

5.1   Function Realization

To verify the feasibility of the proposed model and its services in this paper, building a Hadoop cluster environment by using four ordinary PC based on CentOS6.5, we conducted experiment in network document sharing application system in cloud storage in the self-developed to test specific application examples.

We use four ordinary PC machine to build the cluster for the network document sharing application system, which includes the servers for system services and a Hadoop cluster. The cluster deploy one machine as SS and AS, and another three units as a Hadoop cluster. The operating system installed on PC is CentOS6.5, Java runtime environment is jdk1.7.0_21, Hadoop is hadoop-2.6, the program development platform is IntelliJ IDEA 13.1.2 and the data base is MySQL5.6.

We input "sales budget" for the query keyword and set a user access structure seeing in Fig. 2 for using CP-ABE. Only the users satisfied both in line with the ciphertext decryption policies and user role permission can get plaintext files in the company A. The results verify the data confidentiality and security of access control, as shown in Table 2.

Table 2. Files list for users access

Attributes	Available file number
Manager in change of finance of sales department	1, 2, 3
Manager of sales department	1, 2
Staff of sales department	1
Staff of personnel department	4

5.2 Security Analysis

Confidentiality and integrity of data is the basis for secure cloud storage. UESMCS adopts triple encryption scheme to encrypt user data to ensure the confidentiality of data, by using CP-ABE for encryption key of document file and symmetric encryption algorithm for document files, indexes and query keywords; it uses the MD5 algorithm to ensure data integrity; it brings in the trusted certification authority as a third party, which can store encryption key and user information, solves the key escrow problem and assures information security. The literatures [4, 10] demonstrated security of encryption algorithm and integrity verification algorithm, ensuring unless they have key information and access control authority, otherwise, the adversary cannot peep, tampering, theft and destruction the user data stored in cloud storage platform, and maintain a secure cloud storage platform.

5.3 Performance Analysis

This experiment uses File effectiveness E as the search results evaluation index. We tested 1000 document files. All searched document files can be decrypt effectively for the user by UESMCS. But mostly searched document files can not be decrypt effectively for the user by Non-UESMCS because of inconformity decryption strategy with CP-ABE and consuming flow with invalid files, E is 29%.

6 Conclusions

By building in the Hadoop cluster environment, using symmetric encryption, CP-ABE and MD5 encryption technology, the authors realized a user-controlled encrypted data sharing prototype system in cloud storage. The experiments show that, the proposed model UESMCS in this paper achieves an efficient and secure for sharing document network resources. Next we improve ciphertext access control algorithm to enhance security for storing and accessing resources by the user, while refine analysis of user access record data to provide more accurate system active services.

Acknowledgements. This paper is funded by the National Natural Science Foundation of China under grant numbers 61502163, 61632009, 61472451 and 61379058; the High Level Talents Program of Higher Education in Guangdong Province under Funding Support Number 2016ZJ01; the Hunan Provincial Natural Science Foundation of China under grant numbers 2016JJ5035, 2016JJ305 and 2015JJ3046; the Scientific Research Project of Hunan Province

Department of Education under grant numbers 16C0481, 14A037 and 16A059; the Project of China packaging federation under Funding Support Number 2014GSZJWT001KT010, 17ZBLWT001KT010; the Scientific Research Project of Zhuzhou City Department of science and technology bureau under grant numbers 2016-68-12.

References

1. Armbrust, M., Fox, A., Griffith, R., Joseph, A.D., Katz, R.H., Konwinski, A., Lee, G., Patterson, D.A., Rabkin, A., Stoica, I., Zaharia, M.: Above the clouds: a berkeley view of cloud computing. University of California, Berkeley, Technical report, USB-EECS- 2009-28 (2009)
2. Liu, Q., Wang, G.J., Wu, J.: Time-based proxy re-encryption scheme for secure data sharing in a cloud environment. Inf. Sci. **258**(10), 355–370 (2014)
3. Feng, D.G., Zhang, M., Zhang, Y., Xu, Z.: Study on cloud computing security. J. Softw. **22**(1), 71–83 (2011)
4. Sun, G.Z., Dong, Y., Li, Y.: CP-ABE based data access control for cloud storage. J. Commun. **32**(7), 146–152 (2011)
5. Zhou, Z.B., Huang, D.J., Wang, Z.J.: Efficient privacy-preserving ciphertext-policy attribute based-encryption and broadcast encryption. IEEE Trans. Comput. **64**(1), 126–138 (2015)
6. Jung, T., Li, X.Y., Wan, Z.G., Wan, M.: Privacy preserving cloud data access with multi-authorities. In: Proceedings IEEE Infocom 2013, vol. 12, no. 11, pp. 2625–2633 (2013)
7. Dong, X., Yu, J.D., Luo, Y., Chen, Y.Y., Xue, G.T., Li, M.L.: Achieving an effective, scalable and privacy-preserving data sharing service in cloud computing. Comput. Secur. **42**(5), 151–164 (2014)
8. Yang, K., Jia, X.H., Ren, K., Zhang, B., Xie, R.T.: DAC-MACS: effective data access control for multiauthority cloud storage systems. IEEE Trans. Inf. Forensics Secur. **8**(11), 1790–1801 (2013)
9. Dodis, Y., Vadhan, S., Wichs, D.: Proofs of retrievability via hardness amplification. In: Reingold, O. (ed.) TCC 2009. LNCS, vol. 5444, pp. 109–127. Springer, Heidelberg (2009). https://doi.org/10.1007/978-3-642-00457-5_8
10. Ateniese, G., Kamara, S., Katz, J.: Proofs of storage from homomorphic identification protocols. In: Matsui, M. (ed.) ASIACRYPT 2009. LNCS, vol. 5912, pp. 319–333. Springer, Heidelberg (2009). https://doi.org/10.1007/978-3-642-10366-7_19
11. Zhu, Y., Hu, H.X., Ahn, G.J., Han, Y.J., Chen, S.M.: Collaborative integrity verification in hybrid clouds. Int. J. Cooper. Inf. Syst. **21**(3), 191–200 (2012)
12. Zhu, Y., Ahn, G.J., Hu, H.X., Yau, S.S., An, H.G., Chen, S.M.: Dynamic audit services for outsourced storages in clouds. IEEE Trans. Serv. Comput. **6**(2), 227–238 (2013)
13. Wu, Y.Z., Liu, Q., Li, C.Y., Wang, G.J.: Research on cloud storage based network document sharing. J. Chin. Comput. Syst. **36**(1), 95–99 (2015)

A Cache Consistency Protocol with Improved Architecture

Qiao Tian, Jingmei Li$^{(\boxtimes)}$, Fangyuan Zheng, and Shuo Zhao

College of Computer Science and Technology,
Harbin Engineering University, Harbin, China
lijingmei@hrbeu.edu.cn

Abstract. The effective cache consistency protocol plays an important role in improving the processor performance. This paper designed an improved architecture of consistency protocol for multi-core environment, adding the D-Cache virtual bus to achieve the point-to-point consistency transaction transmission which avoided the bus idle phenomenon caused by the polling query method that the broadcast consistency transaction must be observed. The experimental results show that the architecture can improve the bus utilization.

Keywords: Consistency protocol · Multi-core environment · Virtual bus

1 Introduction

Cache consistency as one of the hot issues in the processor research, it is a technical problem to be solved that determines whether the multi-core technology can be further developed [1]. Therefore, the design of an effective cache consistency protocol to improve the processor performance is of great significance.

The traditional consistency protocols such as bus listening protocol and directory consistent protocol have their own advantages and disadvantages. Based on deep research and analysis, this thesis realized the point-to-point consistent transaction transmission by adding D-Cache virtual bus in the architecture, which improved the effective utilization of bus.

2 Consistency Protocol Optimization

2.1 The Analysis and Optimization of Bus Listening Protocol

The bus listening protocol [2] uses bus to connect processor private cache with the main memory, propagating consistent transaction messages on the bus in broadcast, so the bus is the ordering point, all nodes connected to the bus can observe the messages in same order.

In bus listening protocol, the polling query method [3] that the broadcast consistent transaction must be observed produces bus idle occupancy. Based on the above shortcomings, the D-Cache virtual bus architecture model is added to improve the equipment utilization. The D-Cache virtual bus structure is shown in Fig. 1.

© ICST Institute for Computer Sciences, Social Informatics and Telecommunications Engineering 2018
G. Sun and S. Liu (Eds.): ADHIP 2017, LNICST 219, pp. 21–24, 2018.
https://doi.org/10.1007/978-3-319-73317-3_3

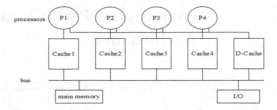

Fig. 1. The system structure with D-Cache virtual bus

The D-Cache virtual bus is used to store directory entry that records data information. By designing and modifying the directory entry, constructing request transaction collection unit, directory entry lookup and update unit and listening response transaction unit, the improved directory entry structure is shown in Fig. 2.

Valid_Bit	Status_Bit	Ident_Bit	Share_Bit	Busy_Bit	Count_Bit

Fig. 2. The directory entry structure

In Fig. 1, raising the location of D-Cache to the private cache of each processor core speeds up the search and reduces the access delay. In Fig. 2, the read and write requests from processor cores are first cached in the request transaction collection unit. The lookup and update unit matches the directory entry in D-Cache with every request, which is identified by Ident_Bit, 1 for hit 0 for miss, after the hit, checking whether Valid_Bit is 1, 1 represents that the entry is valid, otherwise it is invalid; then checking Busy_Bit, 1 represents that the data block is being used, the data block can only be read and wrote until Busy_Bit is 0; when Busy_Bit is 0, the Status_Bit and Share_Bit can get the state of target data and which processor core contains the data in their private cache. When the corresponding read and write requests are met, the entry information will be updated, Count_Bit will be incremented by one, which is used as a reference bit when the data block is replaced, the data block with the smaller number is preferentially replaced.

2.2   Directory Consistency Protocol

The directory protocol uses the directory to store information about the cache data copy, it serves as the ordering point. The requested data is obtained in point-to-point communication after finding the directory. All consistent messages are forwarded through a directory structure. The directory protocol is represented by fully associative directory, limited directory and chained directory [4, 5].

By combining the fully associative directory and chained directory, a new cache consistency protocol of two-level directory structure is proposed. The system architecture is shown in Fig. 3.

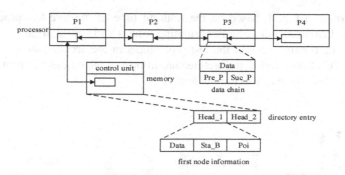

Fig. 3. The two-level directory structure

Each directory entry in main memory consists of Head_1 and Head_2, which consists of Data, Sta_B and Poi. The head node points to first address of shared data. A data chain contains Pre_P and Suc_P is adder to each data block in the private cache.

When a processor core sends read requests, the request first reaches the main memory directory. After matching the data block, the head node sends the data to the processor core, and the private cache of processor is added to the chain of head node.

When a processor core sends write requests, the request also reaches the main memory directory. If Sta_B of head node is the state except "M", firstly, all the data blocks connected to head node should be discarded, then doing write and modifying t Sta_B, finally, the private cache with latest data is connected to the head node. If Sta_B of the head node is "M", it can be wrote directly after transferring the data, and it is not necessary to modify Sta_B, after the completion of write invalidate, the private cache of processor core is connected to the chain which the head node is in.

To sum up, the optimization of cache consistency protocol should from the protocol itself and consider the importance of architecture.

3 Experimental Verification

In order to test the performance of architecture, it is compared with MESI protocol by selecting GEMS system multi-core simulator platform. The thesis uses SPLASH-2 centralized test program LU, Ocean, Radix, FFT and Water-SP to test the performance, as is shown in Table 1.

Table 1. Test procedures

Name of test procedure	Characteristic parameters
LU	512 * 512 matrix
Ocean	258 * 258 ocean
Radix	1M keys, 1024 radix
FFT	256K points
Water	512 molecules

As is shown in Fig. 4, based on the running time of the five test procedures in MESI protocol environment, the unit of running time is CPU cycle. It can be concluded that the average running time of the test procedures in the architecture is 3.84% less than that in MESI. As a result, the architecture improves the efficient utilization of bus and system performance to a certain extent.

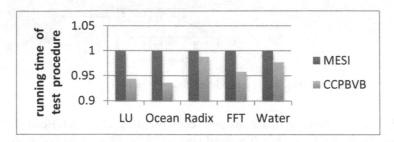

Fig. 4. Comparison of the running time of test procedures

4 Conclusion

Cache consistency problem has become one of the hot issues in multi-core processor research. The paper summarizes the current problem of consistency protocol, the effective use of shared bus resources of bus listening consistency protocol is lack, its broadcast consistent transaction mechanism leads to inadequate use of resources. The directory-based consistency protocol has long access delay. Aimed to the shortcomings of these two consistency protocols, D-Cache virtual bus architecture model in the paper effectively solves the shortcomings of the bus effective utilization. The paper has some shortcomings, which will be further studied and resolved in the following scientific research work.

Acknowledgments. This work is supported by Research on Compiling Technology Based on FPGA Reconfigurable Hybrid System (No. 61003036). The authors would like to thank all of the co-authors of this work.

References

1. Hsia, A., Chen, C.W., Liu, T.J.: Energy-efficient synonym data detection and consistency for virtual cache. Microprocess. Microsyst. **40**(C), 27–44 (2016)
2. Selvin, L.S., Palanichamy, Y.: Push-pull cache consistency mechanism for cooper caching in mobile ad hoc environments. **24**(5), 3459–3470 (2016)
3. Guo, S., Wang, H., et al.: Hierarchical cache directory for CMP. J. Comput. Sci. Technol. **25**(2), 246–256 (2010)
4. Li, G.: Research on Cache Consistency Model in On-chip Multiprocessor Architecture. University of Science and Technology of China, pp. 57–65 (2013)
5. Shu, J., Lu, Y., Zhang, J., et al.: Research study of storage system technology based on nonvolatile memory. Sci. Technol. Rev. (14) (2016)

A Fast Frequency Switching Algorithm for Multi-parameter Fusion Decision Mechanism

Kaizhi Peng[✉], Binbin Xu, Rui Fu, and Xiaoling Liu

Wuhan Maritime Communication Research Institute, Wuhan 430079, China
pengkz722@163.com, 490366845@qq.com,
522721238@qq.com, lain_lxl@163.com

Abstract. In order to improve the transmission performance of the cognitive users in the tactical wireless network of warship formations, this paper we focus on the modeling technique and performance analysis for a fast frequency switching algorithm for Multi-parameter fusion decision. By developing a Multi-parameter fusion decision model, the closure expression of the fast frequency switching delay is derived, then the combined effects of the arrival rates of the primary users' connections and the arrival rates of the secondary users' connections on the cumulative handoff delay distribution is simulated. Based on the analytical results, suitable ship scheduling mechanism can be designed.

Keywords: Cognitive radio · Spectrum handoff · Reactive-sensing mechanism

1 Introduction

Cognitive radio (CR) can improve spectrum efficiency by allowing secondary users to temporarily access primary users' unused licensed spectrum [1–3]. However, due to the spectrum-varying nature of CR network, it is necessary to consider not only the access control and operation, but also the handoff timing, the switching procedure and the target channel should be considered, so the continuity and stability of the service transmission of the cognitive user after spectrum switching is ensured.

Both reactive [4–6] and proactive [7, 8] handoff algorithms are studied in existing works with suitable target channel selection (T.C.S.) procedures. When the primary users' businesses are busy, the pre-designed channels can't be used, the secondary users need to switch channels frequently, so the handoff delay increased, in this situation, the reactive is a better choice. If the arrival rates of the primary users' are small, the secondary user doesn't need to spend time to detect the channel, so the proactive is a better choice. The principle of ship communication is to ensure the reliability of communication on the basis of effectiveness, the goal of this paper is to develop a Multi-parameter fusion decision model, derive the closure expression of the fast frequency switching delay and design a suitable ship communication scheduling mechanism.

G. Sun and S. Liu (Eds.): ADHIP 2017, LNICST 219, pp. 25–32, 2018.
https://doi.org/10.1007/978-3-319-73317-3_4

2 System Model

2.1 System Framework

In this paper, the system framework is shown in Fig. 1, the system is consisting of the primary users and the secondary users. The primary users have the preemptive priority to access channels, while the secondary users have the low-priority to access the unused licensed spectrum of the primary users. In order to ensure the reliability of ship communication, and reduce the spectrum handoff delay, we considers the secondary users are equipped with two antennas, One is used for data and control message transmission and the other is used for idle channel detection, so the availability of the switching channel is ensured. In order to effectively short the extended data delivery time under various traffic arrival rates and service time as well as sensing time, we design an intelligent spectrum selection algorithm.

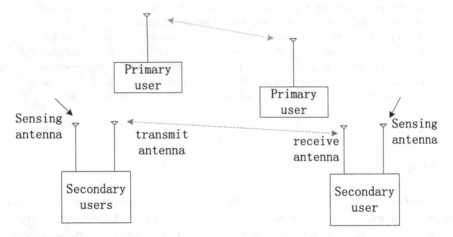

Fig. 1. System framework.

2.2 Multi-parameter Fusion Decision

Compared with two major types of spectrum handoff schemes, Multi-parameter fusion decision reduces the detection time before the data transmission, and then improves the availability of the selected frequencies. The process of the Multi-parameter fusion decision algorithm is as follows (Fig. 2).

The weighted two-threshold spectrum detection algorithm is used to detect whether an primary user arrives. Environment noise module is used to specify local noise detection for channel without service [9]. Primary user occupy channel for a specified time module is used to detect the primary user channel usage in a specified channel and specified time. Secondary user receiver data reception module is used to record the feedback of the channel quality of receiver. Intelligent spectrum selection mechanism module is used to extract the frequency according the different weight factors. Consider various factors to ensure the availability of frequency; the specific formula is as follows:

$$f = f_\varepsilon, \varepsilon = (\max[(\alpha_1 + \beta_1 + \gamma_1 + \theta_1), \ldots (\alpha_M + \beta_M + \gamma_M + \theta_M)]) .\qquad(1)$$

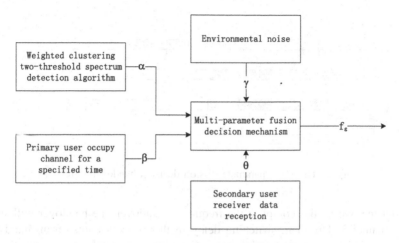

Fig. 2. The Multi-parameter fusion decision algorithm

2.3 Handoff Progress

Spectrum handoff occurs when the primary customers appear in the channel occupied by the secondary customers. In this situation, the secondary customer shall immediately handoff (transit) from the current channel to the target channel. The parameters related to the switching delay are included: (1) the arrival rates and the business duration of the primary user; (2) the arrival rates and the business duration of the secondary user; (3) the duration of the availability of the switching channel. The switching delay consists of the handshaking time and the channel switching time. There is no fixed channel for secondary users, in order to ensure the successful handshake of the secondary user in the initial stage, this paper adopts the common channel way to realize the first handshake of the secondary user. Figure 3 shows an example of Multi-parameter fusion decision spectrum handoff process:

(1) In the beginning, according to the multi-parameter frequency selection algorithm, the secondary users use the historical data and the real-time detection result to select the service initiation frequency, and call the secondary user of the communication object on the common channel, and then complete the first round of communication handshake. For simplicity, assume that the secondary user service is subject to the Poisson distribution, the mean rate is $\lambda_s^{(1)}$, and the service time mean is $E(X_s^1)$.

(2) As shown in Fig. 3, when the secondary user on the channel 1 business is ongoing, while the authorized user, who has the absolutely channel ownership, initiate business. The secondary user detects that the authorized user arrives, the secondary user needs to immediately activate the frequency switching mechanism.

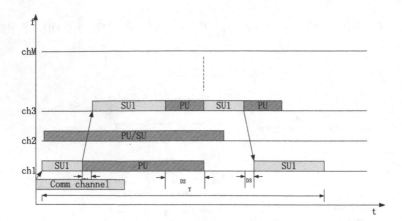

Fig. 3. The Multi-parameter fusion decision handoff progress

After the two parties complete the frequency handover, the handover will switch to channel 3. The main switching delay in this process comes from handshake time and frequency conversion time. For simplicity analysis, assume that the authorized user arrival probability is consistent with the Poisson distribution with mean rates $\lambda_p^{(1)}$ and the business duration is met with mean $E(X_p^1)$.

(3) During the duration of the authorized user service, as shown in Fig. 3, the secondary user can not select the available frequency according to the multi-parameter frequency selection algorithm. The secondary user will remain on channel 3 and immediately start the channel state detection algorithm. When the idle Channel is found, the secondary user will immediately start the frequency switching mechanism to determine whether to switch to new available frequency or not. If the idle channel is of good quality and the idle duration is long, it will switch to the new free channel. Otherwise, the original channel will be maintained until the authorized user has completed the communication.

(4) The above process will continue until the secondary user communication is complete. While after the communication finished, the secondary user will return to the common channel, waiting for the next service.

3   Analysis of Secondary Users' Extended Data Delivery Time

As shown in Fig. 3, the total duration of the secondary user transmission (denoted by ST^k) includes the length of the transmission time (denoted by X_s^k) and the accumulated time of the service (denoted by D^k). The accumulated time is composed of the frequency switching duration and the waiting for the user service time. The formula is shown below:

$$E[ST^k] = E[X_s^k] + E[D^k] .$$ (2)

In order to calculate the accumulated time of the service (denoted by D^k). On the basis of Fig. 3, The proposed Multi-parameter fusion decision handoff progress is established as an L-order state transition diagram, as shown in Fig. 4. Note that the stage i is the set of all possible states at the ith interruption, and the chk is the channel which the secondary user is select to switch, and the end state indicates the secondary user communication ends.

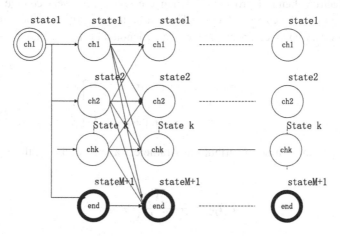

Fig. 4. L-order state transition diagram model

As Fig. 4 shows, for simplified calculations, the secondary user communication duration is consistent with Poisson distribution, the transition probability from states i to j is $P_{i,j}$, and the transition cost from states i to j is $C_{i,j}$. when the target channel is $s_n = (s_1, s_2, \ldots, s_n)$, which default channel is channel $s_0 = k$, the state transition path in Multi-parameter parameter model can be regarded as $(s_0 \rightarrow s_1 \rightarrow s_2 \rightarrow s_3 \rightarrow \cdots \rightarrow s_n \rightarrow M+1)$, so the cumulative handoff delay can be treated as calculating the cumulative transition cost overall possible state transition paths. The specific formula as follows:

$$E[D^k] = \sum_{n=1}^{L} \sum_{\forall s_n \in \Omega^n} [(P_{s_n,M+1} \prod_{i=0}^{n-1} P_{s_i,s_{i+1}})(C_{s_n,M+1} + \sum_{i=0}^{n-1} C_{s_i,s_{i+1}})] ,$$ (3)

where $\Omega = \{1, 2, \cdots, M\}$.

According to Fig. 3, the secondary user initiates a service on channel 3, and then the primary user arrives at probability p. when the primary user arrives, the secondary user will change its channel according to the proposed frequency selection algorithm. As shown is Fig. 3, there is no available channel, so the secondary user will state on channel 3 until the primary user service is completed. Then, the primary user arrives again, the frequency selection algorithm proposes to switch to channel 1 and finally complete the communication process on channel 1. Hence, the state transition probability matrix of the Multi-parameter fusion decision model can be expressed as follows:

$$P = \begin{bmatrix} p^{(1)}\rho^{(3)} & p^{(1)}(1 - \rho^{(3)}) & 1 - p^{(1)} \\ 0 & 0 & 0 \\ p^3(1 - \rho^{(1)}) & p^{(3)}\rho^{(1)} & 1 - p^{(3)} \end{bmatrix}. \tag{4}$$

The cumulative transition cost is composed of the frequency switching duration and the waiting for the user service time. σ_c and σ_s are the total processing time for executing spectrum handoff procedures when the secondary users change to another channel and stay on the current channel. The duration resulting from the transmissions of multiple primary connections at channel k and denoted by Y_p^1. Then, we can have $C_{i,j}$ as follows:

$$C_{i,j} = \begin{bmatrix} \sigma_s + E[Y_p^1] & \sigma_c & 0 \\ 0 & 0 & 0 \\ \sigma_c & \sigma_s + E[Y_p^3] & 0 \end{bmatrix}. \tag{5}$$

According to the Poisson distribution parameters assumed above, the $E[Y_p]$ can be expressed as:

$$E[Y_p] = \frac{E[X_p]}{1 - \lambda_p E[X_p]}. \tag{6}$$

Then

$$p = \frac{\lambda_p}{\lambda_p + \mu_s}. \tag{7}$$

$$\rho = \lambda_p E[X_p] + \frac{\lambda_s}{\lambda_p + \mu_s}\left(1 + \frac{\lambda_p}{\mu_s}\right). \tag{8}$$

According to (3)–(8), the closed-form expression for $E[D^k]$ can be expressed as follows

$$E[D] = \frac{\lambda_p[\sigma_s\mu_s + (E[X_p])^2\lambda_p\mu_s + E[X_p](\lambda_s - \sigma_c\lambda_p\mu_s)]}{(1 - \lambda_p E[X_p])\mu_s^2}. \tag{9}$$

4 Numerical Results

Figure 5 simulates the impact of the primary user arrival probability and the business duration on the cumulative delay of the secondary user transmission. Figure 5 shows the cumulative time of the secondary user increases as the arrive probability λ_p of the primary user increases. The main reason is that the increase in the probability of primary users to arrive, it will lead to secondary user to stop service, and to enable the frequency switch mechanism to determine whether to switch frequency or not. At the same time, it also simulates the influence of the duration of primary user $E[X_p]$ on the cumulative delay of the secondary user. The longer the primary user service time is, the longer the cumulative delay of the secondary users is, due to the increase of the channel occupied by the primary user, and so the secondary users will spend more time to wait or frequently enable the channel selection mechanism.

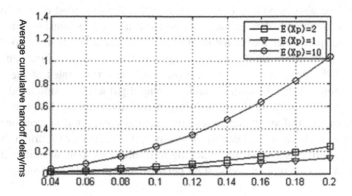

Fig. 5. Average cumulative handoff delay

Figure 6 shows the combined effects of the arrival rates of the primary users' connections and the arrival rates of the secondary users' connections on the cumulative

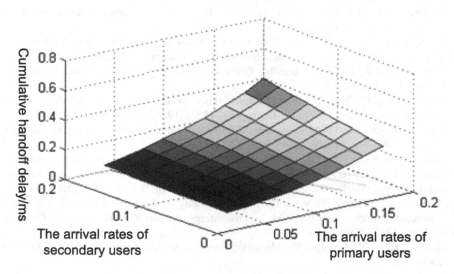

Fig. 6. Cumulative handoff delay

handoff delay distribution. It can be seen from Fig. 5 that the behavior of the primary user' communication has a great influence on the secondary users' performance, with the increase of the primary users' arrival rates, the cumulative handoff delay increase, which is mainly caused by the switching channel cost of the secondary user. The analytical results provide the useful insight for the effect of increasing the efficient time on the transmission performance of the secondary users.

5 Conclusions

In this paper, we also provide a framework to short the extended data delivery time under various traffic arrival rates and service time as well as sensing time. Then, a Multi-parameter parameter model for modeling the connections is developed, and the closed-form expression for handoff delay is expressed, at last the combined effects of the arrival rates of the primary users' connections and the arrival rates of the secondary users' connections on the cumulative handoff delay distribution is simulated. Based on the analytical results, suitable ship scheduling mechanism can be designed. However, the influence of spectral switching on channel capacity gain and system performance degradation has not been studied deeply. Therefore, it is necessary to further explore the influence of cognitive user spectrum switching in future work to achieve the relationship between channel capacity gain and system performance degradation balance.

References

1. Mitola III, J., Maguire, G.Q.: Cognitive radio: making software radios more personal. IEEE Pers. Commun. **6**, 3–18 (1999)
2. Mitola, J.: Cognitive Radio: An integrated Agent Architecture for Software Defined Radio (Ph.D. dissertation). Royal Institute of Technology, Sweden (2002)
3. Haykin, S.: Cognitive radio: brain-empowered wireless communications. IEEE J. Sel. Areas Commun. **23**, 201–220 (2005)
4. Kong, X., Petre, P., Matic, R., Gilbert, A.C., Strauss, M.J.: An analog-to-information converter for wideband signals using a time encoding machine. In: Digital Signal Processing Workshop and IEEE Signal Processing Education Workshop (DSP/SPE), Sedona, AZ, vol. 47, pp. 414–419 (2011)
5. Ning, Z., Song, Q., Peng, Y., Zhang, B.: Interference-aware spectrum sensing mechanisms in cognitive radio networks. Comput. Electr. Eng. **42**(C), 193–206 (2015)
6. Wang, L.: Optimization of MAC-layer multi-user cooperative spectrum sensing mechanism in cognitive radio. Sig. Process. **27**(4), 508–513 (2011)
7. Sasirekha, G.V.K., Bapat, J.: Adaptive model based on proactive spectrum sensing for Emergency Cognitive Ad hoc Networks. In: International ICST Conference on Cognitive Radio Oriented Wireless Networks and Communications, pp. 89–94. IEEE (2012)
8. Chamberl, J.F., Veercivalli, V.V.: The impact of fading on decentralized detection in power constrained wireless sensor networks. In: Proceedings of IEEE ICASSP, Montreal, Cananda, pp. 1286–1290 (2010)
9. Charles Clancy, T., Arbaugh, W.: Measuring interference temperature model. In: IEEE ISIT (2006)

Offline Chinese Signature Verification Based on AlexNet

Cui Wencheng, Guo Xiaopeng$^{(\boxtimes)}$, Shao Hong, and Zou Limin

School of Information Science and Engineering, Shenyang University of
Technology, Shenyang 110870, China
wayneguo279@gmail.com

Abstract. In order to break the limitation of traditional pattern recognition in offline Chinese signature verification, the method of applying machine learning is put forward. First, the offline Chinese signature data set is pre-processed, include removing noises, binarization and normalization. Then the architecture and implementation methods of AlexNet are proposed. The experimental results show the average accuracy of classification has been up to 99.77%, and verification rate is 87.5%.

Keywords: AlexNet · Convolution neural network
Offline signature verification · Writer-dependent

1 Introduction

Biological characteristics of the human body is inherent in the physiological characteristics or behavioral characteristics, physiological characteristics including fingerprints, palm, face, iris, finger vein, etc., behavioral characteristics including gait, sound, handwriting and so on. Signature has a long history as a representative of the individual's identity, and has been widely used in financial and legal industries. Offline signature verification is for static image recognition.

In 2012, Khalajzadeh used convolution neural network (CNN) to verify signatures for Persian [1]. Based on the LeNet-5 architecture, a total of 176 real signatures and a certain number of forged signatures were trained and tested. There were 22 signers. The experimental results showed the accuracy was 99.86%.

Our paper puts forward a method of applying the convolution neural network algorithm AlexNet to recognize offline Chinese signature. Based on the AlexNet, we designed the experimental program. First, preprocessing the signature image, and then, train the writer-dependent classification of real signatures and forged signatures for each signer [2]. Finally, the trained network is used to identify the test set.

2 Pre-processing

The phrase "garbage in, garbage out" is the best summary of data mining and machine learning projects. Data pre-processing is important for image processing. The pre-processing methods include median filtering, OTSU binarization and normalization.

© ICST Institute for Computer Sciences, Social Informatics and Telecommunications Engineering 2018
G. Sun and S. Liu (Eds.): ADHIP 2017, LNICST 219, pp. 33–37, 2018.
https://doi.org/10.1007/978-3-319-73317-3_5

The median filter is a nonlinear smoothing technique, often used to remove noise from an image or signal. It replaces the gray value of each pixel with the median value in its adjacent region. The binarized operation of the filtered signature image is aimed at changing the original image to a purely 'black and white' image with only the pixel value of 0 or 255. The binarization process can significantly reduce the amount of data processing. The size normalization principle is to identity the upper and lower, left and right boundaries of the signature image, and then delete the blanks outside the border and set all images sizes to 227 × 227. Figure 1 is the final pre-processing signature image.

Fig. 1. Final pre-processing signature image.

3   CNN and AlexNet Architecture

In machine learning, a CNN is a feedforward neural network. It performs excellently in large image processing. It is inspired by the cat's cortical structure. The special structure of the convolutional neural network is shared by its weight. It has excellent performance in speech recognition and image processing, and its layout is closer to the actual biological neural network. Their error rate only got 0.23% on the MNIST (Modified National Institute of Standards and Technology) database [3].

AlexNet is designed by Alex Krizhevsky to participate in the 2012 ImageNet Large Scale Visual Recognition Challenge. AlexNet contained only 8 layers, first 5 were convolutional layers, and the next three were fully connected layers. It is trained to classify the LSVRC-2010 ImageNet training set which included 1.3 million high-resolution images, the set are classified into 1000 classes. The structure of AlexNet is shown in Table 1. The first convolutional layer filters the $N \times 227 \times 227 \times 3$ input image, it has 96 kernels, the kernel size is $11 \times 11 \times 3$ size and with a 4 pixels stride. LRN means Local Response Normalization, pool size is 3×3 with a strides of 2 pixels. The second convolutional layer has 256 kernels, its kernel size is $5 \times 5 \times 48$. The third and fourth convolutional layers behind without LRN. The third convolutional layer has 384 kernels, the kernel size is $3 \times 3 \times 256$. While the fourth convolutional layer has 384 kernels, its kernel size is $3 \times 3 \times 192$, and the fifth convolutional layer has 256 kernels, its kernel size also is $3 \times 3 \times 192$. However, the fifth convolutional layer behind with LRN. The first two fully-connected layers have 4096 neurons. Dropout can be more effective to prevent the neural network over-fitting. The last fully-connected layer plus the classifier softmax, the input signature images are divided into two categories [4]. In our experiments, there are a total of 40 signers, each signer has 36 real and 36 forged signature images. Experiments are divided into training and test. Each participant in the training set has 25 real and 25 forged

Table 1. AlexNet structure.

Structure	Size	Other parameters
Input	$N \times 227 \times 227 \times 3$	–
Convolution1	$11 \times 11 \times 3$	96 kernels, Strides = 4
LRN	3×3	Strides = 2
Convolution2	$5 \times 5 \times 48$	256 kernels, Strides = 1
LRN	3×3	Strides = 2
Convolution3	$3 \times 3 \times 256$	384 kernels, Strides = 1
Convolution4	$3 \times 3 \times 192$	384 kernels, Strides = 1
Convolution5	$3 \times 3 \times 192$	256 kernels, Strides = 1
LRN	3×3	Strides = 2^3
Fully-connected1 + dropout	4096	P = 0.5
Fully-connected2 + dropout	4096	P = 0.5
Fully-connected3 + softmax	M	–

signatures. Test set for each signer has 11 real and 11 forged signatures. For each signer, we have a writer-dependent network training, so in the training phase, N in Table 1 is 50 and the test phase N is 22. Whether the test or training, M is 2.

4   Experiment

4.1   Data Set

Domestic researchers are building their own data sets, because there is no public Chinese signature data set. We convene 20 volunteers with stable mentality to set up signature dataset. At the same time, an open Chinese offline signature data set SigComp2011 was provided at the International Document Analysis and Recognition Conference (ICDAR) in 2011 [5], it includes 20 Chinese signers. Together with the SigComp2011, a total of 2880 Chinese signature images are available for experiment.

4.2   Offline Chinese Signature Verification Based on AlexNet

The experimental equipment of this paper is our laboratory equipped desktop, equipped with ubuntu 16.04 system, the Linux configuration of the CPU version of Tensorflow 1.0.0. The machine's CPU parameters are 8-core Intel i7-7700K, 4.2 GHz. Based on the structure of AlexNet, TensorFlow is used to train real signature and forged signature classification. For each signer, the writer-dependent network training took about 40 min, the average accuracy of classification for 40 signers has been up to 99.77%.

After the network training is completed, the trained network is called to identify test set. Each time a signature image is input for network identification, and the network recognizes the authenticity of the image, and respectively output 'yes' or 'no', 'yes' on behalf the real signature, while 'no' stands for forged signature. Table 2 is the result of accuracy (ACC), false accept rate (FAR) and false rejection rate (FRR) of offline Chinese signature verification based on AlexNet.

Table 2. AlexNet verification result.

ACC	FAR	FRR
87.5%	7.5%	5.0%

4.3 Comparison of Offline Signature Verification Methods

We compare the performance of AlexNet with traditional pattern recognition method using in offline Chinese signature verification. The results are shown in Table 3, it includes accuracy and error rate (ERR).

5 Conclusion

The problem to be solved of this paper is how to apply AlexNet to recognize offline Chinese signature. We have done the offline Chinese signature verification experiment on Tensorflow, its Google's open source machine learning library.

The experimental results show that AlexNet's network training classification average accuracy is 99.77%. Through Table 3, offline Chinese signature verification based on AlexNet is better than SVM methods. The accuracy of AlexNet's verification is 87.5%. Compared with the pattern recognition method, although the accuracy is no better than other traditional methods, but this is a new method. The next step is to test the algorithm on the Caltech (foreign) signature dataset and continue to optimize the approach to improve the accuracy.

Table 3. Comparison offline Chinese signature verification methods.

Method	ACC	ERR
Bayesian [6]	89%	11%
KNN [6]	92.5%	7.5%
SVM [7]	83.7%	16.3%
BP Neural Network [8]	90.0%	10.0%
This article proposed AlexNet	87.5%	12.5%

References

1. Khalajzadeh, H., Mansouri, M., Teshnehlab, M.: Persian signature verification using convolutional neural networks. In: International Conference on Pattern Recognition, pp. 851–854. IEEE Press (2000)
2. Hafemann, L.G., Sabourin, R., Oliveira, L.S.: Analyzing features learned for offline signature verification using Deep CNNs. In: International Conference on Pattern Recognition (ICPR), pp. 2389–2994. IEEE Press (2016)
3. Ciregan, D., Meier, U., Schmidhuber, J.: Multi-column deep neural networks for image classification. In: International Conference on Computer Vision and Pattern Recognition (CVPR), pp. 3642–3649. IEEE Press (2012)

4. Krizhevsky, A., Sutskever, I., Hinton, G.E.: ImageNet classification with deep convolutional neural networks. In: International Conference on Neural Information Processing Systems, pp. 1097–1105. IEEE Press (2012)
5. Liwicki, M., et al: Signature verification competition for online and offline skilled forgeries (sigcomp2011). In: International Conference on Document Analysis and Recognition (ICDAR), pp. 1480–1484. IEEE Press (2011)
6. Song, Y.: Research on offline handwritten signature recognition based on Bayes decision theory. Tianjin Normal University (2010)
7. Shasha, X., Jincheng, W., Xiaochu, Q.: Offline Chinese signature verification based on improved support vector machine. J. Electron. Des. Eng. **20**, 17–19 (2012)
8. Arora, A., Choubey, A.S.: Offline signature verification and recognition using neural network. J. Int. Sci. Res. **2**, 196–200 (2013)

An Optimized Method for Turbocharged Diesel Engine EGR Performance Evaluation

Xiang-huan Zu, Chuan-lei Yang$^{(\boxtimes)}$, He-chun Wang,
and Yin-yan Wang

College of Power and Energy Engineering, Harbin Engineering University,
Harbin 150001, China
zuhuan0815@163.com,
{yangchuanlei,wanghechun}@hrbeu.edu.cn,
wyyzxm@sina.com

Abstract. The purpose of this study is to propose a multi-objective decision making optimization method based on subjective and objective empowerment optimization. This paper intend to achieve the evaluation of turbocharged diesel engine EGR performance. First, the main diesel engine EGR parameters were selected as decision target and corresponding experimental data are used as effect sample matrix to establish the initial multi-objective-making model. The characteristics and optimization requirements of turbocharged diesel engine EGR are considered. Secondly, the expert scoring, grey correlation analysis are used to solve the optimized weight vector. Finally, the optimized decision-making model was established to explore the intrinsic objective relationship of EGR evaluation index parameters and give the best evaluation and optimal decision. The results show that the optimized method can successfully solve the turbocharged diesel engine EGR performance evaluation and optimal decision problem, which can provides theoretical support and reference for the further optimization of EGR.

Keywords: Data mining · Performance evaluation · Diesel engine
Exhaust gas recirculation · Optimized model

1 Introduction

As one of the effective ways to reduce NO_X pollutants emissions, exhaust gas recirculation (EGR) has been widely used in marine turbocharged diesel engines. The main process is to introduce a part of exhaust gas into the intake pipe, mixed with fresh air and enter the cylinder to re-enter the combustion process [1–3]. The key to the EGR technology is to introduce enough exhaust gas into the intake pipe and give the best EGR rate according to the different operating conditions of the engine [4, 5]. Due to the effect of different EGR rates on diesel engine performance and emissions is different. Therefore, the power, economy and emission performance of diesel engine must be taken into account in determining the optimal EGR rate. The basic principle of EGR is to reduce NO_X emissions as much as possible, while have a minimal impact of other pollutants emissions.

© ICST Institute for Computer Sciences, Social Informatics and Telecommunications Engineering 2018
G. Sun and S. Liu (Eds.): ADHIP 2017, LNICST 219, pp. 38–49, 2018.
https://doi.org/10.1007/978-3-319-73317-3_6

At present, the general approach is to obtain the operating parameters of the engine through a large number of tests, then analyzing the test results synthetically to specify the corresponding determination principle. Such as Shuai [4], Zhang [5], taking 13 working point particles do not exceed the principle of the original machine. In the determination of the best EGR rate. Because of the subjective judgment and the purpose of the decision-maker is different, the current decision-making principles are not the same. There is a common shortcomings that is subjective factors are too strong and lack a clear theoretical support and guidance. Therefore, it is inevitable that the subjective judgment will bring the error and affect the final selection result. Obviously the EGR performance evaluation can be seen as a typical multi-objective decision-making problems. Therefore, the multi-objective grey situation decision-making method is used. As an important branch of grey theory which is a classic artificial intelligence method, the multi-objective grey situation decision making theory has unique advantages in decision-making problems for selecting the best scheme for a number of programs [6], which has been widely used in aerospace, electronic and other fields because of its low computational complexity and high recognition effect [7–12]. Currently, more and more scholars have considered to seek the optimization of decision-making model [11–13], to improve the reliability of decision-making results, However, different optimization methods are only suitable for some specific issues. By reviewing the relevant information, we have not found the clear literature on the EGR performance evaluation and the optimal EGR rate of the turbocharged diesel engine, and the related theoretical guidance is also less, so it is necessary to explore the subject of this study.

In summary, in order to solve the EGR performance evaluation and optimal decision-making of the turbocharged diesel engine, an optimized multi-objective grey situation decision-making method is proposed. This method makes use of the advantages of traditional grey decision, grey relational analysis, while combining the characteristics and optimization requirements of diesel engine EGR performance, which can explore the intrinsic association between different EGR performance parameters and the ranking of different EGR schemes can be obtained. The results show the this approach can successfully applied to EGR performance evaluation problem and the evaluation results is reasonable, Which has certain theoretical reference and guidance significance for the optimization of turbocharged diesel engine EGR performance.

2 Preliminary Knowledge

2.1 Multi-objective Grey Decision-Making

The main components of the traditional multi-objective grey decision model include event set, strategy set, situation set, decision goal and decision weight.

First, Construct the corresponding set of situations according to the event set and the strategy set. Assume that $A = \{a_1, a_2 \cdots a_n\}$ is the event set, the strategy set is $B = \{b_1, b_2 \cdots b_m\}$, the situation set is $s = \{s_{ij} = (a_i, b_j) \mid a_i \in A, b_j \in B\}$, and the $u_{ij}^{(k)} (i = 1, 2 \cdots, n; j = 1, 2, \cdots m)$ is the effect sample value of the situation under the target.

Secondly, Choose targets and each target needs to determine its effectiveness measure:

$$r_{ij}^{(k)} = \frac{u_{ij}^{(k)}}{\max_i \max_j \{u_{ij}^{(k)}\}} \tag{1}$$

called upper effect measure, which mainly used to measure the degree of albino value deviated from the maximum whitening value;

$$r_{ij}^{(k)} = \frac{\min_i \min_j \{u_{ij}^{(k)}\}}{u_{ij}^{(k)}} \tag{2}$$

called lower effect measure, which mainly for the degree of albino value deviation from the lower limit;

$$r_{ij}^{(k)} = \frac{u_{i_0 j_0}^{(k)}}{u_{i_0 j_0}^{(k)} + \left| u_{ij}^{(k)} - u_{i_0 j_0}^{(k)} \right|} \tag{3}$$

called medium effect measure, where $u_{i_0 j_0}^{(k)}$ is the moderate effect of the specified effect under the target.

These three measures are applicable to different occasions: If you want the situation the bigger the better, you can use the upper effect measure; if you want the smaller the better the loss of the situation, then the lower effect measure can be chose, if you want the effect to be near a specified value, use a medium effect measure.

Thirdly, solve the consistent effect measure matrix of situation set according to the effect measure of each target.

$$R^{(k)} = (r_{ij}^{(k)}) = \begin{bmatrix} r_{11}^{(k)} & r_{12}^{(k)} & \cdots & r_{1m}^{(k)} \\ r_{21}^{(k)} & r_{22}^{(k)} & \cdots & r_{2m}^{(k)} \\ \cdots & \cdots & \cdots & \cdots \\ r_{n1}^{(k)} & r_{n2}^{(k)} & \cdots & r_{nm}^{(k)} \end{bmatrix} \tag{4}$$

where, $r_{ij}^k = (r_{ij}^{(1)}, r_{ij}^{(2)}, \ldots, r_{ij}^{(3)})$ is called the consistent effect measure vector of situation s_{ij} under target k.

The fourth step is to Establish decision weight $\eta_k (k = 1, 2, \cdots s)$, where $\sum_{k=1}^{s} \eta_k = 1$ and solve integrated effect measure r_{ij} and integrated effect measure matrix of situation s_{ij}

$$r_{ij} = \sum_{k=1}^{s} \eta_k \bullet r_{ij}^{(k)} \tag{5}$$

$$R = (r_{ij}) = \begin{bmatrix} r_{11} & r_{12} & \cdots & r_{1m} \\ r_{21} & r_{22} & \cdots & r_{2m} \\ \cdots & \cdots & \cdots & \cdots \\ r_{n1} & r_{n2} & \cdots & r_{nm} \end{bmatrix} \tag{6}$$

At last, if $\max\limits_{1 \le j \le m}\{r_{ij}\} = r_{ij_0}$, then called b_{j_0} is the optimal strategy to event a_i; if $\max\limits_{1 \le j \le m}\{r_{ij}\} = r_{i_0j}$ then called a_{i_0} is the optimal event to strategy b_j; if $\max\limits_{1 \le j \le m}\{r_{ij}\} = r_{i_0j_0}$ then called $s_{i_0j_0}$ is optimal situation.

2.2 Grey Correlation Analysis

Grey relational analysis theory is an important branch of grey system theory [13, 14]. The linearly interpolated method is used to transform the discrete behavior observations of the system factors into the polylines of segmented readings, then construct the model of measure degree according to the geometric feature of the polyline.

The basic steps of the grey relational model are as follows:

Step 1: the original sequence

$$X_0(t) = \{x_0(1), x_0(2), \cdots, x_0(n)\}$$

is specifies the reference data sequence, also called the parent sequence.

$$X_i(t) = \{x_i(1), x_i(2), \cdots, x_i(n)\}$$

is the sequence of data to be compared, also known as the sub sequence;
Step 2: make $\xi_i(k)$ is the correlation coefficient for sequence $X_0(t)$ and $X_i(t)$ at time k:

$$\xi_i(k) = \frac{\min\limits_i \min\limits_k |x_0(k) - x_i(k)| + 0.5 \max\limits_i \max\limits_k |x_0(k) - x_i(k)|}{|x_0(k) - x_i(k)| + 0.5 \max\limits_i \max\limits_k |x_0(k) - x_i(k)|} \tag{7}$$

where 0.5 is the resolution factor, usually between 0–1.
Step 3: Calculate the average of the correlation coefficients at each time of sequence $X_i(t)$, i.e. the degree of correlation of the subsequence $X_i(t)$ to the parent sequence $X_0(t)$:

$$r_i = \frac{1}{N} \sum_{k=1}^{N} \xi_i(k) \tag{8}$$

3 Optimization of Decision-Making Target Weights

In the traditional multi-objective grey decision model, the target weight is usually determined by the subjective weighting method. Although the method can play the expertise or experience of experts or technical staff and has a certain degree of professionalism, it will have an impact on the evaluation decision results because of its great subjectivity and arbitrariness. Therefore, the optimization of the target weight has become the focus of this paper.

3.1 Evaluation Target Selection

First, it is need to establish select the evaluation target. Due to the effect of different EGR rates on the diesel engine combustion and emissions is different, the selection of evaluation indicators should be take into account the combustion and emission performance of the diesel engine as much as possible. In this paper, the fuel consumption rate, in-cylinder explosion pressure, NO_X, smoke and CO were selected as the evaluation targets. Since the main purpose of EGR is to minimize the emission of NO_X pollutants, so define NO_X as the main decision-making target, the other four indicators for the secondary decision-making target.

The determination of the optimal EGR rate is essentially the search for the best compromise between diesel engine combustion and emissions performance, and how this compromise is reflected in the optimization model is the primary consideration. Considering the important role of target weights in decision-making model, in the optimization model, a compromise between diesel engine combustion and emission performance can be achieved By adjusting the target weight vector $\eta_k(k = 1, 2, 3, 4, 5)$, where k respectively on behalf of the fuel consumption rate, cylinder burst pressure, NO_X, smoke and CO.

3.2 Establishment of NO_X Index Weight

Taking into account the main purpose of EGR, which is to effectively reduce the NO_X emissions. Therefore, the expert scoring is used firstly to customize the target weight of NO_X according to the different conditions of the diesel engine. By repeating the trial and reviewing the information, the rules are as follows:

I. When the diesel engine is at a low load conditions (this article defines $\leq 50\%$ load), NO_X emission concentration is low and in order to ensure the stability and economy of diesel engine, it is suitable to choose a lower EGR rate, thus make the NO_X weight $\eta_3 = 0.4$.

II. When the diesel engine is at a high load (this article defines $\geq 50\%$ load), the NO_X emission concentration is high and in order to ensure the necessary emissions, it is suitable to adopt a higher EGR rate, thus make the NO_X weight = 0.5.

3.3 Establishment of All Index Weight

Based on the importance of other indicators and NO_X this paper introduces the gray relational analysis method to solve the other index weights. The corresponding NO_X values (including the original machine value) at different EGR rates were used as the parent sequence, while the other four evaluation indicators corresponding to the value (including the original machine value) as a sub-sequence, then the correlation coefficient $r'_i (i = 1, 2, 3, 4)$ between the other four evaluation indexes and NO_X index was solved by grey relational analysis. At last, the correlation coefficient between the primary and secondary decision goals can be obtained:

$$r_i = \frac{r'_i}{\sum\limits_{i=1}^{4} r'_i} \tag{9}$$

Solve the initial subjective weight vector. Known as η_3 and r_i, the other four decision-making target weight value $\eta_k (k = 1, 2, 4, 5)$ are solved by the formula $r_i(1 - \eta_3)$, and then the initial subjective weight vector is constituted.

4 Establishment of Optimization Model

For EGR performance evaluation and decision making:

Event set $A = \{a_1\}$, i.e. the event is the best EGR rate decision.

Strategy set $B = \{b_1, b_2 \cdots b_m\}$ consist of m decision-making program and b_m represent different EGR rate.

The decision-making evaluation targets are the fuel consumption rate, in-cylinder explosion pressure, NO_X, smoke and CO and their corresponding weights are, $\eta_1, \eta_2, \eta_3, \eta_4$ and η_5.

The situation of each EGR rate is carried out under the same experimental conditions, and $u_{ij}^{(k)}$ is represent the measurement value corresponding to each decision objective under different conditions for different EGR rates. That is, the experimental value of different parameters. As far as EGR performance evaluation indicators are concerned, fuel consumption, cylinder burst pressure, NO_X, CO and soot are the smaller the better, so choose the lower effect measure.

Specific decision modeling steps are as follows:

Step 1: Develop the effect sample matrix $u_{ij}^{(k)} (i = 1, 2 \cdots, n; j = 1, 2, \cdots m)$, which is composed of the experimental data corresponding to different EGR rates at different working conditions. And solve the consistent effect measure matrix according to (1)–(3).

Since the event n = 1 in this article, the effect sample matrix under different targets can be merged into a new matrix:

$$(u_{ij}) = \begin{bmatrix} u_{11} & u_{12} & \cdots & u_{1m} \\ u_{21} & u_{22} & \cdots & u_{2m} \\ \cdots & \cdots & \cdots & \cdots \\ u_{n1} & u_{n2} & \cdots & u_{nm} \end{bmatrix} \qquad (10)$$

where, The abscissa i represents each target and ordinate j represents different EGR rates.

Step 2: Solve the optimized weight vector $\eta_k (k = 1, 2, 3, 4, 5)$.

Step 3: Substituting η_k into (5) to obtain the corresponding comprehensive effect measure matrix.

Step 4: According to the principle of optimal decision, the advantages and disadvantages of different EGR schemes are sorted and the optimal EGR rate is obtained.

5 Test Validation and Result Analysis

5.1 Acquisition of Test Data

In order to verify the effectiveness of the optimization method, taking a certain type of turbocharged diesel engine as the research object.

The main technical parameters of diesel engine are shown in Table 1.

Table 1. Main technical parameters of TBD234V12

Project	Parameter
Power/kW	444 (1800 r/min)
Cylinderbore/mm × stroke/mm	128 × 140
Compression ratio	15:1
Cylinder arrangement	V-shaped 12-cylinder 60° angle
Combustion chamber type	Direct injection w type

The test included low, medium and high three speed test and each speed in turn selected 25%, 50%, 75% load, a total of 9 working conditions, Part of the operating point test data is shown in Table 2. cgr, fc, co, no, soot and cbp represents EGR rate, fuel consumption, CO, NO_X, soot and cylinder burst pressure in Table 2.

5.2 Analysis of Results

I. low load conditions

OP1 and OP2 are the low speed 50% load and medium speed 25% load, respectively. Taking OP1 as an example, EGR rates were 2.2%, 4.6%, 7.5%, 9.8% and 11.5%. The effect sample matrix $u_{ij}^{(k)}$ is base on experimental data under different EGR rates:

Table 2. Part of the operating point test data

OP	cgr	fc	co	no	soot	cbp
OP1	0	236.3	309	1093	0.045	7.6462
	2.2	241.6	316.57	1104.5	0.063	7.2545
	4.6	242.7	335.53	1002.6	0.088	7.2108
	7.5	243.9	366.7	943.5	0.084	7.1393
	9.8	246.9	427.84	890.65	0.12	7.0167
	11.5	248.7	503.62	783.6	0.27	6.9568
OP2	0	230.1	188	825	0.035	6.6859
	1.5	230.5	196.2	783.2	0.041	6.5428
	4.5	234.6	211.3	743.2	0.049	6.3595
	7.8	236.1	229.4	669.1	0.053	6.3052
	9.5	242.9	273.5	543.5	0.09	6.0485
	12.6	244.3	380.6	497.4	0.27	5.9274
OP3	0	212.9	268	1438	0.108	9.5091
	1.7	214.7	286.53	1432	0.11	9.1568
	4.2	217.9	304.76	1351.6	0.13	9.0763
	7.4	218.2	329.89	1185	0.15	8.8016
	9.1	220.8	366.54	1069.4	0.21	8.7569
	11.8	224.3	426.71	994.2	0.33	8.5597
OP4	0	200.4	160	2186	0.093	10.8
	1.6	199.8	156.4	2101	0.1	10.5505
	3.9	202.3	164.2	1894	0.13	10.4165
	7.5	205	172.2	1653	0.148	10.2256
	9.7	209.2	206	1521	0.165	10.0584
	11.1	212.2	312.3	1465	0.32	9.8568

$$(u_{ij}^{(5)}) = \begin{bmatrix} 241.60 & 242.70 & 243.90 & 246.90 & 248.70 \\ 7.2545 & 7.2108 & 7.1393 & 7.0167 & 6.9568 \\ 1104.5 & 1002.6 & 943.50 & 890.65 & 783.60 \\ 0.0630 & 0.0880 & 0.0840 & 0.1200 & 0.2700 \\ 316.57 & 335.53 & 366.70 & 427.84 & 503.62 \end{bmatrix}$$

Among them, the abscissa represents the fuel consumption rate, CO, NO_X, soot and in-cylinder burst pressure respectively. Ordinate j represents different EGR rates, such as the first column representing an EGR rate of 2.2%.

Step 1: first solve the consistent effect measure matrix:

$$(r_{ij}^{(5)}) = \begin{bmatrix} 1.0000 & 0.9955 & 0.9906 & 0.9785 & 0.9715 \\ 0.9590 & 0.9648 & 0.9744 & 0.9915 & 1.0000 \\ 0.7095 & 0.7816 & 0.8305 & 0.8798 & 1.0000 \\ 1.0000 & 0.7159 & 0.7500 & 0.5250 & 0.2333 \\ 1.0000 & 0.9435 & 0.8633 & 0.7399 & 0.6286 \end{bmatrix}$$

Step 2: solve the initial subjective weight vector. Since OP1 belongs to low load operating point, $\eta_3 = 0.4$. Determine the grey association sequence:

Mother sequence:

$$X0 = \begin{bmatrix} 1093 & 1104.5 & 1002.6 & 943.50 & 890.65 & 783.60 \end{bmatrix}$$

Subsequence:

$$X1 = \begin{bmatrix} 236.3 & 241.60 & 242.70 & 243.90 & 246.90 & 248.70 \end{bmatrix}$$
$$X2 = \begin{bmatrix} 7.6462 & 7.2545 & 7.2108 & 7.1393 & 7.0167 & 6.9568 \end{bmatrix}$$
$$X3 = \begin{bmatrix} 0.045 & 0.0630 & 0.0880 & 0.0840 & 0.1200 & 0.2700 \end{bmatrix}$$
$$X4 = \begin{bmatrix} 309 & 316.57 & 335.53 & 366.70 & 427.84 & 503.62 \end{bmatrix}$$

The correlation coefficient between the other four evaluation indexes and the NO_X index are respectively:

$$r_i = \begin{bmatrix} 0.9684 & 0.9926 & 0.7038 & 0.7398 \end{bmatrix}$$

the initial subjective weight vector:

$$\eta_k = \begin{bmatrix} 0.1707 & 0.1749 & 0.4000 & 0.1240 & 0.1304 \end{bmatrix}$$

Step 3: The comprehensive effect measure matrix is solved and the advantages and disadvantages are sorted according to the optimal principle:

$$R = \begin{bmatrix} 0.8766 & 0.8631 & 0.8573 & 0.8539 & 0.8516 \end{bmatrix}$$

It can be seen from the result of OP1 operating conditions, the performance ranking of different EGR rate is:

$$2.2\% > 4.6\% > 7.5\% > 9.8\% > 11.5\%$$

It is shown that the optimal EGR rate is 2.2% for this condition, and when the EGR rate is higher, the comprehensive performance evaluation value decreases obviously, so a smaller EGR rate should be adopted.

Similarly, the performance ranking of different EGR rate at OP2 conditions can be obtained:

$$R = [0.8384 \quad 0.8219 \quad 0.8332 \quad 0.8125 \quad 0.8102]$$
$$1.5\% > 7.8\% > 4.5\% > 9.5\% > 12.6\%$$

which indicates that the optimal EGR rate is 1.5% at this condition, and when the EGR rate is higher, the comprehensive performance evaluation value is obviously decreased.

It can be seen from the result of OP1 and OP2 that a lower EGR rate should be adopted when diesel engine in low or medium speed, low load conditions. Meanwhile, the comprehensive evaluation value is obviously decreased while the EGR rate is higher. Analysis of the reasons is that when at low load, the NO_X pollutant emissions is low, part of the dynamic performance of diesel engines will be consumed if the EGR rate is too high. In order to ensure the economy and power of diesel engines, it is appropriate to reduce the EGR rate.

II. High load conditions

OP3 and OP4 represent the medium speed 75% load and high speed 75% load, respectively. Let = 0.5 and through the simulation calculation, thus the comprehensive effect measure matrix of OP3 and OP4 are as follows:

$$OP3: [0.8324 \quad 0.8323 \quad 0.8675 \quad 0.8821 \quad 0.8886]$$
$$OP4: [0.8392 \quad 0.8470 \quad 0.8890 \quad 0.9024 \quad 0.8604]$$

the performance ranking of different EGR rate at OP3 and OP4 conditions can be obtained:

$$OP3: 11.8\% > 9.1\% > 7.4\% > 1.7\% > 4.2\%$$
$$OP4: 9.7\% > 7.5\% > 11.1\% > 3.9\% > 1.6\%$$

As can be seen from the results of OP3 and OP4, with the increase of EGR rate, the comprehensive evaluation value increases, which indicates that the higher EGR rate should be adopted under high speed and high load conditions.

In summary, it can be seen from the above assessment and decision-making results. When working at the low or medium speed, low load conditions, due to the lower NO_X emission concentration, it is appropriate to use a smaller EGR rate to balance the power and economy of diesel engines. While working at high load conditions, the NO_X emission concentration is high and in order to ensure the emissions performance, a higher EGR rate should be adopt. With the increase in speed and load, it is appropriate to increase the EGR rate. This is consistent with the characteristics of EGR performance of the current turbocharged diesel engine and also shows the effectiveness of the optimization method.

Although the optimization model can be effectively implemented and successfully applied to the EGR performance evaluation and decision making of turbocharged diesel engine, it needs to be further improvement. Such as limited by the test conditions, it is temporarily unable to obtain more work points corresponding to the data, So that there are some defects in the optimization model, such as method of determining the initial subjective weight still need more data points to amend etc., which is also the next step to continue to study.

6 Conclusion

Aiming at the problem of EGR performance evaluation and optimal decision-making of the turbocharged diesel engine, an optimized multi-objective gray situation decision-making method is proposed. This method can integrate the EGR operating characteristics of the turbocharged diesel engine into the optimization model, which makes the final decision result more reasonable.

The results show that when the turbocharged diesel engine is at a low load, the difference between the comprehensive evaluation values of different EGR rates is not significant when the EGR rate is less than 9%, and with the EGR rate increased, the comprehensive evaluation value decreased obviously when the EGR rate is greater than 10%, thus it is appropriate to use a lower EGR rate. When the diesel engine is at high load, when the EGR rate increases to about 7%, the corresponding comprehensive evaluation value increases more significant, thus it is appropriate to use a higher EGR rate.

The results show that the decision result of this method is basically consistent with the performance characteristics of EGR, as well as the current best EGR rate determination principle. So it can be successfully applied to the decision-making problem of optimal EGR rate under different conditions of turbocharged diesel engine.

Acknowledgement. The authors would like to thank the reviewers for their constructive comments. This work is supported by National Science & Technology Plan Projects (2015BAG16B01).

References

1. Asad, U., Zheng, M.: Exhaust gas recirculation for advanced diesel combustion cycles. Appl. Energy **123**, 242–252 (2014)
2. Luján, J.M., Galindo, J., Vera, F., et al.: Characterization and dynamic response of an exhaust gas recirculation venturi for internal combustion engines. Proc. Inst. Mech. Eng. Part D J. Automob. Eng. **221**, 497–509 (2007)
3. Chen, G.-S., Wu, W., Shen, Y.-G., et al.: Influence of different EGR cycle modes on combustion and emission characteristics of heavy-duty diesel engine. Chin. Intern. Combust. Engine Eng. **35**(2), 20–26 (2014)
4. Shuai, Y., Xiuyuan, L., Qijia, Y., et al.: EGR rates optimization rule and experimental study about influence of EGR rates on diesel engine. Trans. Chin. Soc. Agricult. Mach. **37**(5), 30–33 (2006)
5. Zhang, Z.-D., Fang, Y.-B., Chen, Z.-T.: Research and experiments of EGR rates effect on a turbocharged diesel engine. Chin. Intern. Combust. Engine Eng. **37**(5), 30–33 (2006)
6. Alonso, S., Herrera-Viedma, E., Chiclana, F., Herrera, F.: A web based consensus support system for group decision making problems and incomplete preferences. Inf. Sci. **180**, 4477–4495 (2010)

7. Zhou, H., Wang, J., Zhang, H.: Grey stochastic multi-criteria decision-making approach based on prospect theory and distance measures. J. Grey Syst. **29**(1), 15–33 (2017)
8. Zhang, Y., Wang, W., Bernard, A.: Embedding multi-attribute decision making into evolutionary optimization to solve the many-objective combinatorial optimization problems. J. Grey Syst. **28**(3), 124–143 (2016)
9. Liu, S.F., Yuan, W.F., Sheng, K.Q.: Multi-attribute intelligent grey target decision model. Control Decis. **25**, 1159–1163 (2010)
10. Ou, J., Zhang, A., Zhong, L.: Maintenance scheduling of aircrafts based on multi-criteria optimization and preference programming. Syst. Eng.-Theory Pract. **35**(5), 1347–1350 (2015)
11. Yang, B.H., Fang, Z.G., Zhou, W., et al.: Incidence decision model of multi-attribute interval grey number based on information reduction operator. Control Decis. **27**(2), 182–186 (2012)
12. Wang, Y., Du, J., Wang, H., et al.: Grey decision making theory approach to the turbocharged diesel engine. In: Proceedings of 2007 IEEE International Conference on Grey Systems and Intelligent Services, pp. 784–788. IEEE Press, Nanjing (2007)
13. Liu, S.F., Lin, Y.: Grey Information: Theory and Practical Applications. Springer, London (2006). https://doi.org/10.1007/1-84628-342-6
14. Wu, L.F., Wang, Y.N., Liu, S.F.: Grey convex relation and its properties. Syst. Eng.-Theory Pract. **32**(7), 1501–1506 (2012)

Research on User Safety Authentication Based on Biometrics in Cloud Manufacturing

Xiaolan Xie[1,2], Xiao Zhou[3(✉)], and Yarong Liu[1,2]

[1] College of Information Science and Engineering,
Guilin University of Technology,
Guilin 541004, Guangxi Zhuang Autonomous Region, China
[2] Guangxi Universities Key Laboratory Fund of Embedded Technology
and Intelligent Information Processing, Guilin University of Technology,
Guilin 541004, China
[3] College of Mechanical and Control Engineering,
Guilin University of Technology,
Guilin 541004, Guangxi Zhuang Autonomous Region, China
2485782688@qq.com

Abstract. Cloud manufacturing is a use of the network and cloud manufacturing services platform, according to user requirements organize manufacturing resources online (manufacturing cloud), and provide users a new network manufacturing model with various on-demand manufacturing services. Through the design of user access security authentication model, using biometric technology to ensure the access security of users in the cloud environment, to prevent malicious users access to illegal. The point set topological group fractal changing algorithm is used to encrypt biometric information acquired by biometrics, which provides more guarantee for the security authentication of users.

Keywords: Cloud manufacturing · Security authentication · Biometrics
Point set topological group fractal changing algorithm

1 Introduction

Cloud manufacturing technology integrates existing networked manufacturing services technology with cloud computing, cloud security, high-performance computing, networking and other technologies [1]. Cloud manufacturing achieve unified, centralized, intelligent management of all kinds of manufacturing resources (manufacturing hard equipment, computing systems, software, models, data, knowledge, etc.) and provide the available, Immediate, on-demand, safe, reliable, quality and cheap service for the life cycle process. User security certification is the first concern of cloud manufacturing system. In the cloud manufacturing system architecture, the application layer is directly oriented to the user, and the security authentication of the user access is directly related to the security of cloud manufacturing [2, 3]. Biometric identification technology is used to identify biometric and encrypt them at the same time, so as to ensure the user's information security. Biometric cryptography implements the unity of the person's digital identity (who he is) and the physical identity of the person (who he really is).

Key is the most important part of encryption [4]. Point set topological group fractal changing algorithm combined with biological feature information to generate key. At the same time, the biometric points such as face, voice and fingerprint are used as the data source of fractal change, which is unique, and further improves the security of the encryption system [5].

2 Related Introduction

2.1 Cloud Manufacturing

Cloud manufacturing is the enterprise manufacturing resources as the research object, for the purpose of realizing dynamic combination and efficient utilization of resources. Through the Internet of things, Internet technology to achieve comprehensive connectivity and intelligent perception of manufacturing resources; through virtualization technology to build virtual resources cloud pool, and realize the virtualization and service of manufacturing resources. Build a cloud manufacturing service platform with the support of network technology. Publish the personalized requirements of the cloud requester to the manufacturing resource to the platform. Conducting a fast and efficient resource intelligent search and matching by cloud service. The dynamic reconfiguration and utilization of manufacturing resources are rapidly realized by the cloud provider and achieve a new service-oriented network manufacturing model with three win-win situation by cloud request side, cloud service providers and cloud providers.

2.2 Biometrics and Its Risks

When users enter the cloud manufacturing system or access the system resources of different protection levels, the system needs to use some authentication methods to carry out security. Biometric technology is unique individual identification techniques that can be sampled and measured for biological characteristics. Biometric features are acquired by biometrics. There is a risk of biometric information protection, once the user's biometric information was leaked, stolen or tampered with, such as fingerprints or facial features, due to the fixed and only has the biological characteristics, it is difficult to conduct similar password reset remedial measures will likely cause great losses to the users. Therefore, biometric encryption is critical.

2.3 Point Set Topological Group Fractal Changing Algorithm

Firstly, the image data set division, after the division of the subset of hash operations as a random key input, and then get the fractal changing loop operation, the coordinate values of the sub set points after loop operation are obtained, the final output of the pseudo random sequence. The flowchart of the point set topological group fractal changing algorithm is shown in Fig. 1.

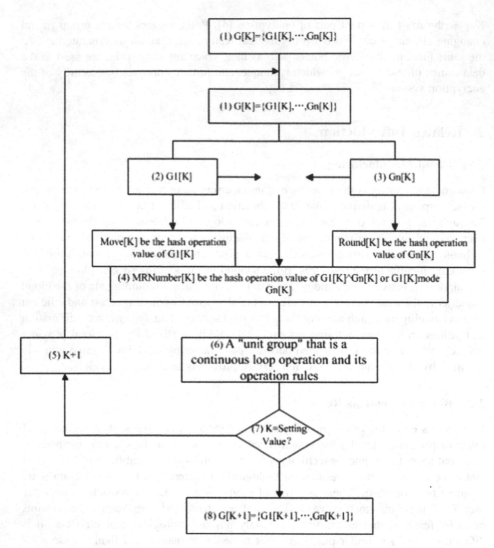

Fig. 1. The flowchart of the point set topological group fractal changing algorithm

3 User Access Security Authentication Design Model in Cloud Manufacturing

The architecture of cloud manufacturing system mainly includes physical resource layer, cloud manufacturing, virtual resource layer, cloud manufacturing core service layer, application interface layer and cloud production application layer. Users in different industries need to access and use various cloud services of cloud manufacturing systems only through cloud manufacturing portals, various user interfaces (including mobile terminals, PC terminals, dedicated terminals, etc.). The two layers in the cloud manufacturing architecture are connected to the outside world, directly to the user. User access security authentication is divided into the user which is bound to platform command access security authentication and the user which is bound to client access security authentication. The authentication process is shown in Fig. 2.

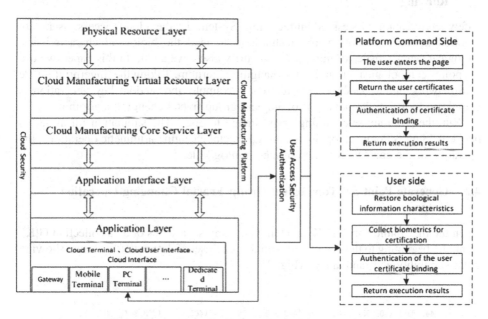

Fig. 2. User access security authentication model in cloud manufacturing

When the user which is bound to platform command access security authentication. First of all, the cloud management platform based on user login web page user information to pass user certificates. If the user does not have a certificate to store user security information, the certificate is returned to the user and pass commands to collect biological information features of users. Then, perform the trusted pattern recognition technology and the certificate signature binding authentication and returns the result of the execution. At last, enters the other service process. If there is a certificate of user security information locally, the binding authentication is performed directly.

When the user which is bound to client access security authentication, client return a certificate's biometric information, then according to public key which is associated with biometric information. The biometric information feature template is restored by using the information characteristic associated with the private key. The platform issues commands to collect user information characteristics. Then, perform the trusted pattern recognition technology and the certificate signature binding authentication and returns the result of the execution. The cloud management platform analyzes binding authentication information, determines the user access, and then provides services.

4   Biological Feature Information Encryption Instance Simulation

4.1   Point Set Topological Group Fractal Changing Algorithm Instance Running

Safety certification process Manufacturing System in the cloud access users are required in the use of biometric technology to read the biological characteristics, biological characteristics of information security also have a risk. In this paper, we use the point set topological group fractal changing algorithm. Taking the fingerprint image of a network public database as a reference example, the random key generation is completed by using the point set topological group fractal changing algorithm.

Run the program, select a fingerprint image to open. The simulation fill in 38, so perform 38 units Point set topological group fractal changing arithmetic operations, the operation of the contents recorded in the "mmlog" file.

4.2   Generate Point Set Topological Group Fractal Changing Operation Value

Open the file "mmlog" by $G1[K]$ and $Gn[K]$ display set a series of data collection $G[K]$. From the beginning to the end, it is shown that each set of data is not the same, showing great variability and randomness (Fig. 3).

```
m = 18
G1[38]: (441,335) (408,352) (408,352) (408,352) (408,352) (408,352) (405,347) (407,350)
(404,346) (407,350) (397,333) (394,328) (400,347) (385,352) (381,306) (363,343) (363,300)
(342,342)
m' = 7
G2[38]: (546,370) (473,415) (476,412) (473,415) (473,415) (473,415) (470,410)
K = 38  f(G1[38])=18    f(G2[38])=860    f(G1[38],G2[38])=846
        Move[38]=8      Round[38]=3      MRNumber[38]=6

m = 18
G1[39]: (407,374) (435,356) (435,356) (435,356) (435,356) (435,356) (439,360) (436,359)
(437,361) (436,359) (446,375) (447,379) (440,361) (456,357) (461,402) (478,367) (477,408)
(498,367)
m' = 7
G2[39]: (431,465) (500,419) (497,421) (500,419) (500,419) (500,419) (504,423)
```

Fig. 3. "mmlog" file content

The range of K the value is 1–38.

Move[K], Round[K], MRNumber[K] numerical range is also from Move[1] = 6, Round[1] = 4, MRNumber[1] = 3, to perform 38 units point set topological group fractal changing arithmetic operations, show Move[38] = 8, Round[38] = 3, MRNumber[38] = 6.

From the file set G[2] series data of G1[2] and G2[2] composed, to set G[39] series data of G1[39] and G2[39] composed, 38 set of G[K] changing data. The first set is the initial data.

5 Conclusion

This paper designs a user access security authentication model in cloud manufacturing, and applies biometric identification technology to user security authentication, which provides security for users to secure access in cloud manufacturing. At the same time, this paper uses the algorithm of point set topological group fractal changing. The biometric information is encrypted by biometric identification technology, and the security key is generated by combining the data of biological features to protect the user's information security, and further protect the security authentication of users in cloud manufacturing. This article has carried on the research safety certification of user in cloud manufacturing, and to ensure the safety of user data such as intrusion detection techniques do not study, this is should pay attention to the subsequent cloud manufacturing safety problems in the research, but also need to carry out research on infrastructure safety and operation management of safety, strengthen the security of cloud manufacturing system. However, the technology of intrusion detection and other technologies to ensure the security of user data has not been studied. This should be the focus of attention in the follow-up research of cloud manufacturing safety. Meanwhile, it also needs to study infrastructure and security, operations management security. To strengthen cloud manufacturing security protection system.

Acknowledgements. This research work was supported by the 'Ba Gui Scholars' program of the provincial government of Guangxi and Guangxi Universities key Laboratory Fund of Embedded Technology and Intelligent Information Processing (Guilin University of Technology).

References

1. Wu, D., Greer, M.J., Rosen, D.W., et al.: Cloud manufacturing: strategic vision and state-of-the-art. J. Manuf. Syst. **32**(4), 564–579 (2013)
2. Wang, X.V., Xu, X.W.: An interoperable solution for cloud manufacturing. Robot. Comput.-Integr. Manuf. **29**(4), 232–247 (2013)
3. Zureik, E., Hindle, K.: Governance, security and technology: the case of biometrics. Stud. Polit. Econ. Soc. Rev. **73**, 113–137 (2016)
4. Moulay, E., Baguelin, M.: Meta-dynamical adaptive systems and their applications to a fractal algorithm and a biological model. Physica D Nonlinear Phenomena **207**(1–2), 79–90 (2005)
5. Hosaka, T.: On boundaries of Coxeter groups and topological fractal structures. Tsukuba J. Math. **35**(2), 153–160 (2009)

An Improved Harris-SIFT Algorithm
for Image Matching

Yu Cao[✉], Bo Pang, Xin Liu, and Yan-li Shi

School of Harbin University of Science and Technology, Harbin 150080, China
759734958@qq.com

Abstract. In view of the feature points extracted by the SIFT algorithm can not fully represent the structure of the object and the computational complexity is high, an improved Harris-SIFT image matching algorithm is proposed. Firstly, the feature points of the image are extracted by Harris corner detection operator. Then, the feature points are described by using the 28 dimension increasing homocentric square window. Euclidean distance is used as the similarity measure function in the matching process. Finally, simulation results show the validity of the improved algorithm, providing a new thought for the research into the image matching.

Keywords: Improved Harris-SIFT algorithm · Corner detection
Homocentric square window · Image matching

1 Introduction

Image matching is a kind of algorithm for finding similar image block, which is mainly based on the similarity and conformity analysis of image content, characteristics, grey degree, etc. [1]. Image matching technology has been applied to 3D Reconstruction [2], target tracking, remote sensing data analysis and many other fields [3, 4]. But it is still a problem to find one with high real-time and high precision from so many existing algorithms at present.

In recent years, there have been numerous image matching algorithms, including Moravec detection operator, Harris detection operator [4] and SUSAN detection operator [5]. SIFT (scale invariant feature transform) algorithm, PCA-SIFT algorithm [6], SVD matching method and Integration image method are new algorithms in modern society. In 2004, Lowe presented SIFT algorithm based on Local invariant descriptors. It has been broadly applied in many scenes with rotating zoom, partial occlusion, scale invariant, etc. [7]. But the feature points extracted by the SIFT operator do not fully represent the actual structure of the object. Beyond that, SIFT descriptors are quite complicated in calculation [8] and weak in real-time performance. On the basis of the above disadvantages, SIFT algorithm is not applicable to the higher requirements [8, 9]. The angle point features extracted by Harris operator is a good indication of the physical characteristics of the object, which is a stable angle point extraction algorithm [10].

This paper discusses the problem of the poor real-time performance of SIFT algorithm, and improves the descriptors of SIFT. In addition, this paper presents an

© ICST Institute for Computer Sciences, Social Informatics and Telecommunications Engineering 2018
G. Sun and S. Liu (Eds.): ADHIP 2017, LNICST 219, pp. 56–64, 2018.
https://doi.org/10.1007/978-3-319-73317-3_8

improved Harris SIFT algorithm in combination with the Harris point detection operators. The simulation results demonstrate the effectiveness of the proposed algorithm.

1.1   Feature Point Detection Algorithm

The basic idea of SIFT algorithm: firstly, the scale space of image is constructed, and the key points are detected by extreme value detection in scale space, and the points with low contrast points and unstable edges are removed. Then the main direction of the key point is determined in scale space, and finally describe the key points, and make the descriptors unique.

1.2   Extreme Value Detection in Scale Space

Scale space is a theory which is simulating multi-scale characteristics to analog image data. SIFT algorithm finds the key points in different scale spaces. And the only linear kernel of scaling transformation is the Gauss convolution kernel. Therefore, the scale space of an image $L(x, y, \sigma)$ is defined as the convolution of a variable scale Gauss's function with the original image. e.g. (1):

$$L(x, y, \sigma) = G(x, y, \sigma) * I(x, y) \tag{1}$$

where: σ is scale parameter.

In order to obtain more stable image features, difference of Gaussians (DoG) is proposed, e.g. (2):

$$D(x, y, \sigma) = L(x, y, k\sigma) - L(x, y, \sigma) \tag{2}$$

where: k is related to the number of layers per dimension s in the scale space, $k = 2^{\frac{1}{s}}$.

In order to obtain the extreme points in the scale space. Each pixel needs to be compared with the 26 points, including the pixel scale, the same scale and the upper and lower scales. If it is the maximum or minimum in its adjacent points, the point is considered to be the extreme point in the scale space.

The key point which is obtained by the method of above-mentioned is the extreme points of discrete space, is not really extreme point. So the DOG function should be fitted of a curve, and then repeatedly interpolated to get continuous space extreme points. And the number of iterations or beyond the image boundary points are removed to obtain accurate positioning. At the same time, the low contrast points and edge unstable points are removed, so that the noise immunity can be enhanced.

1.3   Allocation of Key Points

In order to make the descriptor have rotation invariance, the directional parameters of each key point are obtained according to the gradient direction distribution feature of the neighborhood pixels of feature points. The formula of calculating the modulus $m(x, y)$ and direction $\theta(x, y)$ of the gradient which belongs to the feature points, (3) and

(4). Histograms are used to represent the gradient size and direction of pixels, and the peak direction of the histogram is the main direction of the key points. Using a column at 10 degrees, 0°–360° is divided into 36 columns. We give 8 columns, one of which is the main direction and the other is the auxiliary direction.

$$m(x,y) = ((L(x+1,y) - L(x-1,y))^2 + (L(x,y+1) - L(x,y-1))^2)^{\frac{1}{2}} \quad (3)$$

$$\theta(x,y) = \tan^{-1}\frac{L(x,y+1) - L(x,y-1)}{L(x+1,y) - L(x-1,y)} \quad (4)$$

1.4   Key Point Descriptor Generation

First, the coordinate axis is rotated to be consistent with the main direction of the feature points, so as to ensure rotation invariance. Neighborhood statistics range of SIFT for each of the key points is 16 × 16 pixel window, and divide it into 4 × 4 sub regions, each sub region containing 4 × 4 pixels, and then calculate the gradient of 8 directions in each sub area of the histogram; last sort vector information on the 8 the direction of each sub region in the vector sorted form a 4 × 4 × 8 = 128 dimensional feature descriptor. Such a feature descriptor has the invariance of scale change, geometric deformation and illumination change.

The 128 dimensional descriptor of this algorithm makes the computing complexity and the real-time performance poor, and the detected feature points can not show the physical structure of objects.

2   Improved Harris-SIFT Algorithm

2.1   Detection of Feature Points

The principle of Harris corner detection is: taking a small window to move toward any direction in infinitesimal displacement by centering on target pixel; only when the center of this window is corner that the gray feature values of window change in all directions. According to the variation degrees of gray feature values in each direction, the feature and location information of corners in image can be determined. The gray degree variation is presented by the analytical formula as follows:

$$E(x,y) = \sum w_{x,y}(I_{x+u,y+v} - I_{x,y})^2 = [u \quad v]M\begin{bmatrix}u\\v\end{bmatrix} \quad (5)$$

In this formula, u is the displacement of small window centering on (x, y) in the direction of X; v is the displacement in direction Y; $w_{x,y}$ is Gauss window function; I is function of image gray scale.

Calculating the value of matrix M:

$$M = \begin{bmatrix} I_x^2 & I_x I_y \\ I_x I_y & I_y^2 \end{bmatrix} \tag{6}$$

where I_x and I_y respectively are the gradient values of image pixels in horizontal as well as vertical directions.

Calculating the interest values of each pixel corresponding to original image, which is R value:

$$R = Det(M) - kTr^2(M) \tag{7}$$

where k is experience value taken 0.04–0.06. When the R value in certain point is greater than the given threshold value T, this point is deemed as corner. The threshold value T in this paper is 0.05.

2.2 Description of Feature Points

This paper will adopt neighborhood information to improve descriptor because of its strong anti-noise ability. The layer-by-layer increasing homocentric square window is applied in this paper to describe the neighborhood information of key points. This method divides the neighborhood around key point into 4 regions so as to establish 28 dimension feature point descriptor. The layer-by-layer increasing homocentric square window indicates that, the pixel closer to key point will generate stronger influence on ultimate feature description.

The specific construction method is: taking the window in key point closer to 20×20 pixel as the neighborhood scope of this key point for statistics, and regarding the 4 adjacent neighborhoods as first group; then expanding 2 pixels in each direction of first group and taking this neighborhood circle as second group; expanding 3 pixels in each direction of second group to obtain the corresponding neighborhood circle; expanding 3 pixels in each direction of third group to obtain the corresponding neighborhood circle as shown in Fig. 1. Finally, calculating the gradient accumulated values in 8 directions of pixel in each group. The feature vectors of 1–4 dimensions belong to first group, just as the style a shown in the diagram. The feature vectors in second group are adopted as 5–12 dimensions. I this ways, the feature vectors of 28 dimensions are acquired; such arrangement presents that, the pixel closer to key point will generate stronger influence on feature description. The grayscale accumulated values of pixels within each region is computed and normalized to obtain the feature descriptor with illumination invariants.

The grayscale accumulated values of pixels within each region is computed and normalized to obtain the feature descriptor with illumination invariants. The following formula is acquired by normalizing grayscale accumulated values:

$$\bar{f_i} = f_i \left/ \sqrt{\sum_{i=1}^{4} f_i} \right., \ i = (1, 2, 3, 4) \tag{8}$$

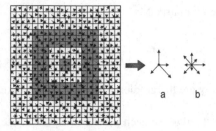

a   b

Fig. 1. Schematic diagram of improved feature descriptor

$$\bar{f}_i = f_i \Big/ \sqrt{\sum_{i=1}^{8} f_i}, \ i = (1,2,3,\cdots 8) \tag{9}$$

where formula (8) is to normalize the grayscale accumulated value of vectors in first group; formula (9) is acquired by normalizing the grayscale accumulated value of vectors in last three groups. Thus, the feature vector of 28 dimension is presented as follows:

$$F_i = (\overline{f_{i1}}, \overline{f_{i2}}, \cdots \overline{f_{i28}}) \tag{10}$$

The improved algorithm descriptor is reduced from 128 dimension to 28 dimension; meanwhile, the contained neighborhood is changed from 16×16 into 20×20 with more neighborhood information, which not only reduced calculated amount, but also avoided the loss caused by decrease of seed points.

2.3   SIFT Feature Vector Matching

The Euclidean distance is adopted as similarity metric function to carry our feature vector matching; k-d tree is utilized to search so as to look for the nearest-neighbor and next nearest neighbor feature points corresponding to each feature points. In these two feature points, if the distance ratio through dividing nearest neighbor by next nearest neighbor is smaller than certain given proportion threshold value, then such pair of matching point is accepted.

3   Experimental Result and Analysis

This paper firstly uses MATLAB programming to realize image matching and the shot pictures for test.

Firstly, the matching of similar image pairs in classical SIFT is research so as to look for the relationship between matching number of image pairs with scale variation of the same article and matching number of similar image pairs; so a threshold value of whether being the image matching number of the same article. The setting of such threshold helps prevent the wrong matching of similar image. The following is the result diagram of matching similar images and the same article in rotation transformation.

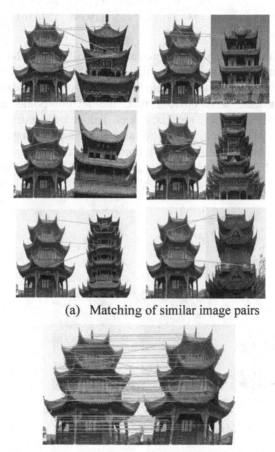

(a) Matching of similar image pairs

(b) Image matching of the same article in rotation transformation

Fig. 2. Matching test of similar image pair

According to a group of test image above, it can be concluded that, the average matching number in the matching of similar image pair in Fig. 2(a) is 5, among which the maximum value 9 and the matching number in the same article is 125. Based on the test of abovementioned ten groups of similar image pairs, the following table is obtained:

According to the results in Table 1, it is concluded that, the more the feature points of articles detected, the more the wrong matching points of image will be. Based on the statistical data of Table 1, this paper sets wrong matching threshold value M = 15. The image with matching point pairs less than 15 will be output as wrong matching.

Table 1. Statistics of similar image pair matching test

Test group	1	2	3	4	5	6	7	8	9	10
Mean value	5	2	8	4	6	5	7	4	6	3
Maximum value	9	6	14	8	11	12	14	9	12	7
Matching number of same object	125	78	143	112	119	98	127	103	136	63

Secondly, the matching verification of improved Harris-SIFT algorithm proposed in this paper is implemented to analyze and compare it with original SIFT algorithm. Figures 3 and 4 respectively are the experimental results of two image pairs; Table 2 is experimental result statistics. It is obvious that, the feature points extracted by improved Harris-SIFT algorithm are corners, which reduced the extraction time of surplus feature points. In addition, the introduction of layer-by-layer increasing homocentric square window greatly reduced computational complexity, enhanced timeliness of original SIFT algorithm, and guaranteed matching correctness.

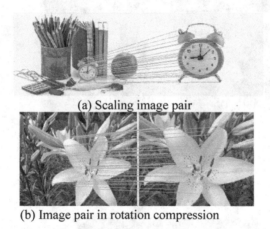

(a) Scaling image pair

(b) Image pair in rotation compression

Fig. 3. Matching of original SIFT algorithm

(1) According to above experimental results, this paper solved three problems of original SIFT algorithm.
(2) By means of multiple matching experiments of similar images, this paper obtained the wrong matching value M = 15; the setting of threshold value can effectively prevent wrong matching of different articles.
(3) This paper adopted Harris corner detection algorithm in the detection stage of feature point, which eliminated many not obvious feature points, reduced computational complexity and enhanced correct matching rate; besides, the corners obtained can better embody article characteristics.
(4) In the stage of feature description, this paper adopted 28 dimension layer-by-layer increasing homocentric square window, which greatly shortened computation time and enhanced matching timeliness.

(a) Scaling image pair

(b) Image pair in rotation compression

Fig. 4. Improved Harris-SIFT algorithm matching

Table 2. Statistics of matching results

Image pair	a			b		
Reduced parameter	Matching number	Matching time/s	Correct matching rate/%	Matching number	Matching time/s	Correct matching rate/%
Original SIFT algorithm	30	0.098	90.0	63	0.134	92.1
Improved Harris-SIFT algorithm	22	0.054	95.5	46	0.085	95.7

4 Conclusion

The SIFT algorithm has the advantages of good scale, rotation, angle and light invariance, which is widely used in image matching. This paper presents an improved Harris SIFT algorithm based on the Harris angle point detection algorithm. The algorithm uses the Harris operator to detect angle points, then improves the descriptor for the SIFT operator. This algorithm describes the character points in a 28-dimensional incremented rectangular-ambulatory-plane descriptor, and finally uses European distance as the measure function to match. Experimental results show that the feature points extracted by the improved algorithm can be a very good reflect the structure of the object, and greatly reduce the matching time, improves the accuracy of matching as well.

Funding Project. This paper is supported by the project of young creative talents training program of Heilongjiang undergraduate higher education institution (UNPYSCT-2015039).

References

1. Zhou, R., Dexing, D., Han, J.: Fingerprint identification using SIFT-based minutia descriptors and improved all descriptor-pair matching. Sensors **13**(3), 3142–3156 (2013)
2. Guo, Y., Sohel, F., Bennamoun, M., et al.: An accurate and robust range image registration algorithm for 3D object modeling. IEEE Trans. Multimedia **16**(5), 1377–1390 (2014)
3. Chen, Y., Shang, L.: Improved SIFT image registration algorithm on characteristic statistical distributions and consistency constraint. Optik-Int. J. Light Electr. Opt. **127**(2), 900–911 (2016)
4. Bay, H., Tuytelaars, T., Van Gool, L.: SURF: speeded up robust features. Comput. Vis. Image Underst. **110**(3), 346–359 (2008)
5. Ke, Y., Sukthankar, R.: PCA-SIFT: a more distinctive representation for local image descriptors. In: IEEE Computer Society Conference on Computer Vision and Pattern Recognition, no. 2, pp. 506–513 (2004)
6. Lowe, D.G.: Object recognition from local scale-invariant features. In: Proceedings of International Conference on Computer Vision, pp. 1150–1157 (1999)
7. Gal, R., Cohen-Or, D.: Salient geometric features for partial shape matching and similarity. ACM (2006)
8. Wang, Y., Hu, J., Han, F.: Enhanced gradient-based algorithm for the estimation of fingerprint orientation fields. Elsevier Science Inc. (2007)
9. Maintz, J.B.A., van den Elsen, P.A., Viergever, M.A.: Evaluation of ridge seeking operators for multimodality medical image matching. IEEE Trans. Pattern Anal. Mach. Intell. **18**(4), 353–365 (2008)
10. Er-Sen, L.I., Zhang, B.M., Liu, J.Z., et al.: The application of SIFT feature matching method in the automatic relative orientation. Sci. Surv. Mapp. **33**(5), 15–16 (2008)
11. Tian, F., Yan, Y.B.: A SIFT feature matching algorithm based on semi-variance function. Adv. Mater. Res. **647**, 896–900 (2013)
12. Zhao, J., Xue, L.J., Men, G.Z.: Optimization matching algorithm based on improved Harris and SIFT. In: International Conference on Machine Learning and Cybernetics, pp. 258–261. IEEE (2010)

Spark Memory Management

Wei Zhang$^{(\boxtimes)}$ and Jingmei Li

College of Computer Science and Technology, Harbin Engineering University,
Harbin 150001, China
zhangwei72@hrbeu.edu.cn

Abstract. In order to obtain detailed information about Spark framework and realize fine grained monitoring of cluster operation information, a performance analysis system is designed. Therefore, the problems of Spark1.6 memory management scheme are researched in depth and improved. The experimental results show that the original memory management scheme is inconsistent with the requirements of Spark's official website. However, the improved memory management scheme not only meets the requirements of Spark's official website, but also makes the application run successfully under the condition of small memory capacity.

Keywords: Spark framework · Memory management · Memory overflow

1 Introduction

As a computing engine that excels in memory computing, memory management in Spark is a very important module [1, 2]. Because of its outstanding memory calculation, putting the application running data in memory as much as possible, the most of the errors in running applications are caused by spark memory overflow. Due to its outstanding memory calculation, the application's running data is stored in memory as much as possible, resulting in most of the errors in running applications from the spark memory overflow.

Through the research on the working mechanism of the distributed platform Spark, a performance analysis system based on Spark log is designed to realize fine grained monitoring of the cluster operation information. On the basis of fine grained monitoring, the memory management of Spark framework is studied deeply and the existing problems are optimized.

2 Performance Analysis System Design

In order to determine the memory efficiency of the system, it is necessary to accurately judge the application details of each stage of execution. So a performance analysis system is designed.

Large data performance analysis system is divided into three main layers and the overall framework is shown in Fig. 1. The first layer is Spark source plug in, which can generate Spark application running log by the tool of the slf4j log and calling

© ICST Institute for Computer Sciences, Social Informatics and Telecommunications Engineering 2018
G. Sun and S. Liu (Eds.): ADHIP 2017, LNICST 219, pp. 65–69, 2018.
https://doi.org/10.1007/978-3-319-73317-3_9

high-precision timing tools of the operating system, methods of Java, etc. The second layer is the data collation layer. The running log generated by Spark is a readable natural language of human oriented. It needs regular expression to extract the data it needs. The original unstructured data is organized into structured data [3], which is convenient for reading on the third level. The third layer is data visualization, which can help users analyze the implementation of the application by drawing the appropriate chart with visualization tools.

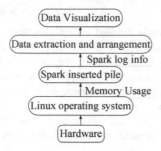

Fig. 1. Spark performance analysis system framework

3 Spark Memory Management

The memory management scheme in this article refers to the new memory management scheme in the Spark1.6 framework [4–6]. The memory management scheme is implemented using dynamic pre-emption, which means that Execution can borrow free Storage memory and vice versa. The borrowed memory is recycled when the amount of memory increases. In memory management, memory is divided into three separate blocks as shown in Fig. 2.

| Spark Memory（Include Storage and Execution Memory，Default:75%） |
| User Memory(Default:25%) |
| Reserved Memory（Default:300M） |

Fig. 2. Unified memory manager in Spark 1.6

By analyzing the memory management scheme, there is a problem that how much memory Execution can borrow from Storage. Storage Fraction is configured on the Spark official website to indicate the memory ratio that Storage occupies at least. To study the Spark memory management scheme, it finds that when storage remaining memory is larger than the difference between Storage's memory and the initial allocated memory, and when Execution needs more memory than it can borrow, then the final borrow memory is equal to Storage of the remaining memory. To update Storage and Execution memory, the now available memory of Storage is equal to the difference between previously owned memory and Storage's remaining memory. Depending on the condition, the now available memory of Storage is smaller than the initial configuration memory, which is inconsistent with the configuration described on the Spark official website. This problem leads to the static configuration algorithm degenerate into an approximate first come first service algorithm. The improved approach is to set the borrowing memory size to the difference between the now available memory of Storage and the initial configuration memory.

4 Experimental Verification

4.1 Memory Management Deficiencies and Improvements

In order to find problems of Spark memory management, it needs to obtain Execution and Storage memory change information. Therefore, the associated log information is added in the Spark framework and memory change information is recorded in the log file. This experiment uses Spark1.6 memory management scheme. The configuration parameters of Spark Memory Fraction and Spark Memory Storage Fraction are 0.75 and 0.5 respectively. Based on the configuration parameters and the 8G size of the committed memory, the Storage memory is calculated to be no less than 2887.5 M.

The Storage Memory change information is obtained by submitting the same PageRank application in the memory management scheme before and after the improvement, as shown in Fig. 3. From the diagram, the memory of the before improved memory management scheme varies with time and the minimum of Storage memory is only 0.297044 M, which obviously does not meet its minimum requirement of 2887.5 M. So there are problems about Execution and Storage memory borrowing from each other. However, memory of the improved memory management program changes in the range of 500 M at different times and memory size is more than 2887.5 M, in line with requirements.

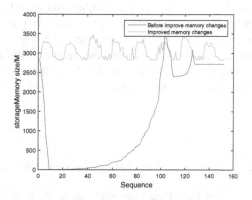

Fig. 3. Memory data changes

To verify the performance of the memory management scheme, the same application is presented and the change is only the size of the executor memory. The running time of PageRank applications before and after the improvement of the Spark memory management scheme is shown in Fig. 4. The performance of the before improved memory management scheme is basically the same as the improved when the memory is relatively large. However, the application in the before improved memory management scheme cannot run properly when the memory size is 7G and 6G, while the improved memory management solution application can still run successfully. Therefore, the overall performance of the improved memory management scheme is superior to that of the before improved memory management scheme.

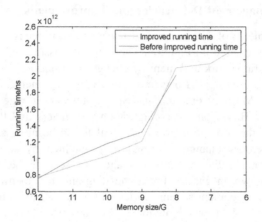

Fig. 4. Application run time

5 Conclusions

The source code and implementation principle of Spark framework are analyzed in this paper. The insufficiency of memory management scheme is proved through experiments and the shortcomings of memory management are improved. The improved memory management scheme not only meets the requirements of Spark's official website for Storage memory configuration, but also has a better performance than the before improved memory management scheme.

References

1. Bosagh, Z.R., Meng, X., Ulanov, A.: Matrix computations and optimization in apache Spark. pp. 31–38 (2015)
2. Sankar, K., Karau, H.: Fast Data Processing with Spark. Packt Publishing, Birmingham (2015)
3. Li, Y., Zhang, X., Tan, R.J., et al.: Establishment of traceability and supervision system for import and export products and its application on import food supervision. J. Food Saf. Qual. **6**, 4312–4317 (2015)

4. Tang, M., Yu, Y., Malluhi, Q.M., et al.: LocationSpark: a distributed in-memory data management system for big spatial data. Proc. VLDB Endow. **9**, 1565–1568 (2016)
5. Park, K., Baek, C., Peng, L.: A development of streaming big data analysis system using in-memory cluster computing framework: Spark. In: Park, J., Jin, H., Jeong, Y.S., Khan, M. (eds.) Advanced Multimedia and Ubiquitous Engineering. LNEE, vol. 393, pp. 157–163. Springer, Singapore (2016). https://doi.org/10.1007/978-981-10-1536-6_21
6. Duan, M., Li, K., Tang, Z., et al.: Selection and replacement algorithms for memory performance improvement in Spark. Concurr. Comput. Prac. Exp. **28**, 2473–2486 (2016)

A Quantitative Model for Analysis and Evaluation of Tor Hidden Service Discovery

Peipeng Liu, Xiao Wang, Xin He, Chenglong Li,
Shoufeng Cao, Longtao He, and Jiawei Zhu[✉]

National Computer Network Emergency Response Technical
Team/Coordination Center, Beijing, China
zhujw.happy@163.com

Abstract. Tor is one of the most popular anonymous communication systems, and its ability of providing receiver anonymity makes *hidden services* more and more attractive. However, with the exposure of illegal contents such as child pornography and drug trades in hidden services, it becomes urgent to make a comprehensive analysis and evaluation of hidden services in the Tor network. In this paper, based on the frequent updates of hidden service descriptors, we proposed an approach to model Tor hidden service discovery as a generalized coupon collector problem with group drawings. Our experiments based on the real Tor network proved the efficiency and feasibility of the proposed model, which proved the possibility of harvesting most of hidden services with a small amount of resources.

Keywords: Tor · Hidden service · Discovery · Coupon collector

1 Introduction

Tor [1] is one of the most popular low-latency anonymous communication systems. Based on globally distributed volunteer-run relays, Tor uses several hops to forward users' messages in a layered-encryption way to prevent an external or internal attacker from correlating the two parties of a communication. Up to November 2016, there are about 7000 running Tor relays and 2000 bridges distributed around the world, and about 2 million users around the world using Tor to protect their communication anonymity [2].

In addition to protecting the client's anonymity, in order to hide the identities of service providers while enabling them to run normal web services, *hidden service* [3] was introduced into Tor in 2004. Recently, with the appearance of illegal contents such as child pornography and drug trades in hidden services, it becomes attractive to realize the current situation of hidden services in Tor network, such as their total number, content distribution, individual popularity and so on. All of these makes hidden service discovery a prerequisite.

In this paper, we model the hidden service discovery by running HSDirs as a generalized coupon collector problem, and based on the proposed model, we

© ICST Institute for Computer Sciences, Social Informatics and Telecommunications Engineering 2018
G. Sun and S. Liu (Eds.): ADHIP 2017, LNICST 219, pp. 70–77, 2018.
https://doi.org/10.1007/978-3-319-73317-3_10

efficiently quantify the relationship between what you have and what you get in terms of hidden service discovery. Contributions in this paper can be summarized as follows:

1. We model the hidden service discovery by modeling HSDirs as a coupon collector problem with group drawings.
2. We quantify the relationship between consumed resources and collected hidden services in the discovery of Tor hidden services, and proved the feasibility of harvesting most of hidden services with a small amount of resources.

Rest of the paper is organized as follows, Sect. 2 introduced the background of Tor and hidden service, and simply summarized previous related work. Section 3 described our approach to model hidden service discovery as coupon collector problem. Section 4 presented our experiment strategies to evaluate the proposed model. Section 5 gave some discussions and Sect. 5 finally concluded the paper.

2   Background

2.1   Tor

Tor, the second-generation onion router [1], is a protocol that intends to anonymize network traffic in a low latency manner. Messages in Tor are forwarded through a multi-hop circuit in a layered-encryption manner, thus preventing a single attacker from knowing both parties of a communication.

With the introduction of *Hidden Service* in 2004 [1], Tor makes it possible for users to hide their locations while offering various kinds of web services, such as web publishing, instant messaging servers and so on. And other Tor users can connect to these hidden services without knowing providers' network identity.

2.2   Related Work

The receiver privacy provided by hidden service attracts more and more users to host web services in Tor network. The rapid growth of Tor hidden services makes it a hot topic in the anonymous research and lots of work have appeared to analyze and evaluate it.

Recently, the exposure of illegal hidden services [4] makes it appealing to analyze the size and content of Tor hidden services. George Kadianakis et al. added a statistics to the Tor software which can report the number of unique .onion addresses observed by a hidden service directory. And then based on these statistics, they extrapolated the total number of .onion addresses. Aiming to enumerate all Tor hidden services, Biryukov et al. described an efficient approach in [5]. They collected hidden services by deploying enough HSDirs based on a *shadowing* technique.

As Tor network grows and more stringent requirements on becoming HSDirs, we will inevitably have to face the predicament of using a small amount of resources to collect hidden services. That is, we have to study these issues:

1. How many hidden services can we discover if we don't have enough HSDir.
2. How many HSDirs are needed if we just want to collect a certain percentage of hidden services.

In this paper, we will present an model to describe the hidden service discovery by running HSDirs, and based on the model, we will quantify the relationship between consumed resources and collected hidden services, and finally give answers to the above questions.

3   Our Approach

In order to quantify the relationship between resources and collected hidden services, we model the discovery of hidden services by running HSDirs as a coupon collector problem. In this section, we will first introduce the coupon collector problem, and then describe our modeling method, and finally deduce the formulas to calculate two key parameters in the model.

3.1   Coupon Collector Problem

In the classical coupon collector problem, all n coupons are obtained with an equal chance of $1/n$. To collect all different coupons, the collector needs to do $\Theta(n \ln n)$ samples on average. In [6], Stadje extended the classical coupon problem to the situation where samples are done with replacement of equiprobable groups of a fixed size g. And in this situation, given a subset $A \subset S$ (S is the set of all different coupons), Stadje deduced the distributions of the number of distinct elements of A after k samples and the sample size necessary to obtain at least say x elements of A. In this paper, we will analyze and evaluate the discovery of hidden services by running HSDirs based on the extended coupon collector problem.

3.2   Discover Hidden Services by Running HSDirs

According to the protocol of Tor hidden service, a hidden service has to publish its descriptors to several HSDirs before can be accessed by any user. Tor relays with the 'HSDir'.flag forms a distributed hash table to store the descriptors published by hidden services. Once descriptor identifiers are determined, the hidden service first arranges HSDirs using their fingerprints in a closed fingerprint circle and then chooses the three closest HSDirs in positive direction (fingerprint values of them are greater than the descriptor identifiers of the hidden service). As a hidden service generates and publishes two replicas of descriptors by default, 2 sets of 3 HSDirs with consecutive fingerprints are chosen to store corresponding descriptors.

It's worth to note that, as each hidden service changes its descriptor identifiers every 24 h, and thus probably changing its responsible HSDirs. A particular HSDir will get an opportunity to discover a particular hidden service whenever the hidden service changes its descriptor identifiers. And this makes it possible to run a few HSDirs to collect more different hidden services over time.

3.3 Modeling

We model the discovery of hidden services by running HSDirs as the extended coupon collector problem with group drawings. We collect a group of hidden services by running several HSDirs everyday, aiming at collecting as many hidden services as possible. Assume the total number of Tor hidden service is S, and the number of hidden services collected by h HSDirs one day is g. Then we can map the discovery of hidden service to coupon collector problem as Table 1.

Table 1. Modeling

Symbols	Coupon collector	Hidden service discovery
S	Total number of coupons	Total number of hidden services
k	Number of samples	Number of days (24 h)
g	Size of coupon group	Number of hidden services collected one day (by h HSDirs)

As shown in Table 1, we take the total number of hidden services as the number of coupons, and due to the specification of Tor hidden service protocol (i.e., hidden service changes its descriptor identifiers every 24 h), we set the sampling interval to one day. Finally, the number of hidden services collected by our h HSDirs in one day corresponds to the size of coupon group in [6].

However, before we can use the conclusion of coupon problem to quantify the relationship between consumed resources and collected hidden services, we have to first specify the values of S and g.

Total number of Tor hidden service. According to the design of Tor hidden service [7], each hidden service generates 2 descriptors with different identifiers, and each descriptor chooses 3 responsible hidden service directories to publish. As both the descriptor identifiers and the fingerprints of HSDirs are generated by SHA1 function, it's reasonable to assume that the probability a descriptor is published to each HSDir is equal[1]. Given the total number of HSDirs N which can be learn from consensus files, the probability that a HSDir receives a particular descriptor is $3/N$, because once the descriptor identifier falls in one of the three intervals before the HSDir in the fingerprint circular, this descriptor will choose the HSDir as one of its responsible HSDirs. Besides, as each hidden service updates its descriptors once per 24 h and generate two descriptors each time, an HSDir thus gets 2 chances to be chosen by one hidden service in one day. According to the Bernoulli trial [9], the probability for a HSDir to store a given hidden service can be calculated as:

$$q = 1 - (1 - 3/N)^2 = 6/N - 9/N^2 \tag{1}$$

---

[1] In [8], George Kadianakis et al. computed the fraction of descriptors that a HSDir is responsible for, and their results showed that the fraction value is very small (0.024%), and there is little difference for this value between different HSDirs.

Thus, given the average number of hidden services collected by an HSDir one day, the total number of hidden services can be estimated by dividing the average number with the above probability.

Size of coupon group. Another parameter in the extended coupon collector problem is the size of coupon group, and in this section, we will estimate the number of hidden services collected by h HSDirs per 24 h, i.e., the size of the coupon group in one sample in the extended coupon collector problem. At first, we make the following definition:

Catch Probability: The probability that a hidden service chooses at least one of the deployed h HSDirs as its responding HSDirs, denoted by p.

At one hand, p is affected by the number of deployed HSDirs. Assume there are h deployed HSDirs and totally N HSDirs. As the fingerprints of the deployed HSDirs can be carefully chosen so that distances of any two deployed HSDirs is larger than 3 in the fingerprint circular. As a result, no descriptor can be published to more than one of the deployed HSDirs. However, with two different descriptors, it's possible for a hidden service to be published to two different deployed HSDirs. Due to the fact that each hidden service updates its descriptors once per 24 h and generate two descriptors each time, a hidden service has two chances to select the deployed HSDirs in one day. As a result, the probability that a hidden service chooses at least one of the h HSDirs as its responsible HSDirs can be given by:

$$1 - (N - 3h)^2/N^2 \tag{2}$$

where $(N - 3h)^2/N^2$ is the probability that neither of the two descriptors of a hidden service chooses one of the deployed h HSDirs as their corresponding HSDirs. Thus, the number of hidden services collected by h HSDirs one day can be estimated by $S * p$.

Once the total number of hidden services and the size of group are known, combining with the conclusions in [6], we can get the expectation of the number of distinct hidden services collected after k days with h HSDirs:

$$E(X_k(S)) = S \left[1 - \left(1 - \frac{g}{S} \right)^k \right] \tag{3}$$

where, S is the total number of hidden services by Formula 1 and g is the number of hidden services collected by h HSDirs one day by $S * p$.

4   Evaluation

We have deployed several HSDirs to collect data to validate our model in early 2015. In this section, we will present our experiments and evaluation, and the results proved the efficiency of our model.

4.1   Experiment Deployment

Four machines have been deployed with 3 locating in American and 1 in Japan, and by configuring 2 Tor instances on each machine, 8 HSDirs are finally operated. We further configured the fingerprints of deployed HSDirs not consecutive so that a same hidden service descriptor would not be published to any two HSDirs we ran. At last, by modifying Tor's source code as [10], we recorded the number of hidden service .onion addresses published to the 8 HSDirs (for the privacy issues, we didn't record the actual .onion addresses).

4.2   Evaluation

By default, hidden services change their responsible HSDirs every 24 h (note that not all hidden services are synchronized, and thus different hidden services may update their descriptor identifiers at different times). We recorded the number of collected hidden services by each deployed HSDir per 24 h, as this makes all hidden services have one chance to update its two descriptors (and thus two chances to choose our HSDirs as its responsible HSDirs) during each statistical period, which matches the requirements of coupon collect problem, i.e., each coupon is collected by same probability in a sample. Figure 1 shows the number of total collected hidden services by each HSDir per day respectively.

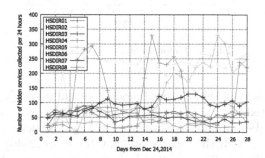

Fig. 1. Hidden services collected by each HSDir per day

Finally, 13337 distinct hidden services are collected by the 8 HSDirs in 28 days. And thus on average $13337/(28*8) = 59.54$ hidden services are collected by each HSDir per day. It's worth to note that the data collected by HSDir5, HSDir6 and HSDir8 is not as stable as the rest 5 HSDirs, and we are still working to find the reasons. When we exclude the data by these three HSDirs, the average hidden services collected by each HSDir per day is $8046/(28*5) = 57.47$, which is almost the same with the previous 59.54. For simplicity, we take 60 as the average number of hidden services collected by one HSDir per day in the following.

Combing with probability Eq. 1, the total number of hidden services is estimated as $60/[1 - (1 - 3/2935)^2] = 29365$, where 2935 is the number of HSDirs in

Tor network got from consensus files, and this result coincides with the statistic (about 30000) announced on Tor network [11] at the writing time.

It's also necessary to evaluate the size of the group of hidden services collected one day to model the hidden service collecting problem as coupon collector problem. As analyzed in Sect. 3.3, we can collect $29365 * (1 - (2935 - 3 * 8)^2 / 2935^2) = 478$ hidden services one day by 8 HSDirs given the total number of hidden services is 29365.

Figure 2 gives the theoretical and the experimental number of accumulated discovered hidden services, where the theoretical value is calculated by Eq. 3 with S set 29365 and g set to 478, while the experimental value is calculated by summing the number of distinct hidden services collected by 8 HSDirs. The result indicates that the proposed model in this paper is consistent with the discovery of hidden service by running HSDirs with a high degree.

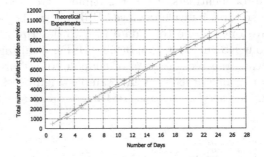

Fig. 2. Theoretical vs experiment

Given the efficiency of the proposed model, we can quantify the relationship between the collected hidden services and the consumed resources, i.e., number of HSDirs and number of days, as illustrated in Fig. 3. Specifically, according to the proposed model, with the estimation that there are 29365 hidden services in total and a HSDir can discover 60 hidden service one day, when 50 EC2 (the

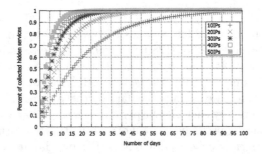

Fig. 3. Conjecture

resources needed to harvest hidden services in [5]) instances are deployed, more than 90% hidden services will be discovered after 10 days.

5 Conclusion

In this paper, we proposed a model based on coupon collector problem to describe Tor hidden services discovery by running HSDirs. The proposed model can efficiently quantify the relationship between consumed resources and collected hidden services. Experiments based on the real Tor network proved the efficiency and feasibility of the proposed model, and can be used to guide the harvesting of hidden services in Tor network with a small amount of resources.

Acknowledgments. This research is funded by National Key Research & Development Plan of China under Grant 2016YFB0801200, 2016YFB0801602 and 2016QY05X1000.

References

1. Dingledine, R., Mathewson, N., Syverson, P.: Tor: The second-generation onion router. Technical Report, DTIC Document (2004)
2. http://metrics.torproject.org
3. https://www.torproject.org/docs/hidden-services.html.en
4. http://en.wikipedia.org/wiki/SilkRoad(marketplace)
5. Biryukov, A., Pustogarov, I., Weinmann, R.: Trawling for Tor hidden services: detection, measurement, deanonymization. In: 2013 IEEE Symposium on Security and Privacy (SP), pp. 80–94. IEEE (2013)
6. Stadje, W.: The collector's problem with group drawings. Adv. Appl. Probab. **22**, 866–882 (1990)
7. https://gitweb.torproject.org/torspec.git/plain/rend-spec.txt
8. https://research.torproject.org/techreports/extrapolating-hidserv-stats-2015-01-31.pdf
9. http://en.wikipedia.org/wiki/Bernoulli_trial
10. https://github.com/DonnchaC/tor/
11. https://metrics.torproject.org/hidserv-dir-onions-seen.html

Research on Compressed Sensing Signal Reconstruction Algorithm Based on Smooth Graduation l_1 Norm

Xuan Chen[✉]

Zhejiang Industry Polytechnic College, Shaoxing, Zhejiang, China
1696450309@qq.com

Abstract. The compressed signal reconstruction of the sensing node has been a hot research topic for the mobile Internet. At present, some reconstruction algorithms finally adopt the minimum l_1 norm optimization algorithm. In order to solve the roughness, poor derivability and other defects of the minimum l_1 norm function, this paper constructs the smooth graduation algorithm based on l_1 norm, proves the monotonicity of the function and the sequence convergence of the optimal solution, and finally verifies the effectiveness of the function through examples. In the simulation experiment, the signal reconstruction algorithm and the classical OMP algorithm were compared, and the results show that it receives better reconstruction effects, small error and high precision.

Keywords: Compressed reconstruction · l_1 norm · Smooth graduation

1 Introduction

In the mobile Internet, the wireless sensor network is characterized by a large number of nodes and large data acquisition and transmission capacity. However, due to its small volume of its own node and the node energy restriction, how to reduce the energy consumption of nodes and prolong the network life cycle is a key challenge confronted by the development and application of the wireless sensor network technology [1, 2]. As a new sampling theory developed in recent years, compressed sensing (CS) [3–5] may achieve the data compression by using the redundancy of the wireless sensor network data, reduce the transmission of redundant information, and provide ideal solutions to reducing the energy consumption of network nodes.

In the compressed sensing theory, the signal reconstruction has become the key to obtaining accurate original signals and produced direct impacts on the measurements required by the reconstruction, i.e., obtaining the transmission data volume required by accurate obtaining of network data. Common signal reconstruction algorithms include the minimum convex optimization algorithm based on l_1 norm and the minimum greedy algorithm based on l_0 norm. The convex optimization algorithm is featured by large calculation and good reconstruction effects, which is represented by Basis Pursuit (BP) [6], Interior-point-iterative Algorithm, Gradient Projection For Sparse (GPSR) [7], Projection onto Convex sets (POCS) [8], Homotopy Algorithm [9] and Least Angle Regression (LARS) [10]. In spite of good reconstruction effects, the convex

© ICST Institute for Computer Sciences, Social Informatics and Telecommunications Engineering 2018
G. Sun and S. Liu (Eds.): ADHIP 2017, LNICST 219, pp. 78–93, 2018.
https://doi.org/10.1007/978-3-319-73317-3_11

optimization algorithm are blocked easily when handling massive signal questions because of high computational complexity and slow computation speed. During the iteration each time, the greedy algorithm selects a local optimal solution to gradually get close to the original signals that are characterized by poor accuracy and high computation speed characteristics, which are represented by that Matching Pursuit (MP) [11], Orthogonal Matching Pursuit (OMP) [12] and Stagewise Orthogonal Matching Pursuit (StOmp) [13]. Literature [14] proposed to first use the arc-tangent function l_0 approximation norm, establish the noisy sparse reconstruction model approximate to l_0 norm, solve the model through quasi-Newton method, and analyze the convergence of the algorithm. Numerical simulations show that the proposed algorithm needs less measurements when reconstructing the sparse vectors and has high accuracy; Literature [15] proposed a new smooth function sequence approximation norm, solve by combining with the gradient projection method, improve the robustness of the algorithm by further proposing to adopt Singular value decomposition (SVD), and achieve the accurate reconstruction of the sparsity signal; Literature [16] put forward the fast smooth norm algorithm - FSL0 algorithm according to the characteristics of Gaussian smoothing function gradient and Hesse matrix as well as basic principles of Newton; Literature [17] utilized the signal sampling value, Laplace prior distribution and Gaussian likelihood model, and derived the signal posterior probability density estimate; finally, converted the MAP estimation process into a weighted iterative L1 norm minimization question, and the signal reconstruction performance had been improved significantly.

The ideal signal reconstruction is to adopt the signal reconstruction based on the minimum l_0 norm. However, this is an NP question, so it is converted into a solution to l_1 minimum norm. Since the minimum l_1 norm is not smooth, this paper constructs, presents and proves the minimum l_1 norm based on the smooth graduation. Simulation results show that the algorithm has better reconstruction effects than the traditional OMP algorithm.

2 Signal Reconstruction Based on Smooth Graduation l_1 Norm

The ideal signal reconstruction is obtained by solving the original reconstruction model or the model based on the minimum l_0 norm [23, 24]. However, this is an NP question, so it is converted to a solution to an l_1 minimum norm. Since this norm is not smooth, this paper constructs a smooth graduation algorithm based on the l_1 norm, describes the monotonicity of the function and the convergence of the optimal solution, and uses this function to perform the signal reconstruction.

2.1 Basic Knowledge

When solving the compressed sensing signal reconstruction, the l_0 norm solution is given as follows:

$$\begin{cases} \min & d(x) = \|x\|_0 \\ s.t. \ Ax = y \end{cases} \tag{1}$$

The l_0 norm is an NP question. It has been proved that signal reconstruction based on the minimum l_0 norm is equivalent to that based on solving the minimum l_1 norm [18, 19]. Therefore, signal-reconstruction questions are handled by solving the minimum l_1 norm with the following model:

$$\begin{cases} \min & d(x) = \|x\|_1 \\ s.t. \ Ax = y \end{cases} \tag{2}$$

2.2   The Improved l_1 Question Model

An algorithm based on the l_1 solution cannot be derived, so Eq. 2 cannot be solved by an algorithm based on massive derivation. Equation 2 is a convex programming question that can be converted to one of linear programming. However, the size of the original question is doubled and the computing space is increased. A solution involving large-scale data is characterized by slow computation speed and poor signal-reconstruction effects. This paper adopts smooth, gradual, and progressive ideas, constructs a smoothing function based on the l_1 norm, studies the monotonicity and optimal sequence, and finally solves Eq. 2.

Assuming Definition 1, when $x \in R^N$, $t > 0$, then

$$F(x) = \|x\|_1 = \sum_{i=1}^{N} |x_i| \quad F_t(x) = \sum_{i=1}^{N} \sqrt{x_i^2 + \frac{c}{t^2}} \tag{3}$$

Theorem 1:

$$\lim_{t \to \infty} F_t(x) = F(x), \ F_t(x) = \sum_{i=1}^{N} \sqrt{x_i^2 + \frac{c}{t^2}}, \ x \in R^N \tag{4}$$

Proof:

$$\begin{aligned} F_t'(x) &= \sum_{i=1}^{N} \frac{1}{2\sqrt{x_i^2 + \frac{c}{t^2}}} \bullet (x_i^2 + \frac{c}{t^2})' \\ &= \sum_{i=1}^{N} \frac{1}{2\sqrt{x_i^2 + \frac{c}{t^2}}} \bullet (\frac{-2c}{t^3}) \\ &= \sum_{i=1}^{N} \frac{-c}{t^3 \sqrt{x_i^2 + \frac{c}{t^2}}} \\ &= \sum_{i=1}^{N} \frac{-c}{t^2 \sqrt{(tx_i)^2 + c}} < 0 \end{aligned} \tag{5}$$

Then, $\{t_k\}$ is a monotonically decreasing integer sequence.
The following proves that $F_t(x)$ is bounded.
For any x and t,

$$
\begin{aligned}
F_t(x) - F(x) &= \sum_{i=1}^{N} \sqrt{x_i^2 + \frac{c}{t^2}} - \sum_{i=1}^{N} |x_i| \\
&= \sum_{i=1}^{N} \left(\sqrt{x_i^2 + \frac{c}{t^2}} - \sqrt{x_i^2} \right) \\
&= \sum_{i=1}^{N} \frac{\frac{c}{t^2}}{\sqrt{x_i^2 + \frac{c}{t^2}} + \sqrt{x_i^2}} \\
&\leq \sum_{i=1}^{N} \frac{\frac{c}{t^2}}{\frac{\sqrt{c}}{t}} \\
&= \frac{\sqrt{c}}{t} N
\end{aligned}
\tag{6}
$$

Therefore $F(x) \leq F_t(x) \leq F(x) + \frac{\sqrt{c}}{t} N$, Because:

$$
\begin{aligned}
\lim_{t \to \infty} \left[F(x) + \frac{\sqrt{c}}{t} N \right] &= \lim_{t \to \infty} F(x) + \lim_{t \to \infty} \frac{\sqrt{c}}{t} N \\
&= F(x) + 0 \\
&= F(x)
\end{aligned}
\tag{7}
$$

This is simplified to

$$
0 \leq F_t(x) - F(x) \leq \frac{\sqrt{c}N}{t}
\tag{8}
$$

Take the limit toward both sides and obtain $\lim_{t \to \infty} F_t(x) = F(x)$. The proof ends.
According to Theorem 1, question 1 can be rewritten as

$$
\begin{aligned}
&\min F_t(x) \\
&s.t.\ Ax = y(t \to +\infty)
\end{aligned}
\tag{9}
$$

Given that there is a continuous real number t, it is very difficult to solve Eq. 9. Through discretization of t, we can obtain

$$
\begin{aligned}
&\min F_t(x) \\
&s.t.\ Ax = y(t_k \to +\infty)
\end{aligned}
\tag{10}
$$

where $\{t_k\}$ is a monotonically increasing integer sequence.

Theorem 2: The existence set $S = \{x \mid F_t(x) \leq F_k(x)\}$ has certain limits. The optimal solution to problem 5 is $x^*(t_k)$, i.e., $t = t_k$, so x^* is the optimal solution of Eq. 1, and $\{x^*(t_k)\}$ existence sub-column converges to x^*.

Proof: Since $F_t(x^*(t_k)) \geq F_t(x^*(t_{k+1})) \geq F_{t+1}(x^*(t_{k+1}))$ and $F_\infty(x) = F(x) \leq F_t(x)$, the combination set S has limits and $\{x^*(t_k)\}$ has a certain limit, so there is a converged sub-sequence $\{x^*(t_k)\}$. When the variable i approaches infinity, $\{x^*(t_k)\} \to \bar{x}$, and it is proved that $\bar{x} = x^*$. Proof by contradiction is as follows:

Assume $\bar{x} \neq x^*, F(x^*) - F(\bar{x}) < 0$.

Taking $\varepsilon_0 > 0$ and assuming $F(x^*) - F(\bar{x}) = -\varepsilon_0$, and $\lim\limits_{t\to\infty} F_t(x) = F(x)$, then

$$\exists I_1 > 0, \ \forall i \geq I_1, \ F_t(x^*) - F(x^*) < \frac{\varepsilon_0}{2} \tag{11}$$

Therefore,

$$F_t(x^*) - F(\bar{x}) = F_t(x^*) - F(x^*) + F(x^*) - F(\bar{x}) < -\frac{\varepsilon_0}{2} \tag{12}$$

Because

$$\lim\limits_{t\to\infty} F_t(x^*(t_k)) = F_\infty(\bar{x}) = F(\bar{x}) \tag{13}$$

Therefore,

$$\exists I_2 > 0, \forall i \geq I_2, F_t(\bar{x}) - F(x^*(t_k)) < \frac{\varepsilon_0}{2} \tag{14}$$

Therefore, $\forall i \geq \max\{I_1, I_2\}$, the following equation can be obtained:

$$F_t(x^*) - F(x^*(t_k)) = F_t(x^*) - F(\bar{x}) + F(\bar{x}) - F(x^*(t_k)) < 0 \tag{15}$$

$F_t(x^*) < F_t(x^*(t_k))$ and $x^*(t_k)$ are obtained as the optimal solution of problem 5, so $\bar{x} = x^*$.

Theorem 3: Problem 6 is a convex programming problem.

Proof: Suppose set $D = \{x \mid Ax = y\}$.

Where A is the matrix of $N \times M$, $x \in R^N, y \in R^M$

For $\forall x^{(1)}, x^{(2)} \in D$ and $\forall \lambda \in [0, 1]$

$$\begin{aligned}
A[\lambda x^{(1)} &+ (1 - \lambda)x^{(2)}] \\
&= \lambda A x^{(1)} + (1 - \lambda) A x^{(2)} \\
&= \lambda y + (1 - \lambda)y \\
&= y
\end{aligned} \tag{16}$$

So $\lambda x^{(1)} + (1 + \lambda)x^{(2)} \in D$. And therefore D is Convex set.

The following proves that the objective function $F_t(x) = \sum_{i=1}^{N} \sqrt{x_i^2 + \frac{c}{t^2}}$, $x \in R^N$ x is a strictly convex function on the set D.

$$
\begin{aligned}
F_t(x + \Delta x) &= \sum_{i=1}^{N} \sqrt{(x_i + \Delta x_i)^2 + \frac{c}{t_k^2}} \\
&\geq \sum_{i=1}^{N} \sqrt{x_i^2 + \frac{c}{t_k^2}} + \sum_{t=1}^{N} \frac{x_i \Delta x_i'}{\sqrt{x_i^2 + \frac{c}{t_k^2}}} \\
&= F_t(x) + \nabla F_t(x)^T \Delta x
\end{aligned}
\tag{17}
$$

So $F_t(x)$ is a convex function on D.

In fact $\nabla^2 F_t(x) = \begin{bmatrix} \frac{t_k}{\sqrt{[(x_1 t_k) + c]^3}} & \cdots & 0 \\ 0 & \ddots & 0 \\ 0 & & \frac{t_k}{\sqrt{[(x_w t_k) + c]^3}} \end{bmatrix} \in R^{N \times M}$ is Positive-definite

matrix.

So $F_t(x)$ is a strictly convex function.

Theorem 4: Suppose $x^*(t_k)$ is the optimal solution of $t = t_k$ for Eq. 10, and x^* is the global optimal solution to problem 2. Therefore, for any $t_k > 0$ and $k \to +\infty$, then

$$
\|x^* - x^*(t_k)\| \leq \sqrt{\max\left\{\frac{2\sqrt{[(x_i t_k)^2 + c]^3}}{t_k^2}\right\}\sqrt{cN}}
\tag{18}
$$

Proof: Select the target function $F_t(x)$. Its $x = x^*(t_k)$ Taylor expansion is

$$
\begin{aligned}
F_t(x) &= F_t(x^*(t_k)) + \nabla F_t(x^*(t_k))^T (x - x^*(t_k)) + \nabla F_t(x^*(t_k))(x - x^*(t_k)) \\
&\quad + o(x - x^*(t_k))^T (x - x^*(t_k))
\end{aligned}
\tag{19}
$$

Given $x = x^*$ and the necessary conditions of the first-order derivative, the following equation can be obtained:

$$
F_t(x) - F_t(x^*(t_k)) = \sum_{i=1}^{N} \frac{1}{2} \frac{t_k}{\sqrt{[(x_i t_k)^2 + c]^3}}(x^* - x^*(t_k))^2 + o(x - x^*(t_k))^T (x - x^*(t_k))
\tag{20}
$$

Because $\nabla^2 F_t(x)$ is a diagonal matrix, the following equation can be obtained:

$$
F_t(x) - F_t(x^*(t_k)) \geq \min\left\{\frac{t_k}{2\sqrt{[(x_i t_k)^2 + c]^3}}\right\}\|x^* - x^*(t_k)\|_2^2
\tag{21}
$$

Because $F_t(x)$ is monotonously decreasing over t, we can obtain the inequality $F_t(x^*(t_k)) - F_{t+1}(x^*(t_k)) < 0$. x^* is the global optimal solution of problem 2, and the following equation can be obtained:

$$F_t(x) - F_t(x^*(t_k)) < 0 \qquad (22)$$

$$\|x^* - x^*(t_k)\|_2^2 \leq \max\{\frac{2\sqrt{[(x_i t_k)^2 + c]^3}}{t_k}\}(F_t(x^*) - F(x^*(t_k)))$$

$$= \max\{\frac{2\sqrt{[(x_i t_k)^2 + c]^3}}{t_k}\}(F_t(x^*) - F(x^*) + F(x^*) - F(x^*(t_k)) \qquad (23)$$

$$+ F(x^*(t_k)) - F_t(x^*(t_k)))$$

$$\leq \max\{\frac{2\sqrt{[(x_i t_k)^2 + c]^3}}{t_k}\}(F_t(x^*) - F(x^*))$$

Substitute Eq. 8 into the above equation to obtain $0 \leq F_t(x^*) - F(x^*) \leq \frac{\sqrt{cN}}{t}$, i.e.,

$$\|x^* - x^*(t_k)\| \leq \sqrt{\max\{\frac{2\sqrt{[(x_i t_k)^2 + c]^3}}{t_k^2}\}\sqrt{cN}} \qquad (24)$$

The proof ends.

Therefore, according to Theorem 2, the algorithm of Eq. 25 is as follows.

Algorithm 1 steps:

Step 1: Enter the matrix A and t_0, the measured value y, the threshold ε, and the step h

Step 2: Given $k = 0, x_0^*(t_0) = A'y$

Step 3: Given $t_k = t_0 + kh$, obtain the optimal solution $x^*(t_k)$ of Eq. 25.

Step 4: Given $\|x^*(t_k) - x^*(t_{k-1})\| > \varepsilon$, set $k = k+1$, return to step 3, and otherwise output $x^*(t_k)$

2.3 Algorithm Examples

Suppose we have $A = \begin{bmatrix} 1 & 0 & 3 & 4 & 5 & 8 & 2 & 3 & -1 & 5 \\ 0 & -10 & 4 & 1 & 2 & 3 & 4 & 7 & 8 & 3 \\ -9 & 15 & 4 & 3 & 8 & 6 & 4 & 7 & 2 & 4 \\ 2 & 5 & 1 & 7 & 6 & 3 & -5 & 0 & 9 & 7 \end{bmatrix}, y = \begin{pmatrix} 1 \\ 4 \\ 2 \\ 5 \end{pmatrix};$

assume $t_k = 10 + 200k$, $F_t(x^*(t_k))$, $\|x^*(t_k) - x^*(t_{k-1})\|_2$, and the computational results of $x^*(t_k)$ can be obtained according to the algorithm solution process, as shown in Tables 1 and 2:

Table 1. Numerical results

k	$F_t(x^*(t_k))$	$\|x^*(t_k) - x^*(t_{k-1})\|_2$
1	1.07768	0.55466
2	1.05858	0.04529
3	1.05232	0.00919
4	1.0492	0.00859
6	1.04569	0.00379
8	1.04352	0.00291
10	1.0432	0.00121

Table 2. Numerical results

k	$x^*(t_k)$
1	$(-0.02517 \quad -0.07485 \quad 0.00241 \quad -0.00669 \quad -0.01147 \quad 0.72901 \quad 0.06089 \quad 0.00701 \quad -0.01242)$
2	$(-0.02519 \quad -0.07131 \quad 0.00129 \quad -0.00361 \quad -0.00621 \quad 0.71601 \quad 0.08321 \quad 0.00401 \quad -0.00653)$
3	$(-0.02521 \quad -0.07129 \quad 0.00091 \quad -0.00312 \quad -0.00521 \quad 0.71982 \quad 0.08643 \quad 0.00261 \quad -0.00489)$
4	$(-0.02521 \quad -0.07129 \quad 0.00091 \quad -0.00312 \quad -0.00521 \quad 0.71982 \quad 0.08643 \quad 0.00261 \quad -0.00489)$
6	$(-0.02497 \quad -0.06751 \quad 0.00041 \quad -0.00125 \quad -0.00219 \quad 0.69758 \quad 0.09999 \quad 0.00239 \quad -0.00231)$
8	$(-0.02492 \quad -0.06763 \quad 0.00038 \quad -0.00101 \quad -0.00149 \quad 0.59501 \quad 0.10152 \quad 0.00099 \quad -0.00108)$
10	$(-0.02516 \quad -0.06731 \quad 0.00029 \quad -0.00103 \quad -0.00129 \quad 0.69371 \quad 0.10371 \quad 0.00081 \quad -0.00128)$

According to Tables 1 and 2, it is feasible to discrete the question, proving that Eq. 10 has effects and demonstrating that the algorithm 1 can achieve signal reconstruction.

3 Reconstructed Signal Algorithm Based on Smooth Approximation Norm l_p

In the previous chapter, we improved the signal reconstruction based on norm l_1 by constructing a smooth approximation function. However, the pseudo-norm $\|x\|_p$ $(0 \leq p \leq 1)$ rather than $\|x\|_1$ is a better approximation of the norm $\|x\|_0$ in the original problem. This chapter adopts the maximum entropy function smooth approximation l_p, proposes the MEFM algorithm, and validates using a one-dimensional signal-reconstruction example.

3.1 Preliminary Knowledge

Restoration signals will sometimes receive better effects by adopting $l_p(0 < p < 1)$ norm optimization than by adopting the l_1 norm optimization method.

The pseudo-norm $\|x\|_p(0 \leq p \leq 1)$ rather than $\|x\|_1$ is more approximate to the norm $\|x\|_0$ in the original problem. The problem model is as follows:

$$\begin{cases} \min d(x) = \|x\|_p \ (0<p<1) \\ s.t. \ Ax = y \end{cases} \tag{25}$$

When choosing the sparse vector to be the global $l_p(0<p<1)$ minimum solution of $Ax = y$, fewer y observations are required than with the l_1 norm optimization method [20]. In addition, existing proved sufficient conditions for lower signal reconstruction requirements than the norm l_1 [21–23]. This paper constructs a smooth approximation function of the norm $l_p(0<p<1)$ by the maximum entropy function, thus realizing the signal reconstruction.

In formula 25 for the $l_p(0<p<1)$ norm minimization, the objective function can be expressed as

$$\|x\|_p = \left(\sum_{i=1}^{n} |x_i|^p \right)^{\frac{1}{p}} = \left[\sum_{i=1}^{n} (\max\{x_i, -x_i\})^p \right]^{\frac{1}{p}} \tag{26}$$

So, formula 25 can be written as

$$\begin{cases} \min \varphi(x) = \left[\sum_{i=1}^{n} (\max\{x_j - x_i\})^p \right]^{\frac{1}{p}} \ (0<p<1) \\ s.t. \ Ax = y \end{cases} \tag{27}$$

where $\varphi(x)$ is the objective function.

Since the objective function in formula 8 is not derivable, the smoothing constraint algorithm cannot be employed. This paper constructs a smoothing function to approximate formula 27 and transforms the problem into a constrained smoothing problem that can be solved using the smooth constraint algorithm.

3.2   Smooth Approximation of the Norm l_p in the Algorithm

The maximum entropy function $\rho^{-1} \ln[\exp(\rho t) + \exp(-\rho t)]$ is a smooth approximation of the maximum function $\max\{t, -t\}$ [24], where $\rho > 0$ and t is a variable. By substituting the function $\max\{x_i, -x_i\}$ for $\rho^{-1} \ln[\exp(\rho x_i) + \exp(-\rho x_i)]$ in formula 27, we obtain the following smoothing problem:

$$\begin{cases} \min \Gamma(x, \rho) = \left[\sum_{i=1}^{n} (\rho^{-1} \ln[\exp(\rho x_i) + \exp(-\rho x_i)])^p \right]^{\frac{1}{p}} \ (0<p<1) \\ s.t. \ Ax = y \end{cases} \tag{28}$$

Lemma 1 [23]. $\forall p \in \{1, 2, \ldots, k\}$, $k \in N$, $g_p(x) : R^n \to R$ is assumed to be a continuously differentiable function,

$$h(x) = \max_{1 \leq p \leq k} [g_p(x)], H(x, p) = \frac{1}{p} \ln \left[\sum \exp(\rho g_p(x)) \right] \tag{29}$$

Then, the function $H(x,p)$ has the following properties:

(1) $\forall x \in R^n$ and $0 < \rho_1 < \rho_2$, there exists $H(x, \rho_1) \geq H(x, \rho_2)$
(2) $\forall x \in R^n$ and $\rho > 0$, there exists $h(x) \leq H(x, \rho) \leq h(x) + \frac{\ln k}{\rho}$
(3) $\forall x \in R^n$ and $\rho > 0$, there exists $\lim\limits_{\rho \to \infty} H(x, \rho) = h(x)$.

Lemma 2: The function $\Gamma(x,p) = ||\frac{\ln(e^{\rho x}+e^{-\rho x})}{\rho}||_p = [\sum\limits_{i=1}^{n}(\frac{\ln(e^{\rho x}+e^{-\rho x})}{\rho})^p]^{\frac{1}{p}}$ $\forall x \in R^n$ and $\rho > 0$, there exists

$$\varphi(x) \leq \Gamma(x, \rho) \leq \varphi(x) + \frac{\sqrt[p]{n}\ln 2}{\rho} \tag{30}$$

where $\varphi(x) = ||x||_p = (\sum\limits_{i=1}^{n}|x_i|^p)^{\frac{1}{p}}$.

Proof: According to Lemma 1, $\forall x \in R^n$, $\rho > 0$, there exists the relation:

$$0 \leq \frac{1}{\rho}\ln[\exp(\rho x_i) + \exp(-\rho x_i)] - \max\{x_i, -x_i\} \leq \frac{\ln 2}{\rho} \tag{31}$$

According to the definitions of $\Gamma(x, \rho)$ and $\varphi(x)$, this paper concludes that

$$\Gamma(x,p) - \varphi(x) = ||\frac{\ln(e^{\rho x}+e^{-\rho x})}{\rho}||_p - ||x||_p$$
$$\leq ||\frac{\ln(e^{\rho x}-e^{-\rho x})}{\rho} - x||_p \tag{32}$$
$$= \left[\sum\limits_{i=1}^{n}(\frac{\ln(e^{\rho xi}+e^{-pxi})}{\rho}) - |x_i|^p\right]^{\frac{1}{p}}$$

According to formula 9, we conclude that

$$0 \leq \Gamma(x, \rho) - \varphi(x) \leq \frac{\sqrt[p]{n}\ln 2}{\rho} \tag{33}$$

The proof ends.

Lemma 3: $\forall x \in R^n, \rho > 0$, there exists

$$\varphi(x) \leq \Gamma(x, \rho) \leq \varphi(x) + \left[\sum\limits_{i=1}^{n}(\frac{\ln 2}{\rho})\right]^{\frac{1}{p}} = \varphi(x) + \frac{\sqrt[p]{n}\ln 2}{\rho} \tag{34}$$

And

$$\lim\limits_{\rho \to \infty} \Gamma(x, \rho) = \varphi(x) = ||x||_p \tag{35}$$

The following hypotheses are assumed for problem 1.

The rank of the matrix A is m, and the variable $x = [x^B, x^N]^T$, where $x^B = (x_1^B, x_2^B, \ldots, x_m^B)$, is the vector corresponding to the basic vector; $x^N = (x_{m+1}^N, x_{m+2}^N, \ldots, x_n^N)^T$ is the vector corresponding to the non-basic variable; B is the m-th column of matrix A corresponding to the basic vector; N is the (n–m)-th column corresponding to the non-basic variable; the matrix $A = [B, N]$; and the feasible region $\{x \mid Ax = y\}$ is not empty.

In the above hypotheses, the constraint condition $Ax = y$ in (1) can be written as

$$Bx^B + Nx^N = y \tag{36}$$

$x^B = B^{-1}(y - Nx^N)$ is available. Substitute x^B into the objective function of problem 3 to transform formula 3 into the following unconstrained problem:

$$\min_{x \in R} M(x^N, \rho) = \Gamma(B^{-1}(y - Nx^N), x^N, \rho) \tag{37}$$

This paper obtains the respective optimal solutions of problems 1 and 2 by using x^* and $x(\rho^*)$.

Algorithm Steps

Step 1: *Take* $(x^N)^0 \in R^{n-m}$ and the error $1 > \beta > 0, \delta \in (0,1)$

Step 2: $\rho^* = \dfrac{\sqrt[n]{n} \ln 2}{\beta(1 - \delta)}$

Step 3: Solve formula 10, i.e., solve the following problem:

$$\min_{x \in R} M(x^N, \rho^*) = \Gamma(B^{-1}(y - Nx^N), x^N, \rho^*) \tag{38}$$

where $M(x^N, \rho^*)$ is the objective function.

The algorithm has the following properties:

Theorem 5: Assume that the optimal solution of problem 12 is $(x^N(\rho^*))^*$ and the point generated by the algorithm satisfies the condition

$$M((x^N)^s, \rho^*) - M((x^N(\rho^*))^*, \rho^*) \le \delta\beta \tag{39}$$

Then $\varphi(x^s) - \varphi(x^*) \le \beta$, where, s is the number of iterations.

Proof: $x^*(\rho^*)$ is the optimal solution of formula 3, i.e.,

$$\Gamma(x^*(\rho^*); \rho^*) \le \Gamma(x^*; \rho^*) \tag{40}$$

From formula 30, we obtain

$$\varphi(x^*) \le \Gamma(x^*; \rho^*) \le \varphi(x^*) + \frac{\sqrt[n]{n} \ln 2}{\rho^*} \; \varphi(x^*(\rho^*)) \le \Gamma(x^*(\rho^*); \rho^*) \le \varphi(x^*(\rho^*)) + \frac{\sqrt[n]{n} \ln 2}{\rho^*} \tag{41}$$

So, we obtain

$$\Gamma(x^*(\rho^*);\rho^*) \leq \Gamma(x^*;\rho^*) \leq \varphi(x^*) + \frac{\sqrt[p]{n}\ln 2}{\rho^*} \tag{42}$$

and

From formula 30, we obtain

$$\varphi(x^s) \leq \Gamma(x^s;\rho^*) \tag{43}$$

By adding formulas 42 and 43, we obtain

$$\varphi(x^s) - \varphi(x^*) \leq \Gamma(x^s;\rho^*) - \Gamma(x^*(\rho^*);\rho^*) + \frac{\sqrt[p]{n}\ln 2}{\rho^*} \tag{44}$$

and from formula 38, we obtain

$$\left.\begin{array}{l} M\big((x^N(\rho^*))^*;\rho^*\big) = \Gamma(x^*(\rho^*);\rho^*) \\ M\big((x^N)^s;\rho^*\big) = \Gamma(x^s;\rho^*) \end{array}\right\} \tag{45}$$

From formulas 39 and 45, we obtain

$$\Gamma(x^s;\rho^*) - \Gamma(x^*(\rho^*);\rho^*) \leq \delta\beta \tag{46}$$

From formulas 45 and 46, we obtain

$$\varphi(x^s) - \varphi(x^*) \leq \delta\beta + \frac{\sqrt[p]{n}\ln 2}{\rho^*} \tag{47}$$

Substituting $\rho^* = \dfrac{\sqrt[p]{n}\ln 2}{\beta(1-\delta)}$ into formula 47, we obtain

$$\varphi(x^s) - \varphi(x^*) \leq \beta \tag{48}$$

The proof ends.

Theorem 6: Assume that $x(\rho) = (x_1(\rho), x_2(\rho), \cdots x_n(\rho))$ is the optimal solution of formula 39. If $\lim\limits_{p\to+\infty} x(\rho)$ exists, we assume $\lim\limits_{p\to+\infty} x(\rho) = x^* = [x_1^*, x_2^*, \cdots, x_n^*]^T$. If there is $x_k^* = 0 (1 \leq k \leq n)$ in $x_1^*, x_2^*, \cdots, x_n^*$, we obtain

$$\lim\limits_{p\to+\infty} \rho x_k(\rho) = 0 \tag{49}$$

Then x^* is the optimal solution to formula 25.

Proof: $\forall x \in R^n$, $\forall \rho > 0$, and we obtain the equation below by Lemma 3:

$$\varphi(x) \le \Gamma(x; \rho) \le \varphi(x) + \frac{\sqrt[\rho]{n} \ln 2}{\rho^*} \tag{50}$$

In formula 30, assuming $\rho \to +\infty$, we can obtain the following equation according to the conditions in Theorem 2:

$$\lim_{\rho \to +\infty} \Gamma(x(\rho); \rho) = \lim_{\rho \to +\infty} \Gamma(x^*; \rho) = \lim_{\rho \to +\infty} \varphi(x(\rho)) = \varphi(x^*) = \|x^*\|_p \tag{51}$$

Since $x(\rho)$ is the optimal solution of formula 3, for the point x satisfying $Ax = y$, we can obtain $\Gamma(x(\rho); \rho) \le \varphi(x; \rho)$.

So,

$$\lim_{\rho \to +\infty} \Gamma(x; \rho) = \varphi(x) = \|x\|_p \ge \|x^*\|_p \tag{52}$$

The following proves to be the feasible solution of problem 3. Since $x(\rho)$ is the optimal solution of formula 9, $Ax(\rho) = y$.

Assume $\lim_{\rho \to +\infty} (x; \rho) = x^*$. Then we obtain $Ax^* = y$, i.e., x^* is the optimal solution of formula 30.

4 Experimental Description

The one-dimensional signal is reconstructed by adopting the proposed algorithm and OMP algorithm. Where, the reconstruction signal sparsity is 6, the signal length is 256, the signal observation M is 64, $f_1 = 50$, $f_2 = 100$, $f_3 = 200$, $f_4 = 400$, $f_s = 800$ and $t_s = 1/f_s$.

$x = 0.3 \sin(2\pi * 50 * t_s * t_s) + 0.6 \sin(2\pi * 100 * t_s * t_s) + 0.1 \sin(2\pi * 200 * t_s * t_s) + 0.9 \sin(2\pi * 400 * t_s * t_s)$, the test results are shown in Fig. 1:

Since the measured values must satisfy $M \ge K \bullet \log(\frac{n}{k})$, when the value of M is 64, the sampling rate M/n is 0.25. Taking taken p as 0.25, β as 0.5 and δ as 0.02, Figs. 2 and 3 shows that these two algorithms receive excellent reconstruction effects. According to Table 3, at the same sampling rate, the signal reconstruction effects of the proposed algorithm are superior to OMP algorithm with small reconstruction errors. Besides, OMP algorithm needs to obtain the known signal sparsity K at running time and the proposed algorithm does not need it, so the proposed algorithm has more convenient computation and high efficiency.

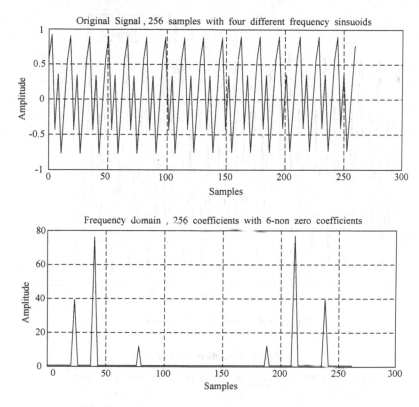

Fig. 1. Original signal and frequency-domain signal

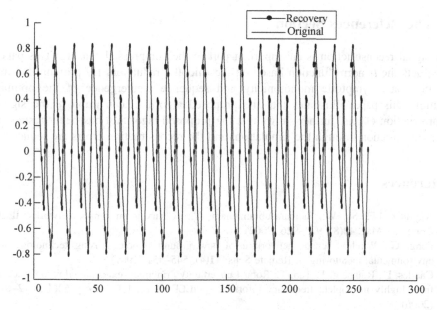

Fig. 2. Proposed reconstruction

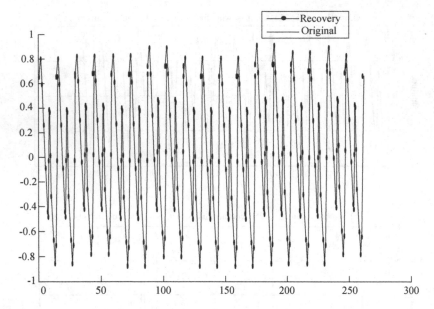

Fig. 3. OMP algorithm reconstruction

Table 3. Reconstruction error

Reconstruction algorithm	Sampling rate	Reconstruction error
OMP	0.25	7.1997e−004
The proposed algorithm	0.25	2.9821e−024

5   The References Section

The signal reconstruction is an important part of the compressed sensing. This paper constructs the l_1 norm function based on the smooth graduation. By proving that the function has asymptotic monotonicity and sequence convergence of the optimal solution, this paper illustrates that the proposed algorithm can improve the signal reconstruction effects, further shows that the proposed algorithm has better results in the reconstruction through the simulation, and the reconstruction errors are reduced.

References

1. Akyildiz, I.F., Su, W., Sankarasubramaniam, Y.: A survey on sensor networks. IEEE Commun. Mag. **40**(8), 923–926 (2002)
2. Peng, G.: Wireless sensor network as a new ground remote sensing technology for environmental monitoring. J. Remote Sens. **11**(4), 545–551 (2007)
3. Candes, E., Romberg, J., Tao, T.: Robust uncertainty principles: exact signal reconstruction from highly incomplete frequency information. IEEE Trans. Inf. Theory **52**(4), 612–616 (2006)

4. Wang, Q.: Compressed sensing for data collection in wireless sensor network. J. Transduct. Technol. **27**(11), 1562–1567 (2014)
5. Dai, Q.-H., Fu, C.-J., Ji, X.-Y.: Research on compressed sensing. Chin. J. Comput. **54**(3), 425–434 (2011)
6. Chen, S., Donoho, D.L., Saunders, M.A.: Atomic decomposition by basis pursuit. SIAM J. Sci. Comput. **20**(1), 33–61 (1999)
7. Kim, S., Koh, K., Lustig, M., et al.: A method for large-scale l1-regularizd least squares problems with applications in signal processing and statistic. IEEE J. Sel. Top. Sig. Process. **1**(4), 606–617 (2007)
8. Blatt, D., Hero, A.O.: Energy-based sensor network source localization via projection onto convex sets. IEEE Trans. Sig. Process. **54**(9), 3614–3619 (2006)
9. Choi, S.H., Harney, D.A., Book, N.L.: A robust path tracking algorithm for homotopy continuation. Comput. Chem. Eng. **20**, 647–655 (1996)
10. Wright, S.J.: Primal-dual interior methods. SIAM (1997)
11. Pati, Y., Rezaifar, R., Krishnaprasad, P.: Orthogonal matching pursuit: recursive function approximation with application to wavelet decomposition. In: 1993 Conference Record of the 27th Asilomar Conference on IEEE Signals, Systems and Computers, pp. 40–44 (1993)
12. Tropp, J., Gilbert, A.C.: Signal recovery from random measurements via orthogonal matching pursuit. IEEE Trans. Inf. Theory **53**(12), 4655–4666 (2007)
13. Donoho, D.L., Tsaig, Y., Drori, I., et al.: Sparse solution of underdetermined systems of linear equations by stagewise orthogonal matching pursuit. IEEE Trans. Inf. Theory **58**(2), 1094–1121 (2012)
14. Wang, J.-h., Huang, Z.-t., Zhou, Y.-y., Wang, F.-h.: Robust sparse recovery based on approximate L0 norm. Acta Electronica Sinica **40**(6), 1185–1189 (2012)
15. Feng, J., Zhang, G., Wen, F.: Improved sparse signal reconstruction algorithm based on SLO Norm. J. Data Acquisit. Process. **31**(1), 178–183 (2016)
16. Ma, S.-x., Zhang, M.-h., Meng, X.: Fast smoothed L0 norm algorithm for compressive sensing reconstruction. Sci. Technol. Eng. **13**(9), 2377–2381 (2013)
17. He, Y.-b., Bi, D.-y., Ma, S.-p., Lu, L., Yue, Y.-s.: Signal reconstruction with probability inference and reweighted iterative L1 norm. J. Optoelectr. Laser **23**(3), 579–587 (2012)
18. Chen, S.B., Donoho, D.L., Saunders, M.A.: Atmoic decomposition by basis pursuit. SIAM J. Sci. Comput. **20**(1), 33–61 (1998)
19. Donoho, D.L., Elad, M., Temlyakov, V.: Stable recovery of sparse overcomplete representations in the presence of noise. IEEE Trans. Inf. Theory **52**(1), 6–18 (2006)
20. Baraniuk, R., Steeghs, P.: Compressive radar imaging. In: Proceedings of Radar Conference, pp. 128–133. IEEE, Washington D.C. (2007)
21. Gribonval, R., Nielsen, M.: Sparse representation in unions of bases. IEEE Trans. Inf. Theory **49**(12), 3320–3325 (2003)
22. Zelinski, A., Wald, L.L., Setsompop, K., et al.: Sparsity-enforced slice-selective MRI RF excitation pulse design. IEEE Trans. Med. Imaging **27**(9), 1213–1229 (2008)
23. Li, X.S., Fang, S.C.: On the entropic regularization method for solving max-min problems with application. Matlietnatical Methods Oper. Res. **46**, 119–130 (1997)
24. Donoho, D.L., Elad, M.: Optimally sparse representation in general (nonorthogoinal) dictionaries via L1 minimization. Proc. Natl. Acad. Sci. U.S.A. **100**(5), 2197–2202 (2003)

Performance Evaluation of Structured Compressed Sensing Based Signal Detection in Spatial Modulation 3D MIMO Systems

Wei Ren[✉], Guan Gui, and Fei Li

College of Telecommunication and Information Engineering,
Nanjing University of Posts and Telecommunications, Nanjing 210003, China
{1215012202,guiguan,lifei}@njupt.edu.cn

Abstract. Signal detection is one of the fundamental problems in three dimensional multiple-input multiple-output (3D MIMO) wireless communication systems. This paper addresses a signal detection problem in 3D MIMO system, in which spatial modulation (SM) transmission scheme is considered results of advantages of low complexity and high-energy efficiency. SM based signal transmission, typically results in the block-sparse structure in received signal. Hence, structured compressed sensing (SCS) based signal detection is proposed to exploit the inherent block sparsity information in the received signal for the uplink (UL). To extend the potential applications in different modulation based systems, this paper analyzes bit error rate (BER) of SCS-based method, in comparison with conventional methods such as minimum mean square error (MMSE) and zero padding (ZF). Simulation results are also provided to show the stable and reliable performance of the proposed SCS-based algorithm under most modulations.

Keywords: Structured compressed sensing · Signal detection
Structured subspace pursuit algorithm · Spatial modulation

1 Introduction

Spatial Modulation (SM) is an attractive technique with low-complexity and high energy-efficient transmission in three dimension (3D) multiple-input multiple-output (MIMO) systems. It is capable of exploiting the indices of transmit antennas as an additional dimension which can invoke for transmitting information, apart from the traditional amplitude and phase modulation (APM) [1]. Unlike the traditional MIMO systems, the SM transmitter in 3D-MIMO systems uses massive transmit antennas with a few number of radio frequency (RF) chains, which significantly improve energy efficiency of the whole system. Because the power consumption and hardware cost highly depend on the number of RF chains [2]. Moreover, with only one or several

This work was supported in part by the National Natural Science Foundation of China grants (No. 61471200 and 61401069).

© ICST Institute for Computer Sciences, Social Informatics and Telecommunications Engineering 2018
G. Sun and S. Liu (Eds.): ADHIP 2017, LNICST 219, pp. 94–102, 2018.
https://doi.org/10.1007/978-3-319-73317-3_12

non-zero components in transmit signal at each slot, the inherent sparsity of 3D-SM-MIMO signals can be utilized in signal detection to reduce computation complexity.

For the novel transmit systems, suitable signal detection algorithms are required to obtain signals. The maximum-likelihood (ML) detector suffers from high complexity which linearly increases with the number of transmit antennas, the number of receive antennas, and the size of the symbol constellation [3]. Linear minimum mean square error (LMMSE)-based signal detector and sphere decoding (SD)-based detector [4] suffer from significant performance loss in SM-MIMO systems [5–7]. To exploit the inherent sparsity of SM signals, compressed sensing (CS) theory can be used to improve the signal detection performance [8, 9]. In [10], CS theory is used for signal detection in large-scale multiple access channels. Paper [11] proposed a structured compressed sensing based signal detector for massive spatial modulation MIMO systems.

To fully extend the applications, this paper analyzes the performance of several compressed sensing signal detectors with different modulation levels in 3D MIMO system. Firstly, we compare the detection performance of several available signal detection algorithms and provide corresponding simulation results. Our simulation study implied that that SSP algorithm based on structured compressed sensing can achieve better performance than others. Additionally, SSP algorithm under different modulation conditions is further analyzed via average bit error rate (BER) standard against with signal to noise ratio (SNR).

The rest of this paper is organized as follows. Section 2 introduces the 3D MIMO system model and Sect. 3 presents structured compressed sensing based signal detection methods. The simulation results and performance analysis of different signal detectors are provided in Sect. 4. Finally, conclusions are drawn in Sect. 5.

2 System Model

In spatial modulation MIMO systems, the transmitter has N_t transmit antennas with $N_a < N_t$ active antennas, and the receiver has N_r receive antennas. The information bit stream is divided into two parts: the first part with $\left\lfloor \log_2 \binom{N_t}{N_a} \right\rfloor$ bits is mapped onto the spatial constellation symbol which indicates different selection schemes of active transmit antennas, and the second part with $\log_2 M$ bits is mapped onto the signal constellation symbols coming from the M-ary signal constellation set (e.g., QAM). Hence, each SM signal carriers the information of $N_a \log_2 M + \left\lfloor \log_2 \binom{N_t}{N_a} \right\rfloor$ bits.

At the receiver, the received signal $\mathbf{y} \in \mathbb{C}^{N_r \times 1}$ can be expressed as $\mathbf{y} = \mathbf{Hx} + \mathbf{w}$, where $\mathbf{x} \in \mathbb{C}^{N_t \times 1}$ is the SM signal transmitted by the transmitter, $\mathbf{w} \in \mathbb{C}^{N_r \times 1}$ is the additive white Gaussian noise (AWGN) vector with independent and identically distributed (i.i.d.) entries following the circular symmetric complex Gaussian distribution $\mathcal{CN}(0, \sigma_w^2)$. $\mathbf{H} = \mathbf{R}_r^{\frac{1}{2}} \tilde{\mathbf{H}} \mathbf{R}_t^{\frac{1}{2}} \in \mathbb{C}^{N_r \times N_t}$ is the correlated flat Rayleigh-fading MIMO channel, entries of $\tilde{\mathbf{H}}$ are subjected to the i.i.d. distribution $\mathcal{CN}(0, 1)$. $\mathbf{R}_r$ and $\mathbf{R}_t$ are the receiver and transmitter correlation matrices respectively [12]. The correlation matrix $\mathbf{R}$ is given by $r_{ij} = r^{|i-j|}$, where r_{ij} is the i-th row and j-th column element of $\mathbf{R}$, and r is the correlation coefficient of neighboring antennas.

Figure 1 shows an example of spatial constellation symbol and signal constellation symbol in spatial modulation 3D-MIMO system. The information bit stream is under both spatial modulation and digital modulation, where spatial modulation increases the energy efficiency and reduces complexity of signal demodulation, and digital modulation improves system throughput.

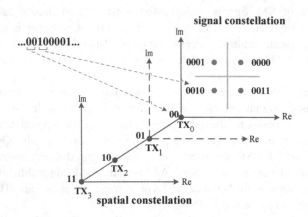

Fig. 1. Spatial constellation symbol and signal constellation symbol in SM 3D-MIMO system, where $N_t = 4$, $N_a = 1$, and 4QAM are considered as for an example.

3 Structured Compressed Sensing Based Signal Detection

3.1 Grouped Transmission Scheme

The SM signal $\mathbf{x}_k = \mathbf{e}_k s_k$ transmitted by the k th user in a time slot consists of two parts: the spatial constellation symbol $\mathbf{e}_k \in \mathbb{C}^{n_t}$ and the signal constellation symbol $s_k \in \mathbb{C}$. Due to only a single RF chain employed at each user, only one entry of $\mathbf{e}_k$ associated with the active AE is equal to one, and the rest of the entries of $\mathbf{e}_k$ are zeros, i.e., we have

$$\text{supp}(\mathbf{e}_k) \in \mathbb{A}, \; \| \mathbf{e}_k \|_0 = 1, \; \| \mathbf{e}_k \|_2 = 1 \tag{1}$$

where $\mathbb{A} = \{1, 2, \ldots, n_t\}$ is the spatial constellation symbol set. The signal constellation symbol comes from L-ary modulation, i.e., $s_k \in \mathbb{L}$, where $\mathbb{L}$ is the signal constellation symbol set of size L. Hence, each user's SM signal carries the information of $\log_2(L) + \log_2(n_t)$ bits per channel use (bpcu), and the overall throughput at the transmitter is $K(\log_2(L) + \log_2(n_t))$ bpcu.

At the transmitter, every G consecutive SM signals are divided into a group. The signals in a group have the same active antenna selection scheme and share the same spatial constellation symbol, i.e.,

$$\text{supp}(\mathbf{x}_k^1) = \text{supp}(\mathbf{x}_k^2) = \ldots = \text{supp}(\mathbf{x}_k^G) \tag{2}$$

where $\mathbf{x}_k^1, \mathbf{x}_k^2, \ldots, \mathbf{x}_k^G$ are SM signal of the k th user in G consecutive symbol slots. Thus they show the feature of structured sparsity, which can be exploited as priori information to improve the performance of the signal detection.

At the receiver, due to the reduced number of RF chains at the BS, only M_{RF} receive antennas can be exploited to receive signals. Since the BS can serve K users simultaneously, the received signal $\mathbf{y}_q \in \mathbb{C}^{M_{RF}}$ for $1 \le q \le Q$ of the q th time slot can be expressed as

$$\mathbf{y}_q = \sum_{k=1}^{K} \mathbf{y}_{k,q} + \mathbf{w}_q = \sum_{k=1}^{K} \mathbf{H}_k \mathbf{x}_k + \mathbf{w}_q \tag{3}$$

where $\mathbf{H}_k \in \mathbb{C}^{M \times n_t}$ is the k th user's MIMO channel matrix. Figure 2 is the illustration of the grouped transmission scheme at the transmitter.

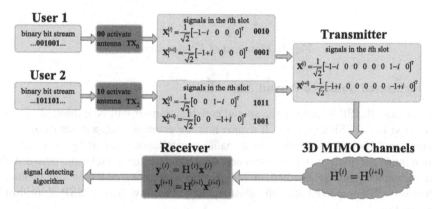

Fig. 2. Illustration of the grouped transmission scheme at the transmitter, where $K = 2$, $N_u = 4$, $N_a = 1$, $G = 2$, $N_t = 8$, $N_r = 4$, and 4QAM are considered.

3.2 Subspace Pursuit Algorithm

The SP algorithm starts by selecting the set of K most reliable information symbols [13, 14]. After each iteration, the estimated support set of size K will be updated according to the correlation between the measurement vector $\mathbf{y}$ and the channel submatrix. Then, the wrong indices will be removed from the estimated support set. The iteration stops when the transient residual is larger than the previous one. The flowchart of SP algorithm is shown in Fig. 3, where input is measurement vector $\mathbf{y}$, channel matrix $\mathbf{H}$, number of active antennas N_a and output is the estimated signal.

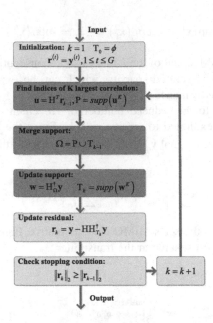

Fig. 3. Flowchart of SP algorithm.

3.3 Structured Subspace Pursuit Algorithm

Different from the SP algorithm, the spatial constellation set will be exploited as priori information in the SSP algorithm. It means that the estimated support set during each iteration should belong to the predefined spatial constellation set. During each iteration, the potential true indices will be obtained according to the correlation between the MIMO channels and the residual in the previous iteration, and then the estimated support set will be updated after the least squares. The flowchart of SSP algorithm is shown in Fig. 4.

It is proved that with the same size of the measurement vector the recovery performance of SCS-based signal detectors is superior to that of conventional CS-based signal detectors [15]. The SSP algorithm can solve multiple sparse signals with the common support set but having different measurement matrices [11].

The description of the SSP algorithm is given as follows:

1. The parameters of input are: the measurement vector y, the channel matrix H, the number of active antennas N_a.

2. In the support merging section, according to the correlation $u^{(t)}$ between the MIMO channels and the residual in the previous iteration, a potential support set P which makes the correlation $u^{(t)}$ largest will be selected from the predefined spatial constellation set.

3. After updating the current support set T_k, wrong indices will be removed and most likely indices will be selected according to the least squares.

4. The parameter of output is the estimated signal $\hat{x}^{(t)} = \left(H_{T_k}^{(t)}\right)^{\dagger}$.

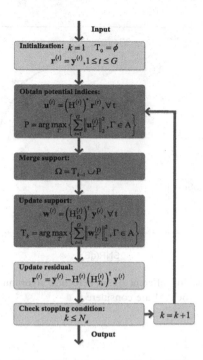

Fig. 4. Flowchart of SSP algorithm.

4 Performance Analysis

The analysis of different signal detecting algorithms including SP, SSP, MMSE and ZF is performed and analyzed using Bit Error Rate (BER) verses Signal to Noise Ratio (SNR) plots in Fig. 5, where $K = 24$, $N_a = 1$, $N_u = 4$, $N_r = 64$, $G = 1$, and 16QAM are considered. One can observe that CS-based signal detectors give better performance than conventional signal detectors, especially when the SNR is comparatively high.

Figure 6 shows BER of SP algorithm and SSP algorithm over different levels of QAM modulation, where $K = 24$, $N_a = 1$, $N_u = 4$, $N_r = 64$, $G = 1$ are considered. From the figure, it is possible to conclude that the performance of SSP algorithm is stable and reliable. Moreover, the lower the level of QAM modulation is, the better the SSP algorithm performs. On the other hand, the SP algorithm suffers from comparatively high performance loss even under modulation of 16 QAM when the SNR is no more than 20 dB.

Figure 7 shows BER of the SSP algorithm over different levels of PSK modulation, where $K = 24$, $N_a = 1$, $N_u = 4$, $N_r = 64$, $G = 1$ are considered. From the figure, it can be observed that the SSP algorithm performs. It is worth noting that BER curves of the proposed algorithm are very close under the modulations of BPSK, QPSK and 8PSK. Also we can deduct that the proposed algorithm can work very well under the low levels of PSK modulation while the BER performance may deteriorate under the high levels such as 32PSK.

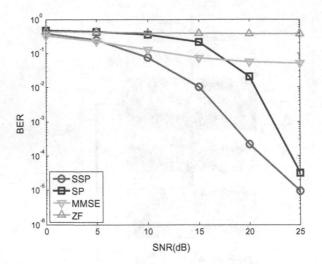

Fig. 5. BER verses SNR plots for different signal detecting algorithm, where $K = 24$, $N_a = 1$, $N_u = 4$, $N_r = 64$, $G = 1$, and 16QAM are considered

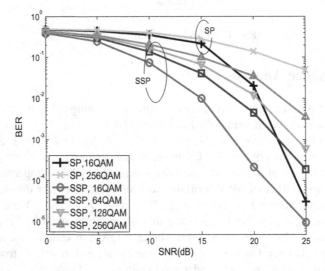

Fig. 6. BER verses SNR plots for SP algorithm and SSP algorithm over different levels of QAM modulation, where $K = 24$, $N_a = 1$, $N_u = 4$, $N_r = 64$, $G = 1$ are considered.

Figure 8 shows BER of SSP algorithm with different sparsity level and a number of received antennas. The figure shows that with larger sparsity level and more received antennas the SSP algorithm performs better.

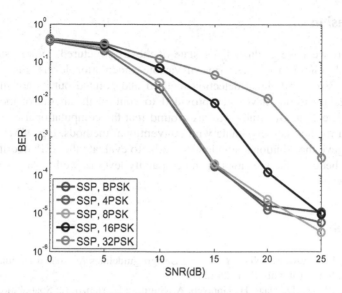

Fig. 7. BER verses SNR plots for SSP algorithm over different levels of PSK modulation, where $K = 24$, $N_a = 1$, $N_u = 4$, $N_r = 64$, $G = 1$ are considered.

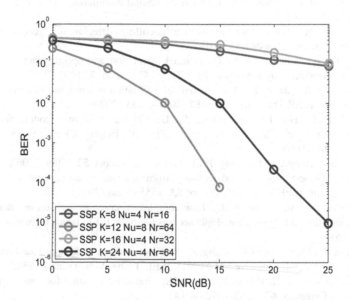

Fig. 8. BER verses SNR plots for SSP algorithm over different sparsity level and number of received antennas.

5 Conclusion

In this paper, we have evaluated the state-of-the-art structured compressed sensing based SSP algorithm in the scenarios of various modulation levels. First of all, we reviewed the structured signal detection method and pointed out its advantage. Secondly, simulation results have been provided to confirm the merits of the proposed methods in detection. Our study was also found that the computational complexity of the proposed method is comparable with conventional methods, e.g. MMSE and ZF. Finally, we gave the additional simulation results to evaluate the SSP algorithm which can perform better in the scenarios of more sparsity level as well as larger number of received antennas.

References

1. Yang, P., Di Renzo, M., Xiao, Y., Li, S.: Design guidelines for spatial modulation. IEEE Commun. Surv. Tutorials **17**, 6–26 (2015)
2. Marco, B., Renzo, D., Haas, H., Ghrayeb, A., Sugiura, S., Hanzo, L.: Spatial modulation for generalized MIMO: challenges, opportunities, and implementation, vol. 102, pp. 56–103 (2014)
3. Zheng, J.: Signal vector based list detection for spatial modulation. IEEE Wirel. Commun. Lett. **1**, 265–267 (2012)
4. Sampaio-Neto, R.: Low-complexity sphere decoding detector for generalized spatial modulation systems. 18, 949–952 (2014)
5. Gao, F., Cui, T., Nallanathan, A.: On channel estimation and optimal training design for amplify and forward relay networks. IEEE Trans. Commun. **7**, 1907–1916 (2008)
6. Gao, F., Zhang, R., Liang, Y.: Optimal channel estimation and training design for two-way relay networks. IEEE Trans. Commun. **57**, 3024–3033 (2009)
7. Cui, T., Gao, F., Ho, T., Nallanathan, A.: Distributed space-time coding for two-way wireless relay networks. In: Proceedings of IEEE ICC, Beijing, China, 19–23 May, 2008, pp. 3888–3892 (2008)
8. Donoho, D.L.: Compressed sensing. IEEE Trans. Inf. Theory **52**, 1289–1306 (2006)
9. Tropp, J.A., Gilbert, A.C.: Signal recovery from random measurements via orthogonal matching pursuit. IEEE Trans. Inf. Theory **53**, 4655–4666 (2007)
10. Garcia-Rodriguez, A., Masouros, C.: Low-complexity compressive sensing detection for spatial modulation in large-scale multiple access channels. IEEE Trans. Commun. **63**, 2565–2579 (2015)
11. Gao, Z., Dai, L., Qi, C., Yuen, C., Wang, Z.: Near-optimal signal detector based on structured compressive sensing for massive SM-MIMO. IEEE Trans. Veh. Technol. **9545**, 1–5 (2016)
12. Wu, X., Claussen, H., Di Renzo, M., Haas, H.: Channel estimation for spatial modulation. IEEE Trans. Commun. **62**, 4362–4372 (2014)
13. Dai, W., Milenkovic, O.: Subspace pursuit for compressive sensing signal reconstruction. IEEE Trans. Inf. Theory **55**, 2230–2249 (2009)
14. Guo, Q., Gui, G., Li, F.: Block-partition sparse channel estimation for spatially correlated massive MIMO systems. In: International Conference on Wireless Communications and Signal Processing (WCSP), Yangzhou, China, 13–15 October, 2016, pp. 1–4 (2016)
15. Duarte, M.F., Eldar, Y.C.: Structured compressed sensing: from theory to applications. IEEE Trans. Sig. Process. **59**, 4053–4085 (2011)

Facial Appearance Description Through Facial Landmarks Computation

Na Liu[1], Hao Ge[1], Lei Song[1,2(✉)], and Huixian Duan[1,3(✉)]

[1] Cyber Physical System R&D Center,
The Third Research Institute of Ministry of Public Security, Shanghai, China
songlei9312@126.com, hxduan005@163.com
[2] Shenzhen Key Laboratory of Media Security,
Shenzhen University, Shenzhen, China
[3] Shanghai International Technology & Trade United Co., Ltd., Shanghai, China

Abstract. Face appearance descriptions are semantic meaningful characteristics and beneficial for face recognition and retrieval. In this paper, we propose a facial appearance description method which can describe the whole face, chin, eyebrow, eye, nose and mouth type separately. The description is obtained through facial landmarks computation and geometry shape estimation of each part. Based on this method, semantic search of face images can be achieved on face dataset. What's more, the large scale dataset can be categorized though the facial appearance description before recognition which can help to improve the recognition accuracy and efficiency.

Keywords: Facial appearance description · Landmarks · Facial type

1 Introduction

Face recognition is playing an increasing significant role in public security since it can help to find the object identity quickly based on the captured face images. Recently with the rapid progress of deep learning, face recognition has made great strides and many deep learning based methods performs better than human levels [1–5].

Although the applications of face recognition under controlled conditions have become mature, there are still some problems in real applications, especially under uncontrolled environment. Firstly, the appearance of face image is likely to be affected seriously due to internal or external variations, such as illumination, partial occlusion, expression variations or image quality problem, and the performance will drop dramatically accordingly [6]. Secondly, the precision of searching a person in large scale face dataset can't be guaranteed. Furthermore, the face image is not able to be captured if there is no surveillance camera, and only the description of witness can provide some clues.

Considering the above several problems, facial appearance description is critical when the face images cannot be used for recognition. Firstly, we can search the person through the facial description when the quality of the face image is not so good for recognition or only the witness oral accounts could be used. What's more, facial appearance description can help to filter the large scale dataset and improve the recognition speed and accuracy.

© ICST Institute for Computer Sciences, Social Informatics and Telecommunications Engineering 2018
G. Sun and S. Liu (Eds.): ADHIP 2017, LNICST 219, pp. 103–108, 2018.
https://doi.org/10.1007/978-3-319-73317-3_13

Related existing work is face attribute prediction which analyzes a series of face related attributes, including age, gender, hair color, hair style, smile intensity, head pose, eye status, etc. Liu et al. construct two face attribute datasets, i.e. CelebA and LFWA [7], by labeling images selected from the database of Celeb-Faces [8] and LFW [9]. Images in CelebA and LFWA are annotated with 40 facial attributes. There are two categories of face attribute recognition research, holistic and local methods. Holistic methods extract the attribute features from the whole image [10]. The performance of holistic methods will be affected by the deformations of objects. On the other hand, local methods first extract the attribute parts and then do attribute recognition based on each part's features [11–14]. The local methods depend on the precision of face and landmark localization.

As we know, the description of facial organs is more stable than other attributes, such as hair style and color, whether or not wearing accessories, etc. However, there is a lack of methods for detailed description of the facial organs. For example, CelebA and LFWA datasets only include one lips type which is big lip. Therefore, in this paper we propose a facial appearance description method, which includes the whole face, eye, nose, mouth, and eyebrow type description. We first detect the landmarks in each face image and extract the whole face and each organ part based on the landmarks locations. Then, we describe the whole face and facial organs type based on the geometrical shape estimation of each part. Specifically the face type is divided into wide face and long face, and the facial organ types are divided into pointy chin, square chin, small eye, big eye, arched eyebrow, straight eyebrow, big nose, small nose, thick lip and thin lip.

The rest of this paper is organized as follows. Section 2 describes the facial appearance description method. In Sect. 3, extensive experiments are performed to examine the effectiveness of the proposed method. Finally, we conclude the paper in Sect. 4.

2   Proposed Method

In this section, we introduce the description method of facial appearance characteristic. It consists of two major stages: landmark detection and facial appearance description.

For face landmark detection, we apply Zhang's tasks-constrained Deep Model [15], which takes face image as input and output the locations of 68 facial landmarks which contain face, eye, eyebrow, lip and nose contour. Illustrations of landmarks are shown in Fig. 1, in which the landmarks are shown as green dots. The advantage of this method is that it is more robust to occlusion and pose variations compared to existing methods.

Fig. 1. Illustration of facial landmarks detection (Color figure online)

After the detection of 68 facial landmarks, we extract each face organs and do quantitative analysis based on the landmarks locations. For the computation convenience, we first define some important keypoints which include glabella point, gnathion, gonion, zygion. In this paper, we use the detected landmarks to approximate these keypoints, especially the glabella point is approximated by the two inner corners of the eyebrows. The illustration of these keypoints are shown on Fig. 2.

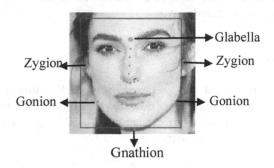

Fig. 2. Illustration of the defined keypoints

After the extraction of each part, we compute the index according to the geometry ratio of each part. The computation is done as following.

Facial index $= \frac{\text{facial height}}{\text{facial breadth}}$, where facial height is the distance from the glabella point to the gnathion, facial breadth is the distance between the left and the right zygion.

Chin index $= \frac{\text{gonion breadth}}{\text{facial breadth}}$, where facial breadth is defined as above and gonion breadth denotes the distance between the left and the right gonion.

Eyebrow index $= \frac{\text{eyebrow height}}{\text{eyebrow breadth}}$, where eyebrow height is the distance between the top and the bottom landmark on the eyebrow, and eyebrow breadth is the distance between the two brow corner points.

Eye index $= \frac{\text{eye height}}{\text{eye breadth}}$, where eye height denotes the distance between the top and the bottom landmark on eyes, eye breadth is the distance from the endocanthion to the ectocanthion.

Nose index $= \frac{1}{2}(\frac{\text{nose breadth}}{\text{facial breadth}} + \frac{\text{nose height}}{\text{facial height}})$, where facial breadth and heigth are defined as in facial index computation formula, nose breadth is the distance of two ala nasi points and nose height is defined as the distance between nasion point and rhinion point.

Mouth index $= \frac{\text{mouth height}}{\text{mouth breadth}}$, where mouth height is the mean of the upper lip and under lip height, mouth breadth is the distance between the two corner points of the mouth.

Based on the index value, we can classify the type of each part. The classes are as follows: the shape of face is divided into wide face and long face, the chin type is divided into pointy chin and square chin, the eye type is divided into big eye and small eye, the eyebrow type is divided into straight brow and arched brow, the nose type is divided into big nose and small nose, the mouth is divided into thick mouth and thin mouth. In other words, the facial characteristics are transformed to standard semantic description through the above method. And on the basis of this, the person can be searched through the facial description when there is only facial characteristic feature can be used. What's more, the large scale dataset can be classified via the description and the recognition task can be done in a smaller set, so the recognition speed and accuracy can be improved accordingly.

3   Experiments

To verify the performance of the proposed method. We first construct a facial description database, by labeling images downloaded from the internet. There are 800 images in total. For each facial type, there are at least 50 images. Figure 3 shows the sample images of each type in the database.

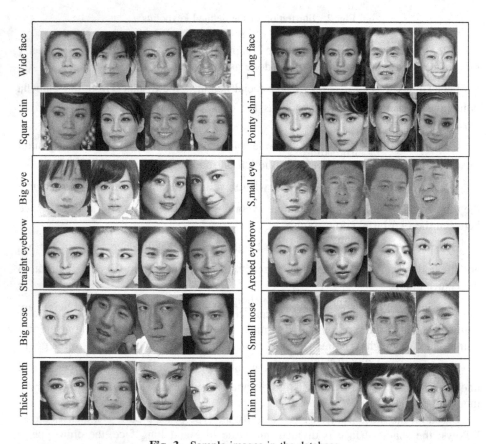

Fig. 3. Sample images in the database

For each type, we selected 30 images for training the description parameters. Then given an image, we can compute the index of each part and determine which type it belongs to. Some experimental results are illustrated in Fig. 4. From the results we can see that through the facial description, the face image can be expressed through standard semantic description. And we can use the descriptions to search the object or classify the large scale database. It should be noted that the facial appearance descriptions may not be accurate in every type classification due to internal or external variations. This is because the appearance of the face image changes due to illumination, partial occlusion, expression variations or image quality problem. So in some cases, the obvious facial features might be correctly described, but the others descriptions may be less accurate. So we should use the more effective descriptions in real applications. And we will do more research on this work.

Long face	Long face	Wide face	Long face
Pointy chin	Pointy chin	Square chin	Pointy chin
Straight eyebrow	Straight eyebrow	Arched eyebrow	Straight eyebrow
Big eye	Big eye	Big eye	Big eye
Big nose	Big nose	Big nose	Small nose
Thick mouth	Thick mouth	Thick mouth	Thin mouth

Fig. 4. Illustration of the experiment results

4 Conclusion

In this paper, we propose a facial appearance description method which is computed through the landmarks computation and geometry shape estimation of each part. It contains the whole face, chine, eyebrow, eye, nose and mouth type description. This work can help to recognize the identity of a person through semantic retrieval when there is only facial feature description can be utilized. In the future, we will study the more elaborate description method and its application in real security applications.

Acknowledgement. The authors of this paper are members of Shanghai Engineering Research Center of Intelligent Video Surveillance. This work is sponsored by the National Natural Science Foundation of China (61403084, 61402116); by the Project of the Key Laboratory of Embedded System and Service Computing, Ministry of Education, Tongji University (ESSCKF 2015-03); and by the Shanghai Rising-Star Program (17QB1401000).

References

1. Taigman, Y., Yang, M., Ranzato, M., Wolf, L.: Deepface: closing the gap to human-level performance in face verification. In: Proceedings of CVPR (2014)
2. Sun, Y., Liang, D., Wang, X., Tang, X.: Deepid3: face recognition with very deep neural networks. arXiv:1502.00873 (2015)
3. Schroff, F., Kalenichenko, D., Philbin, J.: Facenet: a unified embedding for face recognition and clustering. In: Proceedings of CVPR (2015)
4. Parkhi, O.M., Vedaldi, A., Zisserman, A.: Deep face recognition. In: Proceedings of BMVC (2015)
5. Wen, Y., Zhang, K., Li, Z., Qiao, Yu.: A discriminative feature learning approach for deep face recognition. In: Leibe, B., Matas, J., Sebe, N., Welling, M. (eds.) ECCV 2016. LNCS, vol. 9911, pp. 499–515. Springer, Cham (2016). https://doi.org/10.1007/978-3-319-46478-7_31
6. Liu, N., Lai, J.H., Zheng, W.S.: A facial sparse descriptor for single image based face recognition, **93**, 77–87 (2012)
7. Ouyang, W., Li, H., Zeng, X., Wang, X.: Deep learning face attributes in the wild. In: Proceedings of ICCV (2015)
8. Huang, G.B., Ramesh, M., Berg, T., Learned-Miller, E.: Labeled faces in the wild: a database for studying face recognition in unconstrained environments. Technical Report 07–49, University of Massachusetts, Amherst, October 2007
9. Sun, Y., Wang, X., Tang, X.: Deep learning face representation by joint identification-verification. In: NIPS (2014)
10. Razavian, A.S., Azizpour, H., Sullivan, J., Carlsson, S.: CNN features off-the-shelf: an astounding baseline for recognition. arXiv:1403.6382 (2014)
11. Berg, T., Belhumeur, P.N.: Poof: part-based one-vs.-one features for fine-grained categorization, face verification, and attribute estimation. In: Proceedings of CVPR (2013)
12. Luo, P., Wang, X., Tang, X.: A deep sum-product architecture for robust facial attributes analysis. In: Proceedings of ICCV (2013)
13. Zhang, N., Paluri, M., Ranzato, M., Darrell, T., Bourdev, L.: Panda: pose aligned networks for deep attribute modeling. In: Proceedings of CVPR (2014)
14. Bourdev, L., Maji, S., Malik, J.: Describing people: a poselet-based approach to attribute classification. In: Proceedings of ICCV (2011)
15. Zhang, Z., Luo, P., Loy, C.C., Tang, X.: Facial landmark detection by deep multi-task learning. In: Fleet, D., Pajdla, T., Schiele, B., Tuytelaars, T. (eds.) ECCV 2014. LNCS, vol. 8694, pp. 94–108. Springer, Cham (2014). https://doi.org/10.1007/978-3-319-10599-4_7

Research and Implementation of Distributed Simulation System Based on HLA

Weidong Zhang$^{(\boxtimes)}$, Yun Xiao, and Ni Lei

Wuhan Maritime Communication Research Institute, Wuhan 430079, China
67599891@qq.com, 63937073@qq.com, 57512385@qq.com

Abstract. Distributed simulation technology based on HLA is an important direction of simulation development. Based on the HLA technology, this paper put forward an idea about establishing Federation between two different simulating platforms. We developed an interface protocol to communicate with HLA service for Federate, and several network protocols on EXata to simulate the networking process. Finally, the EXata which is good at protocol modeling and the Eagle which is good at movement modeling could interactive through a HLA interface and join in a Federation. In this way, the collaborative simulation of two platforms is realized.

Keywords: HLA · Distributed simulation · EXata

1 Introduction

Distributed simulation is the product of the combination of simulation technology and network technology development [1]. For a large network or a target network with distribution requirements, the distributed simulation method can be used. In this way, the target network can be distributed to multiple computers or simulators, with each one implementing parts of the functions for the network, and we can finally realize interactive dynamic simulation through distributed technologies.

Distributed simulation technology originated from the SIMNET research project which is developed by Defense Advanced Research Projects Agency (DARPA) and the U.S. army in 1983. The United States department of defense modeling and simulation office (DMSO) which is responsible for the simulation in military field put forward the concept of high-level architecture (HLA) in March 1995, and released the HLA specification in August 1996. HLA is a new framework of simulation technology, which defines the relationship between each part of the simulation function, rather than a series of data exchange standards. It defines the rules of the whole process from a higher level of simulation development, modeling and designing.

This paper introduces the basic concept of HLA technology, and realizes a collaborative simulation of two simulation platforms which are good at different simulation functions based on a Federation.

© ICST Institute for Computer Sciences, Social Informatics and Telecommunications Engineering 2018
G. Sun and S. Liu (Eds.): ADHIP 2017, LNICST 219, pp. 109–116, 2018.
https://doi.org/10.1007/978-3-319-73317-3_14

2 Distributed Simulation System Based on HLA

The HLA standard defines the concepts of Federation and Federate. A simulation system combined with simulation subsystems is defined as Federation, and every simulation subsystem is defined as Federate. The core of HLA standard is the HLA rules, Object Model Template (OMT), and interface specification.

According to the HLA rules, all the Federation and Federates should provide their object model following the OMT that are Federation Object Model (FOM) and Federates' Simulation Object Model (SOM). The function of OMT is to provide a standard and documented form which can describe the information of the Federation and Federates' object model. As parts of modeling and simulation repository, both FOM and SOM were stored in the according database and can be used or reused during the executing process [2–6].

2.1 System Composition

Based on the HLA distributed simulation technology [7], this paper describe how to develop HLA interface and functions for EXata (a communication simulating software) and Eagle (a simulation modeling software), in order to make a Federation and realize a system through object type releasing and reflecting method. The system designed as below (Fig. 1).

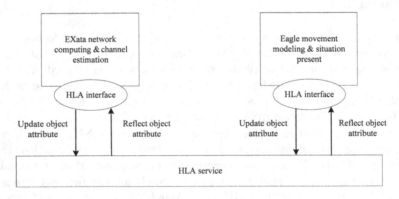

Fig. 1. System composition.

2.2 Functions of Subsystems

EXata mainly completes the work of protocol modeling and course calculating, with its functions as below:

(1) Build up a communication network in the simulate network environment based on a standard or self-defined protocol model, and simulate the whole process of the dynamic executing.
(2) Build up an application modeling based on a currency application model.

(3) Capable for HLA interface, and capable for building Federation, joining Federation, subscribing and releasing.
(4) Update and synchronize of position based on node positon data from HLA service through the process of simulation.
(5) Release the application data from HLA service through the process of simulation.
(6) Compute the network protocol process based on the node positon data, and release the node connection data from HLA service.

Eagle mainly completes the work of opera movement modeling and result rendering, with its functions as below:

(1) Capable for node position and movement modeling.
(2) Capable for HLA interface, and capable for building Federation, joining Federation, subscribing and releasing.
(3) Release the node positon data from HLA service.
(4) Reflect and appear the node connection state from HLA service through the process of simulation.
(5) Reflect and appear the application data from HLA service through the process of simulation.

3 System Implementation

3.1 Runtime Environment

The distributed simulation system adopted MAKRti ver. 4.1.1f as the operation support environment. After MAKRti is installed successfully, there would be a *MAK_RTIDIR* variable added with its value equaling to the installation path of RTI software. Meanwhile, variable *PATH* will include the path to RTI's lib folder and bin folder. Also we need to modify the value of "*setqb RTI_useRtiExec*" from 0 to 1 in the *rid.mtl*, or there would be a mistake when operating.

3.2 Federation Design

This system is developed based on the standard HLA1.3 interface protocol. EXata and Eagle join the same Federation with a name as "*DISP-SYS*", following by the file as "*DISP-STRIVE-RPR.fed*". Besides, every Federate should have its own Federation name as the flag to join the Federation.

3.3 Federation File

The federation file "*DISP-STRIVE-RPR.fed*" in this system is modified based on the basic FOM file form. In the file, we defined the object class and interaction class both are one-way inheritance tree, with the root class of the object class is *ObjectRoot*, and the root class of the interaction class is *InteractionRoot*. A complete name of a class is composed by the name of the root through to the class, separated by "." in the middle.

In addition, the federal file has some necessary object classes for management issues, such as *privilegeToDeleteObject*, etc.

We use some defined classes and create new object class, object class attributes, and interaction classes that we need as below:

(1) ObjectRoot.BaseEntity.WorldLocation
(2) Object-Root.BaseEntity.PhysicalEntity.DamageState
(3) ObjectRoot.BaseEntity.Buffer

3.4 HLA Workflow

We developed a workflow for Federate as shown in the following Fig. 2.

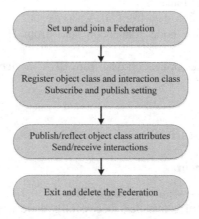

Fig. 2. HLA workflow.

Before the Federation starts running, Federate need to have the function of setting up the HLA configuration, including setting the Federation name, Federation file name, Federate name, and other required files which can be read when the system starts running. At the same time, before the Federate begins to run, it needs to start the RTI software.

After the Federate starts, one of them is supposed to invoke the RTI service "*createFederationExecution*" to establish the Federation, and other Federate will find that the Federation has been established and would not establish the Federation again. Establishing a Federation requires inputting the common Federation file name and the path to the Federation file. Every Federate needs to invoke the RTI service "*joinFederation-Execution*" to join the Federation. After joining the Federation successfully, you can see the established Federation name in the RTI software and the membership of the Federation.

Thereafter, Federate can register their associated object classes, object class attributes, and interaction classes, subscribe to related object class attributes or interaction classes as planning, and publish or send attributes or interaction classes with a publishing authority. Federate gets the object class handle from the RTI service "*getObjectClassHandle*", the attribute handle from "*getAttribute-Handle*", and the interaction classes handle from "*getInteractionClassHandle*". Federate subscribes from the RTI service "*subscribeObjectClassAttributes*" and "*subscribe-InteractionClass*". At last, Federate publish from the RTI service "*publishObjectClass*" and "*publishInteractionClass*". After Federate publish to RTI with corresponding attributes and interaction, RTI will inform the Federate who had subscribed the very attributes. The Federate can receive the message through a callback function. Federate can update object class attributes by invoking RTI service "*updateAttributeValues*", and send interaction by "send-Interaction".

RTI has developed the callback function prototype which should be implemented by Federate themselves, including "*discoverObjectInstance*", "*receiveInteraction*", and so on. In this research, we use simulation node's flag as the object handle, the object class which can update the attribute as the object class handle. Both the object handle and the object class handle can be gotten from RTI through the callback function "*discoverObjectInstance*". Federate members use this handles to build an information library. In the same way, attribute handle and its value can be gotten through the callback function "*reflectAttributeValues*", with which information Federate can acquire the update message of the responsive attribute.

Eventually, a Federate can stop running or exit the Federation from calling the RTI service "*resignFederationExecution*". A Federate can delete the Federation by calling the RTI service "*destroyFederationExecution*", considering there is no other Federate still in the very Federation.

4   Experiments

4.1   Setup and Modeling

We developed a GUI for HLA interface setup, Table 1 show the content of the key parameters which we use in this system. We can set Federation name and Federation file path as below. The file should be edited before building up the Federation. For the EXata software, we gave it a Federate name as "EXata". Similarly, we name the Eagle software as "OSTW_Client" sharing the common Federation name and file.

Figure 3 shows that five simulation nodes were settled on a scene in EXata. The node 1, 2, 4 in one network and node 2, 3, 4, 5 in the other. You can see that a business

Table 1. HLA interface parameters on EXata.

Parameter	Content	Remark
Federation name	DSIP-SYS	Same with Eagle
Federation file path	.fed file storage path	Same file with Eagle
Federate name	EXata	Eagle: OSTW_Client
Entities file path	.hla-entities storage path	
Radios file path	.hla-radios storage path	
Network file path	.hla-network storage path	

flow is configured from node 1 to node 5. Correspondingly, 5 nodes are arranged on the Eagle with node 2 and node 4 settling to move in the opposite directions.

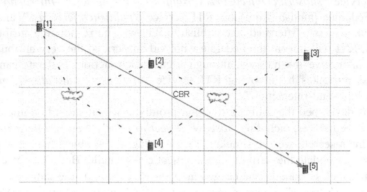

Fig. 3. Network configuration in EXata.

4.2   Simulation Operation

Firstly, we started the RTI software on the both hosts. After executing EXata and Eagle, we can find out that they could join the Federation "DSIP-SYS" successfully. In the running process, the logical connection relationship between the nodes is displayed on Eagle. This connection information was come from EXata through the RTI service. In this way, Eagle makes a synchronized presentation as the results of network protocol calculation on EXata.

Secondly, we started the business flow on EXata. Eagle also got the information through RTI and rendered it on its interface, as shown in the following Fig. 4.

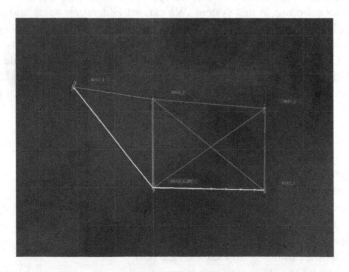

Fig. 4. Sending and receiving business display on Eagle when running.

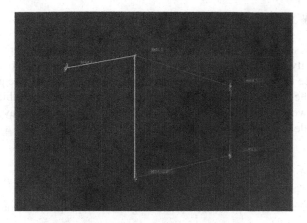

Fig. 5. Display of node moving on Eagle.

When the nodes continue moving as planned in Eagle (as shown in Fig. 5). The corresponding nodes in the EXata also move to the same new location as in Eagle (as shown in Fig. 6). The changed connection information from EXata was published which realized the synchronous change of logical connection on Eagle.

4.3 Result Analysis

In this experiment, we can figure out that developed HLA interface protocol could be used in many different simulation platforms. We made some required functions in HLA service and the simulation platforms to adapt to the needs of users. Our research is an attempt to the use of distributed simulation based on HLA technology, and in the future we would develop more flexible interface protocol to apply to more occasions.

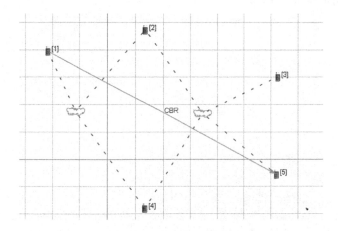

Fig. 6. Nodes synchronize motion on EXata.

5 Summary

The distributed simulation technology conforms to the development trend of the simulation activity from centralized type to distributed interactive type, which has a great significance for the research, design and verification of solving the problem in the complex and integrated system. This technology provides the possibility to realize interoperate between different simulation platforms, and makes the way of simulation activities more flexible [8–10].

References

1. Tian, Z.: Research of sub-water weapon simulation technology based on HLA, NWPU (2004)
2. Kuhl, F., Wealtherly, R., Dahmann, J.: Creating Computer Simulation Systems: An Introduction to the High Level Architecture. Pearson Education, Inc., London (2000)
3. IEEE Std 1516-2000: IEEE Standard for Modeling and Simulation (M&S) High Level Architecture (HLA)-Framework and Rules
4. IEEE Std 1516-2000: IEEE Standard for Modeling and Simulation (M&S) High Level Architecture (HLA)-Object Model Template (OMT) Specification
5. IEEE Std 1516-2000: IEEE Standard for Modeling and Simulation (M&S) High Level Architecture (HLA)-Federate Interface Specification
6. Bo, H.J., Zheng, Q.D., Li, O.L., Xing, S.: Research on the development of distributed simulation application system based on HLA. J. Syst. Simul. 12, 481–483 (2000)
7. Chen, X., Ni, Z.: Research on upgrading of submarine distributed combat simulation system based on HLA. J. Syst. Simul. 19 (2007)
8. Xiao, T., Fan, W.: HLA based integrated platform for collaborative design, simulation and optimization. J. Syst. Simul. 13, 3542–3547 (2008)
9. Zhao, G.: Research on the key technology of fully mechanized coal face safety production of virtual reality system. Xian university of science and technology (2013)
10. Chen, X., Xiong, G., Guo, B., Zhang, H.: Research on multi-disciplinary modeling based on HLA. J. Syst. Simul. 11 (2003)

Study on Rolling Bearing On-Line Health Status Estimation Approach Based on Vibration Signals

Yulong Ying[1], Jingchao Li[2(⊠)], Jing Li[3], and Zhimin Chen[2]

[1] School of Energy and Mechanical Engineering,
Shanghai University of Electric Power, Shanghai, China
[2] School of Electronic and Information, Shanghai Dianji University,
Shanghai, China
lijc@sdju.edu.cn
[3] Zhejiang Huayun Information Technology Co., Ltd., Hangzhou, China

Abstract. As the rolling bearing vibration signal is of nonlinear and nonstationary characteristics, the condition-indicating information distributed in the rolling bearing vibration signal is complicated, and using traditional time domain and frequency domain approaches cannot easily make an accurate estimation for the rolling bearing health status. In this paper, a simple and efficient fault diagnostic approach was proposed to accommodate to the requirements of both real-time monitoring and accurate estimation of fault type as well as severity. Firstly, a four-dimensional feature extraction algorithm using entropy and Holder coefficient theories was developed to extract the characteristic vector from the vibration signals, and secondly a gray relation algorithm was employed for achieving bearing fault pattern recognition intelligently. The experimental study have illustrated the proposed approach can efficiently and effectively improve the fault diagnostic performance compared with the existing artificial intelligent methods, and can be suitable for on-line health status estimation.

Keywords: Rotating machines · Rolling bearing · Vibration signals
Health status

1 Introduction

Rolling bearing is one of main components in various types of rotational machinery (e.g., gas turbine engine, steam turbine engine and electrical machine), and its failure is usually the foremost cause to the failure and breakdown of rotating machines, which results in enormous property loss [1–3]. So as to maintain rotating machine operating reliably, it is important to propose an effective and efficient bearing health status estimation approach. Vibration-based bearing fault diagnosis approaches have attracted broad attention in the near past among all kinds of bearing fault diagnosis methods [4], due to that bearing vibration signals carry abundant machine health status information, which make it possible to extract health status feature vectors using signal processing technology based on vibration signals [5].

© ICST Institute for Computer Sciences, Social Informatics and Telecommunications Engineering 2018
G. Sun and S. Liu (Eds.): ADHIP 2017, LNICST 219, pp. 117–129, 2018.
https://doi.org/10.1007/978-3-319-73317-3_15

Recently, great deal signal processing approaches have been applied for rolling element bearing off-line heath status estimation. As the result of the nonlinear factors, such as stiffness, friction and clearance, rolling bearing vibration signals always bear nonlinear and nonstationary performance at different operating conditions [6]. what's more, bearing vibration signals involve not only the working information related to the bearing itself, but also plentiful information related to other rotating parts of the machine, which in comparison with the former is usually taken as the background noise [7]. The slight bearing health status information may easily be submersed by the background noise due to that background noise is often relatively large. Therefore, the common time domain or frequency domain signal processing approaches may not easily obtain an accurate estimation result about the bearing health status, even the advanced signal processing approaches, e.g., Hilbert transform, fractional fourier transform and wavelet transform [8]. AS the nonlinear dynamics theory develops, many nonlinear analysis techniques have been used to recognize the complicated bearing nonlinear dynamic behavior [9]. The most common manner to extract and refine the health status information from the vibration signals is to combine a few of advanced signal processing approaches (e.g., Hilbert transform [10], wavelet package transform [11], higher order spectra [12] and empirical mode decomposition), to further extract the fault frequency with the aid of empirical judgement by the experts. Recently, the procedure of bearing fault diagnosis is gradually taken as a process of fault pattern recognition with the aid of artificial intelligence (AI) approaches, and its reliability and real-time performance is essentially determined by the effectiveness of the fault feature extraction algorithm and pattern recognition algorithm [13]. In recent years, some entropy based feature extraction algorithms (e.g., hierarchical entropy [14, 15], fuzzy entropy [16], sample entropy [17], approximate entropy [18] and hierarchical fuzzy entropy) were proposed used for extracting fault feature vectors based on the bearing vibration signals. We exploit a four-dimensional feature extraction algorithm using entropy and Holder coefficient theories, which are fit for processing complicated nonstationary and nonlinear problem, for extracting fault feature vectors based on the bearing vibration signals in the paper. When the fault feature extraction is ready, a fault pattern recognition method is required to implement the fault diagnosis automatically [13]. Nowadays, different fault pattern recognition approaches have been proposed for mechanical fault diagnosis, and one of the most common approaches is support vector machines [22] and artificial neural networks [19–21]. However, a large number of samples are needed for the training of ANNs, which may be hard to obtain in the practical applications. The support vector machines are based on statistical learning theory, and have better generalization than artificial neural networks under a smaller number of samples [23]. However, the selection of optimal parameters of SVMs has big effect on the performance of a SVM classifier [23, 24], and thus a multi-class concept [24] or an optimization algorithm has been used to improve the performance of support vector machines. In this paper, so as to balance the issue of accuracy versus real-time performance, a gray relation algorithm was employed to fulfill an intelligent fault pattern recognition based on the extracted four-dimensional feature vector.

The rest of the paper is organized as follows. Firstly, the methodology of the proposed approach is introduced in Sect. 2, and secondly the experimental validation of the proposed approach is illustrated in Sect. 3, and at last the conclusions are presented in Sect. 4.

2 Methodology

In this paper, a simple and efficient fault diagnostic approach was proposed to accommodate to the requirements of both real-time monitoring and accurate estimation of different fault types and in addition different severities for rolling bearing. Firstly, a four-dimensional feature extraction algorithm using entropy and Holder coefficient theories was developed to extract characteristic vectors from the vibration signals, and secondly a gray relation algorithm was used to achieve fault pattern recognition based on the extracted four-dimensional feature vectors.

2.1 Feature Extraction

Entropy is an important concept in the information theory, which is a measure for information uncertainty [25]. Suppose the event set is X, and the probability set for the event set is an n-dimensional probability vector $P = (p_1, p_2, \ldots, p_n)$, and satisfy:

$$0 \leq p_i \leq 1 \tag{1}$$

and

$$\sum_{i=1}^{n} p_i = 1 \tag{2}$$

Then the entropy E is defined as follows:

$$E(P) = E(p_1, p_2, \ldots, p_n) = -\sum_{i=1}^{n} p_i \log p_i \tag{3}$$

Therefore, entropy E can be taken as an entropy function for the n-dimensional probability vector $P = (p_1, p_2, \ldots, p_n)$.

Shannon entropy theory points out that, if there are many possible outcomes for an event and the probability for each possible outcome is $p_i (i = 1, 2, \ldots, n)$, whose sum is equal to 1, then the information obtained from a possible outcome can be expressed by $I_i = \log_a(1/p_i)$, and the information entropy defined for the time series is as follows:

$$S = -k \sum_{i=1}^{N} p_i \log_e p_i \tag{4}$$

when $k = 1$, S stands for a Shannon entropy E_1 and can be used to depict the uncertainty degree of signals.

Based on the definition of Shannon entropy E_1, the definition of Exponential entropy E_2 is also introduced for the feature extraction purpose. Suppose the probability for each possible outcome is p_i, and its information content can be defined as:

$$\Delta I(p_i) = e^{1-p_i} \tag{5}$$

According to the basic entropy definition, the exponential entropy E_2 can be defined as:

$$E_2 = \sum_{i=1}^{n} p_i e^{1-p_i} \tag{6}$$

From Eqs. (5) and (6), it can be seen that compared with conventional information content $\Delta I(p_i) = \log(1/p_i)$, the definition of exponential entropy has the same meaning. The defining domain of $\Delta I(p_i)$ is $[0, 1]$, and $\Delta I(p_i)$ is a monotonic reduction function with the value domain of $[1, e]$. The exponential entropy E_2 is maximal only if the probability of all events is equal.

Holder coefficient can be used to measure the similar degree of two sequences, which may extract signals' features. It is evolved from Holder inequality and the definition of Holder inequality can be described as follows [26, 27]:

For any vector $X = [x_1, x_2, \ldots, x_n]^T$ and $Y = [y_1, y_2, \ldots, y_n]^T$, they satisfy:

$$\sum_{i=1}^{n} |x_i \cdot y_i| \leq \left(\sum_{i=1}^{n} |x_i|^p \right)^{1/p} \cdot \left(\sum_{i=1}^{n} |y_i|^q \right)^{1/q} \tag{7}$$

where $\frac{1}{p} + \frac{1}{q} = 1$ and $p, q > 1$.

Based on the Holder inequality, for two discrete signals $\{f_1(i) \geq 0, i = 1, 2, \ldots, n\}$ and $\{f_2(i) \geq 0, i = 1, 2, \ldots, n\}$, if $p, q > 1$, and $\frac{1}{p} + \frac{1}{q} = 1$, then Holder coefficient of these two discrete signals can be calculated as follows:

$$H_c = \frac{\sum f_1(i) f_2(i)}{\left(\sum f_1^p(i) \right)^{1/p} \cdot \left(\sum f_2^q(i) \right)^{1/q}} \tag{8}$$

where $0 \leq H_c \leq 1$.

Holder coefficient characterizes the similar degree of two discrete signals, if and only if $f_1^p(i) = k f_2^q(i)$, $i = 1, 2, \ldots, n$, in which n denotes the length of the discrete signal and k is a real number, H_c will be the biggest value. In this case, the similar degree of two signals is biggest, which indicates that these two signals belong to the same type of signals; if and only if $\sum_{i=1}^{n} f_1(i) f_2(i) = 0$, H_c get the minimum value, and in this case, the similarity of two signals is smallest, which indicates the signals are irrelevant, and belong to different types of signals.

Rectangular sequence $s_1(i)$ and triangular sequence $s_2(i)$ are selected as reference sequences, and then the Holder coefficient value of the vibration signal to be identified with the two reference signal sequences is obtained as follows:

$$H_1 = \frac{\sum f(i)s_1(i)}{\left(\sum f^p(i)\right)^{1/p} \cdot \left(\sum s_1^q(i)\right)^{1/q}} \tag{9}$$

where the rectangular sequence $s_1(i)$ is as follows:

$$s_1(i) = \begin{cases} s, & 1 \leq i \leq N \\ 0, & else \end{cases} \tag{10}$$

Similarly, H_2 is obtained as follows:

$$H_2 = \frac{\sum f(i)s_2(i)}{\left(\sum f^p(i)\right)^{1/p} \cdot \left(\sum s_2^q(i)\right)^{1/q}} \tag{11}$$

where the triangular sequence $s_2(i)$ is as follows:

$$s_2(i) = \begin{cases} 2i/n, & 1 \leq i \leq n/2 \\ 2 - 2i/n, & n/2 \leq i \leq n \end{cases} \tag{12}$$

2.2   Pattern Recognition

As the basis of gray system theory, the gray relation algorithm is to calculate the gray relation coefficient and relation degree between each comparative feature vector and reference feature vectors based on the basic theory of space mathematics [28].

Suppose the feature vectors (i.e., the four-dimensional feature vector extracted based on entropy and Holder coefficient theories) extracted based on vibration signals, to be identified are as follows:

$$B_1 = \begin{bmatrix} b_1(1) \\ b_1(2) \\ b_1(3) \\ b_1(4) \end{bmatrix}, B_2 = \begin{bmatrix} b_2(1) \\ b_2(2) \\ b_2(3) \\ b_2(4) \end{bmatrix}, \cdots, B_i = \begin{bmatrix} b_i(1) \\ b_i(2) \\ b_i(3) \\ b_i(4) \end{bmatrix}, \cdots \tag{13}$$

where B_i $(i = 1, 2, \ldots)$ is a certain fault pattern to be recognized (i.e., fault types and in addition severities).

Suppose the knowledge base between the health status patterns (i.e., fault types and in addition severities) and fault signatures (i.e., the feature vectors) from a part of samples is as follows:

$$C_1 = \begin{bmatrix} c_1(1) \\ c_1(2) \\ c_1(3) \\ c_1(4) \end{bmatrix}, C_2 = \begin{bmatrix} c_2(1) \\ c_2(2) \\ c_2(3) \\ c_2(4) \end{bmatrix} \cdots, C_j = \begin{bmatrix} c_j(1) \\ c_j(2) \\ c_j(3) \\ c_j(4) \end{bmatrix}, \cdots \quad (14)$$

where C_j ($j = 1, 2, \ldots$) is a known health status pattern (i.e., fault types and in addition severities); c_j ($j = 1, 2, \ldots$) is a certain feature parameter.

For $\rho \in (0, 1)$:

$$\xi\big(b_i(k), c_j(k)\big) = \frac{\min_j \min_k |b_i(k) - c_j(k)| + \rho \cdot \max_j \max_k |b_i(k) - c_j(k)|}{|b_i(k) - c_j(k)| + \rho \cdot \max_j \max_k |b_i(k) - c_j(k)|} \quad (15)$$

$$\xi(B_i, C_j) = \frac{1}{4} \sum_{k=1}^{4} \xi\big(b_i(k), c_j(k)\big), j = 1, 2, \cdots \quad (16)$$

where ρ is a distinguishing coefficient; $\xi\big(b_i(k), c_j(k)\big)$ is the gray relation coefficient of k_{th} feature parameter for B_i and C_j; $\xi(B_i, C_j)$ is the gray relation degree for B_i and C_j. Thereafter B_i is categorized to a certain health status pattern where the maximal $\xi(B_i, C_j)$ ($j = 1, 2, \ldots,$) is calculated.

2.3 Proposed Approach

Totally, the proposed approach for rolling bearing health status estimation is as follows:

(1) The vibration signals from the object rolling element bearing in the rotating machine are sampled under different working conditions, including normal operation condition and various fault types and severities, for the establishment of the sample knowledge base.
(2) Through a four-dimensional feature extraction algorithm using entropy and Holder coefficient theories, the health status feature vectors are extracted from the sample knowledge base.
(3) The sample knowledge base for GRA is established based on the fault symptom (i.e., the extracted feature vector) and the fault pattern (i.e., the known fault types and severity).
(4) The health status feature vectors extracted based on bearing vibration signals to be identified are input into GRA, and the diagnostic results (i.e., fault types and severity) are output.

3 Experimental Validation

All the rolling element bearing vibration signals for analysis are from Case Western Reserve University Bearing Data Center in the paper [29]. The test bearing is a deep groove rolling bearing of 6205-2RS JEM SKF. The related rolling element bearing experimental device consists of a torque meter, a power meter and a three-phase induction motor, and the load power and speed are measured over the sensor, shown in Fig. 1. Over controlling the power meter, the desired torque load can be obtained. The motor drive end rotor is supported over a test bearing, where a single point of failure is set through discharge machining. The fault diameter (i.e., fault severities) includes 28 mils, 21 mils, 14 mils and 7 mils, and the fault types includes outer race fault, the inner race fault and the ball fault. An accelerometer is installed on the motor drive end housing with a bandwidth of up to 5000 Hz, and the vibration data for the test bearing in different operating conditions is collected by a recorder, where the sampling frequency is 12 kHz.

Fig. 1. Experimental setup

The bearing vibration data used for analysis was obtained under the load of 0 horsepower and the motor speed of 1797 r/min. Totally 11 types of vibration signals considering different fault categories and severities are analyzed, seen in Table 1. Each

Table 1. Description of experimental data set

Health status condition	Fault diameter (mils)	The number of base samples	The number of testing samples	Label of classification
Normal	0	10	40	1
Inner race fault	7	10	40	2
	14	10	40	3
	21	10	40	4
	28	10	40	5
Ball fault	7	10	40	6
	14	10	40	7
	28	10	40	8
Outer race fault	7	10	40	9
	14	10	40	10
	21	10	40	11

data sample from vibration signals is made up of 2048 time series points. For those 550 data samples, 110 data samples are chosen randomly for establishment of knowledge base, with the rest 440 data samples as testing data samples (Figs. 2 and 3).

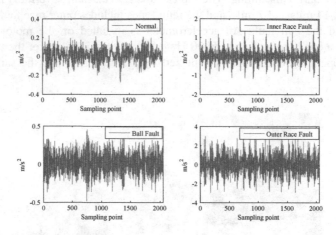

Fig. 2. Rolling bearing normal operating condition and fault conditions with fault diameter 7mils

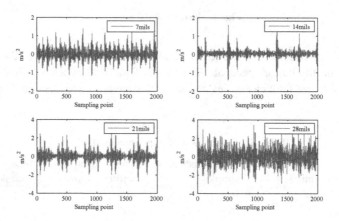

Fig. 3. Bearing inner race fault conditions with various severities

The health status feature vectors extracted from rolling bearing normal operating condition and different fault conditions with 7mils fault diameter over the four-dimensional feature extraction algorithm using entropy and Holder coefficient theories were shown in Figs. 4 and 5 respectively. And the health status feature vectors extracted from rolling bearing inner race fault condition with different severities over the four-dimensional feature extraction algorithm using entropy and Holder coefficient theory were shown in Figs. 6 and 7 respectively.

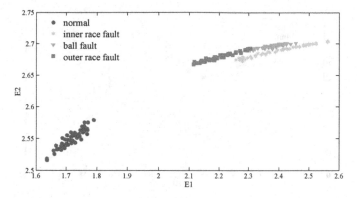

Fig. 4. Entropy features of a random chosen sample from bearing normal operating condition and different fault conditions with fault diameter 7mils

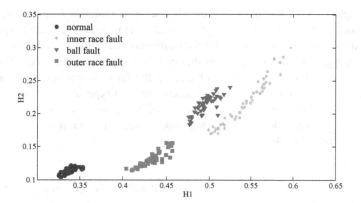

Fig. 5. Holder coefficient features of a random chosen sample from bearing normal operating condition and different fault conditions with fault diameter 7mils

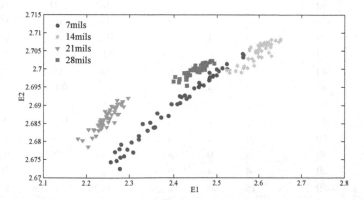

Fig. 6. Entropy features of a random chosen sample from rolling bearing inner race fault condition with various severities

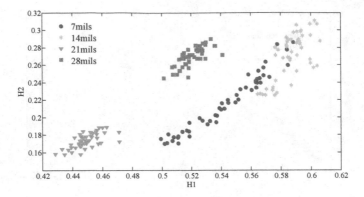

Fig. 7. Holder coefficient features of a random chosen sample from rolling bearing inner race fault condition with various severities

From Figs. 4, 5, 6 and 7, it can clearly be seen that the fault feature vectors extracted based on the rolling bearing vibration signals with different fault types and in addition different severities through the four-dimensional feature extraction algorithm based on entropy and Holder coefficient theory show apparent differences. The sample knowledge base for GRA is established based on the fault symptom (i.e., the extracted feature vector) and the fault pattern (i.e., the known fault types and severity). The fault feature vectors extracted based on the testing rolling bearing vibration signals to be identified are input into GRA, and the diagnostic results (i.e., fault types and severity) are output, shown in Table 2.

Table 2. The diagnostic results by GRA compared with results from references [30, 31]

Label of classification	The number of testing samples	The number of misclassified samples			Testing accuracy (%)		
		[30]	[31]	Proposed	[30]	[31]	Proposed
1	40	0	0	0	100	100	100
2	40	0	0	0	100	100	100
3	40	0	4	2	100	90	95
4	40	3	0	0	92.5	100	100
5	40	0	0	0	100	100	100
6	40	2	4	3	95	90	92.5
7	40	3	0	0	92.5	100	100
8	40	3	4	4	92.5	90	90
9	40	0	0	0	100	100	100
10	40	0	0	3	100	100	92.5
11	40	4	4	0	90	90	100
In total	440	15	16	12	96.59	96.3636	96.9697

The diagnostic results from Table 2, the fault pattern recognition success rate for detecting bearing faulty conditions can reach 100%, and the total fault pattern recognition success rate can reach almost 97%, which shows a certain improvement in diagnostic accuracy compared with the methods from references [30, 31]. The time cost by these methods for one Test Case is shown Table 3 by using a laptop computer with a 2.0 GHz dual processor.

Table 3. The time consumption comparison of these approaches

	[30]	[31]	Proposed
Time consumption/s	0.056695	0.011198	0.002160

From Table 3, the experimental results have demonstrated the proposed approach can be suitable for on-line health status estimation.

4   Conclusion

In this paper, a simple and efficient fault diagnostic approach was proposed to accommodate to the requirements of both real-time monitoring and accurate estimation of fault type as well as severity. The experimental results have many meaningful conclusions as follows:

(1) The proposed approach can accurately and effectively identify the different types of rolling bearing failure and the severity of the fault.
(2) The diagnostic results by the proposed approach show that the fault pattern recognition success rate for detecting bearing faulty conditions can reach 100%, and the total fault pattern recognition success rate can reach almost 97%.
(3) The proposed approach can improve the fault diagnostic performance compared with the existing artificial intelligent methods, and can be suitable for on-line health status estimation.

Acknowledgment. The research of the paper is supported by the National Natural Science Foundation of China (No. 61603239) and (No. 61601281), and the authors are grateful to Case Western Reserve University Bearing Data Center for kindly providing the experimental data.

References

1. Xu, J., Tong, S., Cong, F., et al.: The application of time–frequency reconstruction and correlation matching for rolling bearing fault diagnosis. Proc. Inst. Mech. Eng. Part C. J. Mech. Eng. Sci. **229**, 3291–3295 (2015). https://doi.org/10.1177/0954406215584397
2. Van Hecke, B., Qu, Y., He, D.: Bearing fault diagnosis based on a new acoustic emission sensor technique. Proc. Inst. Mech. Eng. Part O: J. Risk Reliab. **229**(2), 105–118 (2015)

3. Jiang, L., Shi, T., Xuan, J.: Fault diagnosis of rolling bearings based on Marginal Fisher analysis. J. Vib. Control (2012) https://doi.org/10.1177/1077546312463747
4. Zhang, X., Hu, N., Hu, L., et al.: A bearing fault diagnosis method based on the low-dimensional compressed vibration signal. Adv. Mech. Eng. 7(7), 1–12 (2015). https://doi.org/10.1177/1687814015593442
5. Zhang, D.D.: Bearing fault diagnosis based on the dimension–temporal information. Proc. Inst. Mech. Eng. Part J: J. Eng. Tribol. 225(8), 806–813 (2011)
6. Vakharia, V., Gupta, V.K., Kankar, P.K.: Multiscale permutation entropy based approach to select wavelet for fault diagnosis of ball bearings. J. Vib. Control 21, 3123–3131 (2014). https://doi.org/10.1177/1077546314520830
7. Tiwari, R., Gupta, V.K., Kankar, P.K.: Bearing fault diagnosis based on multi-scale permutation entropy and adaptive neuro fuzzy classifier. J. Vib. Control 21(3), 461–467 (2015)
8. Sun, W., Yang, G.A., Chen, Q., et al.: Fault diagnosis of rolling bearing based on wavelet transform and envelope spectrum correlation. J. Vib. Control 19(6), 924–941 (2013)
9. Wang, H., Chen, J., Dong, G.: Fault diagnosis of rolling bearing's early weak fault based on minimum entropy de-convolution and fast Kurtogram algorithm. Proc. Inst. Mech. Eng. Part C: J. Mech. Eng. Sci. (2014). https://doi.org/10.1177/0954406214564692
10. Cai, J.: Fault diagnosis of rolling bearing based on empirical mode decomposition and higher order statistics. Proc. Inst. Mech. Eng. Part C: J. Mech. Eng. Sci. (2014). https://doi.org/10.1177/0954406214545820
11. Liu, Q., Chen, F., Zhou, Z., et al.: Fault diagnosis of rolling bearing based on wavelet package transform and ensemble empirical mode decomposition. Adv. Mech. Eng. 5 (2013). Article no. 792584
12. Yunusa-Kaltungo, A., Sinha, J.K.: Faults diagnosis in rotating machines using higher order spectra. In: ASME Turbo Expo 2014: Turbine Technical Conference and Exposition. American Society of Mechanical Engineers, p. V07AT31A002 (2014)
13. Zhu, K., Li, H.: A rolling element bearing fault diagnosis approach based on hierarchical fuzzy entropy and support vector machine. Proc. Inst. Mech. Eng. Part C: J. Mech. Eng. Sci. (2015). https://doi.org/10.1177/0954406215593568
14. Yan, R., Gao, R.X.: Approximate entropy as a diagnostic tool for machine health monitoring. Mech. Syst. Signal Process. 21(2), 824–839 (2007)
15. Yan, R., Gao, R.X.: Machine health diagnosis based on approximate entropy. In: IMTC 2004. Proceedings of the 21st IEEE Instrumentation and Measurement Technology Conference, vol. 3, pp. 2054–2059. IEEE (2004)
16. Xiong, G., Zhang, L., Liu, H., et al.: A comparative study on ApEn, SampEn and their fuzzy counterparts in a multiscale framework for feature extraction. J. Zhejiang Univ. Sci. A 11(4), 270–279 (2010)
17. Zheng, J., Cheng, J., Yang, Y.: A rolling bearing fault diagnosis approach based on LCD and fuzzy entropy. Mech. Mach. Theory 70, 441–453 (2013)
18. Zhu, K., Song, X., Xue, D.: A roller bearing fault diagnosis method based on hierarchical entropy and support vector machine with particle swarm optimization algorithm. Measurement 47, 669–675 (2014)
19. Samanta, B., Al-Balushi, K.R.: Artificial neural network based fault diagnostics of rolling element bearings using time-domain features. Mech. Syst. Signal Process. 17(2), 317–328 (2003)
20. Jayaswal, P., Verma, S.N., Wadhwani, A.K.: Development of EBP-Artificial neural network expert system for rolling element bearing fault diagnosis. J. Vib. Control 17(8), 1131–1148 (2011)

21. Dong, S., Xu, X., Liu, J., et al.: Rotating machine fault diagnosis based on locality preserving projection and back propagation neural network-support vector machine model. Meas. Control **48**(7), 211–216 (2015)
22. Ao, H.L., Cheng, J., Yang, Y., et al.: The support vector machine parameter optimization method based on artificial chemical reaction optimization algorithm and its application to roller bearing fault diagnosis. J. Vib. Control (2013). https://doi.org/10.1177/1077546313511841
23. Zhang, X.L., Chen, X.F., He, Z.J.: Fault diagnosis based on support vector machines with parameter optimization by an ant colony algorithm. Proc. Inst. Mech. Engi. Part C: J. Mech. Eng. Sci. **224**(1), 217–229 (2010)
24. Hsu, C.W., Lin, C.J.: A comparison of methods for multiclass support vector machines. IEEE Trans. Neural Netw. **13**(2), 415–425 (2002)
25. Li, J., Guo, J.: A new feature extraction algorithm based on entropy cloud characteristics of communication signals. Math. Probl. Eng. **2015**, 1–8 (2015)
26. Li, J.: A novel recognition algorithm based on holder coefficient theory and interval gray relation classifier. KSII Trans. Internet Inf. Syst. (TIIS) **9**(11), 4573–4584 (2015)
27. Li, J.: A new robust signal recognition approach based on holder cloud features under varying SNR environment. KSII Trans. Internet Inf. Syst. **9**(11), 4934–4949 (2015)
28. Ying, Y., Cao, Y., Li, S., Li, J., Guo, J.: Study on gas turbine engine fault diagnostic approach with a hybrid of gray relation theory and gas-path analysis. Adv. Mech. Eng. **8**(1) (2016). https://doi.org/10.1177/1687814015627769
29. The Case Western Reserve University Bearing Data Center. http://csegroups.case.edu/bearingdatacenter/pages/download-data-file. Accessed 11 Oct 2015
30. Li, J., Cao, Y., Ying, Y., et al.: A rolling element bearing fault diagnosis approach based on multifractal theory and gray relation theory. PLoS ONE **11**(12), e0167587 (2016)
31. Cao, Y., Ying, Y., Li, J., et al.: Study on rolling bearing fault diagnosis approach based on improved generalized fractal box-counting dimension and adaptive gray relation algorithm. Adv. Mech. Eng. **8**(10) (2016). https://doi.org/10.1177/1687814016675583

A Novel Individual Radio Identification Algorithm Based on Multi-dimensional Features and Gray Relation Theory

Hui Han[1], Jingchao Li[2(✉)], and Xiang Chen[1]

[1] State Key Laboratory of Complex Electromagnetic Environment Effects on Electronics and Information System (CEMEE), Luoyang 471003, Henan, China
[2] Electronic Information College,
Shanghai Dianji University, Shanghai 201306, China
lijc@sdju.edu.cn

Abstract. With the advent of the Internet of Things, the number of mobile, embedded, and wearable devices are on the rising nowadays, which make us increasingly faced with the limitations of traditional network security control. Hence, accurately identifying different wireless devices through Hybrid information processing method for the Internet of things becomes very important today. To this problem, we design, implement, and evaluate a robust algorithm to identify the wireless device with fingerprints features through integral envelope and Hilbert transform theory based PCA analysis algorithm. Integral envelope theory was used respectively to process the signals first, then the principal component features can be extracted by PCA analysis algorithm. At last, gray relation classifier was used to identify the signals. We experimentally demonstrate effectiveness of the proposed algorithm ixin differentiating between 500 numbers of wireless device with the accuracy in excess of 99%. The approach itself is general and will work with any wireless devices' recognition.

Keywords: Individual radio recognition · Hilbert transform
Integral envelope theory · PCA analysis · Gray relation theory

1 Introduction

Internet of things as an important branch for the information technology, refers to the combination of all kinds of information sensing devices (such as radio frequency identification (RFID) devices, global positioning systems, infrared sensors, laser scanners) with the Internet to form a huge network, whose purpose is to make all the items connected with the network to facilitate the identification and management. Accurately identifying different wireless devices for the Internet of things becomes very important today. It is difficult to draw a conclusion that which factors affect the development of complex system. In 1982, combining the idea of system theory, information theory and cybernetics, Deng proposed the gray system theory, the study object is to extract valuable information by exploiting the limited information from uncertain system with few samples. It can give an effective description of the complex system behavior and development [1].

© ICST Institute for Computer Sciences, Social Informatics and Telecommunications Engineering 2018
G. Sun and S. Liu (Eds.): ADHIP 2017, LNICST 219, pp. 130–136, 2018.
https://doi.org/10.1007/978-3-319-73317-3_16

The gray relational analysis theory (GRA) uses the gray relational grade (GRG) model to calculate and analyze, is an essential concept in the grey system theory. It is the fundamental theory for gray system analysis, prediction and decision. Analyzing a system means that it should distinguish the primary and secondary factors and finding the factors which enhance or restrict the development of system. GRA analyzes the system with few samples by quantifying and ordering the factors. In order to quantify the relationship between factors, various forms of correlation coefficient were proposed, such as canonical correlation coefficient and resemblance correlation coefficient. These coefficients are based on the mathematical statistic theory, so they require a great deal of data because it seems difficult to find out the statistical rules or some kinds of typical probability distribution from few data. But in the practical work, it is hard to meet the requirement, the statistical data are limited and the degree of grey information is large, it is not easy to use the method based on mathematical statistic theory to analyze systems. GRA covers shortcoming to some extent, it has no requirement on the sample size and distribution [2]. The following are some common models: Deng's gray relational grade model, proposed by Deng based on the GRA axioms, known as the most fundamental model [3]; B-type gray relational analysis (B-GRA), given by Wang (1989) according to the proximity and similarity between two objects [4]. The gray absolute relational grade (GARG), proposed by Mei in 1992 based on the adjacency degree of absolute trends and relative trends between the factors' time series curves, the T-type gray relational analysis (T-GRA), produced by Tang in 1995 according to the approaching degree of the relative changing trend between the time series curves of factors [5, 6]. The grey slope relational grade (GSRG), created by Dang in 1994 and later developed by Dang and Sun in 2007 [7, 8]. The generalized relational grade was discussed on generalized interval by Wang and Guo (2005) [9]. Although each kind of relation calculation method is improved, they also have defects. The references [4–6, 10] proposed the defects of grey relational grade and corresponding improvement but the improved relational grade has new defects. This paper proposed a new Hybrid information processing method based on Integral envelope and Hilbert transform theory with PCA analysis theory together to extract the features of individual devices which will establish a good basis for the development of Internet of things.

2   Basic Theory

2.1   Integral Envelope Theory

The signal is integrated at any starting time with a certain length of time, the waveform of the integral value is called the signal integral envelope [11].

If the signal in time domain is:

$$s(t) = A(t) \exp(j(2\pi f_0 t + \varphi(t))) \tag{1}$$

where $A(t)$ is the instantaneous amplitude of the signal, f_0 is the signal carrier frequency, $\varphi(t)$ is the phase modulation function. If $\varphi(t)$ only take 0 and π, the signal is

BPSK signal. If $\varphi(t)$ does not change, the single is carrier frequency signal. Therefore, the If the signal as shown in formula (1) is single carrier frequency signal, the integral envelope can be written as

$$
G^2 = \left| \frac{1}{\Delta T} \int_{t'}^{t'+\Delta T} s(t)dt \right|^2 = \frac{1}{\Delta T^2} \left| \int_{t'}^{t'+\Delta T} \exp(j(2\pi f_0 t + \varphi(t)))dt \right|^2
$$

$$
= \frac{1}{(2\pi f \Delta T)^2}(2 - 2\cos(2\pi f_0 \Delta T)) = \frac{(\sin(\pi f_0 \Delta T))^2}{(\pi f \Delta T)^2} = (\sin c(\pi f_0 \Delta T))^2
$$

(2)

where $\sin c(x) = \frac{\sin(\pi x)}{\pi x}$.

The signal integral envelope G is related to the integral time interval ΔT and the signal carrier frequency f_0, as shown in formula (2). For a fixed frequency signal, when the interval of integration time is fixed, the integral envelope of the signal is a constant value. The G conforms to the rule of $|\sin c(x)|$ function when the signal carrier frequency changes.

If the LFM signal is

$$
s(t) = A \exp(j(2\pi f_0 t + kt^2/2))
$$

(3)

where k is frequency modulation rate. When the interval of integration time is small, the integral envelope process of the LFM signal is equivalent to processing the single carrier frequency signal, and the integral carrier frequency is changed in each integral transformation. So, the waveform of the integral conforms to the rule of $|\sin c(x)|$ function in time domain. When $f_0 \Delta T$ is an integer, the integral envelope of the signal is zero. It is important.

2.2 PCA Analysis Theory

Principal component analysis (PCA) can be described as a regression-type optimization problem. Not only in the data processing, but also in dimensionality reduction, PCA has a wide range of applications [12].

PCA makes the derived variables capture maximal variance over seeking the linear combinations of the original variables. For computing the PCA, we can by obtaining the data matrix's singular value decomposition (SVD). In detail, we have an n-by-p matrix $\mathbf{X}$, here, n is the number of samples and p is the number of variables. In order to generalization, we assume that the means of every column are all 0. The singular value decomposition of $\mathbf{X}$ can be written [13].

$$
\mathbf{X} = \mathbf{U}\mathbf{D}\mathbf{V}^T
$$

(4)

where $\mathbf{D}$ is the singular values of $\mathbf{X}$, an rectangular diagonal matrix which size is n-by-p; $\mathbf{U}$ is the left singular matrix of $\mathbf{X}$, an n-by-n matrix, whose columns are orthogonal unit vectors with the length of n; and $\mathbf{V}$ is the right singular matrix of $\mathbf{X}$, a p-by-p matrix, the columns of which are also orthogonal unit vectors.

We use the singular value decomposition the score matrix $\mathbf{Y}^T$ as

$$\mathbf{Y}^T = \mathbf{X}^T\mathbf{U} = \mathbf{VD}^T\mathbf{U}^T\mathbf{U} = \mathbf{VD}^T \tag{5}$$

It is easily seen that the left singular vectors of $\mathbf{X}^T$ is $\mathbf{V}$, so $\mathbf{Y}^T$ is given by the left singular matrix $\mathbf{V}$ multiplied by the transpose of singular values matrix. The polar decomposition of $\mathbf{Y}^T$ is also expressed as this.

It is no need to form the matrix $\mathbf{X}^T\mathbf{X}$ to calculate the SVD of $\mathbf{X}^T$ in efficient algorithms exist, so calculating a principal component analysis from a data matrix is the standard way for computing the SVD, unless we require a handful of components.

At last, PCA makes the greatest variance according to transforming the data to a new coordinate system, some projection of data which are called the first principle component comes to lie on the first coordinate, and on the second coordinate, the second greatest variance appears, and so on.

Finally, multiply the first l largest singular values and corresponding singular vectors, we can get a truncated $n \times l$ score matrix $\mathbf{Y}_l$ of $\mathbf{Y}$:

$$\mathbf{Y}_l = \mathbf{U}_l^T\mathbf{X} = \mathbf{D}_l\mathbf{V}^T \tag{6}$$

After construction, the size of the transformed data matrices is n-by-l.

3 Simulation and Analysis

The feature extraction algorithm proposed in this paper is used to extract the characteristics of wireless devices, and then gray relation theory was used to classify the signals. The steps of the algorithm are as follows:

Firstly, 50 sets of signals of 10 groups of devices are calculated by integral envelope algorithm respectively, and then instantaneous amplitude features can be obtained as data sets.

Second, the dimensions are decreased based on PCA analysis method. According to the contribution rate of the main components, the corresponding number of principal components are selected as the features to be identified.

At last, gray relation algorithm was used to extract the principal component characteristics of 50 sets of 10 devices in order to classify and identify them. While, 200 sets of data were randomly selected to train and 300 sets of data were selected to test, and the recognition rate was calculated.

According to the above procedures, take two kinds of fingerprint features as example, the algorithm simulation results are shown in Fig. 1:

From the simulation results we can see that, the contribution rate of the first principal component is 89.85%, the contribution rate of the second principal component is 5.69%, so the total contribution rate is 95.54%. According to the definition of PCA analysis, when the contribution rate of principal component is between 85% and 95%, the obtained principal features can approximately represent all the characteristics of the original signal, in order to realize the accurate classification of the signal. Therefore, Fig. 1 shows the two-dimensional principal components of different

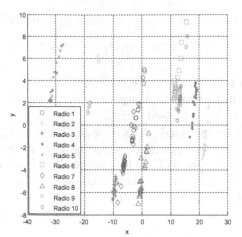

Fig. 1. Two-dimensional principal components of 10 wireless devices' subtle features based on integral envelope algorithm under no-noisy environment

wireless devices' features, where the abscissa x represents the first principal component value and the ordinate y represents the second principal component value. It can be seen that there is a good aggregation degree and interclass separation degree.

And then gray relation algorithm was used to identify the obtained features, and the recognition result is 96.78%, which basically realize the accurately recognize of signals. If the recognition effect needs to be improved, take one more principal components to form three-dimensional features, whose contribution rate is 3.94%. Plus the first two principal components together, the total contribution rate is 99.48%. They can more accurately describe all the characteristics of the original signals. The same method was used to identify the signals, and the recognition rate is 98.33%, comparing with using two principal components, the recognition result is improved.

Similarly, change the simulation condition to 20 dB SNR environment, then using the algorithm proposed in this paper to extract and classify the characteristics of the signals. Simulation results are shown in Fig. 2. Where the abscissa x represents the first principal component value and the ordinate y represents the second principal component value. It can be seen from the simulation results that, some characteristics of wireless devices have a certain degree of overlap, it is difficult to achieve accurately classification.

According to the results of PCA analysis, the contribution rate of the first principal component reached 88.26%, the contribution rate of the second principal component reached 5.39%, and the contribution rate of the third principal component reached 3.95%. Due to the noise added to the signals, the contribution rate of each reduced dimensional principal component are relatively dispersion. So the total contribution rate of the first two principal component features used in Fig. 2 is only 93.65%, and the recognition result obtained by gray relation classifier is 82.67%. In order to improve the recognition result, another principal component is added together, and the total contribution rate is 97.6%, then the recognition result can be calculated as 88.45%.

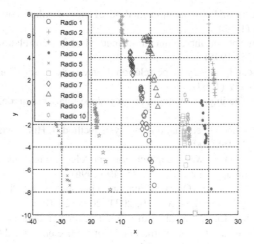

Fig. 2. Two-dimensional principal components of 10 wireless devices' subtle features based on integral envelope algorithm under the SNR of 20 dB environment

4   Conclusion

In this paper we have addressed the fundamental issue of wireless device identification for the Internet of things. We designed, implemented and evaluated the integral envelope theory based PCA analysis algorithm, a technique that can identify the subtle features of wireless devices. Unlike the previous techniques, this algorithm can accurately identify the fingerprints features of different wireless devices. Simulation results show that, the proposed algorithm can recognize the subtle features of signals between 500 numbers of wireless devices with the accuracy in excess of 99%. The approach itself is general and will work with any wireless devices' recognition.

Our evaluation of the strengths and weaknesses of the proposed Hybrid information processing algorithm suggests that it could be especially useful for wireless device's subtle features' identification. And it also can be used in some other related fields such as image processing, fault diagnosis and so on.

Acknowledgements. The research of the paper is supported by the National Natural Science Foundation of China (No. 61603239) and (No. 61601281).

References

1. Liu, S., Forrest, J., Yang, Y.: A brief introduction to grey systems theory. Grey Syst.: Theory Appl. **2**(2), 89–104 (2012)
2. Zhou, X.: The study on grey relational degree and its application. Jilin University Press, Changchun (2007)
3. Deng, J.L.: Grey System. China Ocean Press, Beijing (1988)
4. Wang, Q.: The grey relational analysis of B-mode. J. Huazhong Univ. Sci. Tenchnol. **6**, 77–82 (1989)

5. Mei, Z.: The concept and computation method of grey absolute correlation degree. Syst. Eng. **5**, 43–44+72 (1992)
6. Tang, W.: The concept and the computation method of T's correlation degree. Appl. Stat. Manag. **1**, 34–37+33 (1995)
7. Dang, Y.: The research of grey slope relational grade. Syst. Sci. Compr. Stud. Agric. **10** (Supplement), 331–337 (1994)
8. Sun, Y., Dang, Y.: The improved model of grey slope relational grade. Stat. Decis. **15**, 12–13 (2007)
9. Wang, Q., Guo, L.: Generalized relational analysis method. J. Huazhong Univ. Sci. Technol. (Nat. Sci. Edn.) **8**, 97–99 (2005)
10. Zhang, S.: Comparison between computation models of grey interconnect degree and analysis on their shourages. Syst. Eng. **3**, 45–49 (1996)
11. Liu, X., Si, X., Lu, M., Cai, Z.: Quick estimation to parameters of LPI radar-signals based on integral-envelope. Syst. Eng. Electron. **10**, 2031–2035 (2010)
12. Peng, K., Zhang, M., Li, Q., et al.: Fiber optic perimeter detection based on principal component analysis. In: 2016 15th International Conference on Optical Communications and Networks (ICOCN), pp. 1–3. IEEE (2016)
13. Ying, Y., Cao, Y., Li, S., Li, J., Guo, J.: Study on gas turbine engine fault diagnostic approach with a hybrid of gray relation theory and gas-path analysis. Adv. Mech. Eng. 8(1) (2016). https://doi.org/10.1177/1687814015627769

A New Robust Rolling Bearing Vibration Signal Analysis Method

Jingchao Li[1,2], Yulong Ying[3(✉)], Guoyin Zhang[1], and Zhimin Chen[2]

[1] School of Computer Science and Technology,
Harbin Engineering University, Harbin, China
[2] School of Electronic and Information,
Shanghai Dianji University, Shanghai, China
[3] School of Energy and Mechanical Engineering,
Shanghai University of Electric Power, Shanghai, China
yingyulong060313@163.com

Abstract. As bearing vibration signal is of nonlinear and nonstationary characteristics, and the condition-indicating information distributed in the rolling bearing vibration signal is complicated, a new rolling bearing health status estimation approach using holder coefficient and gray relation algorithm was proposed based on bearing vibration signal in the paper. Firstly, the holder coefficient algorithm was proposed for extracting health status feature vectors based on the bearing vibration signals, and secondly the gray relation algorithm was developed for achieving bearing fault pattern recognition intelligently using the extracted feature vectors. At last, the experimental study has illustrated the proposed approach can efficiently and effectively recognize different fault types and in addition different severities with good real-time performance.

Keywords: Vibration signal processing · Holder theory · Gray relation theory
Fault diagnosis

1 Introduction

Rolling element bearings are commonly used in rotational machines, and usually their failure leads to the machine breakdown, which causes substantial economic losses [1–3]. Vibration-based bearing fault diagnosis approaches have attracted broad attention in the near past as vibration signal holds rich bearing health status information. As the result of the nonlinear factors, such as stiffness, friction and clearance, bearing vibration signals always bear nonlinear and nonstationary performance [4]. what's more, bearing vibration signals involve not only the working information related to the bearing itself, but also plentiful information related to other rotating parts of the machine, which in comparison with the former is usually taken as the background noise [5]. Thus the common time domain or frequency domain signal processing approaches may not easily obtain an accurate estimation result about the bearing health status [6].

Recently, the procedure of bearing fault diagnosis is gradually taken as a process of fault pattern recognition with the aid of artificial intelligence (AI) approaches [7], and its reliability is essentially determined by the effectiveness of the fault feature

© ICST Institute for Computer Sciences, Social Informatics and Telecommunications Engineering 2018
G. Sun and S. Liu (Eds.): ADHIP 2017, LNICST 219, pp. 137–145, 2018.
https://doi.org/10.1007/978-3-319-73317-3_17

extraction. Nowadays, Some entropy based feature extraction methods (e.g., hierarchical entropy [8], fuzzy entropy [9], sample entropy [10] and approximate entropy [11, 12]), were used for extracting fault feature vectors based on bearing vibration signals. Here, we exploit a holder coefficient algorithm, for extracting fault feature vectors based on the vibration signals, so as to improve the performance of traditional feature extraction approaches in the paper.

When the fault feature extraction is ready, a fault pattern recognition method is required to implement the fault diagnosis automatically. The most common approaches are support vector machines [13] and artificial neural networks [14–16]. However, the training of artificial neural networks requires a lot of faulted samples, which are difficult to obtain in practice. The support vector machines are based on statistical learning theory, and have better generalization than artificial neural networks under a smaller number of samples [17]. However, the accuracy of support vector machines is essentially determined by the choice of their optimum parameters [18]. Thereafter, complex multi-class concept [19] or optimization algorithms [14, 18] has been used to improve the effectiveness of SVMs. In this paper, so as to keep a balance between generality and accuracy, a gray relation algorithm was used to achieve fault pattern recognition.

2 Holder Coefficient Algorithm

Holder coefficient can be used to measure the similar degree of two sequences, which may extract signals' features. It is evolved from Holder inequality and the definition of Holder inequality can be described as follows:

For any vector $X = [x_1, x_2, \ldots, x_n]^T$ and $Y = [y_1, y_2, \ldots, y_n]^T$, they satisfy:

$$\sum_{i=1}^{n} |x_i \cdot y_i| \leq \left(\sum_{i=1}^{n} |x_i|^p \right)^{1/p} \cdot \left(\sum_{i=1}^{n} |y_i|^q \right)^{1/q} \tag{1}$$

where $\frac{1}{p} + \frac{1}{q} = 1$ and $p, q > 1$.

Based on the Holder inequality, for two discrete signals $\{f_1(i) \geq 0, i = 1, 2, \ldots, n\}$ and $\{f_2(i) \geq 0, i = 1, 2, \ldots, n\}$, if $\frac{1}{p} + \frac{1}{q} = 1$ and $p, q > 1$, then Holder coefficient of these two discrete signals is obtained as follows:

$$H_c = \frac{\sum f_1(i) f_2(i)}{\left(\sum f_1^p(i) \right)^{1/p} \cdot \left(\sum f_2^q(i) \right)^{1/q}} \tag{2}$$

where $0 \leq H_c \leq 1$.

Holder coefficient characterizes the similar degree of two discrete signals, if and only if $f_1^p(i) = k f_2^q(i)$, $i = 1, 2, \ldots, n$, in which n denotes the length of discrete signal and k is a real number, H_c will be the biggest value. In this case, the similar degree of two signals is biggest, which indicates that the two signals belong to the same type of signals; if and only if $\sum_{i=1}^{n} f_1(i) f_2(i) = 0$, H_c get the minimum value, and in this case, the similarity of two signals is smallest, which indicates the signals are irrelevant, and belong to different types of signals.

Rectangular sequence $s_1(i)$ and triangular sequence $s_2(i)$ are selected as reference sequences, and then the Holder coefficient value of the vibration signals to be identified with the two reference signal sequences is obtained as follows:

$$H_1 = \frac{\sum f(i)s_1(i)}{\left(\sum f^p(i)\right)^{1/p} \cdot \left(\sum s_1^q(i)\right)^{1/q}} \tag{3}$$

where the rectangular sequence $s_1(i)$ is as follows:

$$s_1(i) = \begin{cases} s, & 1 \leq i \leq N \\ 0, & else \end{cases} \tag{4}$$

Similarly, H_2 is obtained as follows:

$$H_2 = \frac{\sum f(i)s_2(i)}{\left(\sum f^p(i)\right)^{1/p} \cdot \left(\sum s_2^q(i)\right)^{1/q}} \tag{5}$$

where the triangular sequence $s_2(i)$ is as follows:

$$s_2(i) = \begin{cases} 2is/N, & 1 \leq i \leq N/2 \\ 2s - 2is/N, & N/2 \leq i \leq N \end{cases} \tag{6}$$

3   Gray Relation Algorithm

As the basis of gray system theory, the gray relation algorithm is to calculate the gray relation coefficient and relation degree between each comparative feature vector and reference feature vectors based on the basic theory of space mathematics [20–23].

Suppose the fault feature vectors (i.e., the two-dimensional feature vector extracted based on Holder coefficient algorithm) extracted based on vibration signals, to be identified are as follows:

$$B_1 = \begin{bmatrix} b_1(1) \\ b_1(2) \end{bmatrix}, \ B_2 = \begin{bmatrix} b_2(1) \\ b_2(2) \end{bmatrix}, \ \ldots, \ B_i = \begin{bmatrix} b_i(1) \\ b_i(2) \end{bmatrix}, \ \ldots \tag{7}$$

where $B_i (i = 1,2,\ldots)$ is a certain fault pattern to be recognized (i.e., fault types and in addition severities).

Suppose the knowledge base between the health status patterns (i.e., fault type as well as severity) and fault signatures (i.e., the feature vectors) from a part of samples is as follows:

$$C_1 = \begin{bmatrix} c_1(1) \\ c_1(2) \end{bmatrix}, \; C_2 = \begin{bmatrix} c_2(1) \\ c_2(2) \end{bmatrix} \dots, \; C_j = \begin{bmatrix} c_j(1) \\ c_j(2) \end{bmatrix}, \dots \tag{8}$$

where $C_j (j = 1, 2, \dots)$ is a known health status pattern (i.e., fault type as well as severity); $C_j (j = 1, 2, \dots)$ is a characteristic parameter.

For $\rho \in (0, 1)$:

$$\xi\big(b_i(k), c_j(k)\big) = \frac{\min\limits_{j} \min\limits_{k} \big|b_i(k) - c_j(k)\big| + \rho \cdot \max\limits_{j} \max\limits_{k} \big|b_i(k) - c_j(k)\big|}{\big|b_i(k) - c_j(k)\big| + \rho \cdot \max\limits_{j} \max\limits_{k} \big|b_i(k) - c_j(k)\big|} \tag{9}$$

$$\xi(B_i, C_j) = \frac{1}{2} \sum_{k=1}^{2} \xi\big(b_i(k), c_j(k)\big), \, j = 1, 2, \dots \tag{10}$$

where ρ is a distinguishing coefficient; $\xi\big(b_i(k), c_j(k)\big)$ is the gray relation coefficient for k_{th} feature parameter for B_i and C_j; $\xi(B_i, C_j)$ is the gray relation degree for B_i and C_j. Thereafter B_i is categorized to the health status pattern where the maximal $\xi(B_i, C_j)(j = 1, 2, \dots,)$ is calculated.

4 Proposed Approach

Totally, the proposed approach for rolling bearing health status estimation is as follows:

a. The vibration signals from the object rolling element bearing in a rotating machine are sampled under different working conditions, including normal operating condition and faulty operating condition with various fault types and severities, for the establishment of the sample knowledge base.
b. Through a two-dimensional feature extraction algorithm based on Holder coefficient theory, the health status feature vectors are extracted from the sample knowledge base.
c. The sample knowledge base for GRA is established based on the fault symptom (i.e., the extracted feature vector) and the fault pattern (i.e., the known fault types and severities).

The feature vectors extracted based on bearing vibration signals to be identified are input into GRA, and the diagnostic results (i.e., fault types and severity) are output.

5 Experimental Validation

All the rolling element bearing vibration signals for analysis are from Case Western Reserve University Bearing Data Center [24] in the paper. The related experimental device consists of a torque meter, a power meter and a three-phase induction motor, and the load power and speed measured by the sensor, seen in Fig. 1. Over controlling

Fig. 1. Experimental setup

the power meter, the desired torque load can be obtained. The motor drive end rotor is supported by a test bearing, where a single point of failure is set through discharge machining. The fault diameters (i.e., fault severities) include 28 mils, 21 mils, 14 mils and 7 mils, and the fault types include outer race fault, the inner race fault and the ball fault. An accelerometer is installed on the motor drive end housing with a bandwidth up to 5000 Hz, and the vibration data for the test bearing in different operating conditions is collected by a recorder, where the sampling frequency is 12 kHz.

The bearing vibration data used for analysis was obtained under the load of 0 horsepower and the motor speed of 1797 r/min. The test bearing is a deep groove rolling bearing of 6205-2RS JEM SKF. Totally 11 types of vibration signals considering different fault categories and severities are analyzed, seen in Table 1. Each data sample from vibration signals is made up of 2048 time series points. For those 550 data samples, 110 data samples are randomly chosen for establishment of knowledge base, with the rest 440 data samples as testing data samples.

Table 1. Description of experimental data set

Bearing condition	Fault diameter (mils)	The number of base samples	The number of testing samples	Label of classification
Normal	0	10	40	1
Inner race fault	7	10	40	2
	14	10	40	3
	21	10	40	4
	28	10	40	5
Ball fault	7	10	40	6
	14	10	40	7
	28	10	40	8
Outer race fault	7	10	40	9
	14	10	40	10
	21	10	40	11

The fault feature vectors extracted from bearing normal operating condition and different fault conditions with 7 mils fault diameter over the two-dimensional feature extraction algorithm using Holder coefficient were shown in Fig. 2.

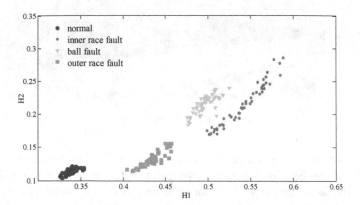

Fig. 2. Holder coefficient features of a random chosen sample from bearing normal operating condition and different fault conditions with fault diameter 7 mils

And the fault feature vectors extracted from bearing inner race fault condition with different severities over the two-dimensional feature extraction algorithm using Holder coefficient were shown in Fig. 3.

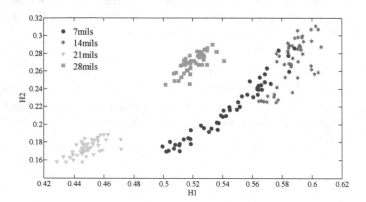

Fig. 3. Holder coefficient features of a random chosen sample from bearing inner race fault condition with various severities

From Figs. 2 and 3, it can be seen that the fault feature vectors extracted from the bearing vibration signals with different fault types and in addition different severities through the two-dimensional feature extraction algorithm using Holder coefficient show apparent differences.

The sample knowledge base for GRA is established based on the fault symptom (i.e., the extracted feature vectors) and the fault pattern (i.e., the known fault types and severities). The feature vectors extracted from the testing bearing vibration signals to be identified are input into GRA, and the diagnostic results (i.e., fault types and severities) are output, shown in Table 2.

Table 2. The diagnostic results by GRA

Label of classification	The number of testing samples	The number of misclassified samples	Testing accuracy (%)
1	40	0	100
2	40	6	85
3	40	0	100
4	40	0	100
5	40	6	85
6	40	6	85
7	40	0	100
8	40	13	67.5
9	40	0	100
10	40	0	100
11	40	0	100
In total	440	31	92.95

The diagnostic results from Table 2 show that the fault pattern recognition success rate for detecting bearing faulty conditions can reach 100%, and the total fault pattern recognition success rate can reach almost 93%. The time cost by the proposed diagnostic approach for one Test Case is within 1.6 ms by using a laptop computer with a 2.0 GHz dual processor.

6 Conclusion

A novel rolling element bearing vibration signal analysis approach using holder coefficient and gray relation algorithm was proposed in the paper. The experimental results have demonstrated that the holder coefficient algorithm is very suitable for rolling bearing fault feature extraction, which can obtain more distinguishing information imaging different health status. And the gray relation algorithm as a pattern recognition technique is very suitable for implementing the rolling bearing fault pattern recognition intelligently under a small number of base samples. Moreover, the proposed approach can efficiently and effectively recognize different fault types and in addition different severities with good real-time performance.

Acknowledgment. The research is supported by the National Natural Science Foundation of China (No. 61603239) and (No. 61601281).

References

1. Van Hecke, B., Qu, Y., He, D.: Bearing fault diagnosis based on a new acoustic emission sensor technique. Proc. Inst. Mech. Eng. Part O: J. Risk Reliab. **229**(2), 105–118 (2015)
2. Jiang, L., Shi, T., Xuan, J.: Fault diagnosis of rolling bearings based on Marginal Fisher analysis. J. Vibr. Control (2012). https://doi.org/10.1177/1077546312463747
3. Xu, J., Tong, S., Cong, F., et al.: The application of time–frequency reconstruction and correlation matching for rolling bearing fault diagnosis. Proc. Inst. Mech. Eng. Part C: J. Mech. Eng. Sci. (2015). https://doi.org/10.1177/0954406215584397
4. Vakharia, V., Gupta, V.K., Kankar, P.K.: A multiscale permutation entropy based approach to select wavelet for fault diagnosis of ball bearings. J. Vibr. Control (2014). https://doi.org/10.1177/1077546314520830
5. Zhu, K., Li, H.: A rolling element bearing fault diagnosis approach based on hierarchical fuzzy entropy and support vector machine. Proc. Inst. Mech. Eng. Part C: J. Mech. Eng. Sci. (2015) https://doi.org/10.1177/0954406215593568
6. Sun, W., Yang, G.A., Chen, Q., et al.: Fault diagnosis of rolling bearing based on wavelet transform and envelope spectrum correlation. J. Vib. Control **19**(6), 924–941 (2013)
7. Tiwari, R., Gupta, V.K., Kankar, P.K.: Bearing fault diagnosis based on multi-scale permutation entropy and adaptive neuro fuzzy classifier. J. Vib. Control **21**(3), 461–467 (2015)
8. Zhu, K., Song, X., Xue, D.: A roller bearing fault diagnosis method based on hierarchical entropy and support vector machine with particle swarm optimization algorithm. Measurement **47**, 669–675 (2014)
9. Zheng, J., Cheng, J., Yang, Y.: A rolling bearing fault diagnosis approach based on LCD and fuzzy entropy. Mech. Mach. Theory **70**, 441–453 (2013)
10. Xiong, G., Zhang, L., Liu, H., et al.: A comparative study on ApEn, SampEn and their fuzzy counterparts in a multiscale framework for feature extraction. J. Zhejiang Univ. Sci. A **11**(4), 270–279 (2010)
11. Yan, R., Gao, R.X.: Machine health diagnosis based on approximate entropy. In: 2004 Proceedings of the 21st IEEE Instrumentation and Measurement Technology Conference, IMTC 2004, vol. 3, pp. 2054–2059. IEEE (2004)
12. Yan, R., Gao, R.X.: Approximate entropy as a diagnostic tool for machine health monitoring. Mech. Syst. Signal Process. **21**(2), 824–839 (2007)
13. Dong, S., Xu, X., Liu, J., et al.: Rotating machine fault diagnosis based on locality preserving projection and back propagation neural network-support vector machine model. Meas. Control **48**(7), 211–216 (2015)
14. Wang, C.C., Kang, Y., Shen, P.C., et al.: Applications of fault diagnosis in rotating machinery by using time series analysis with neural network. Expert Syst. Appl. **37**(2), 1696–1702 (2010)
15. Jayaswal, P., Verma, S.N., Wadhwani, A.K.: Development of EBP-artificial neural network expert system for rolling element bearing fault diagnosis. J. Vib. Control **17**(8), 1131–1148 (2011)
16. Samanta, B., Al-Balushi, K.R.: Artificial neural network based fault diagnostics of rolling element bearings using time-domain features. Mech. Syst. Sig. Process. **17**(2), 317–328 (2003)
17. Zhang, X.L., Chen, X.F., He, Z.J.: Fault diagnosis based on support vector machines with parameter optimization by an ant colony algorithm. Proc. Inst. Mech. Eng. Part C: J. Mech. Eng. Sci. **224**(1), 217–229 (2010)

18. Ao, H.L., Cheng, J., Yang, Y., et al.: The support vector machine parameter optimization method based on artificial chemical reaction optimization algorithm and its application to roller bearing fault diagnosis. J. Vibr. Control (2013). https://doi.org/10.1177/1077546313511841
19. Hsu, C.W., Lin, C.J.: A comparison of methods for multiclass support vector machines. IEEE Trans. Neural Netw. **13**(2), 415–425 (2002)
20. Ying, Y., Cao, Y., Li, S., Li, J., Guo, J.: Study on gas turbine engine fault diagnostic approach with a hybrid of gray relation theory and gas-path analysis. Adv. Mech. Eng. **8**(1) (2016). https://doi.org/10.1177/1687814015627769
21. Li, J.: A novel recognition algorithm based on holder coefficient theory and interval gray relation classifier. KSII Trans. Internet Inf. Syst. (TIIS) **9**(11), 4573–4584 (2015)
22. Li, J.: A new robust signal recognition approach based on holder cloud features under varying SNR environment. KSII Trans. Internet Inf. Syst. (TIIS) **9**(11), 4934–4949 (2015)
23. Li, J., Guo, J.: A new feature extraction algorithm based on entropy cloud characteristics of communication signals. Math. Prob. Eng. **2015**, 1–8 (2015)
24. The Case Western Reserve University Bearing Data Center. http://csegroups.case.edu/bearingdatacenter/pages/download-data-file. Accessed 11 Oct 2015

Two-Dimensional Fractal Dimension Feature Extraction Algorithm Based On Time-Frequency

Wenwen Li$^{(\boxtimes)}$, Zheng Dou, and Tingting Cao

Harbin Engineering University, Harbin 150001, HLJ, China
939021004@qq.com

Abstract. Digital signal modulation recognition is the technology of signal recognition. In the non-cooperative communication field, the technology is used to process signal and extract feature, and recognize the signal. Because of small distance and intersection between feature classes of digital signal fractal box dimension, its difficult to recognize the signal. This paper proposes a new algorithm. This algorithm is based on time frequency image of two dimensional fractal box dimension feature extraction.

Keywords: Modulation recognition · Fractal box dimension
Feature extration

1 Introduction

In recent years, with the rapid development of software radio technology, communication reconnaissance, confrontation and other modern information technology research has become research hotspots [1]. Radio technology plays an important role both in the civil and military fields. Electronic reconnaissance technology is of great importance to the promotion of civil technology and the enhancement of national defense. Wireless communication uses spatial electromagnetic radiation to transmit images, text, sound and other information. The open channel environment makes communication reconnaissance possible [2]. Signal recognition technology has become an important means of electronic reconnaissance. The signal recognition technology realizes the signal identification by extracting the characteristic parameters of the received signal according to the difference between the different signal characteristics. At present, signal recognition algorithm can be divided into two categories [3]. The first category is based on test method of decision theory, the second category is based on statistical model of identification methods [4].

The signal modulation recognition method based on decision theory can theoretically guarantee the optimal recognition results under the Bayes minimum criterion, but this kind of method has very obvious shortcomings. This method requires too much parameter information and has large computational complexity [5]. So it is not suitable for real-time classification of signal modulation recognition. The signal recognition method based on statistical mode can be regarded as a mapping relation. By extracting the effective and stable characteristics of

© ICST Institute for Computer Sciences, Social Informatics and Telecommunications Engineering 2018
G. Sun and S. Liu (Eds.): ADHIP 2017, LNICST 219, pp. 146–153, 2018.
https://doi.org/10.1007/978-3-319-73317-3_18

the signal, the signal is mapped from the time domain space to the feature space. Then the signal is classified and identified by the difference between the signal characteristics. The appropriate classification features and decision criteria have to implement easily. So the algorithm based on statistical mode is more extensive used in the actual project. Fractal theory has been studied in depth in recent years. Fractal theory are applied in many fields such as protein sequences, kinetic structures, liquid structures, DNA sequence analysis, fault diagnosis [6], image processing [7] and so on [8]. In this paper, we propose a two-dimensional box dimension feature extraction method based on time-frequency image. Simulation results show that method proposed in this paper is superior to one-dimensional signal box dimension feature and is suitable for the classification and recognition of multiple signals [9].

2   Research on Fractal Feature of Digital Signal

2.1   Fractal Box Dimension Theory

Fractal dimension is a tool to describe the dimension of the object. Among the many fractal dimension calculation methods, the box dimension algorithm is simple and can calculate the fractal dimension of the object well [10].

Let (X, d) be an object space, M is a non-empty compact set family of X, A is a non-empty compact set in X. For each positive number ε, the number of boxes covering A can be represented by $N(A, \varepsilon)$, the box length is ε, then [7]:

$$N(A, \varepsilon) = \{M : A \subset \sum_{i=1}^{M} N(x_i, \varepsilon)\} \qquad (1)$$

wherein, $x_1, x_2, \cdots, x_M$ are different point and $x_1, x_2, \cdots, x_M$ belong to X. The box dimension is defined

$$D_b = \lim_{\varepsilon \to 0} \frac{\ln N(A, \varepsilon)}{\ln(1/\varepsilon)} \qquad (2)$$

For signal x_i, ε is the time interval of the signal sampling process. In the calculation of box dimension, ε represents the minimum length of the box and the length growth rate of the box. For a box with a length of $k\varepsilon$ to cover the signal, the number of boxes required is:

$$s_1 = max\{x_{k(i-1)+1}, x_{k(i-1)+2}, \cdots, x_{k(i-1)+k+1}\} \qquad (3)$$

$$s_2 = min\{x_{k(i-1)+1}, x_{k(i-1)+2}, \cdots, x_{k(i-1)+k+1}\} \qquad (4)$$

$$s(k\varepsilon) = \sum_{i=1}^{N_0/k} |s_1 - s_2| \qquad (5)$$

In formula (5), $i = 1, 2, \cdots, N_0/k$, $k = 1, 2, \cdots, K$, N_0 is signal truncation length, and $K < N_0$, $s(k\varepsilon)$ is the signal amplitude range, then $N_{k\varepsilon}$ is expressed as:

$$N_{k\varepsilon} = s(k\varepsilon)/k\varepsilon + 1 \qquad (6)$$

For the fitting curve of $\lg k\varepsilon \sim \lg N_{k\varepsilon}$, calculating the box dimension is chosen to select a better linear segment. After the logarithm, formula (7) is available

$$\lg N_{k\varepsilon} = -d_B \lg k\varepsilon + b \tag{7}$$

In formula (7), $k_1 \leqslant k \leqslant k_2$, k_1 is the starting points of the number of boxes. k_2 is the ending points of the number of boxes. The Least-Mean-Square algorithm can be used to calculate the straight slope of the segment. The box dimension of the signal is calculated:

$$D = -\frac{(k_2 - k_1 + 1)\sum_{k=k_1}^{k_2}(\lg k) \cdot \lg N_{k\varepsilon} - \sum_{k=k_1}^{k_2}(\lg k) \cdot \lg N_{k\varepsilon}}{(k_2 - k_1 + 1)\sum_{k=k_1}^{k_2}\lg^2 k - (\sum_{k=k_1}^{k_2}\lg k)^2} \tag{8}$$

2.2   Simulation Experiment

In this paper, we identify four different digital modulation signal types. The modulation signal types include 2FSK, BPSK, 16QAM and MSK. The signal carrier frequency is $f_c = 4\,\mathrm{MHz}$, sampling frequency is $f_s = 4 \times f_c = 16\,\mathrm{MHz}$, signal length is $N_s = 2048$, digital signal symbol rate is $R_s = 1000\,\mathrm{Sps}$, 2FSK signal $f_1 = 1\,\mathrm{MHz}$, $f_2 = 2\,\mathrm{MHz}$. The baseband signal is a random code, the modulated signal is shaped by a rectangular pulse, and the noise is white Gaussian noise. For each type signal, 100 Monte Carlo experiments were performed at SNR $= 0\,\mathrm{dB}$ and SNR $= 10\,\mathrm{dB}$ to generate a sample signal to calculate the mean and variance of the box dimension. Table 1 is the mean and variance of the fractal dimension of the four digital signals. Table Remarks: (mean, variance).

Table 1. The fractal dimension mean and variance of signals

SNR	2FSK		BPSK		MSK		16QAM	
	μ	σ	μ	σ	μ	σ	μ	σ
0 dB	1.510	0.015	1.549	0.015	1.554	0.016	1.601	0.016
10 dB	1.481	0.015	1.607	0.016	1.611	0.016	1.645	0.016

The mean of the signal feature represents the central position of the feature of the digital signal in the feature space and the class separation between the features of the digital signal. The variance of signal characteristics represents the intra class aggregation of the characteristics of digital signals. As can be seen from Table 1, the fractal box dimension between digital signals has less distance between classes, but the variance of its characteristic value is small. It shows that digital signal fractal dimension within the degree of polymerization is good. For digital signals, there is a strong similarity between the time domain waveforms of signals. So it is not very good to extract the signal fractal feature from the fractal box dimension of the signal time domain waveform. Figure 1 is the digital signal box dimension feature curve with signal to noise ratio (SNR).

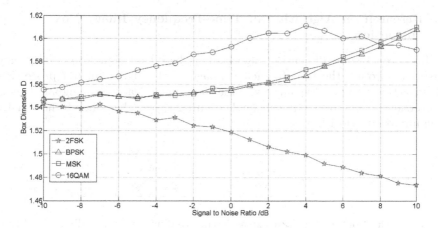

Fig. 1. Digital signal box dimension feature curve with SNR

The signal fractal dimension is a description of the signal dimension. The lower the complexity of the signal, the smaller the box dimension. It can be seen from Fig. 1 that the inter-class distance of fractal box dimension of different signals is small and the characteristic stability is poor. The box dimension curves of different signals have cross phenomena. The fractal box dimension has a good ability to distinguish between 2FSK signals at higher signal-to-noise ratio. But for other digital signals, the inter-class distance between signals is small. It is not conducive to classify and identify digital signals. So, this paper presents a two-dimensional box dimension feature extraction method based on time-frequency image.

3 Research on Two-Dimensional Fractal Dimension Features Based on Time-Frequency Images

Signal time-frequency conversion is to distribute signal energy in signal time-frequency plane. It is a conversion of one-dimensional to two-dimensional. The time-frequency analysis of the signal can effectively reflect the spectral distribution of the signal over time. Compared to the signal's time domain waveform, the time-frequency transformation of the signal can fine describe the local subtle characteristics of the signal. From the simulation results in the previous section, we can see that the difference between fractal dimension features of digital signal time-domain waveforms is not sufficient to be effectively used for the classification of signals and the interclass distance between fractal dimension features is small [11]. The time-frequency diagram of the signal describes the change of signal over time from the two transform fields, which are time domain and frequency domain. Compared to time domain waveform fractal dimension, signal time-frequency characteristics can be better used for signal classification and identification. Therefore, this paper presents a two-dimensional box dimension feature extraction algorithm based on time-frequency image.

3.1 Research on Algorithm of Time-Frequency Image Box Dimension

The improved fractal dimension algorithm is based on signal time-frequency transform, through the time-frequency image of the signal related processing and extracting two-dimensional box dimension image features of signal. This is a conversion of one-to-two-dimensional. Figure 2 shows the concrete flow chart of the improved algorithm.

Fig. 2. Flow chart of fractal feature extraction of two-dimensional box dimension based on time-frequency image

The signal time-frequency transform is the distribution of the signal energy in the time-frequency domain. Therefore, we can convert gray value of the image, according to the signal in the time-frequency domain of the energy value, which is the main work of the time-frequency image preprocessing part.

(1) Normalization

In the time-frequency image preprocessing of digital signals, the larger the energy value of the time-frequency distribution, the larger the gray value in the corresponding image. The difference between the time-frequency transformations of different digital signals results in the dynamic range of the gray value of the time-frequency image is not the same. The size of the gray value have a great impact on the extraction of signal characteristics. Therefore, in order to reduce the balance between the different signals, we need to normalize the gray value of the image preprocessing [5]. $\overline{x}$ and σ^2 are the mean and variance of pixel value [12].

$$\overline{x} = \frac{1}{N} \sum_{i=1}^{N} x_i \tag{9}$$

$$\sigma^2 = \frac{1}{N-1} \sum_{i=1}^{N} (x_i - \overline{x})^2 \tag{10}$$

The gray value of the normalized pixel is:

$$\hat{x} = \frac{x_i - \overline{x}}{\sigma} \tag{11}$$

(2) 2D image box dimension feature extraction

For a digital signal time-frequency grayscale, we set the image size is $M \times M$, and divide the $M \times M$ pixel image into $s \times s$ sub-blocks ($1 \leqslant s \leqslant M/2$, s is an integer), let

$$r = s/M \tag{12}$$

The time-frequency image gray-scale value of the digital signal is a three-dimensional surface in the spatial coordinates. x and y represent the coordinate position of the pixel, and z represents pixel gray value. $x - y$ plane is divided into $s \times s$ squares, which become a $s \times s \times s'$ box. The s' satisfies formula (13):

$$\frac{M}{s} = \frac{G}{s'} \tag{13}$$

G is the total gray scale. We suppose the $max(i,j)$ of the image grayscale in grid (i,j) fall in the kth box. At the same time, the $min(i,j)$ of the image grayscale in grid (i,j) fall in the lth box. Set (i,j) grid boxs box number is $n_r(i,j)$, the number of boxes require to cover the entire image is N_r, then:

$$n_r(i,j) = l - k + 1 \tag{14}$$

The fractal dimension of the image is:

$$D = \lim_{r \to 0} \frac{\log N_r}{\log(1/r)} \tag{15}$$

3.2   Simulation Experiment

In order to verify the feasibility of the algorithm, this paper simulates four kinds of common digital signals, in which simulation conditions are consistent with Sect. 2.2. Each signal is subjected to 100 Monte Carlo experiments at each SNR condition. The signal conducts low-pass filtering, SPWVD time-frequency conversion grayscale transformation and normalization, at last extracting the fractal dimension features of time-frequency images according to the algorithm in this paper. Table 2 is the mean and variance when the time-frequency image fractal features is under the SNR = 0 dB and SNR = 10 dB simulation conditions, and the table notes (mean, variance). Figure 3 is the curve in which signal time-frequency image fractal dimension feature changes with SNR.

Table 2. The fractal dimension mean and variance of signals

SNR	2FSK		BPSK		MSK		16QAM	
	μ	σ	μ	σ	μ	σ	μ	σ
0 dB	1.233	0.013	1.237	0.019	1.233	0.035	1.273	0.019
10 dB	1.230	0.009	1.279	0.012	1.293	0.009	1.300	0.015

It can be seen from Tables 1 and 2 that signal time-frequency image fractal box dimensionality variance is smaller than signal one dimensional fractal box dimension characteristic variance. So it proves that the intra-class polymerization degree of fractal box dimension feature of digital signal time-frequency image is relatively good. From Fig. 3, we can see that 16QAM signal and the other

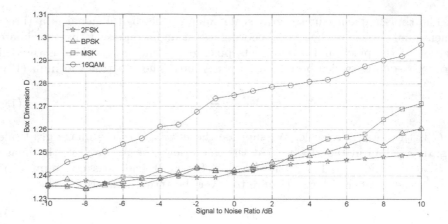

Fig. 3. Signal time-frequency image fractal dimension with SNR

three kinds of signal dimension feature has a clear interclass distance. Compared with the one-dimensional box dimension characteristic curve of digital signal in Fig. 1, the characteristic curve of time-frequency fractal dimension of digital signal is gentle with the change of SNR. For the signal characteristics, it is shown that the time-frequency fractal dimension of the signal is better than the one-dimensional box. Therefore it is more suitable for the signal classification and identification. Comprehensive comparison, the signal time-frequency image feature fractal dimension proposed in this paper is better than signal dimension box dimension features. And it is suitable for classification and recognition of multi-class signal.

4   Conclusion

In this paper, the feature extraction algorithm of digital signal is simulated and improved. For the digital signal fractal box dimension feature distance is small and the box dimension curve has a cross term, it is not suitable for a variety of digital signal classification and recognition. This paper presents a two-dimensional box dimension feature extraction algorithm based on time-frequency image. Simulation results show that the improved algorithm proposed in this paper has a good ability to distinguish 16QAM signals.

Acknowledgments. This paper is funded by the Nation Nature Science Foundation of China (No. 61401115), Nation Nature Science Foundation of China (No. 61301095), Nation Nature Science Foundation of China (No. 61671167). This paper is funded by the International Exchange Program of Harbin Engineering University for Innovation-oriented Talents Cultivation.

References

1. Zhao, Y., Xing, W.: Building a local geomagnetic reference map by the multifractal Kriging based step-by-step interpolation correction method. Appl. Sci. Technol. **06**, 1–5 (2015)
2. Wang, G., Zhang, S., Yan, C., et al.: Probabilistic neural networks and fractal method applied to mineral potential mapping in Luanchuan. In: 2010 Sixth International Conference on Digital Object Identifier, pp. 1003–1007 (2010)
3. Ivanovici, M., Richard, N.: Fractal dimension of color fractal images. IEEE Trans. Image Process. **20**(20), 227–235 (2011)
4. Tang, Z., Yang, X., Li, J.: Study on fractal feature of modulated radio signal. J. Phys. **60**(5), 0564701 (2011)
5. Zhao, C., Ma, S., Yang, W.: Research on spectrum awareness based on fractal box dimension. J. Electron. Inf. Technol. **02**, 475–478 (2011)
6. Chi, F., Hu, Y., Wang, Z.: Feature extraction of turbine blades based on the fractal theory. Appl. Sci. Technol. **04**, 64–69 (2015)
7. Bai, H.: Research on radar emitter signal recognition technology based on time-frequency analysis. People's Liberation Army Information Engineering University (2012)
8. Mokni, R., Kherallah, M.: Novel palmprint biometric system combining several fractal methods for texture information extraction. In: 2016 IEEE International Conference on Systems, Man, and Cybernetics (SMC), pp. 002267–002272 (2016)
9. Zehani, S., Mimi, M., Taleb-Ahmed, A., Toumi, A.: Anisotropy analysis of textures using wavelets transform and fractal dimension. In: 2016 2nd International Conference on Advanced Technologies for Signal and Image Processing (ATSIP), pp. 341–347 (2016)
10. Jarvenpaa, E., Jarvenpaa, M., Wu, M.: Random affine code tree fractals: hausdorff and affinity dimensions and pressure. In: Mathematical Proceedings of the Cambridge Philosophical Society, vol. 100, pp. 297–300 (2017)
11. Latorre, E., Layunta, E., Grasa, L.: Intestinal serotonin transporter inhibition by Toll-like receptor 2 activation. A feedback modulation. PLOS One **11**(12), e0169303 (2016)
12. Tam, S.K.E., Hasan, S., Hughes, S.: Modulation of recognition memory performance by light requires both melanopsin and classical photoreceptors. Proc. Roy. Soc. B-Biol. Sci. **283**(1845) (2016). https://doi.org/10.6084/m9.figshare.4285250.v1

Accurate Decision Tree with Cost Constraints

Nan Wang[1], Jinbao Li[1(✉)], Yong Liu[1], Jinghua Zhu[1], Jiaxuan Su[2],
and Cheng Peng[2]

[1] School of Computer Science and Technology,
Heilongjiang University, Harbin 150080, China
lijbsir@126.com
[2] School of Computer Science and Technology,
Harbin Institute of Technology, Harbin 150001, China

Abstract. A decision tree is a basic classification and regression method that uses a tree structure or model of decisions and their possible consequences, including chance event outcomes, resource costs, and utility. Decision tree is an effective approach for classification. At the same time, it is also a way to display an algorithm. It serving as a classical algorithm of classification has many optimization algorithms. Even though these approaches achieve high performance, the acquirement costs of attributes are usually ignored. In some cases, the acquired costs are very different and important, the acquirement cost of attributes in decision tree could not be ignored. Existing construction approaches of cost-sensitive decision tree fail to generate the decision tree dynamically according to the given data object and cost constraint. In this paper, we attempt to solve this problem. We propose a global decision tree as the model. The proper decision tree is derived from the model dynamically according to the data object and cost constraint. For the generation of dynamic decision trees, we propose the cost-constraint-based pruning algorithm. Experimental results demonstrate that our approach outperforms C4.5 in both accuracy and cost. Even though the attribute acquirement cost in our approach is much smaller, the accuracy gap between our approach and C4.5 is also small. Additionally, for large data set, our approach outperforms C4.5 algorithm in both cost and accuracy.

Keywords: Decision tree · Cost constraint · Machine learning
Algorithm of classification

1 Introduction

Decision tree [1] is an important approach for classification. Existing approaches, such as the LEGAL-tree using genetic algorithms [2], the HTILDE using incremental and anytime methods [3], trees with evaluation function [4], trees utilizing boosting and bagging [5], and some taking use of Cross-validation [6], focus on the selection for features that maximize the performance of the decision-tree-based classification.

Even though these approaches achieve high performance, the acquirement costs of attributes are ignored. In some cases, the acquired costs are very different and important, which should not be ignored. We consider a scenarios.

© ICST Institute for Computer Sciences, Social Informatics and Telecommunications Engineering 2018
G. Sun and S. Liu (Eds.): ADHIP 2017, LNICST 219, pp. 154–165, 2018.
https://doi.org/10.1007/978-3-319-73317-3_19

In individual medical service, decision-tree- based classification could be used for assistant diagnosis. For assistant diagnoses, multiple medical indicators could be applied. Clearly, the costs of these indicators are very different. For example, the cost of body temperature is almost free. As a comparison, PAT-CT is much more expensive. Of course, the diagnosis abilities of these indicators are different. Some people prefer an assistant diagnose of a cold which need not an expensive acquirement cost. So how to select suitable indicators for diagnosis that could not only achieve high accuracy of diagnosis but be acquired within a reasonable cost is a problem.

For the wine dealers, it is important for them to know the origin of the wine so that they can estimate the quality of the wine accordingly. Hence approach of decision-tree-based classification could be used for assistant judgment. For assistant judgment, multiple chemical detections could be applied, and then different detection has different price and influence to the classification of origin. Thus, it is also a problem to select suitable detections that could be performed within a reasonable cost and also provide a high accuracy for the predicted value of origin.

From this scenario, construction techniques for optimal decision trees within the cost constraint are in demand. And such techniques brings following challenges.

- Without attribute costs, the ideal decision tree have two features, less leaf node and smaller tree depth. Since those features affect not only the efficiency but also the accuracy of classification, it has been proved that the construction of an idea decision tree is an NP-hard problem [7, 8]. With the constraint of cost, the problem becomes harder. The algorithm of construction for effective decision tree within tolerable time is the first challenge.
- Since different tasks and purposes of classification may have different cost constraint, a static decision tree does not satisfy those requirements. So the decision tree should change according to the cost constraints.
- In the practical cases, the indicators of zero cost could help to obtain a free decision tree. And users may want to obtain a free decision tree as a first baseline. Hence, those indicators should be used in high priority effectively.

With these challenges, existing approaches cannot be applied to solve this problem. They mainly concentrate on two aspects. One is to find the idea behind decision tree algorithm that aim to maximize accuracy, such as ID3, C4.5 and so on. The other is to induce decision tree that aim to minimize costs of misclassification or costs of obtaining the information in a way they adopt [9].

Even though they can generate effective decision trees with a relative small cost, they still cannot control the costs into a specified range, and also do not have a dynamic mechanism to get a decision tree in a tolerable time with different cost requirements. And as users tend to get the free information first, their methods cannot ensure the attributes with zero cost is located in the first place of the tree.

To achieve the goal of constructing optimal decision tree within the given cost, we develop a novel decision tree model. In this model, we design a novel classification criterion called cost-gain-ratio which combines the cost of attribute and the information gain ratio. And this ratio considers the cost first and attempts to select attribute that cost less.

To obtain a decision tree correctly, this ratio still considers information gain ratio [1] and construction criteria of our decision tree also makes the free indicators can be selected in a high priority during the construction of decision tree. Additionally, we can also choose more information gain when the cost is zero, and it also provides convenience for building the zero-cost-constraint decision tree in the dynamic building tree phase.

With the criteria, we use a top-down greedy approach to select the attributes with the least cost-gain-ratio as the tree node. After building the tree, we utilize a PEP post pruning to avoid problem of overfitting. Then, with the decision tree after PEP pruning as the basic decision tree, we develop a dynamic cost pruning strategy to make the decision tree satisfy different cost constraints. To increase the efficiency, we propose a cost-based pruning strategy based on cost constraint. We have proven that the worst complexity of the dynamic algorithm decreases from O(NK2) to O(N), where N is the size of training set and K is the number of attributes.

The contributions of this paper are summarized as follows.

- We develop a decision tree model. With the model, for a data object, we can get different decision trees with different requirement of cost constraints in a tolerable time.
- We propose a new method to induce a decision tree with a consideration of both the costs and information acquirement.
- We conduct extensive experiments to verify the effectiveness of the proposed methods. From the experimental results, the proposed method could achieve high accuracy within the cost constraint.

The remaining parts of this paper are organized as follows. Section 2 introduces some background knowledge of this paper. Section 4 describes the proposed algorithm in detail. We present the experiments and analysis in Sects. 5 and 6 draws the conclusions and give a future research directions.

2   Background

In this section, we introduce one of the based knowledge of decision tree, PEP (Pessimistic Error Pruning) post-pruning algorithm which is also a part of C4.5.

The main reason for pruning is to reduce the complexity of the decision tree and help prevent overfitting. However, among pruning methods, we choose PEP for the following reasons. Firstly, PEP does not use extra pruning set. Thus, it provides sufficient data for testing. Secondly, this method has valid statistics theoretical foundations. Thirdly, PEP is a powerful pruning strategy and quite efficient in terms of computational effort [10].

In the PEP, as the apparent error rate is optimistically biased, Quinlan [1] add an 0.5 adjustment to PEP pruning in order to provide a more practical error rate. Quinlan considered the event that whether a sample is classified correctly is in a Bernoulli distribution. 1 means correct classification and 0 means wrong classification. Thus, we can get the estimated error rate through samples statistics as

$$e_{subtree} = (\Sigma E_i + 0.5 * L)/\Sigma N_i$$

where E_i is error number of each leaf node, and L is the number of leaf nodes. Then we can estimate mean and variance of error count defined as follows.

$$E_{subtree\_err\_count} = N * e_{subtree} \quad \mathrm{var}_{subtree\_err\_count} = \sqrt{N * e_{subtree} * (1 - e_{subtree})}$$

Then we let a leaf node with most frequent class label Ci in N replace the subtree. Hence the error count becomes E while sample size is still N and its error rate and mean of error count is calculated as follows.

$$e_{new\_leaf} = (E + 0.5)/N \quad E_{leaf\_err\_count} = N * e_{new\_leaf}$$

While the mean of subtree's error count is larger than the mean of new leaf node's error count by a variance, we replace this subtree with a leaf node. We get the following inequality.

$$E_{subtree\_err\_count} - \mathrm{var}_{subtree\_err\_count} > E_{leaf\_err\_count}$$

We have introduced the main idea of the PEP pruning. We will utilize this method in the second step of our method.

3 Overview

3.1 Problem Definition

Definition 1 (Cost of a Decision Tree): The cost of a decision tree is defined as the maximal sum of the acquirement costs of the attributes from root to a leaf, denoted by cost(T). The cost means the maximal acquirement costs of the attributes required for the classification with T.

We denoted the optimal decision tree generated from an attribute set S as Acc(S). The problem is defined formally as follows.

Problem 1. Given a training set S with each tuple having attribute set $S_T = \{T1, T2, ..., Tn\}$, the goal is to find a decision tree model M, such that given a data object o and a cost C, the decision tree T is derived from M with attribute set $SR \subseteq ST$, such that cost $(T(SR)) \leq C$ and $\forall S' \subseteq ST$ with $cost(T(S')) \leq C$, Acc(S') $\leq$ Acc(SR).

3.2 The Overview of the Proposed Method

In this section, we show an overview of our solution. In our solution, the model is a global decision tree with all attributes. For a classification task with a data object and cost constraint, the global decision tree is pruned accordingly. The method contains three steps.

Step 1: We apply a branching strategy to generate a decision tree with all attributes as the model. For the sake of keeping the correctness of decision tree algorithm, we still take IGR (information gain ratio) as a part of choice criterion. It is also one of the standards to judge whether branching should stop, since if IGR of the attribute of class is equal to zero, it means there are only one class in the subset [11]. As we should consider of the cost of attributes. We develop a new branching criterion, CGR (cost gain ratio) as follows, while IGR of T_i is not equal to zero.

$$CGR(T_i) = \frac{\cos t(T_i)}{IGR(T_i)}$$

And In the premise that *IGR* of the class is not equal to zero and sample size is not lower than pre-threshold, then we recuse with the rest of conditional attributes and compared the value of $CGR(T_i)$ with each other, then we use the Greedy Algorithm to find the smallest one to generate the splitting attribute, which means the attribute with the lowest cost for each percentage point of info gain ratio.

For each discrete attribute, a branch is generated according to each value. For each continuous attribute, we attempt to find the best splitting point. The methods of calculating the best split point of continuous attribute and $IGR(T_i)$ is the same in C4.5 algorithm [11].

Step 2: After Step 1, we get a complete decision tree which fits the training data perfectly. Such tree is treated as the model. However, it may be overfitting and becomes inaccuracy on other data set. In order to avoid overfitting, we use re-pruning method which means that when the sample size is lower than a threshold, the decision tree stops to grow. Then, we use the PEP (Pessimistic Error Pruning) post-pruning algorithm of C4.5 since such algorithm does not need extra testing data and have a linear computational complexity. Thus, the pruning is exhaustive.

Step 3: Through Step 2, we get a basic decision tree as the model. All the decision trees are derived from it. Hence when a data object o is to be handled, we perform a second round of pruning according to the required cost constraint and generate a decision tree T. The classification of o is determined based on T.

In practice, we can combine PEP pruning with global decision tree generation, since they could be performed offline and will not affect the experience of individual users. Even though both Step 2 and Step 3 prune the global decision tree, we do not merge them since Step 3 has to be executed online and Step 2 could be performed offline.

4 Algorithms

In this section, we will discuss the algorithms based on the framework introduced in Sect. 3.2. Since Step 2 applies existing method introduced in Sect. 2, we discuss the algorithms in Step 1 and Step 3 in Sects. 4.1 and 4.2, respectively.

4.1   Branching Strategy

This step builds a global decision tree containing all attributes as the basic model and the cost-based pruning strategy will be applied on such model. For the convenience of the pruning in the following steps, the node with small cost tends to locate near to the root such that they are not easy to prune and we make the zero cost attributes on the top of the global decision tree.

The building of global decision tree always starts with the growth of a tree which means a branching strategy among all the attributes. Therefore, we need to deal with all attributes by a criterion called cost-gain-ratio to find the attribute with a smallest cost-gain-ratio as the best splitting attribute. By the best splitting attribute, the data set is divided into several parts. We handle the data set in such way recursively until all the instances belong to one class or the size of sample in each leaf is lower than the threshold. When the recursion finishes, we get the global decision tree.

At first, we introduce a new criterion called cost-gain-ratio *(CGR)* for the generation of global decision tree. Such criterion combines the cost of attributes and the information gain ratio as in C4.5 algorithm (Quinlan [11]). For an attribute T_i, we define that its *CGR* is in direct proportion to the cost (denoted by $cost(T_i)$) and inverse proportion to the information gain ratio. That is,

$$CGR(T_i) = \frac{\cos t(T_i)}{IGR(T_i)} \tag{1}$$

To make *CGR* well-defined, we need first check whether *IGR(Class)* equals to zero. If it equals to 0, such attribute is useless to the classification and could be discarded. An attribute T_i with a smaller $CGR(T_i)$ attempt to be cheaper in cost and more powerful in classification. During the usage *CGR*, the decision tree construction prefers the attribute with small acquirement cost and powerful ability of classification. Specially, for an attribute with zero cost, its *CGR* is 0 and could be selected directly.

The cost is defined according to the application and we need to calculate the information gain ratio. It is defined according to the entropy, which is common used in decision tree and defined as follows.

$$Entropy(C, S) = -\sum_{i=1}^{m} p_i \log p_i \tag{2}$$

Let m denote the number of classes, C denote the attribute, and pi denote the proportion between the amount of *i-th* class instances to the amount of total sample size S.

Since we want to calculate the information gain ratio, which is a ratio of the gain of the attribute to the splitInfo of the attribute in the data set S. The gain of the attribute is the difference between the entropy of class and that of the attribute which is defined as $\sum_{v \in Value(S_t)} \frac{|S_{t,v}|}{|S_t|} Entropy(t_v)$, and the splitInfo of the attribute t is defined as $SplitInfo(t, S) = \sum_{v \in S} -\frac{|S_{t,v}|}{S_t} \log \frac{|S_{t,v}|}{S_t}$ Therefore, according to S, the gain of attribute t is defined as follows.

$$Gain(t, S) = Entropy(C, S) - \sum\nolimits_{v \in Value(S_t)} \frac{|S_{t,v}|}{|S_t|} Entropy(t_v) \qquad (3)$$

where $Value(S_t)$ means all the value of attribute t in data set S, $|S_{t,v}|$ means the number of samples in data set S with attribute $T = v$.

Hence when we got the gain of the attribute, we need to get the information gain ratio, denoted as $GainRatio(T, S)$. For an attribute t in the data set S, $GainRatio(t, S) = \frac{Gain(t,S)}{splitInfo(t,S)}$.

The algorithm selects the attributes greedy according to CGR of all attributes. The pseudo code is shown in Algorithm 1. In this algorithm, the tree is generated recursively.

In this algorithm, Line 1 to Line 9 check recursion stopping condition, including that the dataset S is null (Line 1), no attribute is left (Line 2–3), single attribute is left (Line 4), and the size of the left dataset is smaller than a threshold (Line 5). The loop for selecting the best split attribute is in Line 8–20. Line 21–22 update parameters for next recursion.

In each loop, we compute the entropy of S according to (2) in Line 11, and in Line 12–14, we compute the entropy info and split info of attribute t. Then, in Line 15, we compute the gain info of attribute t according to (3). In Line 18, we compute the info gain ratio and cost gain ratio of attribute according to (1). With Line 16–17, we keep the attribute with the smallest cost-gain-ratio.

Since it is known that classification based on the entropy is reliable, similar as information gain ratio of C4.5 algorithm, CostGrain-Ratio is reasonable.

Note that calculating CostGrainRatio does not increase the time complexity of the algorithm, still linear complexity.

After building a complete decision tree, we can use the PEP method (introduced in Sect. 2) to optimize the tree, and generate the pruned global decision tree as the model.

4.2   Cost Pruning Strategy

In this part, we propose the algorithm for decision tree generation based on the cost constraint. To achieve this goal, we develop a pruning strategy on the global decision tree. The major idea is to traverse all the nodes in the global decision tree. For each node v, we calculate the sum cost of the nodes from the root to r, and judge that whether the sum cost is over the cost constraint. The pseudo code is shown in Algorithm 2.

This method handles the global decision tree nodes from top to bottom. For a specified cost constraint C, we calculate the total cost from root to node and then judge whether the total cost violates the cost constraint in Line 2. If so, we remove the subtree with *node* as the root and only *node* is left (Line 3). Otherwise, we move to the next *node* until all nodes in the tree are visited.

After this step we can get a decision tree with the cost of each root-to-leave path lower than the cost constraint. Hence the cost of the pruned decision tree is within the cost constraint.

Algorithm 1 Formtree(S, T, C, P, Tree)

Input: training dataset S, attributes T, class attribute C, costs P, the decision tree Tree
1: **if** S is null **then return** failure
2: **if** T is null **then**
3:     **return** the node with the most frequent class label C_i in S
4: **if** $|T| \leq 1$ **then return** T
5: **if** $|S| < threshold$ **then**
6:     **return** a leaf node with the most frequent class label C_i in S
7: Tree=$\varnothing$
8: **for** each attribute $t \in T$ where the sample is S **do**
9:     Info(t,S)=0, SplitInfo(t,S)=0;
10:    MinGainRaio=100, node=null
11:    $Entropy(C,S) = -\sum_{i=1}^{m} p_i \log p_i$
12:    **for** $v \in$ value(t,S) **do**
13:        set $S_{t,v}$ as the subset of S where attribute $t=v$
14:        $Info(t,S) = \dfrac{|S_{t,v}|}{S_t} Entropy(t_v)$
15:        $SplitInfo(t,S) = -\dfrac{|S_{t,v}|}{S_t} \log \dfrac{|S_{t,v}|}{S_t}$
16:    Gain(t,S)=Entropy(C,S)-Info(t,S)
17:    $GainRatio(t,S) = \dfrac{Gain(t,S)}{splitInfo(t,S)}$
18:    **if** CostRatio(t,S)<MinGrainRatio **then**
19:        MinGainRatio=CostGrainRatio(t,S); node=t
20:    attach node to Tree;
21: update S, T, C, P
22: Formtree(S, T, C, P,Tree)

Algorithm 2 CostPruning(Tree, n, c)

Input: decision tree Tree, depth of tree n, cost constraint c;
1: **for** node=$nodes_1$ to leaf_node **do**
2:    **if** TotalCostTo($node$)>c **then**
3:        turn subtree of the node to a leaf node with the most
         frequent class label in it

4.3   Algorithm Complexity

As discussed in Sect. 3.2, the branching and PEP pruning are executed at the same time. We denote the number of attribute and tuples in the training set as K and N, respectively. Since each layer only having one attribute, there are K layers in a tree totally. Since each layer of the tree needs to process K attributes and for each attribute, we need to traverse all the tuples in the training set. Hence the time complexity of these two steps is $O(NK2)$. Even though the cost in superlinear, these two steps are executed offline. During each cost pruning, we need to traverse the whole global decision tree a time and the number of nodes in the tree smaller than K. Therefore, the time complexity of online part (Step 3) is $O(K)$.

5   Experiment

In this section, we conduct extensive experiments to evaluate the performance of our algorithm. We compare our approach with C4.5 algorithm. All algorithms are implemented in python by with IDE Py2.7.9 IDLE 2.7.9 and running on the environment of Windows8.1 Pro with Inter CPU 2.39 GHz and 8.00 G RAM. We measure the accuracy, which is ratio of the right classified records to the total records in the testing set. For the convenience of discussions, we define the decision tree after PEP as *PEP tree* and the maximum sum of the acquirement cost of attributes in all paths in the decision tree after PEP as *PEP cost*.

For experiments, we use three data sets from UCI Machine Learning Repository with various applications and properties. Their information is summarized in Table 1. To handle the missing values in the data set, we remove the tuples with 40% missing values and fill the blanks in other tuples with the mean value of other values in the corresponding attribute. For data set H and D, we use the attribute cost in the data set while for data set T, the cost of each attribute is set randomly from 0 to 1000.

Table 1. Information of data set

ID	Data set name	#Training tuples	#Testing tuples
H	Hepatitis	115	34
D	Heart disease	210	70 + 34
T	Thyroid	7980	1192

5.1   Comparisons

In this section, we compare the performance of the proposd algorithm with C4.5. The experimental results are shown in Figs. 1 and 2, respectively.

From Fig. 1, we have two observations. (1) The acquirement cost of attributes used in C4.5 algorithm is 27.8, while the acquirement cost used in our approach is at most 14.8, which is almost half of C4.5 cost. However, the largest gap of these two approaches is about 0.06. (2). The accuracy of our approach increase with cost decreasing when the cost is large and our approach outperforms C4.5 on both cost and accuracy when the cost is small. When the accuracy of our approach is smaller than that of C4.5 by no more than 15%, the cost of C4.5 is about ten times of ours, and sometimes we even get a better accuracy. Our approach outperforms C4.5 in accuracy as the cost is small.

From Fig. 2, we observe that with the data size increasing, the gap between our accuracy and C4.5 is smaller in general by almost 0.02, while the cost of C4.5 which is equal to 584 is nearly 3 times larger than our largest cost (222). And even though at the point of zero, the cost gap of these two approaches 0.12 in accuracy. When the data size increases from 114 to 280, the accuracy of our method increases as the average gap between C4.5 and our algorithm in accuracy is about 0.03 and the cost of C4.5 is 10 times larger than that of our approach.

5.2   Accuracy Vs. Cost Constraint

In this section, we test the relationship between the cost and accuracy. For D, we vary the cost constraint from 0 to 16, since the largest possible cost of decision trees after the cost pruning step is the cost of PEP tree (14.27).

The results are shown in Fig. 4. From Fig. 3, we observe that when the cost constraint is small, the accuracy changes significantly with the cost constraint and is better than those with larger cost constraint. As a comparison, with the cost increasing, the accuracy decreases but becomes stable. When the cost goes up to a point with cost constraint higher than PEP cost (14.27), the accuracy goes down to accuracy of the PEP tree (0.73529) and remains unchanged as the cost will not be over 14.27. Since the cost of any generated decision tree is smaller than PEP cost, the tree will be unchanged when cost constraint gets larger than PEP cost.

We vary the constraint from 0 to 230 step by 10, since the PEP cost is 222.17. And the results are shown in Fig. 4. From Fig. 5, we observe that the accuracy is stable with the changing of cost. We also observe that when the cost constraint is small, the accuracy changes significantly with the cost constraint, similar as that of dataset D.

From the discussion, Figs. 3 and 4 have similar trends and the accuracy converges that of the PEP tree. This is because all decision trees pruned according to the cost is based on the PEP tree. The pruning according to the cost constraint prevents the overfitting furthermore and thus the accuracy of cost-based-pruned decision tree is better than that of PEP tree in most of cases.

From the experimental results, the accuracy of our approach is comparable to C4.5 even though our approach has a pretty small cost constraint. It is caused by the use of new criterion cost gain ratio. Such that we keep all the zero cost attribute first, and the choice of splitting attribute has tend to low-cost attribute. The nodes far from the root tend to have high costs and will be pruned in high possibility.

5.3 The Impact of Attribute Costs

To test the impact of attribute costs, we set the costs to the attributes of T randomly for 5 times and the results are plotted in Fig. 5.

The cost of C4.5 is 200, which is larger than the maximal cost of our approach in the experiment. The cost of our approach and C4.5 is shown in the brackets in the accuracy and C4.5 in the legend, respectively.

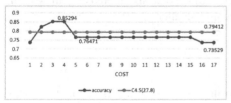

Fig. 1. Comparisons on H

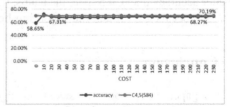

Fig. 2. Comparisons on D

Combing the experimental results in Figs. 1, 2 and 5, we can observe that the accuracy gap is about 11% in Fig. 1 with data size of 149 and 9% in Fig. 2 with data size of 280, and in Fig. 5 the largest gap is no more than 1% with data set of 9172. In Fig. 5(a) and (c), our approach outperforms C 4.5 in both accuracy and cost. Thus, we

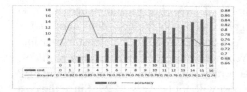

Fig. 3. Cost constraint vs. accuracy on H   **Fig. 4.** Cost constraint vs. accuracy on D

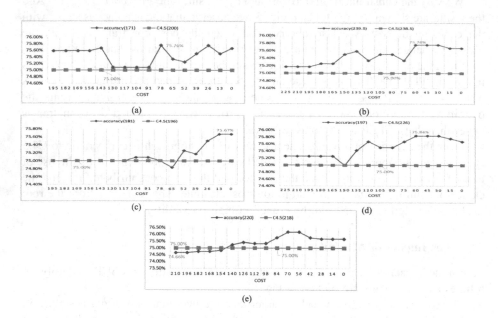

Fig. 5. Experimental results on T

have two conclusions. (1) When the cost constraint is smaller enough, our approach has a better accuracy than C4.5 in all the teams. (2) With the data size increasing, the gap of accuracy between C4.5 and our algorithm become smaller.

6 Conclusion

In this paper, we propose a generation algorithm of cost-based decision tree. The motivation is to solve classification problems with the non-ignorable attribute acquirement cost. To solve this problem, we develop an approach to generate the global decision tree with all attributes as the model. For a given object, the global decision tree is pruned according to the cost constraint. Experimental results demonstrate that for large data sets, our algorithm outperforms C4.5 in both cost and accuracy.

Acknowledgment. This work was supported in part by the National Natural Science Foundation of China (No. 61370222), the Natural Science Foundation of Heilongjiang Province (No. F201430), the Innovation Talents Project of Science and Technology Bureau of Harbin (No. 2017RAQXJ094), and the fundamental research funds of universities in Heilongjiang Province, special fund of Heilongjiang University (No. HDJCCX-201608).

References

1. Quinlan, J.R.: Induction of decision trees. Mach. Learn. **1**(1), 81–106 (1986)
2. Basgalupp, M.P., et al.: LEGAL-tree: a lexicographic multi-objective genetic algorithm for decision tree induction. In: ACM Symposium on Applied Computing, pp. 1085–1090 (2009)
3. Lopes, C.M., Zaverucha, G.: HTILDE: scaling up relational decision trees for very large databases. In: ACM Symposium on Applied Computing, pp. 1475–1479 (2009)
4. Rodriguez, J.J., Alonso, C.J.: Interval and dynamic time warping-based decision trees. In: ACM Symposium on Applied Computing, pp. 548–552 (2004)
5. Ren, C., King, B.R.: Predicting protein contact maps by bagging decision trees. In: International Conference on Bioinformatics, pp. 649–650 (2014)
6. Blockeel, H., Struyf, J.: Efficient algorithms for decision tree cross-validation. J. Mach. Learn. Res. **3**(1), 621–650 (2003)
7. Hong, J.: AE1: an extension matrix approximate method for the general covering problem. Int. J. Parallel Prog. **14**(6), 421–437 (1985)
8. Tu, P., Chung, J.: A new decision-tree classification algorithm for machine learning. In: International Conference on Tools with Artificial Intelligence, pp. 370–377 (1992)
9. Lomax, S., Vadera, S.: A survey of cost-sensitive decision tree induction algorithms. ACM Comput. Surv. **45**(2), 16–25 (2013)
10. Barros, R.C., et al.: Towards the automatic design of decision tree induction algorithms. In: Proceedings of the 13th Annual Conference Companion on Genetic and Evolutionary Computation, pp. 567–574. ACM (2011)
11. Quinlan, J.R.: C4.5: Programs for Machine Learning. Elsevier, Amsterdam (2014)

A Signal Recognition Method Based on Evidence Theory

Xiang Chen[1,2], Hui Han[1,2], Hui Wang[1,2], Yun Lin[1,2(✉)],
Mengqiu Chai[1,2], and Mingyu Hu[1,2]

[1] State Key Laboratory of Complex Electromagnetic
Environment Effects on Electronics and Information System (CEMEE),
Luoyang 471003, Henan, China
linyun_phd@hrbeu.edu.cn
[2] College of Information and Communication Engineering,
Harbin Engineering University, Harbin, China

Abstract. In modern complex communication environment, how to effectively identify signal modulation types has become a hot research topic. Based on information entropy and Dempster-Shafer evidence theory (D-S theory), a new signal modulation recognition algorithm is proposed. Through extracting the information entropy feature and normal test, a new acquisition method of basic probability assignment (BPA) is proposed, and then the D-S theory is used to identify the signals. Simulation results show that the proposed algorithm has a better recognition rate, which has great application value.

Keywords: Signal recognition · Rényi entropy singular entropy D-S theory

1 Introduction

The key technology of non-cooperative signal modulation recognition is feature extraction and classification Recognition. Typical feature extraction methods include instantaneous parameters' extraction [1], higher order cumulants [2], Cyclic spectrum method [3], fractal dimension method [4], etc. [5–7]. In recent years, the research on information theory on feature extraction becomes a hot topic. Information entropy represents the uncertainty of a system, which can be used to measure the uncertainty measure of the signal state distribution, so it provides a theoretical framework for signal characterization description [8]. D-S theory is an important method for reasoning about uncertainty, which can be used for the targets detection, classification and identification [9–11]. In this paper, we extracted the signals' entropy features including the Rényi entropy and singular entropy. In the process of simulation, the influence of symbol and noise are considered, signal symbol is generated randomly, and the Gauss noise is added to the signal. Simulation is carried out for different modulation types of signals, and verified the effectiveness of this method.

© ICST Institute for Computer Sciences, Social Informatics and Telecommunications Engineering 2018
G. Sun and S. Liu (Eds.): ADHIP 2017, LNICST 219, pp. 166–172, 2018.
https://doi.org/10.1007/978-3-319-73317-3_20

2 Preliminaries

2.1 Dempster-Shafer Evidence Theory

The Demptster-Shafer evidence theory is firstly introduced by Dempster and later extended by Shafer, the rule of evidence combination is shown as follows:

Suppose m_1 and m_2 are two mass functions in the same frame of discernment θ; Dempster combines rules of two BPA m_1 and m_2 to yield a new BPA:

$$m(A) = \frac{\sum\limits_{B \cap C = A} m_1(B)m_2(C)}{1-k} \tag{1}$$

$$k = \sum\limits_{B \cap C = \phi} m_1(B)m_2(C) \tag{2}$$

where k is often interpreted as a measure of conflict between the sources. The larger value of k is the more conflicting are the sources, and the less informative is their combination.

2.2 The Rényi Entropy Based on WVD

The Wigner-Ville distribution (WVD) [12] is an efficient time-frequency method for anlyzing the non-stationary signals. In order to eliminate or lessen the cross terms of WVD, the kernel function of WVD is presented and different kernels are used for the uniform Cohen distribution. The smooth Pseudo WVD (SPWVD) is one of these techniques, which is defined as follows:

$$SPWVD_{g,h}(t,f) = \int_{-\infty}^{\infty}\int_{-\infty}^{\infty} g(u)h(\tau)x(t-u+\frac{\tau}{2})x^*(t-u-\frac{\tau}{2})e^{-j2\pi ft}dud\tau \tag{3}$$

where $h(\tau)$ is a rectangular windows and $g(u)$ is smoothing function. The time and frequency windows are adopted to smooth a signal in the two dimensions.

As is well known, Rényi entropy is a measure of complexity, which can be used to estimate the amount of information and complexity of signals, For the continuous form of the two-dimensional probability density distribution, Rényi entropy is defined as follows:

$$R^\alpha(P) = \frac{1}{1-\alpha}\log_2\frac{\int\int f^\alpha(x,y)dxdy}{\int\int f(x,y)dxdy} \tag{4}$$

The time frequency distribution of signal is similar with two-dimensional probability density function $f(x,y)$. So time frequency distribution Rényi entropy can be defined as follows:

$$H_{\alpha,x} = \frac{1}{1-\alpha}\log_2 \iint \left(\frac{SPWVD_{g,h}(t,f)}{\int\int SPWVD_{g,h}(t,f)dfdt}\right)^{\alpha} dtdf \tag{5}$$

2.3 The Rényi Entropy Based on CWT

Wavelet analysis is an effective and important method for non-stationary signals [13]. Different from the traditional Fourier analysis, wavelet packet analysis simultaneously decomposes the low and high frequency of different signals. And then, according to the analyzed type of the signal, wavelet packet analysis self-adaptively chooses the frequency band and confirms the signal resolution at different bands.

Suppose, wavelet transform scale selection is j, the signal is decomposed into low frequency part c_j and high frequency part $d_1, d_2, \ldots, d_j$, using Fourier Transform for each wavelet coefficients.

$$X(k) = \sum_{n=1}^{N} d_i(n)e^{-j\frac{2\pi}{N}kn} \tag{6}$$

The power spectrum $\{S_k, k = 1, 2, \ldots, j+1\}$ of each layer of wavelet coefficients can be calculated by the formula (7).

$$S(k) = \frac{1}{N}|X(k)|^2 \tag{7}$$

Therefore, according to formula above, the p_k can be calculated and the wavelet energy spectrum entropy is shown as follows:

$$H_{WESE} = -\sum_{k=1}^{N} p_k \log_2 p_k \tag{8}$$

2.4 Singular Spectrum Entropy

Singular spectrum entropy [14] is used to describe the signals in the perspective of singularity. Suppose, $X_t = \{x_t^1, x_t^1, \cdots, x_t^L\}$ represents the received signal sequence, it means that the receiver simultaneously collect signals from L different channels. For the signal in the each channel, the signal sampling is $\{x_i, i = 1, 2, L, N\}$, and the sampling number is N. The analysis window M is used to analyze the sampling sequence. Suppose the time delay parameter of analysis window is equal to 1. When the sampling sequence x_i can be divided into segments with the number of $N - M$, which is the matrix A with the dimension of $(N - M) \times M$.

$$A = \begin{bmatrix} x_1 & x_2 & \cdots & x_M \\ x_2 & x_3 & \cdots & x_{M+1} \\ \cdots & \cdots & \cdots & \cdots \\ x_{N-M} & x_{N-M+1} & \cdots & x_N \end{bmatrix} \tag{9}$$

where, the track vector at time i of all the channels is shown as: $\{x_{t+1}^1, x_{t+1}^1, \cdots, x_{t+M}^1, x_{t+1}^1; x_{t+1}^2, \cdots, x_{t+M}^2; \cdots; x_{t+1}^L, \cdots, x_{t+M}^L\}$. Considering the singular decomposition of matrix A, and getting the singular spectrum value $\{\delta_i, 1 \leq i \leq N - M\}$. The δ_i reflects the proportion of corresponding pattern to the total pattern. Based on the information entropy theory, in time domain, the singular spectrum entropy of the signal is shown as follows:

$$H_{SSE} = -\sum_{k=1}^{N} p_k \log_2 p_k \quad P_k = \frac{\delta_i}{\sum_{i=1}^{M} \delta_i} \tag{10}$$

where, P_i is the proportion of ith singular values to the whole singular spectrum value.

3 Experiments

During the simulation process, firstly, we need to train the features of the signal, the feature is $\mathbf{H} = [H_1, H_2, H_3]$, H_1, H_2, H_3 represent three entropy value matrices. Secondly, we extract the entropy features of test signal, we can get h_1, h_2, h_3. At last, we get BPA and make fusion calculation. The whole flow chart shows as Fig. 1.

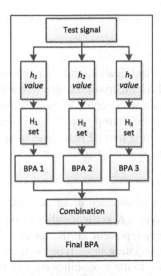

Fig. 1. The simulation flow chart of the system.

Step 1: Entropy features extraction
Information entropy describes the complexity of the signal in different domains, such as time frequency domain, wavelet domain. In this paper, we select the signal $x(t)$ length to 2048 points and the signal symbol is generated randomly to every simulation. The symbol rate $f_d = 1000B$, the carrier frequency $f_c = 4$ kHz, and the sample rate $f_s = 1.6$ MHz.

Actually, due to the presence of noise and the change of symbol, the entropy is unstable even in the same SNR and same sample points. The Fig. 2 are the probability distribution curve of entropy when SNR = 0 dB and SNR = 10 dB.

The entropy probability distribution curves show that the stability of the entropy. Through the entropy test, we can find that the entropy probability consistent with normal distribution. The curve is "fat", that means the entropy has poor stability, otherwise the entropy has better stability.

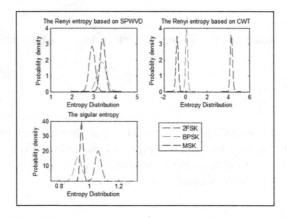

Fig. 2. The probability distribution curves of entropy (SNR = 10 dB).

Step 2: BPA acquisition
In order to realize the signal classification and recognition, we need to get the BPA function. The proposed method incorporates the test sample information with the attribution provided by the training samples to extract the BPA. Through the probability distribution of entropy, the entropy probability obey the normal distribution. Therefore, we define the rules to obtain BPA for test sample by using the relationship between the test data and the normal distribution model. The proposed method as follows:

(1) Calculating the mean μ_i and variance σ_i^2 of entropy value, $i = 1, 2, \ldots, K$, i presents the training signal types, K is the number of types of training signal, K = 3 and the label i respectively represent 2FSK, BPSK, MSK.
(2) Inputting a test signal, calculating three types entropy value $h = [h_1, h_2, h_3]$. The entropy value generation into the probability density function, and we can get the

probability value $p(i = 1, 2, \ldots n)$ through brought into the probability function of different signals $N \sim (\mu, \sigma^2)$, we can get:

$$p = \frac{1}{\sqrt{2\pi}\sigma} \exp\left(-\frac{(h - \mu)^2}{2\sigma^2}\right) \tag{11}$$

$$m(p) = \{m(p_1), m(p_2), \cdots m(p_n)\} = \{p_1, p_2 \cdots p_K\} \tag{12}$$

Through the normalization of $m(p)$, we can get the BPA $m(A)$ function.

$$m(A) = \frac{p_i}{\sum\limits_{i=1}^{n} p_i} \tag{13}$$

Step 3: Fusion calculation

The test signal with MSK signal as an example, calculating three types entropy value $h = [h_1, h_2, h_3]$, generating into the probability density function, we can get the probability value p. After the normalization, we get the BPA function $m_1(A), m_2(A), m_3(A)$, through the D-S theory fusion calculating, it get the final BPA function m.

Step 4: Simulation result

Based on the signal features, D-S classifier is used to classify the signal modulation, the recognition rates of three kinds of digital communication signals are shown in Fig. 3.

As it is shown in Fig. 3, based on three entropy features and D-S classifier, the three different signals can be recognized, and the 2FSK can reach high recognition rate even under low SNR. With the reducing of SNR, the recognition rate of BPSK, MSK decreased. For the modulation mode, the BPSK and MSK belong to digital phase modulation signal, the differences between these two kinds of signals are relatively small, with the effect of noise, the recognition rate of these two kinds of signals can be reduced sharply under low SNR.

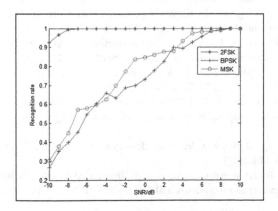

Fig. 3. The recognition rate of digital communication signals.

4 Conclusion

In this paper, a recognition algorithm of communication signal based on entropy features and D-S theory is proposed. Through extracting the entropy and normal test, a new BPA acquisition method is proposed, and D-S theory classifier is used to classify the signals. Simulation result shows, that the new recognition algorithm has a good performance, which can get 90% recognition rate when the SNR is greater than 5 dB.

Acknowledgements. This paper is funded by the National Natural Science Foundation of China (61301095), Nature Science Foundation of Heilongjiang Province of China (F201408). This paper is also funded by the International Exchange Program of Harbin Engineering University for Innovation-oriented Talents Cultivation. Meantime, all the authors declare that there is no conflict of interests regarding the publication of this article.

References

1. Nandi, A.K., Azzouz, E.E.: Algorithms for automatic modulation recognition of communication signals. IEEE Trans. Commun. **46**(4), 431–436 (1998)
2. Guo, J., Yin, H., Jiang, L., Mei, H.: Recognition of digital modulation signals via higher order cumulants. Commun. Technol. **11**, 1255–1260 (2014)
3. Zhu, L., Cheng, H.-W., Wu, L.: Identification of digital modulation signals based on cyclic spectral density and statistical parameters. J. Appl. Sci. **27**(2), 137–143 (2009)
4. Ye, F., Luo, J., Hai, L.: Recognition of radar emitter signal intra-pulse modulation mode based on fractal dimension. Comput. Eng. Appl. **44**(15), 155–157 (2008)
5. Bai, L., Yan, N.: Automatic modulation identification for communication system. Radio Commun. Technol. **37**(4), 59–61 (2011)
6. Cheng, C., He, M.-H., Zhu, Y.: Extracting in-pulse characteristics based on time-frequency reassignment and time-frequency ridge. J. Data Acquis. Process. **23**(1), 95–99 (2008)
7. Jia, C., Li, J.-P., Lu, X.-J.: Study on multi-biometric feature fusion and recognition model. In: International Conference on Apperceiving Computing and Intelligence Analysis, pp. 66–69 (2008)
8. Li, J., Li, Y., Lin, Y.: The application of entropy analysis in radiation source feature extraction. J. Proj. Rockets Missiles Guidance **31**(5), 155–157 (2011)
9. Lei, L., Wang, X., Xing, Y., Bi, K.: Multi-polarized HRRP classification by SVM and DS evidence theory. Control Decis. **28**(6), 861–866 (2013)
10. Luo, X., Luo, H., Zhou, J., Lei, L.: Error-correcting output codes based on classifiers' confidence for multi-class classification. Sci. Technol. Eng. **22**, 5502–5508 (2012)
11. Lin, Y., Wang, C., Ma, C., et al.: A new combination method for multisensor conflict information. J. Supercomput. **72**(7), 2874–2890 (2016)
12. Sucic, V., Saulig, N., Boashash, B.: Analysis of local time-frequency entropy features for nonstationary signal components time supports detection. Digit. Signal Process. **34**, 56–66 (2014)
13. Xue, H., Yang, R.: Morlet wavelet based detection of noninteger harmonics. Power Syst. Technol. **12**, 41–44 (2002)
14. Li, J., Ying, Y.: Radar signal recognition algorithm based on entropy theory. In: 2014 2nd International Conference on Systems and Informatics (ICSAI 2014), pp. 718–723 (2015)

Research on Intelligent Test Paper Based on Improved Genetic Algorithm

Ruitao Nan$^{(\boxtimes)}$ and Jingmei Li

College of Computer Science and Technology, Harbin Engineering University,
Harbin 150001, China
{nanruitao, lijingmei}@hrbeu.edu.cn

Abstract. At present, under the current quality education, the examination is still one of the main measure of teachers' teaching ability and student achievement. At the same time, different levels of examination are different to the test paper. Aiming at the multi-combination of constraints in the test paper, an improved genetic algorithm is proposed, which combines the constraints of the papers effectively, so that the test papers can be maximized to meet the needs of the users.

Keywords: Restrictions · Intelligent test paper · Genetic algorithm
Convergence speed

1 Introduction

Nowadays, the examination is one of the important ways to assess individual ability and talent selection [1]. Among them, the test paper is an important part of the entire test and the quality of the test paper determines the quality of the examination results, the traditional manual method does not work well to ensure the quality of the papers and the scientific rationality of the examination [2]. Based on the above research background, this paper presents an improved genetic algorithm. The algorithm improves the initial population of the test paper by introducing the chaos theory, which ensures a good convergence rate of the test paper population.

2 Analysis of Intelligent Test Paper

The research results of this paper are an improved intelligent test paper based on genetic algorithm. In order to better describe the research results of this paper, the problem of intelligent test is analyzed.

2.1 Constraints on Smart Packets

In fact, the papers are composed of different types of questions, questions and other constraints of the combination of questions, each question has a different attribute constraints [3]. Assuming that a set of papers is made up of questions, each question contains a property, so the test paper can use a matrix, each row represents a question, each column

© ICST Institute for Computer Sciences, Social Informatics and Telecommunications Engineering 2018
G. Sun and S. Liu (Eds.): ADHIP 2017, LNICST 219, pp. 173–176, 2018.
https://doi.org/10.1007/978-3-319-73317-3_21

represents a property of the question. In this paper, the attributes of each question are: difficulty, knowledge points, scores, questions, cognitive level, time, exposure.

2.2　The Objective Function of Intelligent Test Paper

The problem of group volume is a multi-constrained multi-objective combinatorial optimization problem [4]. Before the test paper, set the expected value for the attributes of each test questions. It is hoped that each test question in the composition paper will meet the preset expectation value. However, in the actual process, the actual value will be caused by some reason and user expectations do not match [5]. According to the characteristics of the test paper, the difficulty degree, the cognitive level and the knowledge point constraint condition are selected, and the objective function of the intelligent test group is set as the sum of the constraint error weight in the paper. The formula is (1):

$$f = w_1 \times E_D + w_2 \times E_R + w_3 \times E_Z \tag{1}$$

In Eq. (1), we represent the weight of the index and the sum of the weights is 1, E_D is the error value of the difficulty constraint, E_R is the error value of the cognitive level constraint, and E_Z is the error value of the knowledge point constraint. For each indicator of the weight, the user can be adjusted according to actual needs.

3　Improved Genetic Grouping Algorithm

In this paper, the global convergence rate of the algorithm and the early convergence phenomenon are optimized. By introducing the chaotic selection method, the individual variables of the chaotic test paper are satisfied according to the given test paper constraints and the initial test paper population is composed, These initial test paper population is a rough selection of the individual papers and thus can speed up the genetic algorithm convergence rate.

In the genetic algorithm, the chaotic selection method is introduced in the population initialization of the test paper, the individual variables of chaotic papers are generated by full mapping, and the formula is (2):

$$p_{i+1}(R(m)) = 1 - p_i^2(R(m)) \tag{2}$$

In Eq. (2), m is the number of constraints, $R(m)$ represents the sum of the values of each constraint.

The process of generating the initial population by the chaos selection method is:

(1) Set the initial value of the chaos. Determine the number of constraints on the requested problem is m, and calculate the sum of the values of each constraint as the initial value of chaos.
(2) Produce chaotic individuals. Substituting the initial value of chaos into formula (2) produces a chaotic individual and to determine whether to meet the set constraints, if the agreement is retained, otherwise eliminated.

(3) Until the chaotic sequence conforming to the initial population size is generated, the length of the chaotic sequence is the size of the initial population.

Through the above process, the selection of the individual is directed, the initial population of the test paper is fast and the individual is related to the problem.

4   Experimental Verification

1. In the same experimental parameters set, and asked the number of papers produced each experiment consistent, respectively, SGA, CGA, NCAGA conducted 50 repeated experiments, and randomly selected 10 times.

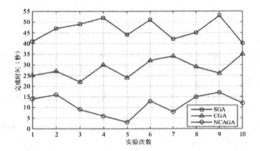

Fig. 1. The average completion time of the three test methods

It can be seen from Fig. 1 that the SGA, CGA and NCAGA show different fluctuations with the increase of the number of experiments. The overall average of the SGA-based method is the highest, the CGA-based method, The method is minimal. Thus, the NCAGA-based method of generating a test paper is faster.

2. Using SGA, CGA, NCAGA three test methods were carried out 50 times repeated experiments and each time only to generate a set of papers, the statistical results shown in Fig. 2.

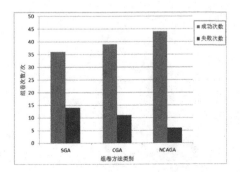

Fig. 2. The results of the three test methods

It can be seen more intuitively from Fig. 2 that the relative difference between the number of successes and the number of failures of each test method is the largest, and the third method has the largest relative difference, which indicates that the success rate of the third method is more Well, the success rate based on the NCAGA method is better than the other two methods.

5   The References Section

The results show that the improved genetic algorithm is a good performance advantage in the success rate of package, time of test paper, quality of test paper, etc., and it is possible to meet the actual needs of users as much as possible.

References

1. Wang, L.: Research on computer intelligent test paper composition based on genetic algorithm. In: International Conference on Machinery, Materials and Information Technology Applications, pp. 1030–1033 (2015)
2. Jacobs, K.: Quantum Measurement Theory and Its Applications. Cambridge University Press, Cambridge (2014). 15–35
3. Yan, S., Guoxing, Y.: A genetic algorithm of test paper generation. In: Computer Science & Education (ICCSE), pp. 897–901. IEEE (2013)
4. Zhang, Y., Zhang, K., et al.: A topic-based computer aided instruction system for programming practice courses. In: International Conference on Social Science, Education Management and Sports Education, pp. 1342–1345 (2015)
5. Liu, Y., Zhang, J.: The development and implementation of intelligent test paper assembling system. In: International Conference on Intelligent Computation Technology and Automation, pp. 777–780. IEEE (2015)

A Fast Cyclic Spectrum Detection Algorithm for MWC Based on Lorentzian Norm

Junwei Peng[1(✉)], Zhiren Han[2], and Jingfang Sun[2]

[1] College of Information and Communication Engineering,
Harbin Engineering University, Harbin 150001, China
pengjunwei@hrbeu.edu.cn
[2] Wuhan Maritime Communication Research Institute, Wuhan 430205, China
hanzr@csic722.com, 32114199@qq.com

Abstract. In order to solve the problem of high sampling rate in the wideband spectrum sensing of cognitive radio, this paper studies the method of cyclic spectrum detection based on the modulation wideband converter (MWC). A novel fast cyclic spectrum detection algorithm of MWC based on Lorentzian Norm is proposed to deal with the influence of some non-ideal factors on the performance of the existing MWC system reconstruction algorithm in physical implementation. Firstly, the objective function for sparse optimization is build based on smoothed L0-norm constrained Lorentzian norm regularization. Then a parallel reconstruction method is implemented in a unified parametric framework by combining the fixed-step formula and the conjugate gradient algorithm with sufficient decent property. Simulation results demonstrate that the proposed algorithm can not only improve the recovery probability of sparse signal, but also has a higher detection probability in low SNR environment compared with traditional reconstruction algorithms.

Keywords: Cognitive radio · Cyclic spectrum detection
Modulated wideband converter · Signal recovery · Impulsive noise

1 Introduction

Ensuring the normal communication of the primary user (PU) is a prerequisite for cognitive radio, therefore, spectrum sensing is very important. Fast and accurately sensing of the whole frequency domain information is the target of spectrum sensing, and it is still a huge challenge for spectrum sensing. Different with the spectrum sensing problem of traditional narrowband systems, cognitive radio needs to complete the dynamic access to broadband. The cyclic spectrum feature detection has stronger ability to resist the uncertainty of the noise power, and can better distinguish the noise and signal than energy detector, so it has a good application prospect [1]. However, traditional detection methods are based on the Nyquist theorem for sampling, such a high-speed ADC design and mass information processing in the broadband spectrum sensing is difficult to achieve [2].

© ICST Institute for Computer Sciences, Social Informatics and Telecommunications Engineering 2018
G. Sun and S. Liu (Eds.): ADHIP 2017, LNICST 219, pp. 177–188, 2018.
https://doi.org/10.1007/978-3-319-73317-3_22

Compressed sensing (CS) is a new kind of compressed sampling technology [3]. Tian and Giannakis introduced CS technology into the broadband spectrum sensing of cognitive radio [4]. Professor Eladar's research group proposed a modulated wideband converter (MWC) with parallel multi-branch structure [5]. Modulated wideband converter can theoretically use existing devices to sample the continuous frequency sparse multiband signal with sub Nyquist sampling and accurately reconstruct the original signal.

In literature [6], it is pointed out that the signal reconstruction of MWC system can be transformed into multiple measurement vectors, which is a generalized form of single measurement vector (SMV) model in CS theory. Eldar and Rauhut demonstrated that the MMV model can significantly improve the probability of successful reconstruction of unknown sparse signals relative to the SMV model algorithm in [7] and [8]. The number of MWC system channels determines the hardware complexity of the device. The literature [9] proposed a reconstruction algorithm based on random projection idea, which reduces the minimum number of channels required for high probability reconstruction. However, there are still large gaps in the performance of the MWC reconstruction algorithm between theory and practice, and it is assumed that different measurement columns meet the joint sparse characteristics. In addition, the reconstruction model does not consider the effect of some non-ideal factors on the performance of the system.

In order to solve the above problems, a fast cyclic spectrum detection algorithm for MWC based on Lorentzian norm (MWC-FCSD) is proposed. For the beginning, the objective function for sparse optimization was built based on matrix smoothed L0-norm. The Lorentzian norm is used to fit the error term of the noise, which effectively suppresses the singular values in the measurement vector and improves the reconstruction precision and robustness. Then, the conjugate gradient method with fixed step is used to solve the parallel optimization problem under the unified parameter framework, which reduces the matrix storage and operation, and improves the convergence speed and efficiency of the algorithm. Finally, the algorithm is applied to the cyclic spectrum detection. The simulation results show the effectiveness of the proposed algorithm.

2   Cyclic Spectrum Estimation Based on Compressive Sensing

2.1   MWC Compressed Sampling

The block diagram of MWC system is shown in Fig. 1. The system uses a parallel multi-channel structure, and each channel consists of a pseudo-random sequence generator, a mixer, a low-pass filter and a low-speed sampler. Different channels of the MWC system are mixed with different pseudo-random ± 1 waveform functions with the same period T_p, so that each frequency band is weighted with different Fourier coefficients to ensure that all the frequency band information can be obtained by low speed sampling.

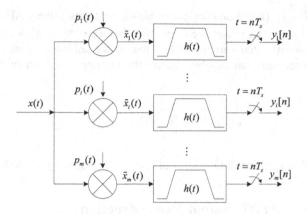

Fig. 1. MWC sampling system block diagram.

According to Fourier analysis, we can get the relationship between $Y_i(e^{j2\pi f T_s})$ and $X(f - lf_p)$:

$$Y_i(e^{j2\pi f T_s}) = \sum_{l=-L_0}^{L_0} c_{il} X(f - lf_p), \tag{1}$$

where $f \in F_s = [-f_s/2, f_s/2]$. c_{il} is the coefficients of Fourier expanding series of $p_i(t)$. To facilitate the analysis of subsequent signal reconstruction process, the combination of all m samplers, we can obtain the following matrix form:

$$Y(f) = \Phi z(f), f \in F_s, \tag{2}$$

where $\Phi_{i,j} = c_{i,j-L_0-1} \in R^{m \times L}$, $Y_i(f) = Y_i(e^{j2\pi f T_s})$, $z_l(f) = X(f - lf_p), f \in F_s$.

2.2 Cyclic Spectrum of Compressed Sampling Signal

To calculate the cyclic spectrum of $x(t)$, we must derive the linear relationship between the cyclic spectrum and the reconstructed signal. The mean of the sequence $x(n)$ is zero and the cyclic spectrum is stable, so the autocorrelation function can be defined as

$$r_x(n, v) = E\{x(nT_s)x^*(nT_s + vT_s)\} = E\{x[n]x^*[n+v]\}, \tag{3}$$

where $r_x(n, v) = r_x(n + kP, v)$, the integer P means the cyclic period

The Fourier coefficient of $r_x(n, v)$ is called Cyclic Autocorrelation Function (CAF). For the sampling length N is limited, so the estimation of CAF can be represented as

$$\tilde{r}_x^{(c)}(a, v) = \{\frac{1}{N} \sum_{n=0}^{N-1-v} r_x(n, v)e^{-j\frac{2\pi}{N}an}\}e^{-j\frac{\pi}{N}av}, \tag{4}$$

where $a \in [0, N-1]$. Based on continuous signal processing, the CAF of the discrete cyclic stationary signal increases the correction factor $e^{-j\pi av/N}$. Although this expression is biased, its estimated variance is less than other unbiased estimates [10].

The cyclic spectrum can be obtained by the Fourier transform of CAF which is represented as

$$s_x^{(c)}(a,b) = \sum_{v=0}^{N-1} \tilde{r}_x^{(c)}(a,v)e^{-j\frac{2\pi}{N}bv}, \tag{5}$$

where $b \in (0, N-1]$ is the digital form of spectral frequency $f = (b/N)f_s$.

3   Problems in MWC Signal Reconstruction

3.1   Arbitary Sparse Structure Model

MWC compressed sampling is equivalent to the projection process as shown in Fig. 2. The spectral shift step f_p determines the final position of each frequency band of $X(f)$ in $z(f)$. So, the original sparse multi-band signal can be reconstructed by tracking the sparsest solution of MMV problem and performing spectral shift.

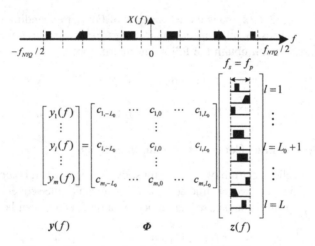

Fig. 2. Illustration for the spectrum of MWC system.

MMV model can be represented below:

$$Y = \Phi Z, \tag{6}$$

where $Z = [z^{(1)}, \cdots, z^{(L)}], z^{(l)} \in R^{N \times 1}$ is consist of L numbers of sparse column vectors, and it is assumed that these vectors have K numbers of common nonzero rows, which means joint K sparse. $Y = [y^{(1)}, \cdots, y^{(L)}], y^{(l)} \in R^{M \times 1}$ is the sampled value matrix. L is the total column number of the measured vectors. MMV reconstruction problem is essentially to obtain the sparsest solution by solving the optimization problem with sparse constraints.

$$\arg\min \sum_{l=1}^{L} ||\mathbf{z}^{(l)}||_{l_0} \text{ st.} \mathbf{y}^{(l)} = \boldsymbol{\Phi}\mathbf{z}^{(l)} \, l = 1, \cdots, L, \tag{7}$$

where $\mathbf{z}^{(l)}$ represents the l-th column vector of matrix $\mathbf{Z}$ and $\mathbf{y}^{(l)}$ represents the l-th column vector of matrix $\mathbf{Y}$. $|| \bullet ||_{l_0}$ represents the l_0 norm. Solving MMV model can be regarded as solving a series of SMV problems with sparseness constraints, which belong to the typical combinatorial optimization problems.

However, in MWC compressed sampling system, the sparseness of different measured columns are arbitrary and the locations of nonzero elements were not consistent, and the joint sparseness assumption of traditional MMV model cannot accurately describe the sparseness of such signals. In this paper, it is assumed that MMV model has arbitrary sparse structure (MMV of Arbitrary Sparse Structure, ASS-MMV), which means the sparseness and support sets of different column vectors matrix do not require the same, conforming the frequency sparseness features of vector $z(f)$ in MWC system.

3.2 Effect of Analog Low Pass Filter

In MWC system, in order to retain the low frequency $f \in [-f_s/2, f_s/2]$ after mixing to achieve low rate sampling, it is required analog low pass filters to complete the anti-aliasing filtering. The relationship between the Fourier transformation of the output sequence $y_i(n)$ and the original signal $x(t)$ in Eq. (5) is established in the case of ideal filtering. However, the actual analog low pass filters have some non-ideal condition, such as the transition band and the passband fluctuation, as showed in Fig. 3.

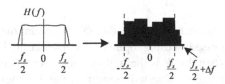

Fig. 3. Influence of transition band of filter on baseband.

Equation (7) represents the MMV model of compressed sensing without noise. However, during the compressed sampling process in MWC system, the measured value matrix can be influenced by noise and interface, because of the aliasing frequency component in filter transition band and the distortion in passband. So the MMV model with noise can be expressed as:

$$Y = \mathbf{\Phi}Z + W , \tag{8}$$

where $\mathcal{W} = [\boldsymbol{w}^{(1)}, \cdots, \boldsymbol{w}^{(L)}], \boldsymbol{w}^{(l)} \in \mathrm{R}^{M \times 1}$, W represents additive noise.

The residual frequency components, located in transition band $[f_s/2, f_s/2 + \Delta f]$ in Fig. 3, were superimposed on the original components in the form of discrete frequency after A/D sampling. So a number of singular points were added to the compressed sample value matrix, and each element in the sample value matrix was directly related to the original sparse signal. In the framework of compressed sensing, noise W was divided into two categories: Gaussian white noise and non-Gaussian impulse noise. In MWC system, the aliasing distortion caused by analog low pass filter transition band sampling belongs to the latter.

4   Cyclic Spectrum Detection Algorithm for MWC

4.1   Sparse Optimization Objective Function

For the MMV solution problem in the noise model, the Eq. (8) can be modified as follows:

$$\arg \min \sum_{l=1}^{L} ||\boldsymbol{z}^{(l)}||_{l_0} + \lambda \mathrm{loss}(\boldsymbol{y}^{(l)} - \mathbf{\Phi}\boldsymbol{z}^{(l)}) , \tag{9}$$

where $\mathrm{loss}(\boldsymbol{y}^{(l)} - \mathbf{\Phi}\boldsymbol{z}^{(l)})$ denoting error term, and $\lambda \geq 0$ is regularization parameters, which controls the balance between allowable error and sparseness. When the W is Gaussian noise, the norm can be used to fit the error term. In this case, (5) has the following expression:

$$\arg \min \sum_{l=1}^{L} ||\boldsymbol{z}^{(l)}||_{l_0} + \lambda ||\boldsymbol{y}^{(l)} - \mathbf{\Phi}\boldsymbol{z}^{(l)}||_2^2 . \tag{10}$$

It can be seen from the analysis in [11] that the minimum mean square error of the signal under the compressed sensing optimal reconstruction is proportional to the variance of the noise. When the W is the impact noise, as it is characterized by a large variance, elements with larger value will appear in the error term. Because there are discrete points, the l_2 norm will linear amplify the impact of residual.

The literature [12] pointed out that when the Lorentzian norm is used to fit the error term, due to the bounded soft-return characteristic of the derivative function, the penalty for the element with large amplitude in the error term is heavier and its effect is the same as the l_1 norm; The penalty of the element with smaller amplitude in the error term is lighter, and its function is the same as the l_2 norm. So it is possible to robustly reduce the effect of the outliers on the reconstruction results. The Lorentzian norm is defined as follows:

$$||u||_{LL_2,\gamma} = \sum_{m=1}^{M} \log(1 + \gamma^{-2}u_m^2), \gamma > 0 , \tag{(11)}$$

where $u \in R^{M \times 1}$ is a column vector, and $|| \bullet ||_{LL_2,\gamma}$ denotes the Lorentzian norm of u, γ is the scale parameter of the Lorentzian norm and determines the robustness of the LL_2 norm to the error term outliers.

In this paper, the Lorentzian norm is used to replace the norm in (10) to fit the error term. The solution of MMV model under impact noise can be expressed as follows:

$$\arg\min \sum_{l=1}^{L} ||z^{(l)}||_{l_0} + \lambda||y^{(l)} - \Phi z^{(l)}||_{LL_2,\gamma} , \tag{12}$$

where $||y^{(l)} - \Phi z^{(l)}||_{LL_2,\gamma}$ denotes the Lorentzian norm of the i-th column reconstruction error term of the sampling matrix.

4.2 ASS-MMV Fast Reconstruction Algorithm

The signal reconstruction of MMV model can be summarized as an optimization problem:

$$L(X) = \sum_{l=1}^{L} ||z^{(l)}||_{l_0} + \lambda||y^{(l)} - \Phi z^{(l)}||_{LL_2,\gamma} . \tag{13}$$

In the formula (13), the norm is pseudo-norm, which is highly discontinuous and cannot be solved by analytic method. It belongs to the NP-Hard problem. The SL0 algorithm approximates the l_0 norm by a class of smooth Gaussian functions, and solves the minimum problem directly by analytic method. This method not only improves the reconstruction probability, but also greatly shortens the computing time. The optimal objective function based on smooth norm and Lorentzian norm is

$$L(Z) = \sum_{l=1}^{L} F_\sigma(z^{(l)}) + \lambda||y^{(l)} - \Phi z^{(l)}||_{LL_2,\gamma} , \tag{14}$$

where $F_\sigma(z^{(l)}) = N - \sum_{i=1}^{N} f_\sigma(z_i^{(l)})$, $f_\sigma(z_i^{(l)})$ denotes Standard Gaussian function

$$f_\sigma(s) = \exp(-s^2/2\sigma^2) , \tag{15}$$

where σ is used to measure the relationship between the accuracy and smoothness of the l_0 norm of the vector s. By the properties of the Gaussian function

$$\lim_{\sigma \to 0} F_\sigma(z^{(l)}) = ||z^{(l)}||_0 \, . \tag{16}$$

The fast reconstruction algorithm of ASS-MMV model uses the characteristics of SL0 algorithm which converge to the vicinity of the optimal value at each σ value, and set the initial least squares solution of sparse vector: $Z_0 = \boldsymbol{\Phi}^H(\boldsymbol{\Phi}\boldsymbol{\Phi}^H)^{-1}Y$. The algorithm reconstructs the multi-vector in parallel with the numerical optimization algorithm under the unified parameter setting framework, and realizes the parallel reconstruction of the MMV signal model with arbitrary sparse structure.

The iterative method is used to solve the optimal solution as (16):

$$z_{k+1} = z_k + a_k d_K, \tag{17}$$

where z_k is the k-th iteration point, d_k is the k-th search direction, a_k is the k-th iterative step. In order to overcome the slow convergence rate of steepest descent method, and high computational complexity and large storage of newton method used in SL0 algorithm, a conjugate gradient algorithm based on fixed step size is adopted in this paper [13].

5 Numerical Experiment

We performed simulations to demonstrate the effectiveness of the MWC-FCSD algorithm. Firstly, the influence of the transition band of analog low-pass filter on the reconstruction performance of MWC-FCSD algorithm, OMPMMV algorithm and MSL0 algorithm are analyzed. Secondly, the reconstruction time of each algorithm is compared. Finally the performance of cyclic spectrum detection is verified. For all the experiments we create sparse multiband signals, which is BPSK modulation signal with different energy E_n, carrier frequency f_n and bandwidth B_n. The carriers f_n for very signal are chosen uniformly at random in $[-f_{NYQ}/2, f_{NYQ}/2]$ with $f_{NYQ} = 10$ GHz. In order to use MATLAB to simulate the sampling process of the analog signal, the sampling rate $10f_{NYQ}$ is used to simulate the analog signal.

The parameters of MWC are configured as follows, $f_s = f_p = 51.28$ MHz, $M = 195$, $L = 2L_0 + 1 = 195$, $E_n \in [1, 3]$, τ_n determined randomly in the effective observation time.

The following simulations are repeated 500 times for each set of parameters setting. The ratio of the number of successes to the number of experiments is taken as the reconstruction success rate which is defined as the recovered support sets is the same as the actual support sets.

A. Influence on performance of transition band of LP filter
In order to evaluate the influence of analog low-pass filter on signal reconstruction performance, we adjust the rectangle coefficients of low-pass filter, and compare the reconstruction success rate of OMPMMV algorithm, MSL0 algorithm and MWC-FCSD algorithm, as shown in Fig. 4. The multiband signals consist of $N = 4$ pairs of bands, and the channel number takes one of the two choices: 30 or 50.

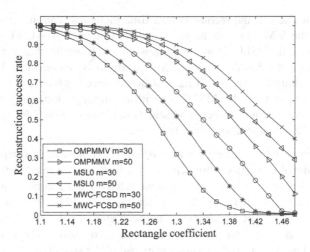

Fig. 4. Reconstruction success rate comparison under different transition bandwidth.

As can be seen from Fig. 4, the larger the rectangular coefficient of the low-pass filter, the smaller the success rate of the reconstruction. This is because the wider the transition band of the low-pass filter, the higher the frequency aliasing of the baseband signal after sampling, that is, the greater the impact noise. Due to the use of the Lorentzian norm fitting error term in MWC-FCSD algorithm, the singular value in the observation vector can be robustly suppressed. It can be seen from Fig. 4 that the reconstruction success rate can be improved by increasing the number of channels. In order to achieve high probability reconstruction (more than 90%), the number of channels and the rectangular coefficient required by MWC-FCSD algorithm, OMPMMV algorithm, MSL0 algorithm, respectively, are $m = 30$ and $r = 1.3$, $m = 50$ and $r = 1.26$, $m = 50$ and $r = 1.26$. In conclusion, our algorithm can effectively improve the reconstruction ability of the MWC system, reduce the number of hardware channels, and the design requirements of the analog low-pass filter transition bandwide.

B. Comparison of reconstruction time under different channels

In this section, we add a set of simulation data of SL0 algorithm based on SMV model to verify the advantages of MMV model in reconstruction speed. The average operation times of the four algorithms are given in Table 1, and the number of channels is set to 24, 26, 28, 30, 32, 34. In addition to $N = 6$, the other parameters are consistent with experiment A.

Table 1. Reconstruction times comparison of several algorithms.

Channel	OMPMMV	MSL0	MWC-FCSD	SMV-SL0
24	0.8361	1.6279	1.8294	19.276
26	0.8527	1.6764	1.8846	19.985
28	0.8704	1.7302	1.9403	20.515
30	0.8918	1.7824	1.9971	21.132
32	0.9174	1.8395	2.0572	21.760
34	0.9352	1.9047	2.1163	22.376

As shown in Table 1, the reconstruction time increases with the number of channels. Based on the MMV model, the reconstruction times of MWC-FCSD algorithm, OMPMMV algorithm, MSL0 algorithm are always much smaller than the of SMV-SL0 algorithm, because the SMV-SL0 algorithm needs to be reconstructed one by one. OMPMMV algorithm has the fastest reconstruction speed, which is a greedy iterative algorithm. Compared with the MSL0 algorithm, although the computational complexity of objective function gradient and search step size of MWC-FCSD algorithm is slightly larger, the reconstruction times are close.

C. Cyclic spectrum detection performance of MWC compression sampling

The detection signal consists of three channels which are occupied at the same time. The cycle spectrum of detection signal reconstructed by our algorithm while $m = 50$ and SNR = 0 dB is shown in Fig. 5. The signals PU1, PU2, PU3 have significant spectral peaks at their cyclic frequencies. The peak and its position information can be used for signal detection and signal modulation recognition. The cyclic spectrum estimation based on compressed sensing makes use of the sparsity of the cyclic spectral domain, which reduces the requirement of sampling rate ($f_{\sum} = mf_s$).

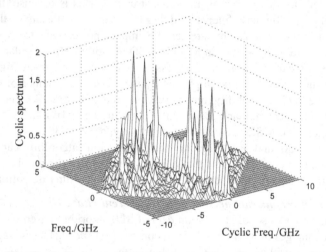

Fig. 5. Cyclic spectrum of the reconstruction signal on m = 50.

Figure 6 shows the detection probability curves for various numbers m of channels and various SNRs. When SNR = 20 dB, $m = 36$, the detection probability Pd is close to 1. When the SNR is lower than 10 dB, the detection probability decreases sharply, which is due to the decline of the cyclic spectrum sparsity under low SNR and lead to deterioration of the reconstruction performance. Meanwhile, the sampling rate can be adjusted according to the SNR, and channel number can be reduced when the SNR is high. The detection probability of the detection probability curve in Fig. 6 is obtained by 500 Monte-Carlo simulations.

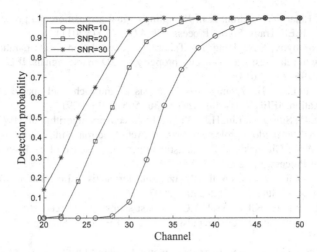

Fig. 6. Cyclic spectrum detection performance of MWC-FCSD algorithm.

6   Conclusion

In this paper, a fast cyclic spectrum detection algorithm for MWC based on Lorentzian norm is proposed. Our algorithm solves the problem that the performance of the existing MWC sub-Nyquist sampling reconstruction algorithm is easy to be influenced by non-ideal factors. Simulation and experimental results show that the algorithm proposed in this paper has the advantages of good reconfiguration performance and few reconstruction channels compared with the existing algorithms. It is not only achieves efficient reconstruction of MWC compression samples with arbitrary sparse structure, but also can effectively reduce the influence of non-ideal factors such as filter transition.

References

1. Mitola, J.I., Maguire, G.Q.J.: Cognitive radio: making software radios more personal. IEEE Pers. Commun. **6**, 3–18 (1999)
2. Kong, X., Petre, P., Matic, R., Gilbert, A.C.: An analog-to-information converter for wideband signals using a time encoding machine. In: Digital Signal Processing Workshop and IEEE Signal Processing Education Workshop (DSP/SPE), Sedona, AZ, vol. 47, pp. 414–419 (2011)
3. Foucart, S., Rauhut, H.: A Mathematical Introduction to Compressive Sensing: Applied and Numerical Harmonic Analysis, vol. 44. Springer, Heidelberg (2013). https://doi.org/10.1007/978-0-8176-4948-7
4. Tian, Z., Giannakis, G.B.: Compressed sensing for wideband cognitive radios. In: IEEE International Conference on Acoustics, Speech and Signal Processing, vol. 4, pp. 1357–1360 (2007)
5. Mishali, M., Eldar, Y.C.: From theory to practice: sub-Nyquist sampling of sparse wideband analog signals. IEEE J. Sel. Top. Signal Process. **4**, 375–391 (2010)

6. Mishali, M., Eldar, Y.C., Elron, A.J.: Xampling: signal acquisition and processing in union of subspaces. IEEE Trans. Signal Process. **59**, 4719–4734 (2011)
7. Fang, H., Vorobyov, S.A., Jiang, H., Taheri, O.: Permutation meets parallel compressed sensing: how to relax restricted isometry property for 2D sparse signals. IEEE Trans. Signal Process. **62**, 196–210 (2013)
8. Eldar, Y.C., Rauhut, H.: Average case analysis of multi-channel sparse recovery using convex relaxation. IEEE Trans. Inf. Theory **56**, 505–519 (2009)
9. Gai, J.X., Fu, P., Sun, J.Y., Lin, H.J., Wu, L.H.: A recovery algorithm of MWC sub-Nyquist sampling based on random projection method. Acta Electron. Sin. **9**, 1686–1692 (2014)
10. Dandawate, A.V., Giannakis, G.B.: Statistical tests for presence of cyclostationarity. IEEE Trans. Signal Process. **42**, 2355–2369 (1994)
11. Candes, E., Tao, T.: Discussion: the Dantzig selector: statistical estimation when p is much larger than n. Ann. Stat. **35**, 2392–2404 (2007)
12. Carrillo, R.E., Barner, K.E., Aysal, T.C.: Robust sampling and reconstruction methods for sparse signals in the presence of impulsive noise. IEEE Trans. Sel. Top. Signal Process. **4**, 392–408 (2010)
13. Huang, J., Zhou, G.: A conjugate gradient method without line search and the convergence analysis. In: Fourth International Conference on Emerging Intelligent Data and Web Technologies, Xi'an, pp. 734–736 (2013)

Trusted Computing Based on Interval Intuitionistic Fuzzy Sets in Cloud Manufacturing

Xiaolan Xie[1,2], Xiaofeng Gu[3], and Xiaochun Cheng[4(✉)]

[1] College of Information Science and Engineering,
Guilin University of Technology, Guilin 541004, Guangxi, China
237290696@qq.com
[2] Guangxi Key Laboratory Fund of Embedded Technology
and Intelligent System, Guilin University of Technology, Guilin 541004, China
[3] College of Mechanical and Control Engineering,
Guilin University of Technology, Guilin 541004, Guangxi, China
gxf199295@163.com
[4] Department of Computer Science, Middlesex University, London, UK
x.cheng@mdx.ac.uk

Abstract. Aiming at the problem that the trust information is not complete in the existing cloud manufacturing and the single model lacks the multi-perspective, the model of the trust evaluation mechanism in the cloud manufacturing environment is established, at the same time, using the interval intuitionistic fuzzy set (IVIFS), this paper proposes a trusted computing model based on interval intuitionistic fuzzy sets in cloud manufacturing. Through experimental analysis, and finally through the results of sorting, to get the optimal solution of trust, which solves the problem that the information in the process of interaction between the demand side and the service side is not complete or the fuzzy uncertainty of the attribute itself is difficult to give the information of accurate preference.

Keywords: Cloud manufacturing · Trust assessment mechanism
Interval intuitionistic fuzzy sets · Trust · Multi-attribute group decision

1 Introduction

In the cloud manufacturing environment, the trust relationship between the subjects is formed in the process of continuous interaction with each other. The results of the trust assessment can visually express whether the information in the information exchange is trustworthy [1, 2]. One of the decisive factors of trust decision-making is trust. We make a comprehensive assessment through the calculation of the trust of the results of its trust. Although there are a lot of trust calculation method, but it is not very good to complete a more comprehensive trust calculation for the trust of such a multi-attribute comprehensive measurement body, and can not describe the trust decision-making state better [3–5], therefore, this paper will study the multi-attribute group decision algorithm of interval intuitionistic fuzzy sets and establish the relevant model of trust degree

© ICST Institute for Computer Sciences, Social Informatics and Telecommunications Engineering 2018
G. Sun and S. Liu (Eds.): ADHIP 2017, LNICST 219, pp. 189–194, 2018.
https://doi.org/10.1007/978-3-319-73317-3_23

calculation in the form of IVIFS (interval intuitionistic fuzzy sets) to avoid that it is difficult to give precise preference information because of incomplete information or the attribute itself Fuzzy uncertainty, etc.

2   Establishment of Trust Degree Calculation Model Based on Interval Intuitionistic Fuzzy Sets

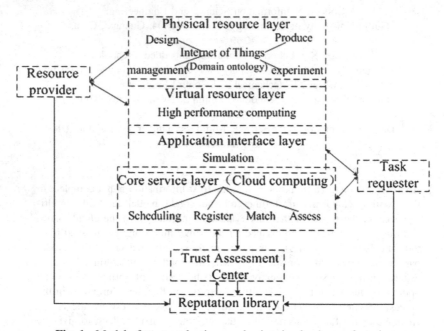

Fig. 1. Model of trust evaluation mechanism in cloud manufacturing

We give the following cloud manufacturing trust evaluation mechanism model in here, as shown in Fig. 1:

2.1   Interval Intuitionistic Fuzzy Entropy and Solution of Group Decision Weight

Entropy measure is an important measure in the research of fuzzy sets theory, which is used to measure the degree of uncertainty of fuzzy sets. For any of the $A = \{(x, \mu_A(x), v_A(x))|x \in X\}$ and $B = \{(x, \mu_B(x), v_B(x))|x \in X\}$, The interval intuitionistic fuzzy entropy E (A) can be defined as follows

$$E(A) = \cos\frac{\mu_A^2(x) - v_A^2(x)}{2}\pi \tag{1}$$

We give the formulan λ_{ij} for calculating the group decision weight by the above formula,

$$\lambda_{ij} = \frac{KC - E_{ij}^l}{k - KC - \sum_l^k E_{ij}^l} (i = 1, 2 \cdots, m; j = 1, 2, \cdots n) \qquad (2)$$

among them, K is the number of group decisions KC is a constant, in general, the value of 1. In principle, the attribute's maximum and minimum weights should be within 1x. Through the decision of the group decision weights λ_{ij}, combined with $IVIFHA_{\omega,w}$ to compute the comprehensive decision matrix of group decision matrix $D_i(i = 1, 2, \cdots k)$, and calculate the attribute weight ω_j, among them, $\overline{E}_{ij} = E(\gamma_{ij})$.

$$\omega_j = \frac{KC - \sum_{i=1}^m \overline{E}_{ij}}{n \times KC - \sum_{j=1}^n \sum_{i=1}^m \overline{E}_{ij}} \qquad (3)$$

2.2 Ranking and Distance Formula of Interval Intuitionistic Fuzzy Numbers

When we can not determine the sorting results are good or bad, we need to use the interval exact function to determine the sort. We set $\alpha_i = \left([a_i^L, a_i^R], [b_i^L, b_i^R]\right)$ $(i = 1, 2, \cdots n)$ is a set of intuitionistic fuzzy numbers in here, the probability of $IS(\alpha_i)$ and $IS(\alpha_j)$ is $p_{ij}(IS) = p(IS(\alpha_i) \geq IS(\alpha_j))$, then we can say the matrix $p(IS) = [p_{ij}(IS)]_{m \times n}$ as follows:

$$p(IS) = \begin{bmatrix} p_{11}(IS) & p_{12}(IS) & \cdots & p_{1n}(IS) \\ p_{21}(IS) & p_{22}(IS) & \cdots & p_{2n}(IS) \\ \vdots & \vdots & \ddots & \vdots \\ p_{11}(IS) & p_{11}(IS) & \cdots & p_{11}(IS) \end{bmatrix} \qquad (4)$$

We calculate the matrix $p(IS)$ from the above formula, we can compare by the following formula:

$$\delta_i^{IS} = \frac{\sum_{j=1}^n p_{ij}(IS) + \frac{n}{2} - 1}{n(n - 1)} i = 1, 2, \cdots, n \qquad (5)$$

2.3 Gray Correlation Coefficient Matrix

According to the comprehensive decision matrix, we can calculate the gray correlation coefficient matrix $(\xi_{ij})_{m \times n}$, the formula is as follows:

$$\xi_{ij} = \frac{\min_{1 \leq j \leq n} \min_{1 \leq i \leq n} d(\gamma_{ij}, \gamma_j^+) + v \max_{1 \leq j \leq n} \max_{1 \leq i \leq n} d(\gamma_{ij}, \gamma_j^+)}{d(\gamma_{ij}, \gamma_j^+) + v \max_{1 \leq j \leq n} \max_{1 \leq i \leq n} d(\gamma_{ij}, \gamma_j^+)} \qquad (6)$$

where the resolution coefficient $v \in [0, 1]$, in general, $v = 0.5$

On the basis of the above formula, we attribute the weighted values of the gray correlation coefficients for each of the alternative attribute values to get the interval gray correlation degree for each alternative:

$$\overline{\xi}_i = \sum_{j=1}^{n} \omega_j \xi_{ij} \tag{7}$$

Using the interval possibility to compare the sorting size of the gray correlation degree of each alternative, and find the sorting result of the corresponding sorting value of the alternatives:

$$\delta_i^{\overline{\xi}} = \frac{\sum\limits_{j=1}^{m} p_{ij}(\overline{\xi}) + \frac{m}{2} - 1}{m(m-1)} \quad i = 1, 2, \cdots, m \tag{8}$$

3 Experiment Analysis

In order to evaluate the effectiveness of the proposed trust calculation model, in this paper, through the relevant manufacturing enterprises to provide gear inspection services on time, economy, processing quality, service attitude, scale of operation of the five demand indicators, we carry out experimental analysis about four attributes for the direct trust, indirect trust, recommended trust, trust attenuation for of each indicator, and get interval intuitionistic fuzzy matrices Di (i = 1,2,3), as follows:

$$D_1 = \begin{bmatrix} ([0.49,0.58],[0.31,0.42])([0.49,0.58],[0.21,0.32])([0.21,0.32],[0.59,0.68])([0.12,0.21],[0.68,0.79]) \\ ([0.59,0.68],[0.21,0.32])([0.68,0.79],[0.12,0.21])([0.68,0.79],[0.12,0.21])([0.32,0.41],[0.38,0.49]) \\ ([0.49,0.58],[0.32,0.41])([0.38,0.49],[0.32,0.41])([0.49,0.58],[0.21,0.32])([0.59,0.68],[0.21,0.32]) \\ ([0.77,0.88],[0.03,0.12])([0.49,0.58],[0.32,0.41])([0.21,0.32],[0.38,0.49])([0.21,0.32],[0.49,0.58]) \\ ([0.59,0.68],[0.21,0.22])([0.32,0.41],[0.38,0.49])([0.67,0.78],[0.03,0.12])([0.49,0.58],[0.31,0.42]) \end{bmatrix}$$

$$D_2 = \begin{bmatrix} ([0.32,0.41],[0.28,0.29])([0.38,0.49],[0.22,0.31])([0.13,0.22],[0.47,0.58])([0.02,0.12],[0.58,0.68]) \\ ([0.59,0.68],[0.21,0.32])([0.58,0.69],[0.02,0.11])([0.48,0.59],[0.02,0.11])([0.31,0.41],[0.39,0.49]) \\ ([0.48,0.59],[0.22,0.31])([0.31,0.41],[0.29,0.39])([0.39,0.49],[0.11,0.21])([0.48,0.59],[0.22,0.31]) \\ ([0.68,0.79],[0.02,0.11])([0.48,0.59],[0.12,0.21])([0.22,0.32],[0.28,0.38])([0.12,0.21],[0.48,0.59]) \\ ([0.48,0.59],[0.12,0.21])([0.29,0.39],[0.21,0.31])([0.59,0.79],[0.01,0.11])([0.39,0.49],[0.21,0.31]) \end{bmatrix}$$

$$D_3 = \begin{bmatrix} ([0.32,0.42],[0.48,0.58])([0.49,0.49],[0.41,0.59])([0.11,0.21],[0.69,0.69])([0.02,0.12],[0.78,0.88]) \\ ([0.48,0.58],[0.32,0.42])([0.59,0.69],[0.21,0.31])([0.59,0.59],[0.31,0.41])([0.32,0.42],[0.48,0.58]) \\ ([0.42,0.42],[0.38,0.48])([0.41,0.49],[0.49,0.51])([0.39,0.49],[0.31,0.41])([0.48,0.58],[0.32,0.42]) \\ ([0.68,0.78],[0.12,0.22])([0.48,0.58],[0.42,0.42])([0.22,0.32],[0.48,0.58])([0.12,0.22],[0.58,0.68]) \\ ([0.48,0.58],[0.32,0.32])([0.21,0.31],[0.39,0.59])([0.58,0.68],[0.12,0.22])([0.39,0.48],[0.31,0.42]) \end{bmatrix}$$

First of all, for the above three matrices, we first use the formula (1) to calculate the attribute entropy of the decision matrix, and then use the formula (2) to calculate the group decision weight λ.

$$\lambda_1 = \begin{bmatrix} 0.34 & 0.35 & 0.33 & 0.32 \\ 0.35 & 0.37 & 0.39 & 0.33 \\ 0.33 & 0.33 & 0.34 & 0.35 \\ 0.40 & 0.33 & 0.33 & 0.32 \\ 0.36 & 0.33 & 0.37 & 0.34 \end{bmatrix}$$

$$\lambda_2 = \begin{bmatrix} 0.33 & 0.33 & 0.31 & 0.28 \\ 0.35 & 0.32 & 0.31 & 0.33 \\ 0.34 & 0.33 & 0.33 & 0.33 \\ 0.31 & 0.35 & 0.32 & 0.33 \\ 0.33 & 0.33 & 0.33 & 0.33 \end{bmatrix}$$

$$\lambda_3 = \begin{bmatrix} 0.34 & 0.32 & 0.36 & 0.40 \\ 0.31 & 0.30 & 0.30 & 0.34 \\ 0.32 & 0.33 & 0.32 & 0.31 \\ 0.29 & 0.32 & 0.35 & 0.36 \\ 0.32 & 0.34 & 0.30 & 0.33 \end{bmatrix}$$

The second step, computing the intuitionistic intuitionistic fuzzy decision matrix by the decision of the group decision weight λ combined with $IVIFHA_{\omega,w}$ operator, at the same time using the formula (3) to calculate the trust-related attribute weight ω:

$$\omega = \begin{bmatrix} 0.24 & 0.26 & 0.25 & 0.25 \end{bmatrix}$$

The third step, according to formulas (4) and (5), the ideal scheme $A^+ = \{\gamma_1^+, \gamma_2^+, \gamma_3^+, \gamma_4^+\}$ is determined by comparing the magnitude of the different scheme attribute values

$$\gamma_1^+ = ([0.72, 0.83] \ [0.00, 0.12]) \quad \gamma_2^+ = ([0.67, 0.77] \ [0.00, 0.18])$$
$$\gamma_3^+ = ([0.63, 0.78] \ [0.00, 0.12]) \quad \gamma_4^+ = ([0.56, 0.66] \ [0.18, 0.29])$$

The fourth step, select the resolution $v = 0.5$, using the formula (6) can be calculated gray correlation coefficient matrix $\xi = [\xi_{ij}]_{m \times n}$

$$\xi = \begin{bmatrix} [0.25, 1.11] & [0.30, 1.56] & [0.21, 0.79] & [0.22, 0.80] \\ [0.32, 1.79] & [0.38, 2.36] & [0.35, 2.36] & [0.30, 1.40] \\ [0.29, 1.38] & [0.27, 1.25] & [0.31, 1.80] & [0.42, 2.36] \\ [0.41, 2.36] & [0.31, 1.77] & [0.24, 0.99] & [0.25, 1.01] \\ [0.33, 1.78] & [0.25, 1.13] & [0.38, 2.36] & [0.37, 2.32] \end{bmatrix}$$

The fifth step, calculate the gray relational degree $\bar{\xi}$ using the formula (7)

$$\overline{\xi} = \begin{bmatrix} [0.25, 1.07] \\ [0.34, 1.99] \\ [0.33, 1.69] \\ [0.30, 1.53] \\ [0.33, 1.89] \end{bmatrix}$$

The sixth step, according to the gray correlation degree obtained above, through the interval possibility degree formula and the alternative probability matrix, finally, using the formula (8) to find the corresponding sort value $\sigma = [0.15 \quad 0.23 \quad 0.21 \quad 0.19 \quad 0.22]$, By final ranking we can determine the optimal trust of different indicators, so as to make the best choice of program A_2.

4 Conclusion

This paper first analyzes the important trust relationship between cloud manufacturing entities. A trusted computing model based on interval-based intuitionistic fuzzy sets in cloud manufacturing is proposed by studying the multi-attribute group decision-making of interval intuitionistic fuzzy sets. Through experimental analysis, Through the optimal solution, the demand side and the service side in the information exchange will be able to get more convincing, more comprehensive trust information. Of course, this study is not particularly deep, there are many deficiencies, hope in the future to continue to carry out more in-depth study.

Acknowledgements. This research work was supported by the 'Ba Gui Scholars' program of the provincial government of Guangxi and Guangxi key Laboratory Fund of Embedded Technology and Intelligent System (Guilin University of Technology) and 2017 autonomous regions of industry and information technology development special funds No. [2017]333.

References

1. Kiliç, M., Kaya, İ.: Investment project evaluation by a decision making methodology based on type-2 fuzzy sets. Appl. Soft Comput. **27**, 399–410 (2015)
2. Liu, B.S., Shen, Y.H., Chen, X.H., et al.: A complex multi-attribute large-group PLS decision-making method in the interval-valued intuitionistic fuzzy environment. Appl. Math. Model. **38**, 4512–4527 (2014)
3. Zhang, X., Xu, Z.: Soft computing based on maximizing consensus and fuzzy TOPSIS approach to interval-valued intuitionistic fuzzy group decision making. Appl. Soft Comput. **26**, 42–56 (2015)
4. Joshi, D., Kumar, S.: Interval-valued intuitionistic hesitant fuzzy Choquet integral based TOPSIS method for multi-criteria group decision making. Eur. J. Oper. Res. **248**(1), 183–191 (2016)
5. Chen, T.Y.: The inclusion-based TOPSIS method with interval-valued intuitionistic fuzzy sets for multiple criteria group decision making. Appl. Soft Comput. **26**, 57–73 (2015)

Topic-Aware Influence Maximization in Large Recommendation Social Networks

Jinghua Zhu[✉], Qian Ming, and Nan Wang

School of Computer Science and Technology, Heilongjiang University,
Harbin, China
zhujinghua@hlju.edu.cn

Abstract. Influence maximization (*IM*) is a problem of finding several influential individuals in a social network so that their influence spread is maximized under certain propagation model. In recommendation social network such as Douban, information diffuses with multiple origins: internal and external influence. Furthermore, pairs of individuals usually have different influence strength on different topics, information, ideas and rumors etc. In this paper, we focus on the topic-aware *IM* problem for large recommendation social networks. We propose a novel TSID propagation model to formulate the multiple topics diffusion in recommendation social networks. We propose TIP algorithm to solve the influence maximization problem under TSID propagation model. Our experiment results show that TSID model can well depict the mix information propagation process in recommendation social network, the TIP algorithm has competitive response time and influence spread.

Keywords: Influence maximization · Topic-aware
Recommendation social network

1 Introduction

Recently, large social networks have sprung up, social network is not only important medium to exchange information, make friends, but also important business platform. Businesses can choose a small part of influential people in social networks, through to provide them with free products, to make them through social networks recommend the product to their friends or family, reaching the largest scope of products with "word of mouth".

The information spread is affected by many factors, including the impact probability between users, the user's preference for information and the impact of the web site to the user. For example: whether or not the user to accept the product will not only be affected by their friends, but also by the push message of web site impact. The web site can be used to get more information through the home page news, sending messages, reminding message and other forms, and the user may be able to accept these messages, then further recommend to their friends. Another one example: to spread different products or ideas in the web site, because the user's different preferences for different types, so the spread effect between the same user is different, propagation process will

© ICST Institute for Computer Sciences, Social Informatics and Telecommunications Engineering 2018
G. Sun and S. Liu (Eds.): ADHIP 2017, LNICST 219, pp. 195–203, 2018.
https://doi.org/10.1007/978-3-319-73317-3_24

inevitably be influenced by user preference. Just as women pay more attention to cosmetics than men, cosmetics marketing should be more dependent on women.

In recent years, many algorithms have been proposed to solve the influence maximization problem, although some algorithms take into account the topic, but did not consider the impact of the web site itself to the user. The web site is an important influence, with the users to promote the spread, can be spread in a number of local areas, and therefore spread faster than the traditional spread process. Considering the social network user's preference, combining with the impact of the site can make the selection more accurate, the spread process can better fit the actual situation. Therefore, this paper extends the SID (Super Influencer Diffusion) diffusion model, and proposes the TSID (Topic-aware Super Influencer Diffusion) diffusion model, which can deal with the topic-aware influence propagation. Based on the TSID model, this paper proposes a TIP (Topic-aware Influence Path) algorithm, according the current activated node transmission, fast calculation the influence of node based on propagation influence path selecting the node with largest marginal gain as seed with greedy thought is inactive node set. This adaptive selection method can faster and broader the spread influence.

To evaluate TIP algorithm, we choose movie reviews in the Douban network as the data set. Douban is a famous domestic social networking sites, services including project recommendation, making friends, comment which is the core service. Because a large number of user provide ratings and reviews, the Douban score has important reference in the minds of users. The experimental results show that the TIP algorithm is more extensive than the existing algorithms, and the time efficiency is high.

The main contributions of this paper are as follows:

- An extended TSID diffusion model is proposed, and the formulas for calculating the internal and external influence probabilities are given.
- The TIP algorithm is proposed, which can adaptively determine the seed set in inactive nodes according to the current communication.
- The comparative experiments on the data set and the result show that the TIP algorithm has a greater impact on the transmission range and less running time.

2   Related Works

Kempe et al. [1] first propose discrete optimization method for the influence maximization, they present a greedy hill-climbing approximation algorithm. Goyal et al. [2] exploited simple paths between neighbor nodes to estimate the influence propagation probability. Lu et al. [3] propose algorithm to get the influence in a range of four hops, they also propose an approximation algorithm to compute influence in the range of at least five hops. You et al. [4] find that under certain incentives, one would build new relationship in the social network to promote the process of information propagation. The above algorithms can deal with the traditional influence maximization problem, but they did not take into account the factors affecting the transmission process.

Barbieri et al. [5] propose TIC model and TLT model to solve the topic-aware influence maximization problem. Zhou et al. [6] propose a two-step mining algorithm

GAUP. Guo and Lv [7] propose EIC model which is based on users' activities and preference and L_GAUP algorithm. Chen et al. [8] find that the majority of seed nodes under multiple topics are derived from the composition of the topic set and they propose C-Greedy algorithm. Zhu et al. [9] propose structural hole based influence maximization algorithm. Chen et al. [10] establish a maximum influence tree to approximate the computational power of the topic based algorithm.

3   Diffusion Model and Problem Statement

3.1   TSID Model

Niu et al. [11] investigate the information diffusion of Douban network and propose SID model. In this paper, we extend SID model to TSID model which is suitable for topic aware influence maximization problem for recommend social network.

In TSID model, there are lots of common user nodes and one super node. Common nodes have two states: active or inactive. Inactive node can be activated by active node at least once, all common nodes can only change state from inactive to active, the opposite is not allowed. The propagation process of TSID model is similar to traditional IC model: Initially, the super node is active and the common nodes are inactive. Then propagation begins. In each time step, the active nodes would influence their neighbors. The super node infect all nodes with probability P_{ex}; other active nodes will infect their neighbor nodes with probability P_{in}. The propagation end when all nodes don't change states anymore.

As shown in Fig. 1, the active nodes (in red) can influence their neighbors with probability P_{in}, and the super node can also influence inactive nodes with probability P_{ex}.

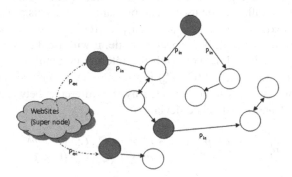

Fig. 1. The TSID model. (Color figure online)

3.2   Influence Probability

(1) *Internal influence probability*
In this paper, P_{in} represents the internal influence probability among users. In this paper, we consider the influence probability not only is related with influence

frequency, but also is correlated with users' similarity. We define the internal influence probability from user u to v as the following formula:

$$p_{uv}^{in} = b \times W_{uv} + (1 - b) \times S_{uv} \tag{1}$$

In the above formula, the internal influence probability p_{uv}^{in} is the weighted linear combination of original uniform probability W_{uv} and the similarity S_{uv} of u and v. The similarity S_{uv} is measured by similar activities of u and v.

(2) *External influence probability*
The external influence probability P_{ex} represents the environment impact from the super influencer such as the website itself. In this paper, we define the external influence probability from super node g on user u as the following formula:

$$p_{gu}^{ex} = c \times A_u + (1 - c) \times D_u \tag{2}$$

In the above formula, c is the harmonic factor. A_u and D_u represent the activeness and dependence of user u. As shown in formula (3), A_u is the number of films that user u has watched divided by the average number of films that have been seen by all users. D_u can be measured by the portion of online time of user u as shown in formula (4).

$$A_u = |S_u| / \overline{|S|} \tag{3}$$

$$D_u = T_u^{on} / T_u^{all} \tag{4}$$

(3) *Topic aware influence probability*
Now, we incorporate the topic mixtures in the diffusion model. Under a specific topic vector t, user u has an influence on user v with probability p_{uv}^t. This probability contains two parts: internal/external probability and user preference correlation under the given topic. As shown in formula (5), if u is a super node, it will use the external probability to active v; otherwise, it will active v with the internal probability. C_u^t represents the preference of user u for topic t. $F(C_u^t, C_v^t)$ represents the preference similarity of user u and v about topic t which can be estimated by the difference between the arithmetic mean of C_u^t and C_v^t and the standard deviation.

$$p_{uv}^t = \begin{cases} a \times p_{uv}^{in} + (1 - a) \times F(C_u^t, C_v^t) \, (u \neq g) \\ a \times p_{gv}^{ex} + (1 - a) \times F(C_g^t, C_v^t) \, (u = g) \end{cases} \tag{5}$$

3.3   Topic-Aware *IM* Problem

Given a graph $G = (V, E, W)$, the recommendation social network graph is described as $G^s = (V^s, E^s, W)$, here $V^s = \{g\} \cup V$, g represents the super node. The edges set $E^s = E \cup E'$, here $E' = \{(g, v_i)\}$ represents the influence from super node g to common nodes.

Given the recommendation social network G^s, topic distribute vector t, and budget k, **topic-aware IM problem** is to choose k seeds, the information propagate from these seeds and the influence spread can be maximized. To get set $S^* = S^*(k,t)$, and $S^* = \arg\max_{|S| \leq k, S \subseteq V}(\sigma(S \cup \{g\}, t))$, $\sigma(S \cup \{g\}, t)$ is the influence spread of S and super node g under topic t.

4 Topic-Aware Influence Maximization Algorithm TIP

4.1 Influence Spread

To compute the influence spread of common node u, we first analyze the ways that u will influence the other nodes. Nodes can be activated directly by user u if there is an edge between them. Nodes can also be activated indirectly by u if there exists path between them. The path from u to v ($v \neq u$) is $p_{u \to v} = \langle u, v_2, \ldots, v_m = v \rangle (m \geq 2)$. The influence probability of path p is:

$$pro(p) = \prod_{i=1}^{m-1} w(v_i, v_{i+1}) \qquad (6)$$

After searching the paths from u, we calculate the influence probability of u on nodes which can be affected by it. Let $\sigma(u)$ be the number of nodes that can be influenced by u. The paths set $Path_{T \to v} = \{p | p = <u, \ldots, v>, u \in T\}$ contains all the paths starting from u. Accordingly, the paths set from node set $T \subseteq V$ to node v is $Path_{u \to T}$. The influence spread of node u is represented as $O_u = \{v | <\ldots, v> \in Path_{u \to v}\}$. The approximate influence of node u is

$$\sigma(u) = 1 + \sum_{v \in O_u} \sigma^v(u) \qquad (7)$$

In the above formula, 1 is the influence of node u itself. $\sigma^v(u)$ is the probability of node u on the specific node $v \in O_u$. Given the path set $Path_{u \to v}$, the influence of u on v is the complement of all paths are failure, the formula is as follows:

$$\sigma^v(u) = 1 - \prod_{p \in Path_{u \to v}} (1 - pro(p)) \qquad (8)$$

The marginal influence of node u is represented as $MI(u) = \sigma(S \cup \{u\}) - \sigma(S)$. The marginal influence of u depends only on the sum of the influence from u to $v \in O_u \cup \{u\}$ as shown in the following formula:

$$MI(u) = 1 + \sum_{v \in O_u \cup \{u\}} MI^v(u) \qquad (9)$$

Here $MI^v(u)$ is marginal influence from u to v, it can be computed as follows:

$$MI^v(u) = \sigma^v(S \cup \{u\}) - \sigma^v(S) \qquad (10)$$

4.2 TIP Algorithm

In the TSID model, the super node can begin to active the user before the seed is selected, nodes that have been activated by the super node cannot be used as the seeds candidate. Super nodes can activate multiple nodes at the same time, these nodes may be far away, they start from different regions of the network at the same time, can quickly affect a wider range of network users.

The pseudo code of TIP algorithm is as follows:

Input: $G=(V^s, E^s, W)$, k, path threshold θ

Output: S seed nodes set

1) $S\leftarrow\phi$, $L\leftarrow\phi$
2) while $|S|<k$
3)   for every $v\in V$
4)   if (v is activated)
5) $L\leftarrow L\cup\{v\}$
6)   endfor
7)   for each $v\in V$
8)   calculate the marginal influence $MI(v)$ of v
9)   endfor
10) $s=\arg\max_{v\in V}MI(v)$
11) $S\leftarrow S\cup\{s\}$; $L\leftarrow L\cup\{s\}$
12) endwhile
   return S

---

5 Experiments

5.1 Dataset

We use Douban network as our data. Douban data contains 485853 nodes and 4409997 edges. Contrast algorithms include C-Greedy and L_GAUP.

5.2 Experiment Results and Analysis

We do experiments to find the optimal threshold value θ trading off between the accuracy and efficiency. Figure 2 shows the effect of the threshold on the accuracy of the algorithm, Fig. 3 shows the impact on the time of the implementation.

As can be seen from Fig. 2, with the decrease of threshold, the influence spread will be increased. But when threshold $\theta = 1/320$, the curve of growth slowed down significantly, that means the stable propagation point is here. Figure 3 shows the running time as the threshold decreases, it first increase a little, later at threshold $\theta = 1/640$ the running time increases quickly. According to the above two figures, TIP algorithm can get the best compromise at $\theta = 1/320$.

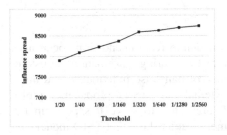

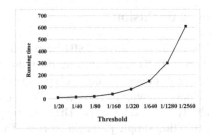

Fig. 2. Influence spread VS θ **Fig. 3.** Running time VS θ

We compare the accuracy and efficiency of TIP, G-Greedy and L_GAUP algorithm by varying the topic distribution. Figures 4 and 5 are respectively the influence spread and execution time of the algorithms. Figures 6 and 7 are the spread and time on multiple topics.

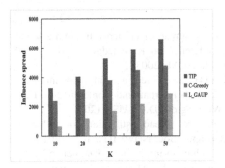

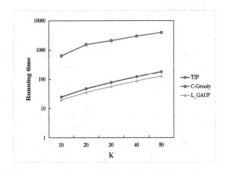

Fig. 4. Running time vs. K with one topic   **Fig. 5.** Running time vs. K with one topic

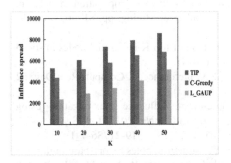

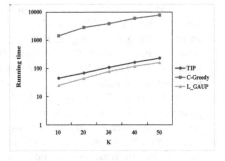

Fig. 6. Influence spread with multiple topic   **Fig. 7.** Running time with multiple topic

As can be seen from Figs. 4 and 5, the spread of TIP algorithm is the largest, this is because it takes into account the impact of the super node. Figures 6 and 7 are the results of the execution time of three algorithms. TIP is two times faster than C-Greedy. We can see that TIP is more effective than traditional algorithm, it can not only ensure the time efficiency but also has a greater influence spread.

6 Conclusion

We propose a novel TSID propagation model in online recommendation social networks. TSID takes into account three impact factors during information diffusion: external influence from website, internal influence of pair wise individuals, and individuals' preference for topics. We induce the external and internal propagation probability in TSID model. Then we propose TIP algorithm to solve this problem by exploiting simple propagation path. The experiment results show that TSID model can well describe mixed topic information propagation for recommendation social networks and TIP performs well in terms of influence spread and response time.

Acknowledgment. This work was supported by the National Science Foundation of China (61632010, 61100048, 61370222), the Natural Science Foundation of Heilongjiang Province (F2016034), the Education Department of Heilongjiang Province (12531498).

References

1. Kempe, D., Kleinberg, J., Tardos, É.: Maximizing the spread of influence through a social network. In: 9th ACM SIGKDD International Conference on Knowledge Discovery and Data Mining, pp. 137–146, Washington, D.C., USA. ACM (2003)
2. Goyal, A., Wei, L., Lakshmanan, L.V.S.: SIMPATH: an efficient algorithm for influence maximization under the linear threshold model. In: 11th International Conference on Data Mining, pp. 211–220. IEEE Computer Society, Washington, D.C., USA (2011)
3. Lu, Z., Fan, L., Wu, W., et al.: Efficient influence spread estimation for influence maximization under the linear threshold model. Comput. Soc. Netw. **1**(1), 1–19 (2014)
4. You, Q., Hu, W., Wu, O.: Influence maximization in human-intervened social networks. In: 24th International Conference on Social Influence Analysis, IJCAI, pp. 9–14, Buenos Aires, Argentina (2015)
5. Barbieri, N., Bonchi, F., Manco, G.: Topic-aware social influence propagation models. In: 5th ACM International Conference on Web Search and Data Mining, pp. 81–90, Brussels, Belgium, New York, USA (2012)
6. Zhou, J., Zhang, Y., Cheng, J.: Preference-based mining of top-K influential nodes in social networks. Future Gener. Comput. Syst. **31**, 40–47 (2014)
7. Guo, J.F., Lv, J.G.: Influence maximization based on preference. J. Comput. Res. Dev. **52** (02), 533–541 (2015)
8. Chen, W., Lin, T., Yang, C.: Real-time topic-aware influence maximization using preprocessing. In: Thai, M., Nguyen, N., Shen, H. (eds.) CSoNet 2015. LNCS, vol. 9197, pp. 1–13. Springer, Cham (2015). https://doi.org/10.1007/978-3-319-21786-4_1
9. Zhu, J., Yin, X., Wang, Y., Li, J., Zhong, Y., Li, Y.: Structural holes theory-based influence maximization in social network. In: Ma, L., Khreishah, A., Zhang, Y., Yan, M. (eds.) WASA 2017. LNCS, vol. 10251, pp. 860–864. Springer, Cham (2017). https://doi.org/10.1007/978-3-319-60033-8_73
10. Chen, S., Fan, J., Li, G.: Online topic-aware influence maximization. Proc. VLDB Endow. **8** (6), 666–677 (2015)

11. Niu, J., Wang, D., Stojmenovic, M.: How does information diffuse in large recommendation social networks? IEEE Netw. **30**(4), 28–33 (2016)
12. Kim, J., Kim, S.K., Yu, H.: Scalable and parallelizable processing of influence maximization for large-scale social networks? In: 29th International Conference on Data Engineering, pp. 266–277. IEEE Computer Society, Washington, D.C. (2013)
13. Liu, X., Liao, X., Li, S., et al.: On the shoulders of giants: incremental influence maximization in evolving social networks. Comput. Sci. (2015)

A Novel Channel Extraction Method Based on Partial Orthogonal Matching Pursuit Algorithm

Wang Xiangjun[✉], Dou Zheng, and Lin Yun

Harbin Engineering University, Harbin 150001, HLJ, China
wangxiangjun0216@hrbeu.edu.cn

Abstract. Channelization has proven to be very successful in digital receivers application, and it is a critical component of reducing the sampling rate process. Compressed sensing has been widely applied to reconstruct sparse signals sampled at sub-Nyquist rate. In this paper, a stable and fast algorithm termed Partial Orthogonal Matching Pursuit (POMP) is proposed for a channelized digital receiver. It is suitable for sparse channels in wide bandwidth. The novel POMP algorithm is analyzed and compared with the conventional channelization method based on polyphase filters, and numerical simulations demonstrate that the POMP detection not only achieves the basic functions of a channelizer, but also outperforms a polyphase channelizer. Moreover, the POMP algorithm is an efficient method to suppress the aliasing and leaking between channels.

Keywords: POMP algorithm · Channelizer · Channel extraction
Compressed sensing

1 Introduction

As the frequency spectrum distribution in the communication environment becomes increasingly complex, digital receivers are required to have a larger bandwidth, and a simple yet efficient channelizer is required to separate the band-of-interest (BOI) at the same arriving time. The original channelization structure consists of a bank of mixers and low-pass filters structure [1], which results in much computational consumption. To reduce computational complexity, Harris researched a polyphase channelizer which is an efficient implementation of the conventional channelizer, and reviewed the procession how a conventional channelizer is converted to a standard polyphase channelizer [2]. Harris summarized the advantages of a multichannel polyphase filter bank: simultaneously performing the uncoupled tasks of down conversion, bandwidth limiting and sampling rate change. Due to the above advantage, the polyphase channelizer structure has been extensively studied. Chen established a polyphase analysis channelizer and a polyphase synthesis channelizer utilizing analysis filter banks and synthesis filter banks respectively [3]. Recently, Kim proposed an

© ICST Institute for Computer Sciences, Social Informatics and Telecommunications Engineering 2018
G. Sun and S. Liu (Eds.): ADHIP 2017, LNICST 219, pp. 204–212, 2018.
https://doi.org/10.1007/978-3-319-73317-3_25

efficient channelizer based on polyphase filter banks and the channels can be arbitrarily resampled to any desired rate [4].

Even though the polyphase channelizer outperforms the traditional channelizer and shows its effectiveness, there inevitably exist aliasing and leaking between channels due to filters' non-rectangular coefficient. Moreover, there are not many signals exist at the same time within a certain bandwidth, especially for some military bands and electronic reconnaissance bands. Hence many channels do not exist any signals, causing many processes in a channelizer to be wasted.

The compressed sensing (CS) theory can exploit the sparseness of the spectrum distribution, and reduce the useless work of the spectrum channelization. The core idea of CS is to recover a lot of useful information with a few linear measurements. The well-known approach has been extensively studied these years in the field of communications, such as sparse channel estimation [5,6], sparse targets detection [7], and cognitive radio [8]. Many algorithms have been proposed to recover sparse signals, and the Orthogonal Matching Pursuit (OMP) algorithm has been widely used due to its implementation simplicity and low computational complexity. The OMP algorithm is a greedy algorithm for sparse approximation in the field of compressed sensing [9].

In this paper, we propose a novel Partial Orthogonal Matching Pursuit algorithm (POMP). As the name implies, we first reconstruct one channel which contains the strongest signal using several atoms in sensing matrix. Then we remove the channel from the whole frequency band. After that we find the next strongest signal and reconstruct the channel contains it, and then remove the second channel. The process is recycled until there is no signal detected. In each cycle the intermediate frequency (IF) signals are equivalent to down-convert to baseband, and the sampling rate is also reduced. The POMP algorithm not only achieves the effect of down-conversion, down-sampling and bandwidth limiting, which are core functions of a polyphase channelizer, but also avoids aliasing and leaking phenomena between channels.

2 Background Knowledge

In this section, we suggest to utilize the location relationship between the signals distributed in spectrum and the corresponding columns in sensing matrix to achieve channel extraction.

The Polyphase Channelizer. The basic functions of a polyphase channelizer are down-conversion, bandwidth limiting, and down-sampling. However, due to the non-ideal characteristic of the filter, there inevitably exist aliasing or blind spot between channels, as shown in Fig. 1.

The channel aliasing will cause the error detection of signals, while the blind spot between channels may lead to the loss of signals' detection. Neither of the phenomena is expected to exist.

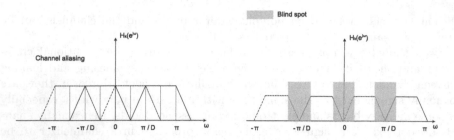

Fig. 1. The aliasing and blind spot phenomena between channels. Both phenomena are caused by the non-rectangular feature of filters.

The OMP Theory. The fundamental problem in compressed sensing (CS) is to recovery a high-dimensional vector x from a small number of linear measurements y [10], the linear measurements are given by:

$$y = \Phi \cdot x = \Phi \cdot \Psi \cdot \theta \tag{1}$$

where $x \in C^{N \times 1}$ denotes the original signal in the time domain in the field of communication, and x is K-sparse under the DFT dictionary matrix Ψ, so $x = \Psi \cdot \theta$. θ is the sparse express of x under the DFT sparse bases. $y \in C^{M \times 1}$ represents the vector obtained by the linear measurements of x, Φ represents the measurement matrix. The sensing matrix A is defined here:

$$A = \Phi \cdot \Psi \tag{2}$$

where $A \in R^{M \times N}$ is also known as the dictionary which contains the atoms that we need in the procession of OMP, and A satisfies the Restricted Isometry Property (RIP) of order $2K$. The core idea of the OMP algorithm is to find a biggest projection of measurement y from the dictionary A. In other words, the atom correlated to the maximum inner product value between sensing matrix A and the current residual needs to be singled out in each iteration. The residual is updated in each iteration, which can be expressed as follows:

$$r_k = y - A\hat{\theta}_k \tag{3}$$

where k represents the iteration times which equals to the sparsity of the signal, and the non-zero items in θ stand for the position where signals exist in the frequency band. We generally use the least square method to minimize the residual r_k. In the process of OMP, we find the fact that,the location of signals, non-zero items in θ and the corresponding atoms in dictionary A is one to one correspondence.

3   POMP Algorithm Model

Based on the theoretical analysis and the issues raised above, this section describes the process of POMP algorithm that we propose for extracting channels containing signals from the BOI. As the projection of y on the dictionary

A corresponds to the position of the nonzero terms in θ. We can use partial atoms in A to extract several channels respectively, instead of reconstructing the whole BOI.

For a BOI within an intermediate frequency band, we first find the position of the strongest signal in the BOI via calculating the inner product values between columns in A and the current residual. The process can be expressed by formula (4).

$$pos = argmax| < A_{pos}, r_k > |, (pos = 1, 2, \cdots, N) \tag{4}$$

where r_k represents the current residual at the kth iteration, and the initial residual is y. A_{pos} denotes the posth atom of the sensing matrix A. $| <, > |$ is the sign of inner product. After recording the atom corresponding to the maximum inner product value, we use partial columns of A to recovery signals in a channel range with the strongest signal as the center of the channel. In other words, the pursuiting range of the OMP algorithm in each iteration is reduced to one channel, rather than the entire BOI. The formulas (5), (6) and (7) are executions for reconstructing one channel, and are operated repeatedly until all signals in a channel are fully recovered, the iteration times is equal to the sparsity of the channel.

$$A_\lambda = argmax| < A_\lambda, r_{k-1} > |,$$
$$((pos - \frac{N}{2 \times chan}) \leq \lambda \leq (pos + \frac{N}{2 \times chan})) \tag{5}$$

$$\hat{\theta}_k = argmin \parallel y - A_\Lambda \theta_k \parallel_2 \tag{6}$$

$$r_k = y - A_\Lambda \hat{\theta}_k \tag{7}$$

The iteration range is determined in formula (5), where $chan$ denotes the amount of the channels, and $\frac{N}{2 \times chan}$ represents half-channel range. The signal is estimated by the least squares method in formula (6), where $\parallel \cdot \parallel_2$ is the sign of L2-norm. $A_\Lambda = A_\Lambda \cup A_\lambda$ represents the support set which is expanded in each iteration. The signification of formula (6) is to make the reconstructed measurement closer to the initial measurement y. Residual is updated in each iteration, as shown in formula (7), the subscript k denotes the iteration time. The iteration ends when k equals to the sparsity k_{max}, where k_{max} represents the amount of signals in each channel.

After recovering a channel, the signals contained in this channel is subtracted from the BOI x, as shown in line (15) in Algorithm 1. The corresponding measurement y has also been updated. The atoms within a channel range is screened out, we set these columns to zero for the purpose of simplicity, so we get a new sensing matrix A, as shown in line (17) in Algorithm 1, where M denotes the measurement times. Then we find the position of the strongest signal from the remained signals, and recover the second channel using partial columns of A, with the strongest signal lies in the center of it. Recycling like this, until the amplitude of the strongest signal we find is less than the threshold Th (Th represents the detection threshold, which is not analyzed here in detail), the whole reconstruction procession ends. We summarize the process in Algorithm 1.

Algorithm 1. POMP algorithm model

1: **input:** ϕ, y,x,A,k_{max},Th,$chan$
   channel number t
2: **initial:** $t = 1$, $A_\Lambda = \emptyset$
3: **while** $\max | < A_{pos}, y > | > Th$ $(pos = 1, 2, \cdots, N)$ **do**
4:    $k = 1$
5:    $r_0 = y$
6:    $pos = argmax| < A_{pos}, y > | \ (pos = 1, 2, \cdots, N)$
7:    **while** $k < k_{max}$ **do**
8:       **find:** $A_\lambda = argmax| < A_\lambda, r_{k-1} > |$,
9:       $((pos - \frac{N}{2 \times chan}) \leq \lambda \leq (pos + \frac{N}{2 \times chan}))$
10:      **enlarge:** $A_\Lambda = [A_\Lambda, A_\lambda]$
11:      $\hat{\theta}_{t_k} = argmin \| y - A_\Lambda \theta_{t_k} \|_2$
12:      **update:** $r_k = y - A_\Lambda \hat{\theta}_{t_k}$
13:      $k = k + 1$
14:    **end while**
15:    **update:** $x = x - \Psi \hat{\theta}_{t_k}$
16:    **update:** $y = \phi \times x$
17:    **update:** $A(:, ((pos - \frac{N}{2 \times chan}) : (pos + \frac{N}{2 \times chan}))) = zeros(M, \frac{N}{chan})$
18:    $t = t + 1$
19: **end while**
20: **output:** the frequency vector per channel θ_t

Based on the algorithm mentioned above, we only need partial columns instead of all columns in sensing matrix A to extract channels which contain signals, as long as the BOI is sparse in frequency. So the iteration number is less than the number required for full band reconstruction. Certainly, with the number of signals increase, and the distribution of them is relatively uniform, the number of channels and iterations will increase accordingly.

4 Numerical Simulations

The POMP algorithm and a ten-channels polyphase channelizer are implemented and simulated in MATLAB. In order to compare the performance of the two methods, we use them to process the same signal which is sparse in frequency domain, and the original signal can be demonstrated in time domain and frequency domain as Fig. 2.

In POMP algorithm, the measurement times M is 64, which is determined by $K \log(N/K)$, and the iteration time in each channel is determined by the sparsity K. In channelization method, there are fifty-percent aliasing between channels. The passband and the stopband of the prototype filter are $f_s/(2 \times 10)$ and $f_s/(2 \times 5)$ respectively, which causes the down-sampling time to be half of the channel numbers. The taps of the polyphase filters are polyphase components of the prototype filter's taps, and the order of the prototype filter is 100.

We process the signal in Fig. 2 utilizing a polyphase channelizer and the POMP method respectively. Then we get results shown in Figs. 3 and 4.

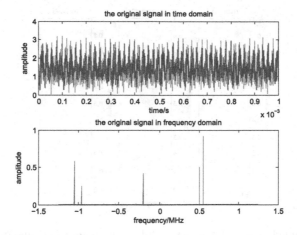

Fig. 2. The original signal in time domain and in frequency domain. The signal is noise-free, complex valued and generated in time domain. The centre frequency is zero, and the sampling rate is 2.5 MHz. The original signal consists of a few single-frequency signals which are generated randomly.

Figure 3 shows the division of the original signal by a ten-channel polyphase channelizer. Due to the aliasing phenomenon, the sampling rate per channel is 0.5 MHz, which is one-fifth of the original sampling rate. We can also notice that the aliasing occurs in the sixth and the ninth channels, which will cause misjudgment to the subsequent signal processing.

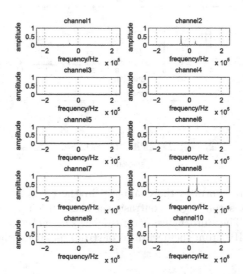

Fig. 3. The division of the original signal by a ten-channel polyphase channelizer. The signals in channel 9 and channel 6 don't exist actually, it is caused by the aliasing between channels.

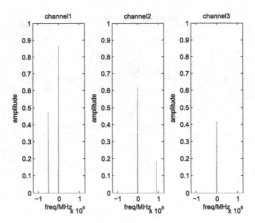

Fig. 4. The channel extracting using POMP algorithm. The amount of channels depends on the number and the intensive degree of signals. Here we need three channels to extract all the signals. The strongest signal in each channel lies in the center of the channel. The three channels are arranged according to the intensity of the center signal.

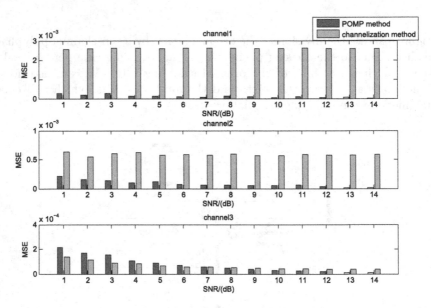

Fig. 5. The first figure contrasts the channel 8 in the channelizer and channel 1 in POMP algorithm. The second figure contrasts the channel 5 in the channelizer and the channel 3 in POMP. The third figure contrasts the channel 2 in the channelizer and the channel 2 in POMP. From the overall reconstruction effect, the POMP algorithm performs better.

Figure 4 shows the extracting of the channels using POMP algorithm. For this simulation experiment, we only need three channels to extract all the signals.

The sampling rate per channel is 0.25 MHz, which is one-tenth of the original sampling rate. The signal locates at the center of each channel are sorted in descending order of energy. We can notice that the POMP algorithm can also achieve the tasks of down-sampling rate, down-conversion, and band limiting. Besides, the aliasing phenomenon has been good to avoid.

We compare the mean square error (MSE) of the signal extracted by the two methods respectively with the original signal at different SNRs. The results are shown in Fig. 5. We notice that the POMP performs significantly better in the first and the second figures. The effect of POMP reconstruction is relatively poor at low SNRs as shown in the third figure, however, with the SNRs increase, the POMP reconstruction errors drop relatively rapid.

These results demonstrate that the performance of the POMP algorithm is better than a polyphase channelizer. We further compare the efficiency of the two methods by calculating the CPU time that the two methods take to reconstruct the whole BOI at different SNRs. The average CPU execution time of the POMP algorithm is 1.618240 s, while the channelizer is 2.086837 s, which demonstrate that the POMP algorithm is more efficient.

5   Conclusion

We study the position relationship among the signal distribution, non-zero items in θ and the corresponding columns in sensing matrix A, and propose the POMP algorithm for extracting channels contain signals from BOI. The proposed algorithm is implemented and simulated, and compared with a ten-channel polyphase channelizer by processing the same signal. The numerical results demonstrate that when the BOI is sparse, the POMP algorithm performs better than a polyphase channelizer. The proposed algorithm not only achieves the tasks of down-convertion, down-sampling and band-limiting, which are core functions for a channelizer, but also avoids the aliasing or leaking that a channelizer may cause.

Acknowledgment. This work is supported by the Key Development Program of Basic Research of China (JCKY2013604B001), the National Natural Science Foundation of China (61301095), the Funda-mental Research Funds for the Central Universities (GK2080260148 and HEUCF1508).This paper is funded by the International Exchange Program of Harbin Engineering University for Innovation-oriented Talents Cultivation.Meantime, all the authors declare that there is no conflict of interests regarding the publication of this article.We gratefully thank of very useful discussions of reviewers.

References

1. Namgoong, W.: A channelized digital ultrawideband receiver. IEEE Trans. Wirel. Commun. **2**(3), 502–510 (2003)
2. Harris, F.J., Dick, C., Rice, M.: Digital receivers and transmitters using polyphase filter banks for wireless communications. IEEE Trans. Microw. Theory Tech. **51**(4), 1395–1412 (2003)

3. Chen, X., Harris, F.J., Venosa, E., Rao, B.D.: Non-maximally decimated analysis/synthesis filter banks: applications in wideband digital filtering. IEEE Trans. Signal Process. **62**(4), 852–867 (2014)
4. Kim, S.C., Bhattacharyya, S.S.: A wideband front-end receiver implementation on GPUs. IEEE Trans. Signal Process. **64**(10), 2602–2612 (2016)
5. Berger, C.R., Zhou, S., Preisig, J.C., Willett, P.: Sparse channel estimation for multicarrier underwater acoustic communication: from subspace methods to compressed sensing. IEEE Trans. Signal Process. **58**(3), 1708–1721 (2010)
6. Chen, P., Rong, Y., Nordholm, S., Duncan, A.J., He, Z.: Compressed sensing based channel estimation and impulsive noise cancelation in underwater acoustic OFDM systems. In: 2016 IEEE Region 10 Conference (TENCON), pp. 2539–2542, November 2016
7. Pan, J., Tang, J.: Sparse targets detection based on threshold orthogonal matching pursuit algorithm. In: 2016 IEEE Sixth International Conference on Communications and Electronics (ICCE), pp. 258–261, July 2016
8. Ridouani, M., Hayar, A., Haqiq, A.: Perform sensing and transmission in parallel in cognitive radio systems: spectrum and energy efficiency. Digit. Signal Process. **62**, 65–80 (2017). http://www.sciencedirect.com/science/article/pii/S1051200416301853
9. Davenport, M.A., Wakin, M.B.: Analysis of orthogonal matching pursuit using the restricted isometry property. IEEE Trans. Inf. Theory **56**(9), 4395–4401 (2010)
10. Wang, J., Shim, B.: Exact recovery of sparse signals using orthogonal matching pursuit: how many iterations do we need? IEEE Trans. Signal Process. **64**(16), 4194–4202 (2016)

Reliability Evaluation of DCell Networks

Xi Wang[1,2]($\boxtimes$), Funan He[1], Yuejuan Han[2], and Lantao You[3]

[1] School of Software and Services Outsourcing,
Suzhou Institute of Industrial Technology, Suzhou 215104, China
wangxi0414@163.com
[2] School of Computer Science and Technology,
Soochow University, Suzhou 215006, China
[3] School of Information Engineering, Suzhou Industrial Park Institute of Services
Outsourcing, Suzhou 215000, China

Abstract. Recently, the reliability evaluation of data center network (DCN) is important to the design and operation of DCNs. Extra connectivity determination and faulty networks structure analysis are two significant aspects for the reliability evaluation of DCNs. The DCell network is suitable for a massive data centers with high network capacity by only using cheap switches. A k-dimensional DCell built with n-port switches, denoted by $D_{k,n}$, is an $(n + k - 1)$-regular graph. In this paper, we firstly prove that the extra-h connectivity of $D_{k,n}$ for $n \geq 2$, $\kappa_h(D_{k,n}) = (k - 1)(h + 1) + n$ if $k \geq 2$ and $0 \leq h \leq n - 1$, and $\kappa_h(D_{k,n}) = (k - 1)(h + 1) + 2n - 2$ if $k \geq n + 1$ and $n \leq h \leq 2n - 1$, respectively. What's more, for any faulty node set $F \subseteq V(D_{k,n})$ with $|F| \leq \kappa_h(D_{k,n}) - 1$, we obtain that there contains a large connected component in $D_{k,n} - F$, and the rest of small connected components have not more than h nodes in total if $k \geq 2$ and $0 \leq h \leq n - 1$ (resp. $k \geq n + 1$ and $n \leq h \leq 2n - 1$). Our result can provide a proper measure for the reliability evaluation of the DCell network when it is used to model the topological structure of a large-scale DCN.

Keywords: DCell network · Reliability · Extra connectivity
Data center network

1 Introduction

With the development of web applications such as email, online search, web game, cloud video, and productivity components such as Map reduce [1] and GFS [2], huge data center network (DCN) with millions of servers will become available in some day. Microsoft implied that Azure, Hotmail, Bing, and some other web services will be storaged by a million servers [3], for instance. With the remorselessly rising in the scale of DCN, the complexity of a DCN can disadvantageously impact its reliability. In order to design and operation of a DCN, proper measures of reliability ought to be sought out. A DCN can be modeled by a simple connected-graph $G = (V(G), E(G))$, where $V(G)$ denotes

© ICST Institute for Computer Sciences, Social Informatics and Telecommunications Engineering 2018
G. Sun and S. Liu (Eds.): ADHIP 2017, LNICST 219, pp. 213–225, 2018.
https://doi.org/10.1007/978-3-319-73317-3_26

the node set with each node denotes a server, and $E(G)$ denotes the edge set with each edge denotes a link between servers, respectively. What's more, switches in a DCN can be identified as transparent devices of network [4]. Therefore, we can measure the reliability of a DCN (network for short) by using the graph parameters of its DCN.

The connectivity of a DCN as a traditional measure for the reliability of DCNs, is the minimum number of nodes eliminated to obtain the graph is disconnected or trivial, which is a worst case. In fact, this measure can accurately reflect the reliability of a small size DCN. However, some DCNs with large size have shown to can tolerate much more server failures while still keep connected. In other words, as one of the measures of reliability, the traditional connectivity would underestimates the ability of reliability of these large DCNs [5].

To counteract the weakness of the connectivity of a simple graph, Harary [6] proposed the definition of the restricted faulty nodes of a graph. Furthermore, Fabrega and Fiol [7,8] introduced the concept of extra connectivity and obtained the extra connectivity of graphs. Given a graph G and a node cut $F \in V(G)$, if each connected component of $G - F$ has not less than $h + 1$ nodes, then F is defined an extra-h node cut. The extra-h connectivity of G is the minimum cardinality of all extra-h node cuts (if exists), can be denoted by $\kappa_h(G)$. In a DCN, the status of the node has meaningless impact on the capability of the rest of graph when all the neighbors of a node are faulty. Thus, it is reasonable of the assumption that there is no isolated node on $G - F$, when we assume it is faulty. What's more, the structure study of an incomplete DCN with a large amount of faulty nodes is closely related to the extra connectivity of a DCN. The large connected component can be used to execute the operation of the DCN not have much capability degrade, when a disconnected DCN with massive faulty nodes contains a large connected component. Therefore, the extra connectivity is great important to the reliability of DCNs [5].

Since a complete graph K_n is nonseparable, $\kappa_h(K_n)$ does not exist with $0 \leq h \leq n - 1$. Furthermore, if G is not a complete graph, then $\kappa_0(G) = \kappa(G)$. Given a nonnegative integer h and graph G, it is quite difficult to calculate $\kappa_h(G)$. As a matter of fact, the existence of $\kappa_h(G)$ is still an open problem so far when $h \geq 1$. Only a little research achievements have been obtained on $\kappa_h(G)$ in some particular graphs [5,9–16]. For example, Zhu et al. [9] and Gu and Hao [10] showed that $\kappa_2(Q_n^3) = 6n - 7$, $\kappa_3(Q_n^k) = 8n - 12$ for $n \geq 3$, where Q_n^3 is the 3-ary n-cube, respectively. Lin et al. obtained that for the n-dimensional alternating group graph AG_n, $\kappa_1(AG_n) = 4n - 11$, $\kappa_2(AG_n) = 6n - 19$, and $\kappa_3(AG_n) = 8n - 28$ for $n \geq 5$ [11]. For any integer $n \geq 6$, Chang et al. proved that the 3-extra connectivity of an n-dimensional folded hypercube is $4n - 5$ [12]. For any integers $n \geq 4$ and $0 \leq h \leq n - 4$, Zhu et al. [5] showed that $\kappa_h(X_n) = n(h+1) - \frac{1}{2}h(h+3)$, where X_n is the n-dimensional bijective connection network. Furthermore, Yang and Lin studied a sharp lower bound of extra-h connectivity of X_n which improves the result in [5] for $n \geq 4$ and $0 \leq h \leq 2n - 1$ [13].

Recently, Guo et al. introduced a server-centric DCN named DCell [4], which have many advantages over traditional tree-based DCN, such as fault-tolerance, scalability, reliability, low cost, and so on. What's more, DCell originated substitutive design considered the server-centric DCNs, and inspired a lot of novel DCN structures such as FiConn [17], BCube [18], and CamCube [19]. Some combinatorial properties of a k-dimensional DCell built from n-port switches, $D_{k,n}$, such as diameter [4], symmetry [20], broadcasting [4], connectivity [4], restricted connectivity [21], node disjoint paths [22], one to one disjoint path covers [23], and Hamiltonian properties [24] have recently been studied. Particulary, these measurement results indicate that a $D_{k,n}$ has excellent combinatorial properties.

In this paper, we have obtained the extra-h connectivity of $D_{k,n}$ for $n \geq 2$, $\kappa_h(D_{k,n}) = (k-1)(h+1) + n$ when $k \geq 2$ and $0 \leq h \leq n-1$ (resp. $\kappa_h(D_{k,n}) = (k-1)(h+1) + 2n - 2$ when $k \geq n+1$ and $n \leq h \leq 2n-1$). What's more, we explore that there contains a large connected component in $D_{k,n} - F$, and the rest of small connected components have not more than h nodes in total if $|F| < \kappa_h(D_{k,n})$ for any two integers $k \geq 2$ and $0 \leq h \leq n-1$ (resp. $k \geq n+1$ and $n \leq h \leq 2n-1$).

This paper is organized in this way: We provide some definitions and preliminaries in Sect. 2. In Sect. 3, the extra-h connectivity of DCells are given. In the end, we conclude this paper in Sect. 4.

2   Preliminaries

We use G to denote a DCN. The node number of G is called the order of G. An edge of G with two end nodes u, v is denoted by (u, v). For any node $v \in V(G)$, let u be a neighbor of the node v or u is adjacent to the node v if $(u, v) \in E(G)$. If $V' \subseteq V(G)$, let $G[V']$ denote the sub-graph of G induced by a node subset $V' \in V(G)$ and let $G - V' = G[V(G) \setminus V']$. Then, let $N_G(V')$ denote the neighbor-set of V' such that $N_G(V') \in V(G-V')$ and let $A_G(V') = V' \cup N_G(V')$.

For $k \geq 0$ and $n \geq 2$, let $D_{k,n}$ denote a k-dimensional DCell built on n-port switches. Then, we use $t_{k,n}$ to denote the order in $D_{k,n}$ with $t_{0,n} = n$ and $t_{i,n} = t_{i-1,n}(t_{i-1,n} + 1)$ for $n \geq 2$, $k \geq 0$, and $i \in \{1, 2, \ldots, k\}$. Let $I_{0,n} = \{0, 1, \ldots, n-1\}$ and $I_{i,n} = \{0, 1, \ldots, t_{i-1,n}\}$ with $i \in \{1, 2, \ldots, k\}$. For any integer $1 \leq l \leq k$, let $V_{k,n}^l = \{u_k u_{k-1} \cdots u_l : u_i \in I_{i,n}$ and $i \in \{l, l+1, \ldots, k\}\}$. The definition of DCell $D_{k,n}$ is adopt from [4].

Definition 1. $D_{k,n}$ is a regular graph with node set $V_{k,n}^0$, where a node $u = u_k u_{k-1} \cdots u_0$ is adjacent to a node $v = v_k v_{k-1} \cdots v_0$ if and only if there exists an integer l with

(1) $u_k u_{k-1} \cdots u_l = v_k v_{k-1} \cdots v_l$,

(2) $u_{l-1} \neq v_{l-1}$,

(3) $u_{l-1} = v_0 + \sum_{j=1}^{l-2} (v_j \times t_{j-1,n})$ and $v_{l-1} = u_0 + \sum_{j=1}^{l-2} (u_j \times t_{j-1,n}) + 1$ with

$l > 1$.

Figure 1 shows the examples of $D_{k,n}$ with some small n and k. It is clear that $D_{k,n}$ is a $(n+k-1)$-regular graph with $t_{k,n}$ nodes. When all the three conditions of Definition 1 hold, we define that two neighbor nodes u, v have a differing bit

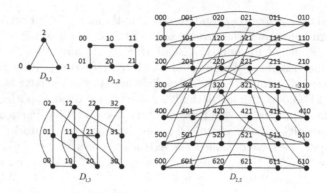

Fig. 1. Examples of $D_{k,n}$: $D_{0,3}$, $D_{1,3}$, $D_{1,2}$, and $D_{2,2}$.

of leftmost at position $l - 1$, denoted by d, the d-neighbor of u can be denoted by $(u)^d = v$ for $d \geq 1$. Usually, if $u = u_k u_{k-1} \cdots u_0$ is a node in $D_{k,n}$, let $(u)_i$ denote the i-th bit of u, and let $\sigma(u, i) = u_k u_{k-1} \cdots u_i$ for any $0 \leq i \leq k$. Clearly, $\sigma(u, 0) = u$. For any $\alpha \in V_{k,n}^l$ with $1 \leq l \leq k$, let $D_{l-1,n}^\alpha$ denote the graph that attained by adding the prefix α to address of every node of one copy of $D_{l-1,n}$. Clearly, $D_{l-1,n} \cong D_{l-1,n}^\alpha$.

In this paper, a set of nodes to be deleted will be denoted as F. Define $F_i = F \cap V(D_{k-1,n}^i)$ and $I = \{i : |F_i| \geq n + k - 2\}$ for each $i \in I_{k,n}$. Furthermore, let $F_I = \bigcup_{i \in I} F_i$, $\bar{I} = I_{k,n} \setminus I$, $D_{k-1,n}^{\bar{I}} = D_{k,n}[\bigcup_{i \in \bar{I}} V(D_{k-1,n}^i)]$, and $F_{\bar{I}} = \bigcup_{i \in \bar{I}} F_i$. These notations will be used throughout the paper.

The following studied results in DCells are helpful in our paper and thus showed as follows.

Lemma 1 [4]. *The connectivity of $D_{k,n}$ is $\kappa(D_{k,n}) = n + k - 1$.*

Lemma 2 [4]. *The order of $D_{k,n}$ satisfies $t_{k,n} \geq (n + \frac{1}{2})^{2^k} - \frac{1}{2}$.*

Lemma 3 [21]. *There exist $t_{k-1,n}$ node disjoint paths joining $D_{k-1,n}^i$ and $D_{k-1,n}^j$ with $i \neq j$.*

Lemma 4 [21]. *Let $F \subset V(D_{k,n})$ denote a faulty node set with $|F| \leq (h + 1)(k - 1) + n$. For any three integers $n \geq 2$, $k \geq 2$, $0 \leq h \leq n - 1$, $D_{k-1,n}^{\bar{I}} - F_{\bar{I}}$ is connected and $|I| \leq h + 1$.*

Lemma 5 [21]. *For any $n \geq 2$, $k \geq 2$, and any $H_0 \subseteq V(D_{0,n}^\alpha)$ and $H_1 \subseteq V(D_{0,n}^\beta)$ such that $\alpha, \beta \in V_{k,n}^1$ and $\alpha \neq \beta$, we have $|N_{D_{k,n}}(H_0) \cap H_1| \leq 1$.*

3   The Extra-h Connectivity of DCells

In fact, the extra-h connectivity for $h = 0$ on $D_{k,n}$ was gotten by Guo et al. [4] for any nonnegative integers $n \geq 2$ and $k \geq 0$. Nevertheless, the extra-h

connectivity for $h \geq 1$ of $D_{k,n}$ has not been obtained yet. In this section, for any integer $n \geq 2$, the extra-h connectivity when $0 \leq h \leq n - 1$ and $k \geq 2$, when $n \leq h \leq 2n - 1$ and $k \geq n + 1$ of $D_{k,n}$ will be studied, respectively.

Lemma 6. *Given an nonnegative integer $n \geq 2$, let $f_n(m) = mn - \frac{m(m-1)}{2}$ be a function of m, $f_n(m) = mn - \frac{m(m-1)}{2}$ is strictly monotonically increasing on m if $1 \leq m \leq n$.*

Proof. If $1 \leq m \leq n$, we can verify that

$$\frac{df}{dm} = n - \frac{1}{2}(2m - 1) = n - m + \frac{1}{2} > 0.$$

Thus, for any nonnegative integers m' and m such that $1 \leq m' < m \leq n$, we have $f_n(m') < f_n(m)$.

Lemma 7. *For any three integers $k \geq 2$, $n \geq 2$, and $0 \leq h \leq n - 1$, let $H \subseteq V(D_{k,n})$ with $|H| = h + 1$. Then, we have $|N_{D_{k,n}}(H)| \geq (k-1)(h+1) + n$.*

Proof. Let $S = \{\sigma(u, 1) : u \in H\} = \{s_1, s_2, \ldots, s_m\}$ with $1 \leq m \leq h + 1$. For any $1 \leq i \leq m$, let $H_i = V(D_{0,n}^{s_i}) \cap H$ and $h_i = |H_i|$. Obviously, $\sum_{i=1}^{m} h_i = |H| = h + 1$. Definition 1 and Lemma 5 implies that any node in H has exactly k neighbor(s) in $D_{k,n} - V(D_{0,n}^{s_i})$, H has at most $\frac{m(m-1)}{2}$ common neighbor(s) in $D_{k,n} - V(D_{0,n}^{s_i})$, and H_i has exactly $n - h_i$ neighbor(s) in $D_{0,n}^{s_i}$ for any $1 \leq i \leq m$. Thus, we have

$$|N_{D_{k,n}}(H)| \geq k(h+1) - \frac{m(m-1)}{2} + \sum_{1 \leq i \leq m} (n - h_i)$$

$$= (k-1)(h+1) + mn - \frac{m(m-1)}{2}.$$

For any m with $1 \leq m \leq h + 1 \leq n$, $mn - \frac{m(m-1)}{2} \geq n$ by Lemma 6. Then, we have

$$|N_{D_{k,n}}(H)| \geq (k-1)(h+1) + mn - \frac{m(m-1)}{2} \geq (k-1)(h+1) + n.$$

Lemma 8. *For any three integers $k \geq 2$, $n \geq 2$, and $0 \leq h \leq n - 1$, and any node set $F \subset V(D_{k,n})$ with $|F| \leq (k-1)(h+1) + n - 1$, $D_{k,n} - F$ contains a large connected component including not less than $t_{k,n} - |F| - h$ nodes.*

Proof. In this lemma, we will prove that by the induction on the integer h. If $h = 0$, $D_{k,n} - F$ is connected since $|F| \leq n + k - 2 < n + k - 1 = \kappa(D_{k,n})$, the result holds. Suppose that the result is correct when $h = \tau - 1$ with $n - 1 \geq \tau \geq 1$. Then, we will show that it is correct for $h = \tau$ ($1 \leq \tau \leq n - 1$). Assume that $H_1, H_2, \ldots, H_m, H_{m+1}$ are total the components of $D_{k,n} - F$, and $|V(H_{m+1})| = \max\{|V(H_1)|, |V(H_2)|, \ldots, |V(H_{m+1})|\}$. By Lemma 4, $D_{k-1,n}^{\bar{I}} - F_{\bar{I}}$ is connected. So $V(D_{k-1,n}^{\bar{I}} - F_{\bar{I}}) \subseteq V(H_{m+1})$. Let $r = |I| \leq \tau + 1$ and

$I = \{\alpha_1, \alpha_2, \ldots, \alpha_r\}$. The lemma holds for $r = 0$ since $D_{k,n} - F = D^{\bar{I}}_{k-1,n} - F_{\bar{I}}$ is connected by Lemma 4. To complete the proof, if $1 \le r \le \tau + 1$, we consider the following three cases.

Case 1. $D^{\alpha_i}_{k-1,n} - F_{\alpha_i}$ is connected for any $1 \le i \le r$.

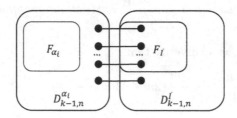

Fig. 2. An illustration for Case 1 in Lemma 8.

By Definition 1, each node in $D^i_{k-1,n}$ for $i \in I$ has accurately one neighbor in $D_{k,n} - V(D^i_{k-1,n})$. For any three integers $k \ge 2$, $n \ge 2$, $1 \le \tau \le n - 1$, and $\alpha_i \in I$, we have

$$|N_{D_{k,n}-V(D^{\alpha_i}_{k-1,n})}(V(D^{\alpha_i}_{k-1,n}) \setminus F_{\alpha_i})| = |V(D^{\alpha_i}_{k-1,n})| - |F_{\alpha_i}| = t_{k-1,n} - |F_{\alpha_i}|$$
$$> (k-1)(\tau+1) + n - 1 - |F_{\alpha_i}| \ge |F| - |F_{\alpha_i}|$$
$$= |F_{\bar{I}}| + (|F_I| - |F_{\alpha_i}|).$$

Thus, we can verify that there exists at least one node of $D^{\alpha_i}_{k-1,n} - F_{\alpha_i}$ to be adjacent to a node in $D^{\bar{I}}_{k-1,n} - F_{\bar{I}}$ for any $\alpha_i \in I$ (see Fig. 2). As a result, $D_{k,n} - F$ is connected. Hence, $D_{k,n} - F$ has a connected component including at least $t_{k,n} - |F| - \tau$ nodes, when $1 \le \tau \le n - 1$.

Case 2. Exactly one subgraph of $D^{\alpha_1}_{k-1,n} - F_{\alpha_1}, D^{\alpha_2}_{k-1,n} - F_{\alpha_2}, \ldots, D^{\alpha_r}_{k-1,n} - F_{\alpha_r}$ is disconnected.

Let $D^{\alpha_\lambda}_{k-1,n}$ be disconnected such that $1 \le \lambda \le r$. According to the Case 1, we can verify that $D_{k,n} - V(D^{\alpha_\lambda}_{k-1,n}) - (F \setminus F_{\alpha_\lambda})$ is connected. So, $V(D_{k,n} - V(D^{\alpha_\lambda}_{k-1,n}) - (F \setminus F_{\alpha_\lambda})) \subseteq V(H_{m+1})$. Then, we have $\bigcup_{i=1}^m V(H_i) \subseteq V(D^{\alpha_\lambda}_{k-1,n} - F_{\alpha_\lambda})$. What's more, we will show that the order in $\bigcup_{i=1}^m V(H_i)$ will not larger than $\tau - 1$. Suppose that the sum orders in $\bigcup_{i=1}^m V(H_i)$ is at least τ. By Lemma 7, we obtain $|N_{D_{k,n}}(\bigcup_{i=1}^m V(H_i))| \ge (k-1)(\tau+1) + n > |F|$, a contraction. Thus, $|\bigcup_{i=1}^m V(H_i)| \le \tau - 1$. Hence, $D_{k,n} - F$ has a connected component including at least $t_{k,n} - |F| - \tau$ nodes, where $1 \le \tau \le n - 1$.

Case 3. Exactly r' subgraphs of $D^{\alpha_1}_{k-1,n} - F_{\alpha_1}, D^{\alpha_2}_{k-1,n} - F_{\alpha_2}, \ldots, D^{\alpha_r}_{k-1,n} - F_{\alpha_r}$ are disconnected, where $2 \le r' \le r$.

Let $\{q_1, q_2, \ldots, q_{r'}\} \subseteq \{1, 2, \ldots, r\}$ such that $D^{\alpha_{q_i}}_{k-1,n}$ is disconnected for any $1 \le i \le r'$. According to the proof of Case 2, we can verify that $D_{k,n} - \bigcup_{i=1}^{r'} V(D^{\alpha_{q_i}}_{k-1,n}) - (F \setminus \bigcup_{i=1}^{r'} F_{\alpha_{q_i}})$ is connected. So, $V(D_{k,n} - \bigcup_{i=1}^{r'} V(D^{\alpha_{q_i}}_{k-1,n}) - (F \setminus \bigcup_{i=1}^{r'} F_{\alpha_{q_i}})) \subseteq V(H_{m+1})$. For any integers $1 \le \tau \le n - 1$ and $1 \le i \le r'$, we have

$$|F_{q_i}| \le |F| - \sum_{1 \le j \le r', j \ne i} |F_{q_j}| \le (k-1)(\tau+1) + n - 1 - (r'-1)(n+k-2)$$

$$\le (k-1)(\tau+1) + n - 1 - (k-1+\tau) \tag{3.1}$$

$$= (k-2)\tau + n - 1$$

and

$$|F \setminus \bigcup_{i=1}^{r'} F_{\alpha_{q_i}}| = |F| - \sum_{j=1}^{r'} |F_{q_j}|$$

$$\le (k-1)(\tau+1) + n - 1 - r'(n+k-2) \tag{3.2}$$

$$\le (k-1)(\tau-1) - (n-1).$$

By the induction hypothesis, $D_{k-1,n}^{\alpha_{q_i}} - F_{\alpha_{q_i}}$ contains a large component $A_{\alpha_{q_i}}$ including not less than $t_{k-1,n} - |F_{\alpha_{q_i}}| - (\tau-1)$ nodes if $1 \le i \le r'$. For any four integers $n \ge 2$, $k \ge 2$, $1 \le \tau \le n-1$, and $1 \le i \le r'$, we can verify

$$|V(A_{\alpha_{q_i}})| \ge t_{k-1,n} - |F_{\alpha_{q_i}}| - (\tau-1)$$

$$\ge (n+\frac{1}{2})^{2^{k-1}} - \frac{1}{2} - ((k-2)\tau + n - 1) - (\tau-1)$$

$$\ge 2(k-1)n - (k-1)\tau - n \ge (k-1)n$$

$$> (k-1)(\tau-1) - (n-1)$$

$$\ge |F \setminus \bigcup_{i=1}^{r'} F_{\alpha_{q_i}}|$$

by (3.1) and (3.2). Therefore, for any nonnegative integer $1 \le i \le r'$, $A_{\alpha_{q_i}}$ is connected to $D_{k,n} - \bigcup_{i=1}^{r'} V(D_{k-1,n}^{\alpha_{q_i}}) - (F \setminus \bigcup_{i=1}^{r'} F_{\alpha_\lambda})$ in $D_{k,n} - F$. That is, we have $V(A_{\alpha_{q_i}}) \subset V(H_{m+1})$. Let $V_{\alpha_{q_i}} = \bigcup_{i=1}^{m}(V(H_i) \cap V(D_{k-1,n}^{\alpha_{q_i}}))$ for any nonnegative integer $1 \le i \le r'$. Then, we will prove the order of $\bigcup_{i=1}^{r'} V_{\alpha_{q_i}}$ will not larger than $\tau - 1$. Furthermore, assume that the total order of $\bigcup_{i=1}^{r'} V_{\alpha_{q_i}}$ is at least τ. By Lemma 7, we have $|N_{D_{k,n}}(\bigcup_{i=1}^{r'} V_{\alpha_{q_i}})| \ge (k-1)(\tau+1) + n > |F|$, a contradiction. Thus, $|\bigcup_{i=1}^{r'} V_{\alpha_{q_i}}| \le \tau - 1$. Hence, $D_{k,n} - F$ has a connected component including at least $t_{k,n} - |F| - \tau$ nodes, where $1 \le \tau \le n-1$.

To sum up, the lemma holds for $h = \tau$. So far, the discussion of the lemma is complete.

Theorem 1. *Given any three integers $n \ge 2$, $0 \le h \le n-1$, and $k \ge 2$, the extra-h connectivity of $D_{k,n}$ is $\kappa_h(D_{k,n}) = (k-1)(h+1) + n$.*

Proof. Let H be a induced subgraph of the number of nodes is $h+1$ in $D_{0,n}^\alpha$ with $\alpha \in V_{k,n}^1$. Let $V' = V(H)$ and $F = N_{D_{k,n}}(V')$, obviously, $D_{k,n} - F$ is disconnected. Definition 1 implies that any node in V' has exactly k neighbors in $D_{k,n} - V(D_{0,n}^\alpha)$ and V' has accurately $n - (h+1)$ neighbors in $D_{0,n}^\alpha - V'$.

Thus, we have $|F| = (h+1)k + n - (h+1) = (h+1)(k-1) + n$. Furthermore, we will prove that the node set F is an extra-h node cut on $D_{k,n}$. Let $u \in V'$ and $\beta = (u)_k$. By Lemma 4, we can verify that $D_{k,n} - (V(D_{k-1,n}^\beta) \cup F)$ is connected. By Definition 1, each node in $D_{k-1,n}^\beta - A_{D_{k-1,n}^\beta}(V')$ has accurately one neighbor in $D_{k,n} - (V(D_{k-1,n}^\beta) \cup F)$. Therefore, $D_{k,n} - F$ contains two components, one of the components is $D_{k,n} - A_{D_{k,n}}(V')$ and the other of the components is H. Accordingly, for any three integers $n \geq 2$, $k \geq 2$, and $0 \leq h \leq n - 1$, we have

$$|V(D_{k,n} - A_{D_{k,n}}(V'))| \geq t_{k,n} - (|V'| + |F|) \geq (n + \frac{1}{2})^{2^k} - \frac{1}{2} - ((h+1)k + n)$$
$$\geq (k+2)n - ((h+1)k + n) \geq n$$
$$\geq h + 1.$$

Then, F is an extra-h node cut of $D_{k,n}$, and thus $\kappa_h(D_{k,n}) \leq (k-1)(h+1) + n$ for three integers $k \geq 2$, $n \geq 2$, and $0 \leq h \leq n - 1$.

Nevertheless, given three integers $n \geq 2$, $k \geq 2$, and $0 \leq h \leq n - 1$, if the number of nodes of each component of $D_{k,n} - F$ is not more than $h + 1$ with $F \subseteq V(D_{k,n})$, then $|F| \geq (k-1)(h+1) + n$ by Lemma 8. So, $\kappa_h(D_{k,n}) \geq (k-1)(h+1) + n$.

Hence, $\kappa_h(D_{k,n}) = (k-1)(h+1) + n$ for the three integers $n \geq 2$, $k \geq 2$, and $0 \leq h \leq n - 1$.

Lemma 9. *For any three nonnegative integers $n \geq 2$, $n \leq h \leq 2n - 1$, and $k \geq n + 1$, and any node sub-set $F \subset V(D_{k,n})$, if $|F| \leq (k-1)(h+1) + 2n - 2$, then, $D_{k-1,n}^{\bar{I}} - F_{\bar{I}}$ is connected and $|I| \leq h + 1$.*

Proof. In the beginning, we prove that $|I| \leq h + 1$. Assume that $|I| \geq h + 2$, according to definition of I, for any three nonnegative $n \geq 2$, $n \leq h \leq 2n - 1$, and $k \geq n + 1$, we have

$$|F| \geq (h+2)(n+k-2) \geq (k-1)(h+1) + 3(n-1) + (n+k-2)$$
$$> (k-1)(h+1) + 2n - 2.$$

In the following, we will show that $D_{k-1,n}^{\bar{I}} - F_{\bar{I}}$ is connected. For any $i \in \bar{I}$, $D_{k-1,n}^i - F_i$ is connected since $\kappa(D_{k-1,n}^i) = n + k - 2$ and $|F_i| \leq n + k - 3$. For any two $D_{k-1,n}^i$ and $D_{k-1,n}^j$ with distinct $i, j \in \bar{I}$, $k \geq 2$, and $n \geq 2$, according to

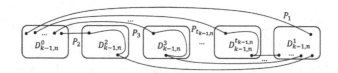

Fig. 3. An illustration of $t_{k-1,n}$ disjoint paths P_1, P_2, ... and $P_{t_{k-1,n}}$ joining $D_{k-1,n}^i$ and $D_{k-1,n}^j$ in Lemma 9.

Lemma 3, there exist $t_{k-1,n}$ disjoint paths P_1, P_2, ..., and $P_{t_{k-1,n}}$ joining $D_{k-1,n}^i$ and $D_{k-1,n}^j$ (see Fig. 3). Then, for any $n \geq 2$, $n \leq h \leq 2n - 1$, and $k \geq n + 1$, we have

$$t_{k-1,n} \geq (n + \frac{1}{2})2^{k-1} - \frac{1}{2} > 2kn \geq (k-1)2n + 2n$$
$$> (k-1)(h+1) + 2n - 2.$$

Thus, we can verify that there exists a path without any failure joining $D_{k-1,n}^i$ and $D_{k-1,n}^j$ in $D_{k-1,n}^{\bar{I}} - F_{\bar{I}}$ for any two distinct $i, j \in \bar{I}$. Then, $D_{k-1,n}^{\bar{I}} - F_{\bar{I}}$ is connected.

Lemma 10. *Given an integer $n \geq 2$, let $g_n(m) = 2mn - \frac{m(m+1)}{2} - n^2 + n$ be a function of m, $g_n(m) = 2mn - \frac{m(m+1)}{2} - n^2 + n$ is strictly monotonically increasing on m if $n + 1 \leq m \leq 2n - 1$.*

Proof. When $n+1 \leq m \leq 2n-1$, we have $\frac{dg}{dm} = 2n - \frac{1}{2}(2m+1) = 2n - m - \frac{1}{2} > 0$. So, for any two positive integers m' and m such that $n + 1 \leq m' < m \leq 2n - 1$, we have $g_n(m') < g_n(m)$.

Lemma 11. *For any three three integers $n \geq 2$, $k \geq n+1$, and $n \leq h \leq 2n - 1$, let $H \subseteq V(D_{k,n})$ and $|H| = h+1$. Then, we have $|N_{D_{k,n}}(H)| \geq (k-1)(h+1) + 2n - 1$.*

Proof. Let $S = \{\sigma(u, 1) : u \in H\} = \{s_1, s_2, \ldots, s_m\}$ with $2 \leq m \leq h + 1$. For any $1 \leq i \leq m$, let $H_i = V(D_{0,n}^{s_i}) \cap H$ and $h_i = |H_i|$. Obviously, $\sum_{i=1}^{m} h_i = |H| = h + 1$. When $2 \leq m \leq n$, similar to the result of Lemma 7, we can verify

$$|N_{D_{k,n}}(H)| \geq (k-1)(h+1) + mn - \frac{m(m-1)}{2}.$$

When $n + 1 \leq m \leq 2n$, let $T_1 = \bigcup_{i=1}^{n} H_i$ and $T_2 = \bigcup_{i=n+1}^{m} H_i$. Definition 1 and Lemma 5 implies that any node in H has exactly k neighbors in $D_{k,n} - \bigcup_{i=1}^{m} V(D_{0,n}^{s_i})$, H_i has exactly $n - h_i$ neighbor(s) in $D_{0,n}^{s_i}$ for any $1 \leq i \leq m$, T_1 has not more than $\frac{n(n-1)}{2}$ common neighbor(s) in $\bigcup_{i=1}^{n} V(D_{0,n}^{s_i})$, and T_2 has not more than $\frac{(m-n)(m-n-1)}{2} + (m - n)$ common neighbors in $\bigcup_{i=1}^{m} V(D_{0,n}^{s_i})$. Thus, we have

$$|N_{D_{k,n}}(H)| \geq k(h+1) + \sum_{i=1}^{m}(n - h_i) - \frac{n(n-1)}{2} - \left(\frac{(m-n)(m-n-1)}{2} + m - n\right)$$
$$= (k-1)(h+1) + 2mn - \frac{m(m+1)}{2} - n^2 + n.$$

For any m with $2 \leq m \leq n$, by Lemma 6, we have

$$mn - \frac{m(m-1)}{2} \geq 2n - 2. \tag{3.3}$$

For any m with $n + 1 \leq m \leq 2n - 1$, by Lemma 10, we have

$$2mn - \frac{m(m+1)}{2} - n^2 + n \geq \frac{n(n+3)}{2} - 1. \tag{3.4}$$

For $m = 2n$, we have

$$2mn - \frac{m(m+1)}{2} - n^2 + n = n^2. \tag{3.5}$$

Thus, by (3.3), (3.4), and (3.5), we have

$$|N_{D_{k,n}}(H)| \geq (k-1)(h+1) + \min\{2n-2, \frac{n(n+3)}{2} - 1, n^2\}$$
$$= (h+1)(k-1) + 2n - 2.$$

So far, $|N_{D_{k,n}}(H)| \geq (k-1)(h+1) + 2n - 1$ for $n \geq 2$, $n \leq h \leq 2n - 1$, and $k \geq n + 1$.

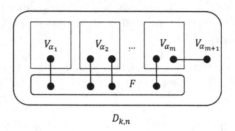

Fig. 4. An illustration of Lemma 12.

Lemma 12. *For any three integers $n \geq 2$, $n \leq h \leq 2n - 1$, and $k \geq n + 1$, and any node sub-set $F \subset V(D_{k,n})$ with $|F| \leq (k-1)(h+1) + 2n - 2$, $D_{k,n} - F$ contains a large component including not less than $t_{k,n} - |F| - h$ nodes.*

Proof. Assume that $H_1, H_2, \ldots, H_m, H_{m+1}$ are all the components of $D_{k,n} - F$, and the number of nodes of H_{m+1} is the largest. By Lemma 9, $D^{\bar{I}}_{k-1,n} - F_{\bar{I}}$ is connected. So, $V(D^{\bar{I}}_{k-1,n} - F_{\bar{I}}) \subseteq V(H_{m+1})$. Let $r = |I| \leq h + 1$ and $I = \{\alpha_1, \alpha_2, \ldots, \alpha_r\}$. Then, let $V_{\alpha_i} = \bigcup_{i=1}^{m} V(H_i) \cap V(D^{\alpha_i}_{k-1,n})$ for any $1 \leq i \leq r$. Furthermore, we will show the order in $\bigcup_{i=1}^{r} V_{\alpha_i}$ does not exceed h. We assume that the sum of orders in $\bigcup_{i=1}^{r} V_{\alpha_i}$ is at least $h + 1$. By Lemma 11, we have $|N_{D_{k,n}}(\bigcup_{i=1}^{r} V_{\alpha_i})| \geq (k-1)(h+1) + 2n - 2 > |F|$, a contraction. Thus, we have $\bigcup_{i=1}^{r} |V_{\alpha_i}| \leq h$ (see Fig. 4). Then, for any $1 \leq i \leq r$, let $A_{\alpha_i} = V(D^{\alpha_i}_{k-1,n} - F_{\alpha_i} - V_{\alpha_i})$, we have

$$|A_{\alpha_i}| \geq t_{k-1,n} - |F| - h \geq (k-1)(h+1) + 2n - 2 > |F|.$$

Therefore, A_{α_i} is connected to $D^{\bar{I}}_{k-1,n} - F_{\bar{I}}$ in $D_{k,n} - F$ and thus $A_{\alpha_i} \subseteq V(H_{m+1})$ for any $1 \leq i \leq r$. Hence, $D_{k,n} - F$ has a connected component including at least $t_{k,n} - |F| - h$ nodes, if $k \geq n + 1$ and $n \leq h \leq 2n - 1$.

Theorem 2. *For any three integers $n \geq 2$, $k \geq n+1$, and $n \leq h \leq 2n-1$, the extra-h connectivity of $D_{k,n}$ is $\kappa_h(D_{k,n}) = (k-1)(h+1) + 2n - 2$.*

Proof. We use H to denote a induced subgraph of order $h+1$ in $D_{k,n}$ with $V(H) = \{\alpha00, \alpha01, \ldots, \alpha0(n-1), \alpha10, \alpha11, \ldots, \alpha1(h-n)\}$, $E(H) = E(D_{k,n}[V(H)])$, and $\alpha \in V_{k,n}^2$. Letting $V' = V(H)$ and $F = N_{D_{k,n}}(V')$, obviously, $D_{k,n} - F$ is disconnected. Then, letting $T = V(D_{0,n}^{\alpha0}) \cup V(D_{0,n}^{\alpha1})$, Definition 1 implies that $\alpha00$ has exactly $k-1$ neighbor(s) in $D_{k,n} - T$, any node in $H - \{\alpha00\}$ has exactly k neighbor(s) in $D_{k,n} - T$, and V' has exactly $2n - h$ neighbor(s) in $D_{k,n}[T] - V'$. Thus, we have

$$|F| = hk + (k-1) + 2n - h = (k-1)(h+1) + 2n - 2.$$

Furthermore, we will prove that F is an extra-h node cut of $D_{k,n}$. Let $u \in V'$ and $\beta = (u)_k$. By Lemma 9, $D_{k,n} - (V(D_{k-1,n}^\beta) \cup F)$ is connected. By Definition 1, every node of $D_{k-1,n}^\beta - A_{D_{k-1,n}^\beta}(V')$ has accurate one neighbor in $D_{k,n} - (V(D_{k-1,n}^\beta) \cup F)$. Therefore, $D_{k,n} - F$ contains two distinct components, one is $D_{k,n} - A_{D_{k,n}}(V')$ and the other is H. Accordingly, for any two integers $n \geq 2$ and $k \geq 2$, we have

$$|V(D_{k,n} - A_{D_{k,n}}(V'))| \geq t_{k,n} - |V'| \geq (n + \frac{1}{2})2^{2^k} - \frac{1}{2} - 2n$$
$$\geq 2kn - 2n \geq 2n^2 > 2n$$
$$\geq h+1.$$

Furthermore, F is an extra-h node cut of $D_{k,n}$, and thus $\kappa_h(D_{k,n}) \leq (h+1)(k-1) + 2n - 2$ for $n \geq 2$, $n \leq h \leq 2n-1$, and $k \geq n+1$.

However, given three integers $n \geq 2$, $k \geq n+1$, and $n \leq h \leq 2n-1$, if the number of nodes of each connected component of $D_{k,n} - F$ is at least $h+1$ with $F \subseteq V(D_{k,n})$, then $|F| \geq (k-1)(h+1) + 2n - 2$ by Lemma 12. So, $\kappa_h(D_{k,n}) \geq (k-1)(h+1) + 2n - 2$.

Hence, $\kappa_h(D_{k,n}) = (k-1)(h+1) + 2n - 2$ when $n \geq 2$, $k \geq n+1$, and $n \leq h \leq 2n-1$.

The reliability a faulty DCN has close relations with its structure. We will determine extra-h connectivity of DCell in the following theorem, use the above results on the structure of a faulty DCell network. The following theorem about the $\kappa_h(D_{k,n})$ follows Theorems 1 and 2.

Theorem 3. *For any positive integer $n \geq 2$,*

$$\kappa_h(D_{k,n}) = \begin{cases} (k-1)(h+1) + n & if\ 0 \leq h \leq n-1\ and\ k \geq 2, \\ (k-1)(h+1) + 2n - 2 & if\ n \leq h \leq 2n-1\ and\ k \geq n+1. \end{cases}$$

By Theorem 3, we will proposed the following theorem:

Theorem 4. *For any $n \geq 2$, $k \geq 2$, and $0 \leq h \leq n-1$ (resp. $n \geq 2$, $k \geq n+1$, and $n \leq h \leq 2n-1$), let $F \subset V(D_{k,n})$ with $|F| < \kappa_h(D_{k,n})$. Then, $D_{k,n} - F$ contains a large connected component and the rest of small connected components have not more than h nodes in total.*

4 Conclusions

Our primary aim of this paper is to explore the boundary problem of node subsets in DCells. In this paper, we determine that the extra-h connectivity of $D_{k,n}$ when $n \geq 2$, $\kappa_h(D_{k,n})$, as follows: (1) $\kappa_h(D_{k,n}) = (k-1)(h+1) + n$ if $k \geq 2$ and $0 \leq h \leq n - 1$; (2) $\kappa_h(D_{k,n}) = (k-1)(h+1) + 2n - 2$ if $k \geq n + 1$ and $n \leq h \leq 2n - 1$. What's more, for any node sub-set $F \subseteq V(D_{k,n})$ with $|F| \leq \kappa_h(D_{k,n}) - 1$, we show that there has a large component in $D_{k,n} - F$, and the rest of small components contain not less than h nodes in total with $0 \leq h \leq n - 1$ and $k \geq 2$ (resp. $n \leq h \leq 2n - 1$ and $k \geq n + 1$). This approach studied in the paper may also be used to research the reliability of other DCNs such as BCube and Ficonn.

Acknowledgment. This paper is supported by National Natural Science Foundation of China (Nos. 61702351 and 61602333), China Postdoctoral Science Foundation (No. 172985), and Natural Science Foundation of the Jiangsu Higher Education Institutions of China (Nos. 17KJB520036 and 16KJB520050).

References

1. Dean, J., Ghemawat, S.: MapReduce: simplified data processing on large clusters. Commun. ACM **51**(1), 107–113 (2008)
2. Ghemawat, S., Gobioff, H., Leung, S.: The Google file system. In: Symposium on Operating Systems Principles (SIGOPS), pp. 29–43 (2003)
3. Anthony, S.: Microsoft now has one million servers (2013). http://www.extremetech.com/extreme/161772-microsoft-now-has-one-million-servers-less-than-google-but-more-than-amazon-says-ballmer
4. Guo, C., Wu, H., Tan, K., Shi, L., Zhang, Y., Lu, S.: DCell: a scalable and fault-tolerant network structure for data centers. In: Special Interest Group on Data Communication (SIGCOMM), pp. 75–86 (2008)
5. Zhu, Q., Wang, X.K., Cheng, G.: Reliability evaluation of BC networks. IEEE Trans. Comput. **62**(11), 2337–2340 (2013)
6. Harary, F.: Conditional connectivity. Networks **13**(3), 347–357 (1983)
7. Fàbrega, J., Fiol, M.A.: Extraconnectivity of graphs with large girth. Discrete Math. **127**(1), 163–170 (1994)
8. Fàbrega, J., Fiol, M.A.: On the extraconnectivity of graphs. Discrete Math. **155**(1), 49–57 (1996)
9. Zhu, Q., Wang, X., Ren, J.: Extra connectivity measures of 3-ary n-cubes. Computing Research Repository (2011). arxiv.org/pdf/1105.0991v1
10. Gu, M., Hao, R.: 3-extra connectivity of 3-ary n-cube networks. Inf. Process. Lett. **114**(9), 486–491 (2014)
11. Lin, L., Zhou, S., Xu, L., Wang, D.: The extra connectivity and conditional diagnosability of alternating group networks. IEEE Trans. Parallel Distrib. Syst. **26**(8), 2352–2362 (2015)
12. Chang, N.W., Tsai, C.Y., Hsieh, S.Y.: On 3-extra connectivity and 3-extra edge connectivity of folded hypercubes. IEEE Trans. Comput. **63**(6), 1594–1600 (2014)
13. Yang, W., Lin, H.: Reliability evaluation of BC networks in terms of the extra vertex-and edge-connectivity. IEEE Trans. Comput. **63**(10), 2540–2548 (2014)

14. Lin, L., Xu, L., Zhou, S., Hsieh, S.Y.: The extra, restricted connectivity and conditional diagnosability of split-star networks. IEEE Trans. Parallel Distrib. Syst. **27**(2), 533–545 (2016)
15. Lin, L., Xu, L., Zhou, S.: Relating the extra connectivity and the conditional diagnosability of regular graphs under the comparison model. Theor. Comput. Sci. **618**, 21–29 (2016)
16. Guo, J., Lu, M.: The extra connectivity of bubble-sort star graphs. Theor. Comput. Sci. **645**, 91–99 (2016)
17. Li, D., Guo, C., Wu, H., Tan, K., Zhang, Y., Lu, S.: FiConn: using backup port for server interconnection in data centers. In: International Conference on Computer Communications (INFOCOM), pp. 2276–2285 (2009)
18. Guo, C., Lu, G., Li, D., Wu, H., Zhang, X., Shi, Y., Tian, C., Zhang, Y., Lu, S.: BCube: a high performance, server-centric network architecture for modular data centers. In: Special Interest Group on Data Communication (SIGCOMM), pp. 63–74 (2009)
19. Libdeh, H., Costa, P., Rowstron, A., O'Shea, G., Donnelly, A.: Symbiotic routing in future data centers. In: Special Interest Group on Data Communication (SIGCOMM), pp. 51–62 (2010)
20. Kliegl, M., Lee, J., Li, J., Zhang, X., Guo, C., Rincon, D.: Generalized DCell structure for load-balanced data center networks. In: International Conference on Computer Communications (INFOCOM), pp. 1–5 (2010)
21. Wang, X., Fan, J., Zhou, J., Lin, C.K.: The restricted h-connectivity of the data center network DCell. Discrete Appl. Math. **203**, 144–157 (2016)
22. Wang, X., Fan, J., Lin, C.K., Jia, X.: Vertex-disjoint paths in DCell networks. J. Parallel Distrib. Comput. **96**, 38–44 (2016)
23. Wang, X., Fan, J., Jia, X., Lin, C.K.: An efficient algorithm to construct disjoint path covers of DCell networks. Theoret. Comput. Sci. **609**(1), 197–210 (2016)
24. Wang, X., Erickson, A., Fan, J., Jia, X.: Hamiltonian properties of DCell networks. Comput. J. **58**(11), 2944–2955 (2015)

Distributed Construction of Fault-Tolerance Virtual Backbone Network for UAV Cluster Network

Kai Tao[✉], Xiaoyun Sun, Kaishi Zhang, and Xiaojun Liu

College of Electrical and Electronic Engineering,
Shijiazhuang Tiedao University, Shijiazhuang 050043, China
taokaitaokai@163.com

Abstract. Unmanned aerial vehicle (UAV) cluster operations adopts the ad-hoc networking, and thus the network performance relates to the virtual backbone network (VBN). Because of the high-speed mobility of UAVs, the topology of UAV network changes frequently, so the VBN must have some fault-tolerant capability. And therefore a distributed fault-tolerant VBN construction algorithm named DKCDS was proposed based on the connected k-dominating sets. Firstly, the CDS was constructed. And then the k-dominating set was constructed based on the maximum independent set, thereby, the connected k-dominating set was finished. Theoretical analysis and simulation showed the DKCDS algorithm could obtain smaller-scaled connected k-dominating backbone network with smaller cost, which means the DKCDS has some application prospect in the filed of UAV cluster operations.

Keywords: UAV cluster · VBN · Distributed · Fault-tolerance

1 Introduction

UAV are paid attention to by the worldwide military due to its unique advantages in recent years. And the UAV cluster operations can expand the search range of single unmanned aerial vehicles, and improve the accuracy of reconnaissance and precision strike capability effectively [1]. Besides, single unmanned aerial vehicle failure or be shot down that will not affect the implementation of the entire collaborative operational plan [2]. Therefore, UAV cluster operations has great development prospects in the military field.

UAV cluster operations requires each node sharing the different target data with one another, so as to carry out the cluster tactical planning effectively, and improve the air combat capability [3]. Due to the limited wireless spectrum resources and the attenuation and interference of the wireless links, the bandwidth resource is the most important network resource for the unmanned aerial vehicle cluster system. And the communication interference between nodes will result in a sharp decline of the network performance due to the limited communication bandwidth [4]. However, the virtual backbone network (VBN) can simplify the routing of UAV cluster network, improve the utilization rate of network resources and reduce the difficulty of network protocol design

© ICST Institute for Computer Sciences, Social Informatics and Telecommunications Engineering 2018
G. Sun and S. Liu (Eds.): ADHIP 2017, LNICST 219, pp. 226–233, 2018.
https://doi.org/10.1007/978-3-319-73317-3_27

effectively. Therefore, it is significant to construct VBN by using distributed algorithm [5]. The problem of virtual backbone construction is usually abstracted as the solution of the connected dominating sets (CDS) based on the graph theory. The study of the VBN construction is focus on how to reduce the VBN scale mostly [6]. However, due to the dynamics of the network topology, which makes the frequent change of the link state [7]. So some virtual backbone redundancy has an important role in improving the network fault tolerance and routing diversity for the UAVs cluster network. However, the existed algorithms based on connected k-dominating set for VBN are centralized almost, and the algorithm cost is high, and also have some limitations. Therefore, a distributed fault-tolerant virtual backbone construction algorithm named DKCDS was proposed based on the connected k-dominating sets based on the preliminary findings in this paper. And this algorithm could obtain smaller-scaled connected k-dominating backbone network with smaller cost, which means the DKCDS has some application prospect in the filed of UAV cluster operations.

2 Mathematical Model

Unit-disk graphs (UDG) are usually used to describe the topology information of wireless ad hoc networks. Assume that all the nodes with the same communication distance are placed in a 2-dimensional plan. If the maximum transmission range is 1, the topology can be modeled as a UDG shown in Fig. 1, from which we can see that there is an edge between any two nodes in the case that their distance is at most one.

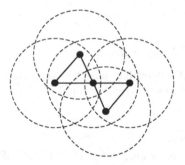

Fig. 1. UDG model.

3 DKCDS Algorithm

3.1 Related Theories

Given graph $G = (V, E)$. Among them, V is the node set and E is the edge set of graph G.

DKCDS algorithm will use the following concepts of graph theory:

k-dominating assume, if any node is dominated by at least k nodes in D, D is called one k- dominating set in figure G.

DKCDS algorithm will use the following graph theory [8]:

Theorem 1. Any maximal independent set (MIS) of G is also its minimum dominating set.

Theorem 2. If B is a k-dominating set of graph G, I is a dominating set of residual subgraph G-B is a $(k + 1)$-dominating set of graph G.

3.2   Algorithm Describe

DKCDS algorithm for constructing k-dominating CDS including three steps: In CDS constructing step, DBCDS distributed algorithm is used to construct the CDS in literature [4]. In the second step the k-dominating set is constructed based on the CDS, the construction of which is compSeted by extending the maximal independent set according to Theorem 2.

The DKCDS algorithm sets the following variables for each node.

(1) Assign unique identifier (ID).
(2) Weight W.

For any node u in the graph, defines its weight as $w(u) = (r(u), ID(u))$, among which $r(u)$ represents the maximum communication distance of node u and ID (u) represents its tag signal. If $w(m) > w(n)$, the node m and n must be satisfied one of the follows cases:

Case 1: $r(m) > r(n)$.
Case 2: $r(m) = r(n)$ and $ID(m) > ID(n)$.

In addition, the DKCDS algorithm sets the parameters LN for each dominating node u. The value of LN value represents the number of neighbor nodes dominating by the node u.

3.2.1   CDS Construction

Constructing a connected dominating set with the DBCDS distributed algorithm in literature [4].

3.2.2   k-Dominating Set Construction

After the construction of CDS, the maximal independent set is extended according to Theorem 2. First of all, each node is assigned a dominating neighbor list $DNList$, which is used to record the dominating neighbor nodes. In addition, $NList$ represents its neighbor node set. Assuming that we can get the maximal independent set is I1 when construct CDS with the DBCDS algorithm and the corresponding connected dominating set is C, and the ith cycle get the dominating set $I_i(2 \leq i \leq k)$. The expansion process is shown in Fig. 2.

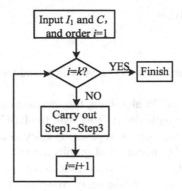

Fig. 2. Constructing k-dominating set flow.

The expending steps are as follows:

Step 1: Set $G' = G - C$
Step 2: Constructing a maximal independent set I_i for G' with the maximum independent set construction algorithm of DBCDS.
Step 3: set $C = C \cup I_i$

After the compSetion of the expansion step shown above, we can get the k-dominating set $I' = C \cup I_2 \cup \ldots \cup I_i \cup \ldots \cup I_k$, and therein I' is the k-dominating CDS set needed to be computed.

Suppose that there are 20 UAV nodes in a UAV cluster network, the nodes are distributed in a 2-dimensional plane that are 100 km × 100 km randomly, and the maximum communication distance of the nodes is 60 km.

Figure 3 shows the results of the DKCDS algorithm for constructing 2-connected k-dominating CDS. In Fig. 3, the nodes 1, 5, 8, 16, 18, 20 constitute a CDS, and the dominating set of the remaining nodes other than the CDS node are $I_2 = \{7, 12, 15\}$, and thus $CDS \cup I_2$ forms a 2-dominating set of the network.

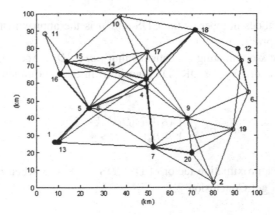

Fig. 3. An example of DKCDS for constructing 2-dominating CDS.

4 Performance Analysis

4.1 Complexity Analysis

Assuming that the nodes number of the network is n, and the maximum value of node degree is Δ.

In the first step of the DKCDS algorithm, the message complexity for constructing CDS is $O(n)$ and the time complexity is $O(n)$ with the DBCDS algorithm. In the first step of the DKCDS algorithm, the message complexity and the time complexity for constructing a maximum independent set of graphs are $O(n)$ by the literature [4]. And thus, the message complexity is $O(n)$ and the time complexity is $O(n)$ for the iterative computation $(k-1)$-dominating set for the set of assignments in the complement graph G in the worst case. And therefore, the message complexity in the worst case is $O(n)$ and the time complexity is $O(n)$ of the second stage. So both of the time complexity and the message complexity of the DKCDS algorithm in the worst case are $O(n)$.

Conclusion 1: Both the message complexity and the time complexity of DKCDS algorithm are $O(n)$.

4.2 Approximation Factor Analysis

Lemma 1: In UDG, any maximum independent set has the relationship with the minimum connected k-dominating set shown as follows:

(1) If $k<5$, $|I| \leq \frac{5}{k}|D_k|$;
(2) If $k \geq 5$, $|I| \leq |D_k|$.

Where, $|D_k|$ represents the nodes number of $|D_k|$ that is the minimum connected k-dominating set, and $|I|$ represents the nodes number of the maximum independent set.

Suppose that opt represents the nodes number of the optimal k-dominating set. C represents the CDS constructed in the first step, so we can get that

$$|C| \leq \rho|D_k| = 8|D_k|, \tag{1}$$

Where, $|C|$ is the nodes number of the CDS and ρ is the approximation factor of the CDS construction problem.

In addition, the k-dominating set satisfies that $opt \geq |D_k|$. According to Lemma 1, the nodes number added by the DKCDS algorithm in the k-dominating set expansion step satisfies that

$$opt \leq \begin{cases} (8 + \frac{5}{k})|D_k| & k<5 \\ 9|D_k| & k \geq 5 \end{cases}, \tag{2}$$

Therefore, the approximation factor of DKCDS are $8 + \frac{15}{k}$ when $k<5$ and 9 when $k \geq 5$. And we can get Conclusion 2.

Conclusion 2: Given k, the approximation factor of DKCDS is constant.

The message complexity reflects the number of information interactions required to construct the virtual backbone network, the time complexity reflects the computational complexity of the algorithm and the approximation factor reflects the size of the virtual backbone network. Besides, the approximation factor is constant indicates that the scale is relatively smaller. Therefore, DKCDS algorithm can adapt to mobile UAV cluster network.

5   Simulation Experiment

Simulation Experiment 1: Suppose that the nodes' maximum communication distance is [100 km, 150 km]. Set $m = 1$, $k = 1$, $m = 1$, $k = 2$ and run the DKCDS algorithm 1000 times, respectively. In each simulation scenario, all the nodes are distributed in a 2-dimensional square plane with 200 km × 400 km area randomly. Figure 4 shows the relationship between the average size of VBN and the number nodes of network.

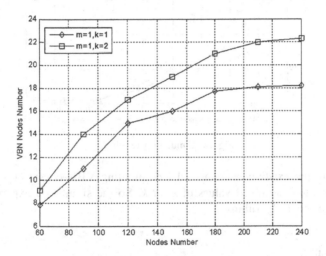

Fig. 4. Simulation result 1.

Figure 4 shows that the nodes number of CDS generated by the DBCDS algorithm increases steadily as the increases of the nodes number of the network, which indicates that any node can communicate with more nodes with the increase of the nodes number in a definite area. When the nodes number reaches or exceeds 170, certain nodes will be able to cover the entire network, so the number of CDS nodes becomes stable.

Simulation Experiment 2: Suppose that all the nodes are distributed in a 2-dimensional square plane with 200 km × 400 km area randomly, and the maximum distance of all the nodes are the same. Set $m = 1$, $k = 1$, $m = 1$, $k = 2$ and run the DKCDS algorithm

1000 times, respectively. Figure 5 describes the relationship between the average nodes number of VBN and the communication distance of the nodes.

Figure 5 shows that these two types of VBN nodes are less and less with increases of the node maximum communication distance, which indicates that fewer nodes can cover the whole network with the increase of the nodes coverage. When the maximum communication distance is 0.75 times or more of the area length, the node coverage almost reaches the area boundary. At least one node can communicate with any other node at the moment. So the nodes number of the connected 1-dominating VBN tends to be the constant 1, and the nodes number of the connected 2-dominating VBN tends to 2 because each node is connected to at least two dominating nodes.

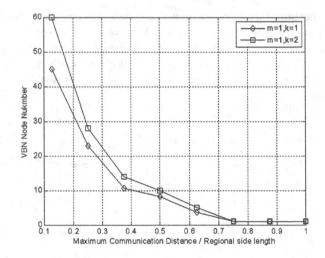

Fig. 5. Simulation result 2.

In addition, the existing m-connected k-dominating VBN construction algorithms are mostly for the determined values of m or k. So the simulation experiment is not compared with other algorithms.

6 Conclusion

Considering the high speed mobility of UAV cluster nodes and the limitation of wireless spectrum resources, a distributed fault-tolerant virtual backbone network based on connected k-domination is proposed to improve the cooperative combat capability. A CDS was constructed based on the previous research, and then k-domination set was constructed. Theoretical analysis showed that the message and time cost of the DKCDS algorithm are $O(n)$ and the approximation factor is constant. That indicated the DKCDS algorithm can get the smaller-scaled VBN with lower communication cost. Simulation results verified the effectiveness of the DKCDS algorithm. As the m-connected virtual backbone network construction cost is very high, the future study will focus on constructing the m-connected k-dominated VBN with lower overhead.

References

1. Au, J.: The Design of a Multi-drone Fleet Control Technology. Nanjing University of Aeronautics and Astronautics, Nanjing (2015)
2. Xu, E., Ding, Z., Dasgupta, S.: Target tracking and mobile sensor navigation in wireless sensor network. IEEE Trans. Mob. Comput. **12**(1), 177–186 (2013)
3. Yi, K.C., Li, Y., Sun, C.H., Nan, C.G.: Recent development and its prospect of satellite communications. J. Commun. **36**(6), 157–172 (2015)
4. Tao, K., Yang, C.L., Shi, H.B., et al.: Distributed construction of virtual backbone network (VBN) for battlefield data link with alien platform. J. Sichuan Univ. (Eng. Sci. Ed.) **46**(2), 111–115 (2014)
5. Thai, M.T., Wang, F., Liu, D., et al.: Connected dominating sets in wireless networks with different transmission ranges. IEEE Trans. Mob. Comput. **6**(7), 721–730 (2007)
6. Mohamed, Y.A., Izzet, F., Senturk, B., Kemal, A.B., et al.: Topology management techniques for tolerating node failures in wireless sensor networks: a survey. Comput. Netw. **58**, 254–283 (2014)
7. Bei, L., Wei, W., Donghyun, K., et al.: On approximating minimum 3-connected m-dominating set problem in unit disk graph. IEEE/ACM Trans. Netw. **99**, 1 (2016)
8. Zhao, Z., Jiao, Z.M., Du, D.Z., et al.: Restoring virtual backbone of wireless sensor network on sensor failure. In: Proceedings of International Conference on Recent Advances in Information Technology (RAIT), Patna, pp. 3–5. IEEE (2016)

Learning the Structure of Dynamic Bayesian Network with Hybrid Data and Domain Knowledges

Haiyang Jia[1,2], Juan Chen[1,2(✉)], and Zhiming Song[3(✉)]

[1] College of Computer Science and Technology, Jilin University,
2699 Ave. Qianjin, Changchun 130012, Jilin, People's Republic of China
{jiahy, chenjuan}@jlu.edu.cn
[2] Key Laboratory for Symbolic Computation and Knowledge Engineering
of Ministry of Education, Jilin University, 2699 Ave. Qianjin,
Changchun 130012, Jilin, People's Republic of China
[3] The Sports Medicine Department, The First Hospital of Jilin University,
2699 Ave. Qianjin, Changchun 130012, Jilin, People's Republic of China
szm3210@163.com

Abstract. Dynamic Bayesian Networks (DBNs) is a powerful graphical model for representing temporal stochastic processes. Learning the structure of DBNs is the fundamental step for parameter learning, inference, application etc. In some cases, such as computational systems biology, learning the structure of DBNs facing the two challenges (1) experimental settings only capture few time series and steady state measurements. (2) the knowledge about DBNs is uncertainty, rare and even with conflict. The paper considers the time series data, steady state and domain knowledge simultaneously, presents a novel algorithm for learning the structure of DBNs. Compare with single source learning, empirical experiment shows that learning with hybrid data and domain knowledges improved the accuracy and effectiveness of the DBNs structure learning.

Keywords: Machine learning · Dynamic system · Bayesian network
Domain knowledge

1 Introduction

Dynamic Bayesian Networks (DBNs), also known as dynamic probabilistic network or temporal Bayesian network, which generalize hidden Markov models and Kalman filters. The DBNs are widely used in many domains such as speech recognition, gene regulatory network (GRN) etc. Learning the structure of DBNs is a fundamental step for parameter learning, inference and application, but learning DBNs is a NP hard problem [1, 2]. In big data scenario, the structure learning is intractable. Despite of the computational efficacy barrier, the training set is also required to be large enough. In some domains, the training set is very noisy and rare, so learning with just one kind of training data is impractical. Domain knowledge may reduce the inherent uncertainty of

© ICST Institute for Computer Sciences, Social Informatics and Telecommunications Engineering 2018
G. Sun and S. Liu (Eds.): ADHIP 2017, LNICST 219, pp. 234–241, 2018.
https://doi.org/10.1007/978-3-319-73317-3_28

the DBNs learning. But the domain knowledge is always uncertainty, unclear and even with conflict. So, combining domain knowledge with training set is a key issue.

This paper presents an algorithm for learning the structure of DBNs with the hybrid data and domain knowledge. The paper is organized as following: Sect. 2 introduces related work and research background; Sect. 3 describes the DBNs learning algorithm; then, Sect. 4 describes the empirical experiment and last section draw the conclusion.

2 Research Background

2.1 (Dynamic) Bayesian Networks

A Bayesian networks (BNs) is a concise representation of joint probability distribution on a set of random variables [3]. A BNs is defined by a structure G and a family of parameters θ, for short $BNs = \langle G, \theta \rangle$. G is a directed acyclic graph (DAG), each node is a random variable in $\mathbf{X} = (X_1, X_2, \ldots, X_n)$, and G encodes the (condition) independencies, θ is the conditional probability distribution (CPD), encoding the conditional distributions of each node and its parent node

$$\theta = \{p(X_i \mid \pi(X_i)) \mid 1 \leq i \leq n\}, \ \pi(X_i) \text{ is the parent nodes of } X_i \tag{1}$$

Briefly, the joint probability distribution represented by BNs is:

$$P(X_1, X_2, \ldots, X_n) = \prod_{i=1}^{n} P(X_i \mid \pi(X_i)) \tag{2}$$

DBNs extend the BNs by modeling the stochastic variables over time [4–6]. Let $\mathbf{X}^t = (X_1^t, \ldots, X_n^t) \ t \in [1, T]$ stand for the random variables $\mathbf{X}$ at time t. Two tiers DBNs, obey first-order Markov rules, which means $P(\mathbf{X}^t | \mathbf{X}^{t-1}, \ldots, \mathbf{X}^0) = P(\mathbf{X}^t | \mathbf{X}^{t-1})$ for all t > 0.

DBNs was composed of two slices: initial network BN^0 and transition network $BN^\rightarrow$. BN^0 encode the probability distribution of $P(\mathbf{X}^0)$, which is the initial state of the temporal process. For each time slice, $BN^\rightarrow$ define the probability of states translate form t−1 to t, $P(\mathbf{X}^t | \mathbf{X}^{t-1})$. With these assumptions, the joint probability distribution of a time series can be written as

$$\begin{aligned}
P(X^0, X^1, \ldots, X^n) &= P(X^0) \prod_{t=1}^{T} P(X^t | X^{t-1}) \\
&= \prod_{i=1}^{n} P(X_i^0 | \pi^0(X_i^0)) \prod_{t=1}^{T} P(X^t | X^{t-1}) \\
&= \prod_{i=1}^{n} P(X_i^0 | \pi^0(X_i^0)) \prod_{t=1}^{T} P(X^t | \pi^\rightarrow(X^t)) \\
&= \prod_{i=1}^{n} P(X_i^0 | \pi^0(X_i^0)) \prod_{t=1}^{T} \prod_{i=1}^{n} P(X_i^t | \pi^\rightarrow(X_i^t))
\end{aligned} \tag{3}$$

Figure 1 gives an example of DBNs. The distribution for this DBNs is

$$P(X^0, X^1, \ldots, X^n) = P(X_1^0)P(X_2^0 \mid X_1^0)P(X_3^0 \mid X_4^0)P(X_4^0 \mid X_1^0)$$

$$\prod_{t=1}^{T} P(X_1^t \mid X_2^{t-1})P(X_2^t \mid X_1^{t-1}, X_4^{t-1})P(X_3^t \mid X_4^{t-1})P(X_4^t \mid X_3^{t-1}) \tag{4}$$

$$BN^0 \qquad\qquad\qquad BN^{\rightarrow}$$

Fig. 1. Example of DBNs

2.2 Literature Review

Structure learning the BNs/DBNs can be considered as the general problem of selecting a probabilistic model that explains a given set of training data. a wealth of literature has been presented that seeks to understand and provide methods of learning structure from data.

Classical approaches for learning the structure can be classified to three main methods: [7] (1) A score-searching approach; (2) A constraint-based approach; (3) A dynamic programming approach;

Score-searching based approach, which define the task as an optimization problem. Based on a scoring function to evaluates different structures G related to a data set D (in the rest D was omitted for the concision). There are many score criteria such as : BD/BDe [8, 9], MDL [10] and BIC [11];

Constraint based approach define the learning task as constraint satisfaction problem. Using conditional independent test to find the independent relationships in data D, then construct a DBNs satisfied such conditional independence [12]. Each approach has its specialty: the constraint based methods are usually more efficient when the number of variables is large. However, when the data is noisy, the score-searching algorithms is more robust.

Aside from the two major techniques of structure learning that have been discussed, there is a third method that is like the score-and-search approach, but does not have the search aspect. These methods use dynamic programming to compute optimal models for a small set of variables and in some cases combine these models.

DBNs, as temporal models, are best learned from temporal data. But in some cases, such as bioinformatics and computational systems biology studies, experimental settings do not always permit collecting massive time series measurements and may only capture few time series and steady state measurements (Steady state measurements can be considered as snapshots of the long-run behavior of a system.), another challenge is that the domain knowledge is uncertain and sparse.

3   Learning Method

3.1   Formalize the Problem

Learning DBNs from steady state, temporal data and domain knowledge can be formalized as maximize the joint distribution:

$$P(\text{DBNs, Evidence}) \tag{5}$$

where Evidence = {Data, Prior knowledge}, Data = {DT,DS}, DT is temporal data, DS is steady state, DBNs = $\{G, \theta\}$ here we only focus on transition network.

3.2   Steady State and Temporal Data

Equation (2) characterizes temporal behavior of DBNs over a given time interval. With the following Eqs. (5) and (6), the DBNs structure learning with Steady state and temporal data was formalized.

$$P(DBN|D_T, D_S) = \frac{P(D_T, D_S|DBN)P(DBN)}{P(D_T, D_S)}$$
$$\propto P(D_T, D_S|DBN)P(DBN) \tag{6}$$

$$P(D|G) = \int_\theta P(D|G, \theta)P(\theta|G)d\theta$$
$$= \int_\theta P(D_T, D_S|G, \theta)P(\theta|G)d\theta \tag{7}$$

Firstly, define some notations: all states for DBNs: $S = \{S_q|q \in [1, N]\}$; Size of S: N;   State   for X_i: $S(X_i) = \{S_k(X_i)|k \in [1, N_i]\}$;   State   for   parent   nodes   of X_i: $S(\pi_i) = \{S_j(\pi_i)| j \in [1, N\pi_i]\}$; $\theta_{i,j,k} = P(X_i^t = S_k(X_i)|X_i^{t-1} = S_j(\pi_i))$. For example: in Fig. 2. Assume all nodes are binary (0,1), then $S = \{(0000), (0001), \ldots\}$; $N = 2^4 = 16$; $S(X_2) = \{0,1\}$, $N_2 = 2$; $\pi_2 = \{X_1, X_3, X_4\}$; $S(\pi_2) = \{(000), (001),$ $(010), (011), \ldots\}$, $N_{\pi_2} = 8$; $\theta_{2,5,1} = P(X_2^t = 1|X_1^{t-1} = 1, X_3^{t-1} = 0, X_4^{t-1} = 0)$.

Let M denote the state transition matrix, each element in M can be calculated with Eq. (8).

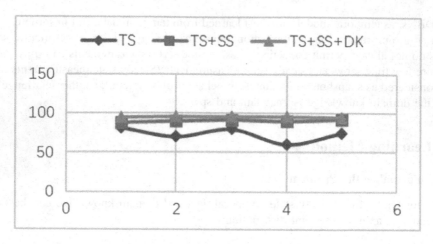

Fig. 2. Accuracy of the experiment. TS-time series; SS-steady state; DK-domain knowledge

$$M_{v,q} = P(\mathbf{X}^t = S_q | \mathbf{X}^{t-1} = S_v) = \prod_{i=1}^{n} P(X_i^t = x_{i,q} | \pi_i^{t-1} = S_{\pi_i,v})$$

$$= \prod_{i=1}^{n} \theta_{i,v_j,q_k} \tag{8}$$

The steady state S^* has the property $S * M = S*$, each element in S^* can be calculated with Eq. (8).

$$\lim_{t \to \infty} M_{v,q}^{(t)} = S_q^*, \text{Where } M_{v,q}^{(r)} = P(X^{t+r} = S_q | X^t = S_v) \tag{9}$$

Theorem: A finite state homogeneous Markov process corresponding to a DBNs, possess a unique stationary distribution, independent of the initial distribution if $\theta_{i,j,k} > 0$, $\forall i \in [1,n]$, $j \in [1, N\pi_i]$, $k \in [1, N_i]$ [13].

The likelihood of a DBNs structure G give both temporal data and steady state is:

$$P(D|G) = \int_{\theta} P(D_T, D_S | G, \theta) P(\theta | G) d\theta \tag{10}$$

where $P(\theta|G) = \prod_{i=1}^{n} P(\theta_i | \pi(X_i)) = \prod_{i=1}^{n} \prod_{j=1}^{N_{\pi i}} P(\theta_{i,j} | \pi_i)$.

The prior distribution is assumed to be Dirichlet distribution (conjugate prior for multinomial), $\boldsymbol{\alpha}$: the prior for $\boldsymbol{\theta}$

$$P(\theta_{i,j}|\alpha,\pi_i) = \frac{1}{B(\alpha)}\prod_{k=1}^{N_i}\theta_{i,j,k}^{\alpha_{i,j,k}-1}, \quad B(\alpha) = \frac{\prod_{k=1}^{N_i}\Gamma(\alpha_{i,j,k})}{\Gamma(\sum_{k=1}^{N_i}\alpha_{i,j,k})} \tag{11}$$

$$\Gamma(x) = \begin{cases} (x-1)! & \text{if x is a positive integer} \\ \int_0^\infty t^{x-1}e^{-t}dt & \text{else} \end{cases}$$

To maxis posteriori $\tilde{\theta}$ with temporal data D_T is straight forward, but for steady state D_S we cannot compute $\tilde{\theta}$ with steady state directly, optimize both G and with D_S is intractable. So, we need an approximation, replace the parameter from steady state with the parameter from temporal data $\tilde{\theta}_S \approx \tilde{\theta}_T$.

3.3 Domain Knowledge

To learning the structure of DBNs means learning both G^0 and $G^{\rightarrow}$. Based on the score-searching approach, we define a score function. Suppose the number of time series is M, the NO. l sample is D_l which has T_l different time point. the score function defined as following:

$$\log P(D|G)$$
$$= \sum_{i=1}^n\sum_{j=1}^{q_i}\frac{\Gamma(\alpha_{i,j})}{\Gamma(\alpha_{i,j}+N_{i,j})}\sum_k^{r_i}\frac{\Gamma(\alpha_{i,j,k}+N_{i,j,k})}{\Gamma(\alpha_{i,j,k})} \tag{12}$$

$$N_{i,j,k}^0 = \sum_{l=1}^M\chi(X_i^0=k,\pi^0(X_i^0)=j|D_l), \quad N_{i,j,k}^{\rightarrow} = \sum_{l=1}^M\sum_{t=1}^{T_l}\chi(X_{ii}^t=k,\pi^{\rightarrow}=j|D_l),$$

$$N_{i,j} = \sum_{k=1}^{r_i}N_{i,j,k}, \text{ if x is a positive integer}, \Gamma(x)=(x-1)!$$

$\alpha_1,\cdots,\alpha_r$ is the hyper parameter for Dirichlet distribution.

The domain knowledge is used to calculate the prior distribution. Domain knowledge about the structure was encoded with matrix K. The initial network K^0: if there should be an edge from v_i to v_j then k_{ij} is 1; if there should not exist an edge k_{ij} is 0, otherwise k_{ij} is -1 for unknown.

$$K^0 = \begin{cases} k_{i,j}^0 = 1, & \text{if } v_i^0 \rightarrow v_j^0 \\ k_{i,j}^0 = 0, & \text{if no edge betwen } v_i^0 \text{ and } v_j^0 \quad i \in [1,n], j \in [1,n] \\ k_{i,j}^0 = -1, & \text{if unknow for } v_i^0 \text{ and } v_j^0 \end{cases} \tag{13}$$

The confidence of the knowledge defined with matrix $C^0 = c_{i,j}^0 \in [0,1]$, the distance matrix D defined as

$$D^0 = Dist(K^0, G^0) = \begin{cases} d_{i,j}^0 = 0, & \text{if } k_{i,j}^0 = -1 \text{ or } k_{i,j}^0 = g_{i,j}^0 \\ d_{i,j}^0 = 1, & \text{if } k_{i,j}^0 \neq g_{i,j}^0 \end{cases} \tag{14}$$

Each structure can be weighted as following:

$$W^0 = \frac{\sum\limits_{i=1,j=1}^{n,n} c_{i,j}^0 d_{i,j}^0}{n^2 - \sum\limits_{i=1,j=1}^{n,n} I(k_{i,j}^0 = -1)}, \quad where \, I(x) = \begin{cases} 1, & if \, x = true; \\ 0, & if \, x = false; \end{cases} \quad (15)$$

For multiple domain knowledge, named the number of knowledge sources Q, there are a set of knowledge matrix and correspond confidence matrix. The weight of the knowledge is defined as $L_1, \ldots, L_Q$, $L_i \in [0, 1]$, $\sum\limits_{i=1}^{Q} L_i = 1$, $i \in [1, Q]$, then the W for the structure G is a weighted average: $W^0 = L_1 * W_1^0 + \ldots + L_Q * W_Q^0$.

The score function is defined as below

$$Score(G) = BI(D, G) - \beta W \quad (16)$$

The β control the ratio that data and domain knowledge effect on learning procedure.

4 Experiment

To test the behavior of the algorithm, several artificial data was generated. DBNs with 10, 30, 50, 100, 200 nodes were generated randomly. Training data were computed with such generative model. Steady state was assumed the state do not change within 30 time steps, time series data and domain knowledge were selected from give model and data respectively, the ratio for training was kept below 20%. The Fig. 2 given the accuracy with different given DBNs learning. The average accuracy was increased from 73.4% to 90.6 with steady state data added and increased another 5% when given domain knowledge.

This paper presents a novel algorithm for learning the structure of DBNs, which consider both time series data, steady state and domain knowledge simultaneously, empirical experiment shows that the proposed algorithm improved the efficiency and the accuracy of the DBNs structure learning.

Acknowledgements. This work is supported by Science and Technology Development of Jilin Province of China (20150101051JC, 20160520099JH), Special Funds of Central Colleges Basic Scientific Research Operating Expenses, Jilin University under Grant 93K172017K04.

References

1. Chickering, D.M.: Learning Bayesian networks is NP-complete. Learn. Data: Artif. Intell. Stat. **112**, 121–130 (1996)
2. Chickering, D.M., Heckerman, D., Meek, C.: Large-sample learning of Bayesian networks is NP-hard. J. Mach. Learn. Res. **5**, 1287–1330 (2004)

3. Pearl, J.: Probabilistic Reasoning in Intelligent Systems: Networks of Plausible Inference. Morgan Kaufmann, San Mateo (1988)
4. Ghahramani, Z.: An introduction to hidden Markov models and Bayesian networks. In: Hidden Markov Models, pp. 9–42. World Scientific Publishing Co., Inc. (2002)
5. Murphy, K.P.: Dynamic Bayesian networks: representation, inference and learning. Ph.D. thesis, University of California, Berkeley (2002)
6. Ghahramani, Z.: Learning dynamic Bayesian networks. In: Giles, C.L., Gori, M. (eds.) NN 1997. LNCS, vol. 1387, pp. 168–197. Springer, Heidelberg (1998). https://doi.org/10.1007/BFb0053999
7. Daly, R., Shen, Q., Aitken, S.: Learning Bayesian networks: approaches and issues. Knowl. Eng. Rev. **26**, 99–157 (2011)
8. Cooper, H.: A Bayesian method for the induction of probabilistic networks from data. Mach. Learn. **9**, 309–347 (1992)
9. David, H., Dan, G., David, M.C.: Learning Bayesian networks: the combination of knowledge and statistical data. Mach. Learn. **20**, 197–243 (1995)
10. Lam, W., Bacchus, F.: Learning Bayesian belief networks: an approach based on the MDL principle. Comput. Intell. **10**, 269–293 (1994)
11. Schwarz, G.: Estimating the dimension of a model. Ann. Stat. **6**, 461–464 (1978)
12. Cheng, J., Greiner, R., Kelly, J., Bell, D., Liu, W.R.: Learning Bayesian networks from data: an information-theory based approach. Artif. Intell. **137**, 43–90 (2002)
13. Lahdesmaki, H., Shmulevich, I.: Learning the structure of dynamic Bayesian networks from time series and steady state measurements. Mach. Learn. **71**, 185–217 (2008)

DLRRS: A New Recommendation System Based on Double Linear Regression Models

Chenglong Li[1], Zhaoguo Wang[2], Shoufeng Cao[1(✉)],
and Longtao He[1]

[1] National Computer Network Emergency Response Technical
Team/Coordination Center of China (CNCERT/CC), Beijing 100029, China
{lichenglong,csf,hlt}@cert.org.cn
[2] School of Computer Science and Technology, Harbin Institute of Technology,
Harbin 150006, Heilongjiang, China
wangzhaoguo@tsinghua.edu.cn

Abstract. Recently, it is difficulty for ordinary users to find their own points of interest when facing of massive information accompanied by the popularity and development of social networks. Recommendation system is considered to be the most potential way to solve the problem by profiling personalized interest model and initiatively pushing potential interesting contents to each user. However, collaborative filtering, one of the most mature and extensively applied recommender methods currently, is facing problems of data sparsity and diversity and so on, causing its effect unsatisfactory. In the article, we put forward DLRRS, a new recommendation system depending on double linear regression models. Compared with the traditional methods, such as item average scores, collaborative filtering, and rating frequency, DLRRS has the best predictive RMSE accuracy and less fluctuation. DLRRS also has high real-time performance, which makes the system complete all the calculations in the time of $\Omega(n)$.

Keywords: Recommendation system · Linear regression · RMSE

1 Introduction

The popularity and growing of social networks have changed the way people passively access information in last several years. And the content generated by users has exploded. For ordinary users, it is difficult to find their own points of interest when facing of massive information. The web portals, such as Yahoo, USA.gov, etc., help users quickly index by sorting information with their attributes. And the search engines, such as Google, Baidu, etc., return the most relevant content by analyzing the queries entered by the user. Although they greatly improve the efficiency of the information accessing, they need for users' close participation, and cannot automatically perceive the users' interests. Moreover, the users are often confused of their real demands, or cannot use keywords to describe his/her own interests. In addition, the results returned from classification and searching technology lack personality which causing poor user experience. By analyzing the user's historical behavior, recommendation system [1]

© ICST Institute for Computer Sciences, Social Informatics and Telecommunications Engineering 2018
G. Sun and S. Liu (Eds.): ADHIP 2017, LNICST 219, pp. 242–249, 2018.
https://doi.org/10.1007/978-3-319-73317-3_29

profiles personalized interest model for each user, and initiatively pushes potential interesting content to the user. Therefore recommendation system is as being the most potential method for solving the information overload issue.

In the article, DLRRS, a new recommender system depending on double linear regression models is presented. With the prepared inputs, DLRRS establishes double linear regression models of the certain score and the highest frequency score of user or item by using the frequency information of the user or the item, and then uses the models to predict the unknown score directly according to the historical score frequency as the system outputs. Compared with the traditional methods, DLRRS has the best predictive accuracy in the term of RMSE and less fluctuation. DLRRS greatly reduces the computational complexity, which makes the system complete all the calculations in the time of $\Omega(n)$. So it is easy to be applied to the actual industrial production. Using the group wisdom and the statistical parameters to estimate the model parameters, DLRRS has a good anti-noise ability. DLRRS also has a good capability of the incremental update, which makes the system complete update to the new user behavior in constant time, leading to high real-time performance.

2 Related Work

A recommender system is defined as: "attempt to recommend the most suitable items (products or services) to particular users (individuals or businesses) by predicting a user's interest in an item based on related information about the items, the users and the interactions between items and users" [2]. Currently, the most widely used personalized recommendation systems mainly depend on the collaborative filtering-based methods. Collaborative filtering systems mainly use two kinds of methods [3]: heuristic-based approaches [4–7] and model-based approaches [8–11].

The heuristic-based methods obtain the user score matrix by making use of the hidden or explicit behavior of the user firstly. And then it calculates the similarity between items or users. Finally, according to the score and similarity of neighbor users or items, the forecast score and the recommended results are achieved. The heuristic-based method could be further divided into user-based approach [12] and object-based approach [13]. Because of its ease of deployment and efficient features, heuristic-based methods are now widely used in commercial systems such as Amazon. However, the sparseness, diversity of data, and other issues make the recommendation performance of heuristic-based methods difficult to improve.

To elevate recommending preciseness, the model-based approaches exploit item scoring matrix for training more accurate scoring models, such as clustering [14, 15], Bayesian belief network [16], Markov decision process [17] and the potential semantic model [18], etc. Although the model-based approach improves the prediction accuracy, they also face problems such as complex model, various parameters and strong dependency on large statistical properties of the data set. The above reasons also cause model-based methods difficult to apply to practical recommendation systems.

In the article, we put forward DLRRS, a new recommender system depending on double linear regression models. DLRRS establishes double linear regression models, and then uses the models to predict the unknown score directly according to the historical score frequency. Compared with the traditional methods, DLRRS has the best predictive accuracy in the term of RMSE and less fluctuation. DLRRS also improves time performance which is easy to be applied to the actual industrial production.

3   The System Implementation of DLRRS

According to the system workflow, DLRRS consists mainly of three parts: data preparation, establishing double linear regression models and prediction result output, described as followings.

3.1   Data Preparation

Firstly, DLRRS requires a certain size of known data to prepare for subsequent modeling and output of the results. Specifically, the data which should be prepared in advance mainly need to include three elements: users, items and user ratings of items. Through the known data, after the subsequent modeling, and calculation the predicted unknown user ratings could be obtained consequently.

3.2   Double Linear Regression Models

In the second step, we use linear regression method to establish double models: a model between the user's highest frequency score and items' scores, and a model between scores of all items and scoring frequency of the corresponding items.

The standard linear regression model is described as following formulas [19]. Given a dataset $\{y_i, x_{i1}, \ldots, x_{ip}\}_{i=1}^{n}$ of n statistical blocks, the model assumes that the relationship between the dependent variable y_i and the p-vector of regressors x_i is linear. With error variable ε_i, the model takes the form:

$$y_i = \beta_0 1 + \beta_1 x_{i1} + \ldots + \beta_p x_{ip} + \varepsilon_i = x_i^T \beta + \varepsilon_i, i = 1, \ldots, n. \tag{1}$$

where T represents the transpose, so that $x_i^T \beta$ is the inner product between vectors x_i and β.

Using the above linear regression method, the first model between the user's score for the items and the user's highest frequency score could be established. And then we could use the model to predict and score non-rated items of the target users. First of all, traverse all users, and each user u makes an n-dimensional vector of the historical ratings of all the evaluated items, where n is the items' count evaluated by the customer u, i.e. $Y_u = [r_{u,i_1}, r_{u,i_2}, \ldots, r_{u,i_k}, \ldots, r_{u,i_n}]$, where r_{u,i_k} represents the customer u's score on item i_k. Then it calculates the highest score in the historical score of the item involved in Y_u and divides the result into the vector X_u in the order of the items in Y_u, i.e. $X_u = [x_{i_1}, x_{i_2}, \ldots, x_{i_k}, \ldots, x_{i_n}]$, where x_{i_k} indicates the highest score for the historical score of the item i_k. Assume Y_u and X_u satisfy the relation $Y_u = \beta_u X_u + \varepsilon_u$, where β_u and ε_u are real numbers. Applying the least squares method [20], the empirical fitting equation of the above relation is described as followings:

$$Y_u = \beta_u X_u + \varepsilon_u$$

$$\begin{cases} \beta_u = \dfrac{L_{uy}}{L_{ux}} \\ \varepsilon_u = \bar{y}_u - \beta_u \bar{x}_u \end{cases} . \tag{2}$$

where $\quad \bar{x}_u = \dfrac{1}{n}\sum\limits_{j=1}^{n} x_{i_j}, \quad \bar{y}_u = \dfrac{1}{n}\sum\limits_{j=1}^{n} r_{u,i_j}, \quad L_{ux} = \sum\limits_{j=1}^{n}(x_{i_j} - \bar{x}_u)^2 = \sum\limits_{j=1}^{n} x_{i_j}^2 - n\bar{x}_u^2 \quad$ and

$L_{xy} = \sum\limits_{j=1}^{n}(x_{i_j} - \bar{x}_u)(r_{u,i_j} - \bar{y}_u) = \sum\limits_{j=1}^{n} x_{i_j} r_{u,i_j} - n\bar{x}_u \bar{y}_u.$

Similarly, we propose the second model between the score of all items and scoring frequency of the corresponding items depending on score conditions to predict scores. First of all, traverse all the items, each object i constitutes an m-dimensional vector Y_i of all the historical score of i, i.e. $Y_i = [r_{u_1,i}, r_{u_2,i}, \ldots, r_{u_k,i}, \ldots, r_{u_m,i}]$, where $r_{u_k,i}$ represents the customer u_k's score on item i. Then it calculates the highest score of the user's historical scores involved in Y_i. And the results make up the vector X_i in the order of the users in Y_i, i.e. $X_i = [x_{u_1}, x_{u_2}, \ldots, x_{u_k}, \ldots, x_{u_m}]$, where x_{u_k} is the highest rated score in the user u_k's historical scores. Assume Y_i and X_i satisfy the relation $Y_i = \beta_i X_i + \varepsilon_i$, where β_i and ε_i are real numbers. Applying the least squares method, the empirical fitting equation of the above relation is described as followings:

$$Y_i = \beta_i X_i + \varepsilon_i$$

$$\begin{cases} \beta_i = \dfrac{L_{iy}}{L_{ix}} \\ \varepsilon_i = \bar{y}_i - \beta_i \bar{x}_i \end{cases} . \tag{3}$$

where $\quad \bar{x}_i = \dfrac{1}{m}\sum\limits_{j=1}^{m} x_{u_j}, \quad \bar{y}_i = \dfrac{1}{m}\sum\limits_{j=1}^{m} r_{u_j,i}, \quad L_{ix} = \sum\limits_{j=1}^{m}(x_{u_j} - \bar{x}_i)^2 = \sum\limits_{j=1}^{m} x_{u_j}^2 - m\bar{x}_i^2, \quad$ and

$L_{iy} = \sum\limits_{j=1}^{m}(x_{u_j} - \bar{x}_i)(r_{u_j,i} - \bar{y}_i) = \sum\limits_{j=1}^{m} x_{u_j} r_{u_j,i} - m\bar{x}_i \bar{y}_i.$

3.3   Prediction Result Output

In the final step, using the recommendation method of linear regression, the previously obtained predicted outcome is merged as the result of the user's evaluation of the items. Firstly, we use the most frequently occurred score X_i of the historical scores of the predicted items as the input of formula (2). Thus the forecast score Y_u is calculated as output. Secondly, we use the most frequently occurred score X_u of the historical scores of the predicted users as the input of formula (3). Thus the forecast score Y_i is calculated as output. In the end, the user u's rating vector on the all undisclosed items is as followings:

$$P_u = \frac{Y_u + Y_i}{2}. \tag{4}$$

Based on the requirements of DLRRS, the system is able to sort and select N items with the highest predicted values in P_u as the final output.

3.4   The Performance Analysis of DLRRS

The actual production environment, especially the large real system with over 100 million users and commodities, which is more time-sensitive, always has a certain demand for the response time of the recommended results. By the analysis of DLRRS system, the modeling process based on the average score of the item only needs to calculate the average score of each item. And the method based on the user and the item rating frequency also requires only a simple calculation of the highest frequency score of each user and the highest frequency of the item. So the modeling time of the system is short. Overall, the method greatly reduces the computational complexity, so that the algorithm is able to complete all the calculations in $\Omega(n)$ time. In summary, the modeling time and prediction time of DLRRS are highly competitive and can meet the requirements of the real system for forecasting time performance.

4   Experiments and Evaluations

4.1   The Dataset of Experiments

To test the performance of DLRRS, the published real dataset MovieLens [21] is used for experimental evaluation is. The MovieLens dataset is a set of film scores graded by a group of users, which is collected by the GroupLens research team at the University of Minnesota from the MovieLens website. The group published three different sizes of datasets. We select the 1 M dataset of MovieLens for experiments, which includes 1 million scores on 3952 films from 6040 users. Each score is an integer between 1 to 5. The value size indicates the users' preference for the certain film. Each user graded at least 20 movies. And the users and the movies are numbered with consecutive integers.

4.2   Evaluation Methods and Indicators

The MovieLens 1 M dataset is randomly divided into training sets and test sets according to certain proportion. Based on the double linear regression models, DLRRS uses the training set of the film score of users, and trains model parameters. Then the system predicts the users' scores on the film in the test sets. The smaller the gap between the forecasted scores and real scores, the higher the prediction accuracy of the recommendation system provides. Therefore, we use Mean Absolute Error (MAE) [3, 22] and Root Mean Square Error (RMSE) [3, 23] to measure the performance of the recommended systems. If the test set contains the actual score r_{ui} of the user u for the movie i, the predicted score given by the DLRRS is p_{ui} $(p_{ui} \in P_u)$, then the definitions of MAE and RMSE are as shown in following equations:

$$MAE = \frac{\sum_{(u,i) \in T} |r_{u,i} - P_{u,i}|}{|T|}. \tag{5}$$

$$RMSE = \sqrt{\frac{\sum_{(u,i) \in T} (r_{u,i} - P_{u,i})^2}{|T|}}. \tag{6}$$

where (u, i) indicates the customer movie pair. T indicates the set of all user movie pairs in the test set. And accordingly, |T| is the number of user movie pairs to be predicted in the test set.

Based on the indicators of MAE and RMSE, we choose some of the most commonly used recommendation methods including the recommendation method based on item average scores (IA), the collaborative filtering method based on items (ICF), the method directly using weighted user rating frequency and item rating frequency (RF) as the contrast references to the DLRRS in the experiments. And in order to compare the tolerances of data sparseness in different recommended methods, we divide the MovieLens 1 M dataset into different proportions of training sets and test sets. The training set ratio increases from 10% to 90% with 10% step size.

4.3   Evaluation Results

For the four recommendation methods, the evaluation of MAE and RMSE are displayed in Figs. 1 and 2. In above figures, each approach shows the maximum, minimum, average values (three horizontal lines) and distribution (the shadow area) of MAE/RMSE result under the conditions of different proportions of training sets.

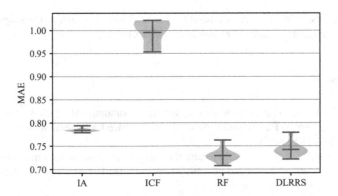

Fig. 1. The MAE comparison result.

From the experiment results, it shows that DLRRS provides the best performance in RMSE comparison, and has a small gap to RF method in MAE comparison. However, compared to the MAE, RMSE enlarges data fluctuation between the forecasted scores and actual scores by squaring. Therefore, DLRRS has the best predictive accuracy in

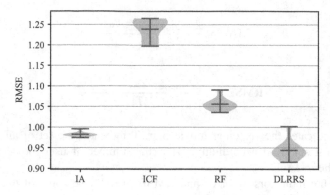

Fig. 2. The RMSE comparison result.

the term of RMSE and less fluctuation, which is superior to the existing collaborative filtering methods. At the same time, it can be seen that the RF accuracy is also high, indicating that the score frequency information has great value for the scoring forecast.

5   Conclusion

In the article, we put forward the DLRRS, a new recommendation system based on double linear regression models, and introduce its system implementation. Compared to other recommended methods such as collaborative filtering, DLRRS has the best RMSE predictive accuracy and less fluctuation. In the future, we will continue to optimize the DLRRS system to enhance its performance in multi-aspects.

Acknowledgments. This research is funded by National Key Research & Development Plan of China under Grant 2016YFB0801200 and 2016QY05X1000.

References

1. Resnick, P., Varian, H.R.: Recommender systems. Commun. ACM **40**(3), 56–58 (1997)
2. Bobadilla, J., Ortega, F., Hernando, A., et al.: Recommender systems survey. Knowl.-Based Syst. **46**, 109–132 (2013)
3. Adomavicius, G., Tuzhilin, A.: Toward the next generation of recommender systems: a survey of the state-of-the-art and possible extensions. IEEE Trans. Knowl. Data Eng. **17**(6), 734–749 (2005)
4. Resnick, P., Iacovou, N., Suchak, M., et al.: Grouplens: an open architecture for collaborative filtering of netnews. In: Proceedings of the 1994 ACM Conference on Computer Supported Cooperative Work, pp. 175–186. ACM (1994)
5. Adomavicius, G., Kwon, Y.: Multi-criteria recommender systems. In: Ricci, F., Rokach, L., Shapira, B. (eds.) Recommender Systems Handbook, pp. 847–880. Springer, Boston (2015). https://doi.org/10.1007/978-1-4899-7637-6_25
6. Wang, F., Zhang, S., Henderson, L.M.: Adaptive decision-making of breast cancer mammography screening: a heuristic-based regression model. Omega (2017)

7. Sun, J., Wang, G., Cheng, X., et al.: Mining affective text to improve social media item recommendation. Inf. Process. Manag. **51**(4), 444–457 (2015)
8. Goldberg, K., Roeder, T., Gupta, D., et al.: Eigentaste: a constant time collaborative filtering algorithm. Inf. Retrieval **4**(2), 133–151 (2001)
9. Hofmann, T.: Collaborative filtering via gaussian probabilistic latent semantic analysis. In: Proceedings of the 26th Annual International ACM SIGIR Conference on Research and Development in Information Retrieval, pp. 259–266. ACM (2003)
10. Jiang, S., Qian, X., Shen, J., et al.: Author topic model-based collaborative filtering for personalized POI recommendations. IEEE Trans. Multimedia **17**(6), 907–918 (2015)
11. Jiang, S., Qian, X., Shen, J., Mei, T.: Travel recommendation via author topic model based collaborative filtering. In: He, X., Luo, S., Tao, D., Xu, C., Yang, J., Hasan, M.A. (eds.) MMM 2015. LNCS, vol. 8936, pp. 392–402. Springer, Cham (2015). https://doi.org/10. 1007/978-3-319-14442-9_45
12. Veena, C., Babu, B.V.: A user-based recommendation with a scalable machine learning tool. Int. J. Electr. Comput. Eng. **5**(5) (2015)
13. Zhang, H.R., Min, F., Shi, B.: Regression-based three-way recommendation. Inf. Sci. **378**, 444–461 (2017)
14. West, J.D., Wesley-Smith, I., Bergstrom, C.T.: A recommendation system based on hierarchical clustering of an article-level citation network. IEEE Trans. Big Data **2**(2), 113–123 (2016)
15. Nilashi, M., Esfahani, M.D., Roudbaraki, M.Z., et al.: A multi-criteria collaborative filtering recommender system using clustering and regression techniques. J. Soft Comput. Decis. Support Syst. **3**(5), 24–30 (2016)
16. Ricci, F., Rokach, L., Shapira, B.: Introduction to recommender systems handbook. In: Ricci, F., Rokach, L., Shapira, B., Kantor, P. (eds.) recommender systems handbook. Springer, Boston (2011). https://doi.org/10.1007/978-0-387-85820-3_1
17. Shani, G., Brafman, R.I., Heckerman, D.: An MDP-based recommender system. In: Proceedings of the Eighteenth Conference on Uncertainty in Artificial Intelligence, pp. 453–460. Morgan Kaufmann Publishers Inc., Burlington (2002)
18. Hofmann, T.: Latent semantic models for collaborative filtering. ACM Trans. Inf. Syst. (TOIS) **22**(1), 89–115 (2004)
19. Linear Regression Method. https://en.wikipedia.org/wiki/Linear_regression
20. Yan, X.: Linear Regression Analysis: Theory and Computing, pp. 1–2. World Scientific, Singapore (2009)
21. The Datasets of MovieLens. https://grouplens.org/datasets/movielens/
22. Karatzoglou, A., Amatriain, X., Baltrunas, L., et al.: Multiverse recommendation: n-dimensional tensor factorization for context-aware collaborative filtering. In: Proceedings of the Fourth ACM Conference on Recommender Systems, pp. 79–86 (2010)
23. Jamali, M., Ester, M.: A matrix factorization technique with trust propagation for recommendation in social networks. In: Proceedings of the Fourth ACM Conference on Recommender Systems, pp. 135–142 (2010)

Chances and Challenges: How to Make a Successful MOOC

Hanbin Wu[1] and Hong Gao[2(✉)]

[1] The Institute of Humanities, Jiangxi University of TCM,
Nanchang, Jiangxi, China
gail74@126.com
[2] The School of Marxism, Jiangxi University of TCM, Nanchang, Jiangxi, China
glen74@126.com

Abstract. As increasingly popular of MOOC (Massive Open Online Course), it is now widely recognized as a powerful strength in the process of educational innovation, which remains its own chances and challenges. MOOC has a great impact on the traditional education, especially the higher education. Universities, colleges and teachers have taken measures to face the challenges by creating their own MOOCs. With an analysis of the existing successful MOOC, ten effective tips we've discovered as follows: (1) Set a Definite Teaching Goal; (2) Make a Detailed Design; (3) Contents First; (4) A Simple and Interesting Title; (5) To Create a Multi-sensory Experience; (6) Light Humor is needed; (7) The Law of "10 to 15 min"; (8) To Tell a Few Good Stories; (9) Your PPT: More Pictures and Charts instead of Words; (10) Just be Yourself. By following these effective skills, it's more likely to create a more attractive and successful MOOC.

Keywords: Effective tips · MOOCs · Design strategy

1 Introduction

MOOC is the abbreviation of Massive Open Online Course. With the development of Internet and Information Technology, MOOC is becoming more prevalent among people especially younger ones in the e-learning era. An educational revolution may happen as nearly all kinds of MOOC appearing in the website platforms like Udacity, Coursera, edX and so on.

Compared with the traditional class, MOOC has many advantages. First of all, MOOC provides us abundant educational resources that anyone can reach it freely and conveniently only if he or she owns an electronic device connected with the Internet such as a computer, a Smart-phone or an tablet PC. Secondly, MOOC is much more impactful and economical than traditional courses. Different from the traditional classes, which can only serve dozens or hundreds of students, MOOC can easily enroll tens of thousands students or even more. Thirdly, as far as the students are concerned, MOOC has a better flexibility and selectivity. Not only can students decide which MOOC they want to take, but also they can choose it anywhere and anytime. Finally, MOOC can help strengthen the interactions between teachers and students. For instance, in a traditional classroom, some students remain high enthusiasm about

G. Sun and S. Liu (Eds.): ADHIP 2017, LNICST 219, pp. 250–256, 2018.
https://doi.org/10.1007/978-3-319-73317-3_30

making a statement while others keep silence unless they are to be asked. Relevantly, during a MOOC, everyone can contribute to the courses with an equal opportunity to submit ideas, comments or questions. Anyone who wants to join the discussion just needs to type their ideas out instead of raising their hands.

Based on these strong points, MOOC has a great effect on the traditional education as well as the higher education, which attributes to much more pressure on teachers. Regarded as a big challenge, MOOC is also viewed as a chance to improve the quality of higher education. Many universities and colleges initiatively adjust themselves to the process by creating and uploading their own MOOC. According to an incomplete statistics, by the June of 2015, 286 Chinese MOOC were available on line. And so many famous universities in China like Peking University, Tsinghua University and Fudan University, have signed a cooperative agreements with international MOOC Platforms such as edX, Coursera and so on to speed up the development of MOOC. A lot of teachers have to redesign their courseware to fit the demand of a MOOC. As a result, the importance has been throwing a light on how to make a successful MOOC.

2 Chances of MOOCs Compared with Traditional Courses

Whether it is called OCW (open course ware), OER (open educational resource), or MOOC (massive open online course), the core change, compared with traditional courses, is to provide open educational resources and open learning process to anyone who has an intention to learn, mostly by free. As a educational revolution in this era, MOOCs have many chances superior to the traditional courses.

2.1 High-Quality Educational Resources

No matter what platform it belongs, MOOC will be assessed and selected before it is presented on line. So most courses offered by MOOC are taught by famous lecturers or teaching team in prestigious universities. In MOOC platform,we can easily find many courses from the top-ranking universities all over the world, such as Harvard University, Stanford University and Massachusetts Institute of Technology, as well as Peking University, Tsinghua University and Fudan University, etc. This means nearly everyone can easily access to these high-quality educational resources by the way of MOOC, which is unthinkable and impossible in the traditional teaching system.

2.2 The Characteristics of Large-Scale

"Massive" is one of characteristics of MOOC, which means in a MOOC it can hold a large-scale participants. Compared with a traditional classroom, which can room at most hundreds of students, a MOOC even can enroll thousands of participants at one time. Take an example, in a MOOC named *Financial Analyses and Decision Making* from Dr Xiao Xing, the professor of School of Economics and Management in Tsinghua University, there are totally 102,000 participants from 201 countries and districts all over the world who signed in the course, and among them 4320 registrants finished the course and obtain the certificate. This is hard to realize in the traditional courses.

2.3   Flexible Ways of Learning

For a learner, MOOC has provided much more flexible ways for their study. In a traditional course, the time and place are always scheduled, and students have to follow them to study. While in a MOOC, people can learn the teaching contents anytime and anyplace only if they have computers or other electronic devices connected with the Internet. Also they can choose to pause, review, fast-forward or repeatedly watch the videos to make sure they've understand the knowledge points thoroughly according to their own present level. Moreover, in a traditional classroom, communication always occurs among few people, when the conversation continues, the rest of class have to remained silent unless they are call upon. On the contrary, most of MOOCs have provided the discussion area, and anyone can join in the conversation by typing their questions or answering other peoples' questions without the need of raising their hands, which can help them to reinforce the knowledge points they've learned, to clarify the misunderstanding, to develop thinking and creativity and to improve their abilities of understand and utilization of the knowledge.

3   The Challenges Faced by MOOCs

Although MOOC has many chances compared with the traditional teaching mode, it also has many challenges. As a result, the development of MOOC has been restricted and faced many difficulties. For example, by far there are no universities or colleges offering the participants with credits for MOOC learning. Degree award and credits for certification raises a real problem for MOOC. In other words, it has a long way to go.

3.1   Low Completion Rate of MOOC

The low completion rate is a common problem for MOOCs. As time went on, a large number of participants have given up their study with unfinished contents of the course which they registered for the first beginning. Recent statistics shows that only 5% to 15% of the enrolled learners can persist to complete a course, and the attrition rate of MOOC is as high as 85% to 95% (Yu 2015). According to a survey, the completion rate of MOOCs is estimated as low as only about 5%–7% (Zheng 2014), which is unimaginable in the traditional courses. This phenomenon of 'alarmingly' low completion rates observed across MOOCs has aroused concerns from the scholars (Halawa et al. 2014).

3.2   Unsystematic Curriculum Design

Although providing various choices for learners, many MOOC platforms only offer different courses instead of organizing them to a systematic curriculum according to a specific major. While in a college or an university, there is a very strict curriculum design to ensure all necessary courses of a major can be scheduled in specific order and time. To realize the goal of talent cultivation, it's very essential and important to make a systematic curriculum design, which should be stipulated by professional development programs.

3.3 Lack of Face-to-Face Communication

The design of the discussion area or forum in a MOOC enables the learners to raise their questions, to share their feelings, to communicate with others by knocking on the keyboard or even through the camera and microphone. This is a convenient and effective way of communication, and people may feel less pressure. However, it is obvious that this way of communication through the screens can't replace a truly, face-to-face communication. In a MOOC, lectures always pay more attention to explain the knowledge points instead of showing their humanistic concern to the students. The lack of face-to-face communication makes a MOOC hardly meet the students' emotion needs.

3.4 The Issue of Teaching Quality Assurance

As we all known, the student-teacher ratio is seriously overweight in a MOOC's massive online learning process. In a MOOC, a few lecturers have to face thousands of students, and they must deal with a lot of things, such as to produce the teaching videos, design issues, upload their courses onto website, join the discussion and maintain the network, and so on. Although they devote most of their energy and time to prepare for the course, it's impossible for them to meet all the needs of so many students. The lack of understanding the real knowledge level and attitude of learners make teaching quality assurance remain a problem. On the other hand, the assessment of teaching effect is very difficult in a MOOC. In order to ensure the teaching quality in a MOOC, these problems such as the effectiveness of the test, to identify the real examinee from the surrogate exam-taker and cheating in the exam, etc. should be solved in the future.

4 How to Make a Successful MOOC

In order to conclude the effective tips of making a successful MOOC, our research group has taken a glance of hundreds of different types of MOOC in the Chinese website (http://www.icourse163.org/). What we have found is that all the popular MOOC own its own specific characteristics and common features. By analyzing these common features of the popular MOOC, we can draw a conclusion that the effective tips of making a successful MOOC can be list as follows:

4.1 Set a Definite Teaching Goal

Before starting the concrete work of making a MOOC, you should ask yourself several questions: What messages do you want to convey to your audience? Who is your target population? How to design your teaching process to fit the different demands of all kinds of students?... and so on. Once you clarified these questions, you will get a specific teaching goal and know how to realize it.

4.2   Make a Detailed Design

The design of a MOOC always includes a teaching objective design, a teaching strategy design and a teaching evaluation design. As for the teaching objective design, we have mentioned above. The teaching strategy design can be divided into a teaching resources collecting strategy, a teaching process strategy and a teaching activity strategy. And the teaching evaluation design can be related to two sides: the evaluation of teaching and learning respectively. All these must be designed carefully and thoroughly.

4.3   Contents First

The contents of the course are always the most important in order to create a successful MOOC. The first concern of people to enroll in a MOOC is whether its contents can fit their needs. In the process of preparing a MOOC,the designer should pay more attention to the contents of the course. Please make sure that contents are the soul of a successful MOOC and should be considered for the first place. All the factors such as the accuracy, completeness, or usefulness related to the contents, should be selected and designed carefully.

4.4   A Simple and Interesting Title

A simple but interesting title as well as the names of its chapters and sections for a MOOC take a very important part. It's a common sense that people prefer to the briefness while problem-solving. It's the interesting things not boring ones that make people easily to understand. Therefore, a simple and interesting title can always catch people's attentions and interests, which is extremely important of people's firstly choosing phrase of a MOOC. Take a MOOC of Fudan University as an example,the name of "Microbes and Human" is much better than the one of "Microbiology". What's more, the name of one of its sections—"How far AIDS from us?" seems much more attractive to people.

4.5   To Create Multi-sensory Experience

As we all known, multi-sensory experience is good for improving the effectiveness of learning. There are many ways you can choose to deepen people's impressions. Making a personal talk-show, presenting some beautiful pictures, telling a few of jokes, inserting a section of video or interview and even making an experiment on the spot as examples. While preparing your teaching process in a MOOC, you should try your best to arouse the sensory channels of the audience as many as possible, because the more their senses involved in the teaching process, the better the teaching effect is.

4.6   Light Humor is Needed

The sense of humor is always an elegant and welcomed personality trait. In some specific situation, the proper light humor can help people to release the metal pressures, melting the embarrassment and even to defuse the conflicts. To bring some light humor in your MOOC can make your presentation more interesting and relaxing, and it can also help you to show your intelligence and confidence while dealing with an academic problem. With the help of some light humor, your students would feel better and enjoy the class.

4.7   The Law of "10 to 15 Minutes"

"10 to 15 min" is a golden law for one section of a MOOC. The period of time is enough for a lecturer to elaborate a theoretic or practical problem, or to express his ideas and attitudes toward an issue. Also, it is the extreme limits that a person focuses his attention on something. Please remember the fact that in the era of Internet, most people who enrolled in a MOOC don't have too much time as well as patience, and the fragmentation of time naturally leads to fragmentation of learning. So make sure to simplify your expression and finish a section with this time limits.

4.8   To Tell a Few Good Stories

Good stories can always stir people's heart, moving them and encouraging them to improve themselves and conquer the difficulties to reach their goals. The skill of telling a few good stories is extremely important in the teaching process of a MOOC. Normally, a story has 4 basic elements: plot, characters, setting and theme. A good story teller often selects the proper story by evaluating these four basic elements. So you can follow that, too. To choose a story for a MOOC, it's always a wise choice to tell a story about your own experience. Peng Kai-ping, professor of Tsinghua University, had been told a good story about fortune-telling based on his own experience in his MOOC "Introduction of Psychology", which gained widely praises by leading the audience to experience the challenge, analyzing the situation and finding a way out.

4.9   Your PPT: More Pictures and Charts Instead of Words

PPT is always an important and essential tool to aid your teaching in a MOOC as well as an traditional teaching process. However, as a lecturer in a MOOC, you shouldn't rely too much on your PPT by preparing a lot of words and characters. Although they are helpful as a hint for your speech, according to the study of educational psychology, PPT with too many words and characters will dramatically weaken the learning interest of the students and let them feel bored. As a replacement, you can prepare more beautiful pictures and elaborate charts in your PPT. Make sure that the purpose of your PPT is to help the students understand your ideas more easily, to find out the logic among the knowledge points and to stimulate their learning enthusiasm. By putting more pictures and charts in your PPT,you have more chance to draw the students' attention and raise the attraction of your MOOC.

4.10   Just be Yourself

When giving your presentation in a MOOC, you just need to be yourself. Never try to put on an act in a MOOC because it's easy for people to recognize a real you. What you need to do is to share your passion and personality fully to your audience. To be yourself can present a real person instead of an actor to people who will choose the course and it will help you to reach a closer relationship with your audience. By doing so, you can gain more trust from your students. Just like an old saying in China, "A student will believe in teachings only when he gets close to his teacher", "just be yourself" can bring even more in a MOOC than that what you have thought.

5 Conclusion

From the analysis above, we can draw a conclusion that nowadays MOOC has played an very important part in our educational system. The popularity of MOOC is a great strength in the process of educational innovation. The storm of MOOC can be a big challenge as well as a big chance. It has even more great impact on the higher education, and we should prepare well to fit the challenge. To make a successful MOOC, these effective tips talked about above are crucial. With the help of these skills, we can create a MOOC more easily and effectively.

References

Anderson, C.: How to give a killer presentation. Harv. Bus. Rev. **6**, 121–125 (2013)

http://www.icourse163.org

Yu, C.J.: Challenges and changes of MOOC to traditional classroom teaching mode. Can. Soc. Sci. **11**(1), 135–139 (2015)

Zheng, X.J.: The rise of MOOC in US universities and its challenge to traditional higher education. Comp. Educ. Rev. **7**, 39 (2014)

Halawa, S., Greene, D., Mitchell, J.: Dropout prediction in MOOCs using learner activity features. eLearning Pap. **37**, 1–10 (2014). http://www.openeducationeuropa.eu/en/article

Peng, K.-P.: Introduction to Psychology. http://www.xuetangx.com/courses/course-v1:TsinghuaX+30700313X+sp/about

Survey on Spectrum Prediction Methods via Back Propagation Neural Network

Zheng Dou, Tingting Cao$^{(\boxtimes)}$, and Wenwen Li

College of Information and Communication Engineering,
Harbin Engineering University, Nantong str. 145, Harbin 150001, China
2457345391@qq.com

Abstract. Spectrum prediction is one of the key technologies of cognitive radio. With the development of electronic warfare, the concept of cognitive electronic warfare has been put forward. At the moment, as one of the key technologies of cognitive electronic warfare, spectrum prediction is also very important. In reality, it is difficult to predict the use of licensed spectrum, and it is more difficult to predict the enemy's spectrum in enemy operations. In this paper, the existing spectrum prediction research is introduced. According to their shortcomings, a method of spectrum prediction is proposed, which improves the BP neural network by using tabu search algorithm.

Keywords: BP neural network · Spectrum prediction · Tabu search

1 Introduction

With the development of communication technology, people are demanding more and more electronic warfare, expecting electronic warfare to have the same thinking and learning ability as people, so people put forward the concept of cognitive electronic warfare. The emergence of cognitive electronic warfare is an inevitable development of electronic warfare technology. In the electronic warfare technology, equipment with a digital, software based on the ability to continue to cognitive (or intelligent) is a matter of course [20]. In the cognitive warfare, the spectrum prediction of the enemy is a prerequisite for interference with enemy communications.

As one of the key technologies of cognitive radio, today's spectrum prediction is mainly to minimize the interference caused by unauthorized users to authorized users, and to find spectrum holes (That is, some bands or timeslots that are not fully used by unauthorized users) to allow unauthorized users use. In this way, the spectrum utilization can be improved. Therefore, in recent years, spectrum prediction has received extensive attention in the field of communication.

At present, the commonly used spectrum prediction method can be attributed to neural network prediction method, regression analysis based forecasting method, based on Markov chain prediction method and data mining

© ICST Institute for Computer Sciences, Social Informatics and Telecommunications Engineering 2018
G. Sun and S. Liu (Eds.): ADHIP 2017, LNICST 219, pp. 257–264, 2018.
https://doi.org/10.1007/978-3-319-73317-3_31

method [11]. Among them, the neural network method has a good non-linear mapping ability, has been applied to the field of cognitive radio. Spectrum prediction played a very good role.

2   Fundamentals

Back Propagation (BP) neural network is a feed-forward artificial neural network model. It can establish a proper mapping relation between input data set and output data set [21]. BP neural network learning process is divided into two processes: positive and reverse transmission. When propagating forward, the input data is passed from the input layer of the network, through the hidden layer, and finally to the output layer. When the output data of the output layer is not equal to the expected value, the reverse propagation of the error is performed. The reverse propagation process of error is that the error is transmitted through the hidden layer to the input layer, the error is distributed in the hidden layer, and the error is distributed to each unit. In the process of forward propagation and backward propagation, we continuously adjust the weights and thresholds to get a better BP neural network.

In the BP neural network model, the application of the single hidden layer network (three layer feed forward network) as shown in Fig. 1 is the most common. It mainly includes input layer, hidden layer and output layer.

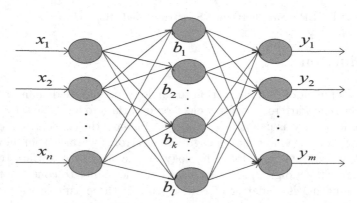

Input layer   Hide layer   Output layer

Fig. 1. BP neural network. Three layers of BP neural network, the eigenvalues $x_1, x_2, ..., x_n$ are input by the input layer, through the hidden layer, and finally to the output layer.

In this 3-layer BP neural network, there are n input neurons, m output neurons, l hidden neurons. The input of each layer is only related to the output of the previous layer. The input of the input layer is $X = (x_1, x_2, ..., x_i, ...x_n)^T$, The output of the output layer is $Y = (y_1, y_2, ..., y_j, ...y_m)^T$. Assume that the connection weights between the ith neurons of the input layer and the kth neurons of the hidden layer is v_{ik}, it is assumed that the connection weight between the kth neuron of the hidden layer and the jth neuron of the output layer is w_{kj}.

It is well known that the ideal activation function is a step function, but the step function is not smooth, discontinuous and other shortcomings, in practice commonly used sigmoid function as an activation function, Sigmoid function mathematical expression:

$$Sigmoid\,(x) = \frac{1}{1+e^{-x}} \tag{1}$$

Assuming that the neurons of the hidden layer and the input layer use the Sigmoid function as the activation function, the training sequence (x_k, y_k), we can give the formula:

$$\tilde{y}_j^k = f(\beta_j - \theta_j) \tag{2}$$

Among them, β_j $(\beta_j = \sum_{k=1}^{l} w_{kj} b_k)$ is represents the input received by the jth neuron of the output layer. θ_j is the threshold of the jth neurons in the output layer. Thus, the mean square error can be expressed as:

$$E_f = \frac{1}{2} \sum_{j=1}^{l} (\tilde{y}_j^f - y_j^f) \tag{3}$$

In the above BP neural network, $(m + n + 1)k + m$ parameters are determined. On the Eq. (3) in the error E_f, we give the learning rate η, there is:

$$\Delta\omega_{kj} = -\eta \frac{\partial E_f}{\partial \omega_{kj}} \tag{4}$$

ω_{kj} first affect the jth output neuron input value β_j, and then affect its output value $\tilde{y}_j^k$, and finally affect E_f, so

$$\frac{\partial E_f}{\partial \omega_{kj}} = \frac{\partial E_f}{\partial (y)_j^k} \cdot \frac{\partial (y)_j^k}{\partial \beta_j} \cdot \frac{\partial \beta_j}{\partial \omega_{kj}} \tag{5}$$

And because the Sigmoid function has the following properties:

$$f'(x) = f(x)(1 - f(x)) \tag{6}$$

According to Eqs. (2) and (3) calculated:

$$\begin{aligned} g_j &= -\frac{\partial E_f}{\partial (y)_j^k} \cdot \frac{\partial (y)_j^k}{\partial \beta_j} \\ &= (y)_j^k (1 - (y)_j^k)(y_j^k - (y)_j^k) \end{aligned} \tag{7}$$

After the calculation, we get the weight between the hidden layer and the output layer. The formula is:

$$\Delta\omega_{kj} = \eta g_j b_h \tag{8}$$

Similarly, we can deduce:

$$\Delta\theta_j = -\eta g_j \tag{9}$$

$$\Delta v_{ik} = \eta e_k x_i \tag{10}$$

$$\Delta\gamma_k = -\eta e_k \tag{11}$$

Among them, γ_k represents the threshold of the kth neurons in the hidden layer. In the formulas 10 and 11, e_k is:

$$
\begin{aligned}
e_k &= -\frac{\partial E_f}{\partial b_k} \cdot \frac{\partial b_k}{\partial \alpha_k} \\
&= -\sum_{j=1}^{m} \frac{\partial E_f}{\partial \beta_j} \cdot \frac{\partial \beta_j}{\partial b_k} f'(\alpha_k - \gamma_k) \\
&= \sum_{j=1}^{m} \omega_{kj} g + j f'(\alpha_k - \gamma_k) \\
&= b_k(1 - b_k) \sum_{j=1}^{m} \omega_{kj} g_j
\end{aligned}
\tag{12}
$$

The goal of the BP neural network is to minimize the cumulative error on the entire training set.

$$E = \frac{1}{n} \sum_{f=1}^{n} E_f \tag{13}$$

So, we have to continue to train the data, adjust the network weights and thresholds [23].

3 Spectrum Prediction and Analysis

In recent years, spectrum prediction is mainly in the field of cognitive radio. The spectrum prediction technology in cognitive radio system mainly includes four aspects: channel state prediction, authorized user activity prediction, radio environment prediction and transmission rate prediction [14]. There is little research on the prediction of spectrum in enemy operations. In the context of the information age, with the development of cognitive electronic warfare technology, the prediction of the enemy spectrum is also particularly important.

In 2005, Zhang et al. conducted a statistical analysis of the wireless signals in the district. Based on the analysis method of Box-Jenkins, Auto Regression (AR), Moving Average (MA) and Autoregressive Integrated Moving Average (ARIMA) models were used to simulate and predict the measured data, and then the model data were analyzed by using the time series analysis method. An error analysis was performed [7]. In 2008, they used SPSS statistical tools and Box-Jenkins modeling method in time series to establish the AR, MA, ARMA (Auto-Regressive and Moving Average) and ARIMA models respectively to analyze and forecast the measured data, and can predict the trend of the wireless signal in the short term [6]. It is possible that they were the first to propose and study spectrum prediction. Since then, the spectrum predicted to enter people's field of vision.

In order to achieve the purpose of improving the spectrum utilization, some people have proposed the use of Markov's method. In 2012, Tang et al. proposed a hybrid spectrum switching algorithm combining passive spectrum switching with active spectrum switching. The algorithm is based on the continuous time Markov chain model of the main user channel, predicts the future state information of the channel, and periodically performs active spectrum switching on the cognitive user who is communicating in accordance with the prediction result. Hybrid spectrum switching algorithm can significantly improve the spectrum utilization of cognitive wireless networks [14]. In 2014, In order to improve the prediction complexity and reduce the prediction complexity, Liu proposes a spectral forecasting method combining the hidden Markov model with the context variable Markov model. This method can eliminate the influence of the spectrum detection error on the prediction performance. Based on the spectral data generated by the queuing model, the validity of the variable-length Markov method based on the context tree is verified in a stable environment and a non-stationary environment, respectively. In this paper, we use the data of the spectrum generated by the queuing model and the discrete time Markov model to verify the validity of the algorithm of the hidden Markov model and the context tree variable length Markov model in the presence of detection error [15]. In 2011, Liu et al. also proposes a dynamic cognitive radio spectrum access technology based on joint probability channel prediction (HMCP) based on hidden Markov model (HMM). The technical scheme can effectively improve the spectrum utilization rate of the cognitive users while reducing the interference of the cognitive users to the authorized users [16].

In the field of spectrum prediction of cognitive radio, the neural network method is often used by people. In 2011, Chen proposed a spectral model combined with the M/M/N queuing model, proposed a method of learning and forecasting the spectral cavity information by using the back propagation neural network, and by using the spectrum analyzer to collect the actual spectrum data as the simulation data, Which verifies the effectiveness of the method [9]. In 2014, Xu et al. proposed a cognitive radio spectrum prediction method based on SVM (Support Vector Machine), which significantly reduced the energy consumption of spectrum sensing, improved the spectrum utilization rate and had a good application prospect in cognitive radio prediction [11]. In 2011, Wang proposed a neural network prediction method. The spectrum of the cognitive radio is predicted by the network and the optimal spectrum is selected for the predicted results [12]. In 2014, Lan et al. Designed a three-step advanced spectrum prediction framework based on the neutral network. The genetic algorithm is used to optimize the neural network. Finally, this method is more suitable for the prediction of cognitive radio than Multi-layer Perceptron (MLP) [5]. In 2015, Huk and Mizera-Pietraszko made an experiment to analyze the predictive performance of Sigma-if neural network and Multi-layer Perceptron (MLP) network. The results show that Sigma-if neural network predicts better performance [4]. In 2011, Xian et al. proposes a chaotic neural network prediction mechanism for the remaining time of the channel state, and uses the chaos prediction to analyze and forecast the remaining time of the channel. The experimental results show that the prediction accuracy can reach more than 90%, which verifies the effectiveness of the prediction mechanism [17]. In 2016, Chen et al. proposed a spectrum support algorithm for weighted support vector machines, which changes the weights of key parameters in support vector machines based on signal reception signal-to-noise ratio and sampling time. The algorithm can improve the accuracy of the support vector in the cognitive radio prediction results [18]. In 2013, Li proposed a neural network spectrum prediction method based on DE-BP. The standard differential evolution (DE) algorithm and the BP algorithm are combined to introduce the neural network-based spectrum prediction, which saves the perception time and reduces the impact of unauthorized users on authorized users [22].

Neural networks have their own advantages in solving non-linear predictive problems, but there are some other ways. In 2014, Xing studied the problem of cooperative spectral state prediction in cognitive radio networks, and proposed a new cooperative spectral state prediction method to improve the accuracy of spectral state prediction [8]. In 2016, Eltholth uses wavelet neural network (WNN) to predict future channel occupancy. And the simulation of 100–200 MHz band is carried out to verify the effectiveness and accuracy of WNN in spectrum prediction [1]. In 2015, Bai et al. proposed the use of genetic algorithm and momentum algorithm to improve the BP neural network, customer service BP neural network shortcomings, and finally, verify the theory [2]. After 2016, Yang et al. also proposed a genetic algorithm to improve the BP neural network model for the field of spectrum prediction [3]. In 2016, Zang has improved the available time prediction algorithm for existing channels, and proposed two kinds of spectrum switching strategies based on the channel available time prediction. Compared with the traditional random passive switching strategy, it can greatly reduce the collision probability between the cognitive user and the authorized user, and can verify its validity [10]. In 2009, Yang et al. proposed a new access mechanism to predict future spectrum activity based on past and current spectrum activity of the primary user, so that the secondary user can access the band with high availability and reduce the possibility of collision with the primary user. It can be seen from the simulation experiment that compared with the traditional access mechanism and the access mechanism without threshold, the proposed scheme can effectively reduce the collision rate between primary and secondary users [13]. In 2012, Li et al., in order to find the airspace and energy domain conditions needed to satisfy the electromagnetic compatibility between the main user network and the cognitive radio network, consider the influence of distance, atmospheric loss and visual distance on the interdiffusion intensity and work efficiency, This method is of great significance for more efficient use of spectrum resources [19].

Cognitive radio spectrum prediction technology has been quite mature, we can learn from these spectrum prediction means, applied to cognitive electronic warfare, lay the foundation for the development of electronic warfare.

4   Conclusion

Although the artificial neural network has developed rapidly in recent years, the artificial neural network is only a simple simulation of the human brain. By summing up the above research results, although there are also neural network algorithm applications, but there is no real solution to some of the problems of neural networks. In this regard, according to the research progress summarized in this paper, we can think of spectrum prediction is expected to be applied in the future Cognitive electronic warfare. By improving the BP neural network by the tabu search algorithm, the BP neural network can improve the convergence rate slowly and easily fall into the local minimum. So as to realize the spectrum prediction in the field of cognitive electronic warfare.

Acknowledgments. This work was supported by the Nation Nature Science Foundation of China (No. 61401115), National Natural Science Foundation of China (No. 61301095), National Natural Science Foundation of China (No. 61671167). And this paper is funded by the International Exchange Program of Harbin Engineering University for Innovation-oriented Talents Cultivation.

References

1. Eltholth, A.A.: Spectrum prediction in cognitive radio systems using a wavelet neural network. In: 2016 24th International Conference on Software, Telecommunications and Computer Networks (SoftCOM), Split, pp. 1–6 (2016)
2. Bai, S., Zhou, X., Xu, F.: Spectrum prediction based on improved-backpropagation neural networks. In: 2015 11th International Conference on Natural Computation (ICNC), Zhangjiajie, pp. 1006–1011 (2015)
3. Yang, J., Zhao, H., Chen, X.: Genetic algorithm optimized training for neural network spectrum prediction. In: 2016 2nd IEEE International Conference on Computer and Communications (ICCC), Chengdu, pp. 2949–2954 (2016)
4. Huk, M., Mizera-Pietraszko, J.: Contextual neural-network based spectrum prediction for cognitive radio. In: 2015 Fourth International Conference on Future Generation Communication Technology (FGCT), Luton, pp. 1–5 (2015)
5. Lan, K., Zhao, H., Zhang, J., Long, C., Luo, M.: A spectrum prediction approach based on neural networks optimized by genetic algorithm in cognitive radio networks. In: 10th International Conference on Wireless Communications, Networking and Mobile Computing (WiCOM 2014), Beijing, pp. 131–136 (2014)
6. Zhang, H., Shou, G., Hu, Y.: Radio signal forecast for mobile network. J. Electron. Meas. Instrum. **04**, 44–48 (2008)
7. Zhang, H.: A method of radio signal forecast for mobile network. Chinese Society of Communications, Youth Work Committee (2006). New Theory of Communication Theory and Technology - Proceedings of the 11th National Youth Communication Conference. China Communications Society Youth Work Committee (2005)
8. Xing, X.: Research on spectrum prediction in cognitive radio networks. Beijing Jiaotong University, Beijing (2014)
9. Chen, B.: Research on spectrum prediction algorithm in cognitive radio system. Beijing University of Posts and Telecommunications, Beijing (2011)

10. Zang, W.: Research on mixed spectrum handoff strategy in cognitive radio based on spectrum prediction. Jilin University, Jilin (2016)
11. Xu, Y., Lu, H., Chen, X.: A SVM based spectrum prediction scheme for cognitive radio. Res. Dev. **11**, 87–92 (2014)
12. Wang, M.: Study on selection strategy of cognitive radio spectrum based on the theory of prediction. North China Electric Power University, Beijing (2011)
13. Yang, X., Yang, Z., Liu, S.: Forecast-based opportunistic spectrum access for cognitive radio networks. J. Chongqing Univ. Posts Telecommun. (Nat. Sci. Ed.) **01**, 14–19 (2009)
14. Tang, W., Yu, H., Li, S.: Mixed spectrum hand off algorithm for cognitive radio based on channel state prediction. Comput. Eng. Appl. **27**, 17–21 (2012)
15. Liu, Q.: Research on spectrum prediction based on markov model in cognitive radio networks. Xidian University, Xian (2014)
16. Liu, Y., Yang, J., Yang, H.: Hidden markov model-based joint probability channel prediction dynamic spectrum access in cognitive radio. J. Shanghai Univ. (Nat. Sci.) **05**, 581–585 (2011)
17. Xian, Y., Yang, Y., Xu, C., Zheng, X.: Spectrum usage prediction based on chaotic neural network model for cognitive radio system. J. Comput. Appl. **12**, 3181–3183+3194 (2011)
18. Chen, H., Chen, J., Gao, Z.: An improved WSVM prediction algorithm in cognitive radio. J. Electron Qual. **05**, 1–4 (2016)
19. Li, X., Zou, S., Xu, L.: Research on EMC prediction of cognitive radio and primary users. Wide Bd. Netw. **17**, 102–105 (2012)
20. Zhang, C., Yang, X.: Elementary study on cognitive electronic warfare. Commun. Countermeas. **02**, 1–4+20 (2013)
21. Zhou, Z.: A survey of the development of BP neural network. Shanxi Electron. Technol. **02**, 90–92 (2008)
22. Li, S.: Research on neural network predictive radio spectrum prediction based on DE - BP neural network. Southwest Jiaotong University, Sichuan (2013)
23. Zhou, Z.: Machine Learning, pp. 97–105. Tsinghua University Press, Beijing (2015)

Prediction Model Based Failure Time Data for Software Reliability

Peng Lin[1,2]([envelope]), Xu Tian[1], Xiaojuan Wang[1], Xu Cao[1], Jiejing Cao[1], Jianli Li[1], and Yan Gong[1]

[1] Software Testing and Evaluation Centre, China Electronic Equipment of System Engineering Institute, Beijing 100141, China
paul-lim@163.com
[2] Academy of Military Sciences PLA China, Beijing 100091, China

Abstract. Since all the defects cannot be detected within a finite software testing process (STP), the failure data should be wisely used to estimate the potential defects for software reliability. Therefore, a standard graphical methodology (GM) model is proposed for software reliability, in which failure data of time domain is utilized to predict the potential defects. First, non homogeneous and compound Poisson process is involved to model the failure time during STP. Then, GM model is utilized to predict the potential defects. Further, the software reliability is estimated based on GM model. Finally, compared with the traditional models, GM model can reach an improvement of 30% relative gain on average.

Keywords: Defect prediction · Poisson process · Data fitting
Software reliability

1 Introduction

As the development of software industry, the scale of software can be increasing day by day. In a typical system environment of software development, the software is programmed by a development term. Once a software release is generated, it should be assigned to a testing term, which should verify the release meets the design specifications restrictly. A software release can be a small program, or a large integrated system consisted by a group of subsystems. The testing term tests the software by applying necessary operation to detect the potential defects, which can find the failures of the software against to the design specifications. Generally, the testing activity is limited by a pre-determined time and a pre-determined number of testers. However, it is not feasible to discover every potential defects in a finite software testing process (STP). Therefore, the software reliability attracts more and more attentions [1–4].

Software reliability can be defined as the probability that a software operates without any failure within a specified time by specified operating. Software reliability can be obtained from the testing progress during the software development

© ICST Institute for Computer Sciences, Social Informatics and Telecommunications Engineering 2018
G. Sun and S. Liu (Eds.): ADHIP 2017, LNICST 219, pp. 265–274, 2018.
https://doi.org/10.1007/978-3-319-73317-3_32

[1]. When one defect is detected and repaired during STP, the potential defects in the code will decrease, which means the defect detection rate is against to the number of detected defects [2] as show in Fig. 1.

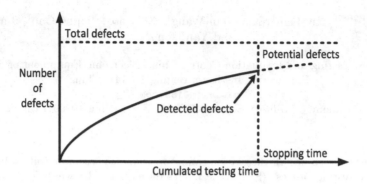

Fig. 1. Defect detection in software testing process.

Based on the detection defects, we can determine whether the program can be released, or more testing time is necessary. The number of failures can be used to estimate the software, which should be reported to our customers before operating the software [3]. The estimation can help us to evaluate the necessary time for software testing.

There are always some constraints limit the software testing time, especially, the constraint of the time-consuming to release a software system under business pressure [4]. Therefore, software reliability modeling is proposed to evaluate both the current and future reliability. In particular, defect prediction can help determine when the software development should be terminated.

Traditional software reliability models can be grouped into three classes.

First, the amount of defects is finite within a finite amount of code [5], by which more code means more defects, so as the defect detection rate too. The amount of detection defects during STP are explicitly made in some models, while others assume that these defects data can be fitted statistically by the software reliability growth model.

Second, a compound Poisson process (CPP) [6, 7] is used to model the clusters of detected defects, where the defects are grouped in a given time interval. CPP not only try to predict the remaining failure rate after a limited testing time, but also can forecast the potential detects after a given STP.

Third, the number of defects is infinite in log Poisson model assumption [8]. Further, Log Poisson models make assumptions that all the detected defects are perfectly repaired. However, it is difficult to evaluate the affection of the model assumptions.

Although infinite assumption is questionable, it is reasonable that the potential defects will exist until be found and repaired [9].

Focus on large-scale software or integrated system within STP, a defect prediction model basing on standard graphical methodology is proposed in this paper, where the defect data of time domain is utilized. Three actual testing data sets of time domain are used to compare GM model with the classical G-O, CPP and M-O models, both the fitting and prediction results of GM model perform better than the others.

2   Poisson Models

2.1   Non Homogeneous Poisson Process

Non homogeneous Poisson process (NHPP) has been proposed as software reliability model [9,10]. The Poisson parameter $\lambda(t)$ (where $t > 0$) in NHPP model is a time dependent function.

Defects of the software cause failures at random times. Assume $N(t)$ is the amount of detected defects within time t, which should be a cumulated testing time (either CPU time or calendar time). Then, let $\lambda(t)$ be the probability of the amount of detected defects within a time interval t. Further, the probability of n failures can be calculated as

$$P\{N(t) = n\} = \frac{\lambda^n(t)}{n!} e^{(-\lambda(t))}. \tag{1}$$

Therefore, $\lambda(t)$ should be the key function in NHPP. There are two kind of NHPP based models, which are G-O model and M-O model [5].

In G-O model [9], let $\lambda(t)$ be the expected amount of total defects, which are detected within time t can be calculated as

$$\lambda(t) = \alpha(1 - e^{(-\beta t)}), \tag{2}$$

where β is the detection rate for each individual defect. The parameter α is the expected amount of total defects in G-O model, and

$$\lambda(t) = \alpha P(t), \tag{3}$$

where $P(t)$ is the cumulative distribution function. Then, $P(0) = 0$, which means that no defect is detected before the software testing process (STP) starts. On the other side, $P(\infty) = 1$, then, $\lambda(\infty) = \alpha$, and α is the amount of total defects, which should be detected after a finite STP.

M-O model [9] assumes that one software may have an infinite number of defects. M-O is a log Poisson model, where the detected number of defects after cumulated testing time t is NHPP. The $\lambda(t)$ in M-O model can be calculated as

$$\lambda(t) = \frac{1}{\theta} \log(\lambda_0 \theta t + 1). \tag{4}$$

Both the operational performance of G-O and M-O depends on the lasting time of STP. Longer STP leads to better performance. Although the time spent in STP delays the product release, which leads to additional costs, the cost of repairing a defect after software release should be more expensive than during STP [7]. Therefore, the defect prediction can be optimal release time to minimize cost by determining STP time.

2.2 Compound Poisson Process

The failures of CPP model are detected and grouped in clusters [11], which are found following a Poisson process. Further, a compounding distribution is used to model the clusters size, which follows a geometric distribution [12]. Further, the amount of detected defects follows a compound Poisson process, and the probability function is given by

$$P\{(N(t) = n)\} = \sum_{k=1}^{m} \frac{(\lambda t)^k}{k!} e^{(-\lambda t)} f^{*k}\{X_1 + X_2 + \cdots + X_k = n\}, \qquad (5)$$

where, $f^{*k}\{X_1 + X_2 + \cdots + X_k = n\}$ is the sum of k independent identically distributed random variables X_i, which follows a distribution function $f(X)$. Since the distribution function $f(X)$ models the size of failures cluster, the mean value can be given by

$$E[N(t)] = \lambda t E[X]. \qquad (6)$$

CPP model is easier to implement, which can adaptively change to fit different projects. The failure rate of CPP model is constant. However, as the failure rate will update time to time, the CPP model can not predict a long time period. Then, the predicted failure rate of CPP is a constant, while it is dependent on time in NHPP model.

3   Prediction Model

A standard graphical methodology (GM) [13] is proposed for defect prediction. There are three steps to realize defect prediction. First, the data of the cumulated failure times should be ascending ordered. Further, the two necessary parameters of the theoretical exponential distribution should be estimated too. Finally, a defect prediction basing on the theoretical distribution can be obtained.

The cumulated failure times are ascending ordered, then, associate a probability with ascending ordered failure time t_i by

$$p_i = \frac{(i - \frac{1}{2})}{n}, \qquad (7)$$

and further associate with the points

$$z_i = (t_i, p_i), i = 1, \cdots, n. \qquad (8)$$

The cumulative distribution function [14] for the two-parameter exponential distribution can be

$$F(t) = 1 - e^{-\frac{t-\mu}{\lambda}}, \qquad (9)$$

where λ is the respected mean, and μ is the respected shift. Then, the $\lambda(t)$ in GM model can be given by

$$\lambda(t) = \alpha e^{-\frac{t-\mu}{\lambda}}. \qquad (10)$$

Further, let $Q(p_i)$ be the theoretical distribution and given by

$$F(Q(p_i)) = p_i. \tag{11}$$

And then,

$$Q(p_i) = F^{-1}(p_i), \tag{12}$$

for the two-parameter exponential distribution,

$$Q(p_i) = -\lambda ln(1 - p_i) + \mu. \tag{13}$$

4   Software Reliability

A software reliability model is defined by NHPP [1,2], where $N(t)$ represents the amount of detected defects by cumulated testing time t during STP. Further, the failure intensity function of the software reliability model is defined by

$$F(t) = \frac{d\lambda(t)}{dt}. \tag{14}$$

The probability of the detected defects $N(t)$ has the value n is given by

$$P\{N(t) = n\} = \prod_i P\{N(t_i) = i\}, i = 1, \cdots, n. \tag{15}$$

Further, the reliability of t_i based on the last failure time t_{i-1} can be obtained as

$$\begin{aligned}
P\{N(t_i)|N(t_{i-1})\} \\
= P\{N(t_i) > i - 1|N(t_{i-1}) = i - 1\} \\
= 1 - P\{N(t_i) \leq i|N(t_{i-1}) = i - 1\}.
\end{aligned} \tag{16}$$

5   Comparison

5.1   Data Sets

Three are three classical models selected to compare with GM model, including G-O, CPP and M-O model. Three actual testing data sets [3,5,15] of time domain are used to estimate the performance of the compared models.

Each data set is sorted and separated into the fitting part and the estimation part. The fitting part data takes a part of 90% percent in the data set, which is the lower part of time domain. The estimation part is about 10% of the data set, which is the higher part of the time domain. The fitting part data is used to compare fitting performance. The estimation part data is used to compare the prediction performance.

The first data set contains 17 defects with cumulated failure time [15], and then, the fitting part has 15 defects and the estimation part has 2 defects. The second data set contains 30 defects [5], in which the fitting part has 27 defects and the estimation part has 3 defects. There are 136 defects in the third data set [3], where the fitting part has the lower 122 defects of time domain and the estimation part has 14 defects.

Therefore, the first data set is the smallest one in the three actual data sets, the second data set is the middle one, and the third data set is the largest one.

5.2   Performance Estimation

The four referenced models are compared on the three actual data sets, and the result of the first data set is shown in Fig. 2.

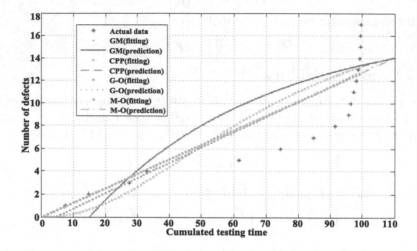

Fig. 2. Performance on the first data set

Further, the second result of the four models is shown in Fig. 3.

At last, the third result of the four models is shown in Fig. 4.

Each fitting curve are separated into two parts. The left part is the fitting result marked with fitting, and the right part is the prediction result marked with prediction.

The mean square error (MSE) is used to compare the performance of the four models, the MSE can be calculated as

$$MSE = \sqrt{\frac{\sum_{i=1}^{n} (e_{t(i)} - p_{t(i)})^2}{n}}, \qquad (17)$$

where $e_{t(i)}$ represents the estimated amount of expected defects at time $t(i)$, which can be a fitting or prediction result. $p_{t(i)}$ represents the real amount of detected defects at time $t(i)$, which can be picked up from the actual testing data sets of time domain.

The results of fitting and prediction performance on the three data sets are demonstrated in Table 1.

On the first data set, the prediction MSE of GM model is the smallest. Although GM model performs the best on the prediction MSE, both the fitting and average MSE are bigger than the other models. Therefore, the average MSE of GM model performs worst on the smallest data set.

Further, the average MSE of GM model is 1.397 on the second data set, which is a little bigger than CPP model, but smaller than the G-O and M-O

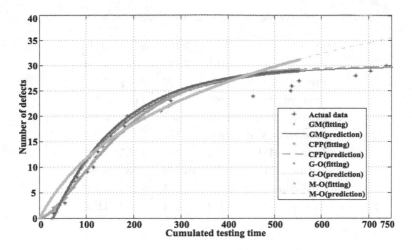

Fig. 3. Performance on the second data set

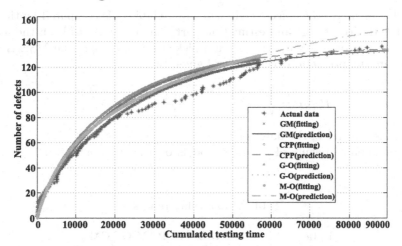

Fig. 4. Performance on the third data set.

model. The third data set is the largest one, the average MSE of GM model is just about 3.950, which is much smaller than the others.

At last, the average MSE of GM model performs the best on the three data sets in the compared models. Since the defect number of the third data set is larger than both the first and second ones, the larger data set could lead to more accuracy. With the number of defects increasing, the performance of GM model should be always better than the other models.

Table 1. Performance results

Data set		G-O	CPP	M-O	GM
1	Fitting MSE	2.210	2.679	2.227	3.211
	Prediction MSE	3.775	3.303	3.841	3.158
	Average MSE	2.993	2.991	3.034	3.185
2	Fitting MSE	2.047	1.668	2.815	1.738
	Prediction MSE	0.934	1.111	5.715	0.957
	Average MSE	1.491	1.389	4.265	1.397
3	Fitting MSE	8.738	10.562	8.532	5.993
	Prediction MSE	2.684	2.881	10.168	1.907
	Average MSE	5.711	6.721	9.350	3.950

5.3 Reliability Estimation

To further estimate the defect prediction, the reliability is compared by the last data of both fitting part and estimation part. The last data of both the fitting part $e_{0.9N}$ and prediction part $e_{1.0N}$ are picked up, and then, the MSE is used to compare the prediction accuracy and given by

$$P_{MSE} = \sqrt{\frac{(\frac{e_{0.9N}}{N} - 0.9)^2 + (\frac{e_{1.0N}}{N} - 1.0)^2}{2}}, \qquad (18)$$

where N is the size of the data set.

The reliability results of the four models on the three actual data sets are shown in Table 2.

Table 2. Reliability results

Data set		G-O	CPP	M-O	GM
1	Fitting $P_{0.9N}$	0.746	0.775	0.742	0.786
	Prediction $P_{1.0N}$	0.754	0.781	0.750	0.787
	P_{MSE}	0.205	0.178	0.209	0.171
2	Fitting $P_{0.9N}$	0.968	0.976	1.043	0.965
	Prediction $P_{1.0N}$	0.986	0.995	1.179	0.989
	P_{MSE}	0.049	0.054	0.162	0.047
3	Fitting $P_{0.9N}$	0.922	0.935	0.950	0.908
	Prediction $P_{1.0N}$	0.964	0.983	1.095	0.974
	P_{MSE}	0.030	0.027	0.076	0.019

On the first data set, both $P_{0.9N}$ and $P_{1.0N}$ of GM model are bigger than the other three models, which means bad performance on the smallest data set.

However, both on the second and third data sets $P_{0.9N}$ and $P_{1.0N}$ of GM model are the smallest ones. Therefore, GM model perform better both on the middle and largest data sets than the three compared models.

Further, P_{MSE} is 0.171, 0.047 and 0.019 respectively. Therefore, P_{MSE} of GM model is the smallest in the compared models, which means the best fitting accuracy at the lasting data of time domain.

Since the GM model performs better both in the performance and reliability results, the relative gain G is formulated as

$$G = \sum_{*=G-O}^{CPP,M-O} \frac{P_{MSE}^* - P_{MSE}^{GM}}{P_{MSE}^*}. \tag{19}$$

The relative gain of GM model on the first data set is 13.15%, 29.90% and 47.10% on the second data set. Then, an average relative gain 30.05% can be reached by GM model, which shows an improvement compared to the classical G-O, CPP and M-O models.

6   Conclusion

A standard GM model is proposed to predict potential defects for software reliability in this paper. By fitting defect data of time domain, both the number of defects and failure rate can be estimated by GM model theoretically. Further, GM model is used to estimate the software reliability during STP, which can help to determine when to terminate the STP and release the software. Finally, three traditional models are compared with GM model on the three actual testing data sets. The performance comparison shows that GM model performs much better than the others, and an average 30% relative gain can be obtained for software reliability estimation.

References

1. Wood, A.: Software reliability growth models: assumptions vs. reality. In: International Symposium on Software Reliability Engineering, pp. 136–141 (1997)
2. Almering, V., von Genuchten, M., Cloudt, G., Sonnemans, P.J.M.: Using software reliability growth models in practice. IEEE Softw. **24**, 82–88 (2007)
3. Musa, J.D., Iannino, A., Okumoto, K.: Software Reliability: Measurement, Prediction, Application. McGraw Hill, New York (1987)
4. Sahinoglu, M., Glover, S.: Economic analysis of a stopping-rule in branch coverage testing. In: International Symposium on Quality Electronic Design, pp. 341–346 (2002)
5. Akuno, A.O., Orawo, L.A., Islam, A.S.: One-sample Bayesian predictive analyses for an exponential non homogeneous Poisson process in software reliability. Open J. Stat. **4**, 402–411 (2014)
6. Sahinoglu, M.: Compound-Poisson software reliability model. IEEE Trans. Softw. Eng. **18**(7), 624–630 (1992)

7. Xianghui, Z., Lin, L., Yafang, H., Lei, Z., Yuangang, Y.: Software reliability measurements based on compound Poisson processes. J. Tsinghua Univ. Sci. Technol. **53**(12), 1743–1749 (2013)
8. Musa, J.D., Okumoto, K.: A logarithmic Poisson execution time model for software reliability measurement. In: International Conference on Software Engineering, pp. 230–238 (1984)
9. Barraza, N.R.: Compound and non homogeneous Poisson software reliability models. In: ASSE 2010–11th Argentine Symposium on Software Engineering, pp. 461–472 (1984)
10. Chang, Y.: An alternative reliability evaluation of non homogeneous Poisson process models for software reliability. Int. J. Qual. Reliab. Manag. **17**(7), 800–811 (2013)
11. Sahinoglu, M., Can, U.: Alternative parameter estimation methods for the compound Poisson software reliability model with clustered failure data. Softw. Test. Verif. Reliab. **7**(1), 35–57 (1997)
12. Barraza, N.R.: Parameter estimation for the compound Poisson software reliability model. Int. J. Softw. Eng. Appl. **7**(1), 137–148 (2013)
13. Chambers, J.M.: Graphical methods for data analysis. Biometrics **40**(2), 493–499 (1983)
14. Aiex, R.M., Resende, M.G., Ribeiro, C.C., et al.: Probability distribution of solution time in GRASP: an experimental investigation. J. Heuristics **8**(3), 343–373 (2002)
15. Lohmor, S., Sagar, B.B.: Overview: software reliability growth models. Int. J. Comput. Sci. Inf. Technol. **5**(4), 5545–5547 (2014)

Automated Segmentation of Carotid Artery Vessel Wall in MRI

Bo Wang[1(✉)], Gang Sha[2], Pengju Yin[3,4], and Xia Liu[1]

[1] School of Automation, Harbin University of Science and Technology,
Harbin 150080, China
{hust_wb, liuxia}@hrbust.edu.cn
[2] School of Computer Science, Northwestern Polytechnical University,
Xi'an 710068, China
shagang@mail.nwpu.edu.cn
[3] School of Life Science and Technology,
XiDian University, Xi'an 710126, China
pengju.yin@outlook.com
[4] Xi'an Realme 3D Co. Ltd., Xi'an 710075, Shannxi, China

Abstract. Automatic or semi-automatic segmentation of carotid artery wall in MRI is an important means of early detection of atherosclerosis. In this paper, a new algorithm is proposed for the automated segmentation of the lumen, outer boundary and plaque contours in carotid MR images. It uses the ellipse fitting to detect the outer wall boundaries. By using the outer wall boundaries as the constraint condition, the lumen is detected using an improved fuzzy C-Means (FCM). The plaque is located by obtaining the area changing of lumen. The experimental results show that our method achieves 95.7% of region overlaps when compared to the gold standard results. This new automated method can enhance reproducibility of the quantification of vessel wall dimensions in clinical studies.

Keywords: Medical image segmentation · Carotid artery MRI
Ellipse fitting · Fuzzy C-Means

1 Introduction

Atherosclerosis is a progressive disease which, at an early stage, is characterized by vessel wall thickening causing outward remodeling, then narrowing of the lumen, and at a later stage by the formation of plaque lesions inside the vessel wall [1]. Medical image segmentation is an important means of early detection of atherosclerosis, through the MR image to detect carotid artery atherosclerotic lesions, the urgent need for an automatic or semi-automatic carotid artery segmentation method to help doctors on the diagnosis of atherosclerosis or treatment. However, MR images are susceptible to factors such as speckle noise, artifacts, and weak boundaries, which result in segmentation failure. Therefore, the design of the highly robust MR carotid artery wall segmentation method is still a challenging problem in the field of medical image processing.

G. Sun and S. Liu (Eds.): ADHIP 2017, LNICST 219, pp. 275–286, 2018.
https://doi.org/10.1007/978-3-319-73317-3_33

Currently, quantitative assessment of the vessel wall dimensions is based on manual tracing of the lumen and outer wall boundaries, which is time-consuming and subject to inter- and intra-observer variation. Consequently, computerized segmentation techniques have been developed to overcome these limitations [2–9]. Petroudi *et al.* [10] put forward the active contour and level set method segmentation vascular access IMC (intima-media complex). The continuous curve is obtained by active contour method to represent the carotid artery boundary, then the energy functional method based on level set boundaries to get blood vessels. But other organizational structures of the blood vessel image often overlaps with carotid artery blood vessels or deformation fuzzy boundaries. This is expected to result in the decline in the method segmentation accuracy greatly. Yang *et al.* [11] put forward by using Hoff round model transformation and dynamic programming method to determine the boundary of the carotid artery, the shape and size of the area to get blood vessels by judging center, but this method is to obtain the outer wall of the carotid artery, not the specific segmentation internal cavity. Menchón-Lara and Sancho-Gómez [12] propose the method based on an artificial neural network of the blood vessels image segmentation, and then machine learning and statistical pattern recognition is used to measure the thickness of the carotid artery middle IMT (Intima Media Thickness). Despite the lining thickness of the carotid artery is measured to identify the location of the plaques, but on the judgement of the size and shape of the plaques have certain limitations.

Accordingly, the purpose of this study was to develop a highly automated image segmentation technique for the detection of the lumen and outer wall boundaries, as well as the contours of the plaques in MR vessel wall images of the carotid artery. The basis of this method is ellipse fitting-based segmentation combined with fuzzy C-Means. The accuracy and reproducibility of this method in measuring the contours and total wall area were implemented using *in vivo* MR images of carotid arteries.

2 Methods

The mainly target of this method is to detect the lumen, outer boundary and plaque contours of carotid artery vessel wall in MR images. The structure of this method is illustrated Fig. 1.

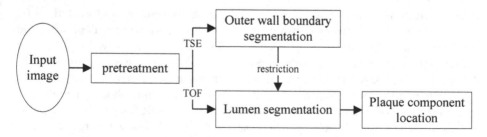

Fig. 1. Overall structure of the method.

2.1 Pretreatment of Carotid Artery Vessel Wall in MRI

Pretreatment is an important part of the process of image segmentation. The input image is distinct from the image acquisition environment. Such as the illumination level and the performance of the device, the image noise, contrast the defect of low doped and so on. In addition, the distance, focal length and other factors lead to vascular uncertainty in the size and position of the image in the middle. In order to ensure the consistency of the vessel size, location and the quality of the carotid artery vessels, the image must be pre-processed.

This algorithm first introduced into the algorithm of pre-processing line gray level stretches, and the gray scale of the original image is converted to [0, 255], the linear stretches is defined as follows:

$$h(x, y) = \frac{255}{(B - A)} (f(x, y) - A).$$ (1)

where A, B is the original image gray scale minimum and maximum, $h(x, y)$ and $f(x, y)$ are the images after and before stretching, respectively.

After the linear stretching of the image from the existence from isolated mutations of the noise point, so the algorithm uses the two-dimensional zero mean discrete Gauss smoothing, which is defined as follows:

$$G(x, y) = \frac{1}{2\pi\sigma^2} e^{-\frac{x^2 + y^2}{2\upsilon^2}}.$$ (2)

Blood vessel location is to obtain the blood vessel position and provide the basis of the following blood vessel segmentation. Image enhancement is to improve the quality of the image, not only to make the image more clearly, and make the image more conducive to computer processing and recognition. The goal of the normalized work is to obtain the same normalized blood vessel images of the same size as the gray scale.

2.2 Outer Wall Boundaries Segmentation

In this paper, the outer wall of the blood vessel is segmented by using ellipse fitting. Firstly, the least squares method is used to find the parameter set.

$$Ax^2 + Bxy + Cy^2 + Dx + Ey + F = 0.$$ (3)

In order to avoid zero solution, the parameters are restricted to A + C = 1. Obviously, the direct application Eq. (3) of the edge detection of the discrete points for the least squares, objective function $f(A, B, C, D, E, F)$, when the objective function values, minimum satisfies:

$$f(A, B, C, D, E, F) = \sum_{i=1}^{x} (Ax_i^2 + Bx_iy_i + Cy_i^2 + Dx_i + Ey_i + F)^2.$$ (4)

$$\frac{\partial f}{\partial A} = \frac{\partial f}{\partial B} = \frac{\partial f}{\partial C} = \frac{\partial f}{\partial D} = \frac{\partial f}{\partial E} = \frac{\partial f}{\partial F} = 0. \tag{5}$$

When there is an impurity in the sample point, result in considerable error of ellipse fitting, cannot meet the accuracy requirements of medical diagnosis. In order to obtain the accurate edge of the vessel boundary, the major a axis, the short b axis and the center point (x, y) of the ellipse is obtained by the ellipse fitting. By changing the setting of a, b and the ellipse angle, many different ellipse can be obtained. Calculate the average gray value of all points on the ellipse, to find the best ellipse as the outer wall boundary of the blood vessels through the gray level of the adjacent ellipse between the Laplace operators.

$$\overrightarrow{P_i} = \frac{\sum_{i=1}^{n} h(x_i, y_i)}{n} \tag{6}$$

$$dp_i = p_i - p_{i-1}. \tag{7}$$

$$ddp_i = dp_i - dp_{i-1}. \tag{8}$$

Although the algorithm uses elliptical model to obtain the outer wall boundary, but there is still a big error in the actual vessel boundary, the images of the external wall of the carotid artery were converted to polar coordinate system, and the x axis in polar coordinates was expressed as the angle of the image in cartesian space(the connection between the points and the origin of the image, and the angle formed by the x axis), angle range of $[-\pi, \pi]$, the y axis represents the radius (image under the cartesian coordinate space in point-to-point distance), the radius of $[0, R]$. The dynamic programming method is to do the best path from the first column to the last column in the polar coordinates.

The definition of the cost function $k(i, j)$ for the final determination of the ellipse to get the most close to the boundary of the vessel wall, which is defined as follows [13]:

$$k(i,j) = w_s s(i,j) + w_g g(i,j) + w_d d(i,j). \tag{9}$$

where (i, j) are the coordinates of a point in polar coordinates. w_s, w_g and w_d are the weight of the corresponding components of the cost function, respectively. s, g and d are the edge strength, the size of the blood vessels, and expectations deviation of gray, respectively.

$$s(i,j) = \frac{\max(y') - y'(i,j)}{\max(y')}. \tag{10}$$

$$g(i,j) = \frac{g_{max} - g(i,j)}{g_{max} - g_{min}}. \tag{11}$$

where max(y') is the maximum gradient value, $y'(i, j)$ is the vertical direction gradient value of each point.

In the polar coordinate image, the value component assigns the same value to the pixel at the same radius length at different angles, unless the swollen shape is an absolute circle, otherwise it cannot appear at the same radius length at different angles. The pixels have the same edge information. It is judged that it belongs to a certain region by obtaining information on the difference in the luminance value between the pixel point and the neighboring point. The new definition of the cost component is $r(i, j)$ instead of $d(i, j)$, which is defined as follows:

$$r(i,j) = \sqrt{G(i,j)^2 + G(i,j-1)^2 - 2G(i,j)G(i,j-1)}. \tag{12}$$

After the end of the optimal path is determined, then the reverse sequence is used to find the pixels of each column in this path.

2.3   Lumen Segmentation and Plaque Location

In this paper, the classical FCM algorithm is improved to extract the blood vessel cavity, the segmentation of the cavity is mainly in the outer wall of the wall based on the extraction of the inner wall and plaque positioning.

Fuzzy C means clustering method is a method of avoiding the problem of setting a threshold, and it can solve the segmentation problem of multiple branches which are difficult to solve. FCM is suitable for the characteristics of the uncertainty and ambiguity of the image. Specific definitions are as follows: FCM divides the data set into C fuzzy group $X = \{x_1, x_2, \ldots, x_n\}$, and seek the clustering center of each group, the value function of non-similarity index reaches the minimum. FCM makes a given data point in (0, 1) between the membership to determine the degree of belonging to each group. However, in accordance with the provisions of the normalization, the membership of a data set and the total is equivalent to 1:

$$\sum_{i=1}^{c} u_{ij} = 1, \forall j = 1, \ldots, n. \tag{13}$$

Then, the value function (or objective function) of FCM is illustrated as follows:

$$J(U, c_1, \ldots, c_c) = \sum_{i=1}^{c} J_i = \sum_{i=1}^{c} \sum_{j}^{n} u_{ij}^m d_{ij}^2. \tag{14}$$

where the u_{ij} value range of the objective function is [0, 1], c_i clustering center for fuzzy group X. $d_{ij} = \|c_i - x_j\|$ is expressed as the i cluster center and the j data point between the Euclidean distance. m is a weighted index, range in [1, ∞), construct a new objective function, which is described as follows:

$$J(U, c_1, \ldots, c_c, \lambda_1, \ldots, \lambda_n) = J(U, c_1, \ldots, c_c) + \sum_{j=1}^{n} \lambda_i (\sum_{i=1}^{c} u_{ij} - 1)$$

$$= \sum_{i=1}^{c} \sum_{j}^{n} u_{ij}^m d_{ij}^2 + \sum_{j=1}^{n} \lambda_i (\sum_{i=1}^{c} u_{ij} - 1) \qquad (15)$$

where λ_i is the Lagrange factor. The first order derivative of all input parameter, the necessary conditions for making the Eq. (14) to the minimum:

$$c_i = \frac{\sum_{j=1}^{n} u_{ij}^m x_j}{\sum_{j=1}^{n} u_{ij}^m}. \qquad (16)$$

$$u_{ij} = \frac{1}{\sum_{k=1}^{c} (\frac{d_{ij}}{d_{kj}})^{2/(m-1)}}. \qquad (17)$$

FCM algorithm is a simple iterative procedure. When the processing mode is running, FCM uses the following steps to determine the clustering center and the membership matrix:

(1) In the (0, 1) interval, the random initial membership matrix U, which satisfies the constraint conditions in the Eq. (13);
(2) Calculate C clustering center by the Eq. (16);
(3) The value function is calculated according to Eq. (14). If it is less than a certain threshold, or is relative to the last value function by altering the amount is less than a threshold, then the algorithm stops.
(4) Using the Eq. (17) to calculate the new U matrix, the return step 2.

In the process of the segmentation of the carotid artery and the location of the plaque, the range of the outer wall of the vessel region restricted to the inner wall partition. By using the improved fuzzy C mean algorithm, the segmentation of the luminal and the patch of MR blood vessel images is carried out, through the same dynamic programming the inner wall contour and patch refinement. Through the analysis of the size of the patch area and the proportion of the internal cavity, the degree of damage of the carotid artery was judged.

3 Experimental and Results Analysis

3.1 Experimental Setup

All of the dataset used in our experiments was from hospital that included 40 MR images containing carotid artery luminal and 70 images of external wall of the carotid artery. Slice spacing is 1 cm. Pixel size is 512×512. The experiments were implemented in the CPU of Intel Core I5 4200M that internal memory is 8 GB. The type of

GPU is NVIDIA GeForce GT 755M, and its memory is 2 GB. Software environment: the operating system is Windows 8.1, MATLAB 2013a.

The same set of data is carried on the gold standard, the common ellipse fitting blood vessel segmentation and the improved ellipse fitting algorithm, compared with the results of the segmentation of blood vessel wall and the segmentation of the inner chamber of the vessel.

3.2 Results and Analysis

Figure 2 shows the result of segmentation the outer wall of the blood vessel of the various algorithms.

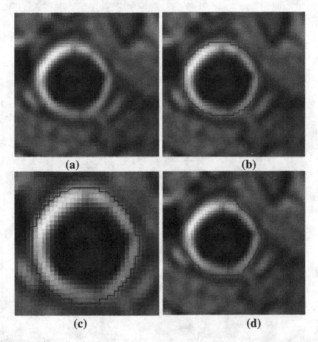

Fig. 2. The result of segmentation the outer wall of the blood vessel of the various algorithms. (a) the original image, (b) the general ellipse fitting result, (c) the improved ellipse fitting result, (d) the gold standard image.

In this paper, an improved analytical method based on the receiver operating characteristic curve is made to analyze the experimental data. *TP* is really positive, *FP* is false positive, *TN* is really negative, *FN* is a false negative. Analysis of the data of the image region overlaps the ratio of the gold standard image and the improved ellipse fitting. *AO* is defined as follows:

$$AO = \frac{TP}{TP + FN + FP} * 100\% \tag{18}$$

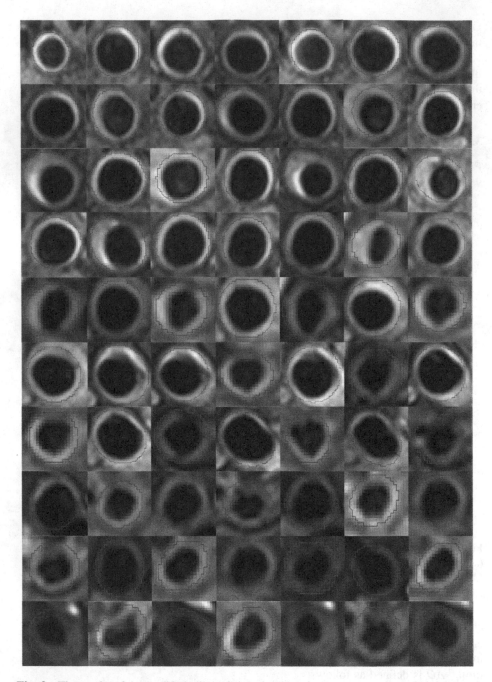

Fig. 3. The results of the modified ellipse fitting algorithm for the segmentation of blood vessel wall.

Figure 2(a) contains the outer boundary of the vessel, the blood vessel boundary was clear and obvious after pretreatment. Figure 2(b) contains the effect of the image of the vessel wall on the segmentation of the common ellipse fitting algorithm. Figure 2 (c) is the result of the improved ellipse fitting algorithm; the effect of the external boundary of the blood vessels obtained by manual segmentation of the gold standard in Fig. 2(d). The *AO* value of the overlap region is 95.7%. The *AO* value of the ordinary ellipse fitting algorithm is 94.6%. We selected 70 sections of the carotid artery blood vessels to segmentation the results as illustrated in Fig. 3.

Figure 4 shows the AO value trend of improved ellipse fitting and ordinary ellipse fitting algorithm.

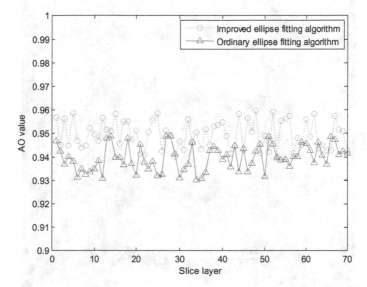

Fig. 4. The AO value trend of improved ellipse fitting and ordinary ellipse fitting algorithm.

From Fig. 4, we can see that the AO value of the modified ellipse fitting algorithm is significantly higher than that of the classical ellipse fitting segmentation algorithm. The contour of the segmentation of the external wall of the carotid artery is limited by the segmentation of the inner chamber. Through the improved FCM algorithm, a series of successive segmentation of the inner segment of the carotid artery is segmented, and Fig. 5 shows the segmentation results.

The location and size of the vascular luminal can be obtained by comparing the segmentation results of continuous carotid artery. In this paper, the cavity ratio q is used for data analysis, which defined as follows:

$$q = \frac{n}{n+b}. \tag{19}$$

where n is the luminal area, b is the plaque area.

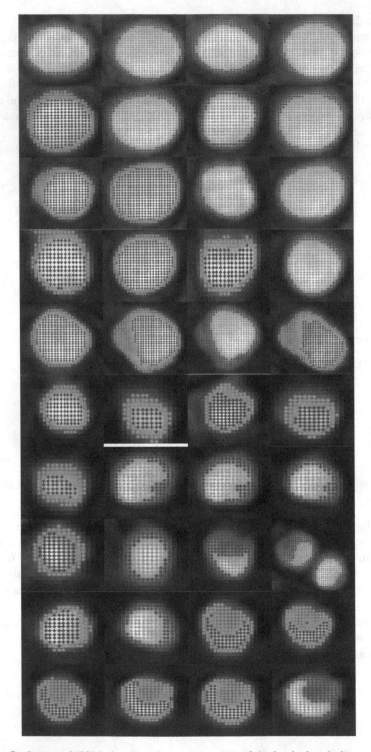

Fig. 5. Improved FCM algorithm for segmentation of the luminal and plaque size.

Figure 6 shows the q ratio of the improved and the ordinary FCM algorithm.

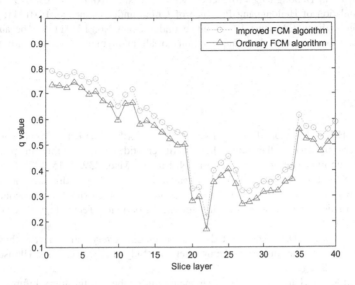

Fig. 6. The q ratio of the improved and the ordinary FCM algorithm.

From Fig. 6, we can see that the percentage of the initial carotid artery plaque area ratio was lower. At this point, the q value is about 0.75. However, with the change of the slice position, the plaque area is gradually increasing, the ratio of the area occupied by the 10th slices was decreased, and the ratio of the inner cavity of the 12th slices was the lowest. At this point, the q value is 0.2189. The proportion of plaque at this time was the largest. Through the upper and lower two curves, we found that the improved FCM algorithm was significantly larger than the ordinary FCM algorithm, which can achieve higher accuracy of plaque location results.

4   Conclusions

In this paper, we propose a method of automatic segmentation and plaque localization of carotid artery based on multi-modal MR images. This method achieved the automatic segmentation of the lumen and outer wall boundaries, as well as the precise position of plaque. Experiments show that this method can ensure the accuracy of vascular segmentation and plaque positioning is relatively close, while shortening the time of segmentation, to achieve the reproducibility. Although this method accurately divides the boundary between blood vessels and plaques, there are still a lot of problems to be solved for plaque component analysis. The next step is to study the specific constituent structure of the segmented patches.

Acknowledgments. This work is supported by the National Nature Science Foundation of China under Grant No. 61672197; the University Nursing Program for Young Scholars with Creative Talents in Heilongjiang Province under Grant No. UNPYSCT-2015045; the Natural Science Foundation of Heilongjiang Province of China under Grant No. F201311; the Foundation of Heilongjiang Educational Committee under Grant No. 12531119. The authors also would like to express their deep appreciation to all anonymous reviewers for their kind comments.

References

1. Barnett, H.J.M., Taylor, D.W., Eliasziw, M.: North American symptomatic carotid endarterectomy trial collaborators benefit of carotid endarterectomy in patients with symptomatic moderate or severe stenosis. N. Engl. J. Med. **339**, 1415–1425 (1998)
2. Mithun, N.C., Das, S., Fattah, S.A.: Automated detection of optic disc and blood vessel in retinal image using morphological, edge detection and feature extraction technique. In: 2013 16th International Conference on Computer and Information Technology (ICCIT), pp. 98–102. IEEE (2014)
3. Polak, J., O'leary, D.: Edge-detected common carotid artery intima-media thickness and incident coronary heart disease in the multi-ethnic study of atherosclerosis. Ultrasound Med. Biol. **4**, S71–S72 (2015)
4. Ogiela, M.R., Hachaj, T.: Automatic segmentation of the carotid artery bifurcation region with a region-growing approach. J. Electron. Imaging **22**, 033029 (2013)
5. Chen, Y., Peng, B., Liu, D.C.: Fully automated ultrasound common carotid artery segmentation using active shape model. Int. J. Signal Process. Image Process. Pattern Recogn. **7**, 99–106 (2014)
6. Emary, E., Zawbaa, H.M., Hassanien, A.E.: Retinal vessel segmentation based on possibilistic fuzzy c-means clustering optimised with cuckoo search. In: 2014 International Joint Conference on Neural Networks (IJCNN), pp. 1792–1796. IEEE (2014)
7. Kundu, A., Chatterjee, R.K.: Morphological scale-space based vessel segmentation of retinal image. In: 2012 Annual IEEE India Conference (INDICON), pp. 986–990 (2012)
8. Jaiswal, V., Tiwari, A.: A survey of image segmentation based on artificial intelligence and evolutionary approach. IOSR J. Comput. Eng. **15**, 71–78 (2013)
9. Vega, R., Guevara, E., Falcon, L.E.: Blood vessel segmentation in retinal images using lattice neural networks. In: Advances in Artificial Intelligence and Its Applications, vol. 8265, pp. 532–544. Springer, Heidelberg (2013). https://doi.org/10.1007/978-3-642-45114-0_42
10. Petroudi, S., Loizou, C., Pantziaris, M.: Segmentation of the common carotid intima-media complex in ultrasound images using active contours. IEEE Trans. Biomed. Eng. **59**, 3060–3069 (2012)
11. Yang, X., Ding, M., Lou, L.: Common carotid artery luminal segmentation in B-mode ultrasound transverse view images. Int. J. Image Graph. Signal Process. **3**, 15 (2011)
12. Menchón-Lara, R.M., Sancho-Gómez, J.L.: Fully automatic segmentation of ultrasound common carotid artery images based on machine learning. Neurocomputing **151**, 161–167 (2015)
13. Timp, S., Karssemeijer, N.: A new 2D segmentation method based on dynamic programming applied to computer aided detection in mammography. Med. Phys. **31**, 958–971 (2004)

Wavelet Threshold Denoising of ACO Optical Lens Image

Ping Xue, Xiangyong Niu[✉], Xiaohui Zhu, Hongmin Wang,
and Jihua Chen

School of Automation, Harbin University of Science and Technology,
Harbin 150080, China
867361996@qq.com

Abstract. In the system of the image defect detection system, during image acquisition and transmission, the salt-and-pepper Noise will adversely affect the subsequent processing and recognition. To eliminate the salt-and-pepper noise effectively, a defect image denoising algorithm based on ant colony optimization wavelet threshold is improved in this paper. Firstly, the basic principle of wavelet denoising is analyzed theoretically, and a compromise threshold function and a GCV optimal threshold selection method are adopted. It uses ant colony algorithm to optimize the wavelet threshold, which greatly improves the speed and accuracy of the optimal threshold. Using standard soft threshold method, GCV threshold optimization method and the ant colony optimization wavelet threshold method, the defect image of the lens is denoised. The results of experiment indicate that the algorithm can remove the salt-and-pepper noise in the image of defective lenses more effectively than the other two algorithms, and improve the accuracy of the lens detection. This algorithm is also suitable for general image denoising.

Keywords: Lens defect image · Wavelet denoising
Ant colony optimization algorithm · Salt-and-pepper noise

1 Introduction

In recent years, Glasses industry have developed by leaps and bounds in our country. Many companies have fabricated optical les detecting system which based on machine vision. However, during the optical lens image capture and transmissing processing, it always brings some noise interference to some degree. It seriously affected the quality of the image because of the precision of the optical lens detection, the noise point that noise interference generate is easily mixed with optical lens' own defections, and submerges the optical lens' own characteristics. Therefore if's necessary to depress the noise processing.

The common ways of denosing can divided into airspace denoising and frequency domain denoising. The traditional airspace denoising way is use template to convolution or ranking to implementation and frequency domain way is usually according to the information of image shows different frequency combination in frequent space, with eliminating or restraining the high frequency part to implement the image

© ICST Institute for Computer Sciences, Social Informatics and Telecommunications Engineering 2018
G. Sun and S. Liu (Eds.): ADHIP 2017, LNICST 219, pp. 287–296, 2018.
https://doi.org/10.1007/978-3-319-73317-3_34

denoising [1]. The traditional image denoising way could damage the image margin detail information when restrain the image noising, and image is blurry after denoising [2]. With the fast progress of the wavelet theory in recent years, wavelet has low entropy, multi-resolution, decor-relation and selection based flexible advantages. Which let wavelet conversion could realize the separation of signal and noise commendabiy, after Mallatt proposed the magnitude of the signal denoising, Donoho and some people proposed the wavelet threshold denoising which according to the multi-scale and the collecting ability of signal energy [3]. However, it is pivotal that using wavelet threshold denoising is to choose threshold function and threshold value. The traditional method of wavelet threshold denoising contains two kinds of ways, one of them is hard one and the other is soft. But the wavelet soft thresholding method has disadvantage, when the soft threshold are greater than the threshold, wavelet coefficients of the noise image will shrink. The hard threshold method can cause pseudo Gibbs phenomenon because the wavelet hard threshold denoising function is discontinuous at the threshold point [4]. Therefore, the reasonable choice of wavelet threshold and wavelet threshold function is very important to denoising effect.

In recent years, many intelligent algorithms have been applied to the threshold optimization of wavelet image denoising, and good results have been achieved. For example, Lin Jie et al. [5] proposed Wavelet Threshold Denoising Based on Particle Swarm Optimization Algorithm. The particle swarm algorithm is used to find the optimal threshold, and the particle fitness function is minimized, and the optimal threshold is obtained. But the algorithm will be caught in the local optimum answer easily and the search accuracy is not high. Zhang and Fang [6] proposed Multi-wavelet Based Adaptive Denoising Method and this algorithm has fast convergence speed and versatility, but it is easy to premature convergence.

In allusion to the problem of the lens defect image acquisition and transmission will generate the salt and pepper noise. The paper proposed a image denoising method which based on ant colony optimization wavelet thredhold. The method uses a compromise threshold function and combines ant colony optimization algorithm to optimize the wavelet threshold. The algorithm can effectively remove the noise in the lens defect image, and restore the characteristics of the defective image itself. It has very good denoising effect, and is beneficial to the post processing and recognition of the lens defects. The algorithm is also applicable to other image denoising.

2   The Basic Theory of Wavelet Denoising for the Lens Defect Image

2.1   The Principle of Wavelet Denoising

The idea of multi-resolution analysis (MRA) was proposed by Mallat in 1988 and the fast algorithm of wavelet analysis and reconstruction was later proposed. It allows us to de-noise noisy images, that is, Mallat algorithm [7]. The principle of the algorithm is that:

If $f(t)$ is the original signal and f_k is the discrete sampling data, and $f_k = c_{0,k}$, then the decomposition formula of the orthogonal wavelet transform of the signal $f(t)$ is:

$$\begin{cases} c_{j,k} = \sum_n c_{j-1,n} h_{n-2k} \\ d_{j,k} = \sum_n d_{j-1,n} g_{n-2k} \end{cases} (k = 0, 1, \cdots N - 1) \qquad (1)$$

$g_{j,k}$ is the scaling factor, and $h_{j,k}$ is the wavelet coefficient, and l, m is Quandrature Mirror Filter (QMF), and J is the decomposition layer number, and N is the discrete sampling point. The reconstruction of wavelet transform is the inverse process of decomposition, and its reconstruction formula is as follows:

$$c_{j-1,n} = \sum_n c_{j,n} h_{k-2n} + \sum_n d_{j,n} g_{k-2n} \qquad (2)$$

After the wavelet decomposition of the noisy signal, the energy of the signal mainly spread in the wavelet range with larger wavelet coefficients, while the energy of the noise spread in the whole wavelet range. Therefore, the amplitude of wavelet coefficients is greater than the amplitude of noise coefficients. It can be said that the wavelet coefficients with larger amplitudes are usually dominated by signals, and the smaller are the noise signals to a large extent. According to the threshold value we set in advance, all wavelet coefficients whose amplitudes are smaller than the threshold are all set to zero, while the wavelet coefficients whose amplitudes are greater than the threshold are retained or properly reduced. Finally, the corresponding wavelet coefficients are transformed into inverse wavelet transform. We can get the de-noised image. The process of wavelet denoising is shown in the following Fig. 1:

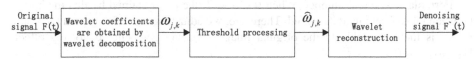

Fig. 1. Flow chart of wavelet denoising

The multi-resolution characteristics of wavelet can decompose signals at different scales, and decompose the signals into different sub signals, so that the signals can be processed by frequency bands. A two-dimensional image with noise is $p(x, y) = b(x, y) + kd(x, y)$. $p(x, y)$ is the noise signal, $b(x, y)$ is the real signal, and $d(x, y)$ is the noise signal. Wavelet denoising is to handle the wavelet coefficients by decomposing the wavelet coefficients, and then suppress the noise signals and restore the real signals.

2.2 Wavelet Threshold Function and GCV Threshold

Using threshold function to deal with the wavelet coefficients, the chosen of wavelet threshold T will influence the denoising effect directly. If the threshold is too small, the de-noised image still has noise, but if the selection is too large, the feature information of the image will be filtered out, which will lead to bias. Therefore, we need to select the appropriate threshold T, and use the threshold function to process the wavelet coefficients and reconstruct the image. In the wavelet analysis proposed by Donoho, the formulas of hard threshold and soft threshold function [8] as:

(1) Hard threshold

$$\omega_{j,k} = \begin{cases} \omega_{j,k} & |\omega_{j,k}| \geq T \\ 0 & |\omega_{j,k}| < T \end{cases} \tag{3}$$

(2) Soft threshold

$$\omega_{j,k} = \begin{cases} \mathrm{sgn}(\omega_{j,k})(|\omega_{j,k}| - T) & |\omega_{j,k}| \geq T \\ 0 & |\omega_{j,k}| < T \end{cases} \tag{4}$$

$\omega_{j,k}$ is the discrete wavelet transform operator, T is the threshold, and $sgn(.)$ is the symbolic function. If the wavelet coefficients are less-than threshold T, it will be represented by zero, and the wavelet coefficients greater than T are reduced by $\omega_{j,k}$.

In the wavelet analysis proposed by Donoho, there are some defects in the hard threshold and the soft threshold. In the hard threshold, because of the discontinuities at T and $-T$, the reconstructed image may suffer from visual anamorphose such as ringing and pseudo Gibbs effect. Although the continuity and smoothness of the soft threshold are good, when $|\omega_{j,k}| \geq T$, the constant deviation between the $\omega_{j,k}$ and $\hat{\omega}_{j,k}$ will lead to the blurring of the reconstructed image.

Therefore, we choose a compromise threshold function:

$$\omega_{j,k} = \begin{cases} \mathrm{sgn}(\omega_{j,k})(|\omega_{j,k}| - \alpha T) & |\omega_{j,k}| > T \\ 0 & |\omega_{j,k}| \leq T \end{cases} \tag{5}$$

Formula: a is a real number. When $0 < a < 1$, the $\omega_{j,k}$ obtained by this method is between the soft and hard threshold. Therefore, we adjust the size of the a and the noisy image is more resemble to the original image. We can get better denoising effect. Usually, $a = 0.5$.

During image acquisition and transmission, the image noise is unstable, the noise is unknown and can not estimate the noise energy. Therefore, the threshold method based on GCV quasi side is selected in this paper [9]. The function expression as:

$$GCV(T_j) = \frac{\frac{1}{N_j} \left\| \omega_j - \omega_{j,T} \right\|^2}{\left[\frac{N_{j0}}{N_j} \right]^2} \tag{6}$$

Formula: N is the number of wavelet coefficients. N_0 is the threshold. The number of wavelet coefficients is zero after the contraction. j is the number of wavelet decomposition.

3   The Application of Ant Colony Optimization Wavelet Threshold (ACOTE) in Image Denoising

3.1   The Basic Theory of Ant Colony Algorithm

Ant colony optimization algorithm, called ant colony algorithm, is an advanced simulated bionic algorithm based on the foraging of ants in nature [10]. Ants can release pheromones when they are foraging, and their companions can sense the presence and intensity of pheromones. Since the beginning of the ant behavior always is random and the number of individuals in the colony is huge. So some ants can always find food, and find the base answer between the nest and the food. Because the path is short, the ants leave more pheromones per unit time, and other ants will choose the shortest path by perceiving the pheromone concentration. Thus, more and more pheromones are added to the path and establish positive feedback, and finally the ant colony is concentrated on the shortest path, and finally the optimal solution is obtained.

Ant colony algorithm (ACO) is a parallel algorithm with strong robustness, few parameter settings and simple setting. It can easily apply to combinatorial optimization problems [11]. The main operation process of ant algorithm in solving the problem is shown below [12]: Suppose that in the t iteration, the probability of ant K from the city i to the city j is $P_{ij}^k(t)$:

$$P_{ij}^k(t) = \begin{cases} \dfrac{\tau_{ij}^\alpha \eta_{ij}^\beta(t)}{\sum\limits_{s \in allowd_k} \tau_{ij}^\alpha \eta_{ij}^\beta(t)} & j \in allowd_k \\ 0 & otherwise \end{cases} \tag{7}$$

Formula: $allowd_k$ is allowed mobile table for the ant K. ι_{ij} is pheromone concentrations of the t iteration on the i and the j. a is the heuristic factor, used to characterize the importance of information, $\eta_{ij} = 1/d_{ij}$. d_{ij} is the distance between two points. β is the expected factor, used to indicate the importance of the i and the j.

When the global ant completes a traversal, the pheromone is updated:

$$\tau_{ij}(t+1) = (1-\rho) \times \tau_{ij}(t) + \Delta\tau_{ij} \tag{8}$$

$$\Delta\tau_{ij} = \sum_{k=1}^m \Delta\tau_{ij}^k \tag{9}$$

Formula: ρ is the pheromone residual coefficient, $0 \leqslant \rho \leqslant 1$, ΔT_{ij} represents the pheromone remain by the ant K in the path between the t iteration and the $t + n$ iteration between the i and the j. The formula used in the ant-cycle model is generally used ΔT_{ij}^k [13]:

$$\Delta\tau_{ij}^k = \begin{cases} Q/L_k, & When\ the\ ant\ K\ passes\ through\ the\ city\ (i,j)\ at\ T\ and\ T+1 \\ 0, & otherwise \end{cases} \tag{10}$$

Formula: Q is pheromone intensity, which affects convergence speed; L_k is the path taken by the ant K in this cycle.

3.2 Wavelet Threshold Denoising Method Based on Ant Colony Optimization

The ant colony optimization wavelet threshold denoising method is as follows:

(1) The wavelet transform and the three-layer decomposition of the image are obtained, and the coefficients of wavelet decomposition are obtained.

(2) The initialization of the ant colony is to assign the initial urban location T_k and initial pheromone concentration τ_{ij} of each ant in the population and to reset the tabu list.

(3) The GCV(T_j) threshold is calculated for each ant in the population using the corresponding wavelet coefficients. When GCV(T_j) is the minimum, the threshold T_j can be considered as the best threshold.

(4) According to formula (7), the transfer probability of each ant is calculated and the ants move according to the calculated probability of movement. Each move adds

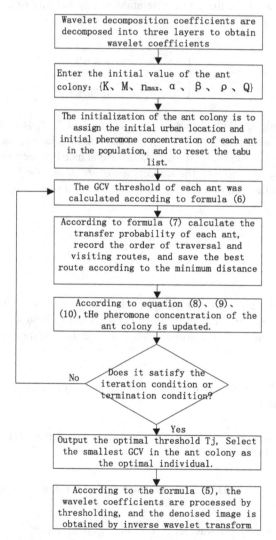

Fig. 2. Low chart of wavelet threshold denoising process based on ant colony optimization

the moving city to the tabu list until the ant has completed its traversal of all the cities. We record the traversal order and the visiting route, and keep the best route according to the minimum distance.

(5) Pheromone concentrations of ants are updated by formula (8), (9) and (10).

(6) The GCV threshold of the ants is calculated again and to determine whether the condition is satisfied. If the condition is satisfied, the optimal solution T_j is output, or else it returns to step 3. The optimal path is obtained and the optimal solution T_j is output until the maximum iterations are reached.

(7) The optimal threshold is used to denoise the image, and then the denoised signal is reconstructed by wavelet transform to get the denoised image.

The parameters of the ant colony algorithm are set as follows: Ant population: $K = 40$, City quantity: $M = 50$, Maximum iterations: $n_{max} = 100$. The flow chart of removing the noise in the optical lens by the wavelet threshold of ant colony optimization is shown in Fig. 2.

4 The Image Denoising Results of the Lens Defect Image

4.1 The Noise Generation and Characteristics of Lens Defect Image

In the detection system of optical lens, the image acquisition of lens general select the method of Dark Field Imaging [14] and the lens defect shows a brighter point in the image. Because of the interference from the outside of the system and the image sensor, the images collected by the CCD camera will have different levels of Salt-and-pepper Noise. Salt-and-pepper Noise is the black and white light dark noise. For optical lenses, filtering not only does not destroy the contours of the image edge, but also needs to make the image clear, which is conducive to subsequent processing. The Salt-and-pepper Noise that appears randomly in the optical image is shown below (Fig. 3).

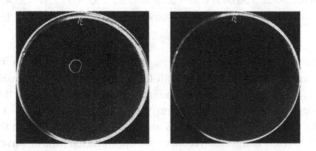

Fig. 3. Random noise of salt-and-pepper in the lens defect image

4.2 Evaluation Criterion of the Lens Defect Image

The experimental environment of this experiment is Matlab R2010b and subjective and objective methods are used in evaluation criteria. The subjective standard is the sharpness of the image and the smoothness of detail, and the objective standard is Peak Signal Noise Ratio (PSNR) and the run time of algorithm as the criterion. The calculation method of PSNR [15] as:

$$PSNR = 10\lg\frac{\delta^2(i,j)}{MSE}$$

$\delta^2(i, j)$ is the variance of the gray value of the denoised image, and MSE is the minimum mean square deviation of the denoised image.

The formula is as follows:

$$MSE = \frac{1}{MN}\sum_{i=0}^{M-1}\sum_{j=0}^{N-1}[f(i,j) - f_0(i,j)]^2$$

M and N is the number of rows and columns of the image, and $f(i, j)$ is the denoised image function, and $f_0(i, j)$ is the original image function.

The object of this experiment is the lens defect image (400 × 400) taken by camera. First, The Salt-and-pepper Noise of 20%–40% is added to the image, and Wavelet base select sym4. We use standard soft threshold denoising (STE), GCV threshold method (GCVTE) and ant colony optimization wavelet threshold algorithm (ACOTE) to denoise and we can get the following experimental data:

Table 1. PSNR of the lens defect image under different intensity noises

Method	Intensity									
	20%		25%		30%		35%		40%	
	PSNR	Time	PSNR	Time	PSNR	Time	PSNR	Time	PSNR	Time
STE	34.042	0.82	34.876	1.14	34.564	1.22	34.345	1.43	34.045	1.66
GCVTE	36.652	6.21	36.045	6.61	35.896	7.01	35.601	7.31	35.454	7.81
ACOTE	39.452	2.21	38.945	2.61	38.696	2.91	38.401	3.21	38.154	3.61

There are the treatment of lens defect image under different strength in the Table 1. The results of experiment indicate that, with the increase of noise intensity, the PSNR decreases gradually, and the processing time increases gradually. Under the same noise, the PSNR processed by ACOTE algorithm is significantly higher than the GCVTE algorithm and the STE algorithm. The GCV method takes a long time in the calculation process, while the ACOTE algorithm reduces the optimization time of wavelet threshold.

It shows the result of adding 25% and 40% salt-and-pepper noise to the lens defect image in the Figs. 4 and 5. The results of experiment indicate that, the ACOTE algorithm and the GCVTE algorithm can effectively remove the salt-and-pepper noise in the image. The STE algorithm is not effective in removing salt-and-pepper noise, so it is difficult to distinguish the salt-and-pepper noise and the defects of the lens itself.

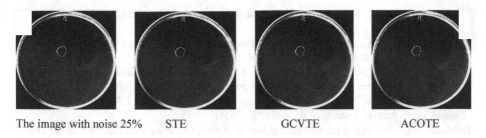

The image with noise 25%   STE   GCVTE   ACOTE

Fig. 4. The treatment result of 25% noise in optical lens

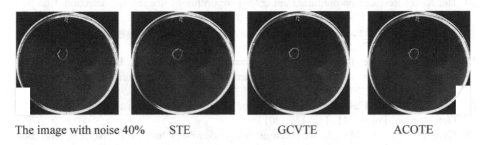

The image with noise 40%   STE   GCVTE   ACOTE

Fig. 5. The treatment result of 40% noise in optical lens

5   Conclusion

Based on a compromise threshold function, combined with ant colony optimization algorithm, the optimal wavelet threshold of image denoising is achieved in this paper. The standard soft thresholding method, the GCV criterion denoising method and the ant colony optimization wavelet threshold algorithm are used to denoise the defective image. The experimental results show that the ant colony optimization wavelet threshold algorithm and the GCV criterion denoising method can remove the salt-and-pepper noise in the defective image more effectively than the standard soft thresholding method, and retain the defect information in the lens image. Ant colony optimization algorithm reduces the optimization time of wavelet threshold, and is beneficial to the post processing recognition of lens defect image.

References

1. Ai, Z., Shi, G.: Wavelet transform used in image denoising. Sci. Technol. Rev. **01**, 102–106 (2010)
2. Li, Z.-S., Li, W.-L., Yao, J.-G., & Yang, Y.-J.: On-side detection of pollution level of insulators based on infrared-thermal-image processing. Proc. CSEE **30**(4), 132–138 (2010)
3. Donoho, D.L.: De-nosing by soft-thresholding. IEEE Trans. Inform. Theory **41**, 613–627 (1995)

4. Ma, G.-B., Xiao, P.-R.: Study on wavelet-based image denoising. Ind. Control Comput. **05**, 91–92 (2013)
5. Lin, J., Sun, S.-X., Wen, W.: Wavelet threshold denoising based on particle swarmal optimization algorithm. Comput. Eng. Appl. **04**, 204–207 (2007)
6. Zhang, L., Fang, Z.-J., Wang, S.-Q., et al.: Multiwavelet adaptive denoising method based on genetic algorithm. J. Infrared Millim. Waves **28**(01), 77–80 (2009)
7. Zhang, F.-J., Zhou, Y., Cao, J.-G.: Fast implementation of MALLAT algorithm and its application. Autom. Instrum. (06), 4–5+27 (2004)
8. Mallat, S.G., Hwang, W.L.: Singularity detection and processing with wavelets. IEEE Trans. Inf. Theory **38**, 617–642 (1992)
9. Zheng, D., Zhou, Y., Jing, N.: Generalized cross validation for wavelet denoising based on GCV rule. Chin. J. Sci. Instrum. **S3**, 2268–2270 (2006)
10. He, X.-H.: Research on optimized ant colony algorithm of image edge detection. Comput. Technol. Dev. **02**, 60–63 (2017)
11. Han, Y., Shi, P.: Image segmentation based on improved ant colony algorithm. Comput. Eng. Appl. **18**, 5–7 (2004)
12. Dorigo, M., Stutzle, T.: Ant Colony Optimization. Bradford Books, Bradford (2004)
13. Zong, Z.: The application and improvement of ant colony algorithm. Appl. Comput. Technol. **01**, 115 (2017)
14. Yao, H., Ma, G.: Flaws detection system for resin lenses based on machine vision. Laser Optoelectron. Process **11**, 112–119 (2013)
15. Gao, Y., Diao, Y., Mao, J.: Research on image denoising based on wavelet optimization threshold. J. Tonghua Teach. Coll. **04**, 25–27 (2011)

Fast Feature Extraction Method for Faults Detection System

Hongmin Wang, Xiaohui Zhu$^{(\boxtimes)}$, Xiangyong Niu, and Ping Xue

School of Automation, Harbin University of Science and Technology,
Harbin 150080, China
1210158334@qq.com

Abstract. The feature extraction based on machine learning is significant in the detection system. The boundary information, the circumference and the area are the essential features in the identification and the classification of flaws. In order to get those information, this paper proposed a novel algorithm to get the boundary information using the boundary tracking, and to make each flaw independent by establishing a balanced binary search tree for data storage. By scanning the image and the image boundaries based on binarization transformation, there is no need to fill the region, nor need to use the chain code to count the number of regions and the boundary information. According to the established balanced binary search tree, we can calculate the number of the pixel of the area of each fault, the edge information of the boundary, and the circumference. The algorithm has the advantages of fast speed, less computation, better noise suppression and accurate results.

Keywords: Image processing · Boundary tracking · Freeman chain code
Balanced binary search tree

1 Introduction

During the manufacturing process of lens, lots of flaws accompanied such as point flaw, plume, scratches, air bubbles etc. At present, our country mainly adopts artificial detection methods. The use of artificial detection wastes a lot of labor, which is based on the experience of quality judgment and fault classification. By the influence of the difference of worker's personal status and experience, the result is subjective and can not be standardized. With the rapid development of national economy, people pay more attention to highly requirement for the quality of optical lenses, and the demand for the lens is becoming bigger and bigger. It's irreversible to realize the automatic detection and classification of flaw for optical lens. In the detection system of lens based on machine vision, it's an essential part of the whole system to obtain feature from the image after binarization processing [1]. SIFI(Scale-invariant feature transform) is a commonly used descriptor as the local characteristics. The SIFT algorithm [2] proposed by LOWE is to find the feature point on different spatial scales, and to calculate the direction of the key point. Those point will not be changed by the light intensity or the affine transformation. To an extent, the SIFI algorithm can solve the problems such as the affine transformation, the projection transformation [3–6], and the target occlusion.

© ICST Institute for Computer Sciences, Social Informatics and Telecommunications Engineering 2018
G. Sun and S. Liu (Eds.): ADHIP 2017, LNICST 219, pp. 297–306, 2018.
https://doi.org/10.1007/978-3-319-73317-3_35

SIFI algorithm is stable. However, due to the massive detection of feature point, it's too complicated and dissipative. SURF (Speeded Up Robust Feature) is more efficient and simple to operate than SIFI. Due to the variable shape of the fault for the lens, both feature descriptor mentioned above are not suitable for the feature extraction of faults for detection system. In a similar way, commonly used Harris corner detection operator and CSS (Curvature Scale Space) corner detection operator do not apply to optical lens fault detection system. Realizing the automation of optical lens fault detection is a process of constantly learning from the artificial detection. According to the quality of the optical lens classification standard, the boundary of the fault information, the area and the perimeter are the main basis of fault detection and classification. Those characteristics can be the input of the neural network and SVM (Support Vector Machine) to learn to identification and classification [7].

2 Edge Following Algorithm Based on Balanced Binary Search Tree

Due to the changeable shape of the optical lens, different kinds and different level of the flaws have different influence on the optical lenses. Taking an example of the scratch, we need the area, perimeter features and all the boundary point to fit the line. In order to obtain these characteristics, there are two commonly used solution as follows.

Plan a: First, detect each edge of image and fill the internal. Second, traverse images, and label each connected domain. In order to label the domain correctly, regard the first point of the traversed domain as the starting point. The region is labeled in a boundary tracking manner until the region is fully labeled. Starting scanning from the beginning of the mark to find the next starting point, unless the whole image is processed.

From this scheme, the digital image after processing, the edges and the internal of each individual fault have the same gray value, and each individual fault's gray value is different. It means that one byte used to describe a digital image pixel can only describe 256 faults. If the number of the faults are more than 256, the more byte are needed to describe a digital image pixel, which causes a waste of space. When to obtain the perimeter or the information of a flaw's boundary, the traverse is needed, which causes the inefficiency.

Plan b: Boundary tracing and described by the chain code.

Chain code is a coded representation of boundary point, using a specific direction and length of links. Scan in the order of the bottom-up, from left to right. Find the edge point named a as a starting point for the edge tracking, and mark it as an already tracking pixels. If another unmarked boundary point b is found, then update the current point to b. Continue to track the edge from point b, until all points are marked [8–12].

From this scheme, it can successfully help track the closed area of the border generally. However, when boundary adhesion appears, lots of the edge points will be missed. If the chain code is to describe the boundary, only the starting point of the boundary points is in absolute coordinates, and the offset of other points is represented by the related direction. If all the boundary points of a fault are needed, it needs to restore the original image by the chain code. Each boundary point needs to be determined according to the location of last point, which causes the edge information processing more complex and inefficiency.

In order to solve the problems above and to improve efficiency, the third plan is proposed here.

Plan c: Boundary tracking method is to scan the image in the order of bottom-up, from left to right. Each flaw is a individual collection with a balanced binary search tree. In order to facilitate the follow-up calculation of the area and the perimeter, the multilevel nested balanced binary search tree is adopted. The map in the STL (Standard Template Library) of c plus plus is referenced to explain. Element of the map appears as a pair with real value and the key value at the same time [13, 14]. In the first layer of the balanced binary search tree, the number of lines i starts from zero as the key value. The independent bank of all the boundary points where i is set in array is the real value. The second floor are unique numbers as key values. To peer number i, there is a corresponding balanced binary search tree as a real value. The tree structure is shown in Fig. 1.

According to the algorithm shown in Fig. 2, the steps of the algorithm are presented as follows:

Step1: Find the edge point from lower left boundary points, current point, as a starting point named s in the border. Mark the starting points. At the same time, put the point into the established balanced binary tree in the first layer.

Step2: Scan from the current point along the scanning direction, as shown in Fig. 3. The default direction is 0. The tracking principle is: If the tracking point is the boundary point, update the point to the new current point, and put the point into the first layer of the established tree. At the same time, change the direction 90° counterclockwise. If the tracking point is not a boundary point, the scan direction will be modified the 45° clockwise.

Step3: Continue to track the boundary from the current boundary point, and repeat the step 2 until the current boundary point backs to the start point s. Set direction 0, and continue to scan the new boundary.

This scheme can make up for both of these scenarios. After a border tracking, all the boundary points are classified by each individual defect. Later, when the boundary information points are extracted, the area and the perimeter are calculated. Only extracted points are needed to scan, without scanning the entire digital image. This improves the efficiency of time and space. Figure 4 is the original image of the scratch section. Figure 5 shows the image after the Fig. 4 traced edge by the plan c. And then we set the stage for the next calculation. In Fig. 4, under the condition of the boundary of a fault information, only three faults in the balanced binary search tree are going to be scanned, and you can get all the boundary of the fault information and feature, instead of scanning the whole image.

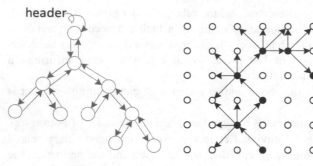

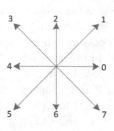

Fig. 1. Structure of tree   **Fig. 2.** Algorithm diagram   **Fig. 3.** 8-direction

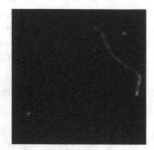

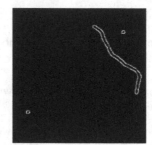

Fig. 4. The original picture of the scratch   **Fig. 5.** The post-processing portion

3 Perimeter Calculation Based on Balanced Binary Search Tree

The length of the closed area connected by a common boundary point center or the sum of regional boundary points can be regarded as the perimeter.

3.1 Kinds of Common Algorithm to Calculate the Perimeter

(1) Using the 8 - direction chain code which is shown in Fig. 6 direction chain code to calculate the perimeter. The serial number in the chain code is even when the number is even code, odd number when odd code. The distance to the odd code is $\sqrt{2}$. The distance to the even code is 1. According to even code number, the odd number of code, its formula is as follows:

$$N = n_o + \sqrt{2}n_e. \tag{1}$$

N is the perimeter. n_e is the number of the even number in code, n_o is the odd number.

Fig. 6. Direction chain code

(2) Use Euclidean distance formula to calculate the perimeter, two points (x_1, y_1) and (x_2, y_2), its formula is as follows:

$$L = \sqrt{(x_1 - x_2)^2 + (y_1 - y_2)^2} \tag{2}$$

L is the perimeter between the two points.

3.2 Improved Algorithm to Calculate the Circumference

When boundary adhesion appears, tracking by traditional boundary tracking method based on chain code, a lot of the edge points will be missed. So Freeman Chain Code is abandoned here. Using Euclidean distance formula to calculate the circumference is complex, time-consuming and space-consuming. So it's not a good choice here. The improved algorithm is based on the balanced binary search tree, which has storied all the boundary point. The number of the corresponding pixels where the line number is i is ni. The total number of boundary points is as follows:

$$L = \sum_{i=0}^{i=N} n_i \tag{3}$$

L is the perimeter of the boundary points.

4 Area Calculation Based on Balanced Binary Search Tree Area

The sum points of the boundary and its total pixels within the element or the area of the integral surrounded by a closed curve can be the area wanted.

4.1 Kinds of Common Algorithm to Calculate the Area [15, 16]

(1) Pixel accumulative method. Calculating area often counts the boundary points and its total pixels within the element. The formula is as follows:

$$S = \sum_{x=0}^{n-1} \sum_{y=0}^{m-1} f(x, y) \tag{4}$$

S is the area wanted. n is line number and m is the row number. $f(x,y)$ gives the gray value of the point (x,y).

(2) On the x-y plane. Using the Green formula to calculate area surrounded by a closed curve. The format is as follows:

$$S = \frac{1}{2} \oint (x dy - y dx) \tag{5}$$

S is the area wanted.

After binarization:

$$S = \frac{1}{2} \sum_{i=0}^{n-1} (x_i(y_{i+1} - y_i) - y_i(x_{i+1} - x_i)) = \frac{1}{2} \sum_{i=0}^{n-1} (x_i y_{i+1} - y_i x_{i+1}) \tag{6}$$

S is the area wanted.

(3) For each individual area, establish the minimum circumscribed rectangle model. The length and width of the rectangle is a and b, then, the format is as follows:

$$S = a \times b \tag{7}$$

S is the area wanted.

By the same token, the maximum and minimum circle model, the average round model, and elliptical model and other model which are equivalent to those model have the similar effect.

4.2 Improved Algorithm to Calculate the Area

Pixel accumulative method is easy, but it is space-consuming. If the area of the flaw is very large, the pixel adds one by one, thus the time of the operation is too long, and it reduce the efficiency of operation in the system. When using the Green theorem, it needs to be carried out by crossover operation point by point, and it's both time-consuming and space-consuming. The improved algorithm is based on the balanced binary search tree, which has storied all the boundary points. The corresponding pixels where the line number is i is on the tree. The format is as follows:

$$S = \sum_{i=0}^{n-1} (y_{imax} - y_{imin}); \tag{8}$$

S is the area wanted. y_{imax} and y_{imin} are the maximum and the minimum, n is the total number of the line.

5 Experimental Results and Analysis

5.1 The Results and Analysis of the Boundary Tracking

The traditional boundary tracking method based on the storage of the 8-direction chain code, when encountered intersection, is easily miss detection. Which will result in the inaccuracy of the data, even lead to the detection failure. Thus graph (a) is the original picture. Graph (b) is the result of the boundary following by the common method based on the Freeman chain code. As is shown in the picture (b), When boundary adhesion appears, tracking by traditional boundary tracking method based on chain code will cause a lot of edge points missed. Graph (c) is the result of the boundary following by the improved algorithm proposed in the paper. The data are stored in established balanced binary search tree. So the boundary tracking algorithm based on the balanced binary search tree is available in this paper.

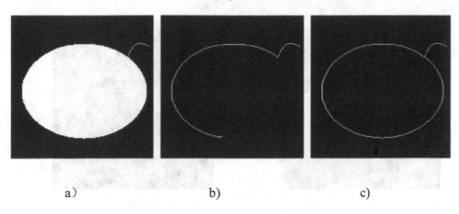

a)   b)   c)

5.2   The Analysis of the Detection Effects for the Optical Lens Detection

Graph (d) is the original picture adopted by the detection system. Graph (e) is the picture of the lens after binarization processing. Graph (f) is the graph (e) after edge following by the algorithm proposed in this paper. The algorithm of boundary tracing can get complete and accurate information of boundary. And by scanning it once, creating a balanced binary search tree for storage, the full boundary information and the data needed for the subsequent feature can be extracted. By reducing the amount of data from the entire digital image to the boundary point of all the defects, the time of calculation is greatly reduced, and the speed of the computation is faster.

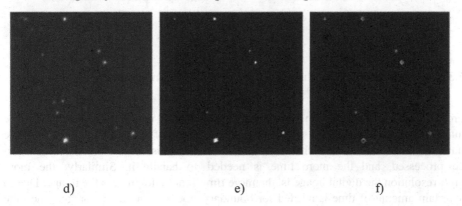

d)   e)   f)

Graph (g) is the original image of the scratch. Graph (h) is the image after being processed by the Sobel operator. Graph (i) is the image processed by the Prewitt operator. The Sobel operator and the Prewitt operator are based on first derivative edge detection operator, through the calculation of the gradient of the image to detect the image edge. So the ability of anti-noise is poor, which brings out a lot of unnecessary points. Graph (j) is the image processed by the LOG operator which produces a large amount of noise and non-demand boundary areas. Therefore, those kinds of edge processing algorithm will not be applied to the rapid feature extraction of optical lens defect.

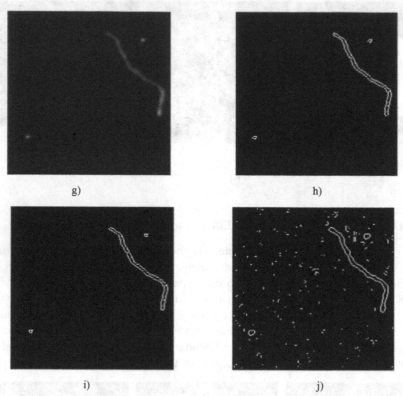

g)   h)

i)   j)

5.3   The Study for the Influence Factors of Digital Image Processing Speed

From the table below, it can be seen that the time of imaging processing has the intimate relationship with the size of the image, the sum of the flaws and the size of the flaw. In the same resolution, the larger size of the image is, the more data is needed to be processed, and the more time is needed to handle it. Similarly, the more high-resolution the digital image is, the more time it takes to process the image. Due to a certain amount of time is needed for boundary tracking and data storage, when the size and resolution are certain, the larger number of defects in the digital image, the more average area of the defects, or the greater average length of the period, the more time it will take to handle the problem. From the Table 1, it is obvious to see that the algorithm proposed this page is much faster than the common method.

Table 1. Detection time of unimproved and improved algorithms

Item value size (pixel)	2592 × 1944	2592 × 1944	2592 × 1944	432 × 324
Detection time of the unimproved algorithm(s)	2.125	3.351	4.142	0.131
Detection time of the improved algorithm(s)	0.712	0.924	1.235	0.026
Sum of the flaws	52	87	116	32
Average perimeter of the flaws (pixel)	1792	1881	1824	52
Average area of the flaws (pixel)	8842	8163	9457	231

6   Conclusion

This paper proposes a edge tracking algorithm based on the balanced binary search tree. Calculate the perimeter and the area of the optical lens by the data storied. The novel algorithm is simplified, and it responds fast. Relying on this method, only once is needed to scan the image based on binarization transformation. It's no need filling area. All the needed message will be extracted, without using Freeman Chain Code.

References

1. Liu, H., Shen, J., Guo, S.: Digital image processing using Visual C++. China Mach. Press **6**, 154–156 (2010)
2. Chen, Y., Shang, L.: Improved SIFT image registration algorithm on characteristic statistical distributions and consistency constraint. Optik-Int. J. Light Electron Opt. **127**(2), 900–911 (2016)
3. Lin, H., Du, P., Zhao, W., et al.: Image registration based on corner detection and affine transformation. In: 2010 3rd International Congress on Image and Signal Processing (CISP), vol. 5, pp. 2184–2188. IEEE (2010)
4. Goodman, J., Weare, J.: Ensemble samplers with affine invariance. Commun. Appl. Math. Comput. Sci. **5**(1), 65–80 (2010)
5. Wang, W., Zhang, D., Zhang, Y., et al.: Robust spatial matching for object retrieval and its parallel implementation on GPU. IEEE Trans. Multimedia **13**(6), 1308–1318 (2011)
6. Wang, P., Chen, Q., Chen, H., et al.: A new affine-invariant image matching method based onSIFT. In: International Symposium on Photoelectronic Detection and Imaging 2013: Infrared Imaging and Applications. International Society for Optics and Photonics, vol. 8907, p. 89072D (2013)
7. Yeh, J.P.: Detecting edge using support vector machine. Adv. Mater. Res. **588**, 974–977 (2012). Trans Tech Publications

8. Sun, X.H.: Digital image processing: the principle and algorithm (2010). (in Chinese). 孙燮华. 数字图像处理: 原理与算法 (2010)

9. Liu, L.L.: New algorithm and its application for edge detection in morphology. J. Infrared Millimeter Waves **17**(5), 386–390 (1998)

10. Zhao, J., Xu, Y., Jiao, Y.: The fast arithmetic study of image edge detection based on the order morphology. Acta Electronica Sinica **36**(11), 2195–2199 (2008)

11. Chuang, C.H., Lie, W.N.: A downstream algorithm based on extended gradient vector flow field for object segmentation. IEEE Trans. Image Process. **13**(10), 1379–1392 (2004)

12. Zhao, Y., Chen, H., Wang, S., et al.: An improved method of detecting edge direction for spatial error concealment. J. Multimedia **7**(3), 262–268 (2012)

13. Jie, H.: The Annotated STL Source. Huazhong University of Science and Technology Press, WuHan (2002). (in Chinese). 侯捷. STL 源码剖析. 华中科技大学出版社 (2002)

14. Tang, J., Millington, S., Acton, S.T., et al.: Surface extraction and thickness measurement of the articular cartilage from MR images using directional gradient vector flow snakes. IEEE Trans. Biomed. Eng. **53**(5), 896–907 (2006)

15. Xie, J., Li, S., Lin, G.: The method of calculating the area and circumference based on the boundary trace. Electron. Technol. Softw. Eng. (9), 119–120 (2014). (in Chinese). 谢家龙, 李林升, 林国湘. 基于边界跟踪的多连通区域面积和周长的计算方法. 电子技术 与软件工程 (9), 119–120 (2014)

16. Zhou, X., Chen, Y., Hu, W.: Tree traversal binary image boundary tracing algorithm based on cross-point. Comput. Appl. Softw. **31**(2), 230–232 (2014). (in Chinese). 周秀芝, 陈洋, 胡文婷. 基于交叉点的树遍历二值图像边界跟踪算法. 计算机应用与软件 **31**(2), 230–232 (2014)

The Influence of Vibration on Performance of Navigation Tasks

Ming-hui Sun[3], Wen-zhao Gu[1,2(✉)], Ming Ding[5], and Xiao-ying Sun[4]

[1] National Space Science Center,
Chinese Academy of Sciences, Beijing 100190, China
guwz2014@163.com
[2] University of Chinese Academy of Sciences, Beijing 100190, China
[3] College of Computer Science and Technology,
Jilin University, Changchun 130022, China
[4] College of Communication Engineering,
Jilin University, Changchun 130022, China
[5] Nara Institute of Science and Technology, Ikoma, Japan

Abstract. In this paper, we explore the efficiency of vibration feedback techniques in pedestrian navigation systems. For vibration feedback technology, many researchers have provided a variety of different modes of vibration, such as vibration belt, vibrating bracelet and vibration shoes. And there are some researchers to discuss the perception of the human body parts, which part is more suitable for vibration feedback. However, there are still some discussion points that are not taken into account, for example, the identification rate of vibration feedback mode in the processes of walking or running. In order to find the answer, we rebuild the vibration feedback mode to have a new experimental evaluation of the identification rate of these vibration modes. We noticed that when using a hand-held vibration feedback device, it can reduce the visual and auditory feedback. On the other hand, because of the rapid development of the current society, the environment is different in different position, so, when getting the maximum recognition rate of vibration pattern, we can't use this vibration navigation replace the existing navigation completely. However, it is a good choice that the kind of high-efficiency vibration feedback navigation system is used as an auxiliary system of the existing navigation.

Keywords: Tactile feedback · Mobile device · Multiple vibration motors

1 Introduction

It is a huge challenge for us to find an appropriate travel path that we want in a strange environment. It usually takes navigation instruments to learn the surrounding environment is what kind of, destination in which and the space position relationship with

Supported by the National Youth Natural Science Foundation of China (No. 61300145), the Postdoctoral Science Foundation of China (2014M561294), the Science and Technology Development Program funded projects of Jilin Province (20150520065JH) and National Key Research and Development Program of China (No. 2016YFB1001300).

© ICST Institute for Computer Sciences, Social Informatics and Telecommunications Engineering 2018
G. Sun and S. Liu (Eds.): ADHIP 2017, LNICST 219, pp. 307–318, 2018.
https://doi.org/10.1007/978-3-319-73317-3_36

the surrounding buildings. In order to become familiar with the unfamiliar environment, many people sometimes need to adapt to the current unfamiliar environment. But when there is no navigation equipment, it is difficult for us to find the path that we want. This makes the application of navigation system become widespread. However, most of current navigation systems use visual feedback or audible feedback manner to pass the navigation information, and the use and application of the scene is relatively single, only the driving trip. It's difficult to apply to the scene, such as walking, which greatly limits the navigation system more widely used.

Tactile vibration has been used another way to provide haptic feedback on touch screen equipment [1–5], when users touch the target on the screen (buttons, drop-down menus, etc.), the device's vibration motor will produce vibration. This way can help users determine whether they touch the target object. Thus, the expression of vibration technology information is an effective mode of human-computer interaction and information delivery methods [6], and as an important delivery channel of information, to make up for the shortcomings and deficiencies in specific conditions (When in a noisy environment and other public places, the navigation voice of navigation system and other surrounding sounds mixed together, making it difficult for the user to identify, which will make voice broadcast efficacy may be greatly reduced or even useless; if the navigation instruments are used in walking, it's not easy to long time staring at the screen to observe the navigation path, which will display the navigation function is not the ultimate role to play; if the headphones are used that based on the voice prompt, which will hinder the whistle sound like vehicle and other sound effects with great navigation). A recent report [11] shows that in smart phone users under the age of 30, 62% of the people encountered serious car accident case since playing with mobile phones not to look at the road, and 43% of people have been aware of this potential threat. It is necessary for us to focus on the road conditions when the vehicle is long. In this case, the use of visual and auditory navigation system has been greatly restricted. And an auxiliary navigation system can be of great help, such as driving travel tasks [12–14] or pedestrian navigation [14–16]. Vibration feedback technology is a good choice for the auxiliary navigation system. The vibration feedback technology can not only help people with normal vision, but also have great help to people who have a disability. This technology can also be used in many ways, such as driving travel and walking, and has broad application prospect.

We found a navigation path by a hand-held device to pass navigation path information to their user. We adopt this kind of form mainly because of the current mobile device and the widespread existence in our daily life, and that can make this kind of technology have great adaptability. Our navigation system includes two types of feedback - speech (semantic) feedback and vibration feedback - to provide between two exact location and path information.

The main contribution of this project is to design and implement a vibration navigation system, which provides navigation path information to users by vibration feedback in many different situations. Our navigation system is composed of a mobile device with a touch screen and a hardware device that generates vibration feedback. The vibration part of the hardware device is placed on the top of the diamond with 4 vibration motors (Fig. 1). When the user takes the device, it can generate different vibration modes according to the different positions of the palm and fingers.

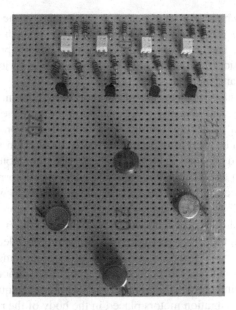

Fig. 1. The hardware parts of vibration navigation system and the location of the four vibration motor

In this paper, we first discuss the research on the information related to the mobile touch screen device and the vibration feedback technology. Secondly, we will describe our prototype system and various vibration modes in this project. Thirdly, we will describe an experiment to detect whether a user can accurately distinguish between different vibration modes, and traveling at different speeds, the system interacts with the user's productivity. Finally, we summarize the whole thesis and plan for the future work.

2 Related Work

Vibration feedback technology has been used as an important interface for the user to interact with the touch screen device and it has been familiar with the majority of users [1, 3, 5]. In this section, we will review the previous vibration tactile feedback technology on mobile devices, and focus on the wealth of information that is intended to convey, rather than a simple vibration. Why do we need vibration feedback? The simple reason is that the feedback is more intuitive, and in many cases, we do not need to look at the screen, we know our own operation effect.

2.1 Vibration Feedback Technology on Mobile Devices

Today, the touch screen has been widely used in a variety of mobile devices, such as smart phones, tablet PCs and music players. Most of these devices provide users with vibration feedback through the vibration motor embedded. Fukumoto and Sugimura may be the first researchers that the vibrators are embedded in the Active Click system [1] for the user to know the details of their touch event on a touch screen. In the Active Click system, it can be used for user to know that they touch a project on the display, and the way of vibration feedback can help to complete a variety of tasks, such as information input [3] and list item selection [2].

For one vibration motor, it can provide a variety of different vibration modes by changing the frequency and intensity of the vibration. Poupyrev et al. Research shows that different vibration modes can convey different information, and the method of vibration feedback can be used to improve the speed of selection in the linear list with the increase of 1/5. And the combination of multiple vibration motor can generate more vibration mode, which can be transmitted to the user more information. On the other hand, the mobile device can be attached to the vibration motor, which can be used to provide vibration feedback to the user, rather than the vibration motor embedded in their own. Brown et al. had placed the multiple vibration motor attached on the participants' arm to obtain the vibration feedback to transmit the calendar information [7].

These projects described have shown that different vibration modes can transmit the different task information to the user. These different vibration modes can be generated by controlling the number of vibration motor, vibration frequency and vibration intensity. The multiple vibration motors placed in the body of the participants will have a greater use of space. However, the placement of multiple vibration motors is also a significant problem. Sahami et al. placed six vibration motors on both sides of the smart phone (three per side) in order to test the accuracy of distinguishing the different vibration mode [8]. In their experiments, the results show that the accuracy of the 8 different vibration modes can be reached by the 70–80%, but they are difficult to distinguish the position of vibration source at each time when a vibration motor is generated, and at that time, the accuracy of the average can only reach 36%.

2.2   Existing Navigation System

Today, navigation system has been widely applied to people daily life. When driving, there will be a vehicle-mounted navigation to guide for us, and when walking, navigation equipment on the mobile device will become essential. These two kinds of common navigation instruments have become an indispensable product of our daily travel, and both of them are used visual feedback and auditory feedback to remind the travel path. Auditory feedback is that the navigation instrument transmit the path information to the user through the voice broadcast function; visual feedback is that a navigation instrument displays the path information on the screen for the users to see and obtain navigation path information. However, both of them have some disadvantages. For example, on the visual feedback, users can't be a long time staring at the screen to observe a navigation path information, the screen can not work for a long time and power supply system will also be a problem difficult to solve; on the other hand, on the auditory feedback, if the user's environment is too noisy, voice broadcast will greatly reduce the efficiency, even be in failure, and if the headphones are used, the sound of great navigation like vehicles whistle sound will be limited, which makes the traveling at a greater risk of environment. Meier et al., who have studied the human sensory perception which part is more suitable for vibration, placed vibration feedback system on the top of the shoes [17] and made a confirmed study, but the study is lack of the research of travel speed.

The application situation of navigation system described above is relatively simple, such as car navigation systems generally only apply to the process of driving velocity or position of great rapid changed, navigation instrument on the mobile device can only have a greater effect on the lower speed of movement. Therefore, the use of them has been limited. However, tactile vibration feedback can play a role in a noisy environment or a variety of moving speed. In a noisy environment, the auditory feedback is limited, but the vibration feedback can be used to provide the travel path information which can not be disturbed by surrounding noise; when in different speeds, the vibration feedback is used to provide travel path information, which can not be limited by the speed of travel, such as driving and walking can use the same navigation instrument. As a consequence, the vibration feedback can play a role in many different situations.

3   System

The vibration navigation system is a kind of navigation system which is designed to be able to be used in different situations and to use the vibration feedback to remind the navigation path information. The difference between the vibration navigation system and the existing navigation system is that it increases the vibration feedback, and uses the voice broadcast and vibration feedback to transmit the path information. In next section, we will describe the hardware part of the vibration feedback and voice broadcast, and the different vibration modes.

4   Hardware

Figure 2 shows the hardware part of our vibration navigation system. Similar with SemFeel [9], we welded a circuit board, the circuit board contains four vibration motors, respectively, in accordance with the upper and lower left and right four directions. The distance between two vibration motors is greater than 1 cm, because there is a study shows that when the distance of two vibration source is not more than 1 cm, if the vibration source is generated, it will be difficult to distinguish which vibration source is [10]. The circuit board is connected with a single chip microcomputer and a Bluetooth module. The single chip microcomputer is used to control the vibration of the motor, the Bluetooth module is used to receive the navigation path information, and the circuit board is connected with a battery box for power supply.

Voice broadcast uses iFLYTEK speech technology broadcasting technology to broadcast. In mobile devices, the path information is transmitted to the iFLYTEK speech technology broadcast module. When obtained the path information, it uses the speech broadcast technology to broadcast to complete auditory feedback function.

Fig. 2. Hardware

5 Interactive

Our vibration navigation system includes software and hardware. The software part is installed on the mobile device, and the starting point and the destination of the navigation path are finished by the software part. After the input is completed, the path planning is performed to obtain the navigation path information which is passed to the hardware to generate vibrations via Bluetooth technology; In the hardware part, the navigation path information is obtained from the software by using the Bluetooth technology, and the information is processed to control the multiple vibration motors to generate different vibration feedback.

When the vibration mode is generated in the hardware device, the different vibration modes can be generated according to the number of vibrator, the order of vibration and frequency and intensity. In our equipment, we use the number of vibration motor and the order of vibration to generate different vibration modes, not to consider the vibration frequency and intensity of these two factors. In the vibration of each vibration motor, we set the vibration time of 500 ms, 1000 ms and 1500 ms, because a longer time of vibration may be not practical.

6 Vibration Feedback Mode

Figure 3 shows that we designed 11 kinds of vibration modes. These vibration modes are divided into four categories: single motor vibrations (left, right), two motor vibrations (upper-right, upper-left, right-upper, left-upper, down-upper), three motor vibrations (right-upper-left, down-upper-left, down-upper-right), four motor vibrations (left-down-right-upper). The 11 kinds of different vibration modes represent different turning when driving or walking. In the following experiments, each vibration motor is only set one kind of vibration intensity in our equipment, because we mainly want to observe the accuracy rate of different vibration modes in various situations, and the recognition degree of vibration feedback mode in many situations.

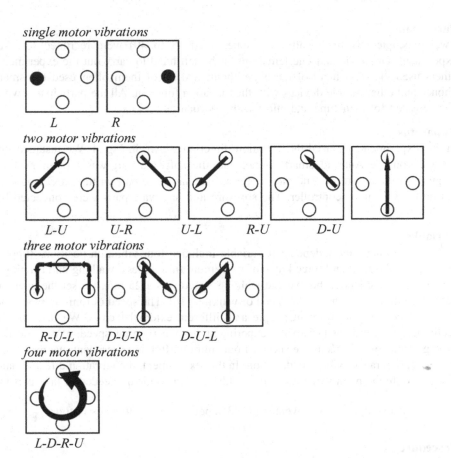

Fig. 3. The eleven kinds of vibration modes (U represents upper, L represents left, R represents right, D represents down)

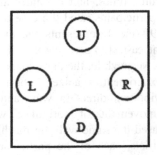

Fig. 4. Vibration direction (U represents upper, L represents left, R represents right, D represents down)

7 Experiment: Recognition Rate of Vibration Direction Under Different Moving Speed

Participants

Twelve people (six male and six female, aged 18 to 40) were recruited for this experiment. One male and one female used the left hand to carry out the experiment, others used the right hand of the experiment, and all of them often used the smart phones and other mobile devices with the vibration function. All the participants were compensated for their time and effort with 20 yuan.

Apparatus

In this experiment, we used the vibration direction shown in Fig. 4. We installed the software on the Android smart phone, and the software part was written in Java language, running on the Android platform. The hardware part written in C language ran on the C51 microcontroller. The software and hardware parts were connected by the Bluetooth.

Variables

In this experiment, the independent variable included four vibration positions (upper, left, right and down) and three kinds of movement (motionless, walking and running). According to the study, the average walking speed was 1.25 m/s, we set the average value for our experiments in the speed of walking [18]. The speed of running would be changed according to different people and different external factors. We had done a preliminary experiment before the experiment for the running speed. We made the average value of 4.5 m/s as the speed of our running. In this experiment, we measured the perception rate of vibration direction. In this experiment, the vibration direction and velocity were the main variables of our study. Each participant needed to take part in:

$$4(\text{directions}) * 3(\text{movements}) * 3(\text{repetitions}) = 36 \text{ trials in total.}$$

Procedure

Before the start of the experiment, we explained the purpose of the experiment and the experimental process to the participants. After the end of the explanation, the participants started to be familiar with the equipment and vibration modes. Each experiment equipment vibrated at least three times, and the interval time was 5 s. After three vibration was completed, the participants rated the ease of perception of the vibration on a 7-point Likert scale [19] (the 1 represents the most difficult to perceive the vibration mode, and the 7 is the easiest to perceive the vibration mode) to record every time the degree of perception. Meanwhile, the participants made an oral evaluation of the vibration mode, and the experiment organizers took notes.

In this experiment, the vibration direction was random. Each direction of the experiment was in the three movements of motionless, walking and running. When walking and running, we all used the same walking machine.

After the end of all the trials, each of the participants would have to fill in a questionnaire (see Fig. 5). In the questionnaire, the participants were asked about the interval of vibration time, the vibration mode, the system's evaluation and

Fig. 5. Questionnaire survey

improvement suggestions and other issues. When the experiment was over, the participants were asked if there is a suggestion or question to the system. It took around one hour for each participant to finish the experiment.

8 Experiment Results

When the speed is less than or equal to 5 km/h, it is in a state of walking, and when the speed is greater than 5 km/h, it is running. After measuring, when the vibration time was 500 ms and the participants were able to feel the vibration, the maximum speed could reach 10.5 km/h. At that time, we had felt weak. On the other hand, when the vibration time was 1500 ms and the participants were able to feel the vibration, the maximum speed could reach 11.2 km/h. At that time, we also had felt weak. In summary, when the traveling speed is less than 10 km/h, the accuracy of vibration perception of the four directions could reach more than 90%. When the traveling speed between the 10 km/h–11 km/h, according to the vibration of long sequence from short to long, the accuracy of vibration perception would gradually reduce. When the speed was greater than 11 km/h, the three vibration time of the current equipment were close to the failure. However, if the vibration time were increased, it will still play a role in vibration perception.

9 Experiment Discussion

The experimental data and conclusions are basically satisfied with the original idea. In this experiment, the accuracy of vibration perception can reach more than 90%, and the error of the vibration perception is caused by the following several points:

(1) Vibrator is stuck to the circuit board, so all the vibration equipment are in vibration. Thus, it is difficult to perceive the vibrator vibration correctly.
(2) In the actual walking process, when the walking speed is faster, but the vibration intensity is weak, the vibration perception is not very obvious.

(3) When the vibration time is too short, vibration perception is not obvious and not easy to distinguish the vibration direction.
(4) The actual initiation voltage of each vibrator is different, when using the same power to supply, the vibration strength is not consistent.

We only need to miniaturize the device and change the vibration time to enhance the user's vibration perception. In addition, we need to further explore the recognition rate of our vibration mode at different speeds of walking process, in order to study the speed of travel and the recognition accuracy of different vibration mode in the case of perceived range.

10 Conclusion and Future Work

Vibration feedback effectively increases the application range of the navigation system, especially when the user can not directly view the touch screen. In this paper, we restore the hand-held vibration feedback device which connect with a plurality of vibrators embedded to explore the recognition rate of vibration feedback modes under different moving speed. Our two experiments showed that the accuracy of the user's identification of the vibration direction can reach about 90% when the travel speed is less than or equal to 10 km/h. For the 11 vibration modes, the accuracy of identification is not high and only about 70%, but the idea or direction is correct, it just need to improve the experimental equipment and experimental steps to improve the identification accuracy of the vibration mode.

We believe that we can accomplish the goal of assisting the existing navigation technology or navigation equipment by improving the identification accuracy of vibration mode, and can provide users with more convenience. The experimental results of this paper show that the design of vibration mode in vibration navigation technology needs to be further improved in order to improve the recognition accuracy of vibration mode. Because the vibration mode is higher, the vibration feedback technology can be better to assist users in navigation. In addition, this navigation can be carried out in a variety of situations to navigate, without considering the changes in the environment (within the carrying capacity of the device). This system can make people's sense focus on a single task, as far as possible to avoid the emergence of a variety of tasks in the same sense. We believe that this vibration navigation system will be used as an auxiliary system for existing navigation system to give many travelers bring great convenience.

In the future work, we will gradually improve the vibration navigation system (for example, to modify the design of vibration mode), in order to improve the recognition accuracy of vibration mode. And we will consider the energy supply of the vibration system, so that it can work for a long time. Meanwhile, we will also apply the vibration feedback mode to more fields, giving more physical meaning to the vibration feedback mode, so that it can be applied in other fields, such as the rapid selection of the touch screen.

Acknowledgement. We would like to thank the School of Computer Science and Technology, Jilin University, for providing us with experimental field and equipment. And we also want to thank the National Youth Natural Science Foundation of China (No. 61300145), the Postdoctoral Science Foundation of China (2014M561294) and the Science and Technology Development Program funded projects of Jilin Province (20150520065JH) to provide funding. This study has been partially supported by National Key Research and Development Program of China (No. 2016YFB1001300).

References

1. Fukumoto, M., Sugimura, T.: Active click: tactile feedback for touch panels. In: CHI Extended Abstracts, pp. 121–122. ACM (2001)
2. Hall, M., Hoggan, E., Brewster, S.: T-Bars: towards tactile user interfaces for mobile touchscreens. In: Proceedings of MobileHCI, pp. 411–414 (2008)
3. Hoggan, E., Brewster, S.A., Johnston, J.: Investigating the effectiveness of tactile feedback for mobile touchscreens. In: Proceeding of CHI, pp. 1573–1582. ACM (2008)
4. Hoggan, E., Anwar, S., Brewster, S.A.: Mobile multi-actuator tactile displays. In: Oakley, I., Brewster, S. (eds.) HAID 2007. LNCS, vol. 4813, pp. 22–33. Springer, Heidelberg (2007). https://doi.org/10.1007/978-3-540-76702-2_4
5. Poupyrev, I., Maruyama, S., Rekimoto, J.: Ambient touch: designing tactile interfaces for handheld devices. In: Proceedings of UIST, pp. 51–60. ACM (2002)
6. Wang, G.: Route guidance for blind based on haptic technology and their spatial congnition. Xinjiang University (2013)
7. Brown, L.M., Brewster, S.A., Purchase, H.C.: Multidimensional tactons for non-visual information presentation in mobile devices. In: Proceedings of MobileHCI, pp. 231–238. ACM (2006)
8. Rantala, J., Raisamo, R., Lylykangas, J., Surakka, V., Raisamo, J., Salminen, K., Pakkanen, T., Hippula, A.: Methods for presenting braille characters on a mobile device with a touchscreen and tactile feedback. IEEE Trans. Haptics 2(1), 28–39 (2009)
9. Yatani, K., Truong, K.N.: SemFeel: a user interface with semantic tactile feedback for mobile touch-screen devices. In: UIST 2009, pp. 111–120. ACM (2009)
10. Palmer, C.I., Gardner, E.P.: Simulation of motion of the skin IV responses of pacinian corpuscle afferents innervating the primate hand to stripe patterns on the optacon. J. Neurophysiol. 64(1), 236–247 (1990)
11. EARSandEYES: Handy im Straßenverkehr: Jüngere unterschätzen das Risiko. Ears and Eyes Creating new Grounds (2014). http://www.earsandeyes.com/en/presse/handy-imstrassenverkehr/?pdf=1
12. Labiale, G.: In-car road information: comparisons of auditory and visual presentations. In: Proceedings of the Human Factors and Ergonomics Society Annual Meeting, vol. 34, no. 9, pp. 623–627. SAGE Publications (1990)
13. Liu, Y.C.: Comparative study of the effects of auditory, visual and multimodality displays on drivers' performance in advanced traveller information systems. Ergonomics 44(4), 425–442 (2001)
14. Zeichner, N., Perry, P., Sita, M., Barbera, L., Nering, T.: Exploring HowMobile Technologies Impact Pedestrian Safety. NYC Media Lab Research Brief (2014)
15. Pielot, M., Boll, S.: *Tactile Wayfinder*: comparison of tactile waypoint navigation with commercial pedestrian navigation systems. In: Floréen, P., Krüger, A., Spasojevic, M. (eds.) Pervasive 2010. LNCS, vol. 6030, pp. 76–93. Springer, Heidelberg (2010). https://doi.org/10.1007/978-3-642-12654-3_5

16. Rümelin, S., Rukzio, E., Hardy, R.: NaviRadar: a novel tactile information display for pedestrian navigation. In: Proceedings of the 24th Annual ACM Symposium on User Interface Software and Technology, pp. 293–302. ACM (2011)
17. Meier, A., Matthies, D.J.C., Urban, B., Wettach, R.: Exploring Vibrotactile Feedback on the Body and Foot for the Purpose of Pedestrian Navigation. ACM (2015)
18. Knoblauch, R.L., Pietrucha, M.T., Nitzburg, M.: Field studies of pedestrian walking speed and start-up time. Transp. Res. Rec.: J. Transp. Res. Board 1538(1), 27–38 (1996)
19. Dawes, J.: Do data characteristics change according to the number of scale points used? An experiment using 5 point, 7 point and 10 point scales. Int. J. Market Res. 50(1), 61–77 (2008)

The Comprehensive Quality Evaluation of Minority Students in Colleges and Universities Based on Principle of Information Entropy

Wu Wang[1], Lina Shan[2(✉)], and Yunjie Gu[2]

[1] Youth League Committee of Inner Mongolia University of Technology,
Huhehot 010051, Inner Mongolia Autonomous Region, China
[2] School of Reserve Officers, Harbin University of Science and Technology,
Harbin 150080, Heilongjiang, China
linashan@126.com

Abstract. The paper does the analysis to the quality character of minority students in Colleges and Universities and there are four evaluation indexes which are suitable for the students: language and communication skills, academic performance and professional skills, personality accomplishment and psychological quality and democratic spirit and patriotism. Based on principle of information entropy, it analyzes the random sample of Inner Mongolia University of Technology graduate and makes use of the entropy to confirm the weight of each evaluation index to the influence of the comprehensive quality. It builds the linear evaluation model to get the comprehensive evaluation index and compares the result calculated by model and the student graduation test to prove the feasible of model with Pearson correlation coefficient.

Keywords: Minority students · Evaluation index
Principle of information entropy · Comprehensive quality

1 Suggest Problems and Confirm the Evaluation Index

The cultivation of the whole quality of the minority nationalities in West China affects the improvement of the western comprehensive quality [1]. Since it is in remote and developing area and most of minorities live in relatively independent region. They live in the cultural atmosphere of the nation, so their cognitive structure has obvious national character, which has an impact on the development of minority students in high school [2]. There are some common situations in the high school.

The normal education part of the minority students is finished in the local minority language before going to high school. The change of language after going into high school must cause difficulty in study and life. The students who are more adaptable to the language environment have obviously stronger ability to accept knowledge, compared with those students with poor language basis.

© ICST Institute for Computer Sciences, Social Informatics and Telecommunications Engineering 2018
G. Sun and S. Liu (Eds.): ADHIP 2017, LNICST 219, pp. 319–325, 2018.
https://doi.org/10.1007/978-3-319-73317-3_37

The basic courses of minority students are opened separately. In the teaching process, methods will be used mostly to finish teaching, such as reducing content, decrease the difficulty and reduce evaluation standard.

Because of the sudden change of culture environment atmosphere and the mutual communication with other nations, the students cannot adapt to the psychology, which has a great shock to their original knowledge to society and the sense of value.

The influence of minority students to different living custom and religion belief. They are very sensitive to nation, religion and belief and it is easy to have friction in communication. Whether they can communicate in high school harmoniously or not would affect their knowledge of national unity, the unity of the motherland.

In summary, the quality education of minority education have specialty. We cannot evaluate the minority students with the method of common high school students, but with these four aspects to have comprehensive evaluation: language and communication skills, academic performance and professional skills, personality accomplishment and psychological quality and democratic spirit and patriotism.

2 The Comprehensive Evaluation Model Based on Principle of Information Entropy

2.1 Information Entropy and Information Entropy Principle

Entropy is an important physical quantity. In the communication principle, the average information of source signal is called as entropy [3]. In information theory, the information entropy shows the degree of disorder of information [4]. The smaller the entropy is, the larger the information effect is; the larger the entropy is, the smaller the information effect is. The definition and formula of information entropy function is:

$$H(\vec{P}) = -\sum_{i=1}^{n} p_i \log_2 p_i \tag{1}$$

$\vec{P} = (p_1, p_2 \cdots p_n)$ stands for the probability vector.

2.2 Comprehensive Evaluation Model

We samples 50 minority students in Inner Mongolia University of Technology randomly and get the single assessment of four aspects (hundred-score system) language and communication skills, academic performance and professional skills, personality accomplishment and psychological quality and democratic spirit and patriotism by counselor and teacher evaluation, academic performance statistics, expert interview. The following picture is the score distribution histogram of 50 students.

Seen from the picture, these score distributions are independent and it has no crossing affect. The comprehensive quality evaluation model can be built with the data combined with principle of information entropy [5]. Following use n stands for student number $(n = 1, 2, \cdots \cdots 50)$ and m stands for index $(m = 1, 2, 3 \ and \ 4)$

2.2.1 Confirmation of Information Entropy

Since all subjects score of the most of the sampling students is higher than 50, it is necessary to normalize the performance of each subject in each random sample to reduce the effect of the invalid information on the results. The specific operation is as follow: the result matrix is normalized and the normalized factor matrix is obtained.

$$z_{ij} = \frac{x_{ij} - x_{min}}{x_{max} - x_{min}} \tag{2}$$

The x_{max} stands for the highest of the single subject. The x_{min} stands for the lowest of the single subject.

According to the definition of entropy, the m subjects score of n students can be evaluation index and the entropy of evaluation index can be confirmed (Fig. 1).

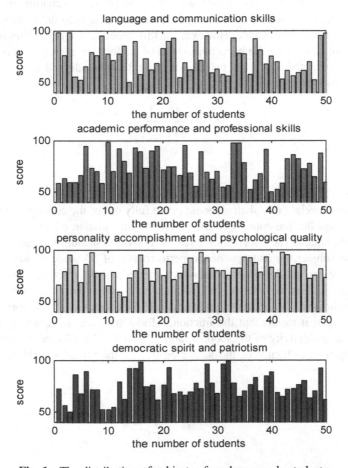

Fig. 1. The distribution of subjects of random sample students

$$H_j = -\frac{1}{\ln n}\sum_{i=1}^{n}(f_{ij}\ln f_{ij}) \tag{3}$$
$$i = 1,2,3\cdots n, j = 1,2,3 \text{ and } 4$$

2.2.2   Revise the Traditional Probability Formula

The traditional probability formula is as follows.

$$f_{ij} = \frac{z_{ij}}{\sum_{i=1}^{n} z_{ij}} \tag{4}$$

To make the H_j meaningful in the probability interval; we suppose that $f_{ij} = 0$. But since the logarithm of 1 is 0, so when $f_{ij} = 1$, $f_{ij}\ln f_{ij}$ equals to zero, which is opposite to the definition of entropy. The reason why there is no such situation in traditional probability formula is that the probability of 1 of the signal is to determine the signal, which has no study significance. However, in this paper $f_{ij} = 1$ represents is a student whose score of subject j is the maximum value of random samples, which is obviously reasonable. Hence, the traditional calculation should not be adopted in the calculation. So the formula is revised as follows.

$$f_{ij} = \frac{1 + z_{ij}}{\sum_{i=1}^{n} 1 + z_{ij}} \tag{5}$$

2.2.3   The Calculation and the Nature of Weight

The principle of weight calculation should make fully use of the concept of information entropy. The smaller the entropy is, the larger the information effect is; the larger the entropy is, the smaller the information effect is. If score distribution presented is for the score of one subject, the entropy of the performance of 50 students will be smaller. Almost no one can get the same score, which means that the fractional division in the process of evaluation is detailed [6]. Almost every point has a distinction, so the objective factor is small, so the weight is larger. If the entropy of the performance of 50 students is larger, it means that the fractional division in the process of evaluation is rough and the subjectivity of the score is larger. So it will be affected by personal play and the subjective influence of the judger easily. So the model should be given less weight [7].

$$\omega_j = \frac{1 - H_j}{m - \sum_{j=1}^{m} H_j} \tag{6}$$

The nature of weight:

$$\sum_{j=1}^{m} \omega_j = 1 \tag{7}$$

We process with 50 random sample and induce the percentile data of four aspects which are language and communication skills ($j = 1$), academic performance and professional skills ($j = 2$), personality accomplishment and psychological quality ($j = 3$), democratic spirit and patriotism ($j = 4$) into MATLAB programming calculation weights [8]. The following are the result.

$$\omega_1 = 0.3248, \; \omega_2 = 0.2970, \\ \omega_3 = 0.1569, \; \omega_4 = 0.2213 \tag{8}$$

2.2.4 Comprehensive Evaluation Model

According to the calculated weight, the comprehensive evaluation model can be described with four element linear equation. The comprehensive quality:

$$Q_i = \sum_{j=1}^{4} \omega_j \cdot x_{ij} \tag{9}$$

3 Comparative Argument

We can use the comprehensive quality model to calculate 50 random samples and compare the result gained from the model and the data gained form the graduation test. The results are shown as following picture (Fig. 2):

The relevance of data of two groups is counted with Pearson correlation coefficient. The Pearson correlation coefficient is also called as product difference correlation (product moment correlation) [9, 10]. It was a method to calculate linear correlation mentioned by the British statistician Pearson in 20 century. The correlation coefficient is larger, the correlation coefficient is more close to 1 and -1; the correlation coefficient is stronger, the correlation coefficient is close to 0, the correlation coefficient is weaker. The formula is as followed:

$$p_{xy} = \frac{N \sum X \cdot Y - \sum X \cdot \sum Y}{\sqrt{N \sum X^2 - (\sum X)^2} \cdot \sqrt{N \sum Y^2 - (\sum Y)^2}} \tag{10}$$

When deviation of the two variables is not zero, the correlation coefficient is defined. Pearson correlation coefficient is suitable for:

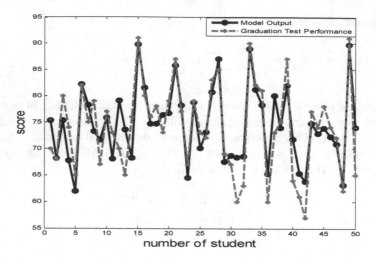

Fig. 2. The compare of graduation test performance and model output result

(1) A linear relationship between the two variables is the continuous data.
(2) The population of the two variables is the normal distribution, or close to the normal one.
(3) The observed values of the two variables are in pairs, and each pair of observations is independent of each other.

Suppose the graduation test result is X and the model calculation result is Y to count the Pearson correlation coefficient of the two by formula and the correlation coefficient is gained. Compare with the table of commonly used Pearson correlation coefficient (Table 1).

Table 1. Commonly used pearson correlation coefficient

Pearson correlation coefficient	Correlation degree
0.8–1.0	Extremely strong correlation
0.6–0.8	Strong correlation
0.4–0.6	Moderate correlation
0.2–0.4	Weak correlation
0–0.2	Extremely weak correlation

It is found that two parties is extremely strong correlation, which says that the model construction is successfully.

4 Conclusion

Clarify the evaluation index of minority students in high school and it is meaningful to build up reasonable evaluation model in the growth of the students and the mutual development of all nations. There are some conclusions gained from the model:

(1) Language communication skills have a lager effect to the development of the students in high school because it affects the improvement of all quality of the student directly. High school should think highly of the disadvantage of language communication and add some language training course.
(2) Besides the academic performance and professional skills, personality accomplishment and psychological quality, democratic spirit and patriotism take larger percentage in the comprehensive quality. High school should think highly of the ideological education to train the correct sense on life, world sense and value sense.

References

1. Wang, D.: POME-based fuzzy optimal evaluation model of water environment. J. Hehai Univ. **30**, 56–60 (2002)
2. Li, J.: The quality character of minority students in colleges and universities. High. Educ. Sci. **4**, 49–54 (2000)
3. Liang, J.Y., Shi, Z.Z.: The information entropy, rough entropy and knowledge granulation in rough set theory. Int. J. Uncertain. Fuzziness Knowl.-Based Syst. **12**, 37–46 (2004)
4. Liang, J., Shi, Z.D., Li, D., Wierman, M.J.: Information entropy, rough entropy and knowledge granulation in incomplete information systems. Int. J. Gen Syst **35**, 641–654 (2006)
5. Zhang, J.Y., Shu, L.X., Chen, S.X., Luan, X.X., Tian, T.: Study on the reserved model of information entropy for the calculation of the amount of nucleus radiant prevention drugs. J. Pharm. Pract. **19**, 765–777 (2008)
6. Huang, D.C.: Study of the comprehensive quality evaluation system for college students. Heilongjiang Res. High. Educ. **5**, 14 (2001)
7. Loucks, D.P., Gladwell, J.S.: Sustainability Criteria for Water Resource System. Tsinghua University Press, Beijing (2002)
8. Liu, Z.Y.: Scientific Computing and MATLAB. Science Press, Beijing (2001)
9. Yin, X.C., Liu, Y.Q.: Reforming experiment teaching to training students' comprehensive quality. Lab. Res. Explor. **2** (2003)
10. Zheng, R.Y, Lin, A.Z, Bao-Fu, L.U.: Reforming traditional mode of practice teaching and strengthening students' comprehensive quality. Res. Explor. Lab. **3** (2004)

An Artificial Neural Network Approach to Student Study Failure Risk Early Warning Prediction Based on TensorFlow

Mi Chunqiao[1,2(✉)], Peng Xiaoning[1,2], and Deng Qingyou[1]

[1] Huaihua University, Huaihua 418000, Hunan, People's Republic of China
michunqiao@163.com, hhpxn@163.com, dengqingyou@163.com
[2] Key Laboratory of Intelligent Control Technology for Wuling-Mountain
Ecological Agriculture in Hunan Province, Huaihua 418000, Hunan,
People's Republic of China

Abstract. Higher education is now facing big challenges about low course study completion and graduation degree completion rate, for which student study failure in course is the main reason. However, the failure in course study is a comprehensive result of various factors and is characterized by uncertainty. Artificial neural network approach is advantageous for dealing with this issue, and in this study we provided such an approach to predicting student study failure risk for early warning in course study based on the TensorFlow platform. In our model, for each student, four input variables: (1) times of login onto the online study system; (2) times of downloading study resource; (3) attendance earned points; and (4) assignment earned points, and one target variable: the final course grade point were collected for network training. At last, by validating with the observed data, consistency is shown between our predicted results and the actual observed data, which indicates that the employed model is a promising approach for identifying at-risk student. It is helpful for educators to timely apply corresponding strategic pedagogical interventions to help at-risk students avoid academic failure, and to effectively improve early warning education management.

Keywords: Artificial neural network · Study failure risk
Early warning prediction · TensorFlow

1 Introduction

Study failure is now a very common phenomenon in college and university education, which can results in failed graduation and unsuccessful job-hunting. However, in today's college and university, there are many existing problems in early warning education, such as very late warning time (usually long after the final examination, or even in the next semester), only single evaluation factor (always only focus on evaluation of the final examination grades), very outdated technology (often done only by hand), etc. So how to quantitively identify the risk of study failure by modern information technologies such as data mining techniques in early time is a very important issue in college education management. Fortunately, with the further development and

© ICST Institute for Computer Sciences, Social Informatics and Telecommunications Engineering 2018
G. Sun and S. Liu (Eds.): ADHIP 2017, LNICST 219, pp. 326–333, 2018.
https://doi.org/10.1007/978-3-319-73317-3_38

application of modern information technology in education, at present many varieties of educational data about student study process have been collected and stored in college and university. Besides, many new data analysis techniques such as big data analysis, learning analytics and data mining methods are becoming more and more widely available in education applications. So it is becoming feasible and a new trend to do further study on early warning risk identification based on data science and machine learning methods.

Some related initial attempts about using data mining methods for prediction of academic performance or study risk can be traced back to the very begin of 2000s [1]. For example, Chen et al. [2] identified potential weak students and profiled student groups based on methods including association rules and decision trees. Morris et al. [3] predicted student final grades and the successful completion of online courses using the method of discriminant analysis. Macfadyen and Dawson [4] detected underperforming students with methods like logistic regression and network analysis. Jay et al. [5] studied the early indicators of student success and failure. Geraldine et al. [6] provided a methodology to classify students using interaction data and predicted first-year students at risk of failing. Kevin and David [7] presented a classification system for detection of poor performers before the end of the course. These related studies provided a useful foundation for early warning prediction of study failure risk and good insights for identify at-risk students. However, the number of studies that can be able to make concept transit into implementation is still few, and there is still little report on application of artificial neural network approach in study failure risk prediction. In addition, most of the current researches mainly focus on modeling and analysis of static historical educational data, while dynamic analysis based on learning process data before the completion of course final examination is insufficient.

The goal of this study is to predict student study failure risk in early time using artificial neural network (ANN) model with TensorFlow platform and Python language, so as to timely identify the at-risk students and improve the efficiency and effectiveness of early warning education in today's college and university.

2 Materials and Methods

2.1 Data Description and Preprocessing

In this study, totally 391 students during the course of "Introduction to Computer Science", "Fundamentals of Computer", "Software Engineering", and "Software Architecture" in 2016 were chosen as study samples. They were from eight different majors. Among the 391 samples, 296(3/4) samples were chosen by random for the network model training, and the remaining 95(1/4) samples were used for validation.

For each student, the daily study process data during the courses were collected from an online study system developed by the authors. These data were used to calculate the value of input variables which could affect student's final performance. The accuracy of student study failure risk prediction depends on the significance of the chosen input variables with respect to their effects on final course grade. There are many factors related to student study performance in a course, of which the student's participation is the most important one that reflects the student's attention and effort spent in the course. In addition to that, the earned points in assignments can reflect student's mastery of course knowledge, and the attendance performance is related to the time and attention that the student spent in the course. Therefore, for each student the following four input variables were chosen: (1) times of login onto the online study system (denoted as X1); (2) times of downloading studying resource (denoted as X2); (3) attendance earned points (denoted as X3); and (4) assignment earned points (denoted as X4). Besides, for each student, the final course grade point was also collected as target variable (denoted as Y), which uses the hundred percentage point system with 60 points as the passing grade. In order to quantify student study failure risk, a three-level risk classification scheme of red (R), yellow (Y), and green (G) was also developed, in which R (serious risk) means actual final grade < 50 points, Y (moderate risk) means $50 \leq$ actual final grade < 60 points, and G (no risk) means actual final grade $\geq$ 60 points.

In practice, the magnitude of different input variables with different units may differ very greatly. So in order to make a balance, the original data have to be preprocessed at first. In our study, all original data including input and output variables were normalized at first using the following expression (1). Where Z is the original data; Z_r is the normalized value; Z_{max} and Z_{min} are the max value and min value of the original data respectively.

$$Z_r = \frac{Z - Z_{min}}{Z_{max} - Z_{min}} \tag{1}$$

2.2   ANN Model and TensorFlow Implementation

The ANN model is a powerful tool in many fields, especially the well-known backward propagation algorithm. A backward propagation network (BPN) with one hidden layer can in a reasonable way approximate an arbitrary non-linear function [8]. So in this study, a three-tiered network construction including one input layer, one hidden layer and one output layer was selected. It is well-known that the generalization of ANN model is both dependent on the network topology and the values of network parameters, like the value of learning rate and so on [9]. But there is no unified solution for network parameter determination, so the trial and error method was used in this study. And the performance of different trials was measured by the value of RRMSE (relative root mean square error) showing in expression (2) and the value of MARE (mean absolute relative error) showing in expression (3), where U is the number of samples; T_α is desired value; O_α is predicted value.

$$\text{RRMSE} = \sqrt{\frac{\sum_{\alpha=1}^{U} (O_\alpha - T_\alpha)^2}{U}} \bigg/ \frac{\sum_{\alpha=1}^{S} T_\alpha}{U} \tag{2}$$

$$\text{MARE} = \frac{\sum\limits_{\alpha=1}^{U} |(O_\alpha - T_\alpha)/T_\alpha|}{U} \tag{3}$$

In order to implement our ANN model, the TensorFlow was used. It is a powerful machine learning platform and APIs, in which the computation is represented by dataflow graphs. It supports a variety of applications, especially for neural network modeling and calculations, helping users easily implement training, optimization and inference. In the current study of this paper, our ANN model included three layers, one input layer having four input nodes, one hidden layer (the hidden node number was to be determined) and one output layer having one output node. The issue of our study is mainly about continuous value prediction, so for hidden layer, the sigmoid activation function can be used, and for output layer, the linear activation function can be used. The main implementation codes by TensorFlow 1.1.0 and Python 3.5.3 are shown in the following (the hidden node number was assumed as 3 for illustration).

The main implementation computer program codes based on TensorFlow and Python

```
import tensorflow as tf
import numpy as np
##input layer
iptlyr_nero_num=4
inputs =
tf.placeholder(tf.float32,[None,iptlyr_nero_num])
##hidden layer
hidlyr_nero_num=3
hidlyr_weights = \
        tf.Variable(tf.random_normal([iptlyr_nero_num,\
        hidlyr_nero_num]))
hidlyr_biases =tf.Variable(tf.zeros([1,hidlyr_nero_num])\
        + 0.1)
hidlyr_wx_plus_b = tf.matmul(inputs, hidlyr_weights) + \
        hidlyr_biases
hidlyr_outputs=tf.nn.sigmoid(hidlyr_wx_plus_b)
##output layer
optlyr_nero_num=1
optlyr_weights = \
        tf.Variable(tf.random_normal([hidlyr_nero_num,\
        optlyr_nero_num]))
optlyr_biases =tf.Variable(tf.zeros([1,optlyr_nero_num])\
        + 0.1)
optlyr_wx_plus_c = tf.matmul(hidlyr_outputs,\
```

```
        optlyr_weights) + optlyr_biases
predictions=optlyr_wx_plus_c
##improvement of error between prediction and observation
##during training
observations = tf.placeholder(tf.float32, [None, 1])
loss = tf.reduce_mean( tf.reduce_sum(tf.square( \
    observations - predictions),reduction_indices=[1]))
learning_rate=0.1
train = tf.train.GradientDescentOptimizer( \
    learning_rate).minimize(loss)
##validation
valid_rrmse = tf.div( \
    tf.sqrt(tf.reduce_mean(tf.reduce_sum(tf.square(\
    observations-predictions),reduction_indices=[1]))))\
    ,tf.reduce_mean(tf.reduce_sum(observations,\
    reduction_indices=[1])))
valid_mare = tf.reduce_mean(tf.reduce_sum(tf.abs(tf.div(\
    predictions - observations,observations)),\
    reduction_indices=[1]))
```

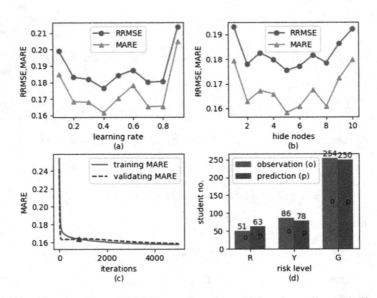

Fig. 1. (a) Learning rate effects, (b) Hidden nodes effects, (c) Iterations effects, (d) The observed and predicted risk results of all students

In order to complete our ANN model, the network parameters at first needed to be tested and optimized with the trial and error method. At the begin, the initial values of learning rate (denoted by η) and training iterations (denoted by n) were chosen by experience as $\eta = 0.01$ and $n = 2000$, and for the initial values of weights and bias in hidden layer and output layer, the values between 0 and 1 were chosen by random. For the value of node number in hidden layer (N_{Hidden}), there is an empirical rule showing in expressions (4) can be used to initialize it, in which N_{Input} is the value of node number in input layer and N_{Output} is that in output layer. In our study, we had $N_{Input} = 4$ and $N_{Output} = 1$, so we used $N_{Hidden} = 3$ as the initial value.

$$N_{Hidden} = (N_{Input} + N_{Output})/2 \qquad (4)$$

So first, we kept $N_{Hidden} = 3$ and n = 2000, and for different values of η the tested errors were shown in Fig. 1(a), from which we got optimized $\eta = 0.4$ with lowest MARE and RRMSE errors. Next, the values of 1–10 were used to determine hidden node number N_{Hidden}, with $\eta = 0.4$ and n = 2000. The tested errors were shown by Fig. 1(b). It was noted that $N_{Hidden} = 5$ was the optimal one. Finally, as the iterations becomes more and more, the MARE of training data will become smaller and smaller, but there will be an over fitting problem, so in conjunction with $\eta = 0.4$ and $N_{Hidden} = 5$, we tested MARE on both training and validating data when changing the number of training iterations. Our criterion of stop training is to get the point when MARE on validating data begins to increase while that on training data still decreases. The tested results were shown in Fig. 1(c), from which we could see that the optimal iterations number was 800, after this point there was an over fitting phenomenon. So we set n = 800 at last.

3   Results and Discussions

After the process of training, the network parameters were determined, and the final optimal values were $\eta = 0.4$, $N_{Hidden} = 5$, and n = 800 for current study. Based on these optimized network parameters, the values of weights and biases in input-hidden layers and hidden-output layers could be determined, which were shown in Table 1. And the corresponding accuracy values of our ANN model on training, validating and total data were shown in Table 2. In which, it was shown that the training data have better accuracy than validating data in general.

Table 1. The values of trained weights and biases of our network model.

The weights between input and hidden layers:				
$W_{11} = -0.315$	$W_{12} = 0.6376$	$W_{13} = -0.0514$	$W_{14} = -0.1973$	$W_{15} = 0.8970$
$W_{21} = -0.2666$	$W_{22} = -0.3215$	$W_{32} = 3.0499$	$W_{24} = -0.7013$	$W_{25} = 0.7192$
$W_{31} = -0.2789$	$W_{32} = -0.6059$	$W_{33} = 0.1020$	$W_{34} = -0.9749$	$W_{35} = -1.1315$
$W_{41} = -0.4460$	$W_{42} = -2.9768$	$W_{43} = 2.4153$	$W_{44} = -1.3014$	$W_{45} = -1.4673$
The biases between input and hidden layers:				
$b_1 = 0.1671$	$b_2 = -0.2705$	$b_3 = -0.3220$	$b_4 = -0.1432$	$b_5 = 0.1837$
The weights between hidden and output layers:				
$W_{11} = -1.2114$	$W_{21} = 1.6841$	$W_{31} = 1.3088$	$W_{41} = 0.6375$	$W_{51} = -0.4901$
The biase between hidden and output layers:				
$c = -0.1908$				

Table 2. The accuracy on training, validating and total data of our network model

	Training	Validating	Total
RRMSE	0.1706	0.1823	0.1735
MARE	0.1575	0.1659	0.1596

		Predicted		
		R	Y	G
	R	39	8	4
Observed	Y	14	67	5
	G	10	3	241

Fig. 2. The risk classification results of all students (Color figure online)

The obtained classification results (prediction) of all students and their actual final grade categories (observation) were shown in Figs. 1(d) and 2. In the observed categories, R (red, serious risk) means actual final grade < 50 points, Y (yellow, moderate risk) means actual final $50 \leq$ grade < 60 points, and G (green, no risk) means actual final grade $\geq$ 60 points.

From Fig. 1(d), we could see that there were 51 R students, 86 Y students, and 254 G students in the observed, while the model resulted in 63 R students, 78 Y students, and 250 G students. Overall, the model could accurately predict every students into the 'R', 'Y' and 'G' category 88.7% (= (39 + 67 + 241)/391) of the time, which is shown in light blue background in Fig. 2. Furtherly, the model made 'Type II' error (predicting an R student as Y or G student, or predicting a Y student as G student) at a rate of only 4.3%, which mean that only 17(= 8 + 4 + 5) out of 391 students were classified to be performing well or near well, but their actual final course grade put them into R or Y category, which is shown in red diagonal background in Fig. 2. The model also made 'Type I' error at a rate of 6.9%, namely putting 27(= 14 + 10 + 3) students out of 391 in the R or Y category while these students actually had passed the course, which is shown in yellow dotted background in Fig. 2. However, as far as the importance of helping student overcome learning difficulties is concerned, in order to identify at-risk student in early time during their course study process, it is somewhat better to mistakenly predict a student as at-risk student than being unable to identify a student who is really at-risk and needs additional help for his/her study. So it is relatively of less concern about Type I error occurrence. In sum, the model used in this study has a good performance in prediction of student study failure risk.

What's more, in order to further test the performance of our obtained model, the determination coefficient (R^2) and paired t-test were used on our total sample data set. First, after calculation we got the determination coefficient value of R = 0.93, showing excellent agreement between the observed data and predicted results. Besides, in the t-test at significance level of α = 0.05, the null hypothesis (H_0: $\rho_1 = \rho_2$) was accepted, where ρ_1 was the mean of observed data and ρ_2 was that of predicted results. It implied that the predicted results had no significance difference from the actual data.

All these results above showed that our obtained network model could well learn the relationship existing between our input and output variables, and it was also reliable in predicting student study failure risk.

4   Conclusions

In constructing neural network model for early warning prediction of student study failure risk, there are some network parameters, like learning rate and training iterations, need to be optimized using a trial and error method [10]. With TensorFlow APIs and Python language, they were easy to be optimized. According to our obtained results predicted by the employed model, college and university educators can implement corresponding pedagogical and learning strategic interventions more timely to help student avoid academic risk. The model is promising in identifying at-risk students who have study difficulties, and makes sense in helping the student who almost failed or failed their courses and may have passed the courses with some earlier learning supports and pedagogical interventions. In sum, all obtained results of this study showed that the neural network model is a reliable and powerful tool to predict student study failure risk. However, further study is also needed, for example more comprehensive input factors should be added, to yield more precision results.

Acknowledgments. The Hunan Province Educational Science 13th Five-Year Planning Program (XJK016QXX003) and the Hunan Provincial Social Science Foundation (17YBQ087) support this study, we are very grateful to them.

References

1. Sandeep, M.J., Erik, W.M., Eitel, J.M.L., et al.: Early alert of academically at-risk students: an open source analytics initiative. J. Learn. Anal. **1**(1), 6–47 (2014)
2. Chen, G., Liu, C., Ou, K., et al.: Discovering decision knowledge from web log portfolio for managing classroom processes by applying decision tree and data cube technology. J. Educ. Comput. Res. **23**(3), 305–332 (2000)
3. Morris, L.V., Wu, S., Finnegan, C.: Predicting retention in online general education courses. Am. J. Distance Educ. **19**(1), 23–36 (2005)
4. Macfadyen, L.P., Dawson, S.: Mining LMS data to develop an early warning system for educators: a proof of concept. Comput. Educ. **54**(2), 588–599 (2010)
5. Jay, B., James, M., Anne, Z., et al.: Using learning analytics to predict at-risk students in online graduate public affairs and administration education. J. Public Aff. Educ. **21**(2), 247–262 (2015)
6. Geraldine, G., Colm, M., Philip, O., et al.: Learning factor models of students at risk of failing in the early stage of tertiary education. J. Learn. Anal. **3**(2), 330–372 (2016)
7. Kevin, C., David, A.: Utilizing student activity patterns to predict performance. Int. J. Educ. Technol. High. Educ. **14**(1), 1–15 (2017)
8. Geng, C., Dandan, L., Haowen, W., Guochang, W.: Analysis and prediction model of financial income in Guangzhou. Stat. Appl. **4**(3), 187–195 (2015)
9. Daniel, B.M., Muttucumaru, S.: Prediction of urban stormwater quality using artificial neural networks. Environ. Model Softw. **24**, 296–302 (2009)
10. Holger, R.M., Graeme, C.D.: The effect of internal parameters and geometry on the performance of back-propagation neural networks: an empirical study. Environ. Model Softw. **13**, 193–209 (1998)

Immune Detector Optimization Algorithm with Co-evolution and Monte Carlo

Xi Liang[✉], Jiang Tao, Sun Guanglu, and Zhang Fengbin

School of Computer Science and Technology,
Harbin University of Science and Technology, Harbin 150000, China
xiliang@hrbust.edu.cn

Abstract. The detector which is devoted to detect the abnormal events in the immune-based instrusion detection system (IDS) is absolutely necessary. But, some problems in the detector set need to be solved before detection, and at the same time, the research in the security vulnerabilities detector optimization is important. In this paper, inspired by the species' co-evolution in nature and the Monte Carlo method, An algorithm of immune detector optimization is presented: co-evolve among detector subsets, estimate the coverage rate by Monte Carlo to end the optimization. Getting a conclusion by the experimental tests is that the security holes can be fewer by the algorithm, and less detectors can be used to achieve more accurate coverage of non-self-space.

Keywords: Instrusion detection system · Artificial immune system
Co-optimization · Detector · Monte Carlo

1 Introduction

Intrusion detection system is a significant component of network security. The basic problems in Intrusion detection can be seen two problems: one is that give an element of the network, the other one is that divide it into normal or abnormal data [1]. Being a classical subfield of artificial intelligence, it is a relatively new territory which is the artificial immune system (AIS) that attempts to create some mechanisms in the biological immune system (BIS) which is a self-adaptive, self-organized, and self-learning protection system [2]. The task of IDS can be considered as analogous to the BIS, while both methods are designed for the detection of abnormal behavior which is in violation of the established policy properly. So, many models and methods in AIS are used in the field of intrusion detection. The immune IDS has achieved great successes [3].

The immune detectors are the most important ingredient in immune IDS, which ensures the detection performances, and gets the candidates through Self-setting tolerance training by the NSA primarily [4]. On the based of the representation method of self and detector: binary and real-valued, NSA is devided into binary NSA (BNS) and real-valued NSA (RNS). BNS is hard to handle many application programs which are normal to be expressed in the real-valued space. So that, the present research mainly focuses on the representation of real-valued [5]. However, because of the randomness and incompleteness of candidates, security holes are difficult to solve effectively (the uncovered nonself space), and spending too much time on the detector generation [6].

© ICST Institute for Computer Sciences, Social Informatics and Telecommunications Engineering 2018
G. Sun and S. Liu (Eds.): ADHIP 2017, LNICST 219, pp. 334–340, 2018.
https://doi.org/10.1007/978-3-319-73317-3_39

For these problems, using the theory of cooperative evolution of biology and the Monte Carlo method for reference, this paper come up with an immune detector optimization algorithm with co-evolution & Monte Carlo, which uses the subsets of detectors to co-optimization by the representative individuals, and assess the scope of the coverage of detectors by the Monte Carlo method to improve detectors' distribution.

The remaining structure of the article is as follows: Sect. 2 is that we analyze the flaw in the detectors and the results. Section 3 introduces the detector optimization algorithm in detail. The experiment was carried out in Sect. 4. Finally, the Sect. 5 is some concluding remarks by the experiment.

2 Problem Analysis

2.1 Holes and Overlapping

The detectors have two problems which are a pair of contradictions: holes and overlapping. For a better coverage, the detectors' number should be large enough which can bring about the overlapping. For less overlapping rate, the detectors should be less which can bring about the holes. In the real-valued space, these problems are unavoidable.

2.2 Problems of Boundary Detectors

In the boundary between self and nonself region, assignment of each detector's radius is a very difficult question. And the detectors can not cover the boundary well which is too narrow, which is referred to boundary holes problem. A classical solution is enlarging radius of these detectors properly. But the "properly" can not be controlled correctly and lead to the intrusion problems which can increase false alarm rate in detection stage. As it was remarked in a previous column, V-detector with boundary-aware by Zhou solves the intrusion better, but the boundary overlapping is worse.

2.3 Multi-area of Self/Detector Set

The self/detector region was almost deemed to be a whole in the real-valued shape-space. However, as a matter of fact, the attribute values of self/detector almost are some statistical data. Therefore, multi areas may make up to be the self/detector region. We should consider this character in optimizing the self/detector for a better result.

3 Detector Co-optimization

After analyzing the main problems which are existing detectors, inspired by the co-evolution of species in nature, a detector co-optimization algorithm with co-evolution & Monte Carlo (abbr. DOCEMC) to be raised: the detectors are divided into different subsets, optimize process within every subset taking advantage of the individuals which are representative in other subsets and select the combination of the every subset to form the final mature detector set in the end. In the process, the Monte Carlo method monitors the coverage of detectors in real time and serves as the "trigger" of algorithm termination. The algorithm can be stated in Fig. 1 and the concrete processes are expatiated as follows:

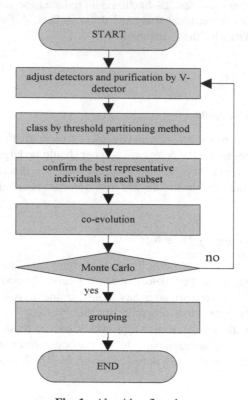

Fig. 1. Algorithm flowchart

Start. Using random method, a candidate is formed and the initial set of detectors is generated: D by RNS.

Adjusting Detectors. For each detector: d_i ($i = 1, 2,..., N_d$), use the closest distance to its self for adjusting its radius:

$$d_i \cdot r = AC\left(d_i, s_i^{nearest}\right) - s_i^{nearest} \cdot r \tag{1}$$

where AC ( ) is the affinity calculation formula.

Purification. Cancel the low-performance samples which are replaced by others using V-detector in every subset.

Classifying. Set the original detector to different subsets $D = \{D_1, D_2, \ldots, D_m\}$. The quantity of subsets are m in the D. Divide the detector set by using the threshold partitioning.

Step 1. Set a threshold Δ for distance. The first original partition is d by taking a random detector: D_1 ($D = D - \{d\}$, $d \in D_1, m = 1$, the m can be confirmed after classifying).

Step 2. For each D_j ($1 \leq j \leq m$), Check the rest of the detectors: d_i ($d_i \in D - Y_{j=1}^m D_j$) by RNS. If the Δ is more than the distance. It means they belong to the same partition ($d_i \in D_j, 1 \leq j \leq m$). If not, take it as a new partition: D_{j+1}, $m+$ $+(d_i \in D_{j+1}, 2 \leq j + 1 \leq m)$.

Step 3. If $D \neq \emptyset$, go to step 2.

Choosing Representatives. Get the central element in the every subset. Afterwards, ensure the individuals which can be best representative to the each of the remaining subsets.

(i) Ensuring the basic element in the every subset. In the every subset, D_i, get the average of each attribute and search out the individual which is the nearest to that average vector as the basic element, d_i.

(ii) Select the best individuals. In the every subset D_i, the best individual which is defined to the each of the remaining subsets is the farthest distance by calculating the distance of the each sample to the each of the remaining subsets: $d_i^j \in D_i$, and $j = 1, 2, \ldots, i - 1, i + 1, \ldots, m$.

Co-evolution. Take advantage of the individuals which can be representative well and the optimization procedure of every subset based on coevolution is realized. In the every subset D_j, use the $d_i^j (i = 1, 2, \ldots, j - 1, j + 1, \ldots, m)$ to count the average vector of d_j and d_i^j, becoming candidate d_0^j. Deal with RNS for self-established tolerance test. If passing the test, its radius will be ascertained by Formula 19, and examined whether other detectors are covered by affinity calculation: eliminate all those covered; if it is a test failure, delete it.

Monte Carlo. If the process is from the formula 2 to the end state, turns to GROUPING.

$$C(D) \approx \frac{\sum_{i=1}^m X_D(x_i)}{m - \sum_{i=1}^m X_S(x_i)} \tag{2}$$

In the detector set, $X_D(x_i)$ shows the number of points. In the self set, $X_S(x_i)$ shows the number of points:

$$X_D(x_i) = \begin{cases} 1, & \text{if } x_i \in D \\ 0, & \text{if } x_i \notin D \end{cases} \tag{3}$$

$$X_S(x_i) = \begin{cases} 1, & \text{if } x_i \in S \\ 0, & \text{if } x_i \notin S \end{cases} \tag{4}$$

Grouping. Put all the subsets $D_j(j = 1, 2, \ldots, m)$ together to be the final set of the mature detectors:

$$D = Y_{j=1}^m D_j \tag{5}$$

4 Experiments

This paper detects the availability of the algorithm by two data sets: using the set of 2-dimensional data to test the optimal intuitive performances; making an examination for the detection performances of the final best detector set and initial detector set by Fisher's Iris Data set.

4.1 Experiments in Two Dimensional Data Sets

The pentagram data set which is often used and contains 198 samples which in pentacle shape is adopted in this experiment [7]. For all the samples of the experiment, they build the set by themselves, which are shown by Fig. 2(a). After the process of RNS, RNS generates 100 detectors, which are shown by Fig. 2(b). By the figure, we can find many security vulnerabilities. Then, 600 detectors are generated by the same method continuously, which are shown by Fig. 2(c). By the figure, we can find the problem of the security vulnerabilities has been reduced, but more detectors produce more inaccurate points. Finally, we used 100 samples by DOCEMC which mentioned above to optimize the detector set, and the result is shown by Fig. 2(d). By the figure, we can find that the quantity of the detectors are reduced (quantity: 43) obviously and the method solves the security vulnerabilities.

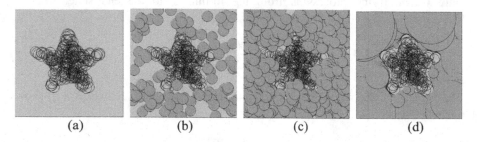

(a)   (b)   (c)   (d)

Fig. 2. Results of detector distribution: (a) initial self set; (b) detectors by RNS (num: 100); (c) detectors by RNS (num: 600); (d) optimized detectors by DOCEMC (num: 43).

4.2   Fisher's Iris Data Set Experiments

The Fisher's Iris data which includes three subsets of data is a famous statistic of Iris flower. Each subset represents one kind of the flower, namely Setosa, Versicolor and Virginica. There are 50 samples in every group, and there are 4 attributes as calyx, calyx width, petal lenth and petal width (units: cm) in each sample. This data set has been used for to the abnormal detection.

Two classes (Versicolor and Virginica) of the data sets are semblable On the distribution through analyzing, however, class Setosa is not the same distribution in spatial. Make the Setosa to be the self-set in the experiment. Veriscolor and Virginica are the exception events. And employ all the data to check the Detector performance. Firstly, produce 100 detectors with RNS as original detector. Secondly, use the algorithm presented in the paper to optimize them. Finally, check the original and optimize detector set with the test sets. Table 1 shows the average of 10 times. As it is shown, RNS-generated intimal detectors have poor performances, while the performences are observably improbed and the detectors have smaller numbers after the optimization.

Tab. 1. The comparison between two detector sets in detecting performances

Algorithm	Detector	Detection rate (%)		False alarm rate (%)	
		Mean	Standard deviation	Mean	Standard deviation
RNS	100	58.4	7.8	8.21	5.5
DOCEMC	37	97.9	1.4	1.97	1.9

5   Conclusions

The optimizing algorithm of the detectors based on Monte Carlo method and co-evolution is proposed in this article. An ideal solution is provided to resolve the deficiencies in real-valued detectors by using the inter-effective relationship between sub-populations to seek the optimal individuals and optimize the subset. The experimental consequences indicate that the algorithm can replace the non-self space with better detecors, sovling the security vulnerabilities and decreasing the quantities of the detecors, making the detector's performance better.

Acknowledgments. This article is supported by the Project of Education Department in Heilongjiang Province (12541130). The author also thanks the reviewers for their helpful comments and suggestions which are improved the article.

References

1. Miao, F., Wang, Z., Guo, Y., et al.: A security threats taxonomy for routing system intrusion detection. In: The 12th International Conference on Computational Intelligence and Security (CIS), pp. 267–270. IEEE (2016)

2. Tabatabaefar, M., Miriestahbanati, M., Grégoire, J.C.: Network intrusion detection through artificial immune system. In: The 11th Annual IEEE International Systems Conference (SysCon), pp. 1–6, April 2017
3. Okamoto, T., Tarao, M.: Toward an artificial immune server against cyber attacks. Artif. Life Robot. **21**(3), 351–356 (2016)
4. Renjie, W., Xiaoling, G., Xiao, Z.: A algorithm of detectors generating based on negative selection algorithm. Lect. Notes Electr. Eng. **375**, 133–139 (2016)
5. Abreu, C.C.E., Duarte, M.A.Q., Villarreal, F.: An immunological approach based on the negative selection algorithm for real noise classification in speech signals. AEU-Int. J. Electron. Commun. **72**, 125–133 (2017)
6. Fouladvand, S., Osareh, A., Shadgar, B., et al.: DENSA: an effective negative selection algorithm with flexible boundaries for self-space and dynamic number of detectors. Eng. Appl. Artif. Intell. **62**, 359–372 (2016). Article in Press
7. UCI Machine Learning Repository: Fisher's Iris Data [DB/OL], 23 December 2009. http://archive.ics.uci.edu/ml/datasets/Iris

Traffic Classification Based on Incremental Learning Method

Guanglu Sun, Shaobo Li, Teng Chen, Yangyang Su, and Fei Lang[(⊠)]

School of Computer Science and Technology,
Harbin University of Science and Technology, Harbin, China
langfei@hrbust.edu.cn

Abstract. Machine learning methods become more and more important in traffic classification, because they are able to explore statistical features to identify encrypted traffic and proprietary protocols. Among many machine learning methods, support vector machine is able to achieve state of the art performance in classifying TCP traffic. However, current support vector machine for traffic classification also shows two limitations: (i) unable to support continuously learning, and (ii) high requirements on both memory and CPU. In this paper, incremental Support Vector Machine method is applied to address these two issues. Experimental results show that the incremental Support Vector Machine method decreases the training time, while still sustains the high accuracy of traffic classification.

Keywords: Traffic classification · Incremental learning
Support vector machine

1   Introduction

Internet traffic classification has attracted a lot of research interests in recent years. The ability to identify flows and their relevant protocols is required for many applications, such as security and QoS.

The traditional methods of traffic classification are based on well-known port numbers and deep packets identifications [1]. They become ineffective to deal with unknown protocols, and even variants of known protocols, because of dynamic port numbers, encrypted payloads, etc.

Since 2004, many machine learning models have been introduced to exploit network behaviors and statistical characteristics to address these issues [2, 3]. Two representative methods have shown outstanding performance at that time. Moore's Bayesian method used two types of Bayesian models and feature selection methods based on the Cambridge open data sets [4]. The Support Vector Machine model

This work was partly financially supported through grants from the National Natural Science Foundation of China (No. 60903083 and 61502123), Scientific planning issues of education in Heilongjiang Province (No. GBC1211062), and the research fund for the program of new century excellent talents (No. 1155-ncet-008).

© ICST Institute for Computer Sciences, Social Informatics and Telecommunications Engineering 2018
G. Sun and S. Liu (Eds.): ADHIP 2017, LNICST 219, pp. 341–348, 2018.
https://doi.org/10.1007/978-3-319-73317-3_40

(SVM) was applied on three types of well-known data sets, CAIDA, LBNL and UNIBS [5]. SVM obtained an average accuracy over 95%, 2.3% over the best performance of Bayesian methods and other methods on the same data sets [1]. As a result, SVM has become a favored method.

Although SVM is able to achieve impressive performance, it shows two main limitations in practice.

(1) **The lack of ability in continuous learning**. Because SVM has a high training complexity [6], it is difficult to update the classification model in-time when identifying new protocols.

(2) **High requirements on both memory and CPU**. More statistical features help us achieve higher accuracy, but they also consume more memory and CPU resources. The large numbers of traffic and protocols will result in a high-dimensional feature space in a backbone network. It demands us to effectively utilize memory and CPU to process these features in a training model.

In this paper, we propose an incremental method to address the above two limitations, by reducing the learn time for model update and efficiently utilizing memory and CPU resources. Incremental Support Vector Machine (ISVM) is instrumental in practical applications of online learning, which is advantageous when dealing with very large or non-stationary data [7, 8]. ISVM incorporates additional training data without re-training from scratch. Traffic classification based on ISVM is better than traditional SVM not only in accuracy, but in the consumption of system resource. The main contributions of this paper are as follows.

- Incremental SVM is firstly applied to classify Internet traffic.
- The update-time for traffic classification is decreased by adopting the ISVM learning model.
- The continual update of traffic classification model is achieved by using the ISVM method.

The remainder of this paper is organized as follows. In Sect. 2, we discuss existing literature related to our work. In Sect. 3, we show the theoretical details of the ISVM method, and explain how to use ISVM to realize the traffic classification in incremental update module. In Sect. 4, we show empirical results on the open real-world data sets to evaluate the effectiveness of ISVM method in traffic classification. In Sect. 5, we conclude the paper.

2 Related Work

As the increasing deployment of many encrypted protocols, port-based and payload-based methods become less attractive while machine learning based methods gain more attention. McGregor et al. firstly used unsupervised machine learning techniques to cluster traffic flows [9].

In this paper, we mainly focus on supervised learning methods used for traffic classification. The supervised machine learning model is built based on the labeled traffic flows, while statistical patterns are abstracted from the flows as the features.

After the adjustment of estimation parameters in the training phase, the model is then used to classify the new traffic flows. Following the above procedure, a lot of machine learning models were implemented in traffic classification. Williams et al. [10] compared five supervised algorithms including naive Bayes with discretization, naive Bayes with kernel density estimation, C4.5 decision tree, Bayesian network and naive Bayes tree, from the aspects of classification accuracy and computational performance. Finamore et al. [11] presented statistical characterization of payload as features and used SVM to conduct traffic classification. Nguyen et al. [12] trained the machine learning models with a set of sub-flows and investigated different sub-flow selection strategies. The accuracy of their models would be maintained when the traffic mixed up bi-directional flows. Ye and Cho [13] proposed an improved two-step hybrid P2P traffic classification with heuristic rules and REPTree model with different levels of features. Li et al. [14] utilized logistic regression model to classify the flows via non-convex multi-task feature selection. They tried a Capped as the regularizer to learn a set of features in traffic flows. Peng et al. [15] verified that 5–7 packets are the best packet numbers for early stage traffic classification based on 11 well-known supervised learning models.

3 Traffic Classification Based on ISVM Model

We first discuss how traffic classification is transformed into a classical classification problem. Consider a set of flows $T = \{t_1, t_2, \ldots, t_n\}$ and a set of application protocols $P = \{p_1, p_2, \ldots, p_i\}$, each flow belongs to one of application protocols $<t_i, p_j>$. Based on the mapping pairs tagged in a training set, the goal of a machine learning model is to find a discriminative function, by which t^* is classified to protocol p^* correctly.

$$p^* = Func(t^*) \quad p^* \in P, \ t^* \text{ is a pending flow} \tag{1}$$

SVM is a discriminative model which has strong theoretical basis and many empirical successes [6]. We introduce SVM in Sect. 3.1, and then present an incremental learning method for SVM and discuss how to solve the two limitations of traditional SVM model in Sect. 3.2.

3.1 SVM Model

SVM is introduced as a binary classification in batch training. We assume the training data and their labels are given as follows:

$$\{(x_1, y_1), (x_2, y_2), \ldots, (x_n, y_n)\}, \ x_i \in \Re^d, \ y_i \in \{+1, -1\}.$$

SVM builds the hyperplane that separates the training data by a maximal margin. The hyperplane is defined by the equation $w \cdot x + b = 0$, where w is a coefficient vector, b is a scalar offset, and the symbol "$\cdot$" denotes the inner product in $\Re^d$, defined as:

$$f(x) = w \cdot x = \sum_{i=1}^{n} w_i x_i \tag{2}$$

Data lying on each side of the hyperplane are respectively labeled as -1 or 1. Through Mercer kernel function $K(x_j, x_k) = \Phi(x_j) \cdot \Phi(x_k)$, e.g. linear, polynomial and RBF kernel, SVM maps the original training data in space X to a higher dimensional space F in order to classify the data that is impossible to be separated in a low dimension space. Using Lagrange interpolation coefficients α_i, Formula (2) is transferred to solve a quadratic programming problem with linear constraints and its dual form with respect to vector $\alpha_i, i = 1 \ldots n$. The final discriminative function is:

$$f(x) = sign(w \cdot \Phi(x) + b) \tag{3}$$

Where $w = \sum_{i=1}^{n} \alpha_i y_i \Phi(x_i)$, $b = -\frac{1}{2} \left(\sum_{x_a, x_b \in \{x_i\}} \sum_{i=1}^{n} \alpha_i y_i \Phi(x_a) \Phi(x_b) \right)$.

SVM optimizes the discriminative function with coefficients using all the training data based on sequential minimal optimization techniques. However, not all the samples but support vectors (SV) (whose coefficients are not equal to zero) decide the hyperplane and the discriminative function. SVs absolutely present the class characteristics of the training data, when kernel function and other coefficients are defined.

3.2   Incremental SVM Model

Because traffic is changing over time in a real network, it becomes a challenge for the traditional SVM model to take new and large-scale new traffic into account, and combine them with the previously trained model. With a large amount of non-stationary data, ambiguous traffic, e.g. different traffic distributions varying over time, is hardly integrated by the traditional SVM model. So it is essential to improve the SVM algorithms to avoid completely retraining with huge CPU and memory overheads.

The ISVM model discards the original training data except of the SVs which are acquired by the last training of SVM model. When the additional new training data is joining, ISVM model combines the new data with the existing SVs, then use the combined data to retain SVM in order to get new SVs. Figure 1 shows the procedure of ISVM model.

Fig. 1. The sketch map of ISVM learning model

3.3   Incremental SVM Model for Multi-class Traffic Classification

Because a protocol set contains more than two classes, the one-against-all approach is utilized to expand the binary SVM model to multi-class SVM model.

The characteristics of flow t_i are described as a vector of statistical features $F_i = \{f_{i1}, f_{i2}, \ldots, f_{im}\}$, which are numeric or discrete values, e.g. packet length. F_i corresponding to x_i can be denoted as $\{(F_i, p_i)\}$, while p_i corresponds to y_i. Based on the model introduced in Sect. 3.2, we use the multi-class ISVM model for traffic classification with training and test modules.

4   Experimental Results and Discussions

4.1   Data Sets and Evaluation Metrics

The data sets with more than 200 features developed by Moore et al. are used in our experiments [4]. For convince, we tag the data sets from M1 to M10. M1 is divided into ten parts in the data sequence for training, the other 9 data sets are used for test.

The metric of True Precision (TP) is used to evaluate the accuracy of the classification in each model. The results are obtained for the whole system instead of per class. The training time is shown with the style of H(hour), M(minute) and S(second). The number of SVs is the occurrence number of SVs in SVM after the current training process.

4.2   Results and Discussions

4.2.1   The Results of Standard SVM Method

We first present the results based on standard SVM by progressively increasing the training data set. In order to reflect the variation of TP, training time, and the number of SVs, ten parts of training data sets are added to the training module one by one. Table 1 shows the results with the standard SVM method. The result in the 10th column shows all the M1 data is added to the training model. In the M1 row, the result is with closing test, because M1 is training data set. The other rows are with open tests. The Average row is the average TP with M2 to M10 data sets.

In Table 1, along with the increasing of training data, the TP is not always increasing. Because SVM is a discriminative model, its performance does not absolutely depend on the increasing of training data, but on the occurrences of SVs. However, the results are promising considering the increasing trends.

On the other hand, the training time and the number of SVs are growing which increases the complexity and the resources consumption of both CPU and memory. In the 10th column, the scale of training data set is 24863. The corresponding training time is 86 h, 44 min and 51 s. Because the categories and the scale of actual traffic are much more than the experimental data set, the model update with large-scale traffic data is difficult for the traditional SVM model and other learning models.

Table 1. The results based on standard SVM.

	1	2	3	4	5	6	7	8	9	10
Time (H:M:S)	0:11:36	0:26:06	0:40:02	1:10:09	4:31:29	8:33:34	19:48:24	39:13:48	62:57:09	86:44:51
SV	20	86	86	130	263	363	540	657	887	1071
M1(%)	87.8	88.1	87.8	88.6	94.8	97.0	98.1	99.2	99.6	99.8
M2(%)	78.0	77.9	79.3	74.7	76.7	78.0	88.8	83.6	77.2	94.4
M3(%)	72.1	71.7	74.3	70.2	77.7	78.2	90.6	89.0	93.7	96.6
M4(%)	83.7	81.9	83.2	80.4	73.8	77.5	93.3	89.8	86.2	97.9
M5(%)	91.7	90.7	91.6	87.2	92.2	84.0	93.3	92.1	93.5	96.4
M6(%)	79.3	83.0	84.8	78.7	62.6	71.9	79.3	84.9	91.6	98.0
M7(%)	81.4	84.1	87.5	89.8	94.6	94.8	95.9	91.4	97.2	97.8
M8(%)	84.3	77.7	84.5	83.2	74.2	76.7	89.0	77.8	72.9	97.7
M9(%)	79.8	73.6	80.2	80.3	72.9	74.0	87.6	79.0	75.7	96.1
M10(%)	89.8	90.5	90.9	88.5	90.3	90.1	89.0	86.2	63.5	91.5
Average(%)	82.9	81.3	84.8	83.1	81.0	81.9	89.9	84.92	80.3	96.0

4.2.2 The Results of ISVM Method

Secondly, we present the classification results of ISVM model. ISVM model can realize continuous learning and reduce the occupation of CPU and memory effectively. We conduct several experiments based on ISVM model by dividing the training data into different proportion. The training model is the incremental SVM algorithm described in Sect. 3.2. The division of training data set and the style of adding training data are described in Sect. 4.1. The statistics of each class is listed in Table 2.

Table 2. The results based on ISVM.

	1	2	3	4	5	6	7	8	9	10
Time (H:M:S)	0:11:40	+0:01:23	+0:01:20	+0:06:13	+0:26:16	+0:34:19	+0:55:43	+1:07:56	+1:16:09	+1:25:25
SV	20	21	20	41	223	299	526	560	711	768
M1(%)	87.80	88.20	87.80	88.80	91.20	96.50	97.00	99.00	98.00	99.40
M2(%)	78.00	71.90	74.00	82.80	85.20	87.40	90.00	90.40	91.70	81.30
M3(%)	72.10	67.40	69.40	80.90	87.30	91.40	96.10	95.30	95.90	96.90
M4(%)	83.70	76.80	79.60	90.40	90.60	92.00	96.00	96.90	97.80	97.80
M5(%)	91.70	86.80	90.40	92.10	91.70	94.00	93.60	97.30	97.10	98.00
M6(%)	79.30	78.50	77.40	84.00	88.40	82.40	60.30	94.00	95.00	97.90
M7(%)	81.40	78.30	81.00	90.00	92.10	94.20	95.40	96.30	97.30	97.70
M8(%)	84.30	72.10	81.20	85.20	91.80	93.10	95.40	94.80	96.20	94.20
M9(%)	79.80	68.00	76.70	83.90	88.90	87.40	91.90	92.00	93.80	91.30
M10(%)	89.80	81.30	87.20	91.20	87.70	84.50	88.50	92.70	92.50	94.50
Average(%)	82.90	75.20	80.40	87.70	89.50	89.50	91.20	94.10	95.00	94.20

4.2.3 Comparison with Two Methods

Table 3 gives the performance comparison with the above two methods. Column (a) is based on the standard SVM. Column (b) is based on ISVM. The number of SVs significantly impacts the performance of SVM model. More SVs usually mean better TP, while more training data often generate more SVs. However, more training data results in the rapid increasing of computational cost. ISVM method decreases the occupancy of CPU and memory with less training data in each training process.

Table 3. The performance comparison with the two methods.

	(a)	(b)
Time (H:M:S)	86:44:51	6:06:24
SV	1071	768
M2(%)	94.40%	81.30%
M3(%)	96.60%	96.90%
M4(%)	97.90%	97.80%
M5(%)	96.40%	98.00%
M6(%)	98.00%	98.00%
M7(%)	97.80%	97.70%
M8(%)	97.70%	94.20%
M9(%)	96.20%	91.30%
M10(%)	91.50%	94.50%
Average(%)	96.00%	94.20%

5 Conclusions

In this paper, we use incremental pattern for identifying TCP traffic, by using incremental learning SVM. We demonstrate the effectiveness of ISVM model in continuous learning and the reduction of CPU and memory usage.

The experimental results show that our solutions are not only more accurate but also CPU and memory efficient. Incremental learning is advantageous when dealing with very large or non-stationary data. As the original training is completed, the incremental learning method has the ability to learning new data continuously without losing the previously trained model.

References

1. Kim, H., Claffy, K.C., Fomenkov, M.: Internet traffic classification demystified: myths, caveats, and the best practices. In: Proceedings of ACM CoNEXT 2008, Spain, 10–12 December 2008
2. Karagiannis, T., Papagiannaki, K., Faloutsos, M.: BLINC multilevel traffic classification in the dark. In: SIGCOMM 2005, USA, 22–26 August 2005
3. Nguyen, T., Armitage, G.: A survey of techniques for Internet traffic classification using machine learning. IEEE Commun. Surv. Tutor. 1–21 (2008)
4. Moore, A., Zuev, D.: Internet traffic classification using Bayesian analysis techniques. In: ACM SIGMETRICS 2005, Banff, Alberta, Canada, June 2005, pp. 50–60 (2005)
5. Este, A., Gringoli, F., Salgarelli, L.: Support vector machines for TCP traffic classification. Comput. Netw. **53**, 2476–2490 (2009)
6. Vapnik, V.: The Nature of Statistical Learning Theory. Springer, New York (1995). https://doi.org/10.1007/978-1-4757-2440-0
7. Syed, N., Liu, H., Sung, K.: Incremental learning with support vector machines. In: Proceedings of IJCAI-1999, Sweden, pp. 352–356 (1999)

8. Laskov, P., Gehl, C., Kruger, S., Muller, K.: Incremental support vector learning: analysis, implementation and applications. J. Mach. Learn. Res. **7**, 1909–1936 (2006)

9. McGregor, A., Hall, M., Lorier, P., Brunskill, J.: Flow clustering using machine learning techniques. In: Proceedings of the Passive Active Network Measurement, pp. 205–214 (2004)

10. Williams, N., Zander, S., Armitage, G.: A preliminary performance comparison of five machine learning algorithms for practical IP traffic flow classification. ACM SIGCOMM Comput. Commun. Rev. **36**(5), 5–16 (2006)

11. Finamore, A., Mellia, M., Meo, M., Rossi, D.: KISS: stochastic packet inspection classifier for UDP traffic. IEEE/ACM Trans. Netw. **18**(5), 1505–1515 (2010)

12. Nguyen, T., Armitage, G., Branch, P., Zander, S.: Timely and continuous machine-learning-based classification for interactive IP traffic. IEEE/ACM Trans. Netw. **20**(6), 1880–1894 (2012)

13. Ye, W., Cho, K.: Hybrid P2P traffic classification with heuristic rules and machine learning. Soft. Comput. **18**(9), 1815–1827 (2014)

14. Li, D., Hu, G., Wang, Y., et al.: Network traffic classification via non-convex multi-task feature learning. Neurocomputing **152**, 322–332 (2015)

15. Peng, L., Yang, B., Chen, Y.: Effective packet number for early stage internet traffic identification. Neurocomputing **156**, 252–267 (2015)

A Clustering Algorithm for the DAP Placement Problem in Smart Grid

Guodong Wang[1](✉), Yanxiao Zhao[1], Yulong Ying[2], Jun Huang[3],
and Robb M. Winter[4]

[1] Department of Electrical and Computer Engineering,
South Dakota School of Mines and Technology, Rapid City, SD 57701, USA
{guodong.wang,yanxiao.zhao}@sdsmt.edu
[2] School of Energy and Mechanical Engineering,
Shanghai University of Electric Power, Shanghai, China
[3] Department of Communication and Information Engineering, Chongqing
University of Posts and Telecommunications, Chongqing 400065, China
[4] Department of Chemical and Biological Engineering,
South Dakota School of Mines and Technology, Rapid City, SD 57701, USA

Abstract. In this paper, we investigate the DAP placement problem
and propose solutions to reduce the distance between DAPs and smart
meters. The DAP placement problem is formulated to two objectives,
e.g., the average distance minimization and the maximum distance minimization. The concept of network partition is introduced in this paper
and practical algorithms are developed to address the DAP placement
problem. Extensive simulations are conducted based on a real suburban neighborhood topology. The simulation results verify that the proposed solutions are able to remarkably reduce the communication distance between DAPs and their associated smart meters.

Keywords: Smart meter · DAP placement · Network partition
Transmission routes

1 Introduction

Smart grid is generally referred to as the next generation power grid which
enables high-speed and two-way communications to increase efficiency, management and reliability of energy resource. Neighborhood area networks play a significant role for the communications in smart grid. A neighborhood area network
is typically composed of smart meters and Data Aggregation Points (DAPs).
Smart meters are responsible for recording energy consumption or billing information of smart houses. DAPs collect the information from different smart
meters and forward it to wide area network gateways. Wireless communications
are recommended for neighborhood area networks due to their advantages in
deployment flexibility and economy efficiency. For a neighborhood area network,
the location of DAPs greatly affects the performance of communications between
DAPs and their associated smart meters. Take the communication distance as an

© ICST Institute for Computer Sciences, Social Informatics and Telecommunications Engineering 2018
G. Sun and S. Liu (Eds.): ADHIP 2017, LNICST 219, pp. 349–359, 2018.
https://doi.org/10.1007/978-3-319-73317-3_41

example. The location of DAPs influences the communication distance between DAPs and smart meters, which further influences the energy consumption, transmission rate, and end-to-end latency in neighborhood area networks. Therefore, it is critical to investigate how to appropriately select locations of DAPs in a neighborhood area network.

The problem of selecting locations for DAPs is termed as the DAP placement problem, which aims to properly choose locations of DAPs and allocate appropriate smart meters to achieve an objective. In the literature, the DAP placement problem is under-explored, and only a few DAP placement strategies are proposed [1,2]. To fill the gap, we have proposed a method to shorten the maximum distance between DAP and smart meters [3]. In this paper, we continue our research and extend the objective of DAP placement problem in neighborhood area networks. Specifically, we develop this problem into two objectives: the average distance minimization and the maximum distance minimization. The first objective is to minimize the average distance between DAPs and smart meters. The second objective is to minimize the maximum distance between DAPs and smart meters. To achieve those goals, we introduce the concept of network partition technique in this paper and clustering based algorithms are developed to address those two problems. In particular, the DAP placement problem is formulated as a network partition problem and a Clustering-based DAP Placement Algorithm (CDPA) is proposed to tackle the DAP placement problem. An actual suburban neighborhood is adopted as a topology to evaluate the performance of our solution. Simulation results verify that the proposed solution is able to significantly reduce the distance between DAP and their associated smart meters.

The rest of the paper is organized as follows. In Sect. 2, the related work is introduced. Section 3 formulates the problem mathematically. In Sect. 4, the proposed new solution is described in detail. Section 5 presents the performance evaluation of the solution. Section 6 concludes this paper

2   Related Work

One of the objectives of the DAP placement is to reduce the deployment cost of DAPs. In [1], the total cost of DAP placement is formulated as the operating time of a network, the cost of installing a DAP and the price of energy consumption. The optimal location of DAP is calculated to minimize the total cost of deploying DAPs in a network. The solution is heavily dependent on the model of cost function, which limits its application in practical systems. In addition, authors of [1] assume one-hop communications from smart meters to DAPs, which may be inapplicable to smart meters that have limited transmission ability. Therefore, it is reasonable to extend the one-hop assumption to a more common situation.

Authors of [2] propose another approach to decrease the deployment cost of DAPs and enable all meters can establish a reliable communication to one or more DAPs. In this paper, the DAP problem is converted to a set covering problem, which is addressed by heuristic approaches. Specifically, a subset of reliable links is pre-constructed based on characteristics of neighborhoods, communication technologies, transmission rates of antennas and their height. The

DAP placement problem is divided into several independent subsets, which is helpful for reducing the execution time and memory for solving the problem.

A smart grid is a large and complex system which consists of power generation, transmission and distribution as well as operations and management such as metering and billing [4]. A huge amount of data needs to be processed and exchanged in a smart grid. Availability of the smart grid requires time latency to be met for different operations and data transmissions [5]. For example, signal of protective actions needs to be generated and transmitted in the order of milliseconds. SCADA data needs to be transmitted within several seconds [6]. The results of [7,8] demonstrate that in a smart grid, the propagation delay of a data packet in the application of fast faults detection should be within the order of tens of milliseconds for a small size network, and 100 ms is acceptable in a medium size network.

In the context of networking, shortest distance path is one of the most common methods adopted for relaying messages in a wide variety of networks [9], since it provides an efficient way to decrease the energy and latency [10,11], which is significant to the overall performance of a network [12–14]. Therefore, in our paper, we focus on a delay-sensitive smart meter network and aim to minimize the communication distance between DAPs and their associated smart meters. In order to fully explore the transmission distance between DAPs and smart meters, we formulate and investigate the problem through two situations. The first situation is to minimize the average distance between DAPs and smart meters. The second one is to minimize the maximum distance between all the DAPs and their associated smart meters. Afterwards, the concept of network partition is introduced in this paper to address the DAP placement problem. Specifically, for a given neighborhood area network, the entire network is divided into subnetworks and DAPs are placed in the locations to minimize the average distance or the maximum distance between DAPs and smart meters. An actual suburban neighborhood is adopted in this paper to evaluate the performance of our solution. Simulation results verify that the proposed solution is able to significantly reduce the distance between DAP and their associated smart meters.

3   Problem Formulation

In this section, we briefly introduce the terminology and definitions that are used in this paper and formulate the DAP placement problem in a smart meter neighborhood area network.

Given a specific suburban neighborhood, let $V = \{v_i\}_{i=1,\cdots,|V|}$, where v_i is the ith smart meter. The location of ith smart meter is denoted by $v_i^l(x_i, y_i)$, where x_i and y_i are the longitude and latitude of smart meters, respectively. The task of DAP placement is to partition the network $\mathrm{G} = (\mathrm{V, E})$ into subnetworks and allocate DAPs to those subnetworks. Denote the set of DAPs by $DAP = \{dap_1, \cdots, dap_k\}$, where k is the number of DAPs. The set of smart meters allocated to dap_i is denoted by $S_i = \{s_0, s_1, \cdots s_{n_i}\}$, where $n_i = |S_i|$, representing the number of smart meters allocated to the ith DAP. Denote the distance between any two nodes by d(u,v) $(u, v \in V)$.

Distance plays a significant role in wireless communications, since it greatly affects the energy consumption and routing optimization [15,16]. For example, in a wireless sensor network, sensors are expected to forward a packet to the neighbor that has the shortest distance to the destination [17,18]. As a special wireless sensor network, DAPs in a neighborhood area network should be placed appropriately to shorten the distance between DAPs and smart meters. Focusing on the distance minimization, there are two objectives regarding the distance between DAPs and smart meters. The first one is the average distance minimization, which stands for minimizing the average distance between smart meters and DAPs. The other one is the worst-case distance minimization, which stands for minimizing the maximum distance between smart meters and DAPs. Those two objectives are formulated as follows.

Average Distance Minimization. The average distance for a DAP placement P' is:

$$D_{avg}(P') = \frac{1}{|V|} \sum_{j=1}^{k} \sum_{s_i \in S_j} \min d(s_i, dap_j) \tag{1}$$

Worst-case Distance Minimization. The worst-case distance for a DAP placement P' is:

$$D_{wc}(P') = \min\{\max\{d(s_i, dap_j)\}\} \tag{2}$$

Denote subnetworks by $A = \{A_i\}_{i=1,\cdots,k}$, then Eqs. (1) and (2) are subjected to:

$$DAP_i, s_i \in A_i, \forall i = 1, 2, \cdots, k \tag{3}$$

The DAP placement problem resembles a facility location problem [19], which is NP-hard and requires heuristic approaches [20]. We investigate the DAP placement problem and seek methods to minimize the distance between DAPs and their associated smart meters. Specifically, two clustering algorithms are developed to address the objectives, which are formulated in Eqs. (1) and (2), respectively. We also evaluate and compare the performance associated with those two objectives and present implications to the DAP placement problem.

4   Clustering-Based DAP Placement Algorithms

In this section, we elaborate how to develop clustering algorithms to partition a neighborhood area network into subnetworks and place DAPs accordingly. Since the DAP placement problem resembles facility location problems, solutions can be borrowed from contexts of clustering algorithms. However, the standard clustering algorithms, e.g., K-means, cannot be directed adopted to address network partition and the DAP placement problem. To facilitate understanding, we first introduce the concept of clustering algorithms and discuss their shortcomings in partitioning a network topology. Afterwards, a clustering-based DAP placement algorithm will be developed to conduct the network partition and the DAP placement. Note that there are two critical parameters in clustering algorithms:

center and centroid. For clarification, the initial nodes which are selected to perform clustering algorithms are termed as center. The actual node, which is eventually found by clustering algorithms, is termed as centroid.

A typical clustering algorithm, e.g., K-means, includes four main steps:

- Initialize k clusters and allocate one center for each cluster using random sampling;
- Allocate nodes into one of the clusters based on Euclidean distance;
- Recalculate centroid for each cluster;
- Repeat step 2 and 3 until there is no change in each cluster.

The standard clustering algorithms cannot be directly applied to network partitions due to the following reasons. First, the Euclidean distance cannot be used in calculating the distance between two nodes, because physical links may not exist in the path of the Euclidean distance. Second, due to the limited transmission range of smart meters, relay smart meters are needed to forward messages from one smart meter to the DAP. Third, the centroid, where DAP is placed, should be chosen from existing smart meters $(DAP_i \in V)$ to guarantee there are routes between the centroid and its associate smart meters.

In this section, we propose a Clustering-based DAP Placement Algorithm (CDPA) to partition a neighborhood area network into subnetworks and place DAPs to appropriate locations. The associated algorithm is presented in Algorithm 1.

The input of CDPA consists of the number (n) of smart meters of a given network, the coordinates of smart meters $(sl_i(x_i, y_i)_{\{i=1,\cdots,n\}})$, the transmission range (r_c) of each smart meter, and the number of DAPs (k). The output of CDPA includes the identification of DAPs (DAP), the set of smart meter clusters (S) and the routing set for each subnetwork (R). Following is the detailed explanation for each step.

The first step of CDPA is to calculate the shortest path of each pair of smart meters among their possible routes. Note that, the distance adopted in this algorithm represents the shortest path distance. In step 2, k smart meters are randomly selected from the network as centers of each cluster to initialize the clustering. In Step 3, smart meters are allocated into different clusters based on their shortest path distances to the k centers. Specifically, smart meters are allocated to the cluster which is closest to the k centers. For each round, since new smart meters are allocated to those k clusters, the cluster center should be recalculated for each cluster. This process is conducted in step 4, which consists of two methods to address different objectives. In step 4 (1), the new cluster center is obtained aiming at minimizing the average distance between cluster members and the center. In contrast, the worst-case situation is achieved in step 4 (2), which aims to minimize the maximum distance between cluster members and the center. The processes of step 3 and 4 are repeated until there is no change in each cluster, as presented in step 5. The output of the algorithm is obtained in Step 6.

Algorithm 1. Clustering-based DAP Placement Algorithm

Input:

(1) n (the number of smart meters)

(2) $SL = \{sl_i(x_i, y_i)\}_{i=1,\cdots,n}$ (the coordinate of smart meters)

(3) r_c (transmission Range)

(4) k (the number of DAPs)

Output:

(1) $DAP = \{dap_i\}_{i=1,\cdots,k}$ (the instance of DAP)

(2) $S = \{s_i\}_{i=1,\cdots,k}$ (the set of smart meters)

(3) $R = \{r_i\}_{i=1,\cdots,k}$ (the routing paths of each subnetwork)

Step 1: Calculate the shortest path distance between any two nodes. (In the rest of this algorithm, distances represent shortest path distances)

Step 2: Initialize k centers ($C = \{c_i\}_{i=1,\cdots,k}$) by randomly selecting k smart meters from S.

Step 3: Distribute the smart meter s_i ($s_i \in S$) to one of the k clusters using the relation,

$$v \in sc_i, \; if \; d(v, c_i) < d(v, c_j), \; \forall j \in \{1, 2, \cdots, k\}$$

where $d(u, v)$ represents the shortest path between smart meter u and v.

Step 4: Update centroids $C' = \{c_i\}_{i=1,\cdots k}$ such that:

(1) the **average distance is minimized** as formulated in Eq. 1, which is termed as ($CDPA_{avg}$).

$$c_i' = v_m, \; if \; \frac{1}{n'} \sum d(v_m, v) = minimum,$$

$$\frac{1}{n'} = size(cluster_i)$$

$$\forall \; m \; , v \; \in cluster_i, \; i = \{1, 2, \cdots, k\}$$

or **(2)** the **maximum distance is minimized** as formulated in Eq. 2, which is termed as ($CDPA_{wc}$).

$$c_i' = v_m, \; if \; Max\{d(v_m, v)\} = minimum,$$

$$\forall \; m \; , v \; \in cluster_i, \; i = \{1, 2, \cdots, k\}$$

Step 5: Repeat steps 3 and 4 until there is no change in each cluster.

Step 6: Save C' to DAP, $\{cluster_i\}_{i=1,\cdots k}$ to S and routing pathes to R.

---

5   Performance Evaluation

In this section, we demonstrate the network partition as well as DAP placement results achieved by CDPA, and evaluate its performance in terms of distance minimization. A real suburban neighborhood is selected from Rapid City, SD, USA, as the neighborhood area network.

5.1   Demonstration of DAP Placement Achieved by CDPA and the Associated Routes

In Sect. 4, CDPA is proposed to conduct network partition and DAP placement. Actually, CDPA consists of two algorithms, $CDPA_{avg}$ and $CDPA_{ws}$, which are adopted to achieve two different objectives as formulated in Sect. 3. Specifically,

$CDPA_{avg}$ targets at minimizing the average distance between DAPs and smart meters. $CDPA_{ws}$ aims at minimizing the maximum distance between DAPs and their associated smart meters. In this subsection, we demonstrate and compare the DAP placement results conducted by $CDPA_{avg}$ and $CDPA_{ws}$, respectively.

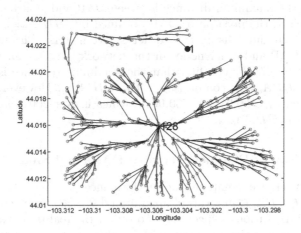

Fig. 1. Demonstration of DAP placement and associated routes achieved by $CDPA_{avg}$

Figure 1 depicts the DAP placement and associated routes achieved by $CDPA_{avg}$. In particular, when only one DAP is deployed in the network, the position of DAP is selected as node 128, which has the smallest sum distance to all other smart meters. The maximum distance among the network is from the DAP (node 128) to node 1, where the distance is 1870.4 m. The average distance between DAP and other smart meters is 549.42 m. The optimal routes from all

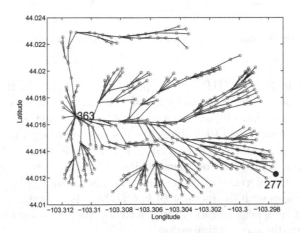

Fig. 2. Demonstration of DAP placement and associated routes achieved by $CDPA_{ws}$

of the smart meters to the DAP are also presented, which are the shortest pathes among all of the possible routes.

The DAP placement result of the $CDPA_{wc}$ is demonstrated in Fig. 2. Compared with $CDPA_{avg}$, the $CDPA_{ws}$ aims to shorten the maximum distance between DAPs and smart meters, so the DAP is preferred to be placed in the location where the maximum distance between DAP and smart meters is minimized. Specifically, the position of DAP obtained by $CDPA_{wc}$ is at node 363, which has the minimum distance to other smart meters. The maximum distance between DAP and other nodes in the network is 1380.4 m, which is from node 363 to node 277. We can find that the maximum distance is significantly decreased by $CDPA_{ws}$ in comparison with $CDPA_{avg}$. However, the average distance achieved by $CDPA_{ws}$ is 760.90 m, which is over 200 m larger than the result achieved by $CDPA_{avg}$.

5.2   Comparison of Distance Between DAPs and Smart Meters

In this subsection, we compare the performance of those two algorithms, $CDPA_{avg}$ and $CDPA_{wc}$, in terms of maximum distance minimization and average distance minimization, respectively. To reflect the real performance of those two algorithms, each of them is executed for 100 times. Cumulative Distribution Functions (CDFs) of those results are plotted and depicted in Figs. 3 and 4, respectively.

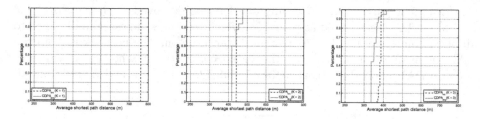

Fig. 3. Average distance between DAPs and smart meters ($CDPA_{avg}$)

As depicted in Fig. 3, $CDPA_{avg}$ outperforms $CDPA_{wc}$ in the average distance minimization, since the majority of the average distance achieved by $CDPA_{avg}$ is smaller than the one achieved by $CDPA_{ws}$, although the difference decreases with the increase of k. Those results further verify that the proposed algorithms $CDPA_{wc}$ and $CDPA_{avg}$ are capable of decreasing the maximum distance and average distance between DAPs and smart meters, respectively. In addition, since the difference of the average distance achieved by $CDPA_{wc}$ and $CDPA_{avg}$ decreases with the increase of k, $CDPA_{wc}$ is recommended to conduct DAP placement in a neighborhood area network due to its better performance in the maximum distance minimization.

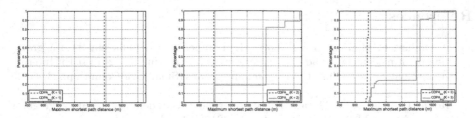

Fig. 4. Maximum distance between DAPs and smart meters ($CDPA_{ws}$) (Color figure online)

In contrast, Fig. 4 depicts the cumulative distribution function of the maximum distance achieved by both $CDPA_{avg}$ and $CDPA_{wc}$, which reveals how the distance between DAPs and smart meters is shortened for each execution. As depicted in Fig. 4, the dashed red curve represents the maximum distance achieved by $CDPA_{wc}$, while the solid green curve is the result achieved by $CDPA_{avg}$. It is clearly observed that $CDPA_{wc}$ outperforms $CDPA_{avg}$ in the maximum distance minimization, since the maximum distance achieved by $CDPA_{wc}$ is smaller than the one achieved by $CDPA_{avg}$.

6   Conclusion

In this paper, we focus on the DAP placement in a smart meter neighborhood area network and aim at minimizing the distance between DAPs and their associated smart meters. To achieve this goal, we formulate this problem and propose two objectives regarding the distance minimization. They are the average distance minimization and the maximum distance minimization. The concept of network partition is introduced in this paper and a clustering-based DAP placement algorithm is developed to tackle the DAP placement problems. Based on this approach, an entire network is divided into subnetworks and one DAP is deployed at an optimal position of each subnetwork. An actual suburban neighborhood is adopted in this paper to evaluate the performance of the proposed solution. Simulation results verify that the proposed solution is able to significantly reduce the distance between DAP and their associated smart meters. At this phase, we only focus on shortening the distance between DAPs and their associated smart meters. Besides distance minimization, there are many other challenges, e.g., energy saving, reliability and resistance to be tackled to pave a way for actual DAP placements in Smart Grid, which will be investigated in the future.

References

1. Aalamifar, F., Shirazi, G.N., Noori, M., Lampe, L.: Cost-efficient data aggregation point placement for advanced metering infrastructure. In: 2014 IEEE International Conference on Smart Grid Communications (SmartGridComm), pp. 344–349 (2014)
2. Rolim, G., Passos, D., Moraes, I., Albuquerque, C.: Modelling the data aggregator positioning problem in smart grids. In: 2015 IEEE International Conference on Computer and Information Technology; Ubiquitous Computing and Communications; Dependable, Autonomic and Secure Computing; Pervasive Intelligence and Computing (CIT/IUCC/DASC/PICOM), pp. 632–639 (2015)
3. Wang, G., Zhao, Y., Huang, J., Winter, R.: On the data aggregation point placement in smart meter networks. In: 2017 26th International Conference on Computer Communication and Networks, pp. 1–6 (2017)
4. Yan, Y., Qian, Y., Sharif, H., Tipper, D.: A survey on smart grid communication infrastructures: motivations, requirements and challenges. Commun. Surv. Tutor. IEEE 15(1), 5–20 (2013)
5. Amin, M.: Challenges in reliability, security, efficiency, and resilience of energy infrastructure: toward smart self-healing electric power grid. In: 2008 IEEE Power and Energy Society General Meeting-Conversion and Delivery of Electrical Energy in the 21st Century, pp. 1–5 (2008)
6. Bennett, C., Wicker, S.B.: Decreased time delay and security enhancement recommendations for AMI smart meter networks. In: Innovative Smart Grid Technologies (ISGT), pp. 1–6 (2010)
7. Sood, V.K., Fischer, D., Eklund, J., Brown, T.: Developing a communication infrastructure for the smart grid. In: 2009 IEEE Electrical Power & Energy Conference (EPEC), pp. 1–7 (2009)
8. Aggarwa, A., Kunta, S., Verma, P.K.: A proposed communications infrastructure for the smart grid. In: Innovative Smart Grid Technologies (ISGT), pp. 1–5, 19–21 January 2010
9. Wang, G., Zhao, Y., Huang, J., Duan, Q., Li, J.: A K-means-based network partition algorithm for controller placement in software defined network. In: International Conference on Communications (2016)
10. Krishnamachari, L., Estrin, D., Wicker, S.: The impact of data aggregation in wireless sensor networks. In: 22nd International Conference on Distributed Computing Systems Workshops, pp. 575–578 (2002)
11. Yilmaz, O., Demirci, S., Kaymak, Y., Ergun, S., Yildirim, A.: Shortest hop multipath algorithm for wireless sensor networks. Comput. Math. Appl. 63(1), 48–59 (2012)
12. Wang, G., Wu, Y., Dou, K., Ren, Y., Li, J.: AppTCP: the design and evaluation of application-based TCP for e-VLBI in fast long distance networks. Future Gener. Comput. Syst. 39, 67–74 (2014)
13. Wang, G., Ren, Y., Dou, K., Li, J.: IDTCP: an effective approach to mitigating the TCP incast problem in data center networks. Inf. Syst. Front. 16, 35–44 (2014)
14. Wang, G., Ren, Y., Li, J.: An effective approach to alleviating the challenges of transmission control protocol. IET Commun. 8(6), 860–869 (2014)
15. Ganesan, D., Govindan, R., Shenker, S., Estrin, D.: Highly-resilient, energy-efficient multipath routing in wireless sensor networks. ACM SIGMOBILE Mob. Comput. Commun. Rev. 5(4), 11–25 (2001)

16. Muruganathan, S.D., Ma, D.C., Bhasin, R.I., Fapojuwo, A.O.: A centralized energy-efficient routing protocol for wireless sensor networks. IEEE Commun. Mag. **43**(3), S8–13 (2005)
17. Goyal, D., Tripathy, M.R.: Routing protocols in wireless sensor networks: a survey. In: 2012 Second International Conference on Advanced Computing & Communication Technologies (ACCT), pp. 474–480 (2012)
18. Pantazis, N.A., Nikolidakis, S.A., Vergados, D.D.: Energy-efficient routing protocols in wireless sensor networks: a survey. IEEE Commun. Surv. Tutor. **15**(2), 551–591 (2013)
19. Drezner, Z., Hamacher, H.W.: Facility Location. Springer, New York (1995)
20. Farahani, R.Z., Hekmatfar, M., Fahimnia, B., Kazemzadeh, N.: Hierarchical facility location problem: models, classifications, techniques, and applications. Comput. Ind. Eng. **68**, 104–117 (2014)

A Fragile Watermarking Scheme of Anti-deleting Features for 2D Vector Map

Guoyin Zhang, Qingan Da, Liguo Zhang, Jianguo Sun$^{(\boxtimes)}$, Qilong Han, Liang Kou, and WenShan Wang

Harbin Engineering University, Harbin, China
sunjianguo@hrbeu.edu.cn

Abstract. This paper proposes a fragile watermarking scheme of anti-deleting features for 2D vector map. The features in vector map are first divided into disjoint groups to ensure the accuracy of tamper localization. In order to locate the batch features deletion attack, we design a feature group correlation technique based on vertex insertion. And a watermark is generated by folding the hash results of the differences of the log-radiuses, which is robust to resist rotation, uniform scaling and translation (RST) operations. And we embed the watermark with a RST invariant watermarking method. Two datasets are constructed for experimentation and the results compared with previous methods indicate that the proposed scheme has good invisibility and high tampering localization accuracy on the feature addition and deletion attack.

Keywords: Fragile watermarking · Tamper localization
2D vector map · Batch features deletion

1 Introduction

During the past decade, the advent of digital maps has had a significant impact on the GPS navigation, digital city, smart transportation and other fields. Unfortunately, data security issues such as malicious tampering and illegal copying have not been well resolved. Then, fragile watermarking technology provides a new way to solve these problems [1,2]. According to the embedding position of the watermark, the fragile watermarking algorithm can be classified into two categories, one is frequency-based method and the other is spatial-based method.

Some algorithms are embedding the fragile watermark in the frequency domain. In [3], the perceived hash value was embedded in the wavelet subband of the carrier data. In [4], a semi-fragile watermarking algorithm based on frequency domain transform embedded the authentication information into high frequency region. These two watermarking strategies can accomplish the purpose of tamper detection, but these algorithms always have high complexity.

There are lots of spatial-based fragile watermarking strategies in previous studies. In [5], for each object in the map, the robust watermark was embedded into its feature points and the fragile watermark was embedded into its

© ICST Institute for Computer Sciences, Social Informatics and Telecommunications Engineering 2018
G. Sun and S. Liu (Eds.): ADHIP 2017, LNICST 219, pp. 360–368, 2018.
https://doi.org/10.1007/978-3-319-73317-3_42

non-feature points. This method implemented the copyright protection and the content authentication for vector maps. In [6], a fragile watermarking scheme was proposed by expanding the Manhattan distances, witch located tampered data with high accuracy [6]. However these two schemes provide less embedded space for the watermark. To solve this problem, Neyman *et al.* created additional vertices for each feature to embed watermarks, they achieved the purpose of locating geometric attacks on received vector map [7]. Nevertheless, the feature rearrangement or vertex reversing operation may disturb the localization ability. In [8], the Douglas algorithm was used to simplify the map before the watermark embedding phase. This method allows users to compress the map, but the contents of the map are damaged to a certain degree. Wang *et al.* used a watermark embedding strategy proposed by Chou and Tseng [9], and designed a signature technique to enhance the localization accuracy [10]. However, these schemes may not be able to detect the batch features deletion attack and then result in passing a dummy authentication.

To solve these problems, we propose a feature group correlation technique to detect the missing group, apply it to the fragile watermarking scheme for 2D geographic data. In this scheme, we divide the spatial features into groups and apply the marking method to each feature. Then we use the correlation mark to mark each feature group. After that, we generate a RST invariant watermark and embed it with the method proposed in [9]. In the watermark authentication phase, we can identify the partial data of the missing group by the correlation mark of the feature group. In order to detect the exact location of the tampered content, the system will compare the extracted watermark with the reproduced watermark. Besides, our watermarking scheme inherits the RST invariance.

2   The Proposed Watermarking Method

Since the polygon feature in the 2D vector map can be seen as a closed polyline, our watermark embedding scheme is designed for polylines. Figure 1 shows the implementation model of our watermarking scheme.

2.1   Pretreatment for Vector Map

To begin with we will provide a brief introduction on the RST invariant fragile watermark embedding method [9]. There are three vertices V_w, T_c and V_n, called the watermark-embedding vertex, the neighboring center and the normalization vertex, respectively. Let $w(0 \leq w < S_w, S_w = 1, 2, 3, ...)$ be the watermark, S_w be an embedding parameter, K_w be a parameter to control the maximum distortion. First, we can obtain the standard quantization $Q_w = \|V_n T^c\| / K_w$. Second, V_w is moved to a new location V_w^e due to quantization operation.

$$V_w^e = V_w - \frac{V_w - T^c}{\|V_w T^c\|} \cdot (\|V_w T^c\| \bmod Q_w). \tag{1}$$

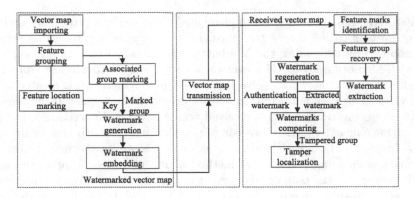

Fig. 1. The implementation model of the proposed fragile watermark algorithm

Third, w is embedded into V_w^e and the watermarked vertex V_w' is obtained,

$$V_w' = V_w^e + \frac{V_w^e - T^c}{\|V_w^e T^c\|} \cdot \frac{Q_w}{S_w} \cdot w. \tag{2}$$

We assume that the length of watermark is L and a vertex carries c watermark bits. The polylines in the map are first divided into disjoint groups. The location ID [10] is used to indicate its group number and the position in the group. The vertices used to indicate the location ID are called mark vertices. Then we assign several extra marks for each group, called correlation mark, to record the information of the adjacent polyline group. The vertices used to indicate the correlation mark are called synergy vertices. For each polyline, we need two mark vertices, two synergy vertices, a normalization vertex and a neighboring center. Since these six vertices can no longer be used to carry the watermark, the total number of vertices on the polyline in which the watermark can be embedded should be at least $\lceil L/c \rceil + 6$. Therefore, the polyline which contains at least $\lceil L/c \rceil + 6$ vertices is an eligible polyline.

Given a vector map with Z polylines, we divide the polyline list into disjoint groups with the grouping method of [10]. Each group has $n(n \geq 1)$ polylines and contains at least one eligible polyline. The number of groups is $N_g = \lceil Z/n \rceil$. The first polyline in each group is an eligible polyline. We call this polyline as a watermark polyline, the second vertex of it as a reference1 vertex and the penultimate vertex of it as a reference2 vertex. We calculate the location ID of the $q^{th}(1 \leq q \leq n)$ polyline in the $p^{th}(0 \leq p \leq N_g - 1)$ group by $m_{p,q} = p \times n + q$.

In order to mark the synergy vertices, we denote the reference1 vertex of the watermark polyline in $G_p(0 \leq p \leq N_g - 1)$ as $v_{1,w}^p(v_{1,w}^{p,x}, v_{1,w}^{p,y})$, the reference1 vertex in the $G_q(q = (p+1) \bmod N_g)$ as $v_{1,w}^q(v_{1,w}^{q,x}, v_{1,w}^{q,y})$. Let s_1^x and s_1^y denote the sign bit of the difference of vertical coordinates and horizontal coordinates between $v_{1,w}^q$ and $v_{1,w}^p$, respectively. When the subtraction result is negative, the sign bit is 1, otherwise, the sign bit is 0. The offset caused by the vertical or horizontal coordinates is divided several times by 2 until the result is less than 1. The times to do the division are denoted as $c_{1,x}$ and $c_{1,y}$. For example, if $\left|v_{1,w}^{q,x} - v_{1,w}^{p,x}\right| < 1$, $c_{1,x}$ is set as 0, otherwise, it is calculated by $\left\lfloor \log_2 \left|v_{1,w}^{q,x} - v_{1,w}^{p,x}\right|\right\rfloor + 1$. The offset values are denoted as Δx_1 and Δy_1,

$$\begin{cases} \Delta x_1 = c_{1,x} \times 10 + s_1^x + \left|v_{1,w}^{q,x} - v_{1,w}^{p,x}\right|/2^{c_{1,x}} \\ \Delta y_1 = c_{1,y} \times 10 + s_1^y + \left|v_{1,w}^{q,y} - v_{1,w}^{p,y}\right|/2^{c_{1,y}} \end{cases}. \qquad (3)$$

Similarly, we denote the offset values between the reference2 vertex in G_q and the one in G_p as Δx_2 and Δy_2. In the subsequent design, we unified use Δx and Δy to represent the correlation marks. For each group, we hide the reference1 vertex's marks of the adjacent group in the watermark polyline, hide the reference2 vertex's marks of the adjacent group in the non-watermark polyline.

2.2 Watermark Embedding

Then, we divide the polyline into five categories: one is composed of more than five vertices (normal), one is composed of five vertices (complex1), one is composed of four vertices (complex2), one is composed of three vertices (complex3) and the other is composed of two vertices (complex4). The embedding results are illustrated in Fig. 2 by way of example. We use $2m_{i,j}$ to indicate the vertex order. The main emphasis is placed on the hidden methods of correlation mark.

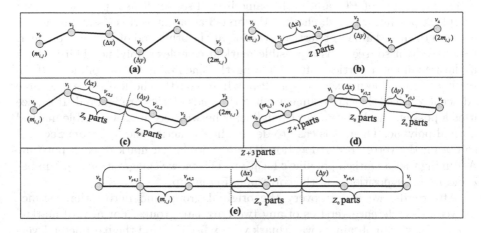

Fig. 2. Method of marking the location for different types of polylines

To embed the correlation mark into the vertex, such as the case in Fig. 2(b), according to Eqs. (1)–(2), we denote the reference vertices' maximum distance between the current group and its correlate group as $dst_{\max}$, define a parameter as $S_w = c_{dst} \times 10 + 2$. The c_{dst} is set as 0 when $dst_{\max}$ is less than 1, otherwise, it is set as $\lfloor \log_2(dst_{\max})\rfloor + 1$. The parameter S_w is the higher limit of the processed offset values. And then a parameter $K_w = len_{\max}/\tau$ is defined, where $len_{\max}$ is the maximum length of the polylines in the vector map M, and τ is the accuracy tolerance of M. We embed Δy into v_2 by regarding the vertices v_1 and v_3 as the normalization vertex and the neighboring center, respectively.

If there is no free vertex to embed the correlation mark, we increase an extra vertex and express the correlation mark through the distance between the vertices. Such as the case in Fig. 2(b), a vertex v_{s1} are inserted between v_1 and v_2. The Euclidean distance between v_1 and v_2 is divided into Z_0 intervals, the number of intervals between v_1 and v_{s1} is equal to Δx, where Z_0 is equal to S_w which is calculated before. After that, Δx is hidden into the polyline.

For a marked group G_i^m with the watermark polyline Pl^m, we see Pl^m's $p(p = \lceil L/c \rceil)$ vertices from v_3 to v_{p+2} as the watermark vertices which is used to embed the watermark, use the rest of the vertices to generate the watermark to obtain a watermark H_i with the method in [10]. According to Eqs. (1)–(2), the reference2 vertex and the reference1 vertex of G_i^m, H_i is embedded in the watermark vertices. Finally, a watermarked vector map M^w is obtained.

2.3   Watermark Authentication

For a polyline Pl^w in received vector map, if the number of vertices on Pl^w is fewer than 6, it is detected as tampered directly. If the number of vertices on Pl^w is greater than 6, we see it as a possible marked normal polyline. If Pl^w has only six vertices, we identify its type with the following rules. First, check if the six vertices of Pl^w are on the same line, if so, see it as a possible marked complex4 polyline. Second, check if the first 3 adjacent vertices starting at one end and the first 4 adjacent vertices starting at the other end of Pl^w are collinear, respectively, if so, see it as a possible marked complex3 polyline. Third, check if the remaining 4 vertices after ignoring the ends of Pl^w are collinear. If so, see it as a possible marked complex2 polyline. Fourth, check if there are three adjacent vertices that are collinear when the ends of Pl^w are ignored. If so, see it as a possible marked complex1 polyline; otherwise, see it as a possible marked normal polyline. Then, it is easy to derive the extraction method from Sect. 2.1 to obtain the vertex order, location ID and correlation mark of each polyline. Assuming that a marked polyline's location ID is m, we can get its group number i and its inner position j in the corresponding group.

Afterwards, we can recovery the original group and derive the distance between the reference vertices of any two correlate groups. For a watermarked group G_i^w, we can obtain its watermark vertex list $V_i^{w\prime}$ and the parameter 1 vertex $v_{r1}{}'$ and the parameter2 vertex $v_{r2}{}'$. We use the input parameter K_w and set the parameter S_w as 2^c. For any watermark vertex $v_j{}'$, the watermark fragment $w_{i,j}{}'$ can be extract from $v_j{}'$. Then according to G_i^w's vertex order, watermark fragments can be connected to obtain the watermark W_i of the current group. Finally, we regenerate the watermark of G_i^w. Comparing the extracted watermark with newly generated one, we can judge whether G_i^w has been tampered.

3   Experiments and Results

We run experiments on a PC with 2.80 GHz, RAM 4.00 GB, Win7 Ultimate, ArcGIS Engine 10.2 and Visual C++6.0. We construct two datasets: one contains 50 maps and the other contains 30 maps. These maps are taken from the resources of ArcGIS. The inputs are set as follows: the number of watermark bit a vertex carries $c = 8$, group size $n = 3$ and the watermark length $L = 128$.

3.1   Verification of Invisibility

Four vector maps of the first dataset are used to show the invisibility of our scheme. They are a British expressway map, a railway map of Taiwan, a lake map of south part of China and an American expressway map. The precision tolerance τ of them are 1300, 200, 500 and 2500, respectively. They are watermarked by the proposed algorithm, the watermarked versions are shown in Fig. 3.

Fig. 3. The watermarked 2D vector maps

We use the average distortion d and the maximum distortion $Maxd$ [10] to measure the objective quality of the received vector map. Table 1 lists the results of three contrast algorithms for the invisibility of each test case and indicates that the introduced distortions do not exceed the tolerance.

3.2   Discussion of Localization Accuracy

We choose a river map from the second dataset to test the tamper localization ability. Figure 4 shows the changes of this original map at different stages of watermarking. The original map in Fig. 4(a) is watermarked by our scheme yielding the watermarked map shown in Fig. 4(b). Afterwards, the watermarked map is manipulated to yield the map in Fig. 4(c). Expressly, we added 3 vertices to region 'A', modified 3 vertices in region 'B', deleted 5 vertices from region 'C' and deleted 3 polylines from region 'D'. The result of authentication can be seen from Fig. 4(d) which used red marks to indicate the located suspicious groups.

In order to test the tamper localization ability of our scheme, we applied the metrics β [2] which expresses the number of polylines detected as tampered after illegal attack. The expectation of β is denoted as $E(\beta)$, which is calculated

Table 1. The objective quality of the received vector map

2D vector map	The method in [7]		The method in [10]		The proposed method	
	$Maxd(m)$	$d(m)$	$Maxd(m)$	$d(m)$	$Maxd(m)$	$d(m)$
British expressway map	783.704	19.380	612.051	1.940	584.446	2.147
Railway map of China Taiwan	121.763	1.509	77.656	0.297	82.392	0.236
Lake map of south part of China	278.748	1.764	152.005	0.282	147.564	0.299
American expressway map	2231.491	52.441	1852.323	21.206	1981.193	25.191

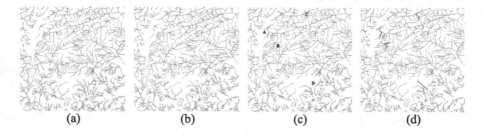

(a)   (b)   (c)   (d)

Fig. 4. The changes of a river map at different watermarked stages (Color figure online)

to compare the localization accuracy of our algorithm with the ones proposed in [7] and [10]. In [7], Neyman *et al.* divide the polylines into disjoint groups based on the number of vertices. But it is hard to evaluate the number of vertices within each polylines. For simplicity, we assume a vector map with 100 polylines is divided into 10 groups, each group has 10 features, the probability of adding/deleting operation of the features in i^{th} group is 1/10. In particular, the probability of the case that a whole group is deleted after removing a small number of features is 0. We assume 10 polylines are missing after the batch features deletion attack. These polylines are in the same group or in two different groups. The probability of these two cases is equal. When we calculate $E(\beta)$ for the method reported in [10], we assume that the probability that the added feature is regarded as a valid feature is 1/2.

Results of the first three attack types in Fig. 5 shows that for the method reported in [7], the feature addition/deletion/rearrangement attacks may cause a different grouping result and a wrong tamper localization. From the performance of vertex reversing, feature rearrangement and RST attacks, we can find that our watermarking strategy is robust to resist these kinds of editing operations. From the comparison of the localization accuracy after the batch features deletion attack, we can see that our scheme can locate the missing group.

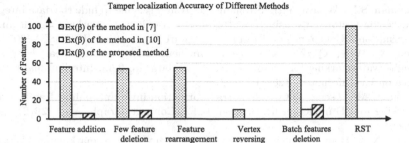

Fig. 5. Tamper localization accuracy of different methods

4 Conclusions

In this paper, we design a digital watermarking method for vector geographic data authentication based on the RST invariant fragile watermark embedding strategy. A grouping method and a feature location marking method are used to ensure the tamper localization accuracy. We design a feature group correlation technique to resist the batch features deletion attack which may lead to passing a dummy authentication. By folding the hash results of the differences of the log-radiuses, our scheme can resist the RST transformations. Furthermore, this watermarking algorithm is robust to resist the feature addition, deletion, rearrangement and vertex reversing attacks.

Acknowledgments. This work was supported by project of NSFC of China (61202455, 61472096, 61501132).

References

1. Wang, N.N., Zhao, X., Xie, C.: RST invariant reversible watermarking for 2D vector map. Int. J. Multimed. Ubiquit. Eng. **11**(2), 265–276 (2016)
2. Wang, N.N., Men, C.G.: Reversible fragile watermarking for 2-D vector map authentication with localization. Comput. Aided Des. **44**(4), 320–330 (2012)
3. Weng, L., Darazi, R., Preneel, B., Macq, B., Dooms, A.: Robust image content authentication using perceptual hashing and watermarking. In: Lin, W., Xu, D., Ho, A., Wu, J., He, Y., Cai, J., Kankanhalli, M., Sun, M.-T. (eds.) PCM 2012. LNCS, vol. 7674, pp. 315–326. Springer, Heidelberg (2012). https://doi.org/10. 1007/978-3-642-34778-8_29
4. Haojun, F.U., Zhu, C., Jian, M.: Multipurpose watermarking algorithm for digital raster map based on wavelet transformation. Acta Geod. Et Cartogr. Sin. **40**(3), 397–400 (2011)
5. Peng, Y., Lan, H., Yue, M.: Multipurpose watermarking for vector map protection and authentication. Multimed. Tools Appl. 1–21 (2017)
6. Neyman, S.N., Sitohang, B., Sutisna, S.: Reversible fragile watermarking baséd on difference expansion using manhattan distances for 2D vector map. Procedia Technol. **11**(1), 614–620 (2013)

7. Neyman, S.N., Wijaya, Y.H., Sitohang, B.: A new scheme to hide the data integrity marker on vector maps using a feature-based fragile watermarking algorithm. In: International Conference on Data and Software Engineering (ICODSE) (2014)
8. Ren, N., Wang, Q., Zhu, C.: Selective authentication algorithm based on semi-fragile watermarking for vector geographical data. In: 22nd International Conference on GeoInformatics (2014)
9. Chou, C.M., Tseng, D.C.: Affine-transformation-invariant public fragile watermarking for 3D model authentication. IEEE Comput. Graph. Appl. **29**(2), 72–79 (2009)
10. Wang, N.N., Bian, J., Zhang, H.: RST invariant fragile watermarking for 2D vector map authentication. Int. J. Multimed. Ubiquit. Eng. **10**(4), 155–172 (2015)

Spatial Spectrum Estimation for Wideband Signals by Sparse Reconstruction in Continuous Domain

Jiaqi Zhen[✉] and Yanchao Li

College of Electronic Engineering, Heilongjiang University,
Harbin 150080, China
zhenjiaqi2011@163.com

Abstract. A novel spatial spectrum estimation method for two-dimensional wideband signals by sparse reconstruction in continuous domain is addressed in this paper. First, Discrete Fourier Transform (DFT) is employed for the data. Then the convex and corresponding dual problems of the data with most power are founded and solved. After that the sparse support sets are decided by semidefinite program and extracting roots. Finally, both of the direction of arrival (DOA) and the primary signals are determined. The proposed idea averts the off-grid effect based on grid partition, and some theoretical results are included to explain the effectiveness of the method.

Keywords: Direction of arrival · Sparse reconstruction · Wideband signals
Continuous domain

1 Introduction

Spatial spectrum estimation through sparse reconstruction is a new kind of direction of arrival (DOA) method arisen in the past few decades [1–5]. Malioutov [6] transformed the DOA estimation into sparse recovery under redundant dictionary, optimized the solution by second-order cone programming. Tang [7] proposed a beam forming method based on sparse characteristic, then reconstruct the signals with orthogonal matching pursuit, but some false peaks exist when there are too many signals. Yin [8] presented the concept of space compression sampling matrix, the signals are sampled, and they are compressed at the same time, then calculated the initial signals and DOA through solving some optimization problems. Basis pursuit [9] and Matching pursuit [10] are both based on $L1$ penalty term. The former has a higher precision, but the

This work was supported by the National Natural Science Foundation of China under Grant No. 61501176 and 61505050, University Nursing Program for Young Scholars with Creative Talents in Heilongjiang Province (UNPYSCT-2016017), China Postdoctoral Science Foundation (2014M561381), Heilongjiang Province Postdoctoral Foundation (LBH-Z14178), Heilongjiang Province Natural Science Foundation (F2015015), Outstanding Young Scientist Foundation of Heilongjiang University (JCL201504) and Special Research Funds for the Universities of Heilongjiang Province (HDRCCX-2016Z10).

© ICST Institute for Computer Sciences, Social Informatics and Telecommunications Engineering 2018
G. Sun and S. Liu (Eds.): ADHIP 2017, LNICST 219, pp. 369–377, 2018.
https://doi.org/10.1007/978-3-319-73317-3_43

computation is complex; the latter is the opposite. In 2013, Carlin [11] employed Bayesian learning for signal recovery, provided a new scheme according to the spatial of solution and timing structure.

Conventional sparse reconstruction technique has lowered the requirement of signal to noise ratio (SNR) and sampling number, but generally speaking, the actual DOAs are not at the grid point. Therefore, Candes and Fernandez [12, 13] studied the super-resolution from samples at the low end of the spectrum, as he reconstructed sources in continuous domain, which had improved the estimation precision to a great extent, but they did not studied how to estimate spatial spectrum for wideband signals according to the theory.

This paper presents a new spatial spectrum estimation algorithm, first, the sources are partitioned into some subbands, then the convex and corresponding dual problems of the data with most power are founded and solved. After that the sparse support sets are decided by semidefinite program and extracting roots. Finally, both of the direction of arrival (DOA) and the primary signals are determined. The proposed algorithm averts the error created by sparse reconstruction based on grid partition, and it has a preferable performance under the circumstance of low SNR and small samples.

2 Array Signal Model

As is shown in Fig. 1, assume that there is an arbitrary array with N sensors in X–Y plane, the origin O is defined as the reference, and the coordinate of these sensors are $(x_n, y_n)(n = 1, 2, \cdots, N)$. Suppose that there are K far-field wideband sources impinging on these sensors, DOAs are $(\phi_k, \theta_k)(k = 1, 2, \cdots, K)$, here ϕ_k and θ_k are the azimuth and elevation respectively, so output of the array is

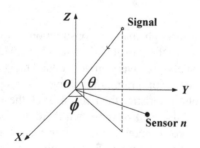

Fig. 1. Array signal model

$$\boldsymbol{y}(t) = [y_1(t), \cdots, y_N(t)]^{\mathrm{T}} = \left[\sum_{k=1}^{K} s_k(t - \tau_{1k}), \cdots, \sum_{k=1}^{K} s_k(t - \tau_{Nk}) \right]^{\mathrm{T}} + [b_1(t), \cdots, b_N(t)]^{\mathrm{T}} \quad (1)$$

where $y_n(t)$ $(n = 1, 2, \cdots, N)$ is the output of the nth sensor, c is the speed of the source, $[b_1(t), \cdots, b_N(t)]$ is the additive Gaussian white noise vector, $b_n(t)$ is the corresponding noise of the nth sensor.

The frequency band is partitioned into G parts, perform discrete Fourier transform (DFT) on $y(t)$, we have:

$$Y(f_g) = A(f_g)S(f_g) + B(f_g) \quad g = 1, 2, \cdots, G \tag{2}$$

Here, $A(f_g)$ is the array manifold of f_g

$$
A(f_g) = [a(f_g, \phi_1, \theta_1), \cdots, a(f_g, \phi_k, \theta_k), \cdots, a(f_g, \phi_K, \theta_K)]
$$
$$
= \begin{bmatrix}
e^{-j2\pi f_g \tau_{11}} & \cdots & e^{-j2\pi f_g \tau_{1k}} & \cdots & e^{-j2\pi f_g \tau_{1K}} \\
\vdots & & \vdots & & \vdots \\
e^{-j2\pi f_g \tau_{n1}} & \cdots & e^{-j2\pi f_g \tau_{nk}} & \cdots & e^{-j2\pi f_g \tau_{nK}} \\
\vdots & & \vdots & & \vdots \\
e^{-j2\pi f_g \tau_{N1}} & \cdots & e^{-j2\pi f_g \tau_{Nk}} & \cdots & e^{-j2\pi f_g \tau_{NK}}
\end{bmatrix} \tag{3}
$$

where $a(f_g, \phi_k, \theta_k)$ is the steering vector of the source from $(\phi_k, \theta_k)(k = 1, 2, \cdots, K)$ at f_g, assume that f_0 is the frequency with the most power and $S(f_g)$ is formed by some spikes [13], then we let

$$\varphi_k(f_0) = \frac{f_0}{c}[1 - (\cos \phi_k \cos \theta_k + \sin \phi_k \cos \theta_k)] \tag{4}$$

so the sparse source $S(f_0)$ can be written

$$
S(f_0) = \begin{bmatrix}
S_1(f_0) \\
\vdots \\
S_k(f_0) \\
\vdots \\
S_K(f_0)
\end{bmatrix} = \begin{bmatrix}
v_1(f_0)\delta_{\varphi_1(f_0)} \\
\vdots \\
v_k(f_0)\delta_{\varphi_k(f_0)} \\
\vdots \\
v_K(f_0)\delta_{\varphi_K(f_0)}
\end{bmatrix} \tag{5}
$$

where $\delta_{\varphi_k(f_0)}$ is the dirac measure at $\varphi_k(f_0)$, let $\{\varphi_1(f_0), \cdots, \varphi_K(f_0)\}$ be the support set of $S(f_0)$, here $\varphi_k(f_0)$ contains DOA of the kth source, $v_k(f_0)$ is its amplitude.

3 Estimation Theory

Assume that the output $Y(f_0)$ is infinite, given a measure $S(\varphi)$, the corresponding Fourier coefficients is

$$q(n, f_0) = \sum_{k=1}^{K} \exp(-j2\pi n\varphi_k(f_0)) v_k(f_0), \quad n = 1, 2, \cdots, N \tag{6}$$

then we have

$$\boldsymbol{Q}(f_0) = \boldsymbol{F}(f_0)\boldsymbol{S}(f_0) \tag{7}$$

where

$$\boldsymbol{Q}(f_0) = [q(1,f_0), q(2,f_0), \cdots, q(N,f_0)]^{\mathrm{T}} \tag{8}$$

and

$$\boldsymbol{F}(f_0) = \begin{bmatrix} \exp(-\mathrm{j}2\pi\varphi_1(f_0)) & \cdots & \exp(-\mathrm{j}2\pi\varphi_K(f_0)) \\ \exp(-\mathrm{j}2\pi \times 2\varphi_1(f_0)) & \cdots & \exp(-\mathrm{j}2\pi \times 2\varphi_K(f_0)) \\ \vdots & \ddots & \vdots \\ \exp(-\mathrm{j}2\pi N\varphi_1(f_0)) & \cdots & \exp(-\mathrm{j}2\pi N\varphi_K(f_0)) \end{bmatrix} \tag{9}$$

We need to solve the following problem so as to recover the original wideband sources

$$\min_{\boldsymbol{S}(f_0)} \|\boldsymbol{S}(f_0)\|_{\mathrm{TV}}, \quad \text{s.t. } \boldsymbol{Q}(f_0) = \boldsymbol{F}(f_0)\boldsymbol{S}(f_0) \tag{10}$$

where $\|\boldsymbol{S}(f_0)\|_{\mathrm{TV}} = \sum_{k=1}^{K} S_k(f_0) = \sum_{k=1}^{K} v_k(f_0)$, thus we can reconstruct the source $\boldsymbol{S}(f_0)$ if the interval between $\varphi_\alpha(f_0)$ and $\varphi_\beta(f_0)$ is larger than $2/f_0$ for $1 \le \alpha, \beta \le N, \alpha \ne \beta$; $k = 1, \cdots, K$ [12].

Assume that sampling number at each frequency is Z, Eq. (2) is changed as

$$\bar{\boldsymbol{Y}}(f_0) = \boldsymbol{A}(f_0)\bar{\boldsymbol{S}}(f_0) + \bar{\boldsymbol{B}}(f_0) \tag{11}$$

that is

$$\bar{\boldsymbol{Y}}(f_0) = [\boldsymbol{Y}(f_0, 1), \cdots, \boldsymbol{Y}(f_0, z), \cdots, \boldsymbol{Y}(f_0, Z)] \tag{12}$$

$\boldsymbol{Y}(f_0, z)$ is the zth snapshots of f_0, $\bar{\boldsymbol{S}}(f_0)$ and $\bar{\boldsymbol{B}}(f_0)$ are respectively the source and noise matrix. It can be deduced from (11)

$$\bar{\boldsymbol{Y}}(f_0) - \bar{\boldsymbol{B}}(f_0) = \boldsymbol{A}(f_0)\bar{\boldsymbol{S}}(f_0) = \boldsymbol{A}(f_0)\boldsymbol{S}(f_0) + \boldsymbol{D}(f_0) \tag{13}$$

Obviously, $\boldsymbol{D}(f_0)$ is the corresponding perturbation, it reflects the error between infinite and finite received data. Combining (13), we can deduce the Fourier coefficients of finite samples

$q(n, f_0)$

$$= \exp\left(-j2\pi n \frac{f_0}{c}\right) (\bar{\mathbf{Y}}_n(f_0) - \bar{\mathbf{B}}_n(f_0))$$

$$= \exp\left(-j2\pi n \frac{f_0}{c}\right) \left(\sum_{k=1}^{K} e^{j2\pi n \frac{f_0}{c}(\cos\phi_k \cos\theta_k + \sin\phi_k \cos\theta_k)} v_k(f_0) + \mathbf{D}(n, f_0) \right) \quad (14)$$

$$= \sum_{k=1}^{K} e^{-j2\pi n \frac{f_0}{c}(1-(\cos\phi_k \cos\theta_k + \sin\phi_k \cos\theta_k))} v_k(f_0) + \exp\left(-j2\pi n \frac{f_0}{c}\right) \mathbf{D}(n, f_0)$$

$$= \sum_{k=1}^{K} \exp\left(-j2\pi n \varphi_k(f_0)\right) v_k(f_0) + \omega(n, f_0)$$

where $\omega(n, f_0) = \exp\left(-j2\pi n \frac{f_0}{c}\right) \mathbf{D}(n, f_0)$, so (14) can be modified as

$$\mathbf{Q}(f_0) = \mathbf{F}(f_0)\mathbf{S}(f_0) + \omega(f_0) \quad (15)$$

here $\omega(f_0) = [\omega(1, f_0), \cdots, \omega(N, f_0)]^{\mathrm{T}}$. Similarly, we can also solve the following problem so as to recover the original sources

$$\min_{\mathbf{S}(f_0)} \|\mathbf{S}(f_0)\|_{\mathrm{TV}} \text{ s.t. } \|\mathbf{Q}(f_0) - \mathbf{F}(f_0)\mathbf{S}(f_0)\|_2 \leq |\varsigma(f_0)| \quad (16)$$

The question (16) is a multiple convex problem and difficult to be disposed, so we need to simplify it by corresponding dual problem [12]

$$\max_{\mathbf{\Phi}(f_0), \mathbf{U}} \left(\mathrm{Re}[\mathbf{Q}^*(f_0)\mathbf{\Phi}(f_0)] - \varsigma(f_0)\|\mathbf{\Phi}(f_0)\|_2 \right) \text{ s.t.}$$

$$\begin{bmatrix} \mathbf{U} & \mathbf{\Phi}(f_0) \\ \mathbf{\Phi}^*(f_0) & 1 \end{bmatrix} \succ, 0 \ \|\mathbf{F}^*(f_0)\mathbf{\Phi}(f_0)\|_{L\infty} \leq 1 \quad (17)$$

here $\sum_{\alpha=1}^{N-\beta} \mathbf{Z}_{\alpha,\alpha+\beta} = \begin{cases} 1, & \beta = 0 \\ 0, & \beta = 1, 2, \cdots, N-1 \end{cases}$, $\mathbf{U} \in C^{N \times N}$ is a Hermitian matrix, and $\mathbf{\Phi}(f_0)$ is the corresponding Lagrangian multiplier for $\mathbf{Q}(f_0) = \mathbf{F}(f_0)\mathbf{S}(f_0) + \omega(f_0)$, we can obtain the parameter according to the semidefinite program [14], which can be solved by the tool in [15].

The following lemma [13] can be used for describing the relation of (16) and (17)

$$\left(\hat{\mathbf{F}}^* \hat{\mathbf{\Phi}}\right)(f_0) = \mathrm{sign}\left(\|\hat{\mathbf{S}}(f_0)\|_{\mathrm{TV}}\right) \quad (18)$$

where $\|\hat{\mathbf{S}}(f_0)\|_{\mathrm{TV}} \neq 0$, $\hat{\mathbf{F}}(f_0)$, $\hat{\mathbf{\Phi}}(f_0)$ and $\hat{\mathbf{S}}(f_0)$ are respectively the estimated vector of $\mathbf{F}(f_0)$, $\mathbf{\Phi}(f_0)$ and $\mathbf{S}(f_0)$.

As $\left\|\hat{S}(f_0)\right\|_{TV} \neq 0$, we can solve absolute value of (18)

$$\left|\hat{F}^*(f_0)\hat{\Phi}(f_0)\right| = 1 \tag{19}$$

thus, the DOAs of the sources can be acquired by combining (4) and (9), then the sources will also be reconstructed by (5). The proposed sparse reconstruction method is implemented in continuous domain, so it can be abbreviated to SCD method.

4 Simulations

Next, several simulations is shown, the center frequency of the sources is 3 GHz, the sensors are places at (0, 0), (−0.15, 0.17), (−0.051, 0.079), (−0.18, 0.063), (−0.068, −0.041), (0.059, 0.21), (0.07, 0.31), (0.041, −0.039), unit is meter. Two-sided correlation transformation (TCT) [16], conventional sparse methods in discrete domain (SDD) [9] and SCD are compared for the simulations, $\varsigma(f_0)$ in SCD is taken as 2. The DOA grids of SDD and searching step size of TCT are both taken as $0.2°$.

4.1 Normalization Spectrum

Assume that four far-field wideband sources impinge on the array with same power from $(20.5°, 80.5°)$, $(30.5°, 70.5°)$, $(40.5°, 60.5°)$,$(50.5°, 50.5°)$, SNR is 3 dB, sampling number at every frequency is 60, the width of the band is 20% of the center frequency, normalization spectrums of the three methods are given in Figs. 2, 3 and 4.

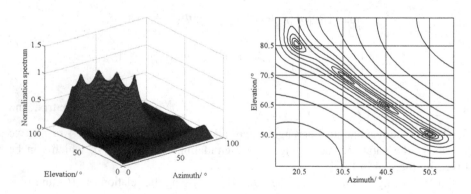

Fig. 2. Normalization spectrum of TCT

4.2 Estimation Error

Figure 5 has shown the estimation error versus SNR when sampling times of each frequency is 60, 400 Monte-Carlo simulations have run for each SNR, as is shown in Fig. 5, the estimation error of SCD is lower than the other two methods.

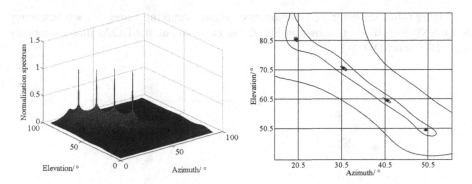

Fig. 3. Normalization spectrum of SDD

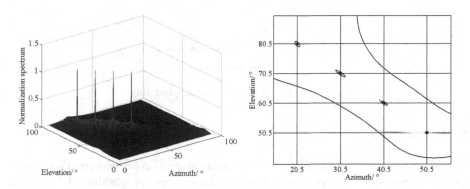

Fig. 4. Normalization spectrum of SCD method

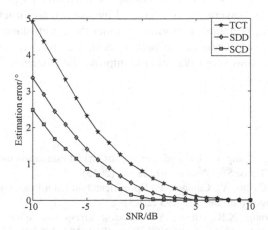

Fig. 5. Estimation error versus SNR

Figure 6 has shown the estimation error versus sampling times of each frequency when SNR is 2 dB, as is shown in Fig. 6, we can estimate the DOAs more accurately than TCT and SDD.

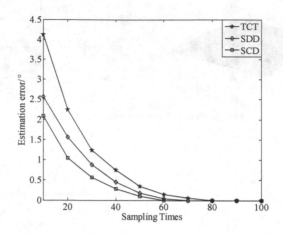

Fig. 6. Estimation error versus sampling times

5   Conclusion

This paper presents a new kind of spatial spectrum estimation for wideband sources by sparse reconstruction in continuous domain, the sources are partitioned into some subbands, then the convex and corresponding dual problems of the data with most power are founded and solved. The sparse support sets are decided by semidefinite program and extracting roots. Both of the DOA and the primary signals are determined. The proposed algorithm averts the error created by sparse reconstruction based on grid partition, and it has a preferable performance under the circumstance of low SNR and small samples. As the process of the optimization, we still have a great amount of computation, how to lower the calculation to improve the efficiency is worthy of going on researching.

References

1. Yang, Z., Xie, L., Zhang, C.: Off-grid direction of arrival estimation using sparse Bayesian inference. IEEE Trans. Sig. Process. **61**, 38–43 (2013)
2. Azais, J.M., De Castro, Y., Gamboa, F.: Spike detection from inaccurate samplings. Appl. Comput. Harmonic Anal. **38**, 177–195 (2015)
3. Amin, M.G., Wang, X.R., Zhang, Y.D.: Sparse arrays and sampling for interference mitigation and DOA estimation in GNSS. Proc. IEEE **104**, 1302–1317 (2016)
4. Dai, J.S., Bao, X., Xu, W.C.: Root sparse bayesian learning for off-grid DOA estimation. IEEE Sig. Process. Lett. **24**, 46–50 (2017)

5. Hu, N., Sun, B., Zhang, Y.: Underdetermined DOA estimation method for wideband signals using joint nonnegative sparse Bayesian learning. IEEE Sig. Process. Lett. **24**, 535–539 (2017)
6. Malioutov, D., Cetin, M., Willsky, A.S.: A sparse signal reconstruction perspective for source localization with sensor arrays. IEEE Trans. Sig. Process. **53**, 3010–3022 (2005)
7. Tang, Z.J., Blacquiere, G., Leus, G.: Aliasing-free wideband beam forming using sparse signal representation. IEEE Trans. Sig. Process. **59**, 3464–3469 (2011)
8. Yin, J.H., Chen, T.Q.: Direction-of-arrival estimation using a sparse representation of array covariance vectors. IEEE Trans. Sig. Process. **59**, 4489–4493 (2011)
9. Heidem, T., Cai, G., Xu, Z.: On recovery of sparse signals via l1 minimization. IEEE Trans. Inf. Theory **55**, 3388–3397 (2010)
10. Pavlidi, D., Griffin, A., Puigt, M.: Real-time multiple sound source localization and counting using a circular microphone array. IEEE Trans. Audio Speech Lang. Process. **21**, 2193–2206 (2013)
11. Carlin, M., Rocca, P., Oliveri, G.: Directions-of-arrival estimation through Bayesian compressive sensing strategies. IEEE Trans. Antennas Propag. **61**, 3828–3838 (2013)
12. Candes, E.J., Fernandez, G.C.: Towards a mathematical theory of super-resolution. Commun. Pure Appl. Math. **67**, 906–956 (2012)
13. Candes, E.J., Fernandez, G.C.: Super-resolution from noisy data. J. Fourier Anal. Appl. **19**, 1229–1254 (2013)
14. Boyd, S., Vandenberghe, L.: Convex Optimization. Cambridge University Press, Cambridge (2004)
15. CVX: MATLAB software for disciplined convex programming, version 1.22. http://cvxr.com/cvx
16. Valaee, S., Kabal, P.: Wideband array processing using a two-sided correlation transformation. IEEE Trans. Sig. Process. **43**, 160–172 (1995)

Improved K-Means Algorithm and Its Application to Vehicle Steering Identification

Hui Qi[1,2(✉)], Xiaoqiang Di[1,2], Jinqing Li[2], and Hongxin Ma[3]

[1] National and Local Joint Engineering Research Center of Space and
Optoelectronics Technology, Changchun University of Science and Technology,
Changchun, China
qihui@cust.edu.cn
[2] School of Computer Science and Technology,
Changchun University of Science and Technology, Changchun, China
[3] Training Department, Aviation University Air Force, Changchun, China

Abstract. K-means is a very common clustering algorithm, whose performance depends largely on the initially selected cluster center. The K-means algorithm proposed by this paper uses a new strategy to select the initial cluster center. It works by calculating the minimum and maximum distances from data to the origin, dividing this range into several equal ranges, and then adjusting every range according to the data distribution to equate the number of data contained in the ranges as much as possible, and finally calculating the average of data in every range and taking it as initial cluster center. The theoretical analysis shows that despite linear time complexity of initialization process, this algorithm has the features of an superlinear initialization method. The application of this algorithm to the analysis of GPS data when vehicle is moving shows that it can effectively increase the clustering speed and finally achieve better vehicle steering identification.

Keywords: K-means · Clustering · Vehicle steering
Vehicle navigation system

An intuitional objective function of clustering algorithms in common use is the Sum of Squares for Error (SSE), which is provided below:

$$SSE = \sum_{i=1}^{K} \sum_{\mathbf{x_j} \in P_i} \|\mathbf{x_j} - \mathbf{c_i}\|_2^2 \tag{1}$$

where: K is the number of clusters, $\mathbf{x_j}$ is the jth datum of this data set, P_i is the ith cluster, $\mathbf{c_i}$ is the center of the ith cluster ($\mathbf{c_i} = 1/|P_i| \sum_{\mathbf{x_j} \in P_i} \mathbf{x_j}$, where $|P_i|$ is the number of data in the ith cluster), $\|.\|_2$ is Euclidean distance. A clustering algorithm is aimed to find the minimum SSE. But because this non-convex optimization is NP-hard [1,2], its approximate solution in polynomial time can only be found at present. K-means algorithm is just such a clustering algorithm. It has

© ICST Institute for Computer Sciences, Social Informatics and Telecommunications Engineering 2018
G. Sun and S. Liu (Eds.): ADHIP 2017, LNICST 219, pp. 378–386, 2018.
https://doi.org/10.1007/978-3-319-73317-3_44

been widely used, as its concept is simple and easy to implement. For instance, K-means algorithm is used in [3] to cluster the GPS data during vehicle driving for identifying whether the vehicle is making a turn or not, and finally to build a learning system of vehicle steering identification based on the architecture of dynamic onboard navigation system. This system sends the GPS data collected by client (onboard terminal) to the server, which, in turn, automatically calculates the steering identification model applicable to the vehicle and returns the model parameters to the client. As the server needs to create a model for many clients, the modeling speed has become an issue of great concern during the server programming, which would influence the server's quality and capability. This paper optimizes the first step of modeling, namely K-means clustering, in order to increase the rate of convergence.

The rest of this paper is organized as follows. Section 1 gives a brief introduction to the research of the initialization of K-means clustering algorithm. Section 2 presents the improved initialization method and the performance it achieves. In Sect. 3 three initialization methods are compared using the field test data and the test results are analyzed. Section 4 concludes this paper.

1   Related Work

K-means clustering algorithm is implemented through two steps: initialization and subsequent iterations. Initialization is to select the initial cluster center, namely c_i of the first iteration, while subsequent iterations are to continuously change the cluster center until it won't change any more or the number of iterations reaches its maximum. As pointed out by [4], K-means clustering algorithm is so sensitive to the cluster center selected during initialization that the selection of a different initial cluster center will influence the algorithm performance. Whats more, improper initialization may result in empty clustering, slower convergence and a higher risk of being caught in the locally optimal solution [5]. Therefore, improving the initialization process has become an important means of K-means performance improvement. In the [4], various initialization methods are analyzed and divided into two categories: linear time complexity and ultra-linear time complexity. The linear method is often non-deterministic or sensitive to sequence [6], while the superlinear method is usually deterministic. In other words, by clustering the same data set repeatedly with the K-means algorithm based on linear initialization, different clustering results will be obtained; by clustering the same data set with the K-means algorithm based on superlinear initialization, only one clustering result will be obtained, no matter how many times the data set is clustered. Therefore, with the superlinear method, only one clustering, rather than repeated clustering to select the optimal clustering result, is needed. Besides, the superlinear method often enables fast convergence of k-means algorithm and applies to the clustering of a large data set. It is just these advantages that attract extensive attention to the superlinear method. For example, in the [7], a variance-based method is proposed to sequence all the data according to the attribute with the maximum variance, then to divide the sorted data into K groups, and finally to choose the middle datum in every group as initial cluster center. In the [8], the kd-tree of data points is built for density estimation, and then the modified maximin method is used to select K cluster centers from the densely generated leaves. In the [9], a robust initialization method is proposed to use a local outlier factor that can prevent an abnormal datum from being taken as cluster center. In the [10], an initialization method with k iterations is proposed to at first establish k sets and then during the ith $(1 \le i \le k)$ iteration, to channel the nearest data pairs from the data sets into the ith set continuously until the number of data in the set exceeds a certain threshold, suggesting the end of the ith iteration and the start of the $(i+1)$th iteration. In the [11], a method based on attribute transformation is proposed to at first change the negative attribute of all the data into positive, then to sequence all the changed data according to their distances to the origin and divide the sorted data into K groups, and finally to choose the middle datum in every group as initial cluster center. The idea of [12] is similar to that of [11], with the exception of using the averages to choose the cluster center. The time complexity of all the above superlinear methods is $O(n \log n)$, except for that in the [10], where the time complexity is $O(n^2)$.

2　Improved Initialization Method

This paper proposes an improved initialization method that uses the ideas of [11,12] for reference and needs to change the negative attribute of all the data in a way shown in [11,12].

After changing the attribute, the calculation of the distances from data to the origin is also needed. But next, unlike the methods in [11,12], the proposed method no longer needs to sequence all the data according to their distances to the origin, but to choose the minimum (d_{min}) and maximum (d_{max}) distances. The time complexity of this step is $O(n)$.

Next, divide the range $[d_{min}, d_{max}]$ into K subranges evenly, each with the following interval:

$$interval = \frac{d_{max} - d_{min}}{K}$$

The range of the ith subrange $(1 \le i \le K)$ is $[d_{i,min}, d_{i,max}]$, where:

$$d_{i,min} = d_{min} + (i-1) \times interval$$

$$d_{i,max} = d_{min} + i \times interval$$

Then group all the data by subrange in the following way. Suppose d_j is the distance from the datum $\mathbf{x_j}$ to the origin, then $\mathbf{x_j}$ is in the range i if $d_{i,min} \le d_j \le d_{i,max}$. During the data grouping, the total of data c_i in every subrange is also counted. The time complexity of this step is $O(n)$.

Next, adjust the range of every subrange. The reason for implementing this step is that the data may be distributed among various subranges so unevenly and differently that the ranges will be empty or composed of abnormal data to finally affect the clustering performance. The method of subrange adjustment is as follows:

Step 1: Define the variables i and p_i, and initialize i as 1 and p_i as 0.

Step 2: If i = K, end the subrange adjustment; otherwise, go to the step 3.

Step 3: Suppose $p_i = p_i + c_i$, $p = p_i + c_{i+1}$, $p_1 = p_i/p$, $p_2 = c_{i+1}/p$, $l_1 = i/(i+1)$ and $l_2 = 1/(i+1)$. To better describe the process of subrange adjustment, the range i and the pre-i ranges may be called by a joint name "pre-i ranges". Then p_i is the total of data in the pre-i ranges, and p is the total of data in the pre-i+1 ranges (or the total of current data). p_1 and p_2 are the ratios between data totals: p_1 is the ratio of the data total of pre-i ranges to current data total, and p_2 is the ratio of the data total in the range i+1 to current data total. By the same token, l_1 and l_2 are the ratios between range lengths: l_1 is the ratio of the total length of pre-i ranges to that of current ranges, and l_2 is the ratio of the length of range i+1 to that of current ranges.

Step 4: If $p_1 > l_1$, it means the data density in the pre-i ranges is bigger than that in the range i+1 so that the pre-i ranges need to be scaled down by $dl = ((p_1 - l_1)/p_1) \times l1$; otherwise, the data density in the pre-i ranges is smaller than that in the range i+1 so that the pre-i ranges need to be scaled up by $dl = ((p1 - l_1)/p_2) \times l2/l1$.

Step 5: Calculate $d_{j,max} = d_{j,max} - d_{j,max} \times dl$ for every pre-i range, where there is $1 \leq j \leq i$.

Step 6: Suppose i = i+1. Then go to the step 2.

The time complexity of subrange adjustment is $O(K^2)$.

Regroup the data by using new subranges, and calculate the average of every group of data, which is just the initial cluster center. The time complexity of this step is $O(n)$.

Here the proposed initialization method comes to an end. Next is the subsequent iterations of K-means algorithm. The total time complexity of this initialization is $O(3n + K^2)$, which is actually linear $O(n)$, as K is a constant and $K \ll n$. But the method proposed by this paper features superlinear initialization rather than linear initialization. In other words, this method is deterministic, because no matter how many times the method is executed, the ranges for the same data set remain unchanged, so does the final clustering result.

The core of the proposed initialization method is subrange adjustment, whose aim is to enable uniform distribution of data in every subrange. This method applies to continuously distributed data, such as the data in [3], as the GPS direction during driving often changes continuously.

The algorithm in this paper, the algorithms in [11,12], and the K-means algorithm based on random initialization are used to cluster one data set in [3] respectively. Suppose m = 4 and K = 4. The learning curve shown in Fig. 1, where the vertical axis is SSE value, can be obtained. In the Fig. 1, "range" is the algorithm in this paper, "median" is the algorithm in [11], "mean" is the algorithm in [12], and "random" is the algorithm based on random initialization. It can be obviously seen from the figure that, the algorithm in this paper converges

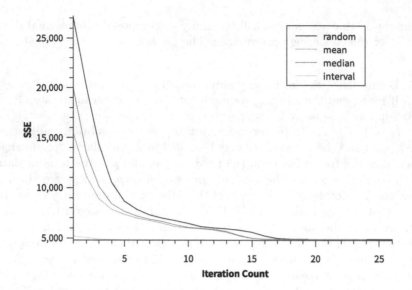

Fig. 1. Learning curves of four K-means clustering algorithms

fastest. In fact, it is iterated for 13 times, the algorithms in [11,12] for 24 times respectively, and the algorithm based on random initialization for 26 times. In addition, the final SSE is 4822.19 in the proposed algorithm and 4884.18 in the other three algorithms respectively.

3   Analysis of Experimental Results

The proposed algorithm can apply to the learning system of vehicle steering identification designed in [3] in order to speed up the identification modeling. To verify the actual application effect of the algorithm, this section introduces it into the learning system designed in [3] and through an experiment, evaluates the performance of the finally generated identification model as well as the execution speed of the algorithm.

The experiment uses the data in [3] for testing. The data are contained in two data sets, each sampled at a frequency of 1 Hz. The sampling mileage of data set 1 is 18.23 km, covering 2960 GPS points; whereas the sampling mileage of data set 2 is 11.58 km, covering 2370 GPS points.

The comparison objects in the experiment include the algorithm in this paper, the algorithms in [11,12], and the K-means algorithm based on random initialization. The comparison indicators include F_1 and the number of subsequent iterations of K-means algorithm, with the former reflecting the performance of identification model and the latter indirectly showing the speed of K-means clustering (i.e. the execution speed of the algorithm).

By testing the data set 1 with the four algorithms respectively, the results in Tables 1 and 2 can be obtained. It is observed from Table 1 that, the proposed

Table 1. F_1 values obtained from testing the data set 1 with the four algorithms

m	K	Random	Algorithm in [11]	Algorithm in [12]	Our algorithm	The best
3	4	0.86792	0.86792	0.86792	0.87711	Our algorithm
3	5	0.78226	0.78226	0.78226	0.87097	Our algorithm
4	4	0.89164	0.92141	0.92141	0.93175	Our algorithm
4	5	0.94461	0.89710	0.89710	0.94461	Our algorithm
5	4	0.93421	0.93421	0.93421	0.80000	Other algorithms
5	5	0.93421	0.95484	0.95484	0.93421	Other algorithms
6	4	0.80000	0.80000	0.80000	0.76316	Other algorithms
6	5	0.95971	0.95971	0.95971	0.82988	Other algorithms

Table 2. Number of subsequent iterations when clustering the data set 1 with the four algorithms

m	K	Random	Algorithm in [11]	Algorithm in [12]	Our algorithm	The best
3	4	26	28	27	18	Our algorithm
3	5	42	41	41	12	Our algorithm
4	4	26	24	24	13	Our algorithm
4	5	36	40	39	12	Our algorithm
5	4	19	21	20	6	Our algorithm
5	5	39	40	39	6	Our algorithm
6	4	23	27	26	5	Our algorithm
6	5	27	29	28	12	Our algorithm

algorithm performs best in 4 of all the 8 models. The average F_1 of the 4 models is 0.90611, 0.02706 higher than the algorithm in the second place; while the average F_1 of the other 4 models is 0.83181, 0.08038 lower than the algorithm in the first place. Besides, when m = 4 or m = 5, the F_1 values of optimal models are all greater than 0.9 and average 0.93941. It can be seen from the Table 2 that, the proposed algorithm is executed much faster and all the models are executed fastest, with 18.9 (or 64.3%) iterations fewer than the algorithm in the second place on average.

By testing the data set 2 with the four algorithms respectively, the results in Tables 3 and 4 can be obtained. It is observed from Table 3 that, the proposed algorithm performs best in 5 of all the 8 models. The average F_1 of the 5 models is 0.93818, 0.07999 higher than the algorithm in the second place; while the average F_1 of the other 3 models is 0.93351, 0.01947 lower than the algorithm in the first place. Besides, when m = 4 or m = 5, the F_1 values of optimal models are all greater than 0.9 and average 0.95117. It can be seen from the Table 4 that,

Table 3. F_1 values obtained from testing the data set 2 with the four algorithms

m	K	Random	Algorithm in [11]	Algorithm in [12]	Our algorithm	The best
3	4	0.84685	0.84685	0.84685	0.90716	Our algorithm
3	5	0.79832	0.79832	0.79832	0.90765	Our algorithm
4	4	0.93617	0.93617	0.93617	0.93293	Other algorithms
4	5	0.85787	0.85787	0.85787	0.94260	Our algorithm
5	4	0.96689	0.96689	0.96689	0.93426	Other algorithms
5	5	0.94631	0.94631	0.94631	0.95973	Our algorithm
6	4	0.92913	0.95588	0.95588	0.93333	Other algorithms
6	5	0.97358	0.97358	0.97358	0.97378	Our algorithm

Table 4. Number of subsequent iterations when clustering the data set 2 with the four algorithms

m	K	Random	Algorithm in [11]	Algorithm in [12]	Our algorithm	The best
3	4	40	40	40	8	Our algorithm
3	5	28	39	39	6	Our algorithm
4	4	19	28	27	5	Our algorithm
4	5	26	38	38	11	Our algorithm
5	4	15	19	19	12	Our algorithm
5	5	16	18	28	10	Our algorithm
6	4	26	18	18	5	Our algorithm
6	5	19	23	23	14	Our algorithm

the proposed algorithm is executed much faster and all the models are executed fastest, with 16.5 (or 62.8%) iterations fewer than the algorithm in the second place on average.

It is observed from the above two groups of test results that, the algorithm proposed by this paper performs best in 9 of all the 16 models. The average F_1 of the 9 models is 0.92393, 0.0418 higher than the algorithm in the second place; while the average F_1 of the other 7 models is 0.87540, 0.05428 lower than the algorithm in the first place. For the m value commonly used in practical application (m = 4 or m = 5), the average F_1 of its optimal models is 0.94529. Moreover, the subsequent iterations of K-means clustering based on the proposed algorithm are significantly reduced, with 16.3 (or 62.7%) iterations fewer than the algorithm in the second place on average. It is thus clear that, the identification model built upon the clustering algorithm proposed by this paper performs basically as well as the other 3 algorithms, while the common identification models using this algorithm perform slightly better but much faster.

4   Conclusion

This paper improves the initialization process of K-means clustering algorithm to effectively reduce subsequent iterations without compromising the clustering performance, which makes it suitable for large-scale data clustering [13,14]. The application of this algorithm to the learning system of vehicle steering identification can speed up the modeling of steering identification and guarantee the performance of identification model. The core concept of this algorithm is to calculate the value range of a data set in a certain aspect and then to reasonably group the data in this range in order to choose the initial cluster center. This paper uses the distances from data to the origin as the criterion of data division, which, in practical use, may be one dimension of those data as well. The selection of this criterion depends mainly on data distribution - an area to be explored more deeply.

Acknowledgment. This work is supported in part by the National High Technology Research and Development Program (863 Program) of China under Grant No. 2015AA015701, the Science and Technology Planning Project of Jilin Province under Grant No. 20150204081GX.

References

1. Aloise, D., Deshpande, A., Hansen, P., Popat, P.: NP-hardness of Euclidean sum-of-squares clustering. Mach. Learn. **75**(2), 245–248 (2009)
2. Mahajan, M., Nimbhorkar, P., Varadarajan, K.: The planar-means problem is NP-hard. Theoret. Comput. Sci. **442**, 13–21 (2012)
3. Qi, H., Liu, Y., Wei, D.: GPS-based vehicle moving state recognition method and its applications on dynamic in-car navigation systems. In: 2014 IEEE 12th International Conference on Dependable, Autonomic and Secure Computing, pp. 354–360 (2014)
4. Celebi, M.E., Kingravi, H.A., Vela, P.A.: A comparative study of efficient initialization methods for the K-means clustering algorithm. Expert Syst. Appl. **40**(1), 200–210 (2013)
5. Celebi, M.E.: Improving the performance of K-means for color quantization. Image Vis. Comput. **29**(4), 260–271 (2011)
6. Arthur, D., Vassilvitskii, S.: K-means++: the advantages of careful seeding. In: Proceedings of the Eighteenth Annual ACM-SIAM Symposium on Discrete Algorithms, Philadelphia, PA, USA, pp. 1027–1035 (2007)
7. Al-Daoud, M.B.: A new algorithm for cluster initialization. Int. J. Comput. Control Quantum Inf. Eng. **1**(4), 1016–1018 (2007)
8. Redmond, S.J., Heneghan, C.: A method for initialising the K-means clustering algorithm using kd-trees. Pattern Recogn. Lett. **28**(8), 965–973 (2007)
9. Hasan, M.A., Chaoji, V., Salem, S., Zaki, M.J.: Robust partitional clustering by outlier and density insensitive seeding. Pattern Recogn. Lett. **30**(11), 994–1002 (2009)
10. Nazeer, K.A.A., Sebastian, M.P.: Improving the accuracy and efficiency of the K-means clustering algorithm. In: World Congress on Engineering, WCE 2009, Hong Kong, China, vol. 1, pp. 308–312 (2009)

11. Yedla, M., Pathakota, S.R., Srinivasa, T.M.: Enhancing K-means clustering algorithm with improved initial centre. Int. J. Comput. Sci. Inf. Technol. **1**(2), 121–125 (2010)
12. Goyal, M., Kumar, S.: Improving the initial centroids of K-means clustering algorithm to generalize its applicability. J. Inst. Eng. (India): Ser. B **95**(4), 345–350 (2014)
13. Broder, A., Garcia-Pueyo, L., Josifovski, V., Vassilvitskii, S., Venkatesan, S.: Scalable K-means by ranked retrieval. In: Proceedings of the 7th ACM International Conference on Web Search and Data Mining, New York, NY, USA, pp. 233–242 (2014)
14. Cap, M., Prez, A., Lozano, J.A.: An efficient approximation to the K-means clustering for massive data. Knowl.-Based Syst. **117**, 56–69 (2017)

Nearest-Neighbor Restricted Boltzmann Machine for Collaborative Filtering Algorithm

Xiaodong Qian$^{(\boxtimes)}$ and Guoliang Liu

Lanzhou Jiaotong University, Lanzhou 730070, China
qianxd@mail.lzjtu.cn, 1185169269@qq.com

Abstract. Based on the restricted Boltzmann machine (RBM) collaborative filtering algorithm in recommendation phase easy to weaken the needs of individual users, and the model has poor ability of anti over-fitting. In this paper, the traditional nearest neighbor algorithm is introduced into the recommendation stage of RBM, use the characteristics of interest similarity, the nearest neighbor's interest is used as the target user's, strengthen the individual needs of users: First, using the traditional K-mean algorithm to find out the user's n nearest neighbors; Then, using nearest neighbor to calculate the probability of users rating grades for the non rating items; Finally, weighted average score probability to the RBM model in the process of recommendation. Using benchmark data set Movielens experimental results show that the improved RBM model with nearest neighbor can not only improve the accuracy of the model results, but also increase the ability to resist over-fitting.

Keywords: Restricted Boltzmann Machine · Nearest neighbor
Collaborative filtering · Accuracy · Over-fitting

Mathematics Subject Classification 2010: 68-W99

1 Introduction

With the rapid development of information technology in social, economic and other areas, data is increasing with hitherto unknown speed, according to the report released by the IDC show that [1], the total network data based on scale, diversity, real-time and low value density will increase from 1.8 ZB in 2011 to 35 ZB in 2020. Faced with such huge data, users can't accurately get information they want: from the point of consumers' view, consumers are overwhelmed by a flood of information, unable to find what they really need or surprise goods; from the point of business' view, the increasing amount of data led to the business can not dig out the user's real interest preferences and can not make accurate recommendations for the user's current interest, gradually lost the trust of users and the viscosity, resulting in the loss of customer resources. The above phenomena show that the increase of the amount of data results in the difficulty of data

© ICST Institute for Computer Sciences, Social Informatics and Telecommunications Engineering 2018
G. Sun and S. Liu (Eds.): ADHIP 2017, LNICST 219, pp. 387–398, 2018.
https://doi.org/10.1007/978-3-319-73317-3_45

mining and reduces the efficiency of information usage, leading to the problem of information overload [2].

At present, recommendation system is one of the most common methods to solve the problem of information overload. Collaborative filtering is the most widely used and successful recommendation strategy. According to the classification of collaborative filtering algorithm by Breese [3], collaborative filtering algorithm is mainly divided into two categories: memory based collaborative filtering and model-based collaborative filtering. The recommended process of memory based collaborative filtering is carried out through the analysis of the whole user item rating matrix, as if the whole score matrix exists in the memory, the core of the method is the calculation of similarity, the similarity calculation method commonly used Pearson Correlation Coefficient [4], Vector Space Similarity [3] and Jaccard Similarity Coefficient. The process of model-based collaborative filtering based on a model obtained by learning user item rating matrix, after the recommendation of the use of the model to replace the original user rating matrix, so the core of this method is to establish a user model, commonly used models including Bayesian Belief Networks model and Clustering model, Regression model, Latent Factor model, Singular Value Decomposition model and Restricted Boltzmann Machine model etc. In recent years, the Restricted Boltzmann Machine (RBM) because of its high accuracy and can be used as the underlying of deep learning, has attracted wide attention of scholars and research.

RBM is a two layer network which is composed of a softmax visible units and a binary hidden units. The RBM model is successfully applied to collaborative filtering recommendation for the first time by Salakhutdinov et al. [5], and puts forward the Conditional Restricted Boltzmann Machine (CRBM) can highlight the importance of rating data; Georgiev and Nakov [6] directly use real values in the visible unit of RBM model as opposed to multinomial variables, reduce the training parameters in the model, and the model can directly deal with the real data; Louppe [7] analysis the impact of various parameters in the RBM model on the Netflix data set and make a detailed comparison and experiment, and in the MapReduce to realize the parallel model; Zhang et al. [8] detailed introduction the RBM model for the training and learning process, parameter selection and evaluation model based on RBM algorithm; Luo [9] analysis of RBM model from the perspective of collaborative filtering, explain the intrinsic link between the RBM and collaborative filtering; He and Ma [10] based on Real_valued CRBM (R_CRBM) training prediction score, and then applied the nearset trusted relationships to the R_CRBM model in the recommended process to improve the accuracy of prediction and parallelization scheme is proposed based on Spark platform; Chen et al. [11] using multi-layer RBM building the depth of structure model, combined the abstract feature extracted from the model with nearest neighbor recommendation method formed a recommendation algorithm which can fast convergence and have high accuracy of recommendation.

This paper analyses from point of the internal principle of the RBM model prediction process view that the excessive growth of partial weight of RBM model is the main cause of poor model discrimination. The poor discrimination of the model leads to the lack of recognition of the individual needs of the user in the final recommendation stage based on the RBM model, thus weakening the user's personalized needs in the recommendation results, eventually resulting in reduced recommendation accuracy. Aiming at the above problems, this paper solves the problem by using the nearest neighbor method, and analyzes the internal mechanism of feasibility used nearest neighbor to improve the prediction accuracy of RBM model, and gives the method to implement the improved model. Unlike Chen Da and He Jieyue, this paper innovatively utilizes the nearest neighbor calculated score probability items which not score by the target user, the probability integrated into the prediction process in RBM model. The experimental results on the MovieLens data sets show that this method can effectively improve the prediction accuracy, it is proved that this method is helpful to solve the problem of poor model discrimination caused by excessive weight growth in RBM model, enhancing the individual needs of the users, improves the recommendation accuracy; at the same time proved by experiments the model of anti overfitting ability has been greatly improved.

The Sect. 2 introduces the collaborative filtering framework based on RBM model, and analyzes the problem existed in the model; Sect. 3 gives the improved RBM model and algorithm description; Sect. 4 show the experimental results of the algorithm and analysis of the results; finally summarized the work of the paper and the existing shortcomings.

2   Collaborative Filtering Framework Based on RBM Model

The main problem of applying RBM model to collaborative filtering algorithm is how to deal with the non scoring items effectively. The literature [5] first improved the visible units of the traditional RBM model, using Softmax cell as a visible units then introduced a special visible units "Missing" to represent the user with no score project, this kind of visible units is not connected with any hidden units. Each user has a separate RBM, but all RBM corresponding to a common hidden unit, and the weights and biases between all RBM are shared (i.e. if the user U_1 and U_2 at the same time scored the film M_1, and the scores were the same, then the two users in visible units and hidden units are used in connection with a same weight). The model is shown in Fig. 1. The RBM model is an energy model, define its energy function that its energy function is Eqs. 1 and 2:

$$E(V,h) = -\sum_{i=1}^{M}\sum_{j=1}^{F}\sum_{k=1}^{K} W_{ij}^k h_j v_i^k + \sum_{i=1}^{M} \log Z_i - \sum_{i=1}^{M}\sum_{k=1}^{K} v_i^k a_i^k - \sum_{j=1}^{F} h_j b_j \quad (1)$$

$$Z_i = \sum_{l=1}^{K} \exp(b_i^l + \sum_{j=1}^{F} h_j W_{ij}^l) \quad (2)$$

where W_{ij}^l is a symmetric interaction parameter between feature j and rating k of movie i; h_j is the binary values of hidden variables j; v_i^k is the user rated movie i as k; a_i^k is the bias of rating k for movie i; b_j is the bias of feature j.

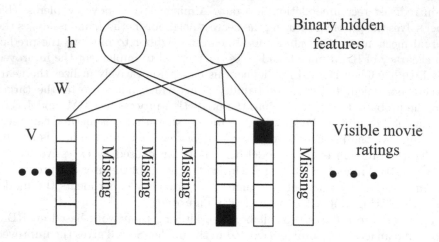

Fig. 1. Restricted Boltzmann Machine used in collaborative filtering

According to the Eqs. 1 and 2, we use the conditional probability (activation probability) for modeling 'hidden' user features h and the conditional probability (activation probability) for modeling 'visible' binary rating matrix V:

$$p(h_j = 1 \,|V\,) = \sigma(b_j + \sum_{i=1}^{M} \sum_{k=1}^{K} v_i^k W_{ij}^k) \tag{3}$$

$$p(v_i^k = 1 \,|h\,) = \frac{\exp(a_i^k + \sum_{j=1}^{F} h_j W_{ij}^k)}{\sum_{l=1}^{K} \exp(a_i^l + \sum_{j=1}^{F} h_j W_{ij}^l)} \tag{4}$$

where $\sigma(x) = 1/(1 + e^{-x})$ is the logistic function.

According to Eqs. 3 and 4 we can see that the training of RBM model is to maximize the generating probability. So we use Eqs. 5, 6 and 7 to update parameters:

$$\Delta W_{ij}^k = \frac{\partial \log p(V)}{\partial W_{ij}^k} = (<v_i^k h_j>_{data} - <v_i^k h_j>_{cd-\text{mod}\,el}) \tag{5}$$

$$\Delta a_i^k = \frac{\partial \log p(V)}{\partial a_i^k} = (<v_i^k>_{data} - <v_i^k>_{cd-\text{mod}\,el}) \tag{6}$$

$$\Delta b_j = \frac{\partial \log p(V)}{\partial b_j} = (<h_j>_{data} - <h_j>_{cd-\text{mod}\,el}) \tag{7}$$

where ∂ is the learning rate. $<\bullet>_{data}$ is an expectation with respect to the distribution defined by the user-rating data, v_i^k is movie i with rating k and h_j is feature j which is computed using Eq. 3. $<\bullet>_{cd-model}$ represents a distribution of samples from running the Gibbs sampler, using Contrastive Divergence (CD) algorithm present by Hinton [12] in 2002.

After training, the Mean Field Method is used to approximate the estimation of a user's score on the non-rating movies.

$$\hat{p}_j = p(h_j = 1 | V) = \sigma(b_j + \sum_{i=1}^{m} \sum_{k=1}^{K} v_i^k W_{ij}^k) \tag{8}$$

$$p(v_i^k = 1 | \hat{p}) = \frac{\exp(a_i^k + \sum_{j=1}^{F} p_j \hat{W}_{ij}^k)}{\sum_{l=1}^{K} \exp(a_i^l + \sum_{j=1}^{F} p_j \hat{W}_{ij}^l)} \tag{9}$$

The key of RBM used in collaborative filtering is how to predict the scores of Missing items. In order to solve this problem, the above model with each user has a separate RBM, all RBM corresponds to a common hidden units, and the weights between visible units and hidden units and the respective bias of all RBM is shared. By using the method of weight and bias sharing is considered the number of movies each user has rated is far less than all the movies, so the number of identical films that have been rated among different users is less, embodied in the model that the weights of the RBM model for different users are only partially overlapped.

However, in practical applications, the data tend to show the characteristics of the "long tail", "popular movie" will be viewed and rated by more users. When a "popular movie(i)" was repeatedly score and score most of r, due to the weight of all users are shared, every user who select the "popular movie" to enter the model training and the weight of w_i^r will be update. The RBM model tends to reconstruct the score of r so that the model is suitable for most users.

3   Improvement RBM and Algorithm Description Based on Nearest Neighbor

For the problems raised in the Sect. 2, analysis of RBM model training and prediction process discovery: in the training phase, the CD algorithm uses the parameter update, while CD algorithm aims at learning the characteristics of reduce the reconstruction error. When the user who scored r for "popular movie(i)" enters the model, in order to reduce the reconstruction error of the model, need the corresponding weight w_i^r is large enough to ensure that the reconstructed data is suitable for most users. Due to the weight sharing, when the score is r for many users, after CD algorithm w_i^r will be updated to very large, and other weight will be significantly less than w_i^r for the movie; in the stage of RBM model, using the mean field method for the prediction of film score, according to Eqs. 8 and 9 we can see the size of the weight can significantly affect the prediction of film scores. When the weight of w_i^r is very large, the prediction score will tend to score r. This makes it difficult to identify some special users, resulting in the model has poor ability to identify and reduce the accuracy of prediction.

Take <the godfather> as an example, many users have seen and its evaluation is very high (assuming that most users score 5 points). In order to reduce the reconstruction error during the learning process of model, learning the weight of w_i^5 will be large to apply to most users. So, namely <the godfather> of the film's score of 5 corresponds to the weight will be great, and the weight will be other scores is very small. When using the RBM model to predict the users who did not see the movie, the majority of the ratings would be 5. This leads to the fact that even users who do not like this kind of movie, but its forecast score will tend to 5 points.

According to the above analysis, reconstruction of CD algorithm in training phase and mean field method in the prediction stage is the main cause of discrimination is poor, so we can consider how to improve from two aspects of the RBM model training and prediction stage. But in the training stage of RBM model has a great influence on the model when changing its parameters, and more suitable parameter learning algorithms are also difficult to find. Therefore, this paper considers the improvement of the model prediction stage, in order to get good results.

The model is based on the mean field method in prediction, which is similar to the prediction results from the global perspective. In order to highlight the individual needs of users, should be from the user's point of view, taking into account the user's own unique interests, similar from the local point of view to strengthen user personalization. It is difficult to find out the unique interests of each user by using the user movie evaluation matrix as the historical data, so an indirect method (nearest neighbor) is used to estimate the user's interest. Users and their nearest neighbors have similar interests, so the interests of the user's nearest neighbor as a user's interest. Still take <the godfather> as an example, if the target user doesn't like this type of film, the target user may score lower on the film (2–3 points), there is a big gap between the apparently predicted by RBM model to score 5 points and the target user's true interest. In the process of model prediction model integration the nearest neighbor. The nearest neighbor, which is similar to the user's interest, does not like the film, they make score the film between 2–3 points, and according to the nearest neighbor prediction target users may also lower the score (2–3 points). Obviously lower score than predicted by the RBM model more accurate. Therefore, this paper considers the nearest neighbor into the RBM model to improve the accuracy of model prediction.

3.1 Improvement Ideas

According to the neighbor, calculate the rating level probability of the target user's un-rating film.

$$p_i^k = \frac{num^k}{sum} \tag{10}$$

where, p_i^k represents the probability of rating k of movie i which target user un-rating (The un-rating films restricted to target users who do not score and score in the nearest neighborhood, the rest of the films that nearest neighbor also did not score the probability of the film was 0); num^k is user number of rating k of movie i in nearest neighbor; sum represents the number of users in the nearest neighbor for all ratings of the movie i.

Then, the probability is added to the RBM model in the prediction process by the form of mixed weighting.

$$Q_i^k = \lambda * p(v_i^k = 1 \,|\hat{p}) + (1 - \lambda) * p_i^k \tag{11}$$

where, $p(v_i^k = 1 \,|\hat{p})$ and p_i^k respectively calculated by Eqs. 9, 10; λ is the weight of the calculated probability of the two calculation methods in the final results.

The estimated value of the target user's score for all the films is calculated based on Q_i^k.

$$R(u, i) = \sum_{k=1}^{K} Q_i^k * k \tag{12}$$

3.2   Algorithm Pseudo-code Description

Step 1. Compute nearest neighbor

Algorithm 1. k-Nearest Neighbor
___
1: Set $Nearest\ Neighbor's\ number \leftarrow n_{neighbor}$;
2: Use Pearson correlation coefficient compute each user's $similarity \leftarrow Sim(i,j)$;
3: Use Top $n_{neighbor}$ users with $Sim(i,j)$ as $user_i$ nearest neighbor;

Step 2. Initialization RBM

Algorithm 2. RBM-Initialize algorithm
___
1: Set Parameter $mini\_batches,\ max\_epoch,\ \theta,\ \rho,\ CD\_step$;
2: Initialize W_{ij}^k with small values sampled from a zero-mean normal distribution;
3: Initialize a_i^k to the log of their respective base rates;
4: Initialize b_j with zeroes.

Determine the training set S, and according to the number of data in mini_batches data, the training sample set is divided into $S = \overset{m}{\underset{i=1}{U}} S_i$ and no intersection between S_i; Adding momentum term to update parameters not only dependent on the gradient direction of the likelihood function in the current sample, but also depends on the direction of the last parameter modification, which helps to avoid premature convergence to local optima. Literature [5] has proved that in the practical application, the parameter step is very small usually can get satisfactory results even in step 1.

Step 3. Training RBM

Algorithm 3. RBM-Training algorithm

1: **repeat**
2: epoch=1:max_epoch
3: **for all** mini_batch of users in S_{batch} and $S_{batch} \in S$ **do**
4:   **for all** *user* $\in S_{batch}$ **do**
5:    Translate the ratings of user to Softmax as visible units v_i^k;
6:    Eq. 3 compute all the hidden units h_j;
7:    Record samples $v_i^k h_j$, v_i^k, h_j
8:    Run CD algorithm to the Gibbs sampler;
9:    **for** $step = 1 : CD\_step$ **do**
10:     Gibbs sampler all the hidden units $<h_j>^{step}$;
11:     Use Eq. 4 compute all the visible units $P(v_i^k = 1|h)$;
12:     Gibbs sampler all the visible units $<v_i^k>^{step}$;
13:     Use Eq. 3 compute all the hidden units h_j;
14:    **end for**
15:    Record samples$<v_i^k h_j>^{step}$, $<v_i^k>^{step}$, $<h_j>^{step}$;
16:   **end for**
17:   Average the first samples to get $<v_i^k \cdot h_j>_{data}$, $<v_i^k>_{data}$, $<h_j>_{data}$;
18:   Average the second samples to get $<v_i^k \cdot h_j>_{cd-model}$, $<v_i^k>_{cd-model}$, $< h_j>_{cd-model}$;
19:   Use Eqs. 5,6,7 compute ΔW_{ij}^k, Δa_i^k, Δb_j;
20:   Update $W_{ij}^k = \rho * W_{ij}^k + \theta * \Delta W_{ij}^k$;
21:   Update $a_i^k = \rho * a_i^k + \theta * \Delta a_i^k$;
22:   Update $b_j = \rho * b_j + \theta * \Delta b_j$;
23: **end for**
24: $epoch = epoch + 1$;
25: Compute the error Err_{epoch};
26: **until** $Err_{epoch-1} - Err_{epoch} > \varepsilon$ or $epoch = max\_epoch$

Step 4. Prediction

Algorithm 4. RBM-Initialize algorithm

1: Translate the ratings of user u to Softmax units;
2: Use Eq. 8 compute $\hat{p}_j$ for all hidden units j;
3: Use Eq. 9 compute $p(v_q^k = 1|\hat{p})$ for all $k = 1, 2..., K$;
4: Use Eq. 10 compute p_i^k;
5: Use Eq. 11 compute Q_i^k;
6: Use Eq. 12 compute $R(u, i)$;

---

4   Experimental Analysis

4.1   Data Sources

The experiment using Matlab 2015b, the data set using MovieLens 100K data set (http://www.grouplens.org) developed by Minnesota University GroupLens research group. Movielens data set is a film rating system, according to user preference score after viewing of the film are scores between 1 5, but also includes the theme of the film and user information. MovieLens 100K includes 943 users, 1682 movies and the score of 100000.

In the experiment, 80% of the data sets were randomly selected as the training set, and the remaining 20% were used as the test set. Each randomly divided data set using the standard RBM collaborative filtering algorithm as compared with the experimental reference algorithm, taking the average of the results of 10 experiments as the final prediction results. The experimental results are compared to test in the training and test sets are exactly the same situation.

4.2   Evaluating Indicator

At present, Root Mean Square Error (RMSE) is common measurement methods for evaluating the accuracy of recommender systems. The formula is as follows:

$$RMSE = \sqrt{\frac{\sum\limits_{(u,i)\in R_{test}} \left(R_{u,i} - \hat{R}_{u,i}\right)^2}{|N_{R_{test}}|}} \tag{13}$$

where, R_{test} is test data set; $R_{u,i}$ is user u actual score for movie i; $\hat{R}_{u,i}$ is user u prediction score for the movie i; $N_{R_{test}}$ represents the number of data in the test data set; The smaller the calculated results of the two evaluation indexes, the higher the accuracy of the recommendation.

4.3   Experimental Results and Analysis

Before the RBM model training and the paper algorithm, we must first determine the parameters of the model. The literature [7,8] on the choice of model parameters are introduced in detail. In this paper, we use the same experimental parameters for the paper algorithm and the RBM algorithm to ensure the accuracy and contrast of the experimental results. And the parameters are set in Table 1.

To determine the values of model parameters, because this algorithm contains the user's nearest neighbor, so it needs to consider the effect of different number of nearest neighbor users on the experimental results. So we need find the optimal user number of nearest neighbor. The calculation results are shown in Fig. 2.

From Fig. 2, the number of users nearest neighbor after reaching 10, its impact on RMSE tends to be stable. Therefore, this paper set up the user's nearest neighbor number to 20.

Table 1. Main parameters of the model

Parameter	Parameter values
Number of hidden units node	60
Weight decay coefficient	0.0005
Weight learning rate	0.001
Bias of visible units learning rate	0.001
Bias of hidden units learning rate	0.01
Iterations times	100
Iterations times of CD algorithm	3

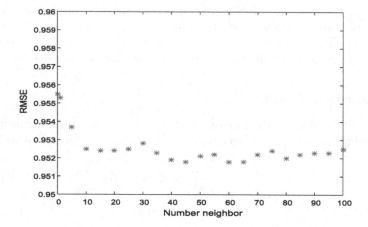

Fig. 2. Effect of different nearest neighbor number on RMSE

Figure 3 show that: the algorithm RMSE value has been less than RBM algorithm RMSE value shows that the accuracy of this algorithm is higher than that of the RBM algorithm; The improvement effect can be seen from Fig. 3, when the number of iterations is smaller and the number of iteration to achieve optimal effect (this is 40–50 times), the improved effect is more obvious. When the number of iterations reached 50, subsequent iterations will cause the overfitting problem and the value of RMSE to become larger. The recommendation accuracy of RBM algorithm will decrease rapidly, while this algorithm the recommendation accuracy decreasing speed was less than that of RBM algorithm. This show that the algorithm against over fitting ability is superior to RBM algorithm. show that: the algorithm RMSE value has been less than RBM algorithm RMSE value shows that the accuracy of this algorithm is higher than that of the RBM algorithm; The improvement effect can be seen from Fig. 3, when the number of iterations is smaller and the number of iteration to achieve optimal effect (this is 40–50 times), the improved effect is more obvious. When the number of iterations reached 50, subsequent iterations will cause the overfitting prob-

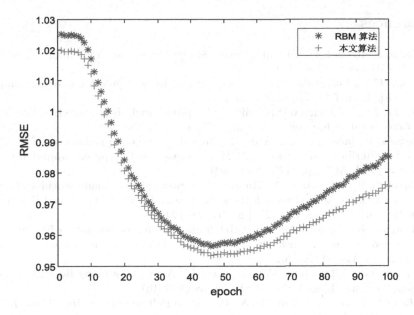

Fig. 3. Contrast experiment between the algorithm and RBM algorithm

lem and the value of RMSE to become larger. The recommendation accuracy of RBM algorithm will decrease rapidly, while this algorithm the recommendation accuracy decreasing speed was less than that of RBM algorithm. This show that the algorithm against over fitting ability is superior to RBM algorithm.

5   Conclusions

A good recommendation algorithm must first ensure the accuracy of recommendation. Therefore, improving the accuracy of recommendation is an important research direction. To provide users with the goods in line with their interests, can increase the user's satisfaction with the recommendation system, enhance the user's adhesion to the recommendation system. In this paper, the nearest neighbor is added to improve the discriminative ability of the RBM model. The experimental results show that the accuracy of the improved RBM model is better than that of the original model, and the over fitting ability of the model is improved. But this method is still not fully reflect the user interest, the target user's interest is calculated according to the nearest neighbor, and there are still some differences between the actual user and the individual interest. In the following work, will consider starting from the user's actual interest, fully tap the user's personal interests.

References

1. Gantz, J., Reinsel, D.: Digital Universe Study: Extracting Value from Chaos. IDC Go-to-Market Services (2011)
2. Wang, G.X., Liu, H.P.: Survey of personalized recommendation system. Comput. Eng. Appl. **48**(746(07)), 66–76 (2012)
3. Breese, J.S., Heckerman, D., Kadie, C.: Empirical analysis of predictive algorithms for collaborative filtering. New Page **7**(7), 43–52 (1998)
4. Resnick, P., Iacovou, N., Suchak, M.: GroupLens: an open architecture for collaborative filtering of netnews. In: ACM Conference on Computer Supported Cooperative Work ACM, pp. 175–186 (1994)
5. Salakhutdinov, R., Mnih, A., Hinton, G.: Restricted Boltzmann machines for collaborative filtering. In: Proceedings of the Twenty-Fourth International Conference on Machine Learning, vol. 227, pp. 791–798 (2007)
6. Georgiev, K., Nakov, P.: A non-IID framework for collaborative filtering with restricted Boltzmann machines. In: International Conference on Machine Learning, vol. 28, pp. 1148–1156 (2013)
7. Louppe, G.: Collaborative Filtering: Scalable Approaches Using Restricted Boltzmann Machine. Liége University Press, Liége (2010)
8. Zhang, C.X., Ji, N.N., Wang, G.W.: Restricted Boltzmann machines. Chin. J. Eng. Math. **32**(2), 159–173 (2015)
9. Lou, H.: Restricted Boltzmann Machines: A Collaborative Filtering Perspective. Shanghai Jiao Tong University Press, Shanghai (2011)
10. He, J.Y., Ma, B.: Based on real-valued conditional restricted Boltzmann machine and social network for collaborative filtering. Chin. J. Comput. **39**(1), 183–195 (2016)
11. Chen, D., Gao, S., Lin, Z.Q.: A survey on recommendation system algorithm based on restricted Boltzmann machine. Software **34**(12), 156–159 (2013)
12. Hinton, G.: Training products of experts by minimizing contrastive divergence. Neural Comput. **14**(8), 1771–1800 (2002)

A Low Energy Consumption Multi-sensor Data Fusion Method for Fan Coil Unit Thermal Performance Test

Cuimin Li[1], Jin Li[2(✉)], Bai Yu[2], and Lei Wang[3]

[1] School of Environmental Science and Engineering,
Suzhou University of Science and Technology, Suzhou 215163, China
li_cuimin@163.com
[2] School of Computer Science and Technology,
Harbin Engineering University, Harbin 150001, China
miaookok@163.com, baiyu@hrbeu.edu.cn
[3] Suzhou Institute of Biomedical Engineering and Technology,
Chinese Academy of Sciences, Suzhou 215163, China
wanglei@sibet.ac.cn

Abstract. The multi-sensor network can acquire and analyze the thermal performance data of fan coil unit and other building systems in real time by means of low energy and high precision sensing technology. It is necessary to compress the thermal data in the data transmission process. Aiming at the data fusion process applied to the thermal performance test system of fan coil unit, a new SMART-RR algorithm with low energy consumption data fusion is proposed. Considering the existence of cyclic repeatability and data redundancy, a time interval data fusion strategy of adding repeatability reduction factor is bedded in the algorithm. The simulation results show that the SMART-RR algorithm is a low energy consumption data fusion algorithm with low data communication volume and high accuracy.

Keywords: Multi-sensor network · Data fusion · Thermal performance test
Low energy consumption · Repeatability reduction

1 Introduction

The fan coil unit consists of fans, coils and filters. It is used as an end device for the air conditioning system. It is distributed in each air-conditioned room and can be treated independently for air. The hot and cold water required for air treatment by the air conditioning room focused on the preparation, through the water supply system to provide the fan coil unit. At present, most of the parameters of the fan coil system are used to cooperate with each other, and the multi-sensor data fusion is needed after acquiring the data.

Multi-sensor data fusion is a combination of data from multiple sensors, and this method could estimate the value of the measured parameters more accurately compared to the data measure method using only a single sensor, but there is still a lot of research work should be applied on the reliability of measurement data [1, 2]. The key

© ICST Institute for Computer Sciences, Social Informatics and Telecommunications Engineering 2018
G. Sun and S. Liu (Eds.): ADHIP 2017, LNICST 219, pp. 399–406, 2018.
https://doi.org/10.1007/978-3-319-73317-3_46

technologies of data fusion are data conversion, data correlation, database and fusion computing, among which fusion computing is the core technology of multi-sensor data fusion system. The general data fusion method is based on the basic principle of data statistics according to the data collected by each sensor to determine the confidence interval of each sensor matrix, and then uses the threshold to measure the degree of correlation between the sensors, but the threshold point to determine the sensor mutual support is a big ambiguity [3–5].

The thermal performance test system of fan coil units is the basis and support for teaching, testing and engineering testing of many disciplines such as construction engineering, environment and energy engineering, and there are many universities and research institutes have built fan coil performance test platform of different scales with corresponding test and control software system. In this paper, the data processing requirements of the thermal performance test system of fan coil are studied, discusses how to extract the multi modal data collected by multi sensor network, and proposes a data fusion method of fan system based on Bayesian network model and inference algorithm.

2 Fan Coil Thermal Performance Test System

There has a number of universities and research institutes have built different scale fan coil performance test platforms with the appropriate test and control software systems. In this paper, based on the original relevant test platform, re-build a complete set of fan coil performance test platform for teaching and research work. The fan coil performance test system topology is shown in Fig. 1.

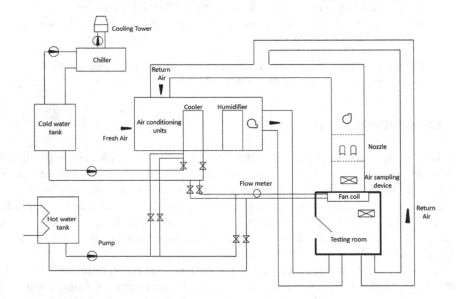

Fig. 1. Fan coil performance test system topology.

2.1 Low Energy Consumption Sensor Node

In the practical application of thermal performance test of fan coil, usually distributes and collects data with low energy and high precision sensor nodes.

First, each sensor node collects the test system thermal performance data with energy-constrained, and the energy consumption of the sensor nodes must be strictly controlled to extend the lifetime of the entire sensor network [6]. The energy of the sensor nodes in the thermal performance test system of the fan coil is mainly consumed in the network communication process, so it is necessary to minimize the data traffic and data redundancy between the sensor nodes.

Secondly, due to the external environment, such as electromagnetic interference, the sensor nodes should collect the data often accompanied by a variety of noise signals, witch reduce the accuracy of the obtained thermal performance data and integrity.

2.2 Data Acquisition Process Based on Multi-sensor Network

Fan coil performance test system is designed for independent design, build the fan coil performance test platform for research and development, and data acquisition Agilent-34970A, digital power meter Yokogawa-WT310 and other hardware work together to collect test room in the fan disk pipe, air conditioning unit inlet and outlet temperature, humidity, pressure, water flow and other technical parameters, real-time record of the node's test data, and through the software system to calculate the corresponding cooling/heating performance indicators.

The thermal data in the fan coil performance test platform is mainly collected by the Agilent 34970A data acquisition and YOKOGAWA WT310 digital power meter. The data interface is connected with the computer supporting the test platform, and the collected test platform thermal data is transmitted to Client application system, that is, the project development of the fan coil performance test system V1.0. The software system can complete the test condition parameter setting, the data record, the test platform real-time monitoring, the data computation processing and the test report generation and the printing function. A fan coil performance test system consisting of a data collector, a digital power meter, a matching computer, and a client application system.

3 Low Energy Data Fusion Method Based on Reproducibility Reduction

Fan coil performance test system in a variety of sensor nodes to obtain fan coil system thermal performance data through the tree sensor network layer by layer upload and fusion, data transmission traffic and encryption and decryption mechanism affect the thermal performance data privacy protection And sensor network energy consumption. In this paper, the sensor network is abstracted into a tree network with three layers. A data fusion algorithm based on repetitive protocol factor is proposed, and the data traffic is reduced by key distribution mechanism.

3.1 Data Fusion Model Based on Tree Structure

The sensor network may be represented by a connected directed graph $G(V, E)$, where the vertex $v(v \in V)$ represents the node in the sensor network and the directed arc $e(e \in E)$ represents the data transmission link between the nodes. A typical sensor network typically consists of three types of nodes: (1) a leaf node consisting of a variety of sensors for collecting and transmitting thermal data from the system; (2) a fusion node, the data transmission node undertaking to collect system thermal data and data fusion (3) QS (Query Server) node, the data analysis node is responsible for the final fusion analysis of the data [7].

The three types of nodes form a tree structure, where the QS node obtains the data fusion result as the root node and provides the basis for further thermal data analysis. The fusion node is responsible for receiving the data from the leaf node and converging the calculation to the root node, the leaf node acquires a variety of modal thermal data and upload to the corresponding node, based on the tree structure of the data fusion process is one-way transmission.

The data fusion function structure currently used in the sensor network can be expressed as the formula (1):

$$f(t) = \theta(d_1(t), \ldots, d_n(t)) \tag{1}$$

where $d_i(t)$, $(i = 1, 2, \ldots, n)$ is the data collected by node i at time t, and operator θ represents the fusion calculation factor, such as count, average, max, min, sum function.

As a sensor network in the field of energy measurement applications, the fan coil performance test system to collect the transmission of thermal data has a certain periodicity characteristics. It can consider the characteristics of the above fields in the design of the data fragmentation and transmission strategy of the sensor network, compress the processing of a large number of periodic data, and collect the change data, thus reducing the data traffic of the sensor network. This paper proposes a data fusion function based on unequal time interval as shown in Eq. (2):

$$f'(t) = \theta(d_1(\Delta t_1), \ldots, d_n(\Delta t_n)) \tag{2}$$

where $d_i(\Delta t_i)$ $(i = 1, 2, \ldots, n)$ is the data collected by the node i in the Δt_i time interval and $t = [\Delta t_1, \ldots, \Delta t_n]$ is the minimum common time period for all node data acquisition time intervals. For periodically significant thermal data, the time interval can be set relatively long, and remove some of the repeated data, which can reduce the data traffic, improve data fusion efficiency.

3.2 Data Fusion Algorithm Based on Reproducibility Reduction Factor

Based on the SMART series algorithm, this paper proposes a data fusion algorithm based on the repetitive reduction factor for the sensor network application.

Data encryption and decryption uses a random key allocation strategy: a key pool containing K keys is generated, and k $(k < K)$ keys are randomly selected; nodes in the sensor network send messages to determine which nodes are assigned the same key, A node with the same key thinks that a data transmission link can be established. If the parent and child nodes in the tree structure are not allocated to obtain the same key, the transmission link can be established by hop-by-hop. As can be seen from the key distribution strategy, if the listener takes the same key distribution scheme, the probability of data being eavesdropped in the sensor network is $p = k/K$. In general, the number of keys in the key pool is set relative to each other, thereby reducing the probability of data being eavesdropped in the sensor network.

The basic structure of the algorithm consists of three main steps: (1) each node divides the collected data into J slices, where $J - 1$ slices are sent to $J - 1$ nodes randomly selected from neighboring node sets; (2) the node receives the fragment data and decrypts it with the shared key; (3) uses the TAG algorithm to carry on the data fusion. Some of the modal data in the sensor network have significant periodic repeatability [8]. The SMART-RC algorithm with repetitive reduction factor is used to divide the data acquisition and transmission time interval into different time slices according to different modal data., And the time slice of the cycle of repetitive data to reduce the amount of data traffic to reduce the sensor network energy consumption.

4 Analysis of Results

In order to verify the performance of the SMART-RR algorithm based on the repetitive convention factor proposed in this paper, we compare the data traffic and accuracy from the data and compare the SMART-RR algorithm with the TAG algorithm and SMART algorithm.

4.1 Data Communication Volume

The data traffic used in the sensor network data fusion algorithm mainly includes node fragment data transmission traffic and data fusion traffic. Data fusion communication is directly related to the network size, that is, the sensor network structure and the number of nodes to determine the data fusion communication fixed. Therefore, the comparison of SMART-RR algorithm and SMART algorithm node data communication volume, which is based on data fragmentation data fusion algorithm, the main communication volume overhead. TAG, SMART, SMART-RR three methods of data traffic shown in Fig. 2, where J is 3.

It can be seen from the simulation results that the data communication volume of SMART and SMART-RR algorithm is smaller than that of TAG algorithm due to the addition of data fragmentation strategy, and because SMART-RR has a certain reduction operation on the existence of repetitive data, data communication volume is further compressed. The relationship between the number of slices and the data communication volume of SMART-RR algorithm is further analyzed. From the simulation results of Fig. 3, it can be seen that the data traffic increases first and then decreases with the increase of J.

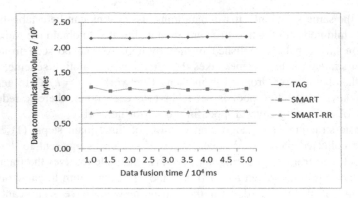

Fig. 2. Data communication volume of TAG, SMART and SMART-RR algorithm

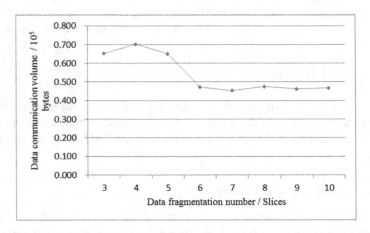

Fig. 3. Data communication volume changes of SMART-RR with the number of slices

4.2 Measurement Accuracy

The SMART-RR algorithm and SMART algorithm proposed in this paper are based on SUM function data fusion calculation [8, 9], the definition of data accuracy is:

$$ma = |D_{QS}|/|\sum D_i| \tag{3}$$

where $|D_{QS}|$ is the amount of data for the root node after fusion, and $|\sum D_i|$ is the amount of raw data collected by all sensor nodes. As shown in Fig. 4, the data accuracy of the SMART-RR algorithm is more sensitive to the number of slices: when $J \geq 5$ the accuracy is significant improved, and the accuracy tends to be stable when $J \geq 8$.

From the simulation analysis of the algorithm data traffic and accuracy, it can be seen that the setting of data segment J in SMART-RR algorithm directly affects the performance of the algorithm, and it should be selected in the practical application according to the specific requirements such as privacy protection.

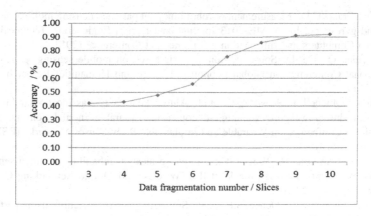

Fig. 4. The accuracy of the SMART RR algorithm varies with the number of slices

5   Conclusions

In this paper, a data fusion algorithm based on repetitive reduction factor is proposed for the data fusion and analysis of sensor networks used in the thermal performance test system of fan coil. It is possible to carry out data for data with dynamic repetition of data cycle Compression, thereby reducing the sensor node data traffic and energy consumption, to extend the sensor network survival time. The performance of the algorithm in data traffic and accuracy is verified by simulation experiment and comparison, which has certain advantages in the field of data acquisition and application of sensor network compared with the same type of algorithm. Further work could study other data fusion strategies and algorithms to collect more practical case analysis algorithm application value.

Acknowledgment. This work was supported by the project of National Import Research Priorities Program (2016YFB0801004), Heilongjiang Province Natural Science Youth Fund (QC2012C116), Jiangsu Province Policy Guidance Program (Research Cooperation)-Prospective Joint Research Project (BY2016049-01), Science and Technology Planning Project of Jiangsu Provincial Department of Construction (2015ZD83) and Natural Science Research Project of Universities of Jiangsu Province (16KJB560015).

Special thanks to referees who provided us constant support and help in a previous version of this article.

References

1. Ghasemzadeh, H., Amini, N., Sarrafzadeh, M.: Energy-efficient signal processing in wearable embedded systems: an optimal feature selection approach. In: 2012 ACM/IEEE International Symposium on Low Power Electronics and Design, pp. 357–362 (2012)
2. Plasqui, G., Bonomi, A., Westerterp, K.: Daily physical activity assessment with accelerometers: new insights and validation studies. Obes. Rev. **14**(6), 451–462 (2013)

3. Vikas, V., Crane, C.D.: Measurement of robot link joint parameters using multiple accelerometers and gyroscope. In: ASME 2013 International Design Engineering Technical Conferences and Computers and Information in Engineering Conference (2013)
4. Wei, Y., Fei, Q., He, L.: Sports motion analysis based on mobile sensing technology. In: International Conference on Global Economy, Finance and Humanities Research (GEFHR 2014) (2014)
5. Ahmadi, A., Mitchell, E., Destelle, F., et al.: Automatic activity classification and movement assessment during a sports training session using wearable inertial sensors. In: 11th International Conference on Wearable and Implantable Body Sensor Networks (BSN 2014), pp. 98–103 (2014)
6. Talasila, M., Curtmola, R., Borcea, C.: Improving location reliability in crowd sensed data with minimal efforts. In: 2013 6th Joint IFIP Wireless and Mobile Networking Conference (WMNC), pp. 1–8 (2013)
7. Carreno, P., Gutierrez, F., Ochoa, S.F., et al.: Supporting personal security using participatory sensing. Concurr. Comput.-Pract. Exp. 27(10), 2531–2546 (2015)
8. He, W., Liu, X., Nguyen, H., et al.: PDA: privacy-preserving data aggregation in wireless sensor networks. In: Proceeding of the 26th IEEE International Conference on Computer Communications, Anchorage, AK, pp. 2045–2053 (2007)
9. Castelluccia, C., Mykletun, E., Tsudik, G.: Efficient aggregation of encrypted data in wireless sensor networks. In: Proceeding of the 2nd Annual International Conference on Mobile and Ubiquitous Systems: Networking and Services, San Diego, USA, pp. 109–117 (2005)

Performance Analysis of Sparsity-Penalized LMS Algorithms in Channel Estimation

Jie Yang[✉], Hao Huang, Jie Wang, Sheng Hong, Zijian Hua,
Jian Zhang, and Guan Gui[✉]

College of Telecommunication and Information Engineering,
Nanjing University of Posts and Telecommunications, Nanjing 210003, China
{jyang, guiguan}@njupt.edu.cn

Abstract. Least mean squares (LMS) algorithm was considered as one of the effective methods in adaptive system identifications. Different from many unknown systems, LMS algorithm cannot exploit any structure characteristics. In case of sparse channels, sparse LMS algorithms are proposed to exploit channel sparsity and thus these methods can achieve better estimation performance than standard one, under the assumption of Gaussian noise environment. Specifically, several sparse constraint functions, ℓ_1-norm, reweighted ℓ_1-norm and ℓ_p-norm, are developed to take advantage of channel sparsity. By using different sparse functions, these proposed methods are termed as zero-attracting LMS (ZA-LMS), reweighted ZA-LMS (RZA-LMS), reweighted ℓ_1-norm LMS (RL1-LMS) and ℓ_p-norm LMS (LP-LMS). Our simulation results confirm the priority of the new algorithm and show that the proposed sparse algorithms are superior to the standard LMS in number scenarios.

Keywords: Gradient descent · Least mean squares · Sparse constraint
Adaptive channel estimation · Compressive sensing

1 Introduction

Second-order statistical errors square based on the least mean square (LMS) algorithm has been considered one of the effective adaptive filtering methods in many applications such as channel estimation and system identification [1, 2], which is a kind of stochastic gradient algorithm. Superior to some other parameter estimation methods, e.g., recursive least squares (RLS) [3] algorithm, the LMS algorithm has the advantage that mass stochastic knowledge of the channel and the input data sequence are not required. Due to its simplicity and easy implementations, the LMS algorithm has been widely applied in signal processing and communications including system detection [4] and channel estimation [5] and so on, without considering any information about the special characteristics of the channel being estimated itself. However, due to the potential sparsity in channels [6–10], some great efforts have been made to develop such LMS algorithms that can employ the potential sparsity and achieve better parameter estimation. The method based on the idea is to add a penalty term to the cost function to perform sparse solution [11, 12]. In a typical fading communication system, the selection of the channel estimation algorithms involves the statistical information

© ICST Institute for Computer Sciences, Social Informatics and Telecommunications Engineering 2018
G. Sun and S. Liu (Eds.): ADHIP 2017, LNICST 219, pp. 407–416, 2018.
https://doi.org/10.1007/978-3-319-73317-3_47

with respect to channels, the expected performance of the used algorithm and its convergence speed.

This paper is organized as follows. First we introduce the communication system model and corresponding linear adaptive algorithms. According to the given model, a standard LMS algorithm and the modifications of the LMS algorithm are provided. Particularly, the sparse channel estimation problem is considered and the sparse CIR is estimated. At last, we confirmed the effectiveness of our study.

2   System Model and Algorithms

Figure 1 shows the system model of a typical communication system in this paper. Assume that the channel vector $\boldsymbol{h} = [h_1, h_2, \ldots, h_N]^{\mathrm{T}}$ where N is the length of the CIR and $(\cdot)^{\mathrm{T}}$ denotes the transposition. $\boldsymbol{h}_k = [h_{1,k}, h_{2,k}, \ldots, h_{N,k}]^T$ denotes the estimate of the vector $\boldsymbol{h}$ at the time step k. $\boldsymbol{x}_k = [x_k, x_{k-1}, \ldots, x_{k-N+1}]^T$ is the input data vector of the system, n_k is the additive noise at the receiver end, d_k is the actual response, $e_k = d_k - \boldsymbol{h}_k^T \boldsymbol{x}_k$ is the error signal, y_k is the system output and $\hat{y}_k$ denotes its estimate.

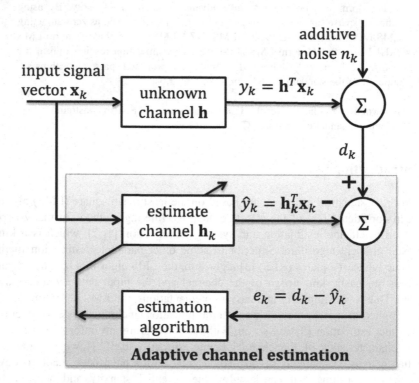

Fig. 1. Block diagram of the communication system.

2.1   Standard LMS Algorithm

Let $L_k = (1/2)e_k^2$ denotes the cost function of the standard LMS algorithm. By minimizing the cost function using the gradient descent method, the parameters of the unknown system can be identified iteratively. Therefore, the iterative equation can be given as

$$h_{k+1} = h_k - \mu \frac{\partial L_k}{\partial h_k} = h_k + \mu e_k x_k \qquad (1)$$

Here, μ is the step size which is among 0 and $\lambda_{\max}^{-1}$, where $\lambda_{\max}$ is the maximum eigenvalue of the covariance matrix of x_k (i.e., $\mathbf{R} = \mathrm{E}[x_k x_k^T]$), which ensures that the standard LMS algorithm converges to the optimum point.

2.2   ZA-LMS Algorithm

If most of the coefficients in the vector h are zeros or insignificant values, then the CIR is called sparse channel. In this case, the l_1-norm of h_k can be used to penalize the non-sparse solutions. Add it to the standard LMS cost function and then we can get the new cost function $L_k^{ZA} = (1/2)e_k^2 + \gamma_{ZA}\|h_k\|_{l_1}$, where $\|.\|_{l_1}$ denotes the l_1-norm of a vector and γ_{ZA} is a corresponding weight for the penalty term. It's remarkable that the new cost function is convex, so that the gradient descent method can be guaranteed to be convergent under some conditions. The corresponding algorithm is called the zero attracting LMS (ZA-LMS) and its iterative formula is

$$h_{k+1} = h_k + \mu e_k x_k - \rho_{ZA} sgn(h_k) \qquad (2)$$

where $\rho_{ZA} = \mu \gamma_{ZA}$ and signum function $sgn(\cdot)$ is denoted as 0 for x = 0, 1 for x > 0, and -1 for x < 0 and $sgn(h_k)$ is the sparse penalty strength of the ZA-LMS.

2.3   RZA-LMS Algorithm

To take more advantage of the sparsity of the channel, we can use the l_0-norm to penalize the non-sparse solutions. However, since l_0-norm penalty has very high computation complexity, a approximate penalty is introduced. And then the cost function becomes

$$L_k^{RZA} = \left(\frac{1}{2}\right)e_k^2 + \gamma_{RZA} \sum_{i=1}^{N} \log(1 + \frac{h_{ki}}{\in_{RZA}'}) \qquad (3)$$

where h_{ki} is the i-th entry of the channel weights h_k. γ_{RZA} and $\in_{RZA}'$ are some positive numbers. Since the logarithmic constraint in (3) that resembles the l_0-norm penalty can describe the sparse channel more accurate, it is expected that the corresponding algorithm which is defined as the reweighted ZA-LMS (RZA-LMS) will gain a more accurate estimation than the ZA-LMS. The iterative formula of the corresponding algorithm is

$$h_{k+1} = h_k + \mu e_k x_k - \rho_{RZA} \frac{sgn(h_k)}{1 + \in_{RZA} |h_k|} \tag{4}$$

where $\rho_{RZA} = \mu \gamma_{RZA} \in_{RZA}$, $\in_{RZA} = 1/ \in'_{RZA}$, absolute value $|\cdot|$, and $\frac{sgn(h_k)}{1+\in_{RZA}|h_k|}$ is the sparse penalty strength of the RZA-LMS.

2.4 LP- LMS Algorithm

In order to further obtain sparse information, p-norm (where p is among 0 and 1) spare function is adopted in LMS-type channel estimation. We called it as for LP-LMS algorithm. The new function is more close to the l_0-norm and as the value of p becomes smaller, it resembles the l_0-norm more. Thus, the cost function of LP-LMS algorithm is given as

$$L_k^{l_p} = \left(\frac{1}{2}\right) e_k^2 + \gamma_p ||h_k||_{l_p} \tag{5}$$

where $||.||_{l_p}$ denotes the l_p-norm of the vector and γ_p denotes the corresponding weight term. It is notice that the cost function (5) is nonconvex and the analysis of the global convergence and consistency of the corresponding algorithm is problematic. However, as it will be seen in the next section, the method based on (5) shows better performance than the RZA-LMS which faces the same problems. Using gradient descent, the update equation based on (5) can be derived as

$$h_{k+1} = h_k + \mu e_k x_k - \rho_p \frac{\left(||h_k||_p\right)^{1-p} sgn(h_k)}{\in_p + |h_k|^{1-p}} \tag{6}$$

where $\rho_p = \mu \gamma_p$, $\in_p$ is some number near to zero and $\frac{\left(||h_k||_p\right)^{1-p} sgn(h_k)}{\in_p + |h_k|^{1-p}}$ is the sparse penalty strength of the l_p-norm penalized LMS.

2.5 RL1-LMS Algorithm

One of alternative way to exploit channel sparsity by using RL1 penalty in accordance with mean square error term. This method considers a penalty term proportional to the reweighted l_1-norm of the coefficient vector. Compared to the standard l_1-norm minimization, this method can get better channel estimation performance. The mentioned cost function above can be written as

$$L_k^{rl1} = \left(\frac{1}{2}\right) e_k^2 + \gamma_r ||s_k h_k||_{l_1} \tag{7}$$

where γ_r is a tradeoff parameter and RL1 row vector s_k are given as

$$[s_k]_i = \frac{1}{\epsilon_r + |[h_{k-1}]_i|}, i = 1, \ldots, N \qquad (8)$$

with small positive parameter ϵ_r. Hence, the RL1-LMS algorithm is derived as

$$h_{k+1} = h_k + \mu e_k x_k - \rho_r \frac{sgn(h_k)}{\epsilon_r + |h_{k-1}|} \qquad (9)$$

where $\rho_r = \mu \gamma_r$ and $\frac{sgn(h_k)}{\epsilon_r + |h_{k-1}|}$ is the sparse penalty strength of the reweighted l_1-norm penalized LMS.

3 Simulation Results

Compared with the standard LMS algorithm, other modified LMS algorithms take the sparsity of the CIR into account. Figure 2(a) is a sparse vector (the number of non-zero values is much smaller than the total length of the vector) diagram. Figure 2(b) shows the sparse penalty strengths for the algorithms tested versus the coefficient component of the estimate h_k of the vector h at the time step k where the CIR is assumed to $h_k = [-1 : 0.001 : 1]$ for all algorithms and p is set to 0.5 in the ℓ_p-norm penalized method. For the ZA-LMS, the sparse penalty strength is zero at the position of zero and is the value of 1 at the non-zero position. Therefore, when the sparse channel vector is disturbed by noise, the value of the sparse position may fluctuate near the value of 0 and the ZA-LMS algorithm can result in obvious errors. However, for the RZA-LMS, the ℓ_p-norm penalized LMS and reweighted ℓ_1-norm penalized LMS, the closer to the value of zero the value of the sparse channel vector coefficient is, the greater the sparse penalty strength is and the higher the probability of taking zero is; the farther away from the value of zero the value of the sparse channel vector coefficient is, the smaller the sparse penalty strength is and the lower the probability of taking zero is. Overall, the sparse penalty strength of the ℓ_p-norm penalized LMS is greater than that of the reweighted ℓ_1-norm penalized LMS and the sparse penalty strength of the reweighted ℓ_1-norm penalized LMS is greater than that of the RZA-LMS.

As is shown in Fig. 3, ZA-LMS, RZA-LMS, the ℓ_p-norm penalized LMS and the reweighted ℓ_1-norm penalized LMS take different regularization parameters to obtain simulation results of MSEs in contrast to the number of iterations respectively in the other same conditions. The step size is set to $\mu = 0.05$ and the signal-to-noise ratio (SNR) is set to 10 dB, which implies that the MSEs are averaged at 2000 simulations. The length of the CIR is 16 and the sparsity level is set to 1, which means that there is only one nonzero tap in the CIR, but the nonzero position is allocated randomly. The other parameters are set to $\epsilon_{RZA} = 10$, $\epsilon_{lp} = \epsilon_{rl1} = 0.05$, $p = 0.5$. Figure 3 shows the convergence speed and the steady state MSE is related to ρ and ρ is larger, the convergence speed is faster but the MSE is also larger at steady state. With ρ decreasing, the MSE of the steady state decreases first, then increases. The minimum steady state MSEs of ZA-LMS, RZA-LMS, the ℓ_p-norm penalized LMS and the reweighted ℓ_1-norm penalized LMS appear in $\rho = 10^{-3}, \rho = 10^{-2}, \rho = 10^{-1}, \rho = 10^0$, respectively.

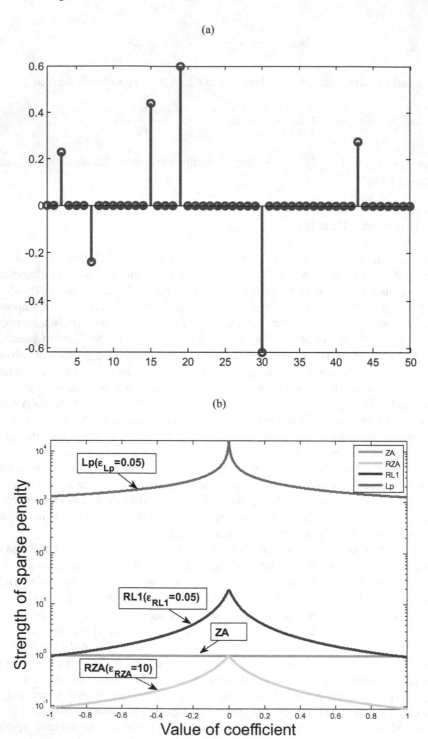

Fig. 2. Strengths of sparse penalty of different estimation algorithms vs number of iterations.

(a)

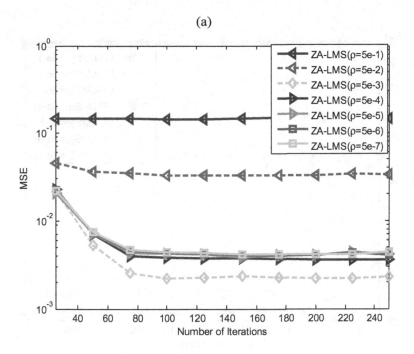

(b)

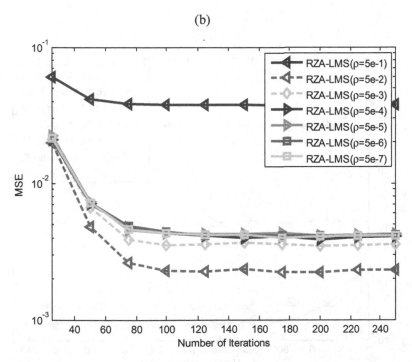

Fig. 3. MSE comparisons with respect to iterations in SNR = 10 dB.

(c)

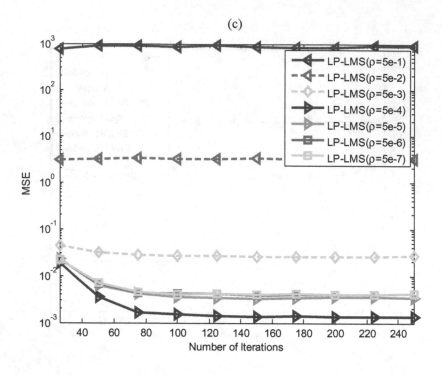

(d)

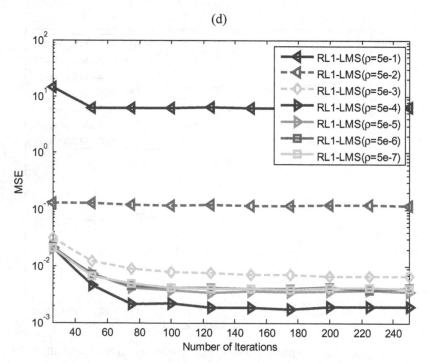

Fig. 3. (*continued*)

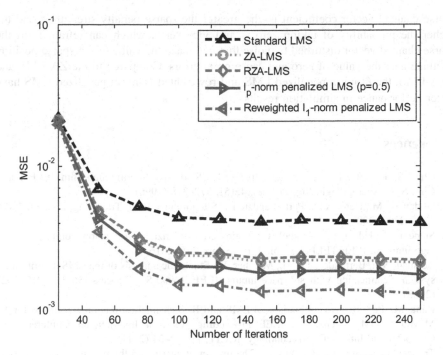

Fig. 4. MSE comparisons with respect to iterations in SNR = 20 dB.

Figure 4 indicates the MSEs of different estimation algorithms with respect to iterations in SNR = 10 dB. The performance of the improved sparse LMS algorithms is compared to that of the standard LMS. The step size is set to $\mu = 0.05$, the signal-to-noise ratio (SNR) is set to 20 dB, the channel length of the CIR is 16, the sparsity level is set to 1 and number of iterations is 2000 times for all LMS algorithms. The other parameters are set to $\epsilon_{RZA} = 10, \epsilon_{lp} = \epsilon_{rl1} = 0.05, p = 0.5$. This can be observed by observing Fig. 4. It is worth noting that both ZA-LMS and RZA-LMS algorithms demonstrate very close performance, while they are much better than LMS. In case of the MSE curves shown in the Fig. 4, it can also be concluded that the reweighted ℓ_1-norm penalized LMS has better performance than the ℓ_p-norm penalized LMS. By examining Fig. 4, it can also be seen that both the reweighted l1-norm and the ℓ_p-norm penalized LMS algorithms have better performance than ZA-LMS and RZA-LMS algorithms.

4   Conclusions

This paper considers the sparsity of the communication system and applies the sparisty to channel estimation with LMS algorithms. Quantitative simulations and analysis indicates that the improved LMS algorithms outperform the standard LMS algorithm with regard to sparse CIR. In addition, for the RZA-LMS, the ℓ_p-norm penalized LMS and reweighted ℓ_1-norm penalized LMS, the closer to the value of zero the value of the sparse channel vector coefficient is, the greater the sparse penalty strength is and the higher the probability of taking zero is and vice versa, which can refrain from the sparse channel vector disturbed by noise that can make the value of the sparse position fluctuate near the value of zero and cause great errors. Compared to the ZA-LMS and RZA-LMS, the ℓ_p-norm penalized LMS and reweighted ℓ_1-norm penalized LMS have better performance in simulation results.

References

1. Chen, S., Kao, Y., Tsai, K.: A new efficient LMS adaptive filtering algorithm. IEEE Trans. Circ. Syst. Analog Digit. Sig. Process. **43**(5), 372–378 (1996)
2. Godavarti, M., Hero, A.O.: Partial update LMS algorithms. IEEE Trans. Sig. Process. **53**(7), 2382–2399 (2005)
3. Stanciu, C., Udrea, M., Anghel, C.: Improved regularization for a low-complexity RLS algorithm. In: IEEE TELFOR, vol. 2, no. 5, pp. 2–5 (2016)
4. Bershad, N.J., Bermudez, J.C.M., Member, S.: Stochastic analysis of the LMS algorithm for system identification with subspace inputs. IEEE Trans. Sig. Process. **56**(3), 1018–1027 (2008)
5. Rana, M.: Performance comparison of LMS and RLS channel estimation algorithms for 4G MIMO OFDM systems. In: IEEE Proceedings of 14th International Conference on Computer and Information Technology, ICCIT, pp. 22–24 (2011)
6. Truhachev, D., Schlegel, C., Yin, D.: The impact of filtering on the resolution of sparsity in channel estimation for OFDM systems. IEEE Ultra Maritime Digital Communications Centre, no. 1 (2016)
7. Zhang, J., Zhang, Y., Yawei, Y., Ruijie, X., Zheng, Q., Zhang, P.: 3D MIMO: how much does it meet our expectation observed from channel measurements? IEEE J. Sel. Areas Commun. **35**(8), 1887–1903 (2017)
8. Zhang, J., Tang, P., Tian, L., Hu, Z., Wang, T., Haiming, W.: 6–100 GHz research progress and challenges for fifth generation (5G) and future wireless communication from channel perspective. SCIENCE CHINA Inf. Sci. **60**(8), 1–16 (2017)
9. Rappaport, T.S., Xing, Y., MacCartney Jr., G.R., Molisch, A., Mellios, E., Zhang, J.: Overview of millimeter wave channel models for fifth-generation wireless networks. IEEE Trans. Antennas Propag. **PP**(99), 1 (2017)
10. Zhang, J., Pan, C., Pei, F., Liu, G., Chen, X.: Three-dimensional fading channel models: a survey of elevation angle research. IEEE Commun. Mag. **52**(6), 218–226 (2014)
11. Taheri, O., Vorobyov, S.A.: Reweighted L1-norm penalized LMS for sparse channel estimation and its analysis. Sig. Process. **104**, 70–79 (2014)
12. Taheri, O., Vorobyov, S.A.: Sparse channel estimation with Lp-norm and reweighted L1-norm penalized least mean squares. In: IEEE ICASSP, 22–27 May 2011, pp. 2864–2867 (2011)

Research on Interference of Conventional Communication Signals

Bekki Sadek, Yun Lin$^{(\boxtimes)}$, and Xiuwei Chi

College of Information and Communication Engineering,
Harbin Engineering University, Heilongjiang 150001, China
linyun_phd@hrbeu.edu.cn

Abstract. This paper, presents the effect of jamming strategies on communication signal by using BPSK and MSK. Jammer can use different
strategies and each one of them has advantages and disadvantages. Who-
ever these two modulations are considered as the most robust digital
modulation technique. They have been widely used, therefore it is very
important to choose the best jamming strategy for this modulation. In
this purpose, it is tested under different kind of jamming namely: single-
tone, multi-tone, broad band noise (BBN) and partial band noise (PBN)
interference channel for its bit error rate performance. Performance of
jamming strategies in this system is analysed and simulated by using
MATLAB program.

Keywords: Communication signals · Jamming effect · Spot jamming
Full band jamming

1 Introduction

The notion says that the electronic warfare (EW) can play big role in military
field back many years ago. Recently, awareness of using EW in communication
field increases dramatically. Nowadays, we are living in time where everything is
directly related to technology. Communication involves our daily life in different
ways that, it is very easy to overlook the multitude of its facets. In the past
methods that used to transmit and receive information between a source and a
user destination took long time. The methods used were analog and digital. As
a result of this delay and by time that analog way is switched rapidly by using
digital communication. In purpose of achieving transmission of this information,
signal is modified into a suitable form before transmitting it over the channel by
a process which known under a name of modulation [1,2].

In this paper, BPSK modulation is used, which is a digital technique. It has a
basic concept on phase shift keying. In addition, the transmitted signal of BPSK
is a sinusoid of fixed amplitude. It has one fixed phase when the data is at one
level and when the data is at the other level the phase is different by 180°. Due to
widely use of BPSK, it is significant and necessary to find the effective jamming
for the BPSK signal [3].

© ICST Institute for Computer Sciences, Social Informatics and Telecommunications Engineering 2018
G. Sun and S. Liu (Eds.): ADHIP 2017, LNICST 219, pp. 417–424, 2018.
https://doi.org/10.1007/978-3-319-73317-3_48

Minimum shift keying (MSK) is a special type of continuous phase-frequency shift keying with h = 0.5 that is used in a number of applications, sometimes called fast frequency shift keying (FFSK). The name minimum refers to the minimum modulation index that allows two FSK signals to be coherently orthogonal, the fast refers to the same given frequency band.

Interference is the sum of all signal contributions that are neither noise not the wanted signal. The interference in communication systems has its effects that can be decisive. It may cause degradation of signal quality and so on. The concept of avoiding interference and increasing range resolution was a familiar concept at the end of the Second World War. Now many anti jamming technologies are in a wide range of applications. In other hand, there is little tendencies on the analysis of BPSK signal jamming pattern. Therefore, this problem is discussed and optimal jamming is analyzed [4].

2   The Principle of BPSK and MSK Signal

A continuous message signal is transformed into a Corresponding sequence of binary symbols by passing three steps: sampling, quantizing and encoding. These binary symbols can be used to modulate a carrier signal. The modulator modifies the carrier by changing its frequency, amplitude and phase. In BPSK, binary symbol 1 and 0 modulation the phase of the carrier. BPSK is a type of digital modulation technique in which we are sending one bit per symbol 0 or a 1 [6].

For example, we can have the following transmitted band-pass symbols:

$$S_1 = \sqrt{\tfrac{2E}{T}} \cos(2\pi f t) \rightarrow represent'1' \tag{1}$$

$$S_2 = \sqrt{\tfrac{2E}{T}} \cos(2\pi f t + \pi) \rightarrow represent'0' \tag{2}$$

Among them, E is the symbol energy; T represents the symbol time period; f represents the frequency of the carrier; By using orthogonalization, we get signal orthonormal basis function, given as:

$$\psi_1 = \sqrt{\frac{2}{T}} \cos(2\pi f t) \tag{3}$$

Hence, the resulting constellation diagram can be given as follows.

We can notice that there are just two in-phase components, and the two waveform of S_1 and S_2 are inverted with respect to one another. Hence, we can use following scheme to design a BPSK modulator:

First of all, digital bits are converted into impulse to add notion of time to them by using NRZ encoder. After that, up-sampling these impulses generate NRZ waveform. Afterwards, the result of NRZ encoder multiple with the carrier (orthonormal basic function) then is carried out to generate the modulated BPSK waveform [7].

Comparing between MSK and BPSK, we find that the MSK signal decreases more rapidly than in BPSK spectral components out of band and BPSK data transmission rate is lower than the MSK data transmission rate [8].

$$S_{MSK} = A_S \cos(2\pi f_c + \frac{\pi a_k t}{2T_b} + \theta_k) \tag{4}$$

f_c represents the carrier frequency, T_b represents the bit width binary baseband signal, θ_k represents the Carrier phase constant symbols.

The minimum frequency difference should be $\triangle f = f_2 - f_1 = 1/2T_b$ to achieve orthogonality condition 2FSK signal (f_1 and f_2 are the carrier frequency for 2FSK signal). The MSK signal can be denoting as $S_{MSK} = \cos[\phi_k(t)]$. Convert it as follows:

$$\frac{d\phi_k(t)}{dt} = \omega_c \pm \frac{\pi}{2T_b} \tag{5}$$

According to this equation the integer times of MSK signal in each symbol period should contain 1/4 carrier cycles. MSK, in particular, has a significant advantage which is known as a continuous phase. No phase discontinuities are a result of changing the frequency of the signal by modulating data signal. This arises as a consequence of the unique factor of MSK that the frequency difference between the logical one and logical zero states is always equal to half the data rate. Whats more, MSK signal has a constant envelope characteristic. MSK modulations wide frequency band and high effectiveness of channel can increase in the frequency hopping spread spectrum communication.

3 Jamming Strategies

Jamming makes use of intentional radio interferences to interrupt wireless communications by adding unwanted signal. Jamming mostly targets attacks at the physical layer but sometimes cross-layer attacks are possible too. In this section, we are going to talk about various types of jamming techniques-each has its own advantages and disadvantages. So this paper makes a detailed analysis of these jamming patterns and considers the broad band jamming, the partial band jamming and the tone jamming. The analysis of the jamming effect needs to rely on JSR. Usually, the jamming-to-signal ratio (JSR) of the receiver determines the impact of the jamming. The main purpose of jamming is to improve the receiver side of the JSR, and then improve the receiver's bit error rate. In the field of military, the jamming effect achieves the requirements when the error rate is bigger than 0.2.

In addition to the above jamming patterns, there are other jamming patterns, such as pulse type jamming, sweep frequency jamming and the smart jamming. These patterns need high technology to achieve and many other factors to consider. For example, the smart jamming technology just interferes a part of the communication to interfere the signal, it can send the false messages to damage communication. So this paper makes a detailed analysis of these jamming patterns and considers the broad band jamming, the partial band jamming and the tone jamming.

3.1   The Broad Band Noise Jamming

Broad band noise jamming is the whole frequency band which is applied to the target station. It is also called full band jamming and it is sometimes called barrage jamming. This kind of jamming is effective against all kinds of anti-jamming communication. This type of jamming increases the background noise level at the receiver, creates a higher noise environment, attacks the Channel capacity of the communication system directly. if we improve the noise emission power that we can get better jamming effect. On other hand, the efficiency of this mode of jamming is very low, and the cost is very high. The jamming is placed between friendly and enemy communication. If this method is used correctly, we can prevent interception of our communication for a period of time.

Since broad band noise jamming generates signals that are similar to broad-band noise, the level of jamming power and is measured in watts/hertz just as background noise is specified. Full band jamming is the best a jammer can do in the absence of any knowledge of the target signal. But, it has also weakness. In the jamming, all the communication in the bandwidth cannot work correctly. Furthermore, it is indispensable to use a large power to interfere communication in a wide frequency band, and it is also bounded by its application to a certain extent.

3.2   The Partial Band Noise Jamming

When the signal is jammed on a single carrier, this gain may be shown by the interference that can be achieved by jamming with the part of the signal rather than by jamming the entire signal in the frequency domain. This is known as partial-band jamming. This strategy is considered more effective than BBN because the jammer uses less bandwidth and more power for the given bandwidth. In this case of jamming, we can set up K as a disturbance coefficient, which indicates that the frequency band of the jamming signal and the frequency band of the whole communication signal are proportional. Hence, the bit error rate can be presented in the following equation:

$$P_e = KP_{e1} + (1 - K)P_{e2} \tag{6}$$

P_{e1} means the bit error rate of the band which has the partial band noise and P_{e2} means the bit error rate of the band which only has the Gauss White Noise. This kind of jamming is very similar to the broad band noise jamming, so we don't discuss it in the paper.

3.3   The Tone Jamming

Tone jamming is one of the main kinds of spot jamming. In this mode of jamming, one or more jammer tones are strategically placed in the spectrum. Where they are placed and their number affects the jamming performance. Depending on the tones transmitted the technique is called single-tone or multi-tone jamming (MTJ).

Single-tone jamming consists of transmitting an unmodulated carrier with an average power J within the spreading bandwidth. In general tone jamming against direct sequence spread spectrum system is very effective because it can offset the receiver end processing gain, which will cause jamming to the spreading process.

The jammer can emit more than one tone, which can be randomly distributed, or at a particular frequency. When these tones are located on adjacent channels, they are called comb like interference. No matter which tone interference is adopted, as long as it can filter through the receiver, it can produce effective interference to the communication signal [5, 9].

4 Jamming in BPSK System

The baseband carrier frequency of BPSK in the paper is 1×10^4 Hz, the sampling frequency is 5×10^4, the rate of bits is 1×10^4. The frequency after digital up conversion is 15 MHz with the White Gaussian Noise of 5 dB. In the discussion of the interference of BPSK system, we first interfere the system with the Broad Band Jamming. Figure 1 shows the jamming effect.

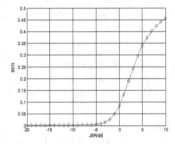

Fig. 1. Broad band noise jamming in BPSK system.

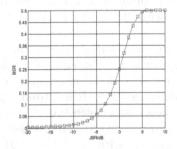

Fig. 2. Single-tone jamming in BPSK system.

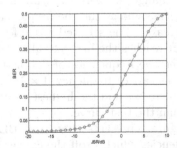

Fig. 3. Multi-tone jamming in BPSK system.

Then, we add a single-tone jamming signal with the same frequency as the BPSK signal, The curve of the error rate changes as the Fig. 2 shows. From Fig. 4 we can get that the jamming effect of single-tone is very good and when the JSR is 0 dB, the BER of communication system can be 0.25.

In the case of multi-tone, the number of tones used is 2 with same power size, and the distance from the center frequency of the communication signal is also the same. The jamming effects are shown in Fig. 3. As a result, we can say that the jamming effect is almost the same with the single tone jamming but the single tone is a little better than multi tone from −5 dB to 5 dB clearly. The transmission of multi tone jamming needs to have higher requirements for the system. Hence we can assume that the selection of single tone jamming efficiency is higher.

5   Jamming in MSK System

The simulation is made under the conditions below. The baseband carrier frequencies of the MSK systems are 9×10^4 Hz and 10.2×10^4 Hz. The rate of bits is 2.4×10^4. The sampling frequency is 1.92×10^5 Hz. The frequency after digital up conversion is 15 MHz with the White Gaussian Noise of 5 dB.

In the discussion of the interference of MSK system, we first interfere the system with the Broad Band Jamming. The Fig. 4 below shows the jamming effect.

Then we will discuss how the different power affects the jamming effect. We first examine the case of single-tone jamming in this section, with fixed frequency attacks the midfrequency. The BER increases as JSR increases. The selected range for SNR was from −20 dB to 10 dB. We notice that BER reaches the highest value which is 0.4836 (Fig. 5).

In this section we examine the case of multi-tone jamming. The number of tones used is 2 with same power size, and the distance from the center frequency of the communication signal is also the same. Due to two picks of MSK frequency we have 3 cases depending on the position of jamming comparing to frequency of MSK.

This Fig. 6 represents change of BER by using multi-tone jamming, with fixed frequencies which is the same as the the frequencies of MSK system. The BER increases as JSR increases. The selected range for SNR was from −20 dB to 10 dB. We see that BER reaches the highest value which is 0.4945.

In the second case when the frequencies of double-tone (low frequency and high frequency) which is off carrier frequency 4×10^3 Hz. We can notice that BER increases when JSR increases and the highest value of BER is 0.4635. This curves in Fig. 7 is lower than the first curve.

The third case this figure represents change of BER by using multi tone jamming, with fixed frequencies which is off the carrier frequency 4×10^3 Hz in the opposite direction above. The BER increases as JSR increases. The selected range for SNR was from −20 dB to 10 dB. We note that BER reaches the highest value which is 0.4703 in Fig. 8.

According to those three figures we notice that the first curve is much higher than the other two curves. According to BER value We can see that the first case is better than the other two when the position of two frequencies of double-tone are between frequencies of MSK modulation. From my point of view multi-tone is the best jamming strategies for MSK modulation when the frequency of jamming signal and MSK signal is the same.

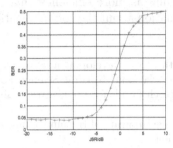

Fig. 4. Broad band noise jamming in MSK system.

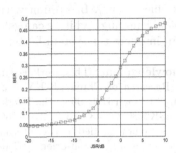

Fig. 5. Single-tone jamming in MSK system.

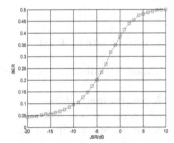

Fig. 6. Multi-tone jamming with spot frequency.

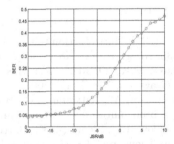

Fig. 7. Multi-tone jamming with the first group of frequency.

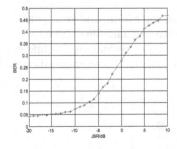

Fig. 8. Multi-tone jamming with the second group of frequency.

6   Conclusion

According to the results of jamming patterns of the ratio of the JSR and the error rate curve diagram above we can assume that the single tone jamming is the most jamming efficiency in BPSK system, and the multi-tone is the most efficiency in MSK system when the frequency of jamming signal and MSK signal is the same, compared with the two methods above the broad band noise jamming is the worst efficient way. In summary, the spot jamming is more efficiency than the full band jamming and if we can get priori information about the communication, we can interfere the system better.

Acknowledgment. This work is supported by the Key Development Program of Basic Research of China (JCKY2013604B001), the National Natural Science Foundation of China (61301095), the Funda-mental Research Funds for the Central Universities (GK2080260148 and HEUCF1508).

This paper is funded by the International Exchange Program of Harbin Engineering University for Innovation-oriented Talents Cultivation.

Meantime, all the authors declare that there is no conflict of interests regarding the publication of this article.

We gratefully thank of very useful discussions of reviewers.

References

1. Poisel, R.A.: Introduction to Communication Electronic Warfare Systems, 2nd edn., p. 35. Artech House, Norwood (2008)
2. Simon, M.K., Omura, J.K.: Spectrum Communication Handbook, pp. 405–749. McGraw-Hill, New York (2002)
3. Annamalai, A., Tellambura, C., Bhargava, V.K.: A general method for calculating error probabilities over fading channels. In: ICC, vol. 1, pp. 36–40 (2000)
4. Peterson, R.L., Ziemer, R.E., Borth, D.E.: Introduction to Spread Spectrum Communications, pp. 368–373. Prentice Hall, Upper Saddle River (1985)
5. Milstein, L.B., Davidovice, S., Schilling, D.L.: The effect of multiple-tone interfering signals on a direct sequence spread spectrum communication system. IEEE Trans. Commun. IEEE J. Sel. Areas Commun. **7**(4), 569–575 (1989)
6. Ziemer, R.E., Tranter, W.H.: Principles of Communications, 5th edn., p. 413. Wiley, New York (2002)
7. Chitode, J.S.: Digital Communication, 2nd edn. (2009)
8. Sen, C.: Digital Communications Jamming (2000)
9. Karkatzounis, K.: Performance evaluation of different jamming strategies over uncoded noncoherent fast FH/MFSK communication systems (2004)

Research on OFDM Carrier Synchronization

Zhaorui Ma$^{(\boxtimes)}$, Zheng Dou, and Zhigang Li

Harbin Engineering University, Nantong Str. 145, Harbin 150001, China
836358835@qq.com

Abstract. OFDM technology is the simultaneous transmission of signals in multiple overlapping channels. In order to correctly receive, the orthogonality of subcarriers must be ensured strictly. However, due to Doppler frequency shift and transceiver of the crystal is not exactly the same, there are certain carrier frequency deviation, which will destroy the orthogonality of the subcarrier wave. The frequency difference influence of phase also has cumulativity, accurate frequency synchronization is the precondition for the normal work of OFDM system. In the text, a typical data-assisted carrier synchronization algorithm is analyzed for the carrier synchronization problem in OFDM system. We studied the improved algorithm which is based on the average algorithm of training symbols, and the performance is compared by simulation analysis. Experiments show that the improved carrier synchronization algorithm is superior to the typical algorithm and has low complexity.

Keywords: OFDM · Frequency deviation · Carrier synchronization
Training symbols · Estimated performance

1 Introduction

There are many researches on the carrier synchronization algorithm at home and abroad. At present, the carrier synchronization algorithm can be divided into two categories according to the data processing [1]: non-data auxiliary class and data assistant class. Non-data-assisted class algorithm is also called blind estimation algorithm. By using the structure of OFDM signal, information is extracted directly from the signal itself (such as cyclic prefix) or after the Fourier transformed spectrum of the signal without using the synchronization parameters from the received signal. And it does not reduce the band utilization, the representative algorithm is based on the cyclic prefix maximum likelihood estimation algorithm [2] (referred to as ML algorithm). The data-assisted method is divided into two parts: the time domain training symbol and the frequency domain training symbol. The concrete realization is that the packet header of the packet is added with an OFDM block dedicated to the frequency offset estimation, such as training symbols or guidance frequency symbols and other additional data information to synchronize the estimation. By changing the pilot or training symbols of the structure, pattern, etc., at the receiving end using related technology to extract synchronization information in the estimation process. This algorithm will reduce the efficiency of system data transmission, and its advantages are fast capture, high precision, suitable for packet data communication.

© ICST Institute for Computer Sciences, Social Informatics and Telecommunications Engineering 2018
G. Sun and S. Liu (Eds.): ADHIP 2017, LNICST 219, pp. 425–432, 2018.
https://doi.org/10.1007/978-3-319-73317-3_49

In the text, a typical data-assisted carrier synchronization algorithm is analyzed for the carrier synchronization problem in OFDM system. We studied the improved algorithm which is based on the average algorithm of training symbols, and the performance is compared by simulation analysis.

2 Typical Data Auxiliary Class Algorithm

OFDM system based on IEEE 802.11a is a typical burst packet transmission system. An OFDM symbol is consists of four pilots and 52 subcarriers. The preamble consists of 10 short training sequences and two long training sequences. Therefore, in the system, we generally use the method of data-assisted. We use the long and short training symbols in the preamble to carry out the carrier frequency offset estimation periodically.

2.1 Carrier Frequency Offset Estimation Technique in Frequency-Domain

In the case there are two identical training symbols need to be transmitted consecutively, and the carrier frequency offset is ε, the relationship between the corresponding two received signals is

$$y_2[n] = y_1[n]e^{\frac{j2\pi n\varepsilon}{N}} \leftrightarrow Y_2[k] = Y_1[k]e^{j2\pi\varepsilon} \tag{1}$$

Among them, $y_1[n]$ is the signal of the transmitter, $y_2[n]$ is the signal of the receiver. Using the relationship in (1), we can estimate the carrier frequency offset

$$\overset{\wedge}{\varepsilon} = \frac{1}{2\pi}\arctan\left\{\frac{\sum_{k=0}^{N-1}\text{Im}[Y_1^*[k]Y_2[k]]}{\sum_{k=0}^{N-1}\text{Re}[Y_1^*[k]Y_2[k]]}\right\} \tag{2}$$

This is the famous method proposed by Moose [3]. Although the estimated carrier frequency offset range of Eq. (2) is $|\varepsilon| \leq 0.5$, when we use training symbols with D repeating styles, the estimated range of the carrier frequency offset can be increased by D times. If the non-zero samples in the frequency domain which need to be averaged is reduced, the MSE performance will deteriorate. In order to calculate Eq. (2), this estimation technique demands a specific cycle time (often referred to as a leading period) to provide continuous training symbols. In other words, in this estimation technique, the preamble period is applied only to the launch training sequence and can't transmit data symbols.

2.2   Carrier Frequency Offset Estimation Technique in Time-Domain

Compared to the time domain algorithm [4], the frequency domain algorithm needs to calculate the DFT of two repetitive symbols, which requires more computation and consumes more hardware resources and time. So for the WLAN receiver in terms of time domain method has a certain advantage. The time-domain method of frequency offset estimation is the maximum likelihood algorithm for data-assisted operation of the receiving time domain signal [5].

Let the transmission signal be $s(n)$, f_{tx} represents the transmission carrier frequency, T_S represents the sampling period, n corresponds to the sampling point; then after RF modulation, the pass band signal complex baseband model

$$y(n) = s(n)e^{j2\pi f_{tx}nT_S} \tag{3}$$

At the receiving end, f_{rx} represents the carrier frequency, the received signal is converted to baseband signal, in the case of sampling frequency deviation is ignored

$$r(n) = s(n)e^{j2\pi f_{tx}nT_S} \cdot e^{-j2\pi f_{tx}nT_S} = s(n)e^{j2\pi \Delta f nT_S} \tag{4}$$

where the deviation of the carrier between transmitted and received is $\Delta f = f_{tx} - f_{rx}$. Assuming D represents the delay between two consecutive repetition symbols and L represents the OFDM symbol length, the delay correlation of the periodic repetition signal is

$$R = \sum_{n=0}^{L-1} r(i+n)r^*(i+n+D)$$

$$= \sum_{n=0}^{L-1} s(i+n)e^{j2\pi \Delta f(i+n)T_S} \cdot [s(i+n+D)e^{j2\pi \Delta f(i+n+D)T_S}]^* \tag{5}$$

$$= e^{-j2\pi \Delta f D T_S} \sum_{n=0}^{L-1} s(i+n)s^*(i+n+D)$$

When the modulus of the autocorrelation R is the maximum, $s(i+n) = s(i+n+D)$, then

$$Z = R_{s(i+n)=s(i+n+D)} = e^{-j2\pi \Delta f D T_S} \sum_{n=0}^{L-1} |s|^2 \tag{6}$$

Theoretically, R should be a real number when the frequency offset is 0. The effect of frequency deviation is reflected in $e^{-j2\pi \Delta f D T_S}$. Therefore, the estimated value of the frequency deviation can be calculated as

$$\Delta f = -\frac{\arg(z)}{2\pi D T_S} \tag{7}$$

This algorithm can estimate the carrier frequency offset by two identical OFDM symbols. L and D is the cumulative length and the delay length. These two quantities are based on the situation. If the short training symbol is selected for carrier frequency offset estimation, then L = D = 16; if long training symbol is selected, L = D = 64. Select the different training symbols, the carrier frequency offset estimation effect is different. At the same signal-to-noise ratio, the accuracy of the long and short training sequences is not the same for the carrier frequency estimation, as is shown in Fig. 1.

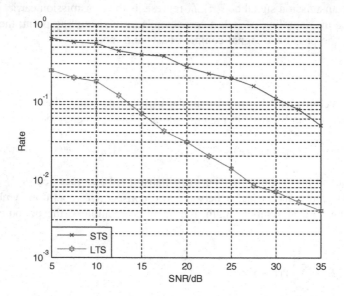

Fig. 1. Carrier frequency offset estimation of time domain algorithm

The Rate represents the percentage of mean square error of estimation of frequency offset among subcarrier spacing. MATLAB simulation of OFDM transmission system to generate the data as the receiving data, set the signal to noise ratio of 5–35 dB, sampling time $T_S = 50$ ns, adding 10 kHz frequency offset to the system. From the simulation results, it is more accurate to estimate the frequency offset as the SNR increases, but the estimation error of the long training sequence is much smaller than that of the short training sequence.

For IEEE 802.11a systems, the ten short training sequence symbols and two long training sequence symbols in the preamble can be used for carrier frequency estimation [6]. However, for short training symbols, the sampling time is 50 ns, the delay D = 16, the maximum frequency error that can be estimated is

$$f_{\Delta\max} = \frac{\pi}{2\pi DT_S} = \frac{1}{2DT_S} = \frac{1}{2 \times 16 \times 50 \times 10^{-9}} = 625 \ (\text{kHz}) \qquad (8)$$

For long training symbols, D = 64, then

$$f_{\Delta max} = \frac{\pi}{2\pi D T_S} = \frac{1}{2D T_S} = \frac{1}{2 \times 64 \times 50 \times 10^{-9}} = 156.2 \text{ (kHz)} \qquad (9)$$

Although the accuracy is high when the long training symbols are used to calculate the frequency offset. However, from the hardware design point of view, the use of long training symbols for frequency offset estimation requires more hardware resources; the most important is the long training symbols can estimate the maximum frequency deviation is too small, only 156.2 kHz. And the short training symbol of the estimated range to 625 kHz, so from the frequency estimation range and the estimated accuracy of the integrated consideration, the use of short training symbols for frequency offset estimation is more reasonable.

3 Estimation Algorithm for Short Training Symbols

Using the repetitive periodicity of short training symbols, the maximum likelihood algorithm is used for carrier synchronization [7, 8]. Assuming that the ideal received signal is $s(n)$, under the influence of the normalized carrier frequency deviation f_Δ, the received signal is

$$r(n) = s(n)e^{j2\pi f_\Delta n T_S} \qquad (10)$$

If the short training symbol period is set D^{STS}, the delay correlation variable C_n can be indicated as

$$
\begin{aligned}
C_n &= \sum_{n=0}^{D^{STS}-1} r(n)r^*(n - D^{STS}) \\
&= \sum_{n=0}^{D^{STS}-1} s(n)e^{j2\pi f_\Delta n T_S}[s(n - D^{STS})e^{j2\pi f_\Delta(n-D^{STS})T_S}]^* \\
&= \sum_{n=0}^{D^{STS}-1} s(n)s^*(n - D^{STS})e^{j2\pi f_\Delta D^{STS} T_S} \\
&= e^{j2\pi f_\Delta D^{STS} T_S} \sum_{n=0}^{D^{STS}-1} s(n)s^*(n - D^{STS})
\end{aligned}
\qquad (11)
$$

According to the maximum likelihood estimation algorithm, the carrier frequency deviation is

$$\hat{f}_\Delta = \frac{1}{2\pi D^{STS} T_S} \arctan[\sum_{n=0}^{D^{STS}-1} s(n)s^*(n - D^{STS})] \qquad (12)$$

In order to improve the accuracy of carrier synchronization, the implementation of multiple estimates using the average

$$\hat{f}_\Delta = \frac{1}{2\pi D^{STS}T_S} \frac{\sum\limits_{i=0}^{N} \arctan(\sum\limits_{n=0}^{D^{STS}-1} s[(i-1) \times D^{STS}+n]s^*[(i-1) \times D^{STS}+n-D^{STS}])}{N}$$

(13)

Firstly, five sets of delay correlations are used to calculate the four points of the correlation and the results [9]. Then, the four-time accumulation and the result are estimated by the angular deviation, and then the average of the angular deviation is estimated, so as to get more accurate angle deviation, as shown in Fig. 2.

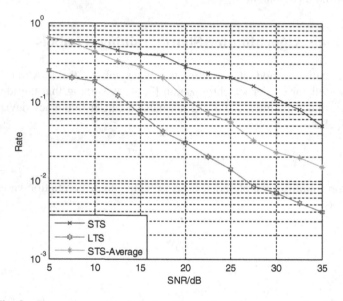

Fig. 2. Comparison of typical algorithm and seeking average algorithm

In the general averaging algorithm, the length of the associated cumulative operation is the length of a short training symbol, so it can only be averaged 9 times in the 802.11a protocol [10]. In order to further improve the accuracy of the frequency offset estimation, from the point of view of averaging, the average of the frequency offset estimates is calculated in the calculation process to obtain more accurate results. Assuming there are M short training symbols, the first two short training symbols are delayed after the correlation operation, with a short training symbol in the sample value, rather than a short training symbol for the unit, the results will be multiplied by the results, constantly related to the cumulative operation.

The delay length is $D = 16$, and the short training symbol is M. According to the characteristics of the relevant cumulative operation, the following improved algorithm is obtained

$$\hat{\Delta f} = -\frac{1}{2\pi DT_S} \frac{\sum\limits_{i=0}^{(M-2)D-1} \arctan(\sum\limits_{i=0}^{D-1} s(n+i) \cdot s(n+i+D))}{(M-2)D} \tag{14}$$

When using 5 short training symbols system carrier synchronization, it can get 48 times the average [11], while ordinary short training symbols for the average algorithm can only seek up to 9 times; In this way, fewer short training symbols can be used to obtain multiple averages, the estimation accuracy of carrier frequency offset will be improved. Under the other conditions remain unchanged, the simulation results of the three algorithms [12], as shown in Fig. 3.

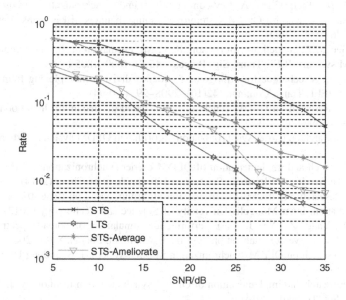

Fig. 3. Comparison between improved algorithm and original algorithm

It can be seen from the above simulation results that the improved averaging algorithm has greatly improved the accuracy of the frequency offset estimation, and it can achieve the ideal effect by estimating the maximum frequency deviation and the estimation accuracy.

4   Conclusion

In this paper, several typical frequency synchronization algorithms are analyzed, and their performance is compared by simulation analysis. Simulation and implementation results show that the error of the improved algorithm is small when compared with the typical algorithm and the averaging algorithm, but the computational complexity is increased. However, compared with the estimation accuracy, the computational complexity increases to a certain extent within the tolerable range, and only the multiplication is used in the hardware implementation. The feasibility of the improved algorithm for frequency offset estimation using short training symbols is verified.

Acknowledgments. This paper is funded by the International Exchange Program of Harbin Engineering University for Innovation Oriented Talents Cultivation, Nation Nature Science Foundation of China (No. 61401115), Nation Nature Science Foundation of China (No. 61301095), Nation Nature Science Foundation of China (No. 61671167).

References

1. Hsieh, M.H., Wei, C.H.: A low-complexity frame synchronization frequency offset compensation scheme for OFDM system over fading channels. IEEE Trans. Veh. Technol. **48**(5), 1596–1609 (1999)
2. Van de Beek, J.J., Sandell, M., Borjesson, P.O.: ML estimation of time and frequency offset in OFDM systems. IEEE Trans. Sig. Process. **45**(7), 1800–1805 (1997)
3. Moose, P.H.: A technique for orthogonal frequency division multiplexing frequency offset correction. IEEE Trans. Commun. **42**(10), 2908–2914 (1994)
4. Zhang, Z.: Research on OFDM synchronization based on maximum likelihood algorithm. Commun. Technol. (2010)
5. Cui, H.: Research on carrier synchronization algorithm in OFDM system. Xi dian University (2015)
6. Xu, J.: Research and implementation of OFDM carrier synchronization algorithm based on 802.11a. University of Electronic Science and Technology of China (2014)
7. Cao, C.: Research on OFDM synchronization algorithm based on IEEE802.11a and FPGA implementation. Inner Mongolia University of Science and Technology (2012)
8. Zhao, D., Yang, Z., Ye, J.: Fast performance simulation of spread spectrum OFDM wideband shortwave communication system. J. Appl. Sci. **36**(10), 8–11 (2009)
9. Cai, X.: Research on OFDM synchronization in burst system. J. Shandong Univ. (Nat. Sci. Ed.) (2016)
10. Cai, L.: Research and implementation of OFDM synchronization technology. J. Xi'an Univ. Electron. Sci. Technol. (2014)
11. Nie, D.: Research on LTE downlink OFDM synchronization. J. Nanjing Univ. Posts Telecommun. (2015)
12. Zheng, J.: Study on synchronization algorithm of broadband wireless OFDM system. Beijing University of Posts and Telecommunications (2008)

Design and Application of Electrocardiograph Diagnosis System Based on Multifractal Theory

Chunkai Zhang, Ao Yin[✉], Haodong Liu, and Jingwang Zhang

Department of Computer Science and Technology,
Harbin Institute of Technology Shenzhen Graduate School, Shenzhen, China
ckzhang812@gmail.com, 1065669324@qq.com,
Haodong.1994@qq.com, Bluesmile2013@hotmail.com

Abstract. At present there are some ECG automatic diagnosis and identification system, which generally have a common characteristic that their research direction is more inclined to time domain analysis and frequency domain analysis. A large number of researchers have proved that ECG signal has multiple fractal characteristics, while using multi-fractal to analyze the chaotic system is also a trend. In this paper, the main research content is ECG automatic identification: ① Design and implementation of a differential threshold method for ECG signal automatic segmentation algorithm, the algorithm can automatically identify a segment of ECG in the ECG cycle, and ignore those ECG cycles, which are not complete ECG signal. ② Propose an algorithm to describe the data classification by using the multifractal theory to describe the data characteristics. The multi-fractal and semi-spectral characteristics of ECG and generalized Hurst exponent are used to train and test the neural network model. The accuracy of classification is 97%. ③ A complete ECG signal annotation system was built, which can automatically identify a segment of ECG sequence with multiple cycles and annotate each cycle. At the same time it can automatically ignored end-to-end incomplete ECG signal of the ECG sequence, that's to say, this system has a better fault tolerance.

Keywords: MFDFA · Scale-free interval · Multifractals · Neural networks

1 Introduction

From many literatures published recently, it can find that most of the research work tend to research the field of ECG (Electrocardiograph) automatic classification in the time domain and frequency domain analysis, while the heart is a complex nonlinear chaotic system, which is affected by many factors. So the form of ECG is very different, the time domain analysis and frequency domain analysis can only give some simple characteristics of the test data from time domain and frequency domain, hence, under the internal factors and external factors together the difference between the original expected results and the actual situation are very big. A large number of researchers have proved that the ECG signal has multiple fractal characteristics, while the use of multi-fractal to analyze the chaotic system is also a trend.

© ICST Institute for Computer Sciences, Social Informatics and Telecommunications Engineering 2018
G. Sun and S. Liu (Eds.): ADHIP 2017, LNICST 219, pp. 433–447, 2018.
https://doi.org/10.1007/978-3-319-73317-3_50

ECG data pre-analysis process is the main research content of the ECG signal noise interference. ECG data preprocessing techniques include a variety of classical filter filtering methods and a variety of modern use of waveform transformation signal processing methods. These pretreatment techniques can be divided into three categories: the classical filter method, the optimized filter method and the high-tech filter method based on wavelet analysis, mathematical morphology and neural network analysis.

Currently, the main research direction of ECG automatic classification and identification is to extract the characteristic waveforms of the ECG signal and its waveform characteristic parameters so as to analyze and diagnose the ECG signal type.

With the development and research of wavelet analysis, neural network, fractal theory and other nonlinear signal processing techniques, the knowledge in these fields is used to analyze the data, which is composed of continuous Q wave, R wave and S wave. Wave group identification has become a new focus of attention. Sahambi et al. [10] proposed a method based on the principle of wavelet transform modulus maxima. The algorithm successfully identifies the waveforms and their associated features in the ECG data, and the algorithm has strong resistance to simulated baseline drift and high frequency noise. Wavelet transform and adaptive matching filter technology are combined to achieve a new QRS complex detection technology, the application of this method after the QRS wave group detection accuracy and detection rate has been greatly improved.

2 Basic Theory

2.1 Fractal Concept

Definition: If a set ensures that the formula (1) holds, then we call the set as a fractal set. For $D_H(A)$ is the Hausdorff dimension of set A, $D_T(A)$ is the geometry dimension of A.

$$D_H(A) > D_T(A) \tag{1}$$

Although the fractal judgment using the definition of formula (1) is correct, there are still some fractal geometries that can be omitted, and it cannot contain some useful fractal geometry.

After scholars continue to theoretical research and practical application, resulting in a variety of views to explain the concept of fractal, to enhance their understanding [16]:

(1) The structure is very detailed, in a small detail, the local implication of all the characteristics of the overall change;
(2) Fractal is actually a feature, which is not only applicable to the geometry, it also is a concept, function, or some kind of signal in a statistical model.
(3) Uncertainty and irregularity, the traditional European geometric language can only analyze its whole or part of the characteristics of the part.

(4) In theory, fractal geometry can be done infinite mosaic, but in reality the nature of fractal geometry is impossible to have an infinite mosaic of the hierarchical structure.

(5) One of the characteristics of self-similarity is the level difference. In general, localities and the whole show good similarity only in the case of hierarchical adjacency; on the contrary, the greater the gap between the levels, the local and the whole show a poor self-similarity, and even come to that they are dissimilar conclusion.

(6) A part of the fractal geometry can be simply defined and analyzed by recursive and iterative methods.

2.2   Fractal Characteristics

Fractal characteristics as mentioned above, the two main properties of fractal are self-similarity and scale-free.

(1) Self-similarity
One of the most representative features of fractal theory is self-similarity. As the fractal definition mentioned in the concept of fractal, the basis for judging whether a thing has fractal properties is whether the thing has self-similarity. Self-similarity refers to the structural characteristics or process characteristics of things in different observation scales, local and overall performance consistent or similar.

(2) No scaling
In the part of the fractal geometry, since the thing has self-similarity, the selected local area is enlarged and transformed, and the local area is compared with the original one by enlarging and transforming. It is found that the original area and the local area in the morphological characteristics of performance similar or consistent, this feature is called scale-free.

2.3   Multi-fractal Data Analysis

In the process of analyzing the data using fractal theory, many researchers are aware of a similar phenomenon [13]: When using the single-fold fractal theory to describe most of the things that exist objectively, the single-fractal theory can only be able to describe the global features, and it lack of the more delicate characterization of local characteristics.

The single-fractal analysis can only describe the global features of time-series data, and lack of a more detailed characterization of the local features. Multifractal analysis, as a single-fractal analysis extension, can effectively deal with such phenomena, and is widely used in Characterization of Time Series.

Mainly using MFDFA method for processing, MFDFA method process:

(1) time series $x_t, t = 1, 2, 3, \ldots, T$;
(2) Calculate the cumulative deviation sequence Y_i:

$$Y_i = \sum_{k=1}^{i} (x_k - \bar{x}), i = 1, 2, 3, \ldots, T \tag{2}$$

(3) Calculate the local root mean square $F(s, v)$: divide the cumulative deviation sequence into N_s segments, each segment length s, the last segment length is $T \bmod s$; then the cumulative deviation sequence Y_i is divided into segments $2 N_s$, each segment length s and the last segment length $T \bmod s$. This is divided into $2 N_s$ segments. Calculate the local root mean square of each segment, and get the root mean square sequence $f(s, v)$

$$f(s, v) = \frac{1}{s} \sum_{i=1}^{s} (Y_{(v-1)s+i} - y_v(i))^2,$$

$$v = 1, 2, 3, \ldots, N_s \tag{3}$$

$$f(s, v) = \frac{1}{s} \sum_{i=1}^{s} (Y_{N-(v-N_s)s+i} - y_v(i))^2,$$

$$v = N_s + 1, N_s + 2, N_s + 3, \ldots, 2N_s \tag{4}$$

$$\bar{x} = \frac{1}{T} \sum_{k=1}^{T} x_k.$$

(4) Calculate the global root mean square $F_q(s)$:

$$F_q(s) = \begin{cases} (\frac{1}{2N_s} \sum_{v=1}^{2N_s} f(s, v)^{\frac{q}{2}})^{\frac{1}{q}}, & q \in R \boxplus q \neq 0 \\ e^{\frac{1}{4N_s} \sum_{v=1}^{2N_s} \ln f(s,v)}, & q = 0 \end{cases} \tag{5}$$

(5) According to formula (5), grouping with different q values, the q value of each group is the same, in the group take different s value to get many, with formula (6) obtaining the H value corresponding to the q value, finally obtains many pairs (q, H).

$$\ln F^2(q; s) = C + H \cdot \ln s \tag{6}$$

If the data is a multifractal time series, H and q are constant, that is, the generalized Hurst exponential graph is a curve; if the data is a single time series, a horizontal straight line.

(6) Calculate the mass index $\tau(q)$:

$$\tau(q) = qH(q) - 1 \tag{7}$$

(7) Calculate the singularity index α:

$$\alpha = \frac{d\tau(q)}{dq} = H(q) + q \cdot H'(q) \tag{8}$$

$$H'(q_i) = \frac{H(q_i) - H(q_{i+1})}{q_i - q_{i+1}} \tag{9}$$

(8) Calculate the singular spectrum $f(\alpha)$:

$$f(\alpha) = q\alpha - \tau(q) = q(\alpha - h(q)) + 1 \tag{10}$$

3 ECG Characteristics Analysis

3.1 Multifractal Analysis

In the MIT heart rate abnormalities database, selecting the five with a complete ECG cycle ECG data. The five ECGs were taken from different categories, such as normal beat (NB), left bundle branch block beat (LB), right bundle branch block heartbeat (RB), premature ventricular contraction (PB), and atrial premature beat (AB) were randomly selected, as shown in Fig. 1. NB signal, sub-picture b is the LB signal, sub-picture c is the RB signal, sub-picture d is the PB signal, and the sub-picture e is the AB signal. In the case of random sampling, for each category, the data is collected for all categories. For example, when we extract the NB signal, the whole is made up of the MIT-BIT database as a whole, that is, the NB signal is composed of the NB signal extracted from the number 100 file to the number 234 file. To the NB signal extracted from the number 234 file. Respectively, on the extraction of five ECG time series are shown as below.

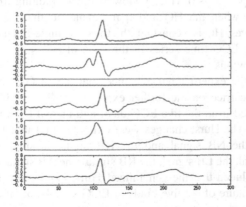

Fig. 1. Five ECG signals

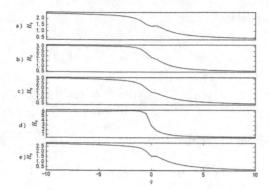

Fig. 2. Five generalized hurst exponential graphs

The generalized Hurst exponent of the NB signal is shown in Fig. 2. The subgraph a is the general Hurst exponent of the NB signal, the subgraph b is the LB signal, and the subgraph c is RB signal, the sub picture d is the PB signal, the sub picture e is the AB signal. From the multifractal method we can see the generalized.

Table 1. Five generalized Hurst exponential changes

Signal	NB	LB	RB	PB	AB
Minimal	0.287	0.575	0.380	0.439	0.296
Maximum	2.338	2.134	2.552	3.763	1.855
Difference	2.050	1.559	2.171	3.325	1.559

Hurst exponent H_q and q can be used as the main basis for judging whether a thing has multifractality. It can be seen from the figure that the generalized Hurst exponents H_q and q of the five electrocardiographic time series have obvious decreasing relations. So we can conclude that the ECG signal is multifractal. In the process of change of q and H_q, we find that when the absolute value of q is greater than 5, the change of generalized Hurst exponent is obviously slowed down. Judging from the multi-fractal method can be seen when the HQ and q independent, that is, no matter how the occurrence of q changes, HQ is a constant, the thing is single-fractal. Therefore, we can draw the conclusion: ECG time series in the case of $-5 \leqslant q \leqslant 5$, the multi-fractal nature is the most obvious.

On the basis of the experimental evidence that the ECG signal has multi-fractal properties, we have carried on the further experiment. In the MIT-BIT database, 50 samples were extracted from the five ECG data, and the MFDFA method was applied to 250 ECG signals. The Hurst changes were extracted in Table 1. From Table 1, the difference between the NB signal and the RB signal is small, and the difference between the NB signal, the LB signal, the RB signal, the AB signal and the PB signal is large. It can be concluded that the generalized Hurst exponent cannot be used as the main classification feature of the five kinds of ECG signals, but it can only play a role of auxiliary ECG signal classification.

3.2   Scale-Free Interval Analysis

From the fractal characteristics of the previous, we can see that things with fractal properties are scale-free characteristics. So in the ECG signal processing, the determination of the scale-free interval is not negligible.

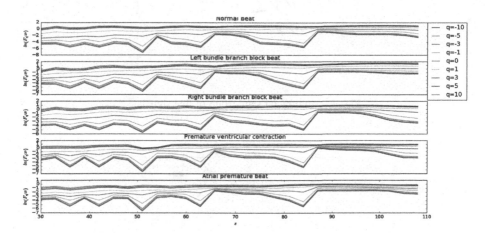

Fig. 3. Analysis of five kinds of signals without scale interval

We also use the data in the scale-free interval analysis of the five signals as the research sample of the scale-free interval, where sub-graph a is the NB signal analysis graph, sub-graph b is the LB signal, sub-graph c is the RB signal, Sub-picture d is the PB signal, sub-picture e is the AB signal, in each sub-graph from bottom to top order q value, that is $-10, -5, -3, -1, 0, 1, 3, 5, 10$. The MFDFA method is applied to each sample data, the scale s is preset between 30 and 110, and the preset value range of the order q is "$-10, -5, -3, -1, 0, 1, 3, 5, 10$". After the MFDFA method, the results shown in Fig. 3. It can be seen that for $q > 0$ and s between 60 and 100, $\ln(F_q(s))$ and s exhibits an obvious linear relationship with s To 100 for its scale-free interval.

3.3   ECG Feature Identification

The scale-free interval obtained in the previous section has obvious problems: when $q > 0$, the resulting multifractal spectrum is a half-spectrum (as shown in Fig. 4). The general multifractal spectrum is a curve with a single peak. Therefore, we assume that the multi-fractal half-spectrum ECG signal can be used as the characteristics of ECG signal.

The MFDFA method was applied to the BMC signal to obtain its multifractal spectrum (Fig. 5). From the multifractal spectrum, we can see that the BMC signal multifractal spectrum is symmetrical, and it can be used half spectrum, but the multi-fractal spectrum derived from the MFDFA method is less symmetry. Nonetheless, we can conclude that the multifractal can be approximated by the multifractal.

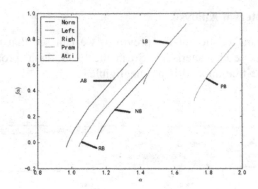

Fig. 4. Multifractal semigroup of five signals

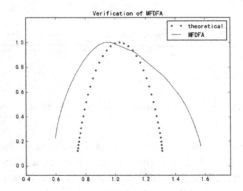

Fig. 5. BMC signal multiple fractal spectrum

4 Neural Network Classification

In this paper, the classification of the ECG signal using the back-propagation algorithm for weight adjustment and threshold adjustment of the feed-forward neural network as a classification model, the BP neural network. As the BP network model in the training process involves more parameters, so we must continue to adjust the parameters of model training, and through the classification of ECG signal classification accuracy rate to determine a set of parameters in the model performance.

4.1 The Number of Features and Classification Results

The MFDFA method was applied to the five ECG signals to obtain its multifractal half-spectrum and its generalized Hurst exponent. The features of multi-fractal half-spectrum and generalized Hurst exponent are divided into four categories:

(1) Basic spectral characteristics
In general use of multifractal spectroscopy for classification of features, the researchers generally use the formula (11) as the eigenvector.

$$feature = \{\alpha_{min}, \alpha_{max}, \Delta\alpha, f_{min}(\alpha),$$
$$f_{max}(\alpha), \Delta f(\alpha)\} = F_0 \tag{11}$$

(2) the basic spectral characteristics and its expansion characteristics
This case contains four extended features in addition to the six eigenvalues in Eq. (11). These four expansion characteristics are $\bar{\alpha}$, $std(\alpha)$, $\bar{f}(\alpha)$ and $std(f(\alpha))$, as in (12). Inside, $\bar{\alpha}$ is the mean value of the sequence α obtained after the MFDFA method, and $std(\alpha)$ is the standard deviation of the sequence, $\bar{f}(\alpha)$ is the mean value of the sequence $f(\alpha)$ obtained after the MFDFA method, and $std(f(\alpha))$ is the standard deviation of the sequence. So the eigenvalues in this case are shown in Eq. (13).

$$F_1 = \{\bar{\alpha}, std(\alpha), \bar{f}(\alpha), std(f(\alpha))\} \tag{12}$$

$$feature = F_0 \cup F_1 \tag{13}$$

(3) Basic spectrum and generalized Hurst exponent
This case contains three generalized Hurst exponential features in addition to the six basic eigenvalues in Eq. (11). The three generalized Hurst exponential characteristics are h_{min}, h_{max} and Δh, as in (14). The minimum value of the generalized Hurst exponent sequence obtained by MFDFA method is the maximum value of the generalized Hurst exponent sequence, and Δh is the difference between h_{max} and h_{min}. So this list contains the eigenvalues as shown in formula (15), which is the union of formulas (11) and (14).

$$F_2 = \{h_{min}, h_{max}, \Delta h\} \tag{14}$$

$$feature = F_0 \cup F_2 \tag{15}$$

(4) Basic spectrum, spectral expansion and Hurst exponent characteristics
In this case, the first three lists are all included, including not only the basic spectral characteristics, but also the extended features of the basic features and the generalized Hurst exponential characteristics, as below formula

$$feature = F_0 \cup F_1 \cup F_2 \tag{16}$$

The above four kinds of lists are applied to the network model which has already been built. For each list, it is trained 30 times. Taking the average value of the iteration times, the mean value of the accuracy and the standard deviation of the accuracy as the standard metrics. The experimental results are shown in Table 2.

Table 2. Number of features and classification results

Feature list	Average of iterative times	Accuracy (%)	Accuracy of the standard deviation
F_0	412	86.93	0.1615
$F_0 \cup F_1$	461	91.47	0.2367
$F_0 \cup F_2$	495	89.17	0.7931
$F_0 \cup F_1 \cup F_2$	498	92.36	0.5783

It can be seen from Table 2 that the increase of the number of features will promote the increase of accuracy, but also increase the time consumption of training. Training time and the number of features is a typical positive correlation, but the number of features and the number of iterations is not a clear linear relationship. From the first list to the second list of accuracy growth than from the first list to the third list of more accurate growth. Comparing the generalized Hurst index of the five ECG signals, the generalized Hurst index of the normal ECG and the generalized Hurst index of the abnormal ECG are obviously different, but the difference of the generalized Hurst index between abnormal electrocardiograms is not very obvious. It can be seen that the generalized Hurst exponent has obvious difference among the groups, but the difference among group is small, so the generalized Hurst index cannot be used as the feature of classification. However, by comparing the multi-fractal half-spectrum of five ECG signals, any one of the five signals has obvious distinguishing characteristics from the other four signals. So the generalized Hurst index can only be used as an auxiliary classification, but it can enhance the classification effect is limited. From the second list to the fourth list and from the third list to the fourth list, it is found that the extended features of the multifractal halftone are better than the generalized Hurst exponent for the network model. Moreover, comparing the first list with the third list, adding the generalized Hurst exponential feature will improve the classification effect of the network model, but at the same time will greatly increase the instability of the network model. A comparison of the second list and the fourth list will also reveal a similar situation. Therefore, although the generalized Hurst exponential feature can enhance the classification effect, it will increase the instability of the model at the same time.

4.2   Hidden Layer and Classification Results

The number of neurons in the hidden layer was set to 10, 20, 30 and 40, respectively, and the neural network model was used to study and validate the data. Under the conditions of the number of neurons in the hidden layer, 30 training and tests were taken, and the mean value of the iteration number, the mean value of the accuracy and the standard deviation of the accuracy were taken as the standard metrics.

As can be seen from Table 3, the number of hidden neurons and the number of iterations will show a typical positive correlation, that is, with the number of hidden neurons increases, the number of iterations will be significantly increased, but the number of elements of hidden layer of neurons and the number of iterations are nonlinear. While the more the hidden neuron are, the longer the network model will learn. As the number of neurons in the input layer increases, the number of loop optimization model parameters will increase correspondingly, meanwhile the time of model learning will increase.

Table 3. Hidden layer and iterative relationship

Number of hidden neurons	10	20	30	40
F_0	412	520	539	610
$F_0 \cup F_1$	461	551	573	683
$F_0 \cup F_2$	495	501	546	661
$F_0 \cup F_1 \cup F_2$	498	532	672	714

It can be seen from Table 4 that the accuracy of the model increases with the number of hidden neurons. However, when the number of neurons in the hidden layer exceeds 30, the increase in accuracy will be significantly reduced. Comparing the first and second lists with the first and the third lists, it is found that the generalized Hurst exponent is not as good as the extended multifractal spectral feature, but the generalized Hurst exponent has the same effect on the iteration number and there is no strong multifractal characteristic. The generalized Hurst exponent and the extended multifractal semi-spectral feature have advantages and disadvantages for the model's lifting. Although extending the multi-fractal half spectrum, the multifractal half-spectrum characteristic is extended. At the same time found that the combination of the two cases, which is in the fourth case, the accuracy will be significantly improved.

Table 4. Hidden layer and accuracy relationship

Number of hidden neurons	10	20	30	40
F_0	86.93	87.46	89.72	90.12
$F_0 \cup F_1$	91.47	94.69	95.34	94.13
$F_0 \cup F_2$	89.17	93.67	94.82	93.87
$F_0 \cup F_1 \cup F_2$	92.36	95.93	97.53	97.02

From Table 5, we can see that with the increase of the number of neurons in the hidden layer, the stability of the model's prediction will be enhanced. At that time, when the number of hidden layer neurons reached 30, the stability decreased slowly.

Table 5. Hidden layer and accuracy standard deviation

Number of hidden neurons	10	20	30	40
F_0	0.1615	0.1729	0.1673	0.1565
$F_0 \cup F_1$	0.2367	0.3764	0.2767	0.2518
$F_0 \cup F_2$	0.7931	0.9123	0.8471	0.7927
$F_0 \cup F_1 \cup F_2$	0.5783	0.6273	0.5573	0.4918

5 ECG Diagnosis System Process

5.1 De-noising

The process mainly for low-frequency noise filtering out high-frequency noise filtering and ECG cycle automatically.

(1) low-frequency noise filter out
The main component of low-frequency noise is the baseline drift interference, so we filter out low-frequency noise in the method used to force the wavelet transform filter noise. Firstly, db5 wavelet is used to decompose the ECG signal. In the process of decomposition, the noise signal (low frequency noise) in the data is filtered by the one-dimensional wavelet coefficient threshold method.

(2) high-frequency noise filter out
High-frequency noise mainly includes two parts of the EMG noise and power-frequency interference noise, so we use high-frequency noise filtering threshold method, the same multi-resolution using db5 wavelet decomposition.

5.2 Automatic Segmentation

The R-wave position is quickly located by the difference threshold method, and then the forward and backward search are carried out at the position of the R-wave, respectively. If the R-wave cannot satisfy the fixed length when the signal is taken forward, that is, if the longest signal that can be obtained is less than, the R-wave is discarded. Likewise, if the R-wave cannot satisfy the fixed length when the signal is taken backward, that is, the longest signal that can be obtained is less than, the R-wave is discarded. Finally, the segments of the electrocardiogram were segmented and the position of the R wave was recorded, and each ECG signal was distinguished by the position of the R wave.

5.3 Feature Extraction

The MFDFA method was used to extract the multi-fractal half-spectrum and generalized Hurst exponent of ECG, which is the formula (16). And the eigenvector is used as the output vector of the neural network classification model.

Table 6. Comparison of model accuracy

Models	NB	LB	RB	PB	AB
Fractal model (%)	95.97	94.04	96.64	98.68	93.33
Chaos model (%)	95.33	95.33	94.00	95.33	91.33
Wavelet model (%)	92.66	92.00	94.00	94.67	90.66

5.4   Classification of Models

The classification model uses a three-layer feedforward neural network, and uses the back propagation algorithm to update the weights and thresholds of each neuron. The training data and test data were used to train the feed-forward neural network model, and a model with 97.5% accuracy was chosen as the classification model of ECG diagnosis system. And two recent ECG diagnosis papers [15, 16] were compared. In [15], the features of ECG waveforms are extracted by using wavelet analysis, and the improved BP neural network algorithm is used to train ECG signals. The average recognition accuracy of this model is 92.8%. The article [16] uses the ECG signal chaos characteristic analysis and the Lyapuov index and so on as the characteristic of the ECG signal, and uses the BP neural network to carry on the classification, this model average recognition accuracy rate reaches 94.53%. The wavelet model and chaos model are compared with the fractal model. The comparison results are shown in Table 6. The results show that the fractal model is better than the wavelet model in classification, especially in the PB signal classification situation to enhance the effect is very obvious. Fractal model is superior to chaotic model in identifying NB, RB, PB and AB signals, especially for PB signals, although the ability to identify LB signals is slightly inferior to chaotic model.

5.5   Data Labeling

After the classification of the model, generate the corresponding data label file. The data in the label file is a matrix, which is the number of complete ECG cycles of the ECG signal. The first column shows the position of the R wave and the second column indicates the ECG period of the R wave. The categories of ECG signals are N, L, R, P and A, representing NB, LB, RB, PB and AB signals, respectively. And then generate the corresponding graph or table from the corresponding data annotation file.

In this paper, the main research content is NB, LB, RB, PB and AB signals, and in reality only these five signals composed of ECG fragments is relatively small, so the ECG fragments mentioned in this article ECG simulator simulation generated. Arranging different types of ECG signals into a sequence, and inputting the sequence into the ECG simulator, and finally generating an ECG fragment. 100 ECG fragments consisting of random arrangement of NB, LB, RB, PB and AB signals, each containing about 5 to 10 cycles. In Table 7, TP denotes the number of cases in which positive cases are judged as positive cases, that is, the actual number of ECG cycles is the same as the system judgment; FP is the number of cases in which negative cases are judged as positive cases, i.e., other kinds of signals FN is the number of cases in which the positive type is judged to be negative, that is, the signal of the current type is judged as the number of signals of other classes by the system; TN is the number of negative cases judged as negative. F1 is calculated by the formula (17).

$$F1 = \frac{2PR}{P+R} \tag{17}$$

The precision rate P and the recall rate R are calculated by the formulas (18) and (19), respectively.

$$P = \frac{TP}{TP + FP} \tag{18}$$

$$R = \frac{TP}{TP + FN} \tag{19}$$

From Table 7 available, the system of the ECG signal recognition ability from strong too weak in turn for the PB signal, RB signal, NB signal, LB signal, AB signal. Although the recognition of the AB signal the weakest, but the recognition rate of the system is still up to 93%.

Table 7. Simulation results

Signal	TP	FP	FN	P	R	F1
NB	143	6	7	0.9597	0.9533	0.9565
LB	142	9	7	0.9404	0.9530	0.9467
RB	144	5	6	0.9664	0.9600	0.9632
PB	150	2	4	0.9868	0.9740	0.9804
AB	140	10	8	0.9333	0.9459	0.9396

References

1. Escalona, O.J., Mitchell, R.H., Balderson, D.E., Harron, D.W.: Fast and reliable QRS alignment technique for high-frequency analysis of signal-averaged ECG. Med. Biol. Eng. Comput. **31**(1), 137–146 (1993)
2. Jané, R., Rix, H., Caminal, P.: Alignment methods for averaging of high-resolution cardiac signals: a comparative study of performance. IEEE Trans. Biomed. Eng. **38**(6), 571–579 (1991)
3. Farrell, R.M., Xue, J.Q., Young, B.J.: Enhanced rhythm analysis for resting ECG using spectral and time domain techniques. In: Proceedings of the IEEE/RSJ International Conference on Computers in Cardiology, Thessaloniki Chalkidiki, Greece, vol. 30, no. 6, pp. 733–736 (2003)
4. Sun, Y., Chan, K.L., Krishnan, S.M.: Characteristic wave detection in ECG signal using morphological transform. BMC Cardiovasc. Disord. **5**(1), 7–19 (2005)
5. Shyu, L.Y., Wu, Y.H., Hu, W.: Using wavelet transform and fuzzy neural network for VPC detection from the Holter ECG. IEEE Trans. Biomed. Eng. **51**(7), 1269–1273 (2004)
6. Kohler, B.U., Henning, C., Orglmeister, R.: The principles of software QRS detection. IEEE Eng. Med. Biol. Mag. **21**(1), 42–57 (2002)
7. Addison, P.S.: Wavelet transforms and the ECG: a review. Physiol. Meas. **26**(5), 155–199 (2005)
8. Chen, H.C., Chen, S.W.: A moving average based filtering system with its application to realtime QRS detection. In: Proceedings of the IEEE/RSJ International Conference on Computers in Cardiology, Thessaloniki Chalkidiki, Greece, pp. 585–588 (2003)

9. Pan, J.P., Tompkins, W.J.: A real-time QRS detection algorithm. IEEE Trans. Biomed. Eng. **32**(3), 230–236 (1985)
10. Sahambi, J.S., Tandon, S.N., Bhatt, P.K.: Using wavelet transforms for ECG characterization: an online digital signal processing system. IEEE Eng. Med. Biol. Mag. **16**(1), 77–83 (1997)
11. Sasikala, P., Wahidabanu, R.S.D.: Robust R peak and QRS detection in electrocardiogram using wavelet transform. Int. J. Adv. Comput. Sci. Appl. **1**(6), 48–53 (2010)
12. Falconer, K.J.: Fractal Geometry: Mathematical Foundation and Applications, pp. 158–159. Wiley, Chichester (1990)
13. Arduini, F., Fioravanti, S., Giusto, D.D.: A multifractal-based approach to natural scene analysis. In: Proceedings of the 1991 International Conference on Acoustics, Speech, and Signal Processing, Piscataway, NJ, USA, pp. 2681–2684 (1991)
14. Cheng, Q.: Generalized binomial multiplicative cascade processes and asymmetrical multifractal distributions. Nonlinear Process. Geophys. **21**(2), 477–487 (2014)
15. Gautam, M.K., Giri, V.K.: A neural network approach and wavelet analysis for ECG classification. In: 2016 IEEE International Conference on Engineering and Technology (ICETECH), pp. 1136–1141. IEEE (2016)
16. Gautam, M.K., Giri, V.K.: An approach of neural network for electrocardiogram classification. APTIKOM J. Comput. Sci. Inf. Technol. **1**(3), 115–123 (2016)

A Precoding Scheme Based on SLNR for Downlink MU-MIMO Systems

Wei Zhang[✉], Wenjie Wo, and Jingjing Duan

College of Information and Communication Engineering,
Harbin Engineering University, Nantong str. 145, Harbin 145001, China
zhangwei@hrbeu.edu.cn

Abstract. The precoding scheme plays an important role in suppressing co-channel interference for downlink multi-user (MU) multiple-input-multiple-output (MIMO) communication systems. The effects of noise are not ignored in precoding scheme based on Signal-to-leakage-and-noise ratio (SLNR) and there are no limits on the number of transmit antennas. In this paper, a modified SLNR-based precoding scheme is presented, which can balance the channel gain for each stream per user by diagonalizating leakage-and-noise and the user's channel matrices simultaneously. Simulation results show that better BER performance can be obtained by the proposed scheme as compared with zero-forcing (ZF) precoding and conventional SLNR solution.

Keywords: Downlink · MU MIMO · SLNR-based precoding · ZF

1 Introduction

In multi-user MIMO systems, precoding technique plays a major role in improving the system performance. The core idea is pre-processing the data to be transmitted by the use of the channel state information (CSI) at the base station, to reduce the co-channel interference (CCI) among users and achieve a higher performance gain. Linear precoding is widely used due to its low complexity [1].

Signal-to-interference-plus-noise ratio (SINR) is always applied as a measure of performance, but it is also a challenge for its coupled problem with precoding matrix and the number of users. In previous studies, so as to solve this problem, zero-forcing (ZF) precoding is proposed to cancel the CCI [2, 3]. The shortcomings of these schemes are the restriction on the number of the receive antennas (RA) and transmit antennas (TA). Furthermore, zero-forcing scheme does not take the effects of noise into consideration [4].

Another criterion, SLNR criterion is first proposed by Sadek et al. [5, 6], which cleverly solved the precoding matrix design problem under the SINR criterion [7]. In view of the SLNR criterion, the precoding scheme is expected to make the received signal power of each active user as large as possible, while the sum of the noise power and the interference power leaked from other users is as small as possible. As a criterion, SLNR is better than SINR [8], for the reason that the SLNR of any user depends only on its own precoding matrix, and has nothing to do with other users' coding matrix. Therefore, it is possible to avoid the nesting problem of optimizing the

© ICST Institute for Computer Sciences, Social Informatics and Telecommunications Engineering 2018
G. Sun and S. Liu (Eds.): ADHIP 2017, LNICST 219, pp. 448–456, 2018.
https://doi.org/10.1007/978-3-319-73317-3_51

precoding matrix of each user, and derive the optimal closed solution of each user's precoding matrix directly. In addition, the precoding scheme which is based on SLNR criterion is no longer constrained by the quantity of system antennas, and thus has a wider application space.

Conventional SLNR-based linear precoding pursues the maximization of SLNR by the use of the generalized eigenvalue decomposition (GED) of the leakage-channel-and-noise covariance matrix among users and the channel covariance matrix [9]. Whereas, in a real communication environment, different users experience different channel fading, and it is difficult to balance the SINR of each user's received signal. The SINR of the users which experience severe channel fading will be much lower [10], thus affecting the overall system performance.

In this paper, the fairness of communication among users in downlink MU-MIMO system is considered, and the precoding scheme is improved. The core idea is reducing the maximum value of SLNR slightly so as to balance the SINR of each user with multiple data streams.

2 System Model

2.1 Downlink MU-MIMO System

The block diagram of a downlink multi-user MIMO system is presented in Fig. 1. The vector $\mathbf{s}_k(n)$ represents the transmitted data of user k at nth time instant, and $\mathbf{w}_k$ represents precoding matrix. Assuming that the downlink MU-MIMO system with K users has N TAs at the base station, and each user in the block diagram has M_K RAs. Then, at time instant n the overall transmit matrix could be expressed as

$$\mathbf{x}(n) = \sum_{k=1}^{K} \mathbf{w}_k \mathbf{s}_k(n) \tag{1}$$

For convenience, the data vector $\mathbf{s}_k(n)$ and precoding matrix $\mathbf{w}_k$ are subject to

$$E|\mathbf{s}_k(n)|^2 = 1, \quad \|\mathbf{w}_k\|^2 = L_k \quad k = 1, 2 \ldots K \tag{2}$$

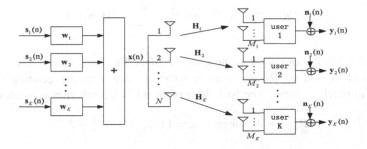

Fig. 1. Downlink MU-MIMO system model

The channel is assumed to be frequency flat faded

$$
\mathbf{H}_k = \begin{bmatrix} h_k^{(1,1)} & \cdots & h_k^{(1,N)} \\ \vdots & \ddots & \vdots \\ h_k^{(M_k,1)} & \cdots & h_k^{(M_k,N)} \end{bmatrix}_{M_k \times N}
\tag{3}
$$

where $h_k^{(r,t)}$ is channel impulse response between the tth$(t = 1, 2, \cdots, N)$ TA and the rth $(r = 1, 2, \cdots, M_k)$ RA at user. Assume that $h_k^{(r,t)}$ obey the complex Gaussian distribution with mean = 0 and variance = 1, i.e., the channel is Rayleigh faded. In this case, the kth$(k = 1, 2, \cdots, K)$ user's received signal at time instant n is

$$
\mathbf{y}_k(n) = \mathbf{H}_k\mathbf{x}(n) + \mathbf{n} = \mathbf{H}_k \sum_{j=1}^{K} \mathbf{w}_j\mathbf{s}_j(n) + \mathbf{n}_k(n)
\tag{4}
$$

where $\mathbf{n}_k(n)$ denotes the additive white Gaussian noise with $\sigma^2 - variance$. So SNR at each RA is

$$
SNR = 1/\sigma^2
\tag{5}
$$

For the convenience of research, we assume that CSI $\mathbf{H}_k(k = 1, 2, \cdots, K)$ is known, and $\mathbf{s}_k(n)$, $\mathbf{H}_k$ and $\mathbf{n}_k(n)$ are assumed to be independent of one another.

2.2   SLNR-Based Precoding System Model

We can expand the expression in (4) into the following form

$$
\mathbf{y}_k(n) = \mathbf{H}_k\mathbf{w}_k\mathbf{s}_k(n) + \mathbf{H}_k \sum_{j=1, j\neq k}^{K} \mathbf{w}_j\mathbf{s}_j(n) + \mathbf{n}_k(n)
\tag{6}
$$

The first term is the signal that the receiver actually needs to receive, while the second term includes the interference signal which is going to leak to other users. SINR of the user k is defined as (omit the time index n for convenience)

$$
SINR_k = \|\mathbf{H}_k\mathbf{w}_k\|^2 / (\mathbf{M}_k\sigma^2 + \sum_{j=1, j\neq k}^{K} \|\mathbf{H}_k\mathbf{w}_j\|^2)
\tag{7}
$$

Choosing SINR expression as the criterion of performance cannot avoid coupled problem with K and $\mathbf{w}_k$ [6]. In order to solve it, zero-forcing precoding has been proposed in previous paper. The basic idea of zero-forcing schemes is to cancel CCI.

$$
\mathbf{H}_k\mathbf{w}_j = \mathbf{0} \quad for \ all \ \ j, k = \{1, 2, \cdots, K\}, j \neq k
\tag{8}
$$

In this way, although the CCI is completely removed, the noise power does not accordingly decrease, and may even be amplified. In addition, in order to let the expression in (8) hold, the following relationship must be satisfied

$$N > \max_i \left\{ \sum_{k=1, k \neq i}^{K} M_k \right\} \qquad (9)$$

Because SINR-based scheme is subject to the above condition, it is necessary to apply a new criterion which takes noise into consideration and will not be limited by constraint condition in (9). SLNR-based scheme can satisfy the above requirements.

SLNR-based precoding system model is illustrated in Fig. 2, where $\|\mathbf{H}_k \mathbf{w}_j s_j\|^2$ $(k = 1, \cdots, j-1, j+1, \cdots, K)$ is defined as leakage from user j to other users. In the above we assume that $E|s_k(n)|^2 = 1$, so SLNR of user k can be defined as

$$SLNR_k = \|\mathbf{H}_k \mathbf{w}_k\|^2 / (M_k \sigma^2 + \sum_{j=1, j \neq k}^{K} \|\mathbf{H}_j \mathbf{w}_k\|^2) \qquad (10)$$

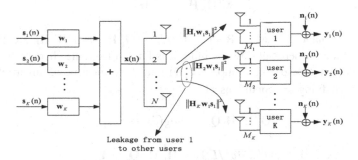

Leakage from user 1
to other users

Fig. 2. SLNR-based precoding system model

Compared with SINR, the SLNR-based scheme calculates the interference of user k to other users, rather than the interference of other users to user k. To maximize every user's SLNR, the precoding matrix $\mathbf{w}_k$ should satisfy

$$\|\mathbf{w}_k\|^2 = L_k \quad k = 1, 2 \ldots K \qquad (11)$$

where L_k denotes the data stream of the user k. In the following, the data stream of every user is assumed equal, and uniformly expressed as L. Then

$$SLNR_k = \frac{Tr(\mathbf{w}_k^H \mathbf{H}_k^H \mathbf{H}_k \mathbf{w}_k)}{Tr(\mathbf{w}_k^H (\frac{M_k \sigma^2}{L} \mathbf{I}_N + \tilde{\mathbf{H}}_k^H \tilde{\mathbf{H}}_k) \mathbf{w}_k)} \qquad (12)$$

$$\tilde{\mathbf{H}}_k = [\mathbf{H}_1, \cdots, \mathbf{H}_{k-1}, \mathbf{H}_{k+1}, \cdots \mathbf{H}_K]^T \qquad (13)$$

The optimization problem of $\mathbf{w}_k$ can be expressed as

$$\mathbf{w}_k^{opt} = \arg \max_{w_k \in \mathbb{C}^{N \times L}} \frac{Tr(\mathbf{w}_k^H \mathbf{H}_k^H \mathbf{H}_k \mathbf{w}_k)}{Tr(\mathbf{w}_k^H (\frac{M_k \sigma^2}{L} \mathbf{I}_N + \tilde{\mathbf{H}}_k^H \tilde{\mathbf{H}}_k) \mathbf{w}_k)} \tag{14}$$

Since the base station simultaneously transmits L spatially multiplexed data streams to all users, co-channel interference includes inter-user interference (IUI) among users and inter-stream interference (ISI) among multiple data streams. So the signal recovered at the receiver of user k is

$$\hat{\mathbf{s}}_k = \frac{(\mathbf{H}_k \mathbf{w}_k)^H}{\|\mathbf{H}_k \mathbf{w}_k\|^2} \mathbf{y}_k = \frac{(\mathbf{H}_k \mathbf{w}_k)^H}{\|\mathbf{H}_k \mathbf{w}_k\|^2} \mathbf{H}_k \mathbf{w}_k \mathbf{s}_k + \frac{(\mathbf{H}_k \mathbf{w}_k)^H}{\|\mathbf{H}_k \mathbf{w}_k\|^2} (\mathbf{H}_k \sum_{j=1, j \neq k}^{K} \mathbf{w}_j \mathbf{s}_j + \mathbf{n}_k) \tag{15}$$

where the first term of the equation is the desired signal and the other term includes noise and the interference. In order to achieve the decoupling of multiple data streams at the receiver of user, the optimization of the precoding matrix problem in (14) needs to satisfy the constraint condition

$$\mathbf{w}_k^H \mathbf{H}_k^H \mathbf{H}_k \mathbf{w}_k = \mathbf{D}_k \tag{16}$$

where $\mathbf{D}_k$ is a diagonal matrix. Both $M\sigma^2/L\mathbf{I}_N + \tilde{\mathbf{H}}_k^H \tilde{\mathbf{H}}_k$ and $\mathbf{H}_k^H \mathbf{H}_k$ are Hermitian matrices, and the former is positive definite. It is known from the characteristics of the generalized eigenvalue decomposition (GED) that there must be an invertible matrix $\mathbf{Q}_i \in \mathbb{C}^{N \times N}$ satisfying the conditions of

$$\mathbf{Q}_k^H \mathbf{H}_k^H \mathbf{H}_k \mathbf{Q}_k = diag(\lambda_1, \cdots, \lambda_N) \tag{17}$$

$$\mathbf{Q}_k^H [(M\sigma^2/L)\mathbf{I}_N + \tilde{\mathbf{H}}_k^H \tilde{\mathbf{H}}_k] \mathbf{Q}_k = \mathbf{I}_N \tag{18}$$

With $\{\lambda_i\}_{i=1}^N$ being sorted in descending order. The column vector of $\mathbf{Q}_i$ and $\{\lambda_i\}_{i=1}^N$ are respectively the generalized eigenvectors and eigenvalues of the matrix $\left\{ \mathbf{H}_k^H \mathbf{H}_k, M\sigma^2/L\mathbf{I}_N + \tilde{\mathbf{H}}_k^H \tilde{\mathbf{H}}_k \right\}$. It has been proved in [3] that the precoding matrix $\mathbf{w}_i$ maximizing the $SLNR_k$ in (14) is given by

$$\mathbf{w}_k^{opt} = \alpha \mathbf{Q}_k \begin{bmatrix} \mathbf{I}_L \\ \mathbf{0} \end{bmatrix} \tag{19}$$

where α is a scalar in order to satisfy $\|\mathbf{w}_k\|^2 = L$, and according to (20), we obtain

$$SLNR_k^{\max} = \sum_{j=1}^{L} \frac{\lambda_j}{L} \tag{20}$$

3   Proposed SLNR-Based Precoding Scheme

In the real communication environment, signals of different users experience different channel fading. And, when is larger than 1, it is difficult to balance the SINR of each user. The severer the channel fading becomes, the lower is the SINR at the receiver, which will affect the overall system performance. In this section, the fairness of communication among users in downlink MU-MIMO systems is considered, and an improved precoding scheme is proposed in the following. In this section, we diagonalize two matrices simultaneously. There must be a full rank matrix which satisfies the conditions in (22) and (23)

$$\mathbf{T}_k^H \mathbf{H}_k^H \mathbf{H}_k \mathbf{T}_k = diag(\beta_1, \beta_2, \cdots, \beta_N) \tag{21}$$

$$\mathbf{T}_k^H (\frac{M\sigma^2}{L} \mathbf{I}_N + \tilde{\mathbf{H}}_k^H \tilde{\mathbf{H}}_k) \mathbf{T}_k = diag(\gamma_1, \gamma_2, \cdots, \gamma_N) \tag{22}$$

where $\{\beta_i\}_{i=0}^M$ are sorted in descending order from 1 to 0, and $\{\beta_i\}_{i=M+1}^N = 0$. In the meanwhile, $\{\gamma_i\}_{i=0}^M$ are sorted in ascending order from 0 to 1, $\{\gamma_i\}_{i=M+1}^N = 1$. Furthermore, elements in $\{\gamma_i + \beta_i\}_{i=1}^N$ are all 1. The precoding matrix is then given by

$$\mathbf{w}_{kp}^{opt} = \varphi \mathbf{T}_k \begin{bmatrix} \mathbf{I}_L \\ \mathbf{0} \end{bmatrix} \tag{23}$$

where φ is a scalar in order to satisfy $\|\mathbf{w}_k\|^2 = L$. And in this way, $SLNR_k$ can be calculated by

$$SLNR_k = \sum_{a=1}^L \beta_a / \sum_{a=1}^L (1 - \beta_a) \tag{24}$$

In contrast with expression in (21), $SLNR_k$ here is a little smaller. But when the number of data streams ≥ 2, $SINR$ of each stream will be more balanced. Denote the $SINR$ of stream l as η_l', then

$$\eta_l' = \varphi^4 \beta_l^2 / \varphi^2 \sigma^2 \beta_l = \varphi^2 \beta_l / \sigma^2 \tag{25}$$

Furthermore, assume that $l > m$, the ratio of SINRs between two data streams l and m can be written as

$$\eta_l' / \eta_m' = \beta_l / \beta_m \tag{26}$$

While in the conventional scheme

$$\eta_l / \eta_m = \lambda_l / \lambda_m \tag{27}$$

Since both $\{\lambda_i\}_{i=1}^N$ and $\{\beta_i/\gamma_i\}_{i=1}^N$ are generalized eigenvalues of $\{\mathbf{H}_i^H\mathbf{H}_i, M\sigma^2/LI_N + \tilde{\mathbf{H}}_i^H\tilde{\mathbf{H}}_i\}$, there must be

$$\{\beta_i/\gamma_i\}_{i=1}^N = \{\lambda_i\}_{i=1}^N \tag{28}$$

We can easily find that

$$(\eta_l'/\eta_m') < (\eta_l/\eta_m) \tag{29}$$

This means that in the proposed scheme, SINR of any two streams is more balanced than that in the original scheme. And the overall BER performance will get better, which will be proved by simulations in the next section.

4   Simulation Results

In this section, first the BER in cases of single user, zero forcing scheme and SLNR-based solution in downlink MU-MIMO systems are simulated. Parameters of simulations are given in Table 1. All simulations are run on the basis of a quasi-static MIMO channel mode. We assume that the CSI is known and the additive white Gaussian noise is subject to σ^2-variance. Furthermore, we assume that the number of RAs belonging to different users is equal. Simulation results are shown in Fig. 3. As known in Sect. 2, when $L = 1$, there is no ISI. Similarly, when the number of users is 1, there is no any IUI. Therefore, there is no doubt that single user scheme's BER performance is the best. Although ZF scheme can reduce CCI to zero, it cannot equalize noise. The SLNR-based scheme takes into account both the noise matrix and the channel impulse response matrix. So its BER performance is better than ZF schemes. In addition, when the number of RAs is 3, i.e. it does not satisfy the expression in (9) so that the worst BER performance is obtained.

In the following simulations, we assume that TA = 8, User = 2 and RA = 3, Fig. 4 illustrates the sum rate and BER performance of the original and the proposed scheme when $L = 1, 2, 3$, where P represents "proposed" and O represents "original". As we can see in the following figures, the sum rate of system with the proposed scheme is less than that of the original scheme. With the increase of L, the gap inbetween becomes gradually smaller, and BER performance gets worse. It is because the interference among data streams increases with L. In summary, with the proposed scheme, the improved over-all error bit performance is obtained on the expense of the sum rate.

Table 1. Simulation parameters

Precoding scheme	L	TA	User	RA of user	Modulation
Single user	1	8	1	3	QPSK
SLNR-based	1	8	3	3	QPSK
ZF, RA = 2	1	8	3	2	QPSK
ZF, RA = 3	1	8	3	3	QPSK

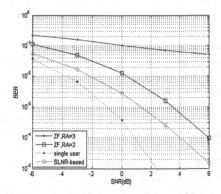

Fig. 3. The BER performance of single user, zero forcing and SLNR-based solution

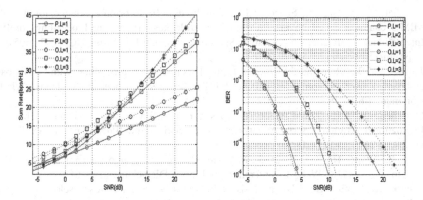

Fig. 4. The BER and sum tate performance of original and proposed schemes

5 Conclusion

The downlink multi-user MIMO system and the traditional SLNR-based system have been detailed in this paper. On this basis, an improved SLNR-based scheme was proposed, which makes the overall BER performance better. The simulation results show that when the number of data streams increase, the BER performance of the proposed scheme is superior to the original scheme, and its sum rate performance gradually catches up with that of original scheme.

Acknowledgment. This work is funded by the International Exchange Program of Harbin Engineering University for Innovation-oriented Talents Cultivation and National Nature Science Foundation of China (No. 61671167, 61301095, 61401114).

References

1. Saeid, E., Jeoti, V., Samir, B.B.: Linear precoding for multi-cell processing multiuser MIMO systems. In: 2012 4th International Conference on Intelligent and Advanced Systems (ICIAS), vol. 1, pp. 259–264. IEEE (2012)
2. Nguyen, V.D., Nguyen, H.V., Shin, O.S.: An efficient zero-forcing precoding design for cognitive MIMO broadcast channels. IEEE Commun. Lett. **20**(8), 1575–1578 (2016)
3. Bashar, M., Eslami, M., Dehghani, M.J.: Zero-forcing precoding with partially outdated CSI over time-varying MIMO broadcast channels. In: 2013 IEEE 77th Vehicular Technology Conference (VTC Spring), pp. 1–5. IEEE (2013)
4. Wiesel, A., Eldar, Y.C., Shamai, S.: Zero-forcing precoding and generalized inverses. IEEE Trans. Sig. Process. **56**(9), 4409–4418 (2008)
5. Sadek, M., Tarighat, A., Sayed, A.H.: A leakage-based precoding scheme for downlink multi-user MIMO channels. IEEE Trans. Wirel. Commun. **6**(5) (2007). Maxwell, C.: A Treatise on Electricity and Magnetism, 3rd edn., vol. 2, pp. 68–73. Clarendon, Oxford (1892)
6. Tarighat, A., Sadek, M., Sayed, A.H.: A multi user beamforming scheme for downlink MIMO channels based on maximizing signal-to-leakage ratios. In: Proceedings of IEEE International Conference on Acoustics, Speech, and Signal Processing (ICASSP 2005), vol. 3, pp. iii/1129–iii/1132. IEEE (2005)
7. James, J.V.B., Ramamurthi, B.: Distributed cooperative precoding with SINR-based co-channel user grouping for enhanced cell edge performance. IEEE Trans. Wireless Commun. **10**(9), 2896–2907 (2011)
8. Swindlehurst, A.L.: Fixed SINR solutions for the MIMO wiretap channel. In: IEEE International Conference on Acoustics, Speech and Signal Processing, ICASSP 2009, pp. 2437–2440. IEEE (2009)
9. Jiang, J., Wang, H., Xie, Y., et al.: MAX-SLNR precoding algorithm for massive MIMO system. In: MATEC Web of Conferences, vol. 56. EDP Sciences (2016)
10. Oturak, A., Öztürk, E.: SINR analysis of FFH/OFDM over frequency selective Rayleigh fading channel. Wireless Commun. Mob. Comput. (2016)

Research on LDPC - CPM Coded Modulation Communication System

Xin Wei$^{(\boxtimes)}$, Zhi-gang Li, and Zheng Dou

College of Information and Communication Engineering,
Harbin Engineering University, Nantong Str. 145, Harbin 150001, China
weixin@hrbeu.edu.cn

Abstract. In order to improve the performance of communication system, using integrated coding and modulation process to balance the design, but after trying, we find it difficult to meet the expected requirements, so joint coding modulation came into being. Continuous phase modulation is a kind of constant-envelope modulation schemes with continuous phase which provides good spectral and power efficiency. In this paper, a continuous phase code modulation system based on soft information propagation is proposed. At first, it decodes the CPM by Soft-out Viterbi Algorithm (SOVA), and then uses the soft belief and the hard decision as the input of the LDPC decoder, and finally gets the simulation results. The simulation results show that the method can reach the performance close to the Shannon limit.

Keywords: CPM · LDPC · SOVA

1 Introduction

The development of multimedia service puts forward new requirements for the validity and reliability of satellite communication system. However, the power and bandwidth of satellite communication system are limited, and how to improve the effectiveness and reliability of satellite communication system under the limited power and bandwidth become an urgent problem to be solved. Since Shannon published the "mathematical theory of communication", coding and modulation technology is critical in any communication system. The role of the channel encoder/decoder is to improve the reliability of digital information transmission, however it will lead to the increased redundancy, then the information transmission rate will be reduced. By increasing the sign set of the modulation signal, it is possible to avoid the decrease in the information transmission rate due to the increased redundancy in the band limited channel. However, if the channel is not only limited frequency, power is limited, expanding the modulation signal symbol set will reduce the Euclidean distance of the signal and reduce the reliability of digital information transmission. This requires a higher gain coding method to compensate for the loss of performance, which will greatly increase the complexity of the code [1]. Therefore, purely increasing the modulation signal symbol set and the increased information redundancy is not an effective way to improve the performance of the communication system. Of course, the integrated coding and modulation process can be balanced design, but after trying to find the

© ICST Institute for Computer Sciences, Social Informatics and Telecommunications Engineering 2018
G. Sun and S. Liu (Eds.): ADHIP 2017, LNICST 219, pp. 457–464, 2018.
https://doi.org/10.1007/978-3-319-73317-3_52

integrated design of the two system performance is still difficult to achieve the desired requirements. Of course, the design can be balanced through an integrated design coding and modulation process, but after trying, we find the integrated design of the system performance is still difficult to achieve the desired requirements. Because when the signal at the receiver is tested, the independent hard decision will be done, the next decoding can not get all the received information, resulting in channel coding gain can not be fully played [2]. Then the idea of joint coding modulation came into being, CPM decomposition method, making CPM as the inner code and the traditional coding cascade, the introduction of iterative detection to improve the system performance has became possible [3].

2 LDPC Codes Introduction

The low density parity (LDPC) code is a class of linear codes named by the sparse features of the parity check matrix, that is, almost all of the elements in H are zero, with only a very small number of nonzero elements. Gallager's first defined binary (N, dv, dc) LDPC code is a linear code with a codeword length of N and a design bit rate of R0 = 1−dv/dc. Each column of the check matrix H contains exactly dv "1" , each line contains just dc "1". Since the parity check matrix satisfying this structural condition is not unique, the LDPC codes with parameters (N, dv, dc) form a set of codes [4]. The following are some commonly used methods in LDPC codes. There are many representations of LDPC codes: (1) check matrix representation; (2) Tanner graph representation; (3) degree function representation. LDPC code construction methods: (1) PEG random configuration method; (2) QC structured construction method. LDPC code decoding method: (1) Sum-product algorithm; (2) BP decoding algorithm, etc. The advantages of LDPC codes are as follows: (1) LDPC decoding algorithm is a parallel iterative decoding algorithm based on sparse matrix. The computational complexity is lower than the Turbo decoding algorithm, and it is easier to implement in hardware because of the parallel structure. (2) LDPC code bit rate can be arbitrarily constructed, flexible; (3) LDPC code has a lower error leveling layer, can be used in wired communications, high-altitude communications and disk storage industry, where the bit error rate requirements are more demanding occasions; (4) its performance approximates the Shannon limit and it is described and implemented simply [5].

3 Continuous Phase Modulation

Continuous phase modulation has the characteristics of constant envelope and continuous phase, which has higher spectral efficiency and power utilization compared with other modulation methods. In addition, due to the memory characteristics, CPM signal has a certain coding gain [6].

3.1 CPM Definition

The transmission signal of the CPM can be defined as

$$s(t, \alpha) = \sqrt{\frac{2E}{T}} \cos(2\pi f_0 t + \varphi(t, \alpha) + \varphi_0), (-\infty \le t \le +\infty) \qquad (1)$$

Among them, E is the symbolic energy, T is the symbol interval, f_0 is the carrier frequency, φ_0 is the initial phase (usually use $\varphi_0 = 0$), $\alpha = (\alpha_0, \alpha_1, \alpha_2, \cdots)$ is sent to the finite length M of the information symbol sequence, $\alpha_i \in \{\pm 1, \pm 2, \cdots, \pm(M-1)\}$, $i = 0, 1, 2, \cdots$, with the same probability $1/M$ (M generally odd), the signal amplitude is constant. It can be seen from the definition of the CPM signal that the additional phase $\varphi(t, \alpha)$ is the result of the common effect of all the symbols before, not only by the single symbol.

Additional phase is

$$\varphi(t, \alpha) = 2\pi h \sum_{i=-\infty}^{\infty} \alpha_i q(t - iT), (-\infty < t < \infty) \qquad (2)$$

$\alpha_i \in \{\pm 1, \pm 2, \cdots, \pm(M-1)\}, (i = 0, \pm 1, \pm 2, \cdots)$ value of the same probability, are $1/M$. h called the modulation coefficient, you can take any real number, but when h takes the number of irrational, CPM system will have numerous states, so h in practical applications should take a rational number, that is, $h = K/P$ (K, P for the quality of integer).

3.2 CPM Phase Status

The phase of the modulation obtained after the introduction of the tilt phase is:

$$\varphi(\tau + nT, \alpha) = R_{2\pi} \left(2\pi \frac{m}{p} R_p \left(\sum_{k=-\infty}^{n-L} u_k \right) \right) + R_{2\pi} \left(4\pi h \sum_{k=0}^{L-1} u_{n-k} q(\tau + kT) \right) + R_{2\pi}(\omega(\tau))$$

$$(3)$$

set $v_n = R_p \left(\sum_{k=-\infty}^{n-L} u_k \right)$, $v_n \in \{0, 1, \cdots, p-1\}$, $S_n = \{v_n, u_{n-1}, u_{n-2}, \cdots, u_{n-L+1}\}$, the phase at this time corresponds to the phase state, and the number of phases of the tilted phase representation has nothing to do with the parity.

$$\begin{cases} \varphi(t, \alpha) = f(S_n, n) = g(\gamma(S_{n-1}, u_{n-1})) \\ N_s = pM^{L-1} \end{cases} \qquad (4)$$

Where the function $g(x)$ is a time-invariant one-one mapping function, the state transition function $\gamma(x, y)$ is also a time-invariant function $\varphi(t, \alpha)$ can be launched for the Markov process [7].

3.3 CPM Model Decomposition

CPM can be decomposed into a Continuous Phase Encoder (CPE) and a Memoryless Modulator (MM) [8].

Memoryless Demodulator (MM). The physical tilted phase can be expressed in the following form:

$$
\begin{aligned}
\bar{\psi}(\tau + nT, u) &= R_{2\pi}[\varphi(\tau + nT, u)] \\
&= R_{2\pi}\left[2\pi h \sum_{i=0}^{n-L} u_i + 4\pi h \sum_{i=P}^{L-1} u_{n-1}q(\tau + iT) + W(\tau) \right] \\
&= R_{2\pi}\left[2\pi h R_P\left[\sum_{i=0}^{n-L} u_i\right] + 4\pi h \sum_{i=0}^{L-1} u_{n-i}q(\tau + iT) + W(\tau) \right], 0 \le \tau < T
\end{aligned}
\tag{5}
$$

Is an item that is independent of the input data. According to Eq. (5), the physical phase of the CPM signal is determined by the input of the MM, so that the output signal is also determined by the input of the MM. The input of the MM can be defined as, $S_n = \{v_n, u_{n-1}, u_{n-2}, \cdots, u_{n-L+1}\}$, here the $v_n = R_p\left(\sum_{k=-\infty}^{n-L} u_k\right)$, the cumulative phase before the time n (besides the moment n). If you use $\bar{\psi}(\tau, S_n)$ to replace $\bar{\psi}(\tau + nT, u)(0 \le \tau < T)$, $s(\tau, S_n)$ replace $s(\tau + nT, u)(0 \le \tau < T)$, you can get:

$$
s(\tau, S_n) = \sqrt{\frac{2E}{T}}\cos(2\pi(\tau + nT)f_1 +
\tag{6}
$$
$$
\bar{\psi}(\tau + S_n) + \varphi_0), 0 \le \tau < T
$$

Phase Encoder (CPE). As noted earlier, according to the next input data u_{n+1} the CPE can update the input of the MM from S_n to S_{n+1}. In $v_n = R_p\left(\sum_{k=-\infty}^{n-L} u_k\right)$ using $n + 1$ to replace n, you can get:

$$
\begin{aligned}
V_{n+1} &= R_P\left[\sum_{i=0}^{n-L+1} u_i\right] = R_P\left[\sum_{i=0}^{n-L} u_i + u_{n-L+1}\right] \\
&= R_P\left[R_P\left[\sum_{i=0}^{n-L} u_i\right] + u_{n-L+1}\right] \\
&= R_P[V_n + u_{n-L+1}]
\end{aligned}
\tag{7}
$$

Obviously, it is possible to obtain the update of the first L components of S_n by the nearest L data shift. In this way, the CPE can calculate the current MM input from formula (7) based on the current data and the input of the previous MM, and MM can calculate the output information according to formula (6).

4   LDPC - CPM System Model

4.1   SOVA Decoding Algorithm

Combined with the literature [9], it is easy to know the 2^s states of a time unit t, taking the i th one as an example. The memory stores the current state S_{ti}, the maximum partial measure $SM([r|v]_{t,i})$ and the partial likelihood code word sequence $V_{t,i}^*$, when entering the current state of the current state. In the iterative process, the grid table is used in the reverse direction, such as the state of m entering $S_{t,i}$ at time $t - 1$, it is respectively $S_{t-1,j=1:m}$.

$$SM\left([r|v]_{t,i}\right) = \max_{j=1:m}\left\{ SM\left([r|v]_{t-1,j}\right) + \log P\left(S_{t,i}|S_{t-1,j}\right) \right\} \tag{8}$$

$$V_{t,i}^* = \left[V_{t-1,i}^*, V_{j\xrightarrow{\text{max}}i}^* \right] \tag{9}$$

SOVA basic operation and Viterbi algorithm are the same, the only difference is that each information bit attaches to a reliability instruction to the hard decision output, that is, soft output. This soft output is $ms = abs(ms_0 - ms_1)$ for binary and multiplied by the ± 1 value representing v. This is similar to SISO, but SISO has both forward and backward. It is envisioned that the method of subtracting the minimum value from the maximum value of SISO is used in Multi-system (Fig 1).

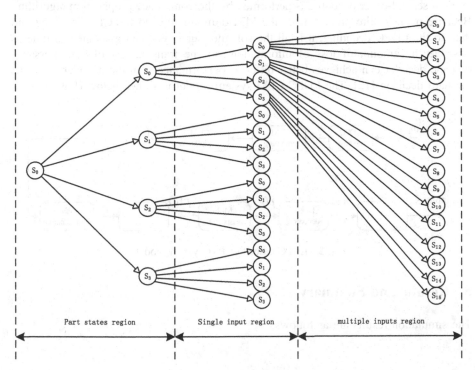

Fig. 1. SOVA messaging

4.2 System Model

CPM modulation is a constant envelope modulation system, which is not sensitive to the non-linear characteristics of the amplifier, allowing the use of non-linear power amplifier, so that the power amplifier can work in a saturated state, for airborne and deep space communications stations and other limited power applications having important significance [10]. The CPM is used as a component code of the concatenated code and the soft message obtained by the soft decoding algorithm is transmitted to the LDPC decoder to make the system have the dual characteristics of the LDPC code and the concatenated code. The system has the following two advantages: 1. The error level is lower, the bit error rate increases with SNR has acute drop characteristics, compared with the SCCPM, the performance is improved significantly. 2. The interleaver does not exist in the system and does not need multiple iterations, the decoding time can be reduced compared with the SCCPM [11].

The decoding process firstly makes demodulation and decoding of the CPM as MM and CPE, respectively. The MM modulator is usually demodulated in a manner of matching the template, and the CPE decoder decodes the relevant values as priori information. The system decoder stores all the CPM waveform template, and demodulation can use these templates in parallel. MM demodulated soft messages are passed directly to the CPE decoder and decoded by the SISO algorithm to pass the posterior probabilities to the LDPC decoder in the form of soft messages. In the LDPC decoder, the soft message provided by the CPE decoder is used as a priori information, and the second-order decoding is performed by the confidence propagation algorithm. Because of the entire process from the MM demodulation to the CPE decoding and then to the LDPC decoding, it is all the soft messages, you can guarantee as little as possible the amount of loss of information, so the transmission of soft messages cascade decoder can achieves better bit error performance than the decoder performs the hard decision [12]. The LDPC-CPM system model is shown below (Fig 2).

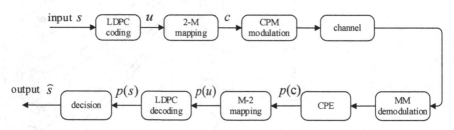

Fig. 2. LDPC cascade CPM system model

5 Results and Summary

The simulation results are as follows:

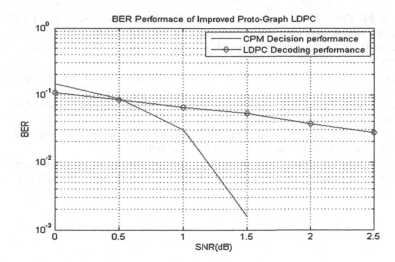

Fig. 3. Simulation results

From the Fig. 3 it can be seen that the LDPC can obtain almost no error decoding when the CPM decision performance reaches 0.03, that is, when $E_b/N_0 = 2$dB, LDPC reaches the waterfall area, which proves that the system designed has excellent performance.

Acknowledgements. This paper is funded by the International Exchange Program of Harbin Engineering University for Innovation Oriented Talents Cultivation, International Science & Technology Cooperation Program of China (2014 DFR10240), National Natural Science Foundation of China (612111070), China Postdoctoral Science Foundation (2013T60346), Harbin Science and Technology Research Projects (P083313026), Natural Science Foundation of Heilongjiang Province (P083014025), Heilongjiang Province Fund Project (F201412), Harbin Science and Technology Bureau project (2013RFLXJ026).

References

1. Bao, M.B., Cheng, S., Pei, Y.C.: New development of channel coding technology. Radio Commun. Technol. **42**(6), 1–8 (2016)
2. Massey, J.L.: Coding and modulation in digital communications. In: The 3rd International Zurich Seminar on Digital Communications, pp. 806–813 (1974)
3. Mazzali, N., Colavolpe, G., Buzzi, S.: CPM-based spread spectrum systems for multi-user communications. IEEE Trans. Wirel. Commun. **12**(1), 358–367 (2013)
4. Shu, C., Li, J.Y., Ya F.W.: IEEE802.16E construction and simulation of standard LDPC codes. In: National Symposium on Signal and Intelligent Information Processing and Application (2016)
5. Dong, F.Y., Hai G.Z.: The theory of LDPC code and application. The People's Post and Telecommunications Press (2008). in Chinese
6. Si, Q.F.: The technology research of continuous phase modulation. Kunming University of Science and Technology, Kunming (2007). in Chinese

7. Messai, M., Colavolpe, G., Amis, K., Guilloud, F.: Robust detection of binary CPMs with unknown modulation index. IEEE Commun. Lett. **19**(3), 339–342 (2015)
8. Rimoldi, B.E.: A decomposition approach to CPM. Inf. Theory IEEE Trans. **34**(2), 260–270 (1988)
9. Shu, L., Sdaniel, J.C.: Error Control Code, 2nd edn. China Machine Press, Beijing (2007). in Chinese
10. Rui, X., Qiang, W., Xi, C.X.: Dynamic iterative stop algorithm in multivariate LDPC - CPM system. Appl. Sci. Technol. **37**(01), 169–174 (2015)
11. Li, X., Ritcey, J.: Trellis-coded modulation with bit interleaving and iterative decoding. IEEE J. Select. Areas Commun. **17**(4), 715–724 (1999)
12. Peng, W., Ling, W., Tao, Y.G., Shun, L.M.: Low complexity soft decision algorithm for Multi-h CPM signal. J. Cent. South Univ. (Natl. Sci. Ed.) **12**, 4869–4873 (2013)

Intelligent Decision Modeling
for Communication Parameter Selection
via Back Propagation Neural Network

Zheng Dou, Yaning Dong, and Chao Li[✉]

Harbin Engineering University, Harbin, China
lichao_heu@hotmail.com

Abstract. Decision-making ability plays a key role in the cognitive radio system. The decision-making engine is expected to decide a suitable radio configuration (modulation mode, coding mode, coding rate, etc.) according to the complex and varying radio environment. In this paper, we propose a decision-making method for the Orthogonal Frequency Division Multiplexing (OFDM) communication system. Through this method, we can select waveform parameters for any channel condition to achieve optimal communication performance via the Back Propagation (BP) Neural Network (NN) regression. The simulation results illustrate the proposed method can provide a reasonable decision surface with various wireless channel condition.

Keywords: Neural Network · Decision making · Cognitive radio
Intelligent radio

1 Introduction

Since Mitola proposed the concept "Cognitive Radio (CR)" in 1999 [1], most of the current CR researches were mainly focusing on spectrum sensing, dynamic spectrum access, etc., to solve the ever-increasing spectrum shortage problem [2,3]. However, when the CR was proposed by Mitola, he has emphasized the importance of the intelligent learning and decision-making characteristics for the cognitive radio [1]. Intelligence should be a core characteristic of cognitive radio. So the next generation of intelligent radio should have the capacity to sense, learn and adapt to the complex electromagnetic environment.

The main function of "learning" in CR is making decision. Optimization based decision-making algorithm has been widely exploited in current researches of intelligent decision-making, and the typical one is Genetic Algorithm (GA). GA is used to search the best system parameters within the given feasible domain according to the designed performance objective function [4]. Christian James Rieser pioneered a biometric-based cognitive radio model (Bio-CR) first [5], and in his doctoral thesis he elaborated on the use of GA to achieve the optimization of cognitive radio configuration parameters. Since then many scholars have

© ICST Institute for Computer Sciences, Social Informatics and Telecommunications Engineering 2018
G. Sun and S. Liu (Eds.): ADHIP 2017, LNICST 219, pp. 465–472, 2018.
https://doi.org/10.1007/978-3-319-73317-3_53

made improvements on this basis, but mainly focused on the improvement of the algorithm performance, such as using the binary quantum particle swarm optimization [6], hybrid binary particle swarm optimization [7], differential evolution [8], bacterial foraging optimization [8] and so on. Note that, when using these optimization algorithms, it requires a multi-objective function of communication performance calculated by the accurate theoretical formula. So these methods only work under the assumption of Additive White Gaussian Noise (AWGN) channel. But when the channel environment is not clear or more complex, we can not get accurate calculation formula. And every time we use an optimized way to make decision, we must spend a lot of time and computing resources.

Another kind of typical intelligent decision-making methods is based on learning (knowledge) [4]. CR system need to analyze and learn from the historical cases through the method of machine learning, dig out potential rules and knowledge, summarize the rules of knowledge, and then make decision based on the rules and knowledge obtained. Related learning algorithms include Neural Networks [9,10], Support Vector Machines (SVM) [11], Bayesian networks [12], etc. [13,14]. At present, this kind of research is still in the infancy.

In this paper, we propose a novel decision-making method to estimate the best modulation type and coding rate OFDM wireless system. In the proposed method, we collect the training sample by sending several training sequence from the transmitter, and utilize these samples to train a Back Propagation (BP) Neural Network (NN) regression model. Last, the fine-trained BP-NN model provide the decision surface which corresponds to the given wireless channel.

2   BP Neural Network

BP-NN is a multi-layer feed-forward NN ordinarily which is trained by the BP algorithm [15,16]. It can achieve the minimum error sum of square by regulating the weight value and threshold value [16]. A basic BP-NN model is shown in Fig. 1.

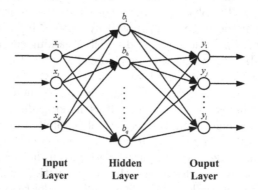

Input Layer   Hidden Layer   Ouput Layer

Fig. 1. A basic BP-NN structure including input layer, hidden layer and output layer.

The BP training process can be described as follows [15, 16]:

Forward propagation stage: The input signal from the input layer propagates through the hidden layer to the output layer, and the weight value and threshold value are fixed. At this stage, the state of each neuron will only affect the next layer of neurons.

Back propagation stage: The error signal is generated by comparing the real output with the desired output. Then the error signal propagates layer-by-layer in the opposite direction. At this stage, the network parameters are continuously regulated by the feedback error. It makes the real network output value closer to the expected one.

The main advantage of BP-NN is that it has strong nonlinear mapping ability [16]. Theoretically, as long as the number of hidden neurons is sufficient, a three-layer BP-NN can approximate a nonlinear function with arbitrary precision.

3   Design of Decision-Making Model

In our method, the objective function is constructed based on the Shannon-Hartley law [17]. It's an evolution of the channel capacity function. And our goal is to find the modulation and coding mode which maximizes the objective function with BP-NN regression. The maximum means the system communication performance is optimal to some extent [17]. The system process is shown in Fig. 2.

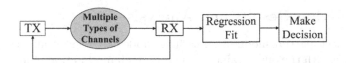

Fig. 2. Decision-making system flow chart.

First, we set up a complete OFDM communication system, modulation modes include binary phase shift keying (BPSK), 4-quadrature amplitude modulation (QAM), ..., 128-QAM, coding mode uses the BCH block code (coding rate from 0 to 1). The main parameters of our OFDM system are shown in Table 1.

Table 1. Main parameters of OFDM system.

Parameter	Value
Available subcarriers	128
Used subcarriers	64
Cyclic prefix	32
Baseband frequency	10 MHz

Select as many channel models as possible to simulate(eg.: AWGN, Rayleigh fading, Rician fading, Plus interference). The objective function related to the modulation-coding modes is defined as follows:

$$c = f(rate) \times f(ber) \tag{1}$$

Here:
$$f(rate) = \log_2(M) \times r_c \tag{2}$$
$$f(ber) = -\log_{10}(ber) \tag{3}$$

where M denotes the modulation order, r_c means the coding rate, ber represents the bit-error rate, $rate$ means the data-transmitted rate.

After that, we choose different values of various channel environment parameters, such as Signal-to-Noise Ratio (SNR), Doppler shift, etc., to collect a large number of sample data in each channel model.

Use BP-NN to regress the objective function $c = f([M, r_c], \mathbf{w})$ (where $\mathbf{w}$ is the channel environment to be regressed). The fitted surface reflects the relationship between transmission performance and different modulation-coding modes in current channel environment. The vertex of the surface means the value of modulation-coding mode which maximizes the objective function.

And we make two constraints to ber as follows:

When $ber < 10^{-6}$, consider that the bit error rate reaches the ideal state, record it as 10^{-6}.

When $ber > 0.1$, consider that the bit error rate is beyond the scope of tolerance, record it as 1.

4   Simulation Results and Analysis

We only select partial modulation-coding modes to regress and compare the fitted surface with the one obtained by mapping all modulation modes (including BPSK, 4-QAM, 8-QAM, 16-QAM, 32-QAM, 64-QAM, 128-QAM) and coding-rate modes (including (8, 15, 22, 29, 36, 43, 50, 64, 71, 78, 92, 127)/127) directly. If the trend is consistent, it verify the correctness of fitting.

The fitted surfaces are shown in Fig. 3. For the convenience of observation, we will use contour lines instead of three-dimensional figure in the following space.

4.1   Simulation in AWGN Channel

As we can see from Fig. 4, when the channel is AWGN (SNR = 20 dB), capacity function approximately reaches the vertex at "128-QAM, R_c=1".

As we can see from Fig. 5, when the channel is AWGN (SNR = 10 dB), capacity function approximately reaches the vertex at "32-QAM, r_c=7/10".

As we can see from Fig. 6, when the channel is AWGN(SNR = 0 dB), capacity function approximately reaches the vertex at "BPSK, r_c=1/5".

In AWGN channels, when the SNR from 20 dB to 0 dB, the modulation-coding options from the high modulation level, large coding rate, to low modulation level, small coding rate. This is basically consistent with the theoretical speculation.

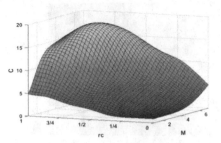

(a) Fitted surface for AWGN
(SNR = 12 dB) channel.

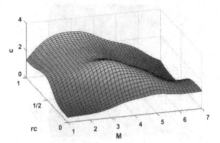

(b) Fitted surface for Rayleigh
(SNR = 12 dB, Fd = 500 kHz) channel.

Fig. 3. Fitting surface examples.

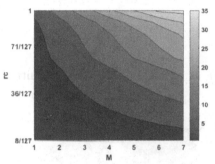

(a) Mapping all modulation-coding
modes in AWGN (SNR = 20 dB) channel.

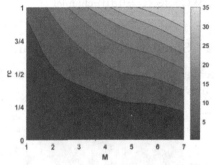

(b) Fitted figure in AWGN (SNR = 20 dB)
channel.

Fig. 4. Relationship between objective function values and modulation-coding modes
in AWGN (SNR = 20 dB) channel.

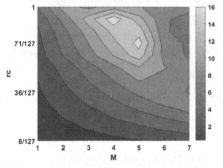

(a) Mapping all modulation-coding
modes in AWGN (SNR = 10 dB) channel.

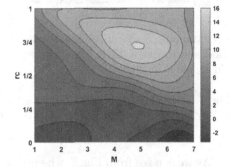

(b) Fitted figure in AWGN (SNR = 10 dB)
channel.

Fig. 5. Relationship between objective function values and modulation-coding modes
in AWGN (SNR = 10 dB) channel.

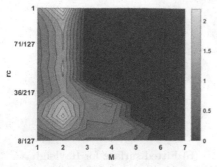
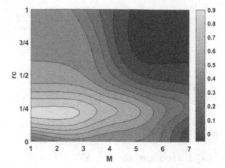

(a) Mapping all modulation-coding modes in AWGN (SNR = 0 dB) channel.

(b) Fitted figure in AWGN (SNR = 0 dB) channel.

Fig. 6. Relationship between objective function values and modulation-coding modes in AWGN (SNR = 0 dB) channel.

4.2 Simulation in Other Channels

Because of the limited space, we use Fig. 7 as an example to show the fitted results for other channels.

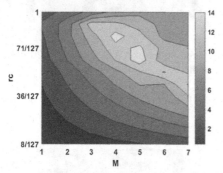
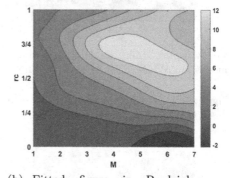

(a) Mapping all modulation-coding modes in Rayleigh (SNR = 20 dB, Fd = 500 kHz) channel.

(b) Fitted figure in Rayleigh (SNR = 20 dB, Fd = 500 kHz) channel.

Fig. 7. Relationship between objective function values and modulation-coding modes in Rayleigh (SNR = 20 dB, Fd = 500 kHz) channel.

As we can see from Fig. 7, when the channel is Rayleigh-fading (SNR = 20 dB, Fd = 500 kHz), capacity function approximately reaches the vertex at "32-QAM, $r_c = 5/8$ ".

From the simulation results we can see that the trend of the fitted surface is basically the same as that of the figure mapping all modulation-coding modes, so the effect of regression is in line with expectations. The fitted surface can reflect the channel environment. However, in the process of fitting, we find that the training of BP-NN is not consistent and it is easy to fall into the local optimum. The fit of the decision surface has uncertainties. Although we select the least mean square error one by fitting ten times, sometimes the fitted error is also large. Therefore, we suggest to use other regression algorithms, such as support vector regression (SVR) (because of the small number of input samples) in the future research.

5   Conclusion

In this paper, we have proposed a decision-making method based on the BP-NN regression model. We made decisions to select the most suitable communication waveform parameters in some channel environment examples. Through our model, we can make a decision and analysis for the complex, undiscovered channel. The simulation results demonstrates the correctness and applicability of the introduced model. In the future research, we will use more other machine learning algorithms to regress, analyze and contrast their regression performance to improve our method.

Acknowledgments. This work is supported by the Nation Nature Science Foundation of China (No. 61671167, No.61401115 and No.61301095). And it is also funded by the International Exchange Program of Harbin Engineering University for Innovation-oriented Talents Cultivation.

References

1. Mitola, J., Maguire, G.Q.: Cognitive radio: making software radios more personal. IEEE Pers. Commun. **6**(4), 13–18 (1999). IEEE Press, New York
2. Ahmed, E., Gani, A., Abolfazli, S., Yao, L.J., Khan, S.U.: Channel assignment algorithms in cognitive radio networks: taxonomy, open issues, and challenges. IEEE Commun. Surv. Tutor. **18**(1), 795–823 (2015). IEEE Press, New York
3. Althunibat, S., Di Renzo, M., Granelli, F.: Towards energy-efficient cooperative spectrum sensing for cognitive radio networks: an overview. Telecommun. Syst. **59**(1), 77–91 (2015). Springer, Heidelberg
4. Wu, C., You, X.J., Yin, M.W.: A survey on intelligent leaning and decision in cognitive radio. Commun. Technol. **143**(11), 21–25 (2010)
5. Rieser, C.J.: Biologically inspired cognitive radio engine model utilizing distributed genetic algorithms for secure and robust wireless communications and networking. Virginia Polytechnic Institute and State University, USA (2004)
6. Zhang, J., Zhou, Z., Gao, W.X., Shi, L., Tang, L.: Cognitive radio decision engine based on binary quantum particle swarm optimization. Chin. J. Sci. Instrum. **32**(2), 451–456 (2011)
7. Xu, H.Y., Zhou, Z.: Cognitive radio decision engine using hybrid binary particle swarm optimization. In: 13th International Symposium on Communications and Information Technologies (ISCIT), pp. 143–147 (2013)
8. Pradhan, P.M., Panda, G.: Comparative performance analysis of evolutionary algorithm based parameter optimization in cognitive radio engine: a survey. Ad Hoc Netw. **17**, 129–146 (2014). Elsevier

9. Dong, X., Li, Y., Wu, C., Cai, Y.: A learner based on neural network for cognitive radio. In: 12th IEEE International Conference on Communication Technology (ICCT), pp. 893–896. IEEE Press, New York (2010)
10. Yigit, H., Kavak, A.: Adaptation using neural network in frequency selective MIMO-OFDM systems. In: 5th International Symposium on Wireless Pervasive Computing (ISWPC), pp. 390–394. IEEE Press, New York (2010)
11. Huang, Y.Q., Jiang, H., Hu, H., Yao, Y.C.: Design of learning engine based on support vector machine in cognitive radio. In: 2009 International Conference on Computational Intelligence and Software Engineering, pp. 1–4. IEEE Press, New York (2009)
12. Huang, Y.Q., Wang, J., Jiang, H.: Modeling of learning inference and decision making engine in cognitive radio. In: Second International Conference on Networks Security, Wireless Communications and Trusted Computing, vol. 2, pp. 258–261. IEEE Press, New York (2010)
13. Bkassiny, M., Li, Y., Jayaweera, S.K.: A survey on machine-learning techniques in cognitive radios. IEEE Commun. Surv. Tutor. 15(3), 1136–1159 (2013). IEEE Press, New York
14. Bourbia, S., Achouri, M., Grati, K., Le Guennec, D., Ghazel, A.: Cognitive engine design for cognitive radio. In: 2012 International Conference on Multimedia Computing and Systems (ICMCS), pp. 986–991. IEEE Press, New York (2012)
15. Li, J., Cheng, J.H., Shi, J.Y., Huang, F.: Brief introduction of Back Propagation (BP) neural network algorithm and its improvement. In: Jin, D., Lin, S. (eds.) Advances in Computer Science and Information Engineering, pp. 553–558. Springer, Heidelberg (2012). https://doi.org/10.1007/978-3-642-30223-7_87
16. Haykin, S.S.: Neural Networks and Learning Machines. Pearson, Upper Saddle River (2009)
17. Clancy, C., Hecker, J., Stuntebeck, E., O'Shea, T.: Applications of machine learning to cognitive radio networks. IEEE Wirel. Commun. 14(4) (2007). IEEE Press, New York

A Cross Domain Collaborative Filtering Algorithm Based on Latent Factor Alignment and Two-Stage Matrix Adjustment

Xu Yu[1], Junyu Lin[2(✉)], Feng Jiang[1], Yan Chu[3], and Jizhong Han[2]

[1] School of Information Science and Technology,
Qingdao University of Science and Technology, Qingdao 266061, China
[2] Institute of Information Engineering, CAS, Beijing 100093, China
linjunyu@iie.ac.cn
[3] College of Computer Science and Technology, Harbin Engineering University,
Harbin 150001, China

Abstract. Sparsity is a tough problem in a single domain Collaborative Filtering (CF) recommender system. In this paper, we propose a cross domain collaborative filtering algorithm based on Latent Factor Alignment and Two-Stage Matrix Adjustment (LFATSMA) to alleviate this difficulty. Unlike previous Cross Domain Collaborative Filtering (CDCF) algorithms, we first align the latent factors across different domains by pattern matching technology. Then we smooth the user and item latent vectors in the target domain by transferring the preferences of similar users and the contents of similar items from the auxiliary domain, which can effectively weaken the effect of noise. Finally, we convert the traditional UV decomposition model to a constrained UV decomposition model, which can effectively keep the balance between under-fitting and over-fitting. We conduct extensive experiments to show that the proposed LFATSMA algorithm performs better than many state-of-the-art CF methods.

Keywords: Cross Domain Collaborative Filtering · Knowledge transfer
Latent Factor Alignment · Constrained UV decomposition model

1 Introduction

In recent years, recommender systems are widely used in e-commerce sites and online social media and the majority of them offer recommendations for items belonging to a single domain. Now collaborative Filtering (CF) [1] algorithm is the most widely used method for recommender systems. However, in real-world recommender systems, the rating matrix is very sparse, which leads to a poor recommendation performance. To alleviate this difficulty, recently a number of Cross-Domain Collaborative Filtering (CDCF) methods have been proposed [2]. They can effectively relieve the sparsity problem in the target domain.

Currently CDCF methods can be categorized into two classes. One class [3–5] assumes shared users or items. The other class contains a limited number of CDCF methods [6, 7] that do not require shared users and items. However, methods in the

© ICST Institute for Computer Sciences, Social Informatics and Telecommunications Engineering 2018
G. Sun and S. Liu (Eds.): ADHIP 2017, LNICST 219, pp. 473–480, 2018.
https://doi.org/10.1007/978-3-319-73317-3_54

second class may not perform well, as they are based on matrix factorization. Matrix factorization techniques fail in the cross-domain recommendation task because the learned latent factors are not aligned over different domains.

In this paper, for the second class, we proposed a CDCF algorithm based on Latent Factor Alignment and Two-Stage Matrix Adjustment (LFATSMA). We first align the latent factors across different domains, so the knowledge transfer from the auxiliary domain to the target domain would be more correct and reasonable. Then we propose a two-stage matrix adjustment method to achieve more effective U and V matrices with the help of the data in the auxiliary domain. Consequently, the prediction performance in the target domain can be improved.

The remainder of this paper is organized as follows: Sect. 2 proposes a method to align the latent factors across different domains. In Sect. 3, we propose the two-stage matrix adjustment method to transfer knowledge from the auxiliary domain to the target domain. We conduct extensive experiments to test the performance of the proposed algorithm in Sect. 4 and conclude the whole paper in Sect. 5.

2   Aligning the Latent Factors

We align the latent factors across different domains by pattern matching technology. As shown in Fig. 1, we **first** construct a mixture rating matrix M_0 by combining the data from the two domains together. The main-diagonal blocks are filled with the rating matrix M_1 in the target domain and the rating matrix M_2 in the auxiliary domain. The off-diagonal blocks are filled with zeros.

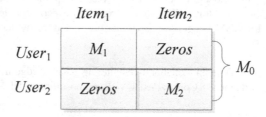

Fig. 1. Constructing a mixture rating matrix

Let n_1 and n_2 denote the size of $User_1$ and $User_2$ respectively. **Then** we decompose M_0, M_1, and M_2 to obtain the latent factors by the UV decomposition model [8]. Let $M_0 = U_0 V_0^T$, $M_1 = U_1 V_1^T$, $M_2 = U_2 V_2^T$, and let f denote the dimensionality of the latent factor space, so the size of U_0 is $(n_1 + n_2, f)$, the size is of U_1 is (n_1, f), and the size of U_2 is (n_2, f). The reason why we construct the mixture matrix M_0 and decompose M_0 is to use it as a reference. Considering that the order of the latent factors in U_0 is unique, we can align the latent factors between the target domain and the auxiliary domain by this order.

Finally, we align the latent factors across the two domains, and return the updated U_1 and U_2.

In Fig. 2, each column vector in U_i ($i = 0$, 1, 2) represents a latent factor. Obviously, for the same latent factor (e.g., SF) in two U matrices, if the users are identical in order, then we can expect the corresponding columns to be with a large similarity. Therefore we can determine whether two latent factors F_i and F_j from two different U matrices are identical according to the similarity of the corresponding columns c_i and c_j.

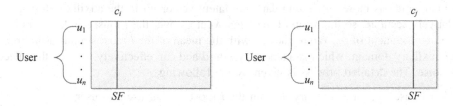

Fig. 2. The same latent factor in two U matrices can be expected to be with a large similarity

Let U_3 denote the upper block of U_0, including the upper n_1 rows, and U_4 denote the lower block of U_0, including the lower n_2 rows. It is clear that each column in both U_3 and U_1 represents the interest values on a latent factor of all the users in the target domain, so we can use U_3 as a reference to align the latent factors of U_1 according to the similarities among columns. In the same way, we can also use U_4 as a reference to align the latent factors of U_2. As U_3 and U_4 correspond to the upper and lower blocks of the same matrix U_0 respectively, so the order of the latent factors in U_3 is the same with that in U_4. As a result, we can align the latent factors of U_1 and U_2.

We align the latent factors by comparing the similarities among columns. Here the similarity can be computed by a cosine measure in the form

$$s(c_i, c_j) = \frac{c_i^T c_j}{\|c_i\|\|c_j\|} \tag{1}$$

For each column c_i in U_1, we compute the similarity between it and the first column C_1 in U_3 by Eq. (1), and denote the column in U_1 with the maximum similarity to C_1 as F_1, and exchange this column with the first column in U_1. Then determine F_2 from the rest columns, and exchange the corresponding column with the second column in U_1. The rest can be done in the same manner. The columns of U_2 can be adjusted in the same way.

In the UV decomposition model, the order of the latent factors in the V matrix is the same with that in the U matrix. Since the orders of latent factors in U_1 and U_2 matrices have been adjusted, if we adjust the orders of latent factors in V_1 and V_2 matrices by the same adjustment process, we can also align the latent factors between V_1 and V_2. As a result, the latent factors between the target domain and the auxiliary domain are aligned, which makes the following knowledge transfer more correct and reasonable.

3   Transferring Knowledge via a Two-Stage Matrix Adjustment

3.1   Weakening the Effect of Noise

For any user u in the target domain, we first choose from the auxiliary domain the l most similar users to user u. Then we compute the mean of the latent vectors over the l most similar users and replace the latent vector p_u with the mean. As the auxiliary domain contains more user rating data, the latent vector $p_{u'}$ in the auxiliary domain is relatively accurate, so the mean of the latent vectors over the l most similar users is a good replacement of p_u. We replace p_u with the mean of the l most similar users from the auxiliary domain, which is a smooth method and can effectively weaken the effect of noise. The detailed process is given by the following.

(1)   Choose from the auxiliary domain the l most similar users to user u
   Let u_a denote a user in the target domain and u_b denote a user in the auxiliary domain. We choose from the auxiliary domain the l most similar users to u_a. Here the similarity can also be computed by a cosine measure that was given in Eq. (1), and accordingly the similarity between u_a and u_b can be computed in the form

$$s(p_{u_a}, p_{u_b}) = \frac{p_{u_a}^T p_{u_b}}{\|p_{u_a}\| \|p_{u_b}\|} \tag{2}$$

(2)   Compute the mean of the latent vectors over the l most similar users
   We compute the mean of the latent vectors over the l most similar users. Let p denote the mean, and p_{u_i} denote the latent vector of the i-th most similar user, $(i = 1, \cdots, l)$. The mean of the latent vectors is defined as

$$p = \sum_{i=1}^{l} p_{u_i} \Big/ l \tag{3}$$

(3)   Replace the latent vector p_u of user u in the target domain with the corresponding p
   Thus we can update the U matrix. In the same manner, we can also update the V matrix.

3.2   Solving a Constrained UV Decomposition Model

Although we transfer important information from the auxiliary domain to smooth the original data in the target domain, there arises a new problem that the updated U and V matrices may not fit the rating data of the target domain accurately. For convenience, we use $U^{(1)}$ and $V^{(1)}$ to denote the first updated matrices. In order to avoid this problem, an intuitive idea is to use $U^{(1)}$ and $V^{(1)}$ as an initial point, and to solve the traditional UV model for a better U and V matrices. However, this may cause a large change of $U^{(1)}$ or $V^{(1)}$. As $U^{(1)}$ and $V^{(1)}$ are obtained by transfer important information from the auxiliary domain, and can effectively weaken the effect of noise, we expect that they are changed as small as possible. To achieve this goal, we convert the traditional unconstrained UV decomposition model into a constrained UV decomposition model in the following form

$$\min_{q*,p*} \sum_{(u,i)\in\kappa} (r_{ui} - q_i^T p_u)^2$$

s.t. $\left\| q_i - q_i^{(1)} \right\|^2$ and $\left\| p_u - p_u^{(1)} \right\|^2$ is as small as possible for any i and u belonging to κ

(4)

We can convert (4) into the following unconstrained optimization problem

$$\min_{q*,p*} \quad F = \sum_{(u,i)\in\kappa} (r_{ui} - q_i^T p_u)^2 + \lambda(\left\| q_i - q_i^{(1)} \right\|^2 + \left\| p_u - p_u^{(1)} \right\|^2) \qquad (5)$$

where $q_i^{(1)}$ and $p_u^{(1)}$ are the item and user latent vectors respectively corresponding to the $V^{(1)}$ and $U^{(1)}$ matrices, and the constant λ is a penalty factor, which penalizes the change between q_i and $q_i^{(1)}$ and the change between p_u and $p_u^{(1)}$. Clearly, the UV decomposition model may arise over-fitting if λ is set to a very small number. On the contrary, it will cause under-fitting if λ is set to a very large number. A proper λ is usually determined by cross-validation. We use $U^{(2)}$ and $V^{(2)}$ to denote the solution of the optimization problem (5). We can also use stochastic gradient descent to achieve $U^{(2)}$ and $V^{(2)}$.

For each given training case, firstly the gradient can be computed in the following form

$$\frac{\partial F}{q_i} = -2\left[e_{ui} p_u - \lambda(q_i - q_i^{(1)}) \right]$$
$$\frac{\partial F}{p_u} = -2\left[e_{ui} q_i - \lambda(p_u - p_u^{(1)}) \right]$$

(6)

where $e_{ui} \overset{def}{=} r_{ui} - q_i^T p_u$. Then we modify the parameters by a magnitude proportional to γ (i.e., the learning rate) in the opposite direction of the gradient, yielding:

$$q_i \leftarrow q_i + \gamma \left[e_{ui} p_u - \lambda(q_i - q_i^{(1)}) \right]$$
$$p_u \leftarrow p_u + \gamma \left[e_{ui} q_i - \lambda(p_u - p_u^{(1)}) \right]$$

(7)

Since the U and V matrices updated in the first adjustment absorb useful information from the auxiliary domain, we use $U^{(1)}$ and $V^{(1)}$ as an initial point in the optimization problem (5). Finally, we can obtain the rating matrix M by computing $M = U^{(2)}V^{(2)T}$.

4   Experiments

In this section, we compare our algorithm to 3 state-of-the-art algorithms. One is a well-known single domain algorithm Funk-SVD (the UV decomposition model), and the other two methods are cross domain methods, namely CBT and RMGM. By comparison with Funk-SVD, we can investigate the effectiveness of transferring knowledge from the auxiliary domain. By comparison with CBT and RMGM, we can investigate the effectiveness of aligning the latent factors across different domains.

4.1   Data Sets

In this part, we use EachMovie and MovieLens data sets.

(1) EachMovie (the auxiliary domain): 500 users and 500 movies are extracted from EachMovie to compose the auxiliary domain.
(2) MovieLens (the target domain): 500 users and 1000 movies are extracted from MovieLens to compose the target domain.

4.2   The Setting of the Compared Methods

(1) Funk-SVD (the UV decomposition model): Here we simply set $f = 50$.
(2) CBT (Codebook transfer): According to the setting in reference [6], the numbers of user and item clusters, K and L, are set to 50.
(3) RMGM (Rating Matrix Generative Model): In order to compare the methods more reasonable and fairer, like CBT, both K and L in RMGM are also set to 50.
(4) **LFATSMA** (the proposed method): In order to compare the methods more reasonable and fairer, like Funk-SVD, the dimension of the latent space is set to 50, and the number l of similar users or items is set to 10.

In the experiments, we set $\gamma = 0.3$ in each algorithm.

4.3   Evaluation Protocol

We use the first 100, 200, and 300 users in the target data set as training data, respectively, and we use the last 200 users as testing data. For each test user, Given5 denotes 5 observed ratings are used for training. Given10 and Given15 are defined in the same way.

We use mean absolute error (MAE) and root mean square error (RMSE) as evaluation metrics in our experiments. MAE is defined as

$$\left(\sum\nolimits_{i \in T} |r_i - \tilde{r}_i|\right)/|T| \tag{8}$$

and RMSE is defined as

$$\sqrt{\sum_{i \in T} (r_i - \tilde{r}_i)^2 / |T|} \tag{9}$$

where T denotes the set of test ratings, r_i is the ground truth and $\tilde{r}_i$ is the predicted rating.

4.4 Results

Table 1 lists the MAE and RMSE scores on MovieLens (ML).

Table 1. MAE and RMSE scores

Training set	Method	MAE			RMSE		
		Given5	Given10	Given15	Given5	Given10	Given15
ML100	Funk-SVD	1.249	1.241	1.234	1.500	1.491	1.481
	CBT	0.692	0.677	0.655	0.893	0.881	0.866
	RMGM	0.694	0.668	0.653	0.895	0.879	0.864
	LFATSMA	**0.633**	**0.605**	**0.561**	**0.860**	**0.826**	**0.775**
ML200	Funk-SVD	1.033	1.093	1.057	1.261	1.329	1.286
	CBT	0.675	0.661	0.644	0.889	0.873	0.861
	RMGM	0.666	0.657	0.632	0.880	0.867	0.849
	LFATSMA	**0.624**	**0.592**	**0.556**	**0.856**	**0.822**	**0.770**
ML300	Funk-SVD	0.918	0.899	0.897	1.178	1.165	1.162
	CBT	0.664	0.659	0.639	0.875	0.869	0.852
	RMGM	0.661	0.663	0.644	0.873	0.876	0.858
	LFATSMA	**0.619**	**0.589**	**0.551**	**0.846**	**0.816**	**0.765**

As shown in Table 1, CBT, RMGM, and LFATSMA all perform better than Funk-SVD on all different configurations. The main reason is that Funk-SVD predicts the ratings only according to the sparse data in the target domain.

As expected, our method performs better than the other two CDCF methods (CBT and RMGM), I think the main reasons are as follows. Firstly, the alignment of latent factors between the target domain and the auxiliary domain makes the following knowledge transfer more correct and reasonable. Secondly, the smooth of the user and item latent vectors in the target domain can effectively weaken the effect of noise. Thirdly, the solution of the constructed constrained UV decomposition model can effectively keep the balance between under-fitting and over-fitting. Consequently, the prediction performance in the target domain can be improved.

5 Conclusion

In this paper, we propose a CDCF algorithm based on Latent Factor Alignment and Two-Stage Matrix Adjustment (LFATSMA). By aligning the latent factors across different domains, and transferring the preferences of similar users and the contents of similar items from the auxiliary domain to the target domain, LFATSMA can effectively alleviate the sparsity problem in the target domain and weaken the effect of noise. Moreover, since we construct a constrained UV decomposition model to control the balance between under-fitting and over-fitting, the effectiveness of the knowledge transfer can be guaranteed. The experimental results have validated the effectiveness of the proposed LFATSMA algorithm.

Acknowledgments. This work is sponsored by the National Natural Science Foundation of China (No. 61402246), a Project of Shandong Province Higher Educational Science and Technology Program (No. J15LN38), Qingdao indigenous innovation program (No. 15-9-1-47-jch).

References

1. Goldberg, D., Nichols, D., Oki, B.M., et al.: Using collaborative filtering to weave an information tapestry. Commun. ACM **35**(12), 61–70 (1992)
2. Berkovsky, S., Kuflik, T., Ricci, F.: Cross-domain mediation in collaborative filtering. In: Conati, C., McCoy, K., Paliouras, G. (eds.) UM 2007. LNCS (LNAI), vol. 4511, pp. 355–359. Springer, Heidelberg (2007). https://doi.org/10.1007/978-3-540-73078-1_44
3. Pan, W., Xiang, E.W., Liu, N.N., et al.: Transfer learning in collaborative filtering for sparsity reduction. In: Twenty-Fourth AAAI Conference on Artificial Intelligence, AAAI 2010, Atlanta, Georgia, USA, July 2010
4. Pan, W., Liu, N.N., Xiang, E.W., et al.: Transfer learning to predict missing ratings via heterogeneous user feedbacks. In: Proceedings of the International Joint Conference on Artificial Intelligence, IJCAI 2011, Barcelona, Catalonia, Spain, July 2011
5. Loni, B., Shi, Y., Larson, M., Hanjalic, A.: Cross-domain collaborative filtering with factorization machines. In: de Rijke, M., Kenter, T., de Vries, A.P., Zhai, C., de Jong, F., Radinsky, K., Hofmann, K. (eds.) ECIR 2014. LNCS, vol. 8416, pp. 656–661. Springer, Cham (2014). https://doi.org/10.1007/978-3-319-06028-6_72
6. Li, B., Yang, Q., Xue, X.: Can movies and books collaborate? Cross-domain collaborative filtering for sparsity reduction. In: Proceedings of the International Joint Conference on Artificial Intelligence, IJCAI 2009, Pasadena, California, USA, pp. 2052–2057. July 2009
7. Li, B., Yang, Q., Xue, X.: Transfer learning for collaborative filtering via a rating-matrix generative model. In: International Conference on Machine Learning, ICML 2009, Montreal, Quebec, Canada, pp. 617–624. June 2009
8. Koren, Y., Bell, R., Volinsky, C.: Matrix factorization techniques for recommender systems. Computer **42**(8), 30–37 (2009)

Abnormal Traffic Flow Detection Based on Dynamic Hybrid Strategy

Yang Liu[✉], Hongping Xu, Hang Yi, Xiaotao Yan, Jian Kang, Weiqiang Xia, Qingping Shi, and Chaopeng Shen

Beijing Institute of Astronautical System Engineering, Beijing, China
yangliu_npu@163.com

Abstract. Efficient and accurate analysis of the traffic data contained in the network is the key measure to detect the abnormal behavior, resist the invasion and protect the information security. In this paper, we make a comprehensive utilization of the characteristics of port mapping identification, payload identification, statistical analysis and SVM machine learning, and propose the dynamic hybrid strategy. Firstly, the machine learning training samples are obtained through port mapping and load feature recognition. Then, on the basis of information gain feature selection, the SVM machine learning model is built and trained. Finally, through the voting mechanism, we achieve comprehensive analysis of the traffic data. The experimental results show that the accuracy of the proposed algorithm is as high as 99.1%, and the number of manual decision analysis is greatly reduced at the same time.

Keywords: Port mapping · Payload feature matching
Dynamic hybrid strategy · Machine learning

1 Introduction

The traffic of the Measurement and Control Network carrying the key information of the system, the majority of abnormal or aggressive behavior will make the system network traffic presents specific differences, through in-depth analysis of the system flow, we can quickly identify non-compliance flow, timely find the information redundancy or abnormal behavior, and ensure the reliability of the data communication network. In 2004, Lang uses port based protocol identification method to obtain pure network traffic, and verifies the effectiveness of the method [1]. In 2006, Liang prove that the port based protocol identification method is not suitable for dynamic port applications, but it still has high accuracy in traditional network applications [2]. In 2012, Lin et al. proposed a method based on packet length distribution and port to identify network traffic. In 2013, Moore reduced the time and space complexity by reducing the length and number of load identification [4]. In 2013, Zhang et al. proposed support vector machine (Support Vector Machine, SVM) and statistical feature classification method [5]. Xiao in 2015 proposed a hierarchical support vector machine method

© ICST Institute for Computer Sciences, Social Informatics and Telecommunications Engineering 2018
G. Sun and S. Liu (Eds.): ADHIP 2017, LNICST 219, pp. 481–488, 2018.
https://doi.org/10.1007/978-3-319-73317-3_55

to solve the classification problem of network flow, and achieve the recognition accuracy of 94%, [6] has achieved good application effect in large networks.

The traffic identification based on port mapping is efficient, however, the error rate is high. Recognition method based on feature matching of load has a high accuracy, but can't identify encrypted traffic. Statistical identification can identify the encryption protocol based on statistical features, but the statistical feature is difficult to select, prone to false positives, and is relatively poor for real-time traffic analysis. The recognition method based on machine learning traffic protocol is intelligent and has high recognition accuracy, but it depends on the correct training data and the appropriate network flow characteristics.

In this paper, we proposed a new method, comprehensively using the port identification, load and precise feature matching, and the accurate statistical identification method to construct the hybrid identification strategy. After obtaining the sample data of more known labels, the support vector mechanism is used to build the self-learning mechanism, constantly update and replace the statistic optimization method. And finally form a self-iteration update network traffic comprehensive recognition mechanism.

2   Traffic Flow Anomaly Detection Based on Dynamic Hybrid Strategy

2.1   Traffic Data Acquisition and Preprocessing

Before flow analysis, the general flow capture tools such as Sniffer, Wireshark, NetFlow, flow-tools and fprobe [7,8], can quickly collect the traffic data. In order to meet the needs of real-time processing, we carry out the flow separation pretreatment according to the five tuple (source IP, destination IP, source port, destination port, transport layer protocol number) before the flow analysis. Flow table is built to store the separated network data. Messages belonging to the same specific data stream have many similar attributes, By calculating the five tuple information of the network packet, we can get the *hash value* as Eq. 1. Packets will be divided into different flow according to the hash value.

$$hash\_index = HASH(I) \tag{1}$$

The information of each stream is saved in the flow table, which provides data support for the flow protocol identification.

2.2   Port Based Identification

In the complex Internet environment, due to the use of dynamic port technology, many applications no longer use the standard port, the accuracy of traditional traffic identification method based on port mapping is reduced greatly. However, most of the protocols or applications still use standard ports for communication in the network environment of the launch vehicle. Traffic data can achieve efficiently identification through the port mapping table (port_table) fast mapping.

$F[*]$ express the port application mapping function.

$$Protocol = F[port\_table] \qquad (2)$$

The specific application in the Measurement and Control Network, through the planning and design of port construction in advance, constructing the port and application mapping table, and using the port mapping to analysis the network data.

2.3   Identification Based on Load Feature Matching

According to the characteristics of the traffic data load, we can judge whether the load has special characteristics or not, and realize the analysis and identification of traffic data. Based on the precise feature matching method, each network packet is split, and the application data is extracted for feature matching. According to the actual characteristics of the launch vehicle network information, firstly, we extract the features and identify the protocol according to the special domain. As shown in formula (2), $G[*]$ express the traffic feature extraction function.

$$Protocol = G[flows] \xrightarrow{matching} protocol\_feature \qquad (3)$$

For example, Protocol_1/0:0xEB_1:0x90_2:0x00_3:0x20, Protocol_2/0: 0x70_2: 0x10_3:0x80 respectively express the feature information of Protocol_1 and Protocol_2, by extracting the protocol fingerprint of traffic data, and using the AC/SRS multi pattern matching algorithm, we can achieve efficient and rapid identification analysis. Process flow is shown in Fig. 1.

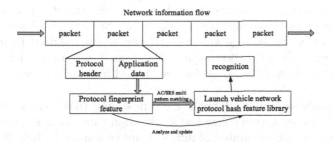

Fig. 1. Traffic identification based on accurate feature matching.

The precision of method based on the feature matching is relatively high, however, the speed is slow because of the need for each packet analysis, besides, the encryption protocol or some special protocol cannot be resolved, it is difficult to achieve analysis.

2.4 Detection and Recognition Based on Statistical Features and Machine Learning Models

In the launch vehicle network, the flow of different applications usually presents some unique statistical characteristics at the network level, such as idle time, the average length of the stream flow density, average packet length, packet interval and so on. For some specific application, application layer features represented by the ratio of source to destination communication data is unique, discrimination can be achieved by joint analysis of multiple dimensions. A large number of studies have shown that the identification based on the statistical characteristics of network traffic data is effective [9–11]. Especially in some specific application scenarios, it can realize the fast identification of encrypted protocols. In 2005, Moore gave a 249 dimensional feature set for summarizing and analyzing network traffic characteristics. Network traffic feature selection is important for the identification, in the actual analysis, some network features contain few information, correlation and redundancy, which has no contribution to the improvement of detection accuracy, but increases the time complexity and space complexity. The feature dimension reduction can be achieved by data feature selection, which can reduce the computational complexity and improve the efficiency of system detection.

The information gain of feature A is defined as the difference between the original information demand and the new demand [12], represented by: $gain(A)$

$$gain(A) = \inf(D) - \inf_A(D) \tag{4}$$

$$= -\sum_1^m p_i \log_2(p_i) - \sum_{j=1}^n \frac{|D_j|}{|D|} \times \inf(D_j),$$

where $p_i = |C_{i,D}| \, / \, |D|$ indicates the nonzero probability that any sample in data set D belongs to C_i, $|D|$ indicates the total sample size, $|C_{i,D}|$ represents the number of samples belonging to class C_i, m is the number of sample classes, $\inf(D)$ represents the average amount of information required to identify the category of tuples D. $\inf_A(D)$ represents the desired information for the classification of tuples in set D based on feature A, and n indicates the number of D_j subsets.

The key problem of network traffic identification is to determine the mapping relationship between network flow and application categories. For the statistical characteristics of a large number of different dimensions, it is difficult to achieve the mapping through the intuitive rules such as threshold. The support vector machine (SVM) method based on the statistical learning theory has strong cognitive ability, especially for small sample learning problems, we can grasp the potential rules of irregular description by statistical learning, and realize the multi feature joint mapping. The basic characteristics and statistical characteristics of network flow are obtained in the unit time after feature selection.

The high dimensional sample feature vector data was constructed as $X = \{x_1, x_2, \ldots, x_l\}$, each network traffic sample can be marked as $D(X, y_i)$, y_i represents the class label for this type of traffic sample, and $y_i \in \{+1, -1\}$. Optimal classification surface used for distinguishing different categories can be expressed by $\vec{w} \cdot \vec{x} + b = 0$ which can make the biggest difference between different categories. Maximizing the interface is equivalent to solving the following optimization problem.

$$\min \quad \frac{1}{2} \sum_{i=1}^{n} w_i^2 \tag{5}$$

$$\text{Subject to} \quad y_i(\vec{w} \cdot \vec{x} + b) - 1 \geq 0, i = 1, \ldots, n, \tag{6}$$

where, n indicates the number of sample, w is not only related to the location of sample points, but also related to the category of samples. Under the constraint of formula (6), the formula (5) can be solved by convex quadratic optimization. For the two classification problem, the SVM discriminant function can be expressed as

$$f(x) = \text{sgn}\{(w, x) + b\} = \text{sgn}\{\sum_{i=1}^{l} \alpha_i \cdot y_i \cdot (x_i \cdot x) + b\}, \tag{7}$$

where α_i indicates the optimized Lagrange operator, (w, b) determining the equation of the classification surface $< w \cdot x > +b = 0$. For the multi classification problem, we design the SVM discrimination model between any two categories. As for k categories it needs C_k^2 categories. For the sample to be classified, the class with the most votes is the category of the sample.

2.5 Network Traffic Anomaly Detection and Analysis Based on Hybrid Strategy

In this paper, we design a hybrid optimization strategy, make a comprehensive utilization of all kinds of detection methods with their advantages to realize the accurate use of network traffic data, and effectively detect the abnormal traffic data. Network traffic anomaly detection and analysis algorithm based on hybrid strategy is shown as follows.

First of all, based on network traffic data distribution on the pretreatment, obtain the preliminary classification results by port mapping identification. At the same time, use the load feature matching to analysis and get the results. Compare the two results and analysis the inconsistent results manually to determine the protocol type. Then we can obtain the label training data for machine learning classification. Next, extract the feature of network traffic and construct the feature vector for machine learning classification. Support vector machine is used for training and learning based on the training data, and the knowledge classification model is obtained. Carry out the training process and test the accuracy constantly until the error rate is lower than the set threshold. Then change the recognition strategy, the identification results of port mapping, load feature matching and machine learning recognition are used to decide the final result by Voting Mechanism. The results are constantly used to train the SVM learning model, and update adaptively. The flow chart of the algorithm is shown in Fig. 2.

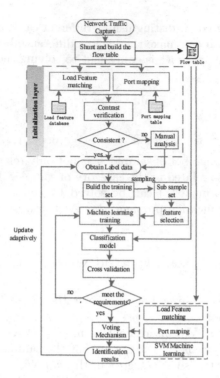

Fig. 2. Flow chart of anomaly detection algorithm.

3   Experiments and Results

In order to verify the applicability of the algorithm based on dynamic hybrid strategy, in this paper, we choose the actual data in the Measurement network of launch vehicle. The network topology of the Measurement network is shown as Fig. 3. Different system devices exchange the instruction and the data with each other through switches. For the test analysis, the whole data of the network can be obtained by the port of the core switch. Main configuration of the computer for experiments is as follows, Intel i5-3450 processor packaged by LGA1155, 4G 1333 DDR3 memory, and 1T SATA 7200r/s mechanical hard drive.

Select a subset of samples and do the feature selection by means of the information gain method described in formula (4), and the threshold parameter used to measure SVM machine learning performance is set to 90%. The experimental data is about 13.2G, and the actual processing time is 2 min 50 s, which can realize real-time data processing. The experimental data were processed with 9742 streams, of which the private network traffic of the network was about 49.18%. In order to verify the effectiveness of the proposed algorithm, the port mapping method and the deep packet detection (DPI) method are compared with the method in this paper. The experimental results are shown in Table 1.

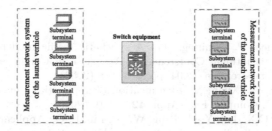

Fig. 3. Network topological of the launch vehicle network.

Table 1. Experimental results.

Methods	Accuracy rate	Proportion of unrecognized flow
Port mapping	84.9%	4.1%
Deep packet detection	92.2%	3.9%
Port mapping with DPI	81.9%	17.5%
Proposed method	99.1%	0.57%

Port mapping with DPI means that the port mapping method is compared with the output result of the DPI. If the results are consistent, then output the results, otherwise, identified as unknown traffic, and need for manual analysis. Inconsistent flows of Port mapping with DPI processed by manual analysis, the accuracy rate can be improved to 99.4 From Table 1, the accurate rates of proposed dynamic traffic identification based on hybrid strategy analysis was 99.1%, far higher than other methods, and the artificial processing required is less than the other three methods. The proposed method not only reduces the manual analysis, but also improves the recognition accuracy rate.

4   Conclusion

In this paper, we propose an algorithm for network anomaly detection based on dynamic hybrid strategy, comprehensively use the port mapping, load feature matching, statistical analysis and machine learning, design a dynamic hybrid strategy, and achieve the identification by using the voting mechanism. Not only ensure the accuracy rate of identification, greatly reduce the manual analysis, but also adaptive update. Greatly improve the intelligence and automation level of the anomaly detection and analysis. In the future, by long term analysis and iterative update of the actual data in the launch vehicle network, the traffic data can be gradually transparent and credible, effectively guarantee the safe and reliable operation of the network system.

References

1. Lang, T., Branch, P., Armitage, G.: A synthetic traffic model for Quake3. In: ACM Sigchi International Conference on Advances in Computer Entertainment Technology, Singapore, June 2004, pp. 233–238 (2004)
2. Liang, C., Jian, G., Xuan, X.: Identification of application- level protocols using characteristic. J. Comput. Eng. Appl. **42**, 16–19 (2006)
3. Lin, Y.-D., Lu, C.N., Lai, Y.-C., Peng, W.-H., Lin, P.-C.: Application classification using packet size distribution and port association. J. Netw. Comput. Appl. **32**, 1024–1030 (2009)
4. Moore, A.W., Papagiannaki, K.: Toward the accurate identification of network applications. In: Dovrolis, C. (ed.) PAM 2005. LNCS, vol. 3431, pp. 41–54. Springer, Heidelberg (2005). https://doi.org/10.1007/978-3-540-31966-5_4
5. Jun, Z., Yang, X., Yu, W., Wanlei, Z., Yong, X., Yong, G.: Network traffic classification using correlation information. J. IEEE Trans. Parallel Distrib. Syst. **24**, 104–117 (2013)
6. Xiao, L., Cheng, L.: State classification algorithm for bus based on hierarchical support vector machine. In: 2015 8th International Symposium on Computational Intelligence and Design (ISCID), Hangzhou, China, vol. 2, pp. 649–652 (2015)
7. Renuka, D.S., Yogesh, P.: A hybrid approach to counter application layer DDoS attacks. Int. J. Crypt. Inf. Secur. **2**, 649–652 (2012)
8. Gao, Y., Zhou, W., Han, J., Meng, D.: An online log anomaly detection method based on grammar compression. Chin. J. Comput. **37**, 73–86 (2014)
9. Wang, C., Zhang, H., Ye, Z., Du, Y.: A peer to peer traffic identification method based on support vector machine and artificial bee colony algorithm. In: 2015 IEEE 8th International Conference on Intelligent Data Acquisition and Advanced Computing Systems: Technology and Applications (IDAACS), Warsaw, vol. 2, pp. 982–986 (2015)
10. Yu, W., Chao, C., Yang, X.: Unknown pattern extraction for statistical network protocol identification. In: IEEE Conference on Local Computer Networks, Clearwater Beach, FL, pp. 506–509 (2015)
11. Chen, T., Liao, X.: An optimized solution of application layer protocol identification based on regular expressions. In: 2016 18th Asia-Pacific Network Operations and Management Symposium (APNOMS), Kanazawa, pp. 1–4 (2016)
12. He, H., Tiwari, A., Mehnen, J., Watson, T., Maple, C., Jin, Y., Gabrys, B.: Incremental information gain analysis of input attribute impact on RBF-kernel SVM spam detection. In: 2016 IEEE Congress on Evolutionary Computation (CEC), Vancouver, BC, pp. 1022–1029 (2016)

Response to Multiple Attack Behaviour Models in Cloud Computing

Xu Liu, Xiaoqiang Di$^{(\boxtimes)}$, Jinqing Li, Huamin Yang, Ligang Cong,
and Jianping Zhao

School of Computer Science and Technology,
Changchun University of Science and Technology, Changchun, China
dixiaoqiang@cust.edu.cn

Abstract. User behaviour models have been widely used to simulate
attack behaviour in the security domain. In this paper, we introduce one
perfect rational and three bounded rational behaviour models to simulate attack behaviour of attack-defense game in cloud computing, and
then discuss defender's response to attacks. We assume cloud provider
as the role of defender is intelligent to collect attack-related information
so that it can predict attack behaviour model, thus the attack behaviour
model is known to defender, we therefore build a single-objective optimization game model to find the optimal virtual machine (VM) monitoring strategy against attacker. Finally, through numerical analysis, we
prove that when the attack behavior model is known, the corresponding
single-objective optimization game solution is better than the other three
solutions.

Keywords: Behaviour model · Attack-defense game
Cloud computing

1 Introduction

Cloud computing provides different services to tenants, such as host service,
storage service, application service and so on. Tenants can access and manage
cloud services as their own computing resources, this kind of open remote mode
is convenient for tenants. Gradually, more and more information is stored in
the cloud platform by tenants, which attracts attackers' attention and brings
serious security threat to IaaS layer that is the foundation layer of cloud platform
[1]. Virtual Machine (VM) is an important IaaS component, it is facing many
security incidents such as invading or destroying VM. In addition, if one VM is
attacked, users who use it or other VMs that communicate with it, and even
its host security will be affected [2]. Therefore, to enhance security of VM has
become a problem of both cloud provider and tenants.

To maintain VMs security, cloud provider often collects information on VMs
in order to design robust defense against attacks. For example, cloud provider
detects intrusion or monitors attack of network system before the invasion of

© ICST Institute for Computer Sciences, Social Informatics and Telecommunications Engineering 2018
G. Sun and S. Liu (Eds.): ADHIP 2017, LNICST 219, pp. 489–496, 2018.
https://doi.org/10.1007/978-3-319-73317-3_56

network system harm and then alerts as soon as it detects invasion or attack [3]. It's noteworthy that monitoring will generate cost such as maintenance resource, budget and so on, according to the statistics that a large data center costs range between \$10 million to \$25 million per year, and maintenance costs up to nearly 80% of the total cost [4]. Hence, monitoring cost can't be ignored, monitoring all VMs may not be the best strategy in consideration of monitoring cost. Since different monitoring strength leads to monitoring resources efficiency for defender, an optimal monitoring strategy balancing cost and monitoring benefit will allow for the saving of the significant resource while minimizing the potential damage inflicted by an unmonitored attack, which is required.

The ultimate objective of monitoring is to respond to attackers. In this paper, we model four types of attack behaviour models: Perfect Rational (PR), (Prospect Theory) PT [5], (Quantal Response) QR [6] and Subjective expected Utility Quantal Response (SUQR) [7], and then analyze how defender will respond to these different attack behaviours in Stackelberg game. In the game, cloud provider playing the role of defender and attacker are two rival game players whose interaction is modelled as repeated games, their payoffs are monitoring or attacking benefit minus operation cost.

From the perspective of defender, if attack behaviour is one of the four models (PR, PT, QR or SUQR), defender will build a corresponding single-objective optimization game model and respond to it according to the game equilibrium strategy.

The main contributions of this paper are as follows:

1. We abstract a trade-off problem between VM monitoring benefit and monitoring cost in cloud computing as a Stackelberg security game problem.
2. The single-objective optimization game equilibrium strategy provides reference to monitor VM for cloud provider.

The structure of this paper is as follows: Sect. 2 introduces the related work researched on single-objective optimization game models; Sect. 3 illustrates the game modelling of the application scenarios and different types of attack behaviour models; Sects. 4 and 5 describe the numerical analysis and summarize this paper.

2   Related Works

There have been many researches about Stackelberg security game based on assumption that attacker is perfect rational, however, sometimes attackers aren't always so perfect rational that they can make the optimal attacking strategy that gives them the maximum utilities. Therefore, more and more researches focus on the bounded rational behaviour model.

1992, Kahneman and Tversky proposed prospect theory (PT) by analyzing behaviour economic, it's innovative that every target's prospect is the composition of value and weight function. 1995, paper [6] first proposed quantal response

(QR) model to control the rationality of the attackers' behaviour by introducing a positive parameter, and then predict the attacking possibility as attacker's response to defender. 2013, paper [7] first put forward subjective expected utility quantal response (SUQR) model, they combined the existing subjective utility functions and QR model proposed before. These three bounded rational user behaviour models are all widely studied. Researches [8,9] summarize and compare the prediction accuracy and performance of PT, QR, SUQR and other user behaviour models used often. These researches mainly focus on the evaluation of prediction accuracy of different attack behaviour models instead of applying them to solve problems.

In order to solve security problems involving different attack behaviours, algorithms [10–13] are designed to calculate the optimal Nash equilibrium strategy based on Stackelberg security game. These researches are concentrated on designing the optimal defense strategy against a single type of attack in a common network environment, however, we apply Stackelberg security game in cloud computing to design VM monitoring strategy based on equilibrium strategy. Meanwhile, many literatures are studied with a restraint that the amount of security resources available is limited [14], different from them, we relax the assumption that security resources are limited since resources in cloud computing are allocated dynamically and relatively cheaper than physical resources.

3   Game Modelling

3.1   Why Use Game Theory?

Game theory is a tool used to analyze how two rival players make decisions from their individual perspectives, especially used more in the security domain recently. We consider a scenario including a cloud provider (the role of defender) and a malicious user (the role of attacker), they belong to two opposing roles without any cooperation. The rivalry between attacker and defender makes their interaction suitable to model as a 1-vs-1 non-cooperative Stackelberg attack-defense game. Attacker selects some or all targets to launch attacks with an attack probability distribution over the target set. Defender tries to monitor VMs that are lean to be attacked in the form of monitoring service time, network traffic peak, data packet content, etc. with a monitor probability distribution over targets set.

In this paper, we focus on finding defender's optimal monitoring probability distribution from a mathematical view instead of monitoring measure. Both attacker and defender will try their best to collect more information about the other side's action. For instance, defender will design monitoring strategy based on attack-related information collected previously, attacker will plan attacking strategy according to the defense-related information collected previously. There will be repeated strategy-making interactions between defender and attacker until a group of monitoring and attacking probability distributions that can satisfy their payoff maximum is reached.

3.2 Payoff

Payoff is the main element in game theory that reflects player's return in every round of action. The payoff of attacker and defender on a target i is shown in Table 1. Two row variables represent attacker's two actions (Attack and Not Attack) and two column variables represent defender's two actions (Monitor and Not Monitor). The payoffs brought to both attacker and defender in each pair of attack and defense action set are separated by commas, the former represents attacker's payoff while the latter represents defender's payoff.

Table 1. Payoff of two players on target i

	Monitor (q_i)	Not monitor ($1 - q_i$)
Attack p_i	$-\alpha P_i^a + (1-\alpha) R_i^a - C_i^a,$ $\alpha R_i^d - (1-\alpha) P_i^d - C_i^m$	$R_i^a - C_i^a,$ P_i^d
Not attack $(1 - p_i)$	$0, -C_i^m$	$0, 0$

The expected payoffs of both attacker and defender are inseparable with respective actions and results thereof (e.g. whether the attacking action is detected by the defender), we use α to define the probability that the attacks are successfully detected. For example, for a target i, if defender monitors that the attacker launches an attack on i, defender will be rewarded by R_i^d; otherwise, defender will be punished by P_i^d. Similarly, attacker will be punished by P_i^a in former case; attacker will be rewarded by R_i^a in later case. The respective expected payoffs of defender and attacker are obtained by accumulating the payoffs from each group of different action set, as shown in Eqs. (1) and (2).

$$U_D(p,q) = \sum_{i \in T} p_i q_i [\alpha R_i^d + (1-\alpha) P_i^d - C_i^m] + p_i(1-q_i) P_i^d$$

$$- (1-p_i) q_i C_i^m = \sum_{i \in T} q_i [\alpha p_i (R_i^d - P_i^d) - C_i^m] + p_i P_i^d \quad (1)$$

$$U_A(p,q) = \sum_{i \in T} p_i q_i [\alpha P_i^a + (1-\alpha) R_i^a - C_i^a] + p_i(1-q_i)*$$

$$(R_i^a - C_i^a) = \sum_{i \in T} p_i [\alpha q_i (P_i^a - R_i^a) + (R_i^a - C_i^a)] \quad (2)$$

Nash Equilibrium: In a game $G = \{s_1, .., s_n; u_1, ..., u_n\}$ with n players, if strategy profile $\{s_1^*, ..., s_n^*\}$ satisfies each player i that s_i^* is the optimal strategy or the strategy that is not worse than other $(n-1)$ strategies, then this strategy profile is called a Nash Equilibrium [15].

In order to find the equilibrium strategy of the Stackelberg game in this paper, we combine the optimization methods of Matlab to develop new algorithm. When attack behavior model is perfect rational, payoff function is linear constrained, we use linprog algorithm; otherwise, we use genetic algorithm (GA).

3.3   Attack Behaviour Model

Attackers are often human beings or agents governed by human beings whose behaviours are not certain. According to recent researches, attack behaviours can be classified into two main categories based on attacker's rationality. If an attacker can design the strategy that provides it the maximum payoff, it will be defined as perfect rational; otherwise, it will be defined as bounded rational. For example, intelligent attackers usually collect information about adversarial information (monitoring strategy or defense measure), but sometimes they can't collect all information, or they aren't always capable of learning defender's exact strategy, which leads that they are unable to design the best strategy that provides them the maximum payoff. In this subsection, we introduce four types of attacker behaviour models that differentiate with attacker's rationality, one perfect rational and three bounded rational: PT, QR, SUQR.

Table 2. Four attack behaviour models

Behaviour model	Attack probability
Perfect Rational (PR)	$p_i = \arg\max U_A, \quad p_i \in [0,1]$
Prospect Theory (PT)	$prospect(i) = \pi(q_i)V * (P_i^a - C_i^a) + \pi(1-q_i)V * (R_i^a - C_i^a)$ $p_i = \frac{prospect(i) - \min(prospect(i))}{\sum_{i=1}^{n}(prospect(i) - \min(prospect(i)))}, \quad \sum p_i = 1$
Quantal Response (QR)	$p_i = \frac{e^{\lambda U_A(q_i)}}{\sum_{j=1}^{n} e^{\lambda U_A(q_j)}}, \quad \sum p_i = 1$
Subjective expected Utility Quantal Response (SUQR)	$p_i = \frac{e^{w_1 R_i^a + w_2 P_i^a + w_3 q_i}}{\sum_{j=1}^{n} e^{w_1 R_i^a + w_2 P_i^a + w_3 q_i}}, \quad \sum p_i = 1$

4   Numerical Analysis

In this section, we will perform numerical analysis of single-objective optimization game solutions on 8 targets in Matlab, we set $R_a, R_d \in [0, 10]$, $P_a, P_d \in [-10, 0]$ used in [12], attack cost C_a and monitor cost C_m both belong to $(0, 1)$. These numbers can be exchanged with money or other units of measurement in a real cloud system. We take two experiments with attack-monitor probability distribution, as well as attacker's and defender's utility.

4.1   Players' Strategy

When attack behaviour model is a single type and known to the defender, the defender will build a corresponding single-objective optimization game. In this subsection, we show attack and monitoring strategy in equilibrium status in Fig. 1.

It can be observed that in Fig. 1(a), when attacker is PR, defender's monitoring strategy is consistent with attacker's strategy; once defender predicts that

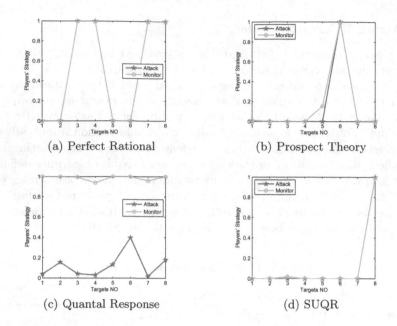

(a) Perfect Rational (b) Prospect Theory

(c) Quantal Response (d) SUQR

Fig. 1. Players' strategy with four attack behaviour models

Table 3. Player's strategy with QR model

Target NO	1	2	3	4	5	6	7	8
Attack	0.0405	0.155	0.043	0.032	0.134	0.398	0.018	0.180
Descend	6th	**3th**	**5th**	7th	**4th**	1st	8th	2nd
Monitor	0.99966	0.99992	0.99565	0.93916	0.99986	0.99995	0.96029	0.99985
Descend	4th	**2nd**	6th	8th	**3th**	1st	**7th**	5th

target NO. 3,4,7,8 will be attacked with a bigger probability, it will monitor these targets; the same trend can be seen in Fig. 1(b), (c) and (d). In Fig. 1(c), the trend isn't clear, hence, we show the specific values in Table 3, it's easy to find that except two items (target 1 and 8) bigger attack probability is, bigger monitoring probability will be; on target 6, attack probability is the biggest among 8 targets and the corresponding monitoring probability is the biggest that is close to 1. In addition, since defender's monitoring probability distribution is between 0.99 and 1 that difference is so small, thus it's acceptable that the order of monitoring probability isn't the same as the order of attack probability. Meanwhile, compared with the other three subfigures, we can observe that, in QR model, attack probabilities on 8 targets are all bigger than 0 and monitoring probability are all close to 1, which reflects that defender is very careful to avoid missing attack.

According to the monitoring probability distribution, cloud provider can design monitoring methods with different strength or defense measures.

4.2   Players' Utility

As shown in Table 4, four row variables represent four attack probabilities that fit in with four attack behaviour models, four column variables represent four monitoring probabilities calculated from four corresponding single-objective optimization games models. Every cell represents defender's utility gained from the corresponding row attacking and column monitoring probability. Take one cell as an example, while attack probability fits in with PR, single-objective optimization solution (Res_PR) gives defender utility valued as 23.4956 that is the biggest value of the four values of its row.

Table 4. Defender's utility with four attack behaviour models

	Res_PR	Res_PT	Res_QR	Res_SUQR
PR	**23.4956**	−11.4183	21.186	1.2972
PT	−6.5044	**6.1938**	3.6514	−5.4841
QR	−4.7896	−1.7931	**3.0629**	−4.5116
SUQR	6.0956	−5.1484	4.5550	**7.1159**

It's seen from the Table 4 that for every attack behaviour model, the corresponding game solution can bring more monitoring utility for defender than the other three game solutions. Since single-objective optimization game focuses on a single clear objective that maximizes defender's utility. Therefore, we conclude that the corresponding game solution may be the best reference for cloud provider to design optimal VM monitoring strategy.

5   Conclusion

In this paper, we solve the utility-based trade-off problem that includes resource consumption and monitoring benefit by formulating Stackelberg security game. Cloud provider and attacker are modelled as two rival roles of defender and attacker in the game. Specially, we model four types of attack behaviours including PR, PT, QR, SUQR and then study how defender responds to these four attack behaviours. Through numerical analysis we prove that defender's monitoring probability on a target is consistent with the probability that it will be attacked, and appropriate game solution can bring defender more utility. Finally, defender responds to attacks by referring to the Nash Equilibrium strategy of the single-objective optimization security game, bigger equilibrium monitoring probability on a target is, more resource or attention will be paid on it.

Acknowledgment. This research is partially supported by research grants from Science and Technology Project of Jinlin province (20150204081GX). The authors are thankful to reviewers that help to improve the quality of this paper.

References

1. Kaufman, L.M.: Can public-cloud security meet its unique challenges? IEEE Secur. Privacy **8**(4), 55–57 (2010)
2. Kamhoua, C.A., et al.: Game theoretic modeling of security and interdependency in a public cloud. In: IEEE 7th International Conference on Cloud Computing, pp. 514–521 (2014)
3. Chen, L., Leneutre, J.: A game theoretical framework on intrusion detection in heterogeneous networks. IEEE Trans. Inf. Forensics Secur. **4**(2), 165–178 (2009)
4. Saha, S., et al.: A novel revenue optimization model to address the operation and maintenance cost of a data center. J. Cloud Comput. **5**(1), 1–23 (2016)
5. Tversky, A., Kahneman, D.: Advances in prospect theory: cumulative representation of uncertainty. J. Risk Uncertainty **5**(4), 297–323 (1992)
6. McKelvey, R.D., Palfrey, T.R.: Quantal response equilibria for normal form games. Games Econ. Behav. **10**(1), 6–38 (1995)
7. Nguyen, T.H., Yang, R., Azaria, A., Kraus, S., Tambe, M.: Analyzing the effectiveness of adversary modeling in security games. In: AAAI (2013)
8. Abbasi, Y.D., et al.: Human adversaries in opportunistic crime security games: evaluating competing bounded rationality models. In: Proceedings of the Third Annual Conference on Advances in Cognitive Systems ACS, p. 2 (2015)
9. Shieh, E.A., et al.: PROTECT: an application of computational game theory for the security of the ports of the United States. In: AAAI (2012)
10. Kar, D., Fang, F., Delle Fave, F., Sintov, N., Tambe, M.: A game of thrones: when human behaviour models compete in repeated Stackelberg security games. In: Proceedings of International Conference on Autonomous Agents and Multiagent Systems, pp. 1381–1390. AAMAS (2015)
11. Yang, R., Ordonez, F., Tambe, M.: Computing optimal strategy against quantal response in security games. In: Proceedings of the 11th International Conference on Autonomous Agents and Multiagent Systems, vol. 2, pp. 847–854. AAMAS (2012)
12. Yang, R., Kiekintveld, C., Ordóñez, F., Tambe, M., John, R.: Improving resource allocation strategies against human adversaries in security games: an extended study. Artif. Intell. **195**, 440–469 (2013)
13. Yang, R., Kiekintveld, C., Ordonez, F., Tambe, M., John, R.: Improving resource allocation strategy against human adversaries in security games. In: IJCAI Proceedings-International Joint Conference on Artificial Intelligence, p. 458 (2011)
14. Qian, Y., Haskell, W.B., Tambe, M.: Robust strategy against unknown risk-averse attackers in security games. In: Proceedings of International Conference on Autonomous Agents and Multiagent Systems, pp. 1341–1349. AAMAS, Istanbul, Turkey (2015)
15. Gibbons, R.: A Primer in Game Theory. Harvester Wheatsheaf, Loughborough (1992)

An Improved Genetic Algorithm on Task Scheduling

Fangyuan Zheng[✉] and Jingmei Li

College of Computer Science and Technology, Harbin Engineering University,
Harbin, China
zhengfangyuan@hrbeu.edu.cn

Abstract. Efficient task scheduling algorithm is critical for achieving high performance in heterogeneous multi-core processors. Because the existing genetic algorithm converges to local optimal solution, so an improved genetic algorithm is proposed to solve the above problems in this thesis. Firstly, the initial population is generated randomly according to the task height value, and then adopting the selection strategy based on competition scale. Finally, the crossover and mutation probability is improved to avoid premature phenomenon. The experiment based on randomly generated graphs shows that the proposed algorithm can improve the efficiency of convergence.

Keywords: Task scheduling · Heterogeneous multi-core processor
Genetic algorithm · Optimal solution

1 Introduction

With the development of computer architecture, chip multi-processor (CMP) [1] becomes the mainstream architecture and provides a platform for high-performance computing. In order to play the parallelism of CMP fully, a good task scheduling algorithm is very important.

Many scholars at home and abroad have carried out many studies on task scheduling, which has been proved to be NP complete [2]. Based on the above research, a new improved genetic algorithm (NIGA) for heterogeneous CMP is proposed, which improves the initial population mode, selection strategy, crossover and mutation probability. The experimental results show that the performance of NIGA is better than genetic algorithm (GA).

2 New Improved Genetic Algorithm

The GA can search the solution in parallel, but it also has the problems of premature and poor stability [3]. In response to the above shortcomings, NIGA is proposed to optimize GA.

© ICST Institute for Computer Sciences, Social Informatics and Telecommunications Engineering 2018
G. Sun and S. Liu (Eds.): ADHIP 2017, LNICST 219, pp. 497–500, 2018.
https://doi.org/10.1007/978-3-319-73317-3_57

2.1 Encoding and Decoding of Chromosomes

Chromosome encoding [4] mode is substring, a substring represents a processor core and each substring contains the number of task which is assigned to the same processor in sequence. Figure 1 is an example of chromosome encoding.

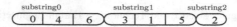

Fig. 1. An example of chromosome encoding

Chromosome decoding and encoding corresponds to each other, decoding is assigning tasks in sequence on the substring of chromosome to the corresponding processor core, then the structure of corresponding task scheduling is constructed.

2.2 Population Initialization and Fitness Function

The individual generation strategy in population is to randomly assign tasks to different processor cores. The tasks on the same core are sorted by the task height. The sequence of tasks with same height is generated randomly. The task height is defined as Eq. (1).

$$h(N_i) = \begin{cases} 0, & if\ pre(N_i) = \phi \\ \max_{N_j \in pre(N_i)} \{h(N_j)\} + 1 & else \end{cases} \tag{1}$$

In NIGA, the quality of individuals is measured with fitness value, the individual with larger value has greater probability to be selected into next generation, and with smaller will be eliminated after some operations. The calculation of fitness is shown in Eq. (2).

$$f(Xi) = \frac{1}{SL(X_i)} \tag{2}$$

In Eq. (2), $SL(X_i)$ represents the scheduling length of individual X_i.

2.3 Selection

After the population initialization, the selection strategy is used to select several individuals randomly, then choosing individual with the highest fitness value to the next step. The difference between initial individuals is large, only the smaller competition scale can guarantee the population diversity. With the individual quality becomes better, the scale becomes larger in order to search the optimal solution globally. The strategy sets the scale double by 20 times, as shown in Eq. (3).

$$K = 2 \times \frac{t}{20}, \quad t \in T \tag{3}$$

2.4   Crossover and Mutation

The main function of crossover is to generate new individual, the mutation operation is mainly to maintain species diversity [5]. If crossover and mutation probability is too large, some individuals with better fitness may be destroyed, it is not conducive to the solution convergence; if the probability is too small, it may not produce new individuals. Therefore, the probability should be adaptive, which can be changed with the fitness value, so as to ensure that individuals with low fitness value have a large probability, and the individuals with high fitness value has a small probability to save excellent individuals. The probability is shown in Eq. (4).

$$P(i) = \begin{cases} P_{\max} & f_i \leq f_{avg} \\ P_{\min} + (P_{\max} - P_{\min}) \cot[\frac{\pi}{4} (\frac{f_i - f_{avg}}{f_{\max} - f_{avg}} + 1)] & f_i > f_{avg} \end{cases} \tag{4}$$

In Eq. (4), $P_{\min}$ and $P_{\max}$ is the minimum and maximum of crossover and mutation probability, $f_{\max}, f_{avg}, f_i$ is the maximum, average and i-th individual of fitness value respectively.

2.5   Termination Conditions

Set the maximum evolution number $T_{\max}$, NIGA is stopped after the certain iterations, then the individual with maximum fitness value is the optimal task scheduling.

3   Experiments

Randomly generated DAG is used as input data, by comparing the scheduling length and algorithm convergence to measure NIGA and GA.

The communication calculation rate (CCR) of DAG is 0.5 and the processor number is 3. The initial calculation parameters of GA and NIGA are: population size $M = 100$, maximum iterations $T_{\max} = 200$. Moreover, P_c of GA is 0.7, P_m is 0.02, the crossover $P_{\min}$ and $P_{\max}$ of NIGA are 0.8 and 0.2 respectively, the mutation $P_{\min}$ and $P_{\max}$ are 0.03 and 0.002 respectively. In order to avoid the randomness, the average of 15 experimental results is used as the test result of scheduling length.

The experiment mainly tests the scheduling length of GA and NIGA with different nodes, the result as shown in Table 1.

Table 1. The scheduling length of GA and NIGA with different nodes

Algorithm	Nodes = 10	Nodes = 20	Nodes = 30
GA	76	104	137
ICLGA	65	89	116

The experiment mainly tests the iterative evolution on same task number (Task Nodes = 20) of GA and NIGA algorithm, the experimental results are shown in Fig. 2.

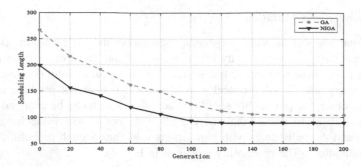

Fig. 2. The iterative evolution of GA and NIGA

From Table 1 and Fig. 2, it can be concluded that the scheduling length of NIGA is shorter than that of GA with the same task nodes, that is, the optimal solution of NIGA is the best, the time of optimal solution is shorter and the convergence speed is faster.

4   Conclusion

The NIGA algorithm is a better task scheduling algorithm based on heterogeneous CMP. It overcomes the shortcomings of GA and improves the scheduling efficiency. NIGA improves the initial population, uses the fitness selection strategy, adopts adaptive crossover and mutation probability to promote the global optimal solution. The experimental results show that the NIGA algorithm has the highest quality of the optimal solution and is faster than GA algorithm.

References

1. Keshanchi, B., Souri, A., Navimipour, N.J.: An improved genetic algorithm for task scheduling in the cloud environments using the priority queues: formal verification, simulation, and statistical testing. J. Syst. Softw. **124**, 1–21 (2016)
2. Akkasi, A.: Genetic algorithm for task scheduling in heterogeneous distributed computing system. **6**(7) (2015)
3. Ahmad, S.G., Liew, C.S., Munir, E.U., et al.: A hybrid genetic algorithm for optimization of scheduling workflow applications in heterogeneous computing systems. J. Parallel Distrib. Comput. **87**(C), 80–90 (2015)
4. Ahmad, S.G., Munir, E.U., Nisar, W.: PEGA: a performance effective genetic algorithm for task scheduling in heterogeneous systems. In: International Conference on High Performance Computing and Communication, 2012 IEEE International Conference on Embedded Software and Systems. IEEE, pp. 1082–1087 (2012)
5. Singh, R.: An optimized task duplication based scheduling in parallel system. **8**(8), 26–37 (2016)

Shared Cache Allocation Based on Fairness in a Chip Multiprocessor Architecture

Dongfang Wang[✉] and Jingmei Li

College of Computer Science and Technology, Harbin Engineering University,
Harbin 150001, China
{wangdongfang,lijingmei}@hrbeu.edu.cn

Abstract. Cache, as the hub between the multi-core processor and the memory, is closely related to the performance of the CMP system. And with the number of processor core increasing, the contention of multi-core for shared cache becomes more intense. Fairness is important to affect the performance of CMP systems, so a Shared Cache allocation method based on fairness is proposed. According to the way of borrow-return, the method assigns Shared Cache to multiple to realize the dynamic balance. The experimental results show that the method significantly improves the system fairness and the system throughput.

Keywords: Multi-core · Shared cache · Fairness · Allocation

1 Introduction

At present, the design of on-chip multi-core (CMP) is widely used in processor design, and the cache structure is also developed from the previous one level cache to multi-level cache design [1]. The paper studies the two level cache. CMP architecture mostly uses private L1 cache and shared L2 cache to improve resource utilization [2]. However, the contention of multi-core for shared cache becomes more intense. There are some problems. On the one hand, due to the interference between threads, one thread may replace another thread's "hot" data, which causes the thread data access failure [3]. On the other hand, because of shared Cache space competition, some that can quickly produce a large number of cache invalidation thread may replace the valid data of other threads, exclusive most or all of the cache space. Therefore, each core uses fair share cache as the research objective, and proposes a shared cache allocation method. The method assign the shared cache to more than one core. And the core which have the phenomenon of frequent data access failure can borrow cache form other cores, paying back after a while.

2 Shared Cache Allocation

Shared Cache allocation is defined as each core privately occupies part of Shared Cache by certain rules. Once a part of the cache space is assigned to a core, the core has control over its cache space. The Shared Cache allocation is divided into static and dynamic. Compared with dynamic allocation, static allocation distribute cache without considering the dynamic demand for cache in program runtime [4]. So dynamic

© ICST Institute for Computer Sciences, Social Informatics and Telecommunications Engineering 2018
G. Sun and S. Liu (Eds.): ADHIP 2017, LNICST 219, pp. 501–504, 2018.
https://doi.org/10.1007/978-3-319-73317-3_58

allocation is better. In the process of shared Cache allocation, fairness affects the performance of the system [5]. If fairness is ignored, certain thread access requests may not be answered for long time, even starvation. Therefore, the paper proposes a shared cache allocation method based on fairness.

There are five 5 metrics defined by kim [6] that measure the fairness of CMP systems.

$$M_1^{ij} = |X_i - Y_j| \quad X_i = \frac{Miss\_shr_i}{Miss\_ded_i} \tag{1}$$

$$M_2^{ij} = |X_i - Y_j| \quad X_i = Miss\_shr_i \tag{2}$$

$$M_3^{ij} = |X_i - Y_j| \quad X_i = \frac{Missr\_shr_i}{Missr\_ded_i} \tag{3}$$

$$M_4^{ij} = |X_i - Y_j| \quad X_i = Missr\_shr_i \tag{4}$$

$$M_5^{ij} = |X_i - Y_j| \quad X_i = Missr\_shr_i - Missr\_ded_i \tag{5}$$

Miss_shr$_i$ denote the number of misses of thread i when it shares the cache with other threads. And Miss_dedi denote miss rate of thread I when it runs alone with dedicated cache. M1is used to balance the increase in the number of cache failures per thread. M2 is the number of cache failures that balance each thread. M3 is used to balance the percentage of thread cache failure rates increasing. M_4 balances cache failure rates for each thread. M_5 is used to balance the cache failure rate due to coordinated running of threads.

To illustrate the problem, N denote the number of date block of cache. M denote the number of core. P$_i$ denote the cache block assignment information table of core$_i$. Q$_i$ denote the cache block debit table of core$_i$. The allocation of shared cache is mainly divided into initialization, borrowing and repayment phases. The specific steps are as follows:

Initialization:

1. Initializes the table Q and table P. Share the shared cache blocks N equally to the M cores. Every core update its cache block assignment information table.

   Lending step:

2. When the core$_i$ sends access request to the Cache, the address of the Cache block is obtained by mapping rules according to the address to be accessed, and judge whether the cache block address is hit in the table P$_i$. if hit, jump step 3.else jump step 7.

3. To determine whether data blocks frequently change in and out, if there is a frequent replacement of data blocks, jump step 4. Else jump step 5.

4. Determine whether the debit table core$_i$ of Q$_i$ is empty, if not empty, then take back the cache block from the debit table Q$_i$, and execute step 5. If the debit table Q$_i$ is empty, then borrow the core$_j$ which has relatively ample cache space cache block

and start the timing. Add these cache block address into P_i and Q_j. And delete these cache block information from P_j and jump step 6.

5. Execute the replacement policy of data, and update the assignment information table P_i of $core_i$.

   Payment step:

6. When the timing reaches the threshold, $core_i$ returned cache block which borrowed from $core_j$ to the $core_j$. And delete the information of borrowed cache block from table P_i and Q_j. Then restore the borrowed cache block information to the table P_j.

3   Evaluation

To evaluate the benefit of the Shared Cache allocation based fairness. We choose a part of SPEC CPU 2006 benchmarks that are memory–intensive. The evaluation is using simulator M5. The CMP cores are set private L1 instruction and data, and shared L2 cache. Processor employs 4-core, Out-of-order, 1 GHz. The Protocol adopts a simple snooping cache coherence protocol. And L1 Cache is designed private 2-way 32 KB DC/32 KB IC block size = 64 B. L2 Cache is designed shared 8-way, block size = 64 B.

3.1   Simulation Result

Figurc 1 shows the throughput (combined IPC) of fairness partitioning and no-fairness partitioning. From the average IPC contrast of each test program in the figure, we can see that the fairness partitioning is better than the no-fairness partitioning. Compared with no-fairness partitioning, IPC of the fairness partitioning improved by 9.7%.

Figure 2 shows system miss rate result which was LRU policy and LRU based on the fair shared cache partitiong. On the whole, the miss rate of system that employs fair shared cache partitioning is obviously decreasing. And the miss rate of LRU that

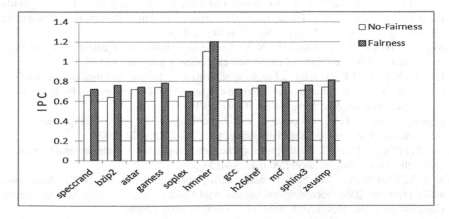

Fig. 1. System throughput comparison

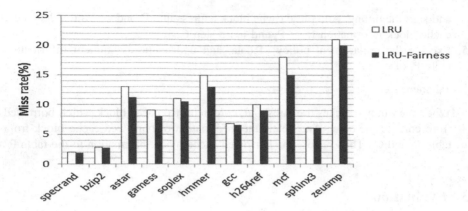

Fig. 2. System miss rate comparison

employs fair shared cache partitioning is decrease by 15% compared with the miss rate of LRU that does not employ shared cache partitioning.

4   Conclusions

The paper has shown the comparison of system throughput and miss rate between shared cache allocation based fairness and no-fair shared cache allocation. The method proposed by the paper uses the fairness as benchmark to realize the dynamic balance of cache allocation. The experimental results show that the IPC of system is greatly improved and the performance of the system is better. And with fair cache partitioning, the OS can assign Shared Cache reasonably to the cores that really need it.

References

1. Pan, A., Pai, V.S.: Runtime-driven shared last-level cache management for task-parallel programs. In: 2015 SC - International Conference for High Performance Computing, Networking, Storage and Analysis, no. 11. IEEE (2017)
2. Mars, J., Hundt, R., Vachharajani, N.A.: Cache contention management on a multicore processor based on the degree of contention exceeding a threshold (2016)
3. Das, S., Kapoor, H.K.: Towards a better cache utilization by selective data storage for CMP last level caches. In: International Conference on VLSI Design and 2016 International Conference on Embedded Systems, pp. 92–97 (2016)
4. Chang, J., Sohi, G.S.: Cooperative cache partitioning for chip multiprocessors. In: International Conference on Supercomputing, pp. 242–252. ACM (2007)
5. Brock, J., Ye, C., Ding, C., et al.: Optimal cache partition-sharing. In: International Conference on Parallel Processing, pp. 749–758. IEEE (2015)
6. Kim, S., Chandra, D., Yan, S.: Fair cache sharing and partitioning in a chip multiprocessor architecture. In: 2004 Proceedings of International Conference on Parallel Architecture and Compilation Techniques, PACT 2004, pp. 111–122. IEEE (2004)

Research on Fast Recognition Algorithm of Golf Swing

Qiao Tian, Jingmei Li[✉], Fangyuan Zheng, and Chao Lv

College of Computer Science and Technology, Harbin Engineering University,
Harbin, China
lijingmei@hrbeu.edu.cn

Abstract. Due to the target recognition algorithm has high time complexity, a fast recognition algorithm of golf gesture based on video sequence is proposed. Firstly, the detector locates the salient region of image, then the gesture detector scans the fraction sequence generated by the video and the sequence is taken as feature data, finally, the linear support vector machine does real-time judgment of the data, thus completing the fast recognition. The experiments show that the recognition speed is over 30 fps and the accuracy of 97% can be achieved on iPhone5s and later version, proving the validity in practical application.

Keywords: Golf gesture recognition · Video sequence · Fraction sequence

1 Introduction

Gesture recognition in video sequence [1, 2] belongs to the research hotspot in computer vision. It is the basic function that auxiliary training equipment must have.

After fully studying the target recognition algorithm [3] based on machine learning, the thesis proposed a golf gesture recognition algorithm based on video sequences, and the experiments verify the algorithm effectiveness in practical application.

2 A Golf Gesture Recognition Algorithm in Video Sequence

The golf gesture recognition in video sequence adopts the machine learning method which is divided into training model and test phase, as shown in Fig. 1.

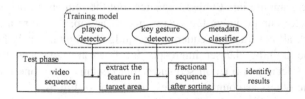

Fig. 1. Schematic diagram of video sequence

G. Sun and S. Liu (Eds.): ADHIP 2017, LNICST 219, pp. 505–509, 2018.
https://doi.org/10.1007/978-3-319-73317-3_59

2.1   Training Model

In training phase, the thesis learns three models: a player detector, several key gesture classifiers and a metadata classifier. These classifiers are shown below.

The player detector is trained by Dollar's fast pedestrian detection algorithm [4] in 2014, it is faster than other recognition algorithms such as HOG + SVM and DMP + SVM [5], because the recognition speed is 30 + fps in natural environment. The labeled player is selected as positive dataset, and the non-human region is as counter dataset. The trained detector acts as player detector, which locates the player in image to reduce the search range and improve the recognition speed, as shown in Fig. 2.

Fig. 2. The location graph of player with player detector

The golf swing action is defined as the combination of key actions, such as swing, back swing, down swing, batting and end swing. The self-created data set is selected to train on the key action classifier which is used to do real-time scoring of the images in the video sequence, the training key actions are selected as positive samples and the others as counter samples, as shown in Fig. 3.

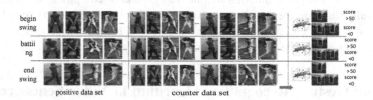

Fig. 3. The key gesture classifier graph in training learn

The key action classifier group learned by training receives many fraction sequences while scanning input video sequence, but the sequence obtained by a single key action detector cannot judge the occurrence of action, therefore a metadata classifier is required, all the fraction sequences are judged simultaneously by a fixed time window L. The training dataset intercepts all fraction sequences through L and regroups them, selecting a fraction sequence that contains only one crest as positive samples, and the others as counter samples, as shown in Fig. 4.

The metadata classifier is learned by linear support vector machine (LSVM), its result is a fraction. This thesis sets the threshold for it, so the "positive" or "negative" judgment action can be simply output.

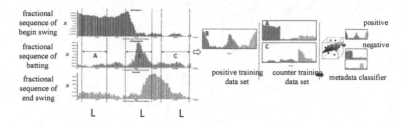

fractional sequence of begin swing

fractional sequence of batting

fractional sequence of end swing

positive training data set   counter training data set   metadata classifier

positive

negative

L   L   L

Fig. 4. Schematic diagram of training metadata classifier

2.2 Test Phase

In test phase, first the player detector locates the salience region of image while inputting the video sequence, and then scanning the video sequence to generate fraction sequence group with the key action classifier group which is trained in the previous phase, as shown in Fig. 5. Then, the metadata classifier is used to judge the fraction sequence obtained by the threshold sliding window, the length of L is got from most cases, sliding in a certain step on all fraction sequences to get the final judgment fraction sequence, as shown in Fig. 6.

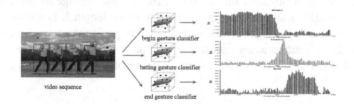

video sequence

begin gesture classifier

batting gesture classifier

end gesture classifier

Fig. 5. The scanning video sequence graph by key gesture classifier

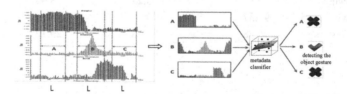

A   B   C

metadata classifier

detecting the object gesture

L   L   L

Fig. 6. The final classify result of metadata classifier

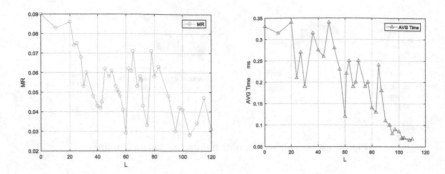

Fig. 7. The corresponding MR and average time with different L

3 Experimental Analysis

The algorithm operating environment: CPU i7, memory 8G, PC with Matlab2016b, and different iphones. The dataset uses UCF Sports and self-created dataset, all the resolution is normalized to 720 × 480. The experiments use 80% of samples as training data, 10% of samples as the validation set and the rest as test set.

In the aspect of golf gesture recognition based on video sequence, the length of sliding window is determined by missile rate (MR) and the average measuring time of each frame. The MR of algorithm with different window length L is shown in Fig. 7. The thesis takes L to 62, uses the precision and recall as performance measurement, and the cross validation method as an assessment method, the recognition frame rate on all iphones is 30 fps. Table 1 shows the experimental results in the motion dataset.

Table 1. The experiment results on UCF dataset

Data type on data set	Precision rate %	Recall rate %	The average time of every frame (ms)
Golf front swing	96.82	93.27	28.94
Golf side swing	97.37	94.87	28.74
Baseball side swing	96.88	83.78	29.12

4 Conclusion

How to reduce the time complexity of target recognition algorithm is an important issue in practical application. The thesis presents a fast golf gesture recognition algorithm based on video sequence. In different phase, player detector, key gesture classifiers and metadata classifier is used to deal with the image in video sequence. The experimental results show that the algorithm runs on iphone5s and later version, the recognition speed is more than 30 fps and the recognition accuracy is 97%, which proves the algorithm validity in practical application.

Acknowledgments. This work is supported by Research on Compiling Technology Based on FPGA Reconfigurable Hybrid System (No. 61003036).

References

1. Dollar, P., Tu, Z., Ponce, P., et al.: Integral channel features. In: BMVC (2009)
2. Ojala, T., Pietikainen, M., Maenpaa, T.: Multiresolution gray-scale and rotation invariant texture classification with local binary patterns. IEEE Trans. Pattern Anal. Mach. Intell. **24**(7), 971–987 (2002)
3. Dalal, N., Triggs, B.: Histograms of oriented gradients for human detection. In: CVPR, vol. 6, no. 2, pp. 886–893 (2005)
4. Dollar, P., et al.: Fast feature pyramids for object detection. IEEE Trans. Pattern Anal. Mach. Intell. **36**(8), 1532–1545 (2014)
5. Wohler, C., Anlauf, J.: An adaptable time-delay neural-networks algorithm for image sequence analysis. IEEE Trans. Neural Netw. **10**(6), 1531–1536 (1999)

Soft Decision Feedback Turbo Equalizer Based on Channel Estimation

Xingyuan You$^{(\boxtimes)}$, Lintao Liu, and Haocheng Ding

Wuhan Maritime Communication Research Institute, Wuhan 430079, China
youxingyuan@hrbeu.edu.cn

Abstract. In order to improve the system BER performance, combining the decoding structure of the feedback iteration in Turbo code, a soft decision feedback equalizer based on channel estimation (CE-SDFE) was proposed. In the initial iteration, CE-SDFE is equivalent to RLS-DFE. In the next iteration, the feedback LLR information is utilized to reconstruct the IQ symbol sequence. The feedback symbol sequence is regenerated by using the IQ symbol sequence and the estimated channel impulse response. We use the weighted sum of the received symbol sequence and the feedback symbol sequence as the input of feedforward filter, and the weighted sum of the soft decision symbol sequence and the reconstructed IQ symbol sequence as the input of feedback filter. The weighting coefficient is generated according to the signal-to-noise ratio and multipath path number. The simulation results show the effectiveness of the proposed algorithm.

Keywords: Channel estimation · Turbo equalizer
Decision feedback equalizer · Iteration

1 Introduction

In wireless communication system, multipath propagation can cause inter-symbol interference (ISI), ISI will cause distortion of the signal, thus affecting the quality of data transmission [1]. In general, the equalizer is used to eliminate the influence of ISI, and then the decoder is used to reduce the bit error rate. Equalizers and decoders are used to eliminate the effects of channel noise and interference, and the independent use of both can guarantee the reliability of communication to a certain extent [2]. However, when the channel environment is poor, to further improve the reliability of the system, we can consider the combination of equalization and decoding to obtain the joint gain, and this joint technology has encountered a significant increase in complexity.

The turbo code [3] proposed in 1993, its feedback iterative decoding structure and its idea of iterative use of soft information provides a new way to solve the high complexity of joint technology. Turbo equalization technology is the use of Turbo code iterative ideas, in the equalization and decoding between the continuous soft information iterative time domain equalization technology, which can greatly reduce the bit error rate [4].

We combined with the feedback structure of feedback iteration in Turbo code and its idea of iterative use of soft information to improve the performance of the receiver.

© ICST Institute for Computer Sciences, Social Informatics and Telecommunications Engineering 2018
G. Sun and S. Liu (Eds.): ADHIP 2017, LNICST 219, pp. 510–519, 2018.
https://doi.org/10.1007/978-3-319-73317-3_60

In this paper, we propose a soft decision feedback equalization based on channel estimation (CE-SDFE). In the initial iteration, CE-SDFE is equivalent to RLS-based decision feedback equalizer (RLS-DFE) [5]. In the next iteration, the feedback LLR information is utilized to reconstruct the IQ symbol sequence. The feedback symbol sequence is regenerated by using the IQ symbol sequence and the estimated channel impulse response. The input of feedforward filter is the weighted sum of the received symbol sequence and the feedback symbol sequence, and the input of feedback filter is the weighted sum of the soft decision symbol sequence and the reconstructed IQ symbol sequence. The weighting coefficient is generated according to the signal-to-noise ratio and multipath path number. The simulation results show the effectiveness of the proposed algorithm.

2 RLS-Based Decision Feedback Equalizer

Decision feedback equalizer [6] consists of two parts: feedforward filter (FFF) and feedback filter (FBF), the structure shown in Fig. 1. The feedforward filter consists of a feedforward transversal filter, which takes the received symbol sequence as input and suppresses the forward ISI linearly. The feedback filter takes the past decision symbol as input and estimates the interference of the preceding symbol to the following symbol.

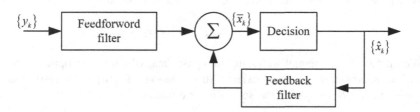

Fig. 1. Decision feedback equalizer.

Thus, the output of the decision feedback equalizer can be represented as

$$\bar{x}_k = \sum_{n=-K_1}^{0} b_n y_{k-n} + \sum_{n=1}^{K_2} b_n \hat{x}_{k-n}, \tag{1}$$

where $\hat{x}_k$ is the estimated value of the kth information symbol, $\{b_n\}$ is the tap coefficient of the filter and $\{\hat{x}_{k-1}, \ldots, \hat{x}_{k-K_2}\}$ is the decision of the previous symbols. The feedforward filter contains $K_1 + 1$ taps, and the feedback filter contains K_2 taps. Here we define $N = K_1 + K_2 + 1$. In the k times, the filter coefficient of DFE is defined as $B_N(k) = [b_{-K_1}, \ldots b_0, \ldots, b_{K_2}]^T$, and the input symbols is defined as $Y_N(k) = [y_{k+K_1}, \ldots y_k, \ldots, x_{k-K_2}]^T$. The matrix form of the DFE output can be expressed as

$$\bar{x}_k = B_N^H(k)Y_N(k). \tag{2}$$

Since the parameters of the wireless channel are variable, the equalizer's tap coefficients must be synchronized to track changes. For the adjustment of the tap coefficient, it is necessary to adopt the adaptive adjustment method, that is adaptive equalization. The RLS algorithm is utilized to optimize $B_N(k)$. RLS algorithm is a special case of Kalman filter algorithm, also known as Kalman algorithm [7]. Kalman filtering is the development of Wiener filtering, which minimizes the trace of the correlation matrix of the filtered state error [8]. Compared with the LMS class algorithm, both the LMS algorithm and the RLS algorithm are based on the least cost function [9], but the choice of the cost function is different. The cost function of the RLS algorithm is

$$\xi(n) = \sum_{k=0}^{n} w^{n-k} |e(k)|^2, \tag{3}$$

where w represents a weighting factor $0 < w < 1$. For RLS-DFE, when the input is the known symbols, the error is defined as

$$e(k) = p_k - \bar{x}_k = p_k - B_N^H(k)Y_N(k). \tag{4}$$

When the input is the known symbols, the error is defined as

$$e(i) = \hat{x}_k - \bar{x}_k = \hat{x}_k - B_N^H(k)Y_N(k). \tag{5}$$

We introduce exponential weighting into past data, which is appropriate when the channel characteristics are time-variant. Minimization of $\xi(n)$ with respect to the coefficient vector $B_N(n)$ yields the set of linear equations

$$R_N(n)B_N(n) = D_N(n), \tag{6}$$

where $R_N(n)$ is the signal correlation matrix of the received symbol sequence which can be represented as

$$R_N(n) = \sum_{k=0}^{n} w^{n-k} Y_N^*(k) Y_N^T(k). \tag{7}$$

and $D_N(n)$ is the cross-correlation vector:

$$D_N(n) = \sum_{k=0}^{n} w^{n-k} \bar{x}_k Y_N^*(k). \tag{8}$$

The solution of Eq. 6 is

$$B_N(n) = R_N^{-1}(n)D_N(n). \tag{9}$$

It is inefficient to solve the set of N linear equations for each new signal component that is received. To avoid this, we proceed as follows. First, $R_N(n)$ may be computed recursively as

$$R_N(n) = wR_N(n-1) + Y_N^*(n)Y_N^T(n), \tag{10}$$

where we call Eq. 10 the time-update equation for $R_N(n)$.

We use the matrix-inverse identity to calculate $R_N^{-1}(n)$:

$$R_N^{-1}(n) = \frac{1}{w}\left[R_N^{-1}(n-1) - \frac{R_N^{-1}(n-1)Y_N^*(n)Y_N^T(n)R_N^{-1}(n-1)}{w + Y_N^T(n)R_N^{-1}(n-1)Y_N^*(n)}\right]. \tag{11}$$

For convenience, we define $P_N(n) = R_N^{-1}(n)$. It is also convenient to define an N-dimensional vector, called the Kalman gain vector, as

$$K_N(n) = \frac{P_N(n-1)Y_N^*(n)}{w + Y_N^T(n)P_N(n-1)Y_N^*(n)}. \tag{12}$$

With these definitions, Eq. 11 becomes

$$P_N(n) = \frac{1}{w}\left[P_N(n-1) - K_N(n)Y_N^T(n)P_N(n-1)\right]. \tag{13}$$

Since

$$B_N(n) = P_N(n)D_N(n). \tag{14}$$

and

$$D_N(n) = wD_N(n-1) + \bar{x}_n Y_N^*(n). \tag{15}$$

The time-update equation of $B_N(n)$ can be represented as

$$B_N(n) = B_N(n-1) + K_N(n)e_N(n). \tag{16}$$

3   Soft Decision Feedback Equalizer Based on Channel Estimation

According to the description of RLS-DFE in the previous section, we propose a soft decision feedback turbo equalizer based on channel estimator based on channel estimation, as it is shown in Fig. 2. In CE-SDFE, the feedforward and feedback filter's tap number are determined based on the estimated channel delay [10]. The input of the equalizer feedforward filter is

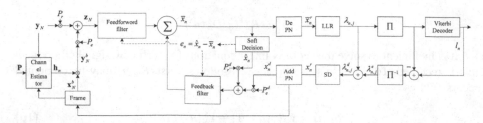

Fig. 2. Soft decision feedback turbo equalizer based on channel estimation.

$$\mathbf{z}_N = P_r \mathbf{y}_N + P_e \mathbf{y}_N^b, \tag{17}$$

where $\mathbf{y}_N$ is the sampled symbol sequence, $\mathbf{y}_N^d$ is the feedback symbol sequence, P_r represents a weighting coefficient of the sampled symbol sequence, P_e represents the weight coefficient of the feedback symbol sequence, P_r and P_e satisfy $P_r + P_e = 1$.

The input of the feedback filter is

$$P_r^d \hat{x}_n + P_e^d x_n^d, \tag{18}$$

where $\hat{x}_n$ represent the soft decision of the equalizer output $\bar{x}_n$, x_n^d represent the feedback data symbol, P_r^d represents the weighting coefficient of $\hat{x}_n$, P_e^d represents the weighting coefficient of x_n^d, P_r^d and P_e^d satisfy $P_r^d + P_e^d = 1$.

In the first iteration, CE-SDFE is equivalent to RLS-DFE, and the concrete steps can be described as:

① Parameter initialization: $P_r = 1$, $P_e = 0$, $\mathbf{y}_N^b = \{0\}$, $P_r^d = 1$, $P_e^d = 0$, The input of feedforward filter is $\mathbf{z}_N = \mathbf{y}_N$; Initialize the equalizer parameters as described in Sect. 2.

② Channel response estimate: The input of channel estimator is a sequence of sampled symbols $\mathbf{y}_N$ and a sequence of known symbols $\mathbf{P}$, and the output of estimator is the channel impulse response $\mathbf{h}_k$. The estimator is implemented using the RLS filter.

③ Adaptive equalization: The input of feedforward filter is $\mathbf{z}_N$, the output is $\bar{x}_n$. When $n \in I_p$, the corresponding reference symbol is a known symbol, the feedback error was

$$e(n) = p_n - \bar{x}_n, \tag{19}$$

The known symbol p_n was the input of the feedback filter;
When $n \in I_d$, the corresponding reference symbol is an unknown data symbol. A soft decision $\hat{x}_n$ was obtain on $\bar{x}_n$, and the feedback error was

$$e(n) = \hat{x}_n - \bar{x}_n, \tag{20}$$

The soft decision result $\hat{x}_n$ is the input of the feedback filter;

④ Decoder: when the equalizer outputs all the data symbols, we need to descramble the data symbol firstly, and obtain $\{\bar{x}_n^r\}$. The second step is to calculate the log-likelihood ratio $\{\lambda_{n,j}\}$ based on $\{\bar{x}_n^r\}$ and channel estimation information. Finally, the deinterleaving and Viterbi deciding are performed on $\{\lambda_{n,j}\}$ to obtain the decoding result $\{l_n\}$.

When the initial iteration is completed, the CE-SDFE needs to adjust the input of the feedforward filter and the feedback filter using the result of demodulation decoding and intermediate information. The specific steps can be described as follows:

① Burst frame symbol sequence reconstruction: First, the priori LLR information is calculated using the decoding results $\{l_n\}$ and $\{\lambda_{n,j}\}$. And then $\left\{\lambda_{n,j}^e\right\}$ and $\{\lambda_{n,j}\}$ will be added to obtain the LLR information $\left\{\lambda_{n,j}^d\right\}$. Then $\left\{\lambda_{n,j}^d\right\}$ is used to reconstruct the data symbol sequence $\{x_n^r\}$, Finally, the sequence $\{x_n^r\}$ is scrambled and framed to reconstruct the burst symbol sequence $\mathbf{x}_N^d$.

② Feedback symbol sequence generation: generated using the estimated channel impulse response $\mathbf{h}_k$ and $\mathbf{x}_N^d$.

③ Calculate the weighting coefficients P_r, P_e, P_r^d, P_e^d: The weight coefficients P_e and P_e^d need to be determined based on the number of channels estimated by the channel, the signal-to-noise ratio and the data symbol modulation: When the number of paths equal to 1,

$$
\begin{aligned}
P_e &= 2Q\left(\sqrt{(2\log_2 L_d)\sin^2\left(\tfrac{\pi}{L_d}\right)\rho}\right), P_r = 1 - P_e \\
P_e^d &= 2Q\left(\sqrt{(2\log_2 L_d)\sin^2\left(\tfrac{\pi}{L_d}\right)\rho}\right), P_r^d = 1 - P_e^d
\end{aligned}
\tag{21}
$$

where $Q(\cdot)$ represents the Q functions, L_d represents the total number of elements in the data symbol map vector set, ρ represents the normalized signal to noise ratio.

When the number of paths is greater than 1,

$$
\begin{aligned}
P_e &= 0, P_r = 1 \\
P_e^d &= 2Q\left(\sqrt{(2\log_2 L_d)\sin^2\left(\tfrac{\pi}{L_d}\right)\rho}\right), P_r^d = 1 - P_e
\end{aligned}
\tag{22}
$$

④ Adaptive equalization: The input of feedforward filter is $\mathbf{z}_N = P_r\mathbf{y}_N + P_e\mathbf{y}_N^b$, the output is $\bar{x}_n$. When $n \in I_p$, the feedback error was

$$
e(n) = p_n - \bar{x}_n,
\tag{23}
$$

The known symbol p_n was the input of the feedback filter;

When $n \in I_d$, the corresponding reference symbol is an unknown data symbol. A soft decision $\hat{x}_n$ was obtain on $\bar{x}_n$, and the feedback error was

$$e(n) = P_r^d \hat{x}_n + P_e^d x_n^d - \bar{x}_n, \tag{24}$$

The input of the feedback filter is $P_r^d \hat{x}_n + P_e^d x_n^d$.

⑤ Decoder: when the equalizer outputs all the data symbols, we need to descramble the data symbol firstly, and obtain $\{\bar{x}_n^r\}$. The second step is to calculate the log-likelihood ratio $\{\lambda_{n,j}\}$ based on $\{\bar{x}_n^r\}$ and channel estimation information. Finally, the deinterleaving and Viterbi deciding are performed on $\{\lambda_{n,j}\}$ to obtain the decoding result $\{l_n\}$.

4   Simulation Results

In this section Monte Carlo simulation result for CE-SDFE are presented to verify the feasibility of the adaptive equalization algorithm. In the simulation, we use the signal frame length of 440, which consist of 128 known 8PSK symbol and 312 data symbols. The adaptive equalization algorithm is simulated by 10000 Monte Carlo experiments using Gaussian channel and fading channel.

Figure 3 shows the bit error rate of the receiver under AWGN channel. In the simulation, the realization of the system need to consider synchronization, parameter estimation and so on. The simulation results show that when the number of iterations is 0 and the bit error rate is 10^{-5}, snr is 8.5 dB. By iteration, The BER performance of this algorithm is improved to 8 dB.

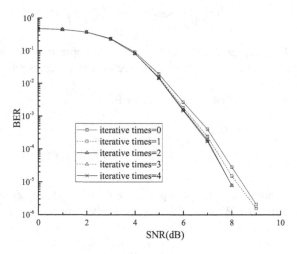

Fig. 3. BER performance for AWGN channel.

Figure 4 shows the convergence performance of the DFE filter when SNR is 5 dB. The simulation has the same channel condition with Fig. 3. The simulation results show that the MSE performance can converge to about 0.2 when the number of iterations is equal to 0. The feedback error is small due to the soft decision of the unknown symbol. When the number of iterations is equal to 4, the MSE can converge to 0.001.

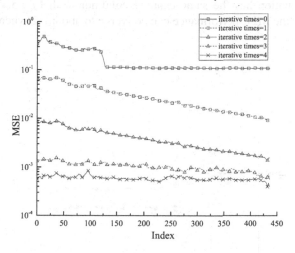

Fig. 4. MSE performance for AWGN channel.

Figure 5 shows the bit error rate of the receiver under fading channel. The fading channel consist of two delay path which have the same power, and the delay is 1 ms.

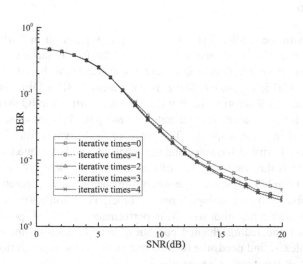

Fig. 5. BER performance for fading channel.

In the simulation, the realization of the system need to consider synchronization, parameter estimation and so on. The simulation results show that when the number of iterations is 0 and the bit error rate is 10−5, snr is 8.5 dB. By iteration, The BER performance of this algorithm is improved to 8 dB. The simulation results show that when the number of iterations is 0 and the bit error rate is 10−2, snr is 15 dB. By iteration, The BER performance of this algorithm is improved to 13 dB.

Figure 6 shows the convergence performance of the DFE filter when SNR is 10 dB. The simulation has the same channel condition with Fig. 5. The simulation results show that the MSE performance can converge to about 0.2 when the number of iterations is equal to 0.

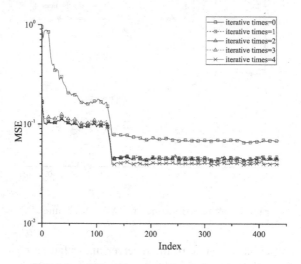

Fig. 6. MSE performance for fading channel.

5   Conclusion

We combined with the feedback structure of feedback iteration in Turbo code and its idea of iterative use of soft information to improve the performance of the receiver. In this paper, we propose a soft decision feedback equalization based on channel estimation. In the initial iteration, CE-SDFE is equivalent to RLS-DFE. In the next iteration, the feedback LLR information is utilized to reconstruct the IQ symbol sequence. The feedback symbol sequence is regenerated by using the IQ symbol sequence and the estimated channel impulse response. The input of feedforward filter is the weighted sum of the received symbol sequence and the feedback symbol sequence, and the input of feedback filter is the weighted sum of the soft decision symbol sequence and the reconstructed IQ symbol sequence. The weighting coefficient is generated according to the signal-to-noise ratio and multipath path number. The simulation results show that the proposed algorithm has improved BER performance and MSE performance under Gaussian channel and fading channel condition, but the iteration increases the computational complexity and needs the relationship between the equalization performance and the number of iterations in practical.

References

1. Eleftheriou, E., Falconer, D.: Adaptive equalization techniques for HF channels. IEEE J. Sel. Areas Commun. **5**(2), 238–247 (1987)
2. Otnes, R.: Evaluation of turbo equalization for the high-rate HF waveforms of STANAG 4539. The Institution of Electrical Engineers. Printed and published by The IEE, Michael Faraday House, Six Hills Way, Stevenage. SG1 2AY, pp. 114–119 (2003)
3. Tuchler, M., Singer, A.C.: Turbo equalization: an overview. IEEE Trans. Inf. Theory **57**(2), 920–952 (2011)
4. Koetter, R., Singer, A.C., Tuchler, M.: Turbo equalization. IEEE Sig. Process. Mag. **21**(1), 67–80 (2004)
5. Bandara, K., Chung, Y.-H.: Reduced training sequence using RLS adaptive algorithm with decision feedback equalizer in indoor visible light wireless communication channel, vol. 2012, pp. 149–154. IEEE (2012)
6. Elgenedy, M.A., Sourour, E., Fikri, M.: Iterative bi-directional Kalman-DFE equalizer for the high data rate HF waveforms in the HF channel, vol. 2013, pp. 1–6. IEEE (2013)
7. Proakis, J.G.: Digital Communications. McGraw-Hill, New York (1995)
8. Wong, W.K., Lim, H.S.: An extended Kalman filter based decision feedback fuzzy adaptive equalizer for power line channel, vol. 2006, pp. 261–266. IEEE (2006)
9. Wang, R., Jindal, N., Bruns, T.: Comparing RLS and LMS adaptive equalizers for nonstationary wireless channels in mobile ad hoc networks, vol. 2002, pp. 1131–1135 (2002)
10. Al-Dhahir, N., Fragouli, C.: How to choose the number of taps in a DFE. In: IEEE Annual Conference on Information Sciences and Systems (CISS 2002) (2002)

Research on Integrity Protection of Data for Multi-server in the Cloud Storage

Guangjun Song[1(⊠)], Dandan Lu[1], and Ming Li[2]

[1] School of Mathematics, Physics and Information Science,
Zhejiang Ocean University, Zhoushan 316022, Zhejiang,
People's Republic of China
song_gj@126.com
[2] College of Computer and Control Engineering,
Qiqihar University, Qiqihar 161006, Heilongjiang, People's Republic of China
lcrb406@163.com

Abstract. Based on existing cloud storage services and remote file synchronization algorithm analysis, a secure cloud storage integration solution is proposed. Its design makes the realization of a cloud-storage-based personal encryption file synchronization and backup system possible. Users can simultaneously manage multiple cloud storage accounts, so that they can synchronize multiple folders and backup at any time. The system can correctly synchronize and backup personal data according to users' needs. Taking advantage of the MD5 algorithm to make encrypted backup file safer, the new mode can prevent the illegal change and disclosure of personal files after synchronization, thus integrity protection of data is achieved, and it becomes easier to manage cloud storage accounts with different servers. Experiments prove the validity and reliability of the system.

Keywords: Cloud storage · MD5 · Cloud sync and backup
Integrity protection

1 Introduction

Cloud computing can conveniently provide users with available resources such as network storage, applications, services and so on. Of them, cloud storage technology offers users a certain capacity of storage space, so that users can upload their data files to the cloud, and they can check, download or sync these files on other terminals or mobile terminals [1, 2]. In recent years, Cloud storage technology has achieved rapid development. To make it easier for users to manage cloud storage accounts of different servers, some cloud storage management platforms have emerged, for example, CarotDAV, Otixo, MultCloud, ZipShare, etc. These cloud storage management softwares provide convenience for users to take full advantage of cloud storage resources. However, data security of cloud storage system has always been a most concerned problem for cloud storage users [3, 4]. Though the cloud storage technology of transfer encryption and storage encryption or other measures have been taken by SSL and AES, etc., data loss, illegal change and other safety problems still exist in cloud storage [5, 6].

© ICST Institute for Computer Sciences, Social Informatics and Telecommunications Engineering 2018
G. Sun and S. Liu (Eds.): ADHIP 2017, LNICST 219, pp. 520–528, 2018.
https://doi.org/10.1007/978-3-319-73317-3_61

These problems have not been satisfactorily resolved by the above-mentioned cloud storage management platforms. Therefore, how can security backup files optionally as required is one of the most pressing problem for cloud storage management platforms. At present, researchers have proposed a variety of solutions to integrity verification of the backup files in cloud [7–10]. However, these fail to meet the actual security needs.

Based on the deficiencies of existing personal cloud storage services, a cloud storage integration solution is presented. That is, users can freely add any personal cloud storage accounts to the system, and can also simultaneously manage several cloud storage accounts of different servers. A backup model combined with compression and MD5 encryption is proposed, which adopts technologies like single or bidirectional selective backup, timing and cycle synchronization. MD5 algorithms are used to generate digital fingerprints of files to identify their tiny changes. Thus, data integrity protection is achieved, the problem of files storage security in cloud computing is better solved.

The paper is organized as follows: The structure and function design of the system are discussed in Sect. 2. The Technology of encryption and Process for backup files are put forward in Sect. 3. The results of simulation and analysis are presented in Sect. 4. Section 5 includes conclusion and further study.

2 System Design

The cloud-storage-based personal encryption file synchronization and backup system is located between open programming interfaces of cloud storage and data access layer.

2.1 System Function Design

The system contains an account database and a client that can run on multiple platforms, mainly including the following functions.

(1) File synchronization: to analyze similarities and differences in local folders and cloud ones, and keep files in the two folders consistent without missing any files.
(2) Account management: users control their multiple cloud storage accounts. They can login, unbind and complete additions and deletions operation of multiple cloud storage services, and get account information of that service. The integration of cloud storage services is achieved by the management of multiple cloud storage accounts.
(3) File backup: to create backup files by compression and MD5 encryption, and simultaneously record this backup time point that could be used as a search point to restore files when needed. The current version of folders is stored in cloud, and the version of the backup file can be retrieved and decrypted through encryption keys so that the model can solve the problem of no backup restore points. By generating digital fingerprints through applying the MD5 algorithm to all files, you can detect whether any changes have been made to this version of the backup files.

(4) Log: the complete log records and content change records are established, including time, file names and type of change.
(5) Common settings: network and system settings, including network proxy settings, bandwidth settings, HTTPS secure transmission mode start using and whether startup.

2.2 System Process Flow

The system implementation process is as shown in Fig. 1. Firstly, users select a cloud storage services platform, login account management module, and create a cloud storage client. Then the system and network parameters of cloud storage client are set in common settings module, and API (Application Programming Interface) control module is called through file synchronization module and simultaneously update local files and cloud files so as to achieve automatic storage and synchronization on multiple cloud storage service platforms. Secondly, file backup module periodically carries on compression, encryption and retrieval for local folder to be backed up, meanwhile checks whether the backup file has been changed. Finally, the performance of API control module is real-time recorded by log module, thereby realizing the security protection for backup files stored in the cloud.

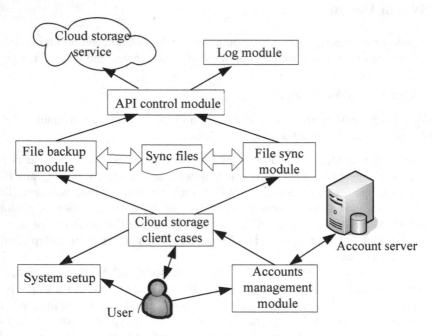

Fig. 1. The system implementation process

3 Encryption Technology and Process

Nowadays, as information security is regarded as an important problem by the society, Cryptography is paying more and more attention. Cryptography is always companioned with Hash functions, which is a kernel of modern Cryptography.

3.1 MD5 Encryption

The full name of MD5 is Message-Digest Algorithm 5 [11], evolving from multiple algorithms, such as, MD2, MD3 and MD4.

The one-way hash function is also called the Hash function [12], which is the core of the MD5 algorithm. Hash function is an important branch of cryptography. It is a non-reversible and one-way cryptosystem which transforms the input of arbitrary length into fixed-length output. Let M be a message with arbitrary length, $h = H(M)$ means the evaluation of M with a one-way hash function, a fixed length value of h is obtained, where h is called the hash value of M. If M is divided into L packets, it is expressed as M_0, M_1, ... M_{L-1}, the length of each packet is m bit, and if the length of the last packet is not enough, it needs to be padded with zeros. A compression function f is reused in the algorithm. It has two inputs, one is the n-bit output h_{i-1} of the previous round and the other is the m-bit input packet M_{i-1}, the output of the compression function f is n bit h_i, and it is the next round of input too. At the beginning of the algorithm, you need to specify an initial input value of n bits IV. The output value with the fixed length in the last round is the final hash value of the entire message. The whole algorithm can be expressed as follows:

$$h_0 = IV \tag{1}$$

$$h_i = f(h_{i-1}, M_{i-1}), \ 1 \leq i \leq L \tag{2}$$

$$H(M) = h_L \tag{3}$$

As Hash is a one-way function, that is we can very easily calculate H from M, while it is difficult to calculate M from the known H. Therefore, it can be only used to encrypt data, yet there is no way to decrypt the encrypted data. MD5 is one of the most widely used Hash algorithm currently, which can convert an arbitrary length byte into a fixed-length string of 128 large integer (message digest), namely H = hash(M), where H is called M's hash value. It is typically applied in two aspects, one is to encrypt user's password by taking advantage of its irreversibility, so as to maintain the security of the system, and the other is to verify the integrity of information. Namely, MD5 takes the entire file as a large text message, generating a unique MD5 message digest. In the process of this document transmission, as long as the contents of the file occur any form of change, and message digest will also change through MD5 computing of that document, thus it can be determined that the received file is not the original one. This design mainly uses the latter. Read reference for a complete description of the MD5 [11].

3.2   System Implementation Steps

Assume that a user has an account of N (N $\geq$ 1) cloud storage service platform, and file backup module in the system adopts MD5 encryption method to encrypt files and generate Message-Digest, uses zip file encryption method to compress files, and uses a MySQL as an account database. System implementation process is as follows:

Step 1. Among N cloud storage service platforms, users can choose any one to login account management module by using his account information in the cloud storage services platform. A cloud storage client is created, and the account information selected in the cloud storage services platforms is stored in the account database.

Step 2. Users make use of common setting module to set the parameters of system and network of the cloud storage client. After the completion of setting the parameters of system and network of the cloud storage client, the system calls the file synchronization module.

Step 3. The methods and directories to be synchronized are selected from both local folders and the cloud in files synchronization module, the local files and cloud files are synchronous updated by the API control module, as shown in Fig. 2:

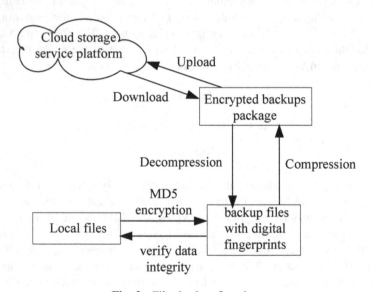

Fig. 2. Files backup flowchart

Step 4. The local files folder to be synchronized in step (3) are periodically carried on compression, encrypted and accessed, and checked the integrity of the files by file backup module.

Step 5. The performances of API control module from step (1) to (4) are real-time recorded by log module.

4 System Tests and Analysis

The correct BibTeX entries for the Lecture Notes in Computer Science volumes can System test platform for PC, and the cloud storage service API of Kanbox is accessed through the campus network. Testing machine configuration is: Intel (R) Core (TM) i7 CPU, 2.80 GHz frequency, 4.00 GB RAM, Windows 7 Home operating system.

4.1 Test on Backup Files

First, the backup efficiency of commonly used files is tested with the same type but different sizes. According to practical experience of backup files, generally speaking, the text file is the most frequently used file type in everyday. For example, the size of txt file is generally ranged 100 KB to 100 MB. Since backup time for less than 1M of file is mostly within 200 ms, so we select a series of files gradually increased from 1M to 100 MB. Those txt files make up data sets that will be used for system performance tests. Figure 3 shows the time of backup system spending on the same type of with different sizes.

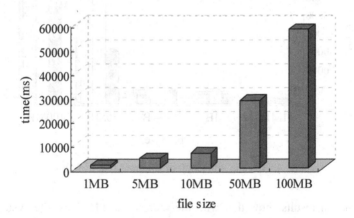

Fig. 3. Backup efficiency of text files

As we can see from Fig. 3, as the file size increases, the longer time it takes to backup system files. Mainly because of larger size, it takes more time for compress and upload larger files, but the backup time of frequently used files between 100 KB– 100 MB is within tolerable range.

We distinguish backup files of different types and sizes. Frequently used file types are txt, doc, ppt, pdf, mp3, jpg, etc., A series of files of different types, whose range of size gradually increased from 1M to100 MB, are selected to make data sets that will be used for system performance tests. Specific file sizes and types are as shown in Table 1.

Test file sets that are selected in Table 1 have certain representativeness. Files larger than 1 GB (rmvb files and other multimedia files) are less used at present, so they

Table 1. Test sets of different types of files

File size (M)	File types				
1	.txt	.ppt	.doc	.jpg	.rar
5	.txt	.mp3	.doc	.jpg	.pdf
10	.txt	.pdf	.doc	.jpg	.wmv
50	.txt	.ppt	.doc	.jpg	.rmvb
100	.txt	.ppt	.doc	.jpg	.rar

will not be included in system tests. Figure 4 shows minimum, maximum and average time that system takes to backup files of different sizes and different types.

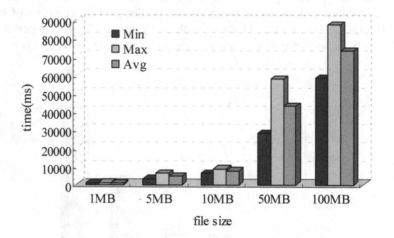

Fig. 4. Backup efficiency of different types of files

Experimental results show that with the increase of file sizes, file system backup time of different types of files presents the overall trend of gradually increase. To backup the same size files in different types, the time it takes fluctuation within a fixed range. That is mainly because it takes different time to compress different file types. Through the analysis of test results, we can see that system backup function is normal.

4.2 Synchronization Performance Comparison on Storage Services

We use resource monitor for network monitoring on Kanbox. The time comparison of certain operation is completed through Kanbox client and the system client respectively, then the performance of the system can be evaluated.

First of all, compare the first round of synchronization, namely initialization, including upload and download. Select 100 synchronize folders, and each one is about 60 MB and contains multi-level files and folders. Followed by adding and deleting file operation, select 100 operating objects, and all of which are about 20 MB files in size.

Finally, select 100 operating objects, all of which are 5 MB files in size to test update operation (Table 2). The average time spent on each operation test is gotten, comparison results are shown as in Fig. 5.

Table 2. Comparison of the performance of different operations

Client	Initialization	Add file	Delete file	Update file
Design model	45346 ms	14124 ms	975 ms	2618 ms
Kanbox	52000 ms	13000 ms	1000 ms	2000 ms

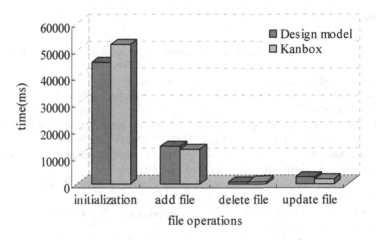

Fig. 5. Comparison of synchronization performance

The test results show that basic operation time of this system and Kanbox are much the same, but the system has a large performance advantage in initialization, namely the first round of synchronized strategy.

5   Conclusions

According to currently existing problems of cloud storage management products, the paper proposed a secure cloud storage integration solution. Its design makes the realization of a cloud storage-based personal encryption file with digital fingerprints synchronization and backup system possible. The system can correctly synchronize and backup personal data as needed, and ensure the safety of files. Through an open API control for cloud storage services, it allows users to simultaneously manage multiple cloud storage accounts and carry on multiple folder reliable synchronization and backup at anytime. The new backup mode uses MD5 algorithm to generate digital fingerprints for backup files, which can effectively prevent changes and tampering of personal files, thus integrity protection of the backup files are achieved. Experimental results show that the system enables users to achieve multiple cloud storage account integration simultaneously and the purpose of synchronizing storage and security management. However, this system synchronization strategy for optimization of conflict processing, mobile terminal services and other issues still need to be improved, which is also an improvement goal of the next step.

Acknowledgments. This work is supported by the National Nature Science Foundation of Zhejiang Province, China, No. LY16F020014, the National Nature Science Foundation of Heilongjiang Province, China, No. F201204 and the Education Department of Heilongjiang Province, China, No. 12531756.

References

1. Zeng, W., Zhao, Y., Ou, K., et al.: Research on cloud storage architecture and key technologies. In: 2nd International Conference on Interaction Sciences: Information Technology, Culture and Human, pp. 1044–1048. ACM, New York (2009)
2. Mell, P., Grance, T.: The NIST definition of cloud computing. J. Natl. Inst. Stand. Technol. **53**, 50–57 (2009)
3. Li, H., Sun, W.H., Li, F.H., et al.: Secure and privacy-preserving data storage service in public cloud. J. Comput. Res. Dev. **51**, 1397–1409 (2014). (in Chinese)
4. Xue, M., Xue, W., Shu, J.W., et al.: A secure storage system over cloud storage environment. J. Comput. **38**, 987–998 (2015). (in Chinese)
5. Julisch, K., Hall, M.: Security and control in the cloud. Inf. Secur. J.: Glob. Perspect. **19**, 299–309 (2010)
6. Feng, D.G., Zhang, M., Zhang, Y., Xu, Z.: Study on cloud computing security. J. Softw. **22**, 71–83 (2011). (in Chinese)
7. Fu, Y.Y., Zhang, M., Chen, K.Q., et al.: Proofs of data possession of multiple copies. J. Comput. Res. Dev. **51**, 1410–1416 (2014). (in Chinese)
8. Wang, H.Q.: Identity-based distributed provable data possession in multicloud storage. IEEE Trans. Serv. Comput. **8**, 328–340 (2015)
9. Liu, C., Yang, C., Zhang, X.Y., et al.: External integrity verification for outsourced big data in cloud and IoT: a big picture. Future Gener. Comput. Syst. **49**, 58–67 (2015)
10. Wang, H.F., Li, Z.H., Zhang, X., et al.: A self-adaptive audit method of data integrity in the cloud storage. J. Comput. Res. Dev. **54**, 172–183 (2017). (in Chinese)
11. Rivest, R.: The MD5 Message-Digest Algorithm. RFC1321, April 1992
12. FIPS PUB 180-1. Secure Hash Standard, April 1995

Implementation of Direction Finding Processor Based on the Novel DOA Estimation with Channel Mismatch Self-calibration

Yan Zou[1,2], Ping Chu[3(✉)], and Xiaoyu Lan[4]

[1] Department of Information and Communicaiton Engineering, Harbin Engineering University, Harbin 150001, China
[2] No. 91404 Army, Qinhuangdao 066000, China
[3] Shenzhen University, Shenzhen 518000, China
chuping1128@gmail.com
[4] Shenyang Aerospace University, Shenyang 110136, China

Abstract. In order to solve the problem that the channel gain-phase mismatch would deteriorate the performance of direction of arrival (DOA) estimation in actual direction finding (DF) system, a novel efficient gain-phase calibration algorithm based on the self-checking signal is proposed in this paper. By injecting a self-checking signal into the actual DF system, the whole calibration process could divide into the off-line pre-calibration and the auto-calibration part. Thus, it could realize the real-time auto-calibration efficiently during the DOA estimation process. Moreover, in order to verify the effectiveness of the proposed method, a practical DF signal processor based on the FPGA and DSP is implemented in this paper, and the experiments are carried out in the anechoic chamber. The experiment result shows that the proposed method could calibrate the gain-phase mismatch in real-time and have higher DOA estimation accuracy.

Keywords: Direction of arrival · Direction finding system · Array calibration
Self-calibration · Multiple signal classification algorithm

1 Introduction

The direction of arrival (DOA) estimation of multiple targets is the most fundamental aspect in array signal processing [1] and has aroused great concern in radar, sonar and wireless communications. The spectrum estimation algorithm with super-resolution performance, such as multiple signal classification (MUSIC) [2] and estimation of signal parameters via rotational invariance techniques (ESPRIT) [3], have been developed greatly for decades. However, these algorithms will fail if the array manifold is not perfectly known due to the gain-phase mismatch between the antennas. Thus, a number of approaches have been proposed to calibrate the mismatch so as to improve the DOA estimation performance [4, 5]. [6] proposed the least squares (LS) array calibration method by using a set of calibration sources whose location are exactly known. Then, the distance between the calibration source and the direction finding (DF) system is investigated in [7].

© ICST Institute for Computer Sciences, Social Informatics and Telecommunications Engineering 2018
G. Sun and S. Liu (Eds.): ADHIP 2017, LNICST 219, pp. 529–537, 2018.
https://doi.org/10.1007/978-3-319-73317-3_62

However, these methods mentioned above would calibrate the array well when the locations of the calibration sources are precisely known, but in practice, the calibration sources may not available in real system. As a result, the self-calibration algorithm has been developed [8, 9]. [8] proposed an alternative iterative method, which could estimate the signal DOAs and the gain-phase error of each channel. And in [9], Kim proposed a blind calibration method by using independent component analysis. In generally, the researches based on self-calibration techniques are difficult to be realized in real time system.

This paper proposed a real-time calibration method based on the self-checking signal. First of all, the calibration work is divided into two parts: the pre-calibration and the real-time self-calibration, separately. The pre-calibration matrix is obtained by setting a signal with the DOA is 0°. Then, the self-calibration matrix will be updated with the help of self-checking signal in the DF system. Moreover, the real DF signal processor is implemented based on the FPGA and DSP. At last, the effectiveness of the proposed method is verified by the practical DF system.

2 Signal Model and the Proposed Method

Consider a scenario in which P narrowband far-field sources are observed by M $(P < M)$ elements, as shown in Fig. 1. The antenna array is assumed to have an UCA structure with the radius d. The noise is assumed to be the additive white Gaussian noise (AWGN).

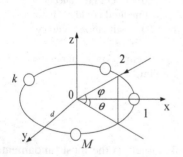
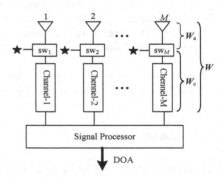

Fig. 1. Uniform circular array diagram.   **Fig. 2.** Diagram of data receiving in DF system.

Assume the incident signals are independent with each other, (θ_i, φ_i) is the azimuth and elevation of the ith $(i < P)$ signal. Therefore, the received array matrix X is modeled as

$$X = A(\theta, \varphi)S + N \tag{1}$$

where A, S and N denote the manifold matrix, signal and noise, respectively. However, when the effect of gain-phase mismatch error is taken into consideration, the actual received array matrix is rewritten as

$$\tilde{X} = WX = WA(\theta, \varphi)S + WN \tag{2}$$

where $W = \mathrm{diag}[g_1 \exp(j\phi_1) \quad g_2 \exp(j\phi_2) \cdots g_M \exp(j\phi_M)]$ is the gain-phase mismatch matrix, and g_i and ϕ_i ($i = 1, 2, \ldots, M$) denote the gain and phase of ith channel, respectively. Then the covariance matrix of $\tilde{X}$ can be expressed as

$$\tilde{R} = \tilde{X}\tilde{X}^{\mathrm{H}} = \begin{bmatrix} \tilde{x}_1\tilde{x}_1^{\mathrm{H}} & \tilde{x}_1\tilde{x}_2^{\mathrm{H}} & \cdots & \tilde{x}_1\tilde{x}_M^{\mathrm{H}} \\ \tilde{x}_2\tilde{x}_1^{\mathrm{H}} & \tilde{x}_2\tilde{x}_2^{\mathrm{H}} & & \tilde{x}_2\tilde{x}_M^{\mathrm{H}} \\ \vdots & & \ddots & \vdots \\ \tilde{x}_M\tilde{x}_1^{\mathrm{H}} & \tilde{x}_M\tilde{x}_2^{\mathrm{H}} & \cdots & \tilde{x}_M\tilde{x}_{1M}^{\mathrm{H}} \end{bmatrix} = \begin{bmatrix} g_1^2 x_1 x_1^{\mathrm{H}} & & \cdots & g_1 g_M \exp(j(\phi_1 - \phi_M)) x_1 x_M^{\mathrm{H}} \\ g_1 g_2 \exp(j(\phi_2 - \phi_1)) x_2 x_1^{\mathrm{H}} & & & \vdots \\ \vdots & & & \vdots \\ g_1 g_M \exp(j(\phi_M - \phi_1)) x_M x_1^{\mathrm{H}} & & \cdots & g_M^2 x_M x_M^{\mathrm{H}} \end{bmatrix} \tag{3}$$

where $\tilde{x}_i$ and x_i denote the received data vector of ith channel when with phase-gain error mismatch and without phase-gain error mismatch, respectively. Assume there is only one signal impinging on the array and the DOA is $0°$, if there is no mismatch between each channel, it is easy to get $x_1 x_1^{\mathrm{H}} = x_i x_j^{\mathrm{H}}$. Let $\tilde{R}_1$ denote the first column of $\tilde{R}$, then from (3), we can get

$$\tilde{R}_1/\tilde{R}_1(1) = [1 \quad g_2/g_1 \exp(j(\phi_2 - \phi_1)) \cdots g_M/g_1 \exp(j(\phi_M - \phi_1))]^{\mathrm{T}}, \tag{4}$$

$$g_i/g_1 \exp(j(\phi_M - \phi_1)) = \tilde{x}_i \tilde{x}_1^{\mathrm{H}}/\tilde{x}_1 \tilde{x}_1^{\mathrm{H}}. \tag{5}$$

It is seen that from (5), if we utilize the classical $0°$ calibration method and consider the first channel as the reference, then (5) is the gain-phase mismatch error of the ith channel. Even though the $0°$ calibration method is an off-line method by utilizing an assistant source, and we only need to obtain the calibration matrix once before estimating the DOA. However, in actual DF system, the channel mismatch is mainly caused by active devices, e.g. amplifier, whose performance would fluctuate with surrounding environment, such as temperature, running hour, etc. As a result, we could divide the error matrix W into two parts, W_a and W_c, as shown in Fig. 2. W_a denotes the error matrix caused by the passive devices, while W_c caused by the active devices. W, W_a and W_c are diagonal matrix and they have the following relationship,

$$W = W_a W_c, \tag{6}$$

$$W_a = \mathrm{diag}[g_{a1} \exp(j\phi_{a1}) \quad g_{a2} \exp(j\phi_{a2}) \cdots g_{aM} \exp(j\phi_{aM})] = g_{a1} \exp(j\phi_{a1}) \cdot W_a', \tag{7}$$

$$W_c = \mathrm{diag}[g_{c1} \exp(j\phi_{c1}) \quad g_{c2} \exp(j\phi_{c2}) \cdots g_{cM} \exp(j\phi_{cM})] = g_{c1} \exp(j\phi_{c1}) \cdot W_c' \tag{8}$$

where $W_a' = \mathrm{diag}[1 \cdots g_{aM}/g_{a1} \exp(j(\phi_{aM} - \phi_{a1}))]$, g_{ai}, ϕ_{ai} ($i = 1, 2, \ldots, M$) denote the gain error and phase error between the antenna and received channel, respectively. And $W_c' = \mathrm{diag}[1 \cdots g_{cM}/g_{c1} \exp(j(\phi_{cM} - \phi_{c1}))]$, g_{ci}, ϕ_{ci} ($i = 1, 2, \ldots, M$) denote the gain error and phase error between received channel and the digital signal processor, respectively. Then, (6) could be rewritten as

$$W = W_a W_c = g_{a1} g_{c1} \exp(j(\phi_{a1} + \phi_{c1})) \cdot W_a' W_c' = g_1. \exp(j\phi_1) \cdot W' \qquad (9)$$

where $W/= W_a' W_c'$, and $W_a' = W' W_c'^{-1}$. Because W', W_a' and W_c' are all diagonal matrix, then

$$W_a'(i, i) = W'(i, i)/W_c'(i, i). \qquad (10)$$

It is seen from (10), W_a' will be obtained once we got W' and W_c'. Hence, in order to obtain W_c' and realize real time self-calibration, a self-checking signal denoted by "★" is injected into the DF system, shown as in Fig. 2. It is seen that, when to receive the signal from the antenna is decided by a Single-pole Double Throw Switch (SPDT) sw$_i$ ($i = 1, 2..., M$), and the self-checking signal would be received at the following edge of the signal pulse that we interested. As the self-checking signal is injected into each channel at the same time, we could utilize the received self-checking signal data to calibrate the gain-phase mismatch between channels. Thus, the received data of self-checking signal with mismatch error could be presented as

$$\tilde{X}_c(t) = W_c X_c(t). \qquad (11)$$

From (3) and (4), we could get

$$g_{ci}/g_{c1} \exp(j(\phi_{cM} - \phi_{c1})) = \tilde{x}_{ci} \tilde{x}_{c1}^H / \tilde{x}_{c1} \tilde{x}_{c1}^H. \qquad (12)$$

Then,

$$\begin{aligned} W_c' &= \mathrm{diag}[1 \quad g_{c2}/g_{c1} \exp(j(\phi_{c2} - \phi_{c1})) \cdots g_{cM}/g_{c1} \exp(j(\phi_{cM} - \phi_{c1}))] \\ &= \mathrm{diag}[1 \quad \tilde{x}_{c2} \tilde{x}_{c1}^H / \tilde{x}_{c1} \tilde{x}_{c1}^H \cdots \tilde{x}_{cM} \tilde{x}_{c1}^H / \tilde{x}_{c1} \tilde{x}_{c1}^H] \end{aligned} . \qquad (13)$$

Setting the incident signal angle is $0°$, and according to (10), (12) and (13), the pre-calibration matrix W_a' could be expressed as

$$W_a'(i, i) = W'(i, i)/W_c'(i, i) = (\tilde{x}_i \tilde{x}_1^H / \tilde{x}_1 \tilde{x}_1^H)/(\tilde{x}_{ci} \tilde{x}_{c1}^H / \tilde{x}_{c1} \tilde{x}_{c1}^H). \qquad (14)$$

As a result, the proposed calibration method can be summarized as follows: (1) Set an incident signal with the DOA is $0°$, and record the received data of the incident signal and the self-checking signal. (2) By (14), calculate the pre-calibration matrix W_a'. (3) According to (13), calculate W_c' by considering the first channel as the reference, and obtain W by (9). (4) Obtain $\tilde{X}$ with (2), and estimate the DOA with MUSIC algorithm. Repeat step (3)–(4), we can estimate the DOA with a higher accuracy in real time.

3   Design and Implementation of the DF Signal Processor

As shown in Fig. 3, the DF system consists of two parts: microwave front-head and digital signal processor. The microwave front-head, which contains 5 channels, is responsible to process the received analog signal. The digital signal processor is comprised of 4 processors, which are wide-band digital channelizer, signal sorting processor, narrow-band digital receiver and DF signal processor, respectively. It is worth to note that, the DF signal processor is the mainly contribution in this paper and in the next, we will introduce the processor based on the hardware and software design, respectively.

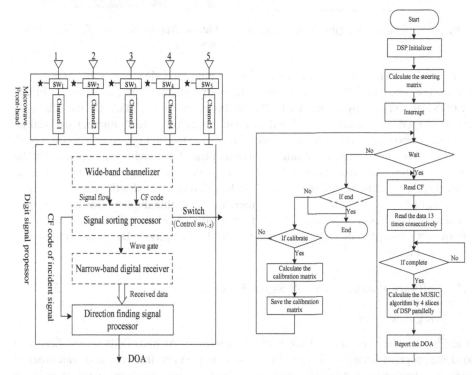

Fig. 3. Block diagram of the DF system

Fig. 4. Software flow chart of the DF signal processor

3.1   Hardware Design of the DF Signal Processor

The task of the DF signal processor is to process the received signal data, estimate the DOA of the incident signal and report the angles to the host finally. The block diagram of the DF signal processor is shown is Fig. 5.

As shown in Fig. 5, the PDS120 is used for the processor to communicate with other processors. In order to improve the calculation speed, four slices of ADSP TS201 process the received data in parallel, besides, they share data and communicate with each other by adopting the tight coupling mode to share the bus line. A slice of FPGA

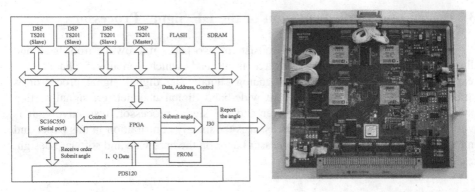

Fig. 5. Diagram of the DF signal processor

Fig. 6. Appearance of the DF signal processor

of virtex-4 is responsible for the logic control, data reception and transmission, and control test, etc. Then, the I, Q data, received from 5 channels, is transferred to FPGA by PDS120, and read by the master DSP after the extension in FPGA. On the one hand, the master DSP is mainly used for data communication, source number estimation, eigen decomposition, spectrum function calculation in the first quadrant, spectrum peak searching, the global extremum judgement, angel transform and result sending. On the other hand, the other three slave DSPs are used to calculate the spectrum function in the other three quadrants, search the peak of the function and transfer the extremum value in each quadrant to the master DSP, and then, the final global extremum value will be decided by the master DSP. At last, the final estimated result (DOA) is converted by FPGA and reported to the servo system through J30. The physic DF signal processor is shown in Fig. 6.

3.2   Software Design of the DF Signal Processor

(1) Work flow of the system

The Fig. 4 is the flow chart of the hardware program. At first, DSP is initialized and load the program from the FLASH. In the next step, enable interrupt and wait order of central computer to start work. However, if the order is not to start work, then judge whether to end the work. If the order is to end the work, then the DF processor will end work. Otherwise, if the order is channel calibration, we will calculate the calibration matrix and save it, then the program will return to the original location and wait order to start. Once receiving the order to start work, it will read the carrier frequency (CF) code from the signal sorting processor, estimate the DOAs and report the final DOA result.

(2) Working principle of the MUSIC algorithm in DSP

As mentioned above, there are four slices of DSP, one master DSP and three slave DSPs. And the three slave DSPs are response for the peak searching of the 2nd, 3rd, 4th quadrant, respectively. When the master DSP start to work, it will calculate the calibration matrix by utilizing the self-checking signal data, and then share the esti-mated source number, noise subspace and the real-time calibration matrix in the broadcast area for other three slave DSPs to use. As the time efficiency is always an essential problem that we concern, some remarks are given as follows:

Remark 1: The three slave DSPs first calculate the component of the steering matrix that independent of signal frequency. And then calculate the reminder after the signal frequency is provided by the master DSP.

Remark 2: It is well known that the spectrum peak searching is an exhaustive step. In order to solve this problem, we first find the spectrum peak in a coarse step, e.g. 4°, and then we improve the accuracy of our result with a smaller step, e.g. 2°. In this way, the estimated DOAs will be more accurate and it will consume less time as well.

4   Performance Test and Analysis

In this section, some test results are presented to illustrate the performance of the proposed method based on the actual DF system. The antenna array is a uniform circular array (UCA) with 5 sensors, the radius is 180 mm. Setting the DOA of the incident signal is 0°, according to (14) and the received data, we can get the pre-calibration matrix is diag [1.0, 1.9266exp(j10.0181°), 2.2830exp(j129.4431°), 1.0203exp(−j21.6611°), 1.9311exp(−j16.8094°)].

Figure 7 presents the MUSIC spectrum based on the real data with three methods. They are the method without calibration, 0° calibration method and the proposed method, respectively. The DOA of the incident signal is (0°, 80°), the snapshot is 100. As shown in Fig. 7(a), the estimated DOA is (72.0°, 23.5°), which is far bias from the true angle. Similarly, the estimated DOAs with 0° calibration and the proposed method are (−3.95°, 81.52°) and (−1.02°, 79.52°), respectively. Obviously, the proposed cal-ibration method has a higher accuracy in the actual system.

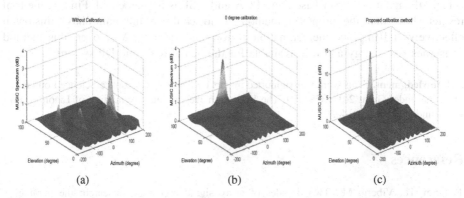

Fig. 7. MUSIC spectrum of DOA estimation under the condition of (a) without calibration (b) 0° calibration method (c) proposed calibration method

Table 1 illustrates the DOA estimation results of the two methods with different frequency and one incident angel. The snapshots are 100. As shown in Table 1, the channel mismatch has a great negative influence on the estimation performance. However, compared with the conventional 0° calibration method, the proposed method can realize the dynamic calibration and has better estimation performance.

Table 1. The DOA estimation result of two methods with different frequency (degree)

DOA	2 GHz		4 GHz	
	0° calibration	Proposed method	0° calibration	Proposed method
25	27.00	24.60	26.40	25.40
20	21.40	20.80	19.60	20.20
15	16.20	15.40	15.80	15.80
10	10.80	10.20	10.80	10.60
5	5.60	4.60	5.60	5.40
0	0.80	−0.40	0.40	0.20
−5	−4.80	−5.40	−4.60	−4.80
−10	−11.60	−10.60	−9.20	−10.60
−15	−16.80	−16.00	−15.20	−15.40
−20	−21.00	−20.60	−19.80	−20.20
−25	−26.40	−25.80	−26.00	−24.80

5 Conclusion

In actual DF system, the active device of the receiver would cause the gain-phase mismatch among sensors and that will seriously deteriorate the performance of the DOA estimation algorithm based on the spatial spectrum estimation. In this paper, a novel self-calibration gain-phase mismatch calibration method is presented and the actual DF signal processor based on FPGA and DSP is implemented. Finally, the trial results show that the proposed method could calibrate the gain-phase mismatch effectively and improve the estimation performance greatly. Moreover, this method consumes less energy and it is available for the actual real-time DF system.

Acknowledgment. This work was supported in part by National Aerospace Science Foundation of China under Grant 2015ZC54010; The Education Department Foundation of Liaoning Province under Grant L2014059.

References

1. Krim, H., Viberg, M.: Two decades of array signal processing research: the parametric approach. J. IEEE Sig. Process. Mag. **13**, 67–94 (1996)
2. Schmidt, R.O.: Multiple emitter location and signal parameter estimation. J. IEEE Trans. Antenna Propag. **34**, 276–280 (1986)

3. Mathews, C.P., Kailath, T.: ESPRIT-estimation of signal parameters via rotational invariance techniques. J. IEEE Trans. Sig. Process. **42**, 2395–2407 (1994)
4. Schmid, C.M., Schuster, S., et al.: On the effects of calibration errors and mutual coupling on the beam pattern of an antenna array. J IEEE Trans. Antennas Propag. **61**, 4063–4072 (2013)
5. Cao, S.H., Ye, Z.F., Xu, X.: A hadamard product based method for DOA estimation and Gain-Phase error calibration. J. IEEE Trans. Aerosp. Electron. Syst. **49**, 1224–1233 (2013)
6. Pierre, J.: Experimental performance of calibration and direction-finding algorithms. In: International Conference on Acoustics, Speech and Signal Processing, pp. 1365–1368. IEEE Press (1991)
7. Henault, S., Antar, Y.M., Rajan, S., et al.: Impact of experimental calibration on the performance of conventional direction finding. In: International Conference on Electrical and Computer Engineering, pp. 1123–1128. IEEE Press (2009)
8. Weiss, A.J., Friedlander, B.: Eigenstructure methods for direction finding with sensor gain and phase uncertainties. J. Circ. Syst. Sig. Process. **9**, 271–300 (1990)
9. Kim, J.: Blind calibration for a linear array with gain and phase error using independent component analysis. J. IEEE Antennas Wirel. Propag. Lett. **9**, 1259–1262 (2010)

Computationally Efficient 2D DOA Estimation for Cylindrical Conformal Array

Xiaoyu Lan[1(✉)] and Yan Zou[2,3]

[1] Shenyang Aerospace University, Shenyang 110136, China
lanxiaoyu1015@gmail.com
[2] Harbin Engineering University, Harbin 150001, China
[3] No. 91404 Army, Qinhuangdao, China

Abstract. A computationally efficient two-dimensional (2D) direction of arrival (DOA) estimation method based on cylindrical conformal antenna array is investigated in this paper. By dividing the entire array into several sub-arrays and transforming every sub-array to virtual uniform rectangular array (URA) via interpolation technique, the generalization propagator method (GPM) without eigen-decomposition is employed to estimate the noise subspace accurately and quickly. Furthermore, in order to lower the computational complexity of the 2D spectral peak searching, a rank reduction (RARE) method based on URA is utilized to solve the 2D DOAs by successive 1D spectrum functions. At last, some numerical simulations verified the superiority of the proposed method.

Keywords: Conformal antenna array · Direction of arrival
Interpolation technique · Generalization propagator method
Rank reduction algorithm

1 Introduction

The conformal array is usually referred to an array amounted with sensors on the curvature surface [1]. The conformal array has many advantages that contains reduction of aerodynamic drag, wide-angle coverage, space saving, reduction of radar cross-section and so on [2]. Due to this flexibility, conformal array has many promising applications in a variety of fields such as radar, sonar, airborne, ship-borne and wireless communication [3].

Among various of techniques for conformal array, the direction of arrival (DOA) estimation has attracted a lot of interests. However, in contrast to the ordinary array, the distinct electromagnetic characteristics of conformal array leads to an tough problem of DOA estimation owing to the curvature of the carrier surface. As a result, the DOA algorithm such as multiple signal classification (MUSIC) [4] and estimation of signal parameters via rotational invariance techniques (ESPRIT) [5] and other conventional methods are not suitable for conformal array directly. Besides, because of the "shadow effect" of the metallic

© ICST Institute for Computer Sciences, Social Informatics and Telecommunications Engineering 2018
G. Sun and S. Liu (Eds.): ADHIP 2017, LNICST 219, pp. 538–545, 2018.
https://doi.org/10.1007/978-3-319-73317-3_63

cylinder, not all of the sensors can receive the signal and which will degrade the detection performance dramatically. In view of these problems, many DOA algorithms have been investigated recently. [6] proposed a higher accuracy DOA estimation via parallel factor analysis (PARAFAC). A general transformation procedure based on geometric algebra is proposed in [7] and the author estimated the parameters by ESPRIT too. [8] introduced a new perspective to shadowing effect and utilized rank reduction (RARE) method to obtain better estimation performance. In order to detect more signals than sensors, [9] firstly utilized the array extension character of the nested array to improve the degree of freedom (DOF) of the array. However, the references mentioned above need eigen-decomposition or 2D spectral peak searching, which will bring much computational complexity to the actual system.

The contribution of this paper is developing a fast DOA estimation method based on cylindrical conformal array. By dividing the whole array into sub-arrays, the interpolation technique is exploited to map each sub-array to an uniform rectangular array (URA). Then, the DOAs are estimated based on the efficient Generalization propagator method (GPM) [10] algorithm without any eigen-decompositon. Besides, the proposed method only requires several 1-D spectrum peaking searchings to estimate the 2D DOAs. Moreover, the estimated parameters are automatically paired together without extra operation.

2   The Signal Model of the Conformal Array

Consider D narrowband far-field signal sources that impinge on an arbitrary 3D conformal array of M directional sensors. Assume $k_0 = 2\pi/\lambda$ and λ is the wavelength of the signal source, the snapshot data model is established in [11], and the corresponding array steering vector is given by

$$\mathbf{a}(\theta, \phi) = [r_1 e^{-jk_0 \mathbf{p}_1 \cdot \mathbf{u}}, r_2 e^{-jk_0 \mathbf{p}_2 \cdot \mathbf{u}}, ..., r_M e^{-jk_0 \mathbf{p}_M \cdot \mathbf{u}}]^T \tag{1}$$

$$r_i = (g_{i\theta}^2 + g_{i\phi}^2)^{1/2}(k_{i\theta}^2 + k_{i\phi}^2)^{1/2} cos(\theta_{igk}) = |g_i||p_l|cos(\theta_{igk})$$
$$= \mathbf{g}_i \cdot \mathbf{q}_l = g_{i\theta}k_\theta + g_{i\phi}k_\phi \tag{2}$$

where θ and ϕ are the elevation and azimuth angles, respectively. $\mathbf{p}_i = [x_i, y_i, z_i]$, $i=1,2,...M$ denotes the position vector of the ith sensor, $\mathbf{u} = [sin\theta cos\phi, sin\theta sin\phi, cos\phi]^T$ denotes the propagation vector. r_i is the response of unit signal by the ith element in the global coordinate system. As shown in Fig. 1(b), $\mathbf{u}_\theta$ and $\mathbf{u}_\phi$ are unit vectors, k_θ and k_ϕ are the polarisation parameters of signal, $\mathbf{g}_i$ is the pattern of the ith element, $\mathbf{q}_i$ is the direction of the electric field, θ_{igk} denotes the angle between vector $\mathbf{g}_i$ and vector $\mathbf{q}_i$. The critical step is the transform from global coordinate to local coordinate and More details can be found in [11]. Thus, the snapshot data model of conformal array antenna can be expressed as

$$\mathbf{X}(n) = \mathbf{G} \cdot \mathbf{AS}(n) + \mathbf{N}(n) = (\mathbf{G}_\theta \cdot \mathbf{A}_\theta \mathbf{K}_\theta + \mathbf{G}_\phi \cdot \mathbf{A}_\phi \mathbf{K}_\phi)\mathbf{S}(n) + \mathbf{N}(n)$$
$$= \mathbf{BS}(n) + \mathbf{N}(n) \tag{3}$$

where $\mathbf{B} = \mathbf{G} \cdot \mathbf{A}$, $\mathbf{G}$ is the antenna response matrix, $\mathbf{A}$ is the $M \times D$ full-rank steering matrix, $\mathbf{S}(n)$ denotes the $D \times 1$ source waveforms and $\mathbf{N}(n)$ is the $M \times 1$ additive noise which is spatially white and statistically independent from the signal source.

3   The Proposed Method

3.1   Cylinder Conformal Array Structure and the 2D Array Interpolation Technique

The configure of the cylindrical conformal antenna array is given in Fig. 1(a), where the sensors are uniformly distributed over the surface of the cylinder. Due to the "shadow effect", which could degrade the DOA estimation performance dramatically because of the incomplete steering vector, the sub-array divided technique is utilized in this paper. Firstly, we divide the whole array into 6 sub-arrays, and each sub-array covers a sector of $\pi/3$. Thus, we could always find a sub-array and all the sensors of this sub-array can receive the signal from any direction. Then, the combination of all sub-arrays will cover all the possible impinging signals. Because the array structure and the DOA estimation process are the same for each sub-array, only one sub-array shown in Fig. 1(a) is considered throughout this paper.

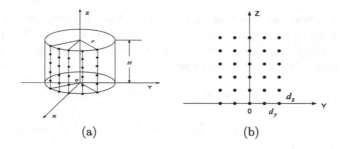

(a)   (b)

Fig. 1. (a) Cylindrical conformal array. (b) Interpolated array.

The 2D interpolation technique is used here to mitigate the effects of imperfect conformal array response, such as the diversity of the sensor's response, mutual coupling effect and so on. The principle of interpolated array is to transform the true conformal array response $\mathbf{B}$ to the desired virtual array respoone $\tilde{\mathbf{A}}$ by define an interpolation matrix $\mathbf{T}$ within the field of view [12], as shown in Fig. 1(b). This process can be expressed as

$$\mathbf{T}^H (\mathbf{G} \cdot \mathbf{A}) = \tilde{\mathbf{A}}. \tag{4}$$

Obviously, we cannot calculate a pert $\mathbf{T}$ because the solution of (4) is not close-form. Thus, The equation of $\tau = \left\| \tilde{\mathbf{A}} - \mathbf{T}^H (\mathbf{G} \cdot \mathbf{A}) \right\| / \|\mathbf{G} \cdot \mathbf{A}\|$ is used to evaluate the interpolation accuracy. When τ is small enough, for example, 0.01, then $\mathbf{T}$ can be accepted. A stable and accurate method to solve the $\mathbf{T}$ is proposed in [13]. It is observed that it will cost much time in calculating the interpolation matrix $\mathbf{T}$ if the size of the sector $[\Theta, \Phi]$ and number of interpolation are very large. However, we only need to calculate the matrix $\mathbf{T}$ once and it also can be done off-line and stored in the system so that it won't increase the computation burden when estimating the DOA parameters.

3.2   DOA Estimation Method Based on GPM and RARE

In the last section, we transform the conformal array to a virtual URA firstly, as shown in Fig. 1(b). The URA has $M = M_y \times M_z$ sensors, and the sensor's space along y axis and z axis are d_y and d_z, respectively. For simplicity, we define $d_y = d_z = \lambda/2$. Then, the steering vector of the URA $\tilde{\mathbf{A}}$ is given by

$$\tilde{\mathbf{A}}(u, v) = [\tilde{\mathbf{a}}(u_1, v_1), \tilde{\mathbf{a}}(u_2, v_2), ..., \tilde{\mathbf{a}}(u_D, v_D)] \tag{5}$$

where $\tilde{\mathbf{a}}(u, v) = \tilde{\mathbf{a}}_y(u) \otimes \tilde{\mathbf{a}}_z(v)$, $\tilde{\mathbf{a}}_y(u) = [1, e^{-j(2\pi/\lambda)d_y u}, ..., e^{-j(2\pi/\lambda)d_y(M_y-1)u}]^T$, $\tilde{\mathbf{a}}_z(v) = [1, e^{-j(2\pi/\lambda)d_z v}, ..., e^{-j(2\pi/\lambda)d_z(M_z-1)v}]^T$. And $u = sin\theta sin\phi$ and $v = cos\theta$ are the direction variables relative to the y-axis and z-axis, respectively. Then, according to (3), the original conformal array manifold $\mathbf{B}(u, v)$ can be rewritten as

$$\mathbf{B}(u, v) = \mathbf{G} \cdot \mathbf{A} = \mathbf{F}\tilde{\mathbf{A}}(u, v) \tag{6}$$

where $\mathbf{F} = (\mathbf{T}^H)^{-1}$. Denote $\mathbf{B}(u, v)$ as $\mathbf{B}$ which is decomposed as

$$\mathbf{B} = [\mathbf{B}_1 \mathbf{B}_0 \mathbf{B}_2]^T \tag{7}$$

where $\mathbf{B}_1 \in \mathbb{C}^{L \times D}$, $\mathbf{B}_0 \in \mathbb{C}^{D \times D}$, $\mathbf{B}_2 \in \mathbb{C}^{(M-L-D) \times D}$, $L = 0, ..., M - D - 1$. Note that $\mathbf{B}_0$ is a nonsingular matrix, so two propagator matrices exist and satisfy $\mathbf{B}_1 = \mathbf{P}_{1L}^H \mathbf{B}_0$, $\mathbf{B}_2 = \mathbf{P}_{2L}^H \mathbf{B}_0$. Define a block matrix $C_L^H \in \mathbb{C}^{(M-D) \times M}$, which is given by

$$\mathbf{C}_L^H = \begin{bmatrix} -\mathbf{I}_L & \mathbf{P}_{1L}^H & \mathbf{0} \\ \mathbf{0} & \mathbf{P}_{2L}^H & -\mathbf{I}_{M-L-D} \end{bmatrix} \tag{8}$$

It is easy to know that $\mathbf{C}_L^H \mathbf{B} = 0$. Then, divide the array output matrix $\mathbf{X}(t)$ as

$$\mathbf{X}(t) = [\mathbf{X}_1 \mathbf{X}_0 \mathbf{X}_2]^T. \tag{9}$$

Assume the noise is zero in (3), we can get $\mathbf{X}_1 = \mathbf{P}_{1L}^H \mathbf{X}_0$, $\mathbf{X}_2 = \mathbf{P}_{2L}^H \mathbf{X}_0$. Then, the covariance matrix of $\mathbf{X}(t)$ can be expressed as

$$\mathbf{R} = E(\mathbf{X}\mathbf{X}^H) = E(\mathbf{X}[\mathbf{X}_1^H \ \mathbf{X}_0^H \ \mathbf{X}_2^H]) = [\mathbf{D} \ \mathbf{E} \ \mathbf{F}] \tag{10}$$

where $\mathbf{D} \in \mathbb{C}^{M \times L}$, $\mathbf{E} \in \mathbb{C}^{M \times D}$, $\mathbf{F} \in \mathbb{C}^{M \times (M-L-D)}$. And we have

$$\mathbf{D} = E(\mathbf{XX}_1^H) = E(\mathbf{XX}_0^H)\mathbf{P}_{1L} = \mathbf{EP}_{1L} \tag{11}$$

$$\mathbf{F} = E(\mathbf{XX}_2^H) = E(\mathbf{XX}_0^H)\mathbf{P}_{2L} = \mathbf{EP}_{2L} \tag{12}$$

where $\mathbf{E} = E(\mathbf{XX}_0^H)$. However, when considering the noise, the propagator matrix can be estimated by the following minimization problem

$$J_1 = min \|\mathbf{D} - \mathbf{EP}_{1L}\|_F^2, \quad J_2 = min \|\mathbf{F} - \mathbf{EP}_{2L}\|_F^2. \tag{13}$$

The optimal solution of J_1 and J_2 are given by

$$\mathbf{P}_{1L} = (\mathbf{E}^H\mathbf{E})^{-1}\mathbf{E}^H\mathbf{D}, \mathbf{P}_{2L} = (\mathbf{E}^H\mathbf{E})^{-1}\mathbf{E}^H\mathbf{F}. \tag{14}$$

The DOAs can be obtained by solving the following spectrum function,

$$f(u,v) = (\mathbf{B}(u,v)^H\mathbf{C}_L\mathbf{C}_L^H\mathbf{B}(u,v)) = 0 \tag{15}$$

In order to utilize the full information contained in the received data, reconstruct $\mathbf{C} = [\mathbf{C}_0, ..., \mathbf{C}_{i-1}, \mathbf{C}_{M-D-i+1}, ..., \mathbf{C}_{M-D}]$, where $1 \leq i \leq \lfloor \frac{M-D+1}{2} \rfloor$ [10]. Therefore, (15) can be rewritten as

$$f(u,v) = (\mathbf{B}(u,v)^H\mathbf{CC}^H\mathbf{B}(u,v)) = 0 \tag{16}$$

In fact, the larger the i, the DOA estimation performance will be better, but it will consume much time too. As a result, we prefer to choose the value according practical need. However, it can be seen from (16) that the function requires to perform an exhaustive 2D spectrum speak searching of both u and v, which leads to very high computational complexity. Hence, in order to reduce computation burden, the spectral RARE technique is employed here. It follows from (6) that we can easily get

$$\mathbf{B}(u,v) = \mathbf{F}[\tilde{\mathbf{a}}_y(u) \otimes \tilde{\mathbf{a}}_z(v)] = \mathbf{F}[\mathbf{I}_y \otimes \tilde{\mathbf{a}}_z(v)]\tilde{\mathbf{a}}_y(u). \tag{17}$$

The Eq. (16) can be rewritten as

$$f(u,v) = \tilde{\mathbf{a}}_y^H(u)\mathbf{Z}(v)\tilde{\mathbf{a}}_y = 0 \tag{18}$$

where

$$\mathbf{Z}(v) = [\mathbf{I}_y \otimes \tilde{\mathbf{a}}_z(v)]^H\mathbf{F}^H\mathbf{CC}^H\mathbf{F}[\mathbf{I}_y \otimes \tilde{\mathbf{a}}_z(v)]. \tag{19}$$

Since $\tilde{\mathbf{a}}_y(u) \neq 0$, (18) holds true only if $\mathbf{Z}(v)$ reduces rank. Generally speaking, $\mathbf{Z}(v)$ is a full-rank matrix, but the $\mathbf{Z}(v)$ will reduce rank when v is the true DOA. As a result, $\mathbf{Z}(v)$ will reach a minimum value when v coincides with the true DOA v_i. Therefore, we could have

$$f(v) = 1/min(\mathbf{Z}(v)). \tag{20}$$

Utilizing the $\{\hat{v}_i\}_{i=1}^{D}$ estimated by (20), the corresponding angles $\{\hat{u}_i\}_{i=1}^{D}$ can be estimated by searching the highest peaks of the following function

$$f(u) = \frac{1}{\|[\mathbf{F}(\tilde{a}_y(u) \otimes \hat{a}_z(v_i))]^H \mathbf{C}\|^2}, \quad i = 1, 2, ..., D. \tag{21}$$

At last, the elevation and azimuth angles $(\theta_i, \phi_i)_{i=1}^{D}$ can be obtained by

$$\theta_i = cos^{-1}(v_i), \quad \phi_i = sin^{-1}(\frac{u_i}{sin(\theta_i)}). \tag{22}$$

Remark: Compared with the traditional 2D spectral spectrum algorithm based on subspace decomposition, the method proposed in this paper avoids eigen-decomposition that reduces much computational burden. Besides, we replace the exhaustive 2D spectrum peak searching with successive 1D searchings, which further reduces the calculation cost significantly. In addition, the estimated azimuth and elevation can be paired automatically.

4   Simulations and Results

In order to illustrate the performance of the proposed method, some simulations are taken out in comparison with the traditional MUSIC algorithm and GPM. Because of the symmetry of the array, only one sub-array of the conformal array is utilized in the following simulations. As is shown in Fig. 1(a), the sub-array consists of 30 elements located uniformly and covers a sector of $\pi/3$. Therefore the angle between each two adjacent sensors is $\pi/6$, the height of the cylinder array $H = 5\lambda/2$ and the radius $r = 2\lambda$. As shown in Fig. 1(b), the corresponding interpolated array is composed of 6 rows and 5 columns with $d_x = d_y = \lambda/2$ and the interpolation error $\tau = 0.18$. We take 100 numbers of Monte Carlo trials in the following figures.

As shown in Fig. 2, the root-mean-square-error (RMSE) varying with the SNR and the snapshots are investigated. Assume there are two incident sources, and the DOAs (θ, ϕ) are $(52°, -8°)$ and $(68°, 8°)$, respectively. Assume the snapshots are 500, the RMSE curve versus SNR is plotted in Fig. 2(a) of three methods. Then, let SNR is 10 dB, the RMSE versus snapshots is given in Fig. 2(b). The RMSE values are obtained by running 100 Monte Carlo simulations. It can be seen from the Fig. 2, the performance of the three methods are improved with increased SNR and snapshots. But the estimation accuracy of the proposed method is not as good as MUSIC and PM with low SNR and small snapshots. However, when the SNR is greater than 5 dB and the snapshots is larger than 70, the performance of the proposed algorithm outperforms MUSIC and PM. That's because we adopt the interpolation technique that transforms the original conformal array to a more clear planar array only if the interpolation error τ is small enough.

Assume the DOAs are given by $(60°, 0°)$ and $(65°, 0°)$, the resolution performance is examined by the probability of successful detection in Fig. 3. Let the snapshots are 500, the resolution performance varying with SNR is given in

Fig. 3(a), and the resolution performance varying with snapshots when SNR is 10 dB is given in Fig. 3(b). From the Fig. 3, we can see that the proposed method is better than GPM but worse than MUSIC algorithm with low SNR and small snapshots. However, with the SNR and snapshots is larger, the resolution performance of the MUSIC and proposed algorithm are contiguous.

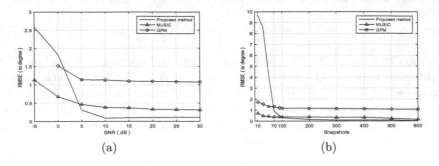

Fig. 2. (a) The RMSE versus SNR. (b) The RMSE versus snapshots.

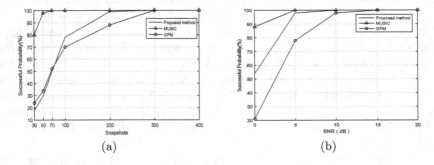

Fig. 3. (a) The successful probability versus snapshots. (b) The successful probability versus SNR.

5   Conclusion

In this paper, we have demonstrated an efficient 2D DOA algorithm for cylindrical conformal array. In this method, in order to avoid "shadow effect" of the metallic cylinder, the array is divided into several sub-arrays. Then, the interpolation technique is applied to transform the curved arrays to URA with omni-directional elements. Next, by combining the GPM and RARE method together, the signal's DOAs could be solved accurately and quickly. Rather than estimate the DOAs by the 2D spectrum peak searching, the proposed algorithm can obtain the 2D DOAs by several 1D peak searching, which reduce the computational complexity greatly. Moreover, the azimuth and elevation can be paired automatically.

Acknowledgement. This work was supported in part by National Aerospace Science Foundation of China under Grant 2015ZC54010, Education Department Foundation of Liaoning Province under Grant L2014059, National Natural Science Foundation of China under Grant 61571309 and 61101161, Research Foundation of Liaoning Provincial Science and Technology Department under grant 2015020097.

References

1. Josefsson, P., Persson, L.: Conformal array antenna theory and design. IEEE Trans. Antennas Propag. (2005)
2. Comisso, M., Vescovo, R.: Fast co-polar and cross-polar 3D pattern synthesis with dynamic range ratio reduction for conformal antenna arrays. IEEE Trans. Antennas Propag. **61**(1), 614–626 (2013)
3. Tsui, K.M., Chan, S.C.: Pattern synthesis of narrowband confromal arrays using iterative second-order cone programming. IEEE Trans. Antennas Propag. **58**(6), 1959–1970 (2010)
4. Schmidt, R.O.: Multiple emitter location and signal parameter estimations. IEEE Trans. Antennas Propag. **34**(3), 276–280 (1986)
5. Roy, R., Kailath, T.: ESPRIT-estimation of signal parameters via rotational invariance techniques. IEEE Trans. Acoust. Speech Signal Process. **37**(7), 984–995 (1989)
6. Wan, L.T., Si, W.J., Liu, L.T., Tian, Z.X., Feng, N.X.: High accuracy 2D-DOA estimation for conformal array using PARAFAC. Int. J. Antennas Propag. **2014**, 1–15 (2014)
7. Zou, L., Lasenby, J., He, Z.: Direction and polarisation estimation using polarised cylinder conformal arrays. IET Signal Proc. **6**(5), 395–403 (2011)
8. Yang, K., Zhao, Z.Q., Yang, W., Nie, Z.P.: Direction of arrival estimation on cylinder conformal array using RARE. J. Syst. Eng. Electron. **22**(5), 767–772 (2011)
9. Alinezhad, P., Seydnejad, S.R., Moghadam, D.A.: DOA estimation in conformal arrays based on the nested array. Digit. Signal Proc. **62**(22), 5930–5939 (2014)
10. Liu, S., Yang, L.S., Huang, J.H., Jiang, Q.P.: Generalization propagator method for DOA estimation. Prog. Electromagn. Res. **37**, 119–125 (2014)
11. Wang, B.H., Guo, Y., Wang, Y.L., Lin, Y.Z.: Frequency-invariant pattern synthesis of conformal array antenna with low cross-polarisation. IET Microw. Antennas Propag. **2**(5), 442–450 (2008)
12. Yang, P., Yang, F., Nie, Z.P.: DOA estimation with sub-array divided technique and interpolated esprit algorithm on a cylindrical conformal array antenna. Prog. Electronagn. Res. **103**, 201–216 (2010)
13. Xu, K.J., Nie, W.K., Feng, D.Z., Chen, X.J., Fang, D.Y.: A multi-direction virtual array transformation algorithm for 2D DOA estimation. Signal Proc. **125**, 122–133 (2016)

Blind Source Separation for Multi-carrier Efficient Modulations Using MIMO Antennas

Zhimin Chen[1], Jingchao Li[1], Peng Chen[2(✉)], and Pu Miao[3]

[1] Shanghai Dianji University, Shanghai 201306, China
[2] Southeast University, Nanjing 210096, China
chenpengdsp@seu.edu.cn
[3] Qingdao University, Qingdao 266071, China

Abstract. In this paper, the blind source separation (BSS) problem in the multi-carrier efficient communication system is considered, and a novel joint approximative diagonalization of eigenmatrix (JADE)-based multiple-input and multiple output (MIMO) model is proposed to separate the mixed signal that the antennas received. Then, the special impacting filter (SIF)-based demodulation method is adopted to demodulate the separated signals. Additionally, different from the traditionally efficient demodulation method, the proposed method can achieve higher communication capacity and spectrum utilization by combining the MIMO technology and JADE-based separation algorithm. Simulation results show that the JADE-based MIMO efficient communication system can separate the mixed signals efficiently, reduce the symbol interference and significantly improved the system performance by using the multiple antennas.

Keywords: Blind source separation · Efficient modulation · JADE MIMO

1 Introduction

The efficient modulation, which has good flexibility, univerality and anti-jamming characteristics, was first proposed by Wu [1,2]. Unlike the ultra wide band communication, the efficient modulated signal is sine-like, the symbol "0" is modulated by N sine carrier cycles and the non-zeros has phase change during the K ($K \ll N$) carrier cycles in the N carrier cycles, the waveform of the modulated signal is shown in Fig. 1. As the sine has a impulse sharp in the frequency domain, the sine-like efficient modulated signal has the similar characteristics, which can achieve high band efficiency and high-speed data transmission within quite narrow bandwidth [3,4]. Up until now, various efficient modulation methods have been proposed, such as the variable phase shifting keying (VPSK), enhanced VPSK, very minimum shifting keying (VMSK), pulse position phase reversal keying (3PRK), missing cycle modulation (MCM), suppressed cycle modulation (SCM), and minimum sideband modulation (MSB), etc. [5–9]. The above modulations have a same characteristic, that is "asymmetric".

© ICST Institute for Computer Sciences, Social Informatics and Telecommunications Engineering 2018
G. Sun and S. Liu (Eds.): ADHIP 2017, LNICST 219, pp. 546–554, 2018.
https://doi.org/10.1007/978-3-319-73317-3_64

The demodulation of the efficient signal is based on the special digital impacting filter (SIF) [10–13]. The SIF is a kind of digital IIR filter that has one pair of zeros and multiple pair of poles, the frequency response of the SIF was shown in Fig. 2. When the SIF works on the proper frequency, it can convert the phase change to amplitude impacting and remove the most noises at the same time. As the output signal reveal obvious amplitude different, we can use simple threshold detection method to demodulate the signals in the intermediate frequency, which can avoid down-conversion to baseband to demodulate the signals. However, the SIF can not demodulate the non-orthogonal multi-carrier signals. [14] proposed a blind source separation method to separate the mixed signals, which can assistant the demodulation and achieve significant effect. Since the multiple-input and multiple-output (MIMO) can provied more spatial diversity, combine the MIMO and the BSS algorithm to separate the mixed carriers may be an feasible solution [15–18]. As the multi-carrier efficient system is non-orthogonal, we can use the SIMO scheme to decrease the symbol interference. In this paper, we first give the system model of the SIMO multi-carrier system. Then, we propose two BSS algorithms, one is based on the Kalman filtering (KF), the other one is the joint approximative diagonalization of eigenmatrix (JADE) algorithm. Finally, we give the simulation results and conclude the paper.

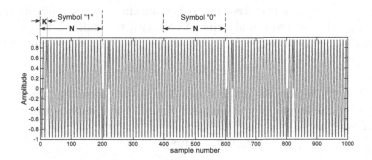

Fig. 1. Waveform of the efficient modulation signal

The organization of this manuscript is as follows. In Sect. 2, the system model of the MIMO efficient communication with interference is described. Next, in Sect. 3, the blind source separation algorithm and Kalman filtering method is proposed to demodulate the mixed signals. Section 4 gives the simulation results. Finally, Sect. 5 concludes the paper.

The notations used in this work are defined as follows. Symbols for vectors (lower case) and matrices (upper case) are in bold face. I_N, $\mathcal{N}\left(0, \sigma_n^2 I\right)$, $(\cdot)^T$, $(\cdot)^H$, diag $\{\cdot\}$, $*$ and $\lfloor \cdot \rfloor$ denote the $N \times N$ identity matrices, the Gaussian distribution with zero mean and covariance being $\sigma_n^2 I$, the transpose, the conjugate transpose (Hermitian), the diagonal matrix, the convolution and the floor function, respectively.

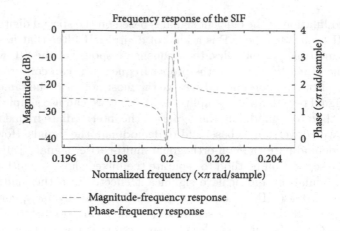

Fig. 2. Frequency response of the special impacting filter

2   System Model of the SIMO Communication with Interference

The SIMO communication system considered in this section is shown in Fig. 3, where the communication system has one transmit antenna and multi receive antennas, and the receive signal is interfered with the independent signal. The number of the receive antennas is Q. The transmitted signal can be expressed as

$$\mathbf{s} = \mathbf{s}_1 + \mathbf{s}_2 + \ldots + \mathbf{s}_P, \tag{1}$$

where $\mathbf{s}_p \in \mathbb{R}^{L \times 1}$ denotes the efficient signal with the carrier frequency being f_p, and L denotes the length of the sampling signal. The receive signal $\mathbf{y}_q \in \mathbb{R}^{L \times 1}$ at the qth antenna is

$$\mathbf{y}_q = a_q \mathbf{s} + b_q \mathbf{s}_I + \mathbf{n}_q, \tag{2}$$

where a_p denotes the channel attenuation between the transmitter and the qth receive antenna, b_p denotes the channel attenuation between the interference and the qth receive antenna, $\mathbf{s}_I$ denotes the interference signal and $\mathbf{n}_q$ denotes the additive white Gaussian noise (AWGN). Then we can obtain the matrix of the receive signal

$$\mathbf{Y} = \mathbf{a}\mathbf{s}^T + \mathbf{b}\mathbf{s}_I^T + \mathbf{N}, \tag{3}$$

where

$$\mathbf{Y} \triangleq \left(\mathbf{y}_1, \mathbf{y}_2, \ldots, \mathbf{y}_Q\right)^T. \tag{4}$$

3   Demodulation of the Efficient Modulation Signals

In this work, we propose two approaches to demodulate the multi-carrier signal with the interference, one is based on the Kalman filtering (KF) [19], the other one is based on the joint approximative diagonalization of eigenmatrix (JADE) algorithm, and each approach has two steps:

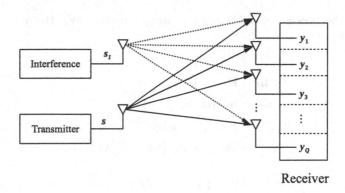

Fig. 3. The system model of the SIMO communication with interference

1. Separate the multi-carrier signal from the interfered receive signal based on the blind source separation (BSS);
2. The demodulation of the multi-carrier signal by the SIF.

The lth column of the receive signal $\mathbf{Y}$ denotes as $\mathbf{y}_l \in \mathbb{R}^{Q \times 1}$, and

$$\mathbf{y}_l = \mathbf{A}\mathbf{x}_l + \mathbf{n}_l, \tag{5}$$

where $\mathbf{A} \triangleq (\mathbf{a}, \mathbf{b})$, $\mathbf{x}_l \triangleq \begin{pmatrix} s_l \\ s_{I,l} \end{pmatrix}$, $\mathbf{n}_l$ denotes the noise, s_l and $s_{I,l}$ respectively denote the lth entry of the transmit signal $\mathbf{s}$ and interference signal. During the process of the BSS, the separating matrix $\mathbf{B}_l \in \mathbb{R}^{2 \times Q}$ is adopted to separate the mixture signal $\mathbf{y}_l$, and we can obtain the separated signal $\mathbf{z}_l \in \mathbb{R}^{2 \times 1}$

$$\mathbf{z}_l = \mathbf{B}_l \mathbf{y}_l. \tag{6}$$

In the theory of the BSS, the separating matrix $\mathbf{B}_l$ includes two parts, i.e., the prewhitening matrix $\mathbf{U}_l \in \mathbb{R}^{2 \times Q}$ and the weight matrix $\mathbf{W}_l \in \mathbb{R}^{2 \times 2}$, and

$$\mathbf{B}_l = \mathbf{W}_l^T \mathbf{U}_l. \tag{7}$$

3.1 The Separation of the Multi-carrier Signal Based on the BSS via the KF Algorithm

We first attain $\mathbf{v}_l \triangleq \mathbf{U}_l \mathbf{y}_l$ by the prewhitening matrix $\mathbf{U}_l$, where $\mathbf{v}$ is the normalized white vector with the zero mean and unity covariance $\mathcal{E}\left\{\mathbf{v}_l \mathbf{v}_l^T\right\} = I$. The LMS-type prewhitening matrix is adopted

$$\mathbf{U}_l = \mathbf{U}_{l-1} + \lambda_l \left[I - \left(\mathbf{U}_{l-1} \mathbf{y}^l \right) \left(\mathbf{U}_{l-1} \mathbf{y}^l \right)^T \right] \mathbf{U}_{l-1}, \tag{8}$$

where λ_l is a leaning rate.

During the process of obtaining the weight matrix $\mathbf{W}_l$, the KF method is adopted [20]

$$\mathbf{d}_l = g(\mathbf{W}_{l-1}^T \mathbf{v}_l) \tag{9}$$

$$\mathbf{h}_l = \mathbf{K}_{l,l-1} \mathbf{d}_l \tag{10}$$

$$\mathbf{m}_l = \mathbf{h}_l / \left(\mathbf{d}_l^T \mathbf{h}_l + Q_l \right) \tag{11}$$

$$\mathbf{K}_{l+1,l} = \mathbf{K}_{l,l-1} - \mathbf{m}_l \mathbf{h}_l^T \tag{12}$$

$$\mathbf{W}_l^T = \mathbf{W}_{l-1}^T + \mathbf{m}_l \left(\mathbf{v}_l^T - \mathbf{d}_l^T \mathbf{W}_{l-1}^T \right), \tag{13}$$

where $\mathbf{K}_{l,l-1} = \mathcal{E}\left\{ \left(\mathbf{W}_l^T - \hat{\mathbf{W}}_l^T \right) \left(\mathbf{W}_l^T - \hat{\mathbf{W}}_l^T \right)^T \right\}$, $Q_l = \| \mathbf{v}_l - \mathbf{W}_{l-1} \mathbf{d}_l \|_2^2$ and $g(t) = t - \tanh(t)$.

3.2 The Separation of the Efficient Signal from the Interfered Receive Signal Based on the BSS via the JADE Algorithm

The separation of the multi-carrier signal from the interfered receive signal based on the BSS via the JADE algorithm is described in Algorithm 1. Statistical performance is achieved by involving all the cumulants of order 2 and 4 while a fast optimization is obtained by the device of joint diagonalization [21,22].

4 Simulation Results

First, we evaluate the proposed methods of the multi-carrier efficient signal demodulation, and the simulation parameters are given in Table 1. To show the simulation results more clearly, we set 4 sub-carrier and use the M-ary efficient signal as the sources. Additionally, these parameters are the same for the simulations in the following contents, if there is no additional statement.

Table 1. Simulation parameters

Parameter	Value
The M-ary efficient signal	$M = 2$
Carrier frequencies	$10e^6 \, 10.005e^6 \, 10.002e^6 \, 10.001e^6$
Sample frequency	$10 \times 10e^6$
Symbol length N	$N = 100$
Phase change length K	$K = 2$
Transmit antennas	1
Received antennas	4

In the proposed methods of the signal demodulation, two steps are included, where at the first step the mixed signal is separated and at the second step a

Algorithm 1. The BSS based on the JADE

1: Calculate the prewhitening matrix $\mathbf{U}$ from the covariance matrix $\mathbf{R}_y$ of the receive signal, and the prewhitening matrix should satisfy the follow condition

$$\mathbf{UA} = \mathbf{V}, \tag{14}$$

where $\mathbf{V}$ is an unitary matrix. Then we can obtain the prewhitening matrix $\mathbf{U}$ from the subspace decomposition of $\mathbf{R}_y$

$$\mathbf{U} = \left[\left(\lambda_1 - \sigma_n^2 \right)^{-\frac{1}{2}} \mathbf{g}_1, \left(\lambda_2 - \sigma_n^2 \right)^{-\frac{1}{2}} \mathbf{g}_2 \right]^H, \tag{15}$$

where λ_1, λ_2 are the two maximal eigenvalues of $\mathbf{R}_y$, $\mathbf{g}_1$ and $\mathbf{g}_2$ are the corresponding eigenvector. σ_n^2 is the variance of noise, which is the mean value of the left eigenvalues.

2: Obtain the whiten signal $\mathbf{v}_l$

$$\mathbf{v}_l = \mathbf{U}\mathbf{y}_l = \mathbf{U}\left(\mathbf{A}\mathbf{x}_l + \mathbf{n}_l \right) \tag{16}$$
$$= \mathbf{V}\mathbf{x}_l + \mathbf{U}\mathbf{n}_l.$$

3: The matrix of the fourth-order cumulant of the whiten signal is defined as

$$\{\mathbf{Q}\left(\mathbf{P}\right)\}_{ij} = \sum_{k,r=1}^{2} \text{cum}\left\{ v_i, v_j^H, v_k, v_r^H \right\} P_{rk}, \tag{17}$$

where P_{rk} denotes the rth and kth column of an arbitrary non-zeros matrix $\mathbf{P} \in \mathbb{R}^{2\times 2}$, and $\{\mathbf{Q}\left(\mathbf{P}\right)\}_{ij}$ denotes the ith and jth column of the fourth-order cumulant $\mathbf{Q}\left(\mathbf{P}\right)$. The fourth-order cumulant can be expressed as

$$\text{cum}\left\{ v_i, v_j^H, v_k, v_r^H \right\} = \mu_4 \left\{ v_i, v_j^H, v_k, v_r^H \right\}$$
$$- \mu_2 \left\{ v_i, v_j^H \right\} \mu_2 \left\{ v_k, v_r^H \right\} - \mu_2 \left\{ v_i, v_k \right\} \mu_2 \left\{ v_j^H, v_r^H \right\}$$
$$- \mu_2 \left\{ v_i, v_r^H \right\} \mu_2 \left\{ v_j^H, v_k \right\}, \tag{18}$$

where $\mu_4 \left\{ v_i, v_j^H, v_k, v_r^H \right\} = \frac{1}{L} \sum_{l=1}^{L} v_{l,i} v_{l,j}^H v_{l,k}^H v_{l,r}$, $\mu_2 \left\{ v_i, v_j^H \right\} = \frac{1}{L} \sum_{l=1}^{L} v_{l,i} v_{l,j}$, $\mu_2 \left\{ v_k, v_r^H \right\} = \frac{1}{L} \sum_{l=1}^{L} v_{l,k} v_{l,r}$, $\mu_2 \left\{ v_i, v_k \right\} = \frac{1}{L} \sum_{l=1}^{L} v_{l,i} v_{l,k}^H$, $\mu_2 \left\{ v_j^H, v_r^H \right\} = \frac{1}{L} \sum_{l=1}^{L} v_{l,j} v_{l,r}$, $\mu_2 \left\{ v_i, v_r^H \right\} = \frac{1}{L} \sum_{l=1}^{L} v_{l,i} v_{l,r}$, $\mu_2 \left\{ v_j^H, v_k \right\} = \frac{1}{L} \sum_{l=1}^{L} v_{l,j}^H v_{l,k}$.

4: From the eigen decomposition of $\mathbf{Q}\left(\mathbf{P}\right)$, we can attain the approximation of $\mathbf{V}$

$$\mathbf{Q}\left(\mathbf{P}\right) = \hat{\mathbf{V}}\mathbf{\Sigma}\hat{\mathbf{V}}^H. \tag{19}$$

5: The separated signal is

$$\mathbf{z}_l = \hat{\mathbf{V}}^H \mathbf{U}\mathbf{y}_l. \tag{20}$$

SIF is adopt to filtering the signals. At the first step, the BSS for 4 carriers with interference in the SIMO scenario is shown in Fig. 4, in order to show the separation more clearly, Fig. 4 only give 2 sub-carrier's results, and we can see that the mixed signals with interference can be separated successfully.

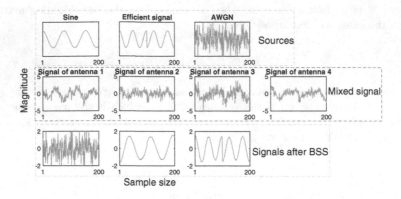

Fig. 4. The BSS separation process of the mixed signals

Additionally, the demodulation processes with the SIF are also shown in Fig. 5. As the demodulation results are sensitive with the first step, in the practical communication system, the number of the sub-carriers is constraint. For example, 4 signals are used in our simulation, and 20 signals are used in practice. Then, use the threshold determination to obtain the demodulator results. As shown in Fig. 5, we can see the final output signals can achieve better performance at the whole duration. Figure 6 shows the BER performance of the proposed system, from Fig. 6, we can see that the BER performance of each sub-carrier is affected by the carrier interval. Since we use one sample frequecy and the SIF must work in proper range, the performances of each sub-carrier is different, the best is the sub-carrier 1 and others decent orderatly. However, even the subcarrier 4, can still obtain satisfactory performance.

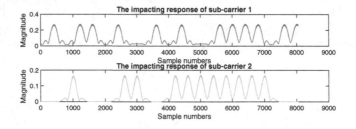

Fig. 5. The demodulation of the sub-carriers with the SIF

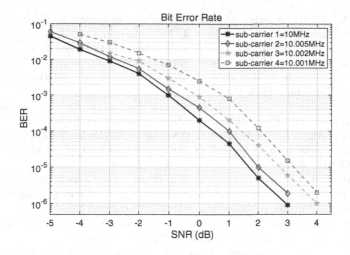

Fig. 6. BER performance of the system

5 Conclusions

In this work, the demodulation for multi-carrier signals has been considered. The system model has been established for the multi-carrier MIMO efficient system. Kalman filtering and JADE algorithms have been adopted to separate the mixed carriers and the inerferences. Moreover, a novel two-step method has been proposed to demodulate the subcarriers and to improve the demodulation performance. The simulation results show that the demodulation performance can be significantly improved by adopting the BSS and MIMO. Future work will concentrate on the waveform optimization for multiple transmit antennas in the multi-carrier efficient system.

Acknowledgment. This work was supported in part by the National Natural Science Foundation of China (Grant No. 61601281 and No. 61603239).

References

1. Wu, L.: UNB modulation in high speed space communications. In: Proceedings of the SPIE International Society Optical Engineering, Wuhan, vol. 6795(Part One), pp. 679510-1–679510-6, November 2007
2. Wu, L., Feng, M., Qi, C.: On BER performance of EBPSK-MODEM in AWGN channel. Sensors **10**(4), 3824–3834 (2010)
3. Wu, L., Feng, M.: Recent patents on ultra narrow band modulations. Recent Pat. Signal Process. **1**(1), 36–47 (2011)
4. He, F., Wu, L.: Analysis of power spectrum of continuous phase waveforms for binary modulation communications. In: Proceedings of the International Conference Ultra Modern Telecommunications and Workshops, St. Petersburg, Russia, pp. 1–5, October 2009

5. Feng, M., Wu, L.: Special non-linear filter and extension to Shannon's channel capacity. Digit. Signal Process. Rev. J. **19**(5), 861–873 (2009)
6. Jin, Y., Wu, L., Wang, J., Yu, J.: A new detector in EBPSK communication system. J. Southeast Univ. Engl. Ed. **27**(3), 244–247 (2011)
7. Feng, M.: Research on key problems in high-efficiency modulation. Ph.D. thesis, Southeast University (2008)
8. Chen, X.: Research on detection and channel coding of efficient modulation communication system. Ph.D. thesis, Southeast University (2013)
9. Zhang, P., Wu, L.: A realization method for multi-carrier MPPSK modulations. Progress in mechatronics and information technology. Appl. Mech./Mater. **462–463**, 615–618 (2013)
10. Feng, M., Wu, L., Gao, P.: An EBPSK demodulator based on ANN detection. In: International Conference on Informational Science and Engineering, ICISE-Proceedings, Hangzhou, China, pp. 969–972, December 2010
11. Feng, M., Wu, L., Gao, P.: From special analogous crystal filters to digital impacting filters. Digit. Signal Process. Rev. J. **22**(4), 690–696 (2012)
12. Ying, P., Wu, L.: New scheme of MPPSK modem. J. Southeast Univ. Engl. Ed. **42**(2), 204–208 (2012)
13. Zhu, R., Wu, L.: Nonlinear geometric feature equalizers based on minimum bit error rate criterion for EBPSK communications. In: Proceedings of the SPIE International Society Optical Engineering, Article no.: 67951D (2007)
14. Chen, Z., Wu, L.: Blind source separation of dual-carrier MPPSK signal based on smoothed pseudo wigner distribution. In: Proceedings of the 9th International Symposium on Communication Systems, Networks and Digital Signal, Manchester, UK, pp. 664–667, October 2014
15. Chen, Z., Wu, L., Chen, P.: Efficient modulation and demodulation methods for multi-carrier communication. IET Commun. **10**(5), 567–576 (2016)
16. Chen, Z., Wu, L.: Design of special impacting filter for multicarrier ABPSK system. Math. Probl. Eng. Article ID: 921932 (2013)
17. Chen, Z., Wu, L.: The dual carrier ABSK system based on a FIR bandpass filter. Sensors **14**(3), 5644–5653 (2014)
18. Chen, P., Qi, C., Wu, L., Wang, X.: Estimation of extended targets based on compressed sensing in cognitive radar system. IEEE Trans. Veh. Technol. **66**(2), 941–951 (2017)
19. Chen, P., Qi, C., Wu, L.: Antenna placement optimisation for compressed sensing-based distributed MIMO radar. IET Radar Sonar Navig. **2**(11), 285–293 (2017)
20. Mirzaei, F.M., Roumeliotis, S.I.: A Kalman filter-based algorithm for IMU-camera calibration: observability analysis and performance evaluation. IEEE Trans. Rob. **24**(5), 1143–1156 (2008)
21. Cardoso, J.F., Souloumiac, A.: Blind beamforming for non Gaussian signals. IEE-Proc.-F **140**(6), 362–370 (1993)
22. Cardoso, J.F.: High-order contrasts for independent component analysis. Neural Comput. **11**(1), 157 (1989)

Author Index